Music in Tolkien's Work and Beyond

Music in Tolkien's Work and Beyond

edited by
Julian Eilmann
& Friedhelm Schneidewind

2019

Cormarë Series No. 39

Series Editors:
Peter Buchs • Thomas Honegger • Andrew Moglestue • Johanna Schön • Doreen Triebel

Series Editor responsible for this volume: Doreen Triebel

Library of Congress Cataloguing-in-Publication Data

Julian Eilmann & Friedhelm Schneidewind (eds.):
Music in Tolkien's Work and Beyond
ISBN 978-3-905703-39-9

Subject headings:
Tolkien, J.R.R. (John Ronald Reuel), 1892-1973
Music
Fantasy
Interdisciplinary Perspectives
Middle-earth
The Lord of the Rings
The Hobbit
The Silmarillion

Cormarë Series No. 39

First published 2019

© Walking Tree Publishers, Zurich and Jena, 2019

All rights reserved. No portion of this book may be reproduced, by any process or technique, without the express written consent of the publisher

Set in Adobe Garamond Pro and Shannon by Walking Tree Publishers

Cover illustraion 'Gunnar in the Snakepit' by Anke Eissmann (copyright by the artist, published by permission of the artist)

Board of Advisors

Academic Advisors

Douglas A. Anderson (independent scholar)

Patrick Curry (independent scholar)

Michael D.C. Drout (Wheaton College)

Vincent Ferré (Université de Paris-Est Créteil UPEC)

Dimitra Fimi (University of Glasgow)

Verlyn Flieger (University of Maryland)

Thomas Fornet-Ponse (Rheinische Friedrich-Wilhelms-Universität Bonn)

Christopher Garbowski (University of Lublin, Poland)

Mark T. Hooker (Indiana University)

Andrew James Johnston (Freie Universität Berlin)

Rainer Nagel (Johannes Gutenberg-Universität Mainz)

Helmut W. Pesch (independent scholar)

Tom Shippey (University of Winchester)

Allan Turner (Friedrich-Schiller-Universität Jena)

Frank Weinreich (independent scholar)

General Readers

Johan Boots

Jean Chausse

Friedhelm Schneidewind

Isaac Juan Tomas

Patrick Van den hole

Johan Vanhecke (Letterenhuis, Antwerp)

Acknowledgments

This volume is part of Walking Tree Publishers' continued endeavour to promote and publish high-quality research on a wide variety of topics related to the works of J.R.R. Tolkien. Thematically, it is a follow-up to *Music in Middle-earth*, which was published by Walking Tree Publishers in 2010, and it expands on and goes beyond the topics discussed therein. In order to make the research accessible to a wider audience, the present volume is published in English (by Walking Tree Publishers) and German (under the title *Musik in Tolkiens Werk und darüber hinaus* by Edition Stein und Baum). Many authors wrote their contributions in both languages; the papers of the others have been translated professionally for this purpose.

Our thanks go to all those who worked with us to make this volume possible – most prominently, of course, the contributors, but also the two volume editors, Julian Eilmann and Friedhelm Schneidewind, who initiated this project and who proved conscientious and enthusiastic collaborators.

A great 'thank you' also to Larissa Zoller and Sophia Mehlhausen, who were in charge of the layouting and proofreading of the text, respectively. The cover art is the work of Anke Eissmann, whose illustrations to the works of Tolkien and other authors have gained international recognition. Also, I want to thank my colleagues at Walking Tree Publishers, Andrew Moglestue, Peter Buchs, Johanna Schön, and Thomas Honegger, who did a great job with the quality management of the layout, the proofing, and who made sure that all the numerous administrative tasks involved in producing a book were taken care of efficiently and responsibly.

Jena on the Saale, August 2019
Doreen Triebel, Series Editor

Contents

Julian Eilmann & Friedhelm Schneidewind
Introduction
"I love music": The Musicality of the Philologist — i

TOLKIEN AND MUSIC

Chiara Bertoglio
Polyphony, Collective Improvisation, and the Gift of Creation — 3

Michaël Devaux & Guglielmo Spirito
Laments and Mercy:
Tolkien and Liturgical Music — 29

Nancy Martsch
Middle-earth Improv:
Song Writing and Improvisation in Tolkien's Works — 59

Łukasz Neubauer
"What news from the North?": The Compositional Fabric, Intricate
Imagery and Heroic Christian Character of the "Lament for Boromir" — 77

Jörg Fündling
"Go forth, for it is there!"
An Imperialist Battle Cry behind the Lament for Boromir? — 111

THE POWER OF MUSIC

Elizabeth A. Whittingham
"A Matter of Song":
The Power of Music and Song in Tolkien's Legendarium — 135

Bradford Lee Eden
"The Scholar as Minstrel":
Word-music and Sound-words in Tolkien's "New Works" — 159

Lynn Forest-Hill
Tolkien's Minstrelsy:
The Performance of History and Authority — 175

Maureen F. Mann
Musicality in Tolkien's Prose — 207

Petra Zimmermann
"A deep silence fell":
Silence and the Presentation of 'Voices' in Tolkien — 235

Music of Different Texts and Characters

Renée Vink
Dance and Song: "The Lay of Leithian" between
"The Tale of Tinúviel" and "Of Beren and Lúthien" — 257

Jennifer Rogers
Music and the Outcast:
Songs of the Wanderer in Tolkien's Time-Travel Fragments — 277

Angela P. Nicholas
Aragorn, Music and the "Divine Plan" — 301

Sabine Frambach
"Where you hear song, you may rest at ease":
The Music of the Evil Ones in Middle-earth — 329

Instruments in Middle-earth

Heidi Steimel
An Orchestra in Middle-earth — 345

John Holmes
Nis me ti hearpun hygi:
Harping on One String in Middle-earth — 359

Allan Turner
The Horns of Elfland — 387

Rainer Groß
Portatives in Middle-earth:
A Speculative Approach to Organ Instruments in Tolkien's Work — 399

Music beyond Tolkien

Anja Müller
The Lords of the Rings:
Wagner's *Ring* and Tolkien's "Faërie"   413

Patrick Schmitz
"True Music in the Words":
A Comparative Analysis of the Function of Music in Tolkien's
The Lord of the Rings and Rothfuss' *Kingkiller Chronicles*   435

Tobias Escher
Of Home Keys and Music Style Guides:
Orchestral Scores for Tolkien-based Video Games   447

Introduction

Introduction

"I love music": The Musicality of the Philologist

Music plays a crucial role in Tolkien's mythology and his tales contain many songs as well as musicians, musical performances and instruments. If we imagine how creation is literally achieved through divine music at the beginning of Tolkien's *Silmarillion*, we can assess that music indeed is the foundation for all the tales and stories that unfold in Middle-earth in all the centuries to come. And although the author himself did not play an instrument and said of himself in one of his letters that he had "little musical knowledge," he nonetheless "c[a]me of a musical family", "married a musician", admitted that "music gives me great pleasure and sometimes inspiration" and ultimately confessed: "I love music" (all Scull/Hammond, *Reader's Guide* 815).

Reflecting on the influence of music on his literary work, Tolkien comes to the conclusion that "such music as was in me [as a child] was submerged (until I married a musician), or transformed into linguistic terms" (ibid.). Tolkien thus points to an important fact that everyone dealing with music in his work must consider: The author's prose itself, his careful use of sounds, words and sentences, has musical qualities, which underlines the vital literary musicality of the philologist Tolkien. We can, therefore, only agree with Tolkien scholar Maureen Mann, who – in accordance with fantasy writer Ursula K. LeGuin – points to the aesthetics of Tolkien's language, which demands to be read aloud:

> The narrative prose of such novelists [like Tolkien] is like poetry in that it wants the living voice to speak it, to find its full beauty and power, its subtle music, its rhythmic vitality (LeGuin, quoted in Mann in this volume on page 217)

> There is both rhyme and reason behind the very popular habit of Tolkien's readers to gather and read aloud his prose. (Mann, ibid.)

Mann's enlightening paper "Musicality of Tolkien's Prose" is just one highlight in our book *Music in Tolkien's Work and Beyond*, which is broad in scope with 21 different approaches to the title's topic. The book is the successor to the well-received 2010 volume *Music in Middle-earth*, No. 20 of the Cormarë Series, which drew the attention of Tolkien scholarship to the importance of music in Tolkien's work. It contained "four sections that highlight the variety of perspectives [and thus offers] a considerable spectrum of different views on the role of music in Tolkien's work and his reception" (Thomas Fornet-Ponse, *Inklings-Jahrbuch* 28, 2010). As the title of this follow-up volume, *Music in Tolkien's Work and Beyond*, suggests, the book simultaneously follows the path of analyzing the use and significance of music and musical elements in Tolkien's literary texts while also considering the broader context, such as adaptations and other authors and composers.

The 21 articles are written by 12 women and 10 men from different countries and thus offer many different perspectives on the phenomenon of music and song. The papers feature a multitude of different academic approaches, e.g. musicological, philosophical or theological, which not only look at music itself but also at poetry, song and instruments. The contributions are divided into five sections: "Tolkien and Music", "The Power of Music", "Music of Different Texts and Characters", "Instruments in Middle-earth" und "Music beyond Tolkien".

Section I: "Tolkien and Music"

In five papers, section I presents Tolkien's view on older musical styles and liturgy as well as an analysis of the element of improvisation of songs and the writing of words to tunes in *The Hobbit* and *The Lord of the Rings*. Two papers offer different perspectives on the "Lament for Boromir".

Chiara Bertoglio opens section I with her study on the standing of Tolkien's description of the Ainur's music in relation to Ilúvatar's theme with respect to the historical development of polyphony in the Western Middle Ages, taking into account the relationship between *cantus firmus* and early *organa*, the practice of improvised polyphony, and the role of the composer of classical polyphony. She discusses the symbolic aspect of polyphony, also with references to the writings of theorists of music and theologians from the late Middle Ages, as well as polyphony's potential for simultaneously symbolizing the community of the believers, their communion, and their diversity, mirroring the unity-in-plurality of the Christian Trinity.

Michaël Devaux and Guglielmo Spirito give an overview about liturgical music of Tolkien's time, with a focus on its possible influence on his conception of Elvish music. Guglielmo Spirito reconstructs the pieces of chant Tolkien used to hear at mass and offers a spiritual appreciation of the theme of laments and mercy from the *Kyrie* in Tolkien's work. Michaël Devaux defines sacred and liturgical music from a canonical point of view at the beginning of the 20th century. He also details the historical context of liturgical music in the Oratory of Birmingham and the history of the pieces of Gregorian chant Tolkien referred to in his texts or even recorded.

Nancy Martsch focuses on the improvisation of songs and the writing of words to tunes in *The Hobbit* and *The Lord of the Rings*: first treating these stories as authentic fictional history, translated by Tolkien, to observe how the characters created their songs; and then treating the stories as feigned history written by Tolkien to examine how he created the songs himself. Martsch also examines previously created poems interpolated into *The Lord of the Rings* and songs which Tolkien created (and sang) elsewhere.

Łukasz Neubauer and Jörg Fündling both deal independently with the "Lament for Boromir" and come to striking conclusions: Neubauer looks at the poem's compositional fabric, intricate imagery and heroic Christian character and examines the often complex nature of elegiac verses in *The Lord of the Rings*. Fündling uses Rudyard Kipling's poem "The English Flag" (1891) to contextualize Tolkien's lament in the British political tradition. Fündling concludes that Tolkien used the framework and, partly, the moods of the very first instance of Kipling's imperialist verse for his own purpose.

Section II: "The Power of Music"

The five articles in section II deal with the evocative power of and the authority given by music and song. The section starts with Elizabeth Whittingham's discussion of the use of music and song by the characters in *The Silmarillion*. She focuses on different aspects like the Great Music in the *Ainulindalë* or

Fëanor's suggestion that being remembered in song will somehow justify what the Elves will suffer, a perspective that Manwë seems to corroborate. Song is even used in battle and as a means of leveling a fortress. These uses along with its creative ability are distinctly different from those in the popular works and indicate that music is the most powerful force in Tolkien's universe and essential to the beings of Middle-earth.

Brad Eden uses the most recent of Tolkien's (posthumous) publications (*The Legend of Sigurd & Gudrún*, *The Fall of Arthur*, *Beowulf*, *The Story of Kullervo*, *The Lay of Aotrou & Itroun*, and *A Secret Vice*) to explicate how Tolkien favored a strong relationship between music and language, specifically using terms like sound-words, word-music, sound symbolism and sound aesthetics.

Lynn Forest-Hill considers the functions of the many instances of 'informal', or non-professional minstrelsy in *The Lord of the Rings* and highlights the essential importance of the informal oral dissemination of history in Middle-earth for racial and social integration. Forest-Hill argues that Tolkien historicizes the relationship between oral and textual versification in ways that challenge notions of textual authority and status, and that he thereby claims the absolute authority of the creative process by smuggling into print versions of *Silmarillion* material which is the subject of informal minstrelsy.

Using statements from *A Secret Vice*, the "Essay on Phonetic Symbolism", and Tolkien's *Letters*, Maureen Mann examines Tolkien's prose style in light of his own comments about the significance of phonetics and the role of sound in communicating meaning, as well as the role of mellifluous expressions to enhance or help formulate the comprehension of meaning. The methodology applies historical interrogation and textual analysis using traditional rhetorical devices from public speaking to identify rhythmic emphasis and sound repetition which create musicality.

Petra Zimmermann explores the dichotomy of silence and voices in Tolkien's work. She discusses how silence is crucial in two contexts: on the one hand as silence experienced in nature in landscape descriptions, and on the other hand in the field of (musical) presentations of poems. Zimmermann argues that for Tolkien silence (almost) always serves as a background for the sounding of multifarious 'voices' – either of voices from nature or of voices from the characters of the novels who recite a poem or sing a song. The paper explores how these 'voices' are presented against the background of silence and how Tolkien achieves to draw the reader into the narrative world through the interaction of silence and voices.

Section III: "Music of Different Texts and Characters"

The topic of section III focuses especially on the Lay of Leithian, Tolkien's time travel fragments as well as Aragorn and the music of evil characters in Middle-earth. Renée Vink opens this section and shows in her paper how, over the years, Tolkien turned "Beren and Lúthien" from a story dominated by dance into one in which music and song gradually began to take over until only one dancing scene remained. But it was the most important one, and the most personal to Tolkien himself.

Tolkien's time-travel fragments, *The Lost Road* and *The Notion Club Papers*, contain several songs which seem disconnected from the two texts' main narratives. However, Jennifer Rogers' ethnomusicological study of these songs shows how the music in *The Lost Road* and *The Notion Club Papers* hints to some of the stories' central themes: mortality and belonging. Rogers analyzes these songs and their singers in cultural context and argues that Tolkien uses music to draw a clear picture of the singers' personal and communal identities as they explore ideas of mortality within the texts. The same ethnomusicological approach is then applied to contemporary primary world songs in order to argue for the characteristic ability of music to discuss questions of mortality while defining the personal and communal identities inherent to those questions.

Angela Nicholas examines the different aspects of music (vocal and instrumental) and verse in relation to the life and character of Aragorn, considering him as a musician and poet in his own right, as someone who understands and appreciates music and poetry, and as the subject of songs and verses. Particular attention is paid to his circumstances and emotions, thus gaining psychological insight into the nature of his struggles and hardship. Overall, the discussion is set within the context of the significance of music in Aragorn's Maian/Elven ancestry and background, and in his role in Tolkien's legendarium.

Sabine Framberg draws our attention to the dichotomy of evil characters in Middle-earth and music. While music and song are mostly associated with positive aspects like joy and artistry, Framberg explains what kind of instruments are preferred by evil beings and how creatures like orcs make use of music in their own wicked way.

Section IV: "Instruments in Middle-earth"

The four papers in section IV deal with instruments in Middle-earth, especially the harp – following a different approach than the papers in "Music in Middle-earth" –, the horns of Elfland and portativs, i.e. small organs.

Tolkien's Middle-earth has inspired many musicians to compositions, both vocal and instrumental. Heidi Steimel's paper introduces readers to a set of classical orchestral works by Carey Blyton, Johan de Meij, Aulis Sallinen, Craig H. Russell and Martin Romberg. Steimel examines the effect orchestral music has in evoking emotions and bringing listeners to Middle-earth. As these compositions come from outside the secondary world and do not intend to sound as if they were authentically played within the context of the story, they are therefore different from music composed for Tolkien's poems and add variety to the mix of folk music, heavy metal, and film soundtracks which are popularly heard by Middle-earth fans.

John Holmes examines the harp as a metonym for poetry in Tolkien's Middle-earth. In a passage from the Old English *Seafarer*, recollected in a dream by a character in Tolkien's *The Notion Club Papers*, the harp in the poem becomes an emblem of ancient music and language itself, calling to the modern mind in an inexplicable way. That ancient music provides the "Door to Other Time" Tolkien found in Fairy Story – as does language itself. A study of an Old English translation of Psalm 137 ("By the Waters of Babylon") suggests that the harp already had such associations in Judeo-Christian tradition. Tolkien's philological comments on the word "harp" in an (undated) lecture to the Lincoln Musical Society illuminate the role of the harp image in Tolkien's creative imagination.

Introduction

As Allan Turner points out in his paper, the arguably most iconic line of English poetry to evoke the world of the imagination just on the edge of consciousness is "The horns of Elfland faintly blowing" from "The Princess" by Tennyson. The paper follows the tradition from Tennyson to Lord Dunsany's *The King of Elfland's Daughter* to Tolkien's Elves who are associated with songs that operate more on the unconscious mind than the conscious. Tolkien's essay accompanying *Smith of Wootton Major*, which has been little regarded by criticism so far, gives a clue that access to the world of Faërie depends on the willingness of mortals to make music of their own that can resonate in harmony with the immortal tones. Turner argues that echoes of this can be found in *The Lord of the Rings*.

From the perspective of an organist and creator of individually designed portative organs, Rainer Groß finally offers a speculative study on organ building in Middle-earth. He focuses on a small organ, the so called 'portative organ' or 'organetto', which is described in different examples by its medieval design and its possible appearance in Middle-earth.

Section V: "Music beyond Tolkien"

Finally, section V opens the window even more to other places beyond Middle-earth. Anja Müller takes a new approach to studying Tolkien and Wagner, a topic that has interested Tolkien scholars like Renée Vink, who also contributes to the present volume (see above), for many years. Müller examines the analogies and differences that can be traced between the two eponymous rings of power. A second chapter reads Wagner's *Oper und Drama* together with Tolkien's "On Faerie-stories", exploring the question in how far Wagner's idea of a music drama as *Gesamtkunstwerk* actually approaches the genre of "fantasy drama," which Tolkien believed to be impossible.

Patrick Schmitz compares the function of music in Patrick Rothfuss' *Kingkiller-Chronicles* with *The Lord of the Rings*. In doing so, similarities and differences between Tolkien's seminal work and the well-regarded piece of new fantasy literature are revealed.

Tobias Escher concludes the section and the book with his study of orchestral scores for Tolkien-based video games, a medium for adaptations often overlooked by literary scholarship. This paper reveals and discusses musical elements used and compares them to Tolkien's own writings about music and related subjects.

We hope that readers take delight in the rich variety of topics and approaches to music in Tolkien's work and beyond. As this book project is like its predecessor a joint venture between Walking Tree Publishers and the Edition Stein und Baum there are some articles which have been originally published in German or English and had to be translated into the respective language for the publication. We are very thankful to the translators who took their precious time to come up with wonderful translations in which they tried to keep the individual style of the original paper wherever possible. Without their help the challenging undertaking of publishing the books in two languages with 21 papers would not have been possible to realize. The great number of papers presented here is also responsible for the fact that the editing and translation process took us much longer than intended and expected. We, therefore, would like to thank all contributors for their support, patience, and continuous loyalty during the four years of putting together this volume. The German volume will be published in the Edition Stein und Baum by the Mannheim publisher Wolkenmühle-Verlag Daniela Osietzki. Those interested in the original German papers can find them there.

We wish our readers a pleasant journey through the fascinating realm of music and song in Tolkien's work (and beyond).

August 2019
Julian Eilmann & Friedhelm Schneidewind

TOLKIEN AND MUSIC

Chiara Bertoglio

Polyphony, Collective Improvisation, and the Gift of Creation

Abstract

Tolkien's creation myth, as transmitted in the *Silmarillion* and in other sources, describes the Ainur's singing as a form of collective polyphonic improvisation. This singing derives from the themes "declared" by Ilúvatar, which are – it will be argued – a form of divine self-revelation (and therefore of knowledge) imparted to the Ainur within the framework of a personal relationship with the God. The beauty of the Ainur's improvisation thus depends on their revealed knowledge of the creator's mind, on their loving attitude to Him and to their brethren, and on their acceptance of the rules and limitations of created beings as a gift which enables their singing to achieve its fulfillment and perfection. This approach, as will be discussed, is Tolkien's development of topics and imagery abundantly found in religious, literary, musical and mythological sources of the past.

Introduction

The entire, fascinating narrative of Tolkien's *legendarium* seems to spring from the pages of the *Ainulindalë*, whose creation myth opens the *Silmarillion* and has been published, in an earlier version, in the first *Book of Lost Tales*. Tolkien readers are familiar with this epic-sounding tale, which has frequently been discussed under literary, philosophical, theological and musical viewpoints, and yet has still much to reveal and to offer to our reflection. The powerful image of matter and history coming forth from the Ainur's music and vision embodies and symbolises the beauty, power and rationality of the creating being(s). The Ainur's songs unfold from Ilúvatar's theme; their distinctive melodies are at once variations and developments of the original theme, and yet are embedded, from the outset, in Ilúvatar's initial "declaration".

In this paper, I will first recall briefly the content of the opening pages of the *Ainulindalë*, pointing out a few details which may require further attention;

then, in a comparatively lengthy section, I will cite from a number of theological, literary and musical sources which will provide the necessary background for a more thorough comprehension of Tolkien's creation myth. We will see that certain of its features can be traced back to primeval mythologies and traditional tales, principally originating in the British Islands, but sharing elements with non-European lore. Other traits are deeply inscribed in the Western culture, with its Greek, Latin and Christian heritage (in particular the concept of cosmological "harmony" as the musical expression of the universal order). In consideration of Tolkien's Christian background, I will dedicate some space to specifically theological views of harmony, as a characterizing feature of the "city of God" and of the heavenly society of the blessed. In their blissful condition, angels and saints rejoice in God and in His other creatures, and know each other in and through their knowledge of God. This is a gift, progressively bestowed on them, and yet by definition inexhaustible, since no created being can penetrate the fullness of God's mystery. These theological concepts, which have shaped the Western depiction and understanding of everlasting and eternal life in heaven, are also at the roots of literary creations which may have been known to Tolkien and can therefore have inspired, at least in part, his fascinating vision of the Ainur's song.

This multidisciplinary framework, which will have no ambition or pretence to thoroughness, and is simply to be intended as a selected – though significant – sample, is however the necessary cultural background for my ensuing discussion of early polyphony. That section aims at providing readers with a musicological perspective which delineates the forms of Western medieval polyphony and how they dovetailed with improvised practices. The role of *cantus firmus* in several polyphonic styles, the challenges, techniques and strategies of collective improvisation and the relationship of these musical aspects with the overall topics of knowledge, creativity and epistemology will be discussed in turn.

Though I will constantly attempt to direct the reader's attention to the relevance of the issues under discussion to a deeper understanding of Tolkien's *Ainulindalë*, the last section of this essay will show more explicitly how the multiple and diverse facets of the preceding exposition concur in creating a unified whole, and how these numerous viewpoints are indispensable for gaining a comprehensive understanding of Tolkien's creation myth.

Framing the *Ainulindalë*

Indeed, this myth presents several interpretive challenges, many of which have been extensively discussed in Tolkien scholarship, while others have perhaps been slightly neglected. For instance, it is rather common to refer to Ilúvatar's "song": however, Tolkien is very careful to avoid all singing-related terms when referring to Ilúvatar, who is constantly said to speak ("And he spoke to them, propounding to them themes of music") or declare ("[Ilúvatar] declared to them a mighty theme", "Of the theme I have declared to you": *S* 15).[1] How are we to understand the "declaration" of a "theme of music"? As I will argue later, this singular choice may signify the transmission to the Ainur of a form of *knowledge*, rather than an immediately *poietic* (or musical) activity by Ilúvatar.

The themes he "propounds" to the Ainur are given to them; the Ainur first sing individually, "for each comprehended only that part of the mind of Ilúvatar from which he came, and in the understanding of their brethren they grew but slowly", and then "they came to deeper understanding, and increased in unison and harmony" (*S* 15). Then Ilúvatar asks the Ainur to "adorn" the theme of the Great Music, and the Ainur's singing progressively unfolds in "endless interchanging melodies woven in harmony" (*S* 15); and, after Melkor brings discord in the Music, prompting Ilúvatar to respond with new themes which embody Melkor's variations within them, the Music is brought to an ending "in one chord" (*S* 17.)[2] The nature of this chord has frequently gone unquestioned by the commentators: is it an abrupt ending, an "interrupted music"? Or is it a powerful musical "resolution" of the tension created in the earlier music, as the very use of the term "chord" seems to imply?[3] While I do not pretend to offer a definitive answer to this question, which was probably left purposefully open by the author, I suggest a Biblical model for this passage. Just as the Book of Job may have given to Tolkien the idea of creation happening "while the morning stars sang together and all the angels[4] shouted together" (Job 38.7), the divine theophany described in the same book may represent an equivalent to Tolkien's chord. The Hebrew God reveals Himself in his power and incomprehensible wisdom to Job, and

---

1 Cf. *LT I* 52, where just one initial reference is made to Ilúvatar "singing [the Ainur] into being".
2 I have discussed the topic of Tolkien's "musical theodicy" in Bertoglio, "Dissonant Harmonies."
3 For a discussion of the semantic field of "chord" and its related terms, see Spitzer 88.
4 Hebrew: "sons of God".

brings to an end his friends' endless discussions on the problem of evil by simply revealing his mysterious omnipotence. For Christians, the question left open in the Book of Job finds its answer on the Cross: the problem of evil cannot be fully comprehended outside the framework of Christ's incarnation, death and resurrection, so – in the provisional absence of this full revelation – it has to be contemplated in the awe of created beings in front of their Creator. Thus, since Tolkien avoids explicit references to Christianity in his *legendarium*, the Ainur's music is driven to a chord which demonstrates Ilúvatar's omnipotence, but at the same time does not entirely conclude the music, leaving a space open for a future revelation, a new music which will be sung by all creation at the end of times.

It ought also to be taken into account that the *Ainulindalë* is fictionally described by Tolkien as an *Elven* creation myth (*L* 147; cf. Flieger 51). Indeed, the *legendarium* constantly refers to the Elves' vocation/temptation to be the preservers of beauty (cf. Milbank 7): so, in my opinion, it is particularly fitting that a *musical* myth should be the form in which the Elves express their deepest beliefs about the origin and meaning of the world, since music lives only in the present, is a syntax of time and yet eludes all attempts to be congealed and fixed. In a reality outside time, such as that of the divine mind, all moments are simultaneously present in an eternal instant; the unfolding and revelation of the divine thought in the comprehension of the created beings is a translation from the atemporal to the temporal, symbolised by the most temporal of all arts, music.

It is therefore my goal to reflect on some musical implications of these first few pages of the *Silmarillion*, to illustrate their relationship with earlier literary, philosophical and theological writings, and to compare them with the actual history of musical composition, improvisation and polyphony in the Western world. While space limits will constrain my exposition to sketchy references, I wish to clarify that, in most cases, I cannot establish with any certainty whether Tolkien was familiar with any individual possible source of influence; however, given his academic accomplishment and omnivorous reading, I think that many of them were known to him and may have inspired, at least as a background atmosphere, his creation of the *Ainulindalë*.

Creation Myths and the Harmony of the Spheres

Music plays a role in several creation myths, some of which, interestingly, originated in the British Islands. While the Anglo-Druidic *Barddas* is considered by scholars to be essentially a forgery, Tolkien the author may have been fascinated by its imagery: here God, "alone in the universe [...] said His own name, and the voice was so beautiful that the universe burst into being with sound, light and form".[5] The "melodious sweetness" of God's voice makes "nonentity [...] rejoice into life."[6] Similar myths are found in the New Hebrides (Leeming 1: 336), while Irish myths give order and ratio to the world through music and *poiesis* (*ibid.* 152). Along with Maya and Hopi "musical" myths (Larsen 12), which may or may not have been known to Tolkien, the cultural connections between Britain and India may have favoured his knowledge of the Hindu tales of the god Prajāpati, which show significant analogies with the *Ainulindalë*,[7] and those of the *Gandharvas*, superhuman singers who have many points in common with the Ainur.[8]

Along with ancestral mythology, Tolkien the scholar was certainly aware of the innumerable declinations of the Pythagorean theme of *harmonia mundi* and of the music of the spheres (whose relationship with the *Ainulindalë* has already been studied, e.g. in Eden 2003). In Plato's *Republic* (617b), the spheres revolve around Necessity: upon them, eight Sirens are seated, and sing each a note, making harmony together.[9] Ptolemy (*Harmonics*, III.3) locates harmony between Nature and Divinity, binding it to Reason: "For it belongs eternally to the gods, who remain forever the same" (in Godwin 23).

Along with well-known authors such as Plotinus or Boethius, this topic was discussed by late-medieval writers such as Jacques de Liège (c.1260-a.1330), whose insights are particularly fascinating. For him, the "citizens of heaven [...] have this music in perfection", since they "no longer contemplate God in a glass darkly through any exterior representation, but behold him directly, face to face"[10] (in

---

5 Leeming 1: 274. Cf. Williams 1: 47, 250-253, 259.
6 Williams 1: 259.
7 Cf. *Satapatha Brahmana*, Part III (SBE 41), 6.1.1, in Eggeling: 143ff; *Agnistoma* (JB. I-68) in Bodewitz 38.
8 Cf. Wilkins 362.
9 These Sirens are interpreted as gods by Macrobius, author of the fifth century CE (in Godwin 66). He also writes that "it is natural for everything that breathes to be captivated by music since the heavenly Soul that animates the universe sprang from music" (in Godwin 67-68).
10 Cf. 1 Cor. 13.12; 2 Cor. 3.18.

Godwin 133). Here Jacques touches upon the subject of knowledge, which, as I suggested earlier, is a key-concept for understanding Ilúvatar's "declarations" and the music of the Ainur. In this overarching harmony, which is made of "connection and unshakable concord among themselves and with God", the angels "receive [...] the divine illuminations and revelations", and see "the specific nature of everything else: their order, connection and concord" (in Godwin 134). Jacques is also careful to distinguish between his depiction of this heavenly music and Boethius' *musica mundana*, since Boethius, in Jacques' opinion, refers to "natural, mobile and sensible things", while Jacques to "metaphysical [...] and transcendent things" (in Godwin 136). Thus, the vision of God is transmitted as a form of knowledge and is expressed through a perfect, eternal music.

Giorgio Anselmi (b.1386-c.1443), living a century after Jacques, described the "holy throngs of blessed spirits", who "contend in song and in the ineffable beauty of their rivalling hymns" (in Godwin 146). Anselmi's description of the singing Seraphim (the highest order of angels) is very close to that of Tolkien's Ainur: "They exceed all the other orders of angels in wisdom and power and bliss, and also in joy; they [...] are called 'burning' because, having a fuller participation in the divine light, they are vouchsafed a more intense flame of love and joy and perfection. [...] [Their sphere] is the realm of eternal heaven, inaccessible to any creature of a lower one. This circle truly includes the melody of all those beneath it, utterly excelling all harmony" (in Godwin 150-151). For him, "the very soul of this great heavenly motion [...] will conform in its harmonious sound to those divine spirits, so that all the different consonant notes may combine with one another". Still, these consonances will be continuously varied, "sounding now a fourth, now a fifth, now an octave" (in Godwin 148), and the angels (with whom he identifies the Platonic Sirens), sing songs which "sound grander and more beautiful by their very diversity" (in Godwin 150). I will later discuss how this description of varied and improvised consonances fits perfectly with the contemporaneous creations in improvised polyphony.

In the seventeenth century, these concepts were abundantly discussed and originally reinterpreted by Athanasius Kircher (c.1601-1680). He wrote that "the seven planets sing with the Earth a perfect four-part harmony, in which dissonance is combined so artistically with consonance that it gives forth the sweetest chords in the world" (in Godwin 274). This harmony in diversity, which seems in fact to need diversity in order to be harmony, is guaranteed by the action of the "Harmost Nature", who distributes "celestial songsters in various choirs": while they are "different in sound", they "conspire in a consonant-dissonant union, ornamenting the world with their diversity and witnessing to the ineffable wisdom of that supermundane Harmost" (in Godwin 275). Those familiar with Tolkien's *Ainulindalë* will probably be impressed by the similarity between Kircher's musical cosmology (with its "consonant-dissonant union", the "ornamentation" and the "witness to the ineffable wisdom" of the God) and that described in the *Silmarillion*.

This varied, harmonious and complex polyphony is also described, more than a century later, by Johann von Dalberg (1760-1812), who portrays Urania's ruling of the "circling of the spheres", while "the silent night and the young day rejoice in the magic of her melodious voice". Directed by Urania, "the solemn melody of the creation sounds forth in antiphonal choirs", while both heavens and morality "are tones of the universal symphony", created, ordered and tuned by an "all-uniting Spirit" (in Godwin 336).

Theology

If several of the Christian writers among the authors quoted above understood the Platonic myth as a depiction of the heavenly city, some theologians expressed similar views in a different fashion. A figure which no Christian writer and scholar may ignore is, undoubtedly, that of St. Augustine. In his *Expositions on the Psalms* (150.5), Augustine explains the musical metaphor of the organ "to signify that [the saints] sound not each separately, but sound together in most harmonious diversity". Indeed, for Augustine, "even then [in heaven] the saints of God will have their differences, accordant, not discordant, that is, agreeing, not disagreeing, just as sweetest harmony arises from sounds differing indeed, but not opposed to one another". This heavenly harmony in diversity is made possible by the loving knowledge that the blessed creatures have of each other and of God himself. In his *City of God* (XXII.29.6), Augustine discusses how the citizens of heaven (human beings and angels) will know God and will know each other in the contemplation of God:[11] as I will discuss later, this knowledge

---

11 Similar concepts are discussed by Augustine in *On Care for the Dead* (14.17 and 15.18). I am grateful to Professor Alison Milbank for her valuable reading suggestions and thought-provoking ideas.

is indispensable for a harmonious musical understanding. If this applies to the redeemed world (the music "to come", in Tolkien's myths), even the primeval act of creation undergoes a similar process in Augustine's view. As Houghton (175ff.) correctly points out, the "five-part internal structure" of the divine creation as seen by Augustine in his *De Genesi ad litteram* (6.14.25-6.18.29) is the simultaneous happening of "God's eternal intention to create", creation "in the minds of the angels of a knowledge of what is to be made", creation proper (in reality or causal reason), the angels' beholding of creation and "God's eternal support of the Creation through the Holy Spirit". Thus, Augustine depicts the eschatological reality as a harmonious concert of diverse voices, whose possibility lies in the mutual knowledge given to the blessed by their contemplation of God; that same knowledge "in God" was present in the creative act, when some comprehension of God's deliberation and action were transmitted to the angels.

Along with Augustinian influences, Thomist perspectives are of course clearly distinguishable in Tolkien's vision. In his *Summa* (SIII.92), St. Thomas Aquinas discusses how the angels may know God, and the ultimate unknowability of God's essence: his account of this heavenly epistemology seems to provide a clear model for Tolkien's description of the Ainur's knowledge of the mind of Ilúvatar and of their brethren (cf. also Halsall 42). Moreover, the Ainur know and behold creation in the three degrees of Music, Vision and Being (cf. *S* 15, 17, 20): these seemingly mirror the three attributes of Beauty in Aquinas' view (if we interpret *consonantia* as referring to Music, *claritas* to Vision and *integritas* to Being: cf. I.q39.a8). On this ground, Collins (261) and McIntosh (*Ainulindalë* 63) have argued that the Thomist view of the created world expressed in Tolkien's *Ainulindalë* can hardly be construed as an actualization of a Platonic Great Chain of Being implying a progressive loss of perfection: rather, the creation of Being after Music and Vision represents the "realization, perfection or actualization of form" (ibid.).

A similar perspective, but with a fascinating "musical" resonance, is found in the writings of Aquinas' contemporary, St. Bonaventura. In the *Prologue* to his *Breviloquium* (2.4),[12] he compares the Bible to an "artfully composed song", where, in the "succession of events", it is possible to behold "the diversity, multiplicity

---

12 The cited translation interprets Bonaventure's Latin *carmen* as "poem", which is of course a legitimate translation. However, since most poetry was sung at Bonaventure's time, I think it possible to translate it as "song".

and symmetry, the order, rectitude and excellence of the many judgments that proceed from the divine wisdom governing the universe". Bonaventura also asserts that, "just as no one can appreciate the loveliness of a song unless one's perspective embraces it as a whole, so none of us can see the beauty of the order and governance of the world without an integral view of its course."[13] Bonaventura's symbolic language suggests a form of knowledge which is "musical" in its unfolding, and yet has something of Ainur's all-encompassing Vision: as we will later see, the condition for musical improvisation in polyphony is a knowledge whose "perspective embraces [the song] as a whole".

Literature

Bonaventura's language, with its combination of poetry and theology, leads us to the final part of this section, where I will suggest a few literary excerpts by authors writing in English, which may have had some bearing on Tolkien's shaping of the *Ainulindalë*. For example, Milton's *At a Solemn Music* is a reinterpretation of Plato's mythical Sirens, who sing for "him that sits" on the "saphire-colour'd throne", in the company of spirits and angels. The earthly beings join "with undiscording voice", as they "once [...] did, till disproportion'd sin [...] / Broke the fair musick that all creatures made / To their great Lord". Notwithstanding the discordance brought in the music by evil, as by Melkor among the Ainur, Milton, similar to Tolkien, contemplates a greater music to come: "O may we soon again renew that Song / And keep in tune with Heav'n, till God ere long / To his celestial consort us unite, / To live with him and sing in endles morn of light" (in Quiller-Couch 309).

A closely-related image is found in *A Litany* by John Donne, who, in stanza XIV, depicts "this universal quire / That Church in triumph, this in warfare here, / Warm'd with one all-partaking fire", which calls unto mind Tolkien's Imperishable Flame as well as the "integral view" seen in Bonaventura. Later (stanza XXIII), Donne beseeches the Lord to hear the sinners' prayer, since "to Thee / A sinner is more music, when he prays, / Than spheres' or angels' praises be / In panegyric alleluias" (Donne, *Poems* 174ff). Though Donne's language is explicitly Christian, here too we find a consistent use of musical metaphors

---

13 Translation as found in McIntosh, *Bonaventure* with adaptations.

to symbolise both the holy harmony and its disruption through sin. The same author employed an analogous metaphor in one of his *Sermons* (Donne, *Sermons* 2: 170, n. 7), where he states that "God made this whole world in such a uniformity, such a *correspondency*, such a *concinnity* of parts that it was an *Instrument, perfectly in tune*: we may say, the trebles, the highest strings were disordered first; the best understandings, angels and men, put this instrument out of tune". As in Tolkien and in the Christian teaching, evil is said to have begun with the "highest" intellects, here assimilated to "the trebles", whose discordance caused the corruption of the whole harmony.

Better known than Donne's *Sermons* is certainly Shakespeare's *Merchant of Venice* (V.1), where the centuries-old image of the harmony of the spheres is evoked by the "orb" which "in his motion like an angel sings, / Still quiring to the young-eyed cherubins" (Shakespeare 169): the harmony "is in immortal souls", but their being incrusted by a "muddy vesture of decay" makes them unable to hear it. It is however to the pre-Romantic poet Edward Young that I will now turn for one of the most impressive anticipations of Tolkien's *Ainulindalë*: in his *Night Thoughts*, Young describes "The song of Angels, all the melodies / Of choral gods". Since angels, unlike humans, are not in need of redemption, the angels are paradoxically less blessed than the redeemed sinners: "View man, to see the glory of your God! / Could angels envy, they had envied here; / And some did envy; and the rest, though gods, / Yet still gods unredeem'd (their triumphs man, / Tempted to weigh the dust against the skies), / They less would feel, though more adorn, my theme. / They sung [sic] creation (for in that they shared); / How rose in melody, that child of love!" (Young 74). The "envy" of angels for humans (which is described by Tolkien as Melkor's malignant jealousy and other Ainur's enchanted and admiring gaze), the "less felt" *adornment* of God's theme by the angels, the "sung creation" which rises in melody are all fascinating parallels to Tolkien's *Ainulindalë*, and – rather probably – sources of inspiration for its author.

The Ainur's Music and the History of Polyphony

While not all of the above-mentioned references may have been known to Tolkien, there is positive proof that he was familiar with two other sources, which constitute therefore an ideal bridge between the literary/philosophical framework I have hitherto sketched and the musical discussion which will follow. Amid Tolkien's scholarly writings, *A Middle English Vocabulary* (*ME*) is a valuable practical tool for interpreting the anthology of fourteenth-century English literature collected by Sisam. Among other musical terms in *ME*, the definition of "Gle, Glew" is – in my opinion – particularly interesting (*ME* 62). It is described as "(skill in) making music, minstrelsy", and the lemma is illustrated with a quote from a poem by Robert Mannyng of Brunne: "*made hem glew*, directed their singing" (cf. Sisam 5 and *ME* 62). This definition is preceded by another meaning of the word, i.e. "mirth, pleasure, play", thus establishing a significant connection between music-making and mirth, the skill of "directing [a choir's] singing" and "pleasure, play."[14] We will see that this semantic link is interestingly developed in Tolkien's *Ainulindalë*.

In *ME* (41), Tolkien also lists the technical term *deschaunt*, which is found in Wycliffe's *Of feigned contemplative life*: "And of schort tyme thane [weren] more veyn iapis founden: deschaunt, countre note, and orgon, and smale brekynge, that stirith veyn men to daunsynge more than [to] mornynge."[15] Sisam's endnote to this Wycliffe quote (Sisam 246) discusses the technique of the discant: though the definition does not correspond to the achievements of today's musicology, and makes no mention of improvised practices, it is however basically correct, and we can safely assume that Tolkien knew it well.

Early Polyphonic Forms

Wycliffe was condemning the increasing use of polyphonic techniques in the church music of his time: I will now sketchily summarise a few of them, with particular attention to those practised in Britain. In England, written sources describe discant against a plainsong since the fourteenth century: it consisted of an upper voice, moving note-against-note above the *cantus firmus*; dissonances were forbidden, perfect consonances (fifths and octaves) had to avoid parallel motion, and imperfect consonances were recommended (we may recall here the

---

14 In *ME*, there is also the interesting definition of "hoppit" as "leapt", and "hoppyng" as "dancing". Thus, the very etymology of the Hobbits' name is connected with music and dancing (*ME* 73).
15 Sisam 123: "And shortly more vain delusions were found: discant, counterpoint and *organum*, and small breakings [of the voice], which stir vain men to dancing more than to mourning" (my modernization).

intervals listed in Anselmi's musical/cosmological depiction: in Godwin 150). On the Continent, starting with the thirteenth century, two-part discant was progressively enriched with further voices: these were "composed not simultaneously in relation to each other, but either independently or each one in relation to the tenor alone" (Flotzinger I.4). Thus, even in composed music of the thirteenth century, polyphony was created "by adding one line at a time to a previously worked-out melody, each of the added lines agreeing with this melody but not necessarily with each other" (Horsley II.2.i), and therefore it closely resembled – both in technique and in its aural shape – improvised polyphony. We may note the primacy of the *cantus firmus* in determining the overall structure of polyphony, since every individual added melody had to be in relationship with it, while the relationships among secondary melodies were looser and less determining.

The polyphonic form most typical for medieval England was the *faburden*, which may be loosely defined as a kind of improvisation with strict rules, or performance without a written score. Here, the original *cantus firmus* was sung by the middle voice (Mean or Mene); "faburden" was also the name of the *lower* voice, which moved in thirds and fifths under the plainchant, while a third upper voice, the treble, "could be added at the fourth above [the plainsong] with no risk of collisions. The result would sound, superficially, like the familiar progressions of English discant" (Trowell 52-53). Thanks to a system of mental transpositions (the "sights", a word fascinatingly reminiscent of Tolkien's "vision"), faburden singers could practise a kind of music "in which many sing together, but none of the singers produces those sounds which the notes on the page indicate", as Erasmus described it (in Miller 341). In sum, several of the early polyphonic techniques were based on a system of rules which enabled singers to "improvise" together: pitches were not defined beforehand (and thus the result was different from what we would call "performance of a written score"), but at the same time the range of possible choices was so limited that it allowed several singers to "improvise" together. As the Pseudo-Tunstede (c.1350) described it, "as long as you are discanting beneath the plainchant, no one may discant above, unless he is previously acquainted with the pitch-levels of the lower voices, because all of the upper voices must make consonance with the lowest" (in Besser Scott 347).

Collective Improvisation

Indeed, this brief digression on early polyphonic techniques aims at showing how multivoiced "improvisation" could be realized: the singers/improvisers had to behold a fixed *cantus firmus* (which could be read from a choir book or known by memory) and a rigid set of rules, the compliance with which allowed a certain freedom in the choice of pitches and, at the same time, a consonant aural result. As Horsley (II.2.i) puts it, "the problem of improvising a melody to fit with a given chant required a technical knowledge of vertical consonance and dissonance and of the melodic materials available in the diatonic system. Furthermore, while at first the improvising singer may have relied on his memory of the chant to which he was adding a counter-melody, the improvisers eventually saw this chant in some sort of visual notation so that they could anticipate its notes".

Fascinatingly, improvised polyphony was considered as a typical feature of Welsh music already in the twelfth century (and we know Tolkien's particular interest in medieval Wales). Giraldus Cambrensis, writing in the 1190s, described the practices of Welsh musicians as follows: "When they make music together, they sing their tunes not in unison, as is done elsewhere, but in parts with many simultaneous modes and phrases. Therefore, in a group of singers (which one very often meets within Wales) you will hear as many melodies as there are people, and a distinct variety of parts; yet they all accord in one consonant and properly constituted composition" (in Sternfeld 1: 264). Here too it may be inferred that Tolkien the medievalist may have known this work and the description quoted above, which would therefore provide a fascinating model for the music of the Ainur.

Indeed, as Nettl points out ("Thoughts" 4), the very concept of improvisation is seemingly self-explanatory, but becomes elusive when one tries to pinpoint it. For this reason, he prefers to describe it in terms of practices rather than of an opposition of written and unwritten: research on musical improvisation "deals with concepts of risk, competence, dealing with unexpected situations and making positive use of mistakes" (Nettl, "Improvisation" I.1). This leads us again to the music of the Ainur, and particularly to the theme of their knowledge of each other, which is the prerequisite for their ensemble music-making. Ilúvatar's themes, which create a musical dialogue with the rebellious melodies of Melkor and ultimately embody them – even if reluctantly – in the Music, can be seen as a transcendent version of the human "dealing with unexpected situations and making positive use of mistakes" quoted above; at the same time, since we may suppose that the Ainur would only attempt to sing together when certain of a beautiful result, the element of "risk" in their improvisation would be consequently downplayed.

Collective improvisation is also practised in jazz, where the term is employed "where some or all members of a group participate in simultaneous improvisation of equal or comparable 'weight'": therefore it "implies a degree of equality between all the players in the ensemble" (Kernfeld III.2), in contrast with the hierarchical concept of soloist and accompanist(s) which characterizes most improvisations in jazz music. As in the early polyphony discussed above, it is far easier to obtain an aurally satisfying result when only one musician is free to improvise, and the other(s) perform a known scheme, tune or harmony, upon which the improvised part can move with a certain freedom. When two or more musicians actually improvise together, and there is equality among them, "no matter how intimately they know one another's work, some agreed decisions about the progress of a piece are normally necessary"; thus, "certain prearranged schemes, such as the sequence in which soloists should play and the signals by which players will communicate decisions, are usually followed" (Kernfeld III.3).

Improvisations vs. Models

In jazz music, thus, the improvising musicians constantly refer to "prearranged schemes", such as, for example, harmonic and chordal sequences. A topic central to the musicological debate on improvisation is in fact that of the relationship between an improvisation and its *model*. As Nettl ("Improvisation" I.3) puts it, a model is a "point of departure used as the basis of performance. No improvised performance is totally without stylistic or compositional basis. The number and kinds of obligatory features (referred to here as the 'model') vary by culture and genre". Since models, as said, may take a variety of shapes according to their historical-geographical context, a particular culture's concept of musical improvisation may be very different from another. The same scholar, writing on Indian music, observes that "the improviser, when he performs a variety of versions of one mode (*raga, dastgah, maqam,* etc.) is really doing precisely that – performing a version of something, not improvising upon something. In other words, he is giving a rendition of something that already exists, be it a song or a theoretical musical entity. And its basic 'table of contents' is set" (Nettl, "Thoughts" 9). Thus, the model of an improvisation may be "actual music [...] performed without improvisation", or "material that the musician learns but does not execute in a true performance", or a "largely theoretical subject matter, consisting of verbal instructions and exercises" (ibid. 16). In the case of Western medieval improvised polyphony, "the model may be a tune sung by one voice (against which the other is to improvise) and a set of allowable harmonic intervals as well as their characteristic sequences" (ibid. 12).

The relationship between a model and its improvised "version", therefore, is culturally determined; in consequence, the artistry of an improvised music is culturally evaluated in terms of the listeners' expectations. Here, too, we may find contrasting viewpoints: for example, listeners of the collective improvisations of Javanese *gamelan* appreciate most those improvisers who move most from their model (Nettl, "Improvisation" I.2). In other cultures, instead, "the musician who is highly creative and tries to avoid using the points of reference and the building blocks of the model is chastised for his ignorance of the model" (Nettl, "Thoughts" 18-19). Thus, Melkor's deviation from Ilúvatar's model can be seen either as a proud and illegitimate rebellion, which destroys the Ainur's harmony, or as a creative achievement. Since the Ainur are enacting a collective improvisation, indeed, their abiding to the "model" is crucial for the maintenance of an overall harmony, as I will discuss more deeply in the following pages.

The "model", whatever its nature, is therefore both a help and a limit for the creativity of the improviser. Busse Berger (215) has studied the mnemonic techniques used by orators in the classical antiquity and by musical improvisers in the Middle Ages, and has established that the elaboration of speech, as well as of musical improvisations, is based on the memorization of "a background grid of places, say an architectural structure", which is then visualized when the speech is delivered. "Thus", for Busse Berger, "the art of memory is a kind of imaginary writing". This combination of imaginary visualization, memory, creativity and aural result is in turn highly relevant both to polyphonic improvisation (as, for instance, in faburden singing, with the "sights") and to the Ainur's music, where music and vision are intimately intertwined. (Fascinatingly, however, Caporaletti [106] points out that the etymology of "improvisation" refers to *in-provideo*, i.e. something that cannot be "foreseen"). If a visualized or otherwise retained model is indispensable for the creation, elaboration and delivery of a verbal or musical composition which is not read contextually to its performance, the models for improvisation can also be seen as limits or limitations to the improviser's fantasy.

In our society, which prizes autonomy and self-determination above most other values, limits and limitations have an inherently negative connotation. However, both in the "real" Middle Ages when polyphony was created and in the fictional epic past of Tolkien, limits are given to created beings for their own good, as the boundary within which they can flourish in fullness. As argued by Montemaggi with reference to Dante's Ulysses, who defies the Pillars of Hercules which delimit human knowledge, these Pillars are a gift. They are "a reminder that ultimate comprehension of the world is not even in principle available to human beings": all alternative construal of their reality implies misunderstanding "what it means to say 'God', or the fact that God is love". Thus, they remind us that the individual's "pursuit of knowledge" should "never lose sight of the proper dynamics of community" (Montemaggi 73-74).

A completely free improvisation is possible only in the absolute absence of relationships: in fact, even a solo improviser who is singing according to his or her own fantasy will do this within a framework of rules (at least those of pitch and rhythm) which will make his or her improvisation meaningful and therefore intelligible for the listeners. Absolute freedom implies incommunicability. The Ainur's improvisation must therefore take into account their relationship with Ilúvatar and with the themes ("models") he "declares" to them, and the contemporaneous musical intentions of their brethren. Polyphonic improvisation is therefore deeply relational.

It is also a kind of game or play, where rules are given and accepted for the purpose of mutual enjoyment. Here, Tolkien's awareness of the Middle-English meaning of "glew" (see above) as "play/mirth" and as a kind of musical conducting comes to the fore, and can be compared to Dante's use of "*gioco*" (play, game) to depict the blessed life (*Purgatorio* 28.96; *Paradiso* 20.117). This "gioco" is the framework within which "the flourishing of virtue, of the dynamics of community" are made possible (Montemaggi 76). Music has indeed the gratuitous enjoyment of beauty which characterizes play in its highest essence, and which can therefore be seen as a symbol for the contemplation of God. As Mazzotta (227) suggests, commenting on Dante, "As the creation of the soul is grounded in God's play activity, this view of God means that to play is to accept rules established by God; it also means that man is not to play God, but to be content with God's play as he lets the soul play". Playfulness, thus, transforms both rules and limits into gifts enabling creativity and freedom.

As I have elsewhere demonstrated,[16] Dante's perspective faithfully echoes Augustine's view of a perfect society (*City of God* XIX.13): "The peace of the celestial city is the perfectly ordered and harmonious enjoyment of God and one another in God". The musical concept of harmony is further developed in its aural implications in the same work by Augustine (II.21), where he suggests that the concord of diversity is not just the actual reality of the heavenly city, but also the ideal model for a peaceful earthly society. We have seen in the preceding sections that the possibility of harmonizing diversity was a trait commonly acknowledged by writers discussing polyphony as a symbol for perfect societies (earthly or heavenly); it is fascinating that this same view is found already in the (possible) surprising mention of polyphony by John Scotus Eriugena, writing as early as the ninth century (cf. Spitzer 41). On the other hand, one of the greatest modern Catholic theologians, Hans Urs von Balthasar, has defined Truth as being "symphonic", and described it in tones highly reminiscent of the Ainur's concert: "In his revelation, God performs a symphony, and it is impossible to say which is richer: the seamless genius of his composition or the polyphonous orchestra of Creation that he has prepared to play it. [...] The unity of the composition comes from God". For Balthasar, in a fashion similar to the Ainur's at the beginning of their musical attempts, musicians tuning up their instruments before the concert "stand or sit next to one another as strangers"; but later "they realize how they are integrated. Not in unison, but what is far more beautiful – in sym-phony". And it is precisely by means of limits that the symphony is made possible: "Today's situation [...] is characterized by an impatient tugging at the framework of a unity that is felt to be a prison. Isn't it unjust that a melody is trapped within a triple fugue, and

---

16 See Bertoglio, "Dante, Tolkien, and the Supreme Harmony."

that the law of the fugue governs how it shall develop – and even determines its original shape?" (Balthasar 7-8). In every polyphonic work, be it composed or improvised, the very fact of singing or playing together implies reciprocal limitations; these are, however, the necessary condition for all relationality and for the very existence of a polyphonic composition such as a fugue.

This relational aspect – which is at the root of our discussion of collective improvisation – was also conceived in musical terms by another great modern theologian, the Lutheran Dietrich Bonhoeffer, who maintained that our love for God should be the *cantus firmus* of our lives, with all other loves, relationships and interests constituting a counterpoint to it: "Where the *cantus firmus* is clear and plain, the counterpoint can be developed to its limits. [...] I wanted to tell you to have a good, clear *cantus firmus*: that is the only way to a full and perfect sound, when the counterpoint has a firm support and can't come adrift or get out of tune, while remaining a distinct whole in its own right" (Bonhoeffer 106).

Cantus Firmus and Polyphony

In comparison with other forms of musical composition and improvisation, therefore, early polyphony was grounded on the *cantus firmus*, to which an improvised/composed second voice could be added, note against note (discant), or which could be framed by the lower and upper melodies extemporaneously created by faburden singers, or which could be sung in long values, upon which more elaborated melodies created lighter musical garlands (*organum melismaticum*). Since in early polyphony most *cantus firmus* were taken from the liturgical plainchant repertoire, the *cantus firmus*' role in determining the most important features of the polyphonic composition corresponded to the religious sacredness of the plainchant repertoire. The *cantus firmus* was not only the root of the eventual composition, but its germinating force; since all parts had to relate themselves with it, the *cantus firmus* could be seen as embodying the entire range of musical possibilities, as comprising in potency all of its polyphonic developments.

Moreover, polyphonic composition embodies a concept of plurality which not only reconciles diversity and variety in unity, but also gives a multi-dimensional breadth (and therefore a significant enrichment in meaning) to the individual lines concurring in it. As Lippmann (59ff) suggests, listeners form a set of expectations about the development and unfolding of monodic singing (unaccompanied individual melodies), while the interplay of two or more melodies intertwining in polyphonic music both challenges and delights the attentive hearer: listeners' expectations "can be divided into two or three separately flowing channels of consciousness", which have also "intercommunication and mutual influence", so that "there is a unifying total consciousness along with the streams of individualized experience". Thus, a polyphonic composition is an organic whole which both encompasses and transcends the single melodies, and at the same time partially transfigures them through their very interplay, which gives them new meanings and direction.

At the same time, in early polyphony, the architectural role of the *cantus firmus* was pivotal for the entire musical concept, so that the derivate parts could be aurally equal to it, but were causally secondary: and this applied to improvised polyphony as well. In the case of *super librum* improvisation (i.e. the extemporaneous addition of parts to the *cantus firmus*), the given plainchant constituted the fixed frame, the pillars of the work, which the added voices ought to respect, with which they had to conform and which therefore largely determined their shape. When Vicente Lusitano, in 1553, first codified the centuries-old techniques of polyphonic improvisations, he suggested to his readers some schemes in long note-values, which constituted a kind of note-against-note structure which could be superimposed to the given *cantus firmus*; these patterns could afterwards be ornamented in the fashion of the *organum melismaticum*. Other techniques of polyphonic improvisation were more complex, as the improvised canons described by Gioseffo Zarlino (302ff): here, as Horsley (II.2.i) puts it, "the leading singer must know all the possible combinations at specific times over precise pitches, and those following him must have good ears and memories". These techniques, as well as those regulating improvised variations, were extremely sophisticated and allowed musicians to improvise together without tonal clashes, as surprising as it may be, for us, that "two, three, or even four singers could anticipate each other's moves" (Busse Berger 162).

When the musicians improvising polyphonically were particularly skilled, knew each other well, and employed the improvisation techniques properly, the result was however impressive: it gave to listeners the impression of an almost superhuman foreknowledge of each other's musical intentions.

This magical or transcendent feeling is beautifully conveyed in a treatise (1274) by Elias Salomo (c.1229-c.1294), which is also illustrated by a fascinating image which could be taken as a depiction of the Ainur's music. In Salomo's description (Ch. 30), the four singers are led by a *rector* (conductor), and their parts all relate to the bass, entering in progression from the lowest to the highest; eye-contact is indispensable. The attached image shows the four singers disposed as to form a crescent ("*ad modum lunae*", thus with an explicit cosmological reference) around a choir book where the *cantus firmus* is visible by all. As Ferand (318) points out, the visual arrangement is such "that they are – literally – 'bound' by the rules and directions, laid down for the first time, for four-part singing". To enhance the cosmological significance of the drawing, the singers wear robes embroidered with crescents or stars. Both the *cantus firmus* and the treatise's rules, therefore, constitute the net of references and models which makes the improvised polyphony possible; these laws are not seen as a straightjacket forcedly imposed onto the singers' freedom, but rather as their chance to create, with their music, an aural equivalent of the cosmological order symbolized by their robes and position.

Polyphony, Relationship, and Knowledge

It is now my goal to gather the threads which have been left loose in the preceding pages, and to offer an interpretation of the *Ainulindalë* which takes into account the complex web of cultural, musical and theological sources cited above. Ilúvatar's themes can be seen as the Ainur's *cantus firmus*. His themes have a sacredness which corresponds to the liturgical origin of the plainchant repertoire used as the *cantus firmus* of early medieval polyphony. They constitute the pillars which at the same time delimit and permit the Ainur's creativity. Ilúvatar's communication of the themes to the Ainur is also a self-revelation of this divine character; it is the establishment of an intellectual and personal relationship which is based on the Ainur's freedom and intelligence, both of which are in turn gifts of the God. The initial self-knowledge of the Ainur is therefore determined by their relationship with their creator: each Ainu has some knowledge of the "part" of the mind of Ilúvatar whence he or she originates. Thus, even the Ainur's "I" cannot be conceived outside their "I-Thou" relationship with their creator.

Being creatures, the Ainur can neither aim to nor have full knowledge of Ilúvatar's mind: as maintained by Augustine and Aquinas with reference to the angelic and blessed spirits, it is not in the nature of created beings to have the possibility of "comprehending", quite literally, the mind of their creator. By responding to Ilúvatar's call to life and to (secondary) creativity, the Ainur start to make music, at first individually; in so doing, they reveal themselves to their brethren, who, consequently, grow both in the knowledge of each other and of Ilúvatar himself. The more an Ainu hears of another's music, the more their reciprocal knowledge increases; this cannot be done outside a relational framework, since an Ainu's singing is the aural embodiment of his or her deepest being, which is freely given and offered to the others. When an Ainu sings, he or she is responding to the primeval call of Ilúvatar (and thus is deepening his or her loving relationship with the creator) but at the same time is revealing his or her intimate being to the other Ainur.

Their attempts to sing together, at first with some shyness and then more confidently, depend on their reciprocal knowledge: as I hope to have demonstrated in the preceding pages, the possibility of improvising polyphonically without clashes is entirely dependent on the singers' reciprocal knowledge and to their melodies' relationship with the model (which was constituted by the *cantus firmus* and the improvisation rules in the early polyphony of the Western Middle Ages). These rules were intended in a fashion similar to that of game-rules: nobody would enjoy a game with no rules, since there would be no meaning and no purpose in playing. The same applies to music: the spontaneous emission of sounds expressing only the individual musician's occasional fancy produces a chaotic, disordered, nonsensical and ultimately disagreeable cacophony. Melkor fails to see the given rules and theme as a gift: he wants to affirm his own singing not only in defiance of Ilúvatar, but also in a hegemonic position with respect to his brethren. Instead of a collective improvisation played on a ground of equality, he wants to establish his standing as a soloist, to whom the other musicians must be subordinated as accompanists. This would increase his share of creative "freedom", at the expense of the others, whose music must become subservient to his own.

The image of polyphonic singing, thus, is a marvelous symbol for a number of theological and philosophical truths. It points out the gratuitous and creative beauty of a "playful" activity which has – seemingly – no other purpose beyond itself and the enjoyment it gives to both players and listeners. It underpins the relational quality of all knowledge, be it the knowledge of God or that of created beings. It indicates a model for these relationships: when the given model or theme is respected, all players can express themselves in fullness and thus achieve their individual and social fulfilment. Polyphony is more beautiful than any individual melody taken by itself, and its aesthetic value is greater than the sum of its parts; thus, by renouncing the temptation of individual power, which affirms itself at the expenses of another being, the individual is in fact empowered, since the single melody is incorporated within a greater, higher and more beautiful reality. Complex polyphonic improvisation is only possible, therefore, when there is full and loving knowledge of the intentions of all performers: and this knowledge, which has the simultaneity and instantaneity of vision, can only be contemplated in the mind of a superior, divine Being. Thus, Music, Vision and Being are distinct moments of Tolkien's narration, but they also are the three simultaneous embodiments of a concord of knowledge, beauty and creativity. And – it could be added – though Ilúvatar is described differently from the Christian Triune God, these three features strikingly correspond to some traits which have traditionally been ascribed to the three divine Persons of the Christian Trinity: the Father as Creator, the Son as Logos/Wisdom, the Holy Spirit as Gift/Beauty. For Christians, indeed, it is precisely in the "polyphonic" nature of God that all harmony of relationships originates and can be found. So, even if Tolkien's myths purposefully and constantly avoid explicit references to the Christian dogmas, the Christian worldview is beautifully expressed, in symbols, by his fascinating narrative.

About the Author

CHIARA BERTOGLIO (Turin, 1983) is a concert pianist, musicologist and theologian. She graduated in piano at the Conservatory of Turin, in Switzerland and at the Accademia di Santa Cecilia in Rome; she obtained Master's Degrees in musicology (Venice and Rome) and a PhD in Music (Birmingham), followed by two Master's Degrees in theology (Rome and Nottingham). She is the author of several books and monographs, including *Reforming Music. Music and the Religious Reformations of the Sixteenth Century* (De Gruyter: 2017). Her website is www.chiarabertoglio.com.

List of Abbreviations of Tolkien's Works

L	*The Letters of J.R.R. Tolkien*
LT I	*The Book of Lost Tales, Part One*
ME	*A Middle English Vocabulary*
S	*The Silmarillion*

Bibliography

ALIGHIERI, Dante. *La Divina Commedia di Dante Alighieri*. http://bit.ly/2mdUewW. 23 May 2017.

AQUINAS, Thomas. *Summa Theologiae*. http://bit.ly/2qRwrFM. 23 May 2017.

AUGUSTINE OF HIPPO. *The City of God*. http://bit.ly/2oMCVpm. 23 May 2017.

De Genesi ad litteram libri duodecim. http://bit.ly/2qg5Qyn. 23 May 2017.

Expositions on the Psalms. http://bit.ly/2rwDGDP. 23 May 2017.

On the Care of the Dead. http://bit.ly/2q7GU0P. 23 May 2017.

Bertoglio, Chiara. "Dissonant Harmonies: Tolkien's musical theodicy." *Tolkien Studies* 15 (2018): 93-114 (doi:10.1353/tks.2018.0007).

"Dante, Tolkien e la musica delle sfere." *Tolkien e i classici II*. Eds. Roberto Arduini, Cecilia Barella, Giampaolo Canzonieri and Claudio A. Testi. Rome: Eterea, 2018, 55-67.

"Dante, Tolkien, and the Supreme Harmony." *Tolkien and the Classics*. Eds. Roberto Arduini, Giampaolo Canzonieri and Claudio A. Testi. Zurich and Jena: Walking Tree Publishers, 2019, 83-96.

BESSER SCOTT, Ann. "The Beginnings of Fauxbourdon: A New Interpretation." *Journal of the American Musicological Society* 24/3 (1971): 345-363.

BODEWITZ, Hendrik Wilhelm (ed.). *The Jyotiṣṭoma Ritual*. Leiden: Brill, 1990.

BONAVENTURE. *Prologue to the Breviloquium*. http://bit.ly/2qfW3IM. 23 May 2017.

BONHOEFFER, Dietrich. *Letters and Papers from Prison*. Ed. Eberhard Betge. London: SCM Press, 2017.

BUSSE BERGER, Anna Maria. *Medieval Music and the Art of Memory*. Berkeley, CA: University of California Press, 2005.

CAPORALETTI, Vincenzo. *I processi improvvisativi nella musica: un approccio globale.* Lucca: Libreria Musicale Italiana, 2005.

COLLINS, Robert. "'Ainulindalë': Tolkien's Commitment to an Aesthetic Ontology." *Journal of the Fantastic in the Arts* 11 (2000): 257-265.

DONNE, John. *The Poems of John Donne.* London: Lawrence & Bullen, 1896. http://bit.ly/2qRAQc2. 23 May 2017.

The Sermons of John Donne. Eds. George Potter and Evelyn Simpson. Berkeley, CA: University of California Press, 1953-1962.

EDEN, Bradford Lee. "The 'Music of the Spheres': Relationships between Tolkien's *The Silmarillion* and Medieval Cosmological and Religious theory." *Tolkien the Medievalist.* Ed. Jane Chance. New York City, NY and London: Routledge, 2003, 183-93.

EGGELING, Julius (trans.). *Satapatha Brahmana*, Part III. Delhi: Motilal Banarsidass, 1894. http://bit.ly/2rdCo0V. 23 May 2017.

FERAND, Ernst Th. "The 'Howling in Seconds' of the Lombards: A Contribution to the Early Polyphony." *The Musical Quarterly* 25/3 (July 1939): 313-324.

FLIEGER, Verlyn. *Interrupted Music: The Making of Tolkien's Mythology.* Kent, OH and London: The Kent State University Press, 2005.

FLOTZINGER, Rudolf. "Discant I. Discant in France, Spain and Germany. 4. Discant in three and four voices." *The New Grove Dictionary of Music and Musicians.* https://grovemusic.github.io. 23 May 2017.

GODWIN, Joscelyn. *The Harmony of the Spheres. A Sourcebook of the Pythagorean Tradition in Music.* Rochester: Inner Traditions, 1992.

HALSALL, Michael. "A Critical Assessment of the Influence of Neoplatonism in J. R. R. Tolkien's Philosophy of Life as 'Being and Gift'." PhD thesis, University of Nottingham. 2015.

HORSLEY, Imogene. "Improvisation. II. Western Art Music. 2. History to 1600. i. Ensemble improvisation." *The New Grove Dictionary of Music and Musicians.* https://grovemusic.github.io. 23 May 2017.

HOUGHTON, John William. "Augustine in the cottage of lost play: the Ainulindalë as asterisk cosmogony." *Tolkien the Medievalist.* Ed. Jane Chance. New York City, NY and London: Routledge, 2003, 171-182.

KERNFELD, Barry. "Improvisation. III. Jazz. 2. Solo and collective improvisation." *The New Grove Dictionary of Music and Musicians.* https://grovemusic.github.io. 23 May 2017.

LARSEN, Kristine. "'Behold Your Music!': The Themes of Ilúvatar, the Song of Aslan, and the Real Music of the Spheres." *Music in Middle-earth.* Eds.

Heidi Steimel and Friedhelm Schneidewind. Zurich and Jena: Walking Tree Publishers, 2010, 11-28.

LEEMING, David. *Creation Myths of the World: An Encyclopedia.* Santa Barbara: ABC CLIO, 2010.

LIPPMANN, Edward A. *The Philosophy & Aesthetics of Music.* Lincoln, NE and London: University of Nebraska Press, 1999.

LUSITANO, Vicente. *Introduttione facilissima et novissima de canto fermo.* (Venice: Marcolini, 1558). https://books.google.it/books?id=dlg8AAAAcAAJ&printsec=frontcover&hl=it&source=gbs_ge_summary_r&cad=0#v=onepage&q&f=false. 23 May 2017.

MAZZOTTA, Giuseppe. *Dante's Vision and the Circle of Knowledge.* Princeton, NJ: Princeton Legacy Library, 1993.

McINTOSH, Jonathan. "Ainulindalë: Tolkien, St Thomas, and the Metaphysics of Music." *Music in Middle-earth.* Eds. Heidi Steimel and Friedhelm Schneidewind. Zurich and Jena: Walking Tree Publishers, 2010, 53-74.

"Bonaventure and the Music of the Ainur." Blog entry. 20 Oct. 2012. http://bit.ly/2rPucQC. 23 May 2017.

MILBANK, Alison. "In a Dark Wood: Tolkien and Dante." Paper read at The School of English, Trinity College Dublin, Sept. 21st-22nd, 2012 (courtesy of the author).

MILLER, Clement A. "Erasmus on Music." *The Musical Quarterly* 52/3 (1966): 332-349.

MONTEMAGGI, Vittorio. "In Unknowability as Love. The Theology of Dante's Commedia." *Dante's Commedia: Theology as Poetry.* Eds. Vittorio Montemaggi and Matthew Treherne. Notre Dame, IN: University of Notre Dame Press, 2010, 60-94.

NETTL, Bruno. "Improvisation. I. Concepts and practices. 1. Concepts." *The New Grove Dictionary of Music and Musicians.* https://grovemusic.github.io. 23 May 2017.

"Thoughts on Improvisation: A Comparative Approach." *The Musical Quarterly* 60/1 (1974): 1-19.

QUILLER-COUCH, Arthur Thomas (ed.). *The Oxford Book of English Verse.* Oxford: Clarendon Press, 1919. http://bit.ly/2qRfCLh. 23 May 2017.

SALOMO, Elias. "Scientia artis musicae." *Scriptores ecclesiastici de musica sacra potissimum.* Ed. Martin Gerbert. 3 vols. 1784. Hildesheim: Olms, 1963. http://bit.ly/2rQ1UFA. 23 May 2017.

SHAKESPEARE, William. *The Merchant of Venice*. Cambridge: Cambridge University Press, 1987 (2003).

SISAM, Kenneth (ed.). *Fourteenth Century Verse and Prose*. Oxford: Clarendon Press, 1921.

SPITZER, Leo. *Classical and Christian Ideas of World Harmony*. Baltimore, MD: The Johns Hopkins Press, 1963.

STERNFELD, Frederick (ed.). *History of Western Music*. New York City, NY: Praeger, 1973.

TOLKIEN, J.R.R. *The Book of Lost Tales, Part One* (The History of Middle-earth 5). Ed. Christopher Tolkien. London: Unwin Hyman; Boston, MA: Houghton Mifflin, 1987.

The Letters of J.R.R. Tolkien. Ed. Humphrey Carpenter, with the assistance of Christopher Tolkien. London: George Allen & Unwin; Boston, MA: Houghton Mifflin, 1981.

A Middle English Vocabulary. Designed for use with Sisam's *Fourteenth Century Verse and Prose*. Oxford: At the Clarendon Press, 1922.

The Silmarillion. Ed. Christopher Tolkien. London: George Allen & Unwin; Boston, MA: Houghton Mifflin, 1977.

TROWELL, Brian. "Faburden and Fauxbourdon." *Musica Disciplina* 13 (1959): 43-78.

VON BALTHASAR, Hans Urs. *Truth is Symphonic: Aspects of Christian Pluralism*. San Francisco, CA: Ignatius Press, 1987.

WILLIAMS "Ab Ithel", John. *The Barddas of Iolo Morganwg*. Llandovery: Roderic, 1862. http://bit.ly/2q7Zd67. 23 May 2017.

WILKINS, William Joseph. *Hindu Mythology, Vedic and Puranic*. Calcutta and Simla: Thacker, Spink & co., 1913. http://bit.ly/2qSDo7P. 23 May 2017.

YOUNG, Edward. *Young's Night Thoughts*. Ed. George Gilfillan. Edinburgh: J. Nichol, 1853. http://bit.ly/2rwW3IX. 23 May 2017.

ZARLINO, Gioseffo. *Le istitutioni harmoniche*. 3rd ed. Venice: De Franceschi, 1573. http://bit.ly/2qLto1I. 23 May 2017.

Michaël Devaux & Guglielmo Spirito

Laments and Mercy: Tolkien and Liturgical Music

Abstract

The aim of this article is to offer an overview of Tolkien and the liturgical music of his time, with a focus on its possible influence on the Tolkienian conception of Elvish music. Guglielmo Spirito has reconstructed, focusing on the *Kyrie eleison*, the pieces of chant Tolkien used to hear at mass in Birmingham, Oxford and during his holidays in Assisi (1955). He also offers a spiritual appreciation of the themes of laments and Mercy from the *Kyrie* in Tolkien's texts. The larger content of what is sacred music and liturgical music from a canonical point of view at the beginning of the 20th Century is defined by Michaël Devaux, who also details the historical context of liturgical music in the Oratory of Birmingham and the history of the pieces of Gregorian chant Tolkien referred to in his texts or himself recorded.

> *The distraction fit, lost in the shaft of sunlight,*
> *The wild thyme unseen, or the winter lightning*
> *Or the waterfall or music heard so deeply*
> *That is not heard at all but you are the music*
> *While the music lasts.*
> T.S. Eliot

How impressively, in those last few lines, Eliot evokes the power of music! For music in an almost miraculous way can communicate, at times, not only aspects of the meaning but also something of the innermost beauty of Christian prayer. Our inner heart is awakened and quickened. We find ourselves being instinctively drawn forward by the beauty of the sound and by the beauty of truth, and drawn, while the music lasts, to give our full and rapt attention to even the quietest echo of the Eternal Word, the smallest trace of the source of all beauty, the God whom Gerard Manley Hopkins calls "beauty's self and beauty's giver" (see Murray 43-44).

There is music in general, but there is also the music specifically devoted to worship in Church. For centuries, Old Roman, Byzantine, and Gregorian chants assumed this way to pray to God. For us, the question is: what about Tolkien and that music, mainly liturgical music and Gregorian chant? Did he consider it only a *pleasant* music to be listened to rest at home, or also as the *sacred music* of the Church, or even as a *pattern* for something in Middle-earth?[1] And if so, what does it mean? What are the chants he takes with him into his works of imagination? On one hand, everybody knows that Tolkien was a devout and practicing Catholic, and on the other hand, many think that his imaginary world(s) remain(s) distinct from his personal faith. We'll scrutinize such affirmations. Biographical testimonials in the letters (e.g. *L* 172) are nothing but a cross for the hermeneutic of the *opus magnum*, to restrict the question to *The Lord of the Rings*. Tolkien began the creation of Arda with (angelic) music. But what kind of music did he like? We know that he experienced Opera quite late when he was in Venice, Italy, during the summer of 1955.[2] So let us have a look at the relation between Tolkien and liturgical music in order to reflect on the richness of such a source for identifying some key elements of his creativity.

Such a perspective first of all requires defining what liturgical music is. On this basis, we'll found our inquiry on biographical elements to shed light on his religious education and the context of the music of the Church at that time. We can thus see what sacred music Tolkien used to listen to when he was in Oxford and when he travelled (mainly in Italy). We'll finish by showing what the influence of Gregorian chant music on Elvish music was. Three of Tolkien's linguistic and literary creations will here be analysed from our point of view: the Elvish translation of the *Litany of Loreto* (in fact the verse of the *Kyrie eleison*), *Namárië*, and *The Homecoming of Beorhtnoth*. We will see that Tolkien had a special feeling for laments and Mercy.

Sacred Music, Liturgical Music, and Religious Music

We can quickly explain what liturgical music is. Confusion often occurs today even among (unaware) believers and practicing Catholics. If you are not able to distinguish sacred music, liturgical music, and religious music, you

---

1 Alas for us the relevant study by Bradford Lee Eden, "Gregorian Chant as Influence on Tolkien's Development of Lyric and Song", delivered at Kalamazoo, 40th International Congress on Medieval Studies, May 2005, is still unpublished.
2 "He [J.R.R. Tolkien] had had hitherto little opportunity to enjoy opera" (Priscilla Tolkien viii, cf. Devaux 16).

might assume that what would be fun around a campfire for young scouts is pertinent and deserves to take place in the church during Mass. An elementary religious instruction could avoid such an aberration. Between the time Tolkien was a child, learning and deepening (with Fr. Morgan) his religion and what the Church of (his) God teaches, and the time of the publication of his *Hauptwerk*, the Vatican published several texts on the question on which we are focusing.

First of all, in 1903 a text (on which we'll say more in the next section) says that "Sacred music should consequently possess, in the highest degree, the qualities proper to the liturgy, and in particular *sanctity* and *goodness of form*, which will spontaneously produce the final quality of *universality*" (emphasis added).[3] The main category is this: sacred music. There are several kinds of sacred music–branches from that tree trunk–with regard to the three qualities just emphasised. The *highest* degree of sanctity, art, and universality go to Gregorian chant (ibid.). A lower but still *excellent* degree is recognized as classic polyphony (e.g. Palestrina; ibid., § 4). Third is modern music (e.g. Viennese Masses) if it has "excellence, sobriety and gravity"[4], removing profane music and theatricality from the service of religion. So modern music is accepted with conditions: it has to be artistic, not too demonstrative (and so external of the mystery), and taking really seriously the sacrifice on the altar.

During Christmas 1955, Pope Pius XII in the encyclical *Musicæ Sacræ Disciplina* reaffirmed that the main category remains sacred music. But he said that "the highest honor and praise must be given to 'liturgical' music" (*musica "liturgica"*, § 35), distinguishing it from "'religious' music" (*musica "religiosa"*). The first one takes place at Mass and divine office. The second one is dedicated to "music which is not primarily a part of the sacred liturgy, but which by its power and purpose greatly aids religion"[5]. Often religious music is sung with lyrics in a vernacular language. Hymns and canticles in English can, for example, be helpful in learning aspects of God, and so be a kind of catechism. For its part, Gregorian chant, with its sanctity, is of course liturgical music (§ 42).

---

3 "*Ex quo evenit ut musica sacra omnibus muneribus liturgiae praedita sit, praesertim sanctitate, bonitate formarum quibus et universalitas oritur.*" (Pius X, *Tra le sollicitudini*, § 3).
4 <https://adoremus.org/1903/11/22/tra-le-sollecitudini>. accessed 23rd Feb. 2018.
5 "*Nihilominus illa quoque musica magni habenda est quae, etsi sacrae Liturgiae non praecipue inservit, argumento tamen et fine religionem valde iuvat, ideoque iure merito musica 'religiosa' nuncupatur.*" (§ 36).

The Context of Liturgical Music during Tolkien's Education in Birmingham (1905-1911)

Music at the Oratory of Newman

When Tolkien lost his mother in November 1904, he was (with his brother Hilary) put under the guardianship of Fr. Morgan at the Oratory of Birmingham. They lived with their aunt Beatrice Suffield at 25 Stirling Road in the quarter of Edgbaston in Birmingham until the summer of 1907. The oratory was thought of as their real home. Alternatively, they both served in the morning Mass for Father Francis at Our Lady's altar in the chapel of the Oratory (cf. Ferrández Bru 156; *L* 395). There, Tolkien first learned the Italian pronunciation of Latin (see Drout 298b). From 1908, they lived at the home of Louis Faulkner, where there were musical evenings. In March 1910, Tolkien wrote the devotional pamphlets *The Stations of the Cross* and *The Seven Words of the Cross*. It gives an idea of the spiritual context he was in. In April and December 1910 and July 1911, he attended concerts at King Edward's School, which could show the interest for music he had at this moment.

The sacred music he could have frequently listened to was the Sunday High Mass sung at the Oratory of Birmingham. What was the tradition of music at the Oratory? We know that when Saint John Henry Newman gave his preference for choir performances of pieces by his favourites composers, Beethoven would be in first place, followed by Haydn, Mozart, and Cherubini. At the Oratory, he first introduced the boys to Corelli and Romberg (see Bellasis 13 *sqq.*). Newman himself didn't seem to be delighted by Gregorian chant: "In Gregorian music, Newman could see no beauty whatever [...] An exception must be made in favour of those familiar chants occurring in the Mass" (Hutton 234). He even thought Gregorian music was one of the "inchoate sciences" (63). But what was the Gregorian chant which Newman knew? When he published that text (1858), it was just the beginning (in 1856) of its restoration through the decisions of Dom Guéranger in St Peter Abbey in Solesmes, France (see Combe 11), and Newman only met Guéranger once, later, in 1860 (see Miquel 286).

In England, The Plainsong and Medieval Music Society, was founded in 1888, and began issuing its publications two years later. But things changed worldwide in sacred music in 1903, just before Tolkien, as an orphan, attended Mass regularly at the Oratory. Indeed, the publication of *Tra le sollecitudini* (1903), a *motu proprio* by Pope Pius X, and soon after the *Graduale de Tempore et de Sanctis* (1908), gave an idea of the magisterial situation throughout the Catholic world. The influence of the monks of Solesmes was winning over the whole Church. We know that in 1905, 80% of all chant books sold used the rhythmic signs of Solesmes (see Mitchell 900)! At the Vatican in 1910, the Superior School of Sacred Music (known today as the Pontifical Institute for Sacred Music) was founded, and in 1911 it was approved by Pius X's Brief *Expleverunt desiderii*; it became 'Pontifical' in 1914, and its name was changed through the *Deus scientiarum Dominus* by Pius XI in 1931 (see Hayburn 295 sqq.).

What was the situation at the Oratory of Birmingham? The ideas of Solesmes (namely of Dom Mocquereau) were in vogue in the archdiocese of Birmingham. The Archbishop Edward Ilsley requested Laurentia McLachlan to write a *Grammar of Plainsong*, published in 1905. It was the main manual for learning Gregorian until 1929, and Dom Mocquereau helped her to write it. Were other oratories following this way? We know that the Oratory of London only changed its mind on that point in 1935 (see Muir, *Roman Catholic Church Music* 209), but what about the Oratory of Birmingham? Henry Bird Collins (who converted to Catholicism in 1898) became an organist at the Oratory in 1915 and "faithfully worked for the revival of Gregorian chant along the same lines as Dom Guéranger" (Crouan ch. 14; cf. Oscar Thompson 443). He was an expert on early English musical notation (see Blatchly & Wilson 15a). But Tolkien left the Oratory in 1911. While he stayed there, it was William Sewell who directed the music at the Oratory in the quarter of Edgbaston (see Nicholls 8), and from 1903 he also directed the Birmingham Musical Society. He notably composed the *Mass of St. Philipp Neri*, a Magnificat, and the anthems *O salutaris hostia* and *Tantum ergo* (Humphreys & Evans 303a). As Henry Washington says in his article "The Oratory Musical Tradition":

> At a time when papal representations concerning musical propriety were being widely respected the Oratory musicians continued to specialise in the masterpieces of the Classical period. [...] efforts were being made to conform to Papal authority as long as the classics were not to be abandoned. The Masters

of Beethoven, Schubert, Cherubini and the rest were drastically dismembered (164-5).

The context of the Birmingham Oratory is then twofold: first, the principle of ultramontanism (following the Pope) was in contradiction with the second one, that the music which the founder (Newman) recommended was modern! Sewell, although he is reputed to have belonged to the Cecilian movement (reacting to the relegation of the Gregorian chant to the second place), introduced modern features in his *Mass of St. Philipp Neri* (see Muir, "Sacred Sound for a Holy Space" 55). So Tolkien may have learned some Gregorian pieces and could have appreciated recitative in the singing of the Preface of the Canon during Mass. Was he at that time really immerged in a context of listening and learning Gregorian chant, as it can be understood, through the restoration of Solesmes?

The *Kyrie Eleison* at Birmingham

The following is the list of the *Kyrie* at the Oratory of Birmingham, sorted in alphabetical order. We'll explain after this list why such a focalization is relevant for Tolkien's thought, but we find it more accurate to present here the list of *Kyrie eleison* from the Masses Tolkien, with his mother and brother, had heard from 1902 to 1911.

1902
(16 different Masses)

Beethoven in C.
Cherubini in A.
Gounod, M., *Solennelle*.
Haydn no. 1, 4, 16
Hummel in B flat, in D.
Kalliwoda (Kalivoda).
Mozart no. 2, 12, 13.
L. Niedermeyer in B minor.
Palestrina, *Missa Brevis*.
Piel in D minor.
C. Reissiger in E flat.

1903 (8)

H. B. Collins (organist at Oratory).
Ebner in G.
Gounod, *Sacré Cœur*.
Haydn no. 4.
Hummel in E flat.
Mendelssohn.
Piel, *St Anthony Padua*.
Victoria, *Missa Quarti Toni*.

1904 (7)

Ebner, M., *de Spiritu Sancti, Missa Solemnis*.
Haller, *Missa Septima*.
Palestrina, *Æterna Christi munera*.
Perosi, M., *Patriarchalis*.
Witt in C. op. 12, *St Lucy*.

1905 (7)

Goller in E flat, *St Stephen*.
Haller, *Missa Tertia*.
Hassler, *Dixit Maria*.
Mitterer, M., *Dominicalis II, VI*.
Palestrina, *Papae Marcelli*.

1906 (6)

F. Anerio, *Hor le tue forze adopra*.
Haller, *St Michael Arch*.
Mitterer, M., *Festiva, St Charles Borromeo, St Joseph*.
Terry, *St Gregory*.

1907 (4)

Ebner, *in Solemnio, de Nativitate*.
Palestrina, *Assumpta est Maria*.
Sewell, *St Philip Neri*.

1908 (4)

Goller, *St Gerard Majella*.
Haller, *St Cecily*.
Sewell, *Mass in A flat, St Philomena*.

1909 (3)

Ett in A.
Filke in E minor.
Palestrina, *Jesu noster Redem*.

1910 (2)

Griesbacher, *St Godehard*
Gerhard Jakob Quadflieg, *St Anthony*.

1911 (3)

Bruno Stein no. 11.
Peter Griesbacher, *Stella Maris*.
Joseph Rheinberger in F minor.
Palestrina, *Dies sanctificatus*.

In this list, compiled thanks to the help of Daniel Joyce from Birmingham's Oratory, we see no Gregorian Mass at all. But the reduction from 16 to 2 or 3 different Masses played is for us a sign that Gregorian chant took place after 1903. This is very likely the place Tolkien first learnt it.

The *Kyrie Eleison* in Tolkien's Adult Life

What is the *Kyrie Eleison*?

Let's focus on the *Kyrie eleison*. We hear it so often. We utter it so often – so much as to suspect that it recapitulates, perhaps, the basic character of Christian spiritual life. In every Liturgical office it is often repeated. We meet it everywhere, in the happy and sad events of existence, sung by the church at weddings, baptisms, funerals – whatever the circumstances, one cannot miss such a cry. Not surprisingly, this exclamation has inspired enormous musical creativity; no other part of the liturgy has attracted composers in a so vast, multi-faceted, and varied a composition. Every mood, joyful, exultant, heartbroken, sad, and hopeful, finds its expression in the singing of the *Kyrie*, from pre-Gregorian chants to Baroque compositions and beyond. There are hundreds if not thousands of different *Kyries*.

Kyrie eleison (there being an *i*, close to the French *u*), which goes from the chest (where the *Ky* is born), passing and passing again into the throat and the point of the palate (by the rolled *r* in front of the *l*) to the forehead and the head (by the *l* but especially the *n* and its final resonance), has an architectural sound in the body that is exceptional. Repetition produces an ascending spiral movement in the concentration of the vibration, which goes from the place of the heart towards the forehead and the top of the head; this repetition can be as fast as you want. On the other hand, in Latin, *Domine miserere nobis*, the fast repetition is impossible, there is no architectural sound, and one begins to lisp; therefore the *Kyrie eleison*, a perpetual prayer, repeated hundreds of times, was to remain in Greek.

We see the importance of the acoustic dimension in the ancient liturgy; the sacred song, the Gregorian chant, is founded on principles. This repetition of the *Kyrie* is powerful, awakening the inner body by the touch of sonorous vibration; a fine vibration of the body of prayer which will help its awakening and which will bring it to the contemplation of the Lord in a concentration that the Sound, the Icon, and all the liturgical Art arouse and maintain. Then, becoming superfluous, the song withdraws, delivering the soul to a silence which is truly wonderful; *Kyrie eleison* (see Reznikoff 8-9).

The words *have mercy* are used – said or sung – in all Christian Churches from both East and West, and they are the response of the people to all the petitions suggested by the celebrant. In the Eastern Churches the use is much wider, and repeated over and over again through the Divine Liturgy, as the people sing their supplications; it is possible to cover every inside and outside event. Thus this wondrous prayer becomes all embracing and universal.

Our modern translation "have mercy" is a limited and insufficient one. The word *mercy* in English is the translation of the Greek word *eleos*, and it has the same ultimate root as the old Greek word for oil or, more precisely, olive oil; a substance which was used extensively as a soothing agent for bruises and minor wounds. The oil was poured onto the wound and gently massaged in, thus soothing, comforting, and making whole the injured part (see the parable of the Good Samaritan, Lk 10.33). The Hebrew word, which is translated as *eleos* (mercy) is *hesed*, and it means "steadfast love", long-suffering love. The Greek words for "Lord have mercy" are "*Kyrie eleison*" – that is to say, "Lord, soothe me, comfort me, take away my pain, show me your steadfast love and your compassion!"

Thus *have mercy* does not refer so much to justice or acquittal but to the infinite loving kindness of God and his compassion for his suffering children. We follow the example of the Canaanite woman who cried out to Jesus: "Have mercy on me, Lord (*eleison me, Kyrie*)" (Mt 15.22), and of a father who came up to him and kneeling before him said: "Lord, have mercy (*Kyrie, eleison*) on my son" (Mt 17.15). It is in this sense that we pray "Lord, have mercy" (see Williams 130).

For these reasons, we wondered what *Kyries* Tolkien knew during his lifetime. The first way to answer (before the list of those we were able to check) is by reading Tolkien, being attentive to the prayers he mentions, and tracking them in Liturgy.

> If you don't do so already, make a habit of the "praises". I use them much (in Latin): the *Gloria Patri*, the *Gloria in Excelsis*, the *Laudate Dominum*; the *Laudate Pueri Dominum* (of which I am specially fond), one of the Sunday psalms; and the *Magnificat*; also the Litany of Loreto (with the prayer *Sub tuum præsidium*). If you have these by heart you never need for words of joy. It is also a good and admirable thing to know by heart the Canon of the Mass, for you can say this in your heart if ever hard circumstance keeps you from hearing Mass. (*L* 66; cf. Scull and Hammond 2-B, 1072-1073)

So, we have two main places where the *Kyrie* is to be found: the Litany and the Mass. The litany type of prayers of the congregation, with its petitions intoned by a deacon and with its *Kyrie eleison* as the response of the people, has been in use since the 4th century. This use of the *Kyrie* still survives at the beginning of the Litanies outside of the Mass and has so at the beginning of every Eucharistic celebration in the Roman rite of the Catholic Church since the 5th century.

The Litany of the Blessed Virgin Mary is a Marian litany originally approved in 1587 by the Franciscan Pope Sixtus VI. It is also known as the *Litany of Loreto* for its first-known place of origin, the Shrine of Our Lady of Loreto (Ancona, Italy). The most ancient printed copy hitherto discovered is that of Dillingen in Germany, dating from 1558. The litany was probably published and circulated in Germany by Saint Petrus Canisius. The Dillingen copy is entitled: *Letania Loretana. Ordnung der Letaney von unser lieben Frawen wie sie zu Loreto alle Samstag gehalten* ("Order of the Litany of Our Lady as said every Saturday at Loreto"). This Litany starts with a triple couple (2x3) of responsorial invocations, a Latin transliteration from the Greek Κύριε ελέησον. In the Tridentine Mass Tolkien mainly knew, the evocations occur thrice (3x3).

The *Kyrie Eleison* at Oxford (1930s and Beyond)

Let's have a look now at the situation in Oxford in 1911 when Tolkien was a student and, after World War I and the Leeds period of teaching, from 1925 when he came back as a Fellow. We'll once again give the list of the *Kyrie eleison* he used to listen to and sing there, but before we will contextualize the question of liturgical music in Oxford during Tolkien's life.

He attended mostly St. Gregory & St. Augustine, Blackfriars (Dominicans), and St. Anthony of Padua. More precisely, as a student, he sometimes attended Mass at St. Aloysius (Woodstock Road), which was served by Jesuits at that time. But he wasn't actively practising (see Blackham ch. 9). He himself later said of the following period that "out of wickedness and sloth I almost ceased to practice my religion – especially at Leeds, and at 22 Northmoor Road" (*L* 340), so during the years 1920-9. So we reach the very beginning of the 1930s. At that time (1929), the Blackfriars in Oxford, just after the priory was established as a House of studies for Dominicans in England, welcomed the first seminar of the *Society of Saint Gregory* on Gregorian chant (see Ainslie 42-43, 50). At the end of the 1930s, Oxford University elected the Catholic Egon Joseph Wellesz in the faculty of music. He was an authority on Byzantine music and Gregorian chant (see Kennedy and Kennedy 914 b). Tolkien may have at least heard about him from another Byzantinologist among the Inklings, the Dominican Gervase Matthew.

At St. Aloysius, after the Oxford Oratory, Fr. Josep Welch OP, from Blackfriars, wrote us that there are no records preserved:

> I have checked with our archivist and I'm afraid there is no record at all of the music that was sung in our church at that time. In any case, it seems more than a little likely that Tolkien came to weekday Masses here sometimes but usually went to St Gregory & Augustine's church on Sundays when he lived in Summertown and then St Anthony's when he moved to Headington. He rarely, if ever, came here for Sunday Masses as far as we can tell.

At St. Gregory & St. Augustine (see Scull and Hammond 2-B, 928), three Gregorian Masses were usual: *Deus Genitor Alme*, *De Angelis*, and *Orbis Factor*. Tolkien used to go there from 1930 to 1953. His son, John, was there ordained as a Catholic Priest (even if his first Mass took place at St. Anthony of Padua). If there was not regular use of Gregorian in the Oratory of Birmingham, at least he regularly attended Masses with Gregorian there.

With the Blackfriars (see Scull and Hammond 2-B, 918), among the rituals of *Tenebræ* (we'll see the importance of this Office in the next section), the Litany-like prayers are sung at the foot of the High Altar by the cantors on Maundy Thursday with the *Lord, have mercy* (in Greek & Latin). From the *Graduale*

Ordinis Praedicatorum (1950), here is the list (with page references) of the (13) Masses Tolkien could have known there:

- *pro Defunctis* (115*)
- *in Festis solemnibus* (126*)
- *in Totis Duplicibus communibus et Dominicis majoribus* (132*)
- *in Duplicibus et Dominicis minoribus* (135*)
- *in Tempore Paschali* (138*)
- *in Sabbatis, Festis et Octavis B.V.M.* (139*)
- *in Semiduplicibus et Simplicibus* (143*)
- *Profestis diebus* (145*)
- *Cantus et Graduali Romano deprompti*:
    in Festis solemnibus 2 (149*)
    in Festis solemnibus 3 (*De Angelis*, 152*)
    in Dominicis Adventus et Quadragesimae (161*)
    in Duplicibus et Dominicis minoribus (162*).

At St. Anthony of Padua in Headington, Oxford (see Scull and Hammond 2-B, 928):

'Modern' (12 Masses)	Gregorian (12)
Sir Richard Runciman Terry (1865-1938, an English organist, choir director, and musicologist), *Short Mass in C*, no. 4, *For Unison Chorus*, *Mass* no. 3, on the theme *Veni Sancte Spiritus*, *Mass of Saint Dominic*.	I. *Lux et Origo* (Eastertide)
	II. *Fons bonitatis* (On Solemn Feasts 1)
	III. *Deus sempiterne* (On Solemn Feasts 2)
	IV. *Cunctipotens Genitor Deus* (On Double Feasts 1)
Fr. Ludovico Viadana, OFM Obs (1560-1627), *Mass l'Hora Passa*.	V. *Magnae Deus potentiae* (On Double Feasts 2)
Vinzenz Goller (1873-1953, South Tyrol, a composer and church musician), *Missa in hon. St. Stephani Protomartyris*, *Missa in honorem B.M.V. de Loreto*. <https://youtu.be/vbPY2ll6n8g>	VIII. *De Angelis* (On Double Feasts 5)
	IX. *Cum jubilo* (On Feasts of Our Lady 1)
	X. *Alme Pater* (On Feasts of Our Lady 2)
James Lyon (1735-1794, an American composer), *Mass of Saint Christopher* no. 1, *Mass of Saint Jude*, no. 2.	XI *Orbis factor* (On Sundays throughout the year)
	XV. *Dominator Deus* (On Simple Feasts)
Wolfgang Amadeus Mozart (1756-1791), *Missa brevis* in B.	XVII. *Mass for the Dead* (On Sundays in Advent and Lent)
Dom Gregory Murray, OSB (1905-1992, an organist and composer), *A People's Mass*.	
Joseph Egbert Turner, OSB (1853-1897, gifted English organist, singer, and composer), *Mass of the Good Shepherd in F Minor*, no. 4. <https://youtu.be/f9mXhpfg2WU>	

So it was at St. Gregory & St. Augustine (1930-1953), at St. Anthony (1953-1968), and with the Blackfriars that Tolkien could have confirmed his habit of hearing and singing Gregorian melodies. The balance between modern (a category of the *motu proprio* of 1903) and Gregorian music is perfect (as far as our extensive research can show).[6]

The *Kyrie Eleison* in Assisi (1955)

We can add here the information we found about the Festivals Tolkien attended in Assisi. One example of Tolkien's love for the Litany comes from this travel, on August 7th, 1955:

> Abbey of San Pietro to attend Benediction, 'wickedly (and vainly) intending to miss *rosario*'. (...) We had rosary, very well said, and entirely in Latin to my pleasure and surprise: it seemed altogether familiar to the people, though most were poor (to all appearances). The *Litany of Loreto*, also in Latin. There was a small organ and the congregation sang, in this small bright corner of the large austere dark church. It was homelike and delightfully familiar. (Scull and Hammond 1, 494)

At the Basilica of San Francesco, he attended Mass at least twice, on August 7th and 8th, 1955 (see Scull and Hammond 1, 493-494):

> In Assisi one might say that some times all the bells are ringing, and at all times some bells are ringing. (...) [They] go to high Mass in the upper church at San Francesco at 10.00 a.m., "marvellously sung by the friars in the choir in the beautiful church ablaze with Giotto frescoes".

Tolkien and Priscilla attended Mass at the Basilica of San Francesco before breakfast. Tolkien heard most of another Mass at the Tomb of St. Francis, 'beautifully said'. In those years, the famous composer Fr. Domenico Stella, OFM Conv (1881-1956), was producing his last works: the *Missa Dies Sanctificatus, tribus vocibus in aequalibus et organo comitante concinenda* (1954) was sung.

At the Basilica of Santa Chiara on August 12th, 1955, Tolkien and Priscilla decided to attend High Mass. Beginning at 10:35, a procession of friars, hal-

---

[6] Through the Italian Tolkienist Oronzo Cilli, Guglielmo Spirito sought the help of Daniel Joyce, archivist of the Oratory at Birmingham. Thanks to his kind availability and generosity, they were able to rebuild the Mass Settings sung at the Oratory between 1902 and 1911. Somehow in a similar way, with the help of an Italian friend in Oxford, Mirco Meniconi, and the organists and choirmasters of the churches which Tolkien attended (Fr. John Saward at St. Gregory & St. Augustine, Fr. Matthew Jarvis (OP) and Fr. Josep Welch (OP) at Blackfriars, and Tom Czepiel at St. Anthony), we were able to check a fair amount of music in the cupboards, and so identify about 40 *Kyries* that were played and sung during the celebrations in those years. Analogically, with the help of the Director of the Musical Chapel of the Basilica of St. Francis in Assisi, Fr. Giuseppe Magrino (OFM Conv), we were able to find some of the music used in Assisi, both at San Francesco and at Santa Chiara, during 1955.

berdiers, trumpeters, guards, and officials entered, followed by the celebrant, Cardinal Micara.

> The great choir of friars sang magnificently, to my thinking, with enormous controlled power – capable of lifting the roof even of Santa Chiara instantaneously and without effort. […] I was startled when, just as the choir crashed into the Patrem Omnipotentem of the Creed, a large Italian woman shouted out *Giorgio!* with a force that must have reached the Cardinal in spite of the choir. But it had no effect on Giorgio. He had to be fetched – from the Tomb, while his small sister sat on the floor at my feet and played with a toy … Personally I found the fanfare of trumpets at the first Elevation very impressive and not at all improper at so high a ceremony. But it was a pity that Cardinal Micara had not a note of music, and could not even manage the Pater Noster. (see Scull and Hammond 1, 497)

For the solemnity of Saint Clare, the Mass sung was most probably the *Missa in honorem Sanctae Clarae Assisiensis, 4 vocum cum organo*, composed in 1953 for the seventh centenary of her death by the prestigious Fr. Licinio Refice (1883-1954). Having tracked the *Kyrie eleison* during Tolkien's life, we will next study it in his own works of imagination – in Middle-earth but also elsewhere. There are the Laments, and the Mercy they convey.

The *Kyrie Eleison* in Middle-earth?

Mercy in Middle-earth

The Catholic daily Mass, we can assume, was one of Tolkien's sources for the great themes of pity and mercy in his life and work (see Wendling). In the Liturgy, the whole history of salvation continues to happen in the celebration. Time is redeemed and made free of decay, and the ritual hides and reveals the access to the new life in Christ, in the harmony of a new creation – already, though not yet.

Standing before the abysses of the divine mercy, the faithful can only proclaim the awareness of their own radical poverty, which immediately becomes a plea for help and a cry of rejoicing – *Kyrie eleison!* – on account of an even more generous salvation, since from the abyss of his own wretchedness such salvation is unthinkable. This is why the plea for forgiveness and the glorification of God form a substantial part of liturgical prayer. "*The Eucharist is the culmination of this prayer experience*" (Saint John Paul II, *Orientale Lumen* 10).

To grasp something of the richness of content that "mercy" had for Tolkien, it is now pertinent to look at his own account of creation, where already harmony, sorrow, and mercy are woven together in the drama of our beautiful wounded world:

> In the beginning Eru, the One, who in the Elvish tongue is named Ilúvatar, made the Ainur of his thought; and they made a great Music before him. In this Music the World was begun; for Ilúvatar made visible the song of the Ainur, and they beheld it as a light in the darkness. And many among them became enamoured of its beauty, and of its history which they saw beginning and unfolding as in a vision. Therefore Ilúvatar gave to their vision Being, and set it amid the Void, and the Secret Fire was sent to burn at the heart of the World; and it was called Eä. (S 27)

> Then again Ilúvatar arose, and the Ainur perceived that his countenance was stern; and he lifted up his right hand, and behold! a third theme grew amid the confusion, and it was unlike the others. For it seemed at first soft and sweet, a mere rippling of gentle sounds in delicate melodies; but it could not be quenched, and it took to itself power and profundity. And it seemed at last that there were two musics progressing at one time before the seat of Ilúvatar, and they were utterly at variance. The one was deep and wide and beautiful, but slow and blended with an immeasurable sorrow, from which its beauty chiefly came. (S 17)

Nienna is one of the Queens of the Valar. She epitomizes Mercy, Compassion, and Healing, and so was also one of the few Valar who sided with the release of Melkor the Evil One from his bondage, being compassionate of his suffering yet unaware, as Manwë, highest of the Valar, was of his unfailing evil.

> She is acquainted with grief, and mourns for every wound that Arda has suffered in the marring of Melkor. So great was her sorrow, as the Music unfolded, that her song turned to lamentation long before its end, and the sound of mourning was woven into the themes of the World before it began. But she does not weep for herself; and those who hearken to her learn pity, and endurance in hope. She brings strength to the spirit and turns sorrow to wisdom. (S 31)

Tolkien emphasizes that *Pity* and *Mercy* were essential in his sub-created world: "It is the pity of Bilbo and later Frodo that ultimately allows the Quest to be achieved" (*L* 191). Frodo "(and the Cause) were saved – by Mercy: by the supreme value and efficacy of Pity and forgiveness of injury" (*L* 251-2). Gandalf's rebuke of Frodo for wishing death upon Gollum in *The Fellowship of the Ring* is obliquely attributed in *The Silmarillion* to Gandalf's having been a disciple of Nienna, a Queen of the Valar, in Valinor: "Wisest of the Maiar was Olórin [Gandalf] [...] His ways took him often to the house of Nienna, and of her he learned pity and patience" (*S* 34). Nienna, the patron of mercy, gave him tutelage. As one of the Maiar, Gandalf would have participated in the Music of the Ainur at the creation of the world, when the compassion (*eleos*) of Nienna, mighty among the Valar, was woven into the fabric of the world. *Mercy* is woven into the very reality of our universe and is one of the sounds that heal the harmony of our wounded world. Somehow we may feel as if we where "*inside a song, if you take my meaning*", as Sam said to Frodo at Cerin Amroth (*LotR* 360, book II, ch. 6). *This musical perception of mercy is a distinctive feature of Tolkien's feelings, and we think that it tells us something of his experience of the* Kyrie eleison.

It is a mystery of goodness and mercy, a mystery of love our minds can hardly begin to grasp, a divine compassion and care for the very aspect of our lives which seems most hopeless and most lost, which transform us into someone full of joy and radiance. "Blessed are the merciful for they shall obtain mercy" (Mt 5.7). Tolkien would describe this event as a *Eucatastrophe* (see *L* 100). A synonym might be what C.S. Lewis described as "a severe mercy" (Vanauken 210).

Elvish Translation of the *Kyrie Eleison*

During the second half of the 20th century, significant reforms were made in Roman Catholic worship. Tolkien approved of these in the abstract, but he felt a little dislocated and even a little sad for his era. Most notably, the "Latin rite" was replaced with the vernacular, and liturgical texts were extensively revised. Tolkien for his part could not see the point of abandoning Latin in the Mass. His grandson, Simon Tolkien, recalled going to church with him in Bournemouth, where he made all the responses very loudly in Latin while the rest of the congregation answered in English (see Scull and Hammond 2-B, 1073).

The petition *Kyrie eleison* is sometimes retained without alteration, sometimes translated, and sometimes expanded. This began in ancient times, as early as the 5th century (for instance, Armenians sing it translated). There is evidence of its use by the converted Germanic tribes, as the Vandals of North Africa pray "Frôja armês" (*Domine Miserere*) (Jungmann 335 n. 11).

Tolkien's translation of the *Litany of Loreto* prayer into Quenya, composed sometime in the 1950s, was first published in the "Words of Joy (Part Two)" article in *Vinyar Tengwar* 44 (12). Tolkien did not provide an English translation of the prayer. Here we are interested only in the first line of Tolkien's Quenya translation of the *Litany of Loreto* prayer:

> *Heru órava omessë:* Lord, have mercy on us.

The first word is the noun *heru* (also *hér*; VT 41, 9), "lord", followed by the aorist form of the verb *órava*, "to have mercy". The last word *omessë*, "on us", is the locative form (-*ssë*, "on") of the pronoun *me*, "us". The significance of the prefix *o-* is unclear, but Wynne, Smith, and Hostetter suggested that it might be the preposition *ó* (VT 44, 15), though its translation elsewhere as "with" does not seem appropriate here. It could instead be the prefix *o-*, "together", though this does not fit well either.

In later lines, Tolkien wrote *(o)messë* indicating the prefix was optional. In fact, it is absent in the original form, *Kyrie eleison*: other ways would have been *Kyrie eleison imas (on us)*. *Der Voghormiá, Kyrie eleison* in Armenian, gives an outstanding sense of similar musicality with the Quenya. The recent creation (1980) by the Armenian master Khoren Mekanejian is somewhat amazing.[7]

Elvish Poetry, Monks of Ely, and Gregorian Chant

Namárie and *Lamentations of Jeremiah Prophet*

Turning to another Elvish text Tolkien sung (and not only wrote) belonging to Middle-earth, we can look at (from the point of view here adopted) the longest text in Quenya: *Namárie*.

---

7 *Khorenian Divine Liturgy*, Label Khoren Mekanejian, May 2017, CD 2, track 8; see <https://youtu.be/rGOdNqRerOA>, published on Feb. 9th, 2014, and <http://sharakanner.blogspot.com/>, accessed Feb. 23rd, 2018.

The Lament was performed in the show *The Road Goes Ever On* created by Donald Swann, whom Tolkien met on May 30th, 1965. He approved five of the six settings Swann submitted to him, placing restrictions on and in fact having a specific idea about *Namarië*. It's well known that Tolkien "hummed a Gregorian chant" (Swann, *Road* vi; cf. Swann, *Swann's Way* 207) to illustrate what he had in mind. Priscilla Tolkien says:

> My father loved the monastic tradition of Gregorian Plain Chant and was much concerned with the giving up of Latin in Church services, since it had been for so many centuries the universal language of Western Christianity. I remember when the English performer and composer Donald Swann first met my father in my house in the 1960s in order to perform for him his song cycle, *The Road Goes Ever On*, [...] when it came to the Elvish poem "*Namárië*, Galadriel's Lament and Farewell," my father demonstrated how he wished this to be sung in the mode of Plain Chant. (viii-ix)

Swann took notes at this very moment (of the melody), and after asked Tolkien for some further explanations.[8] The Professor sent the musician a letter on June 7th, making "some notes on the 'chant' which might assist you. But they are too elaborate (though reduced)."[9] At that time, he had already himself recorded years before a "plainchant" version when he was in George Sayer's home for a few days in late August, 1952 (cf. Scull and Hammond 2-B, 1063; Hammond with Anderson, 384-5). It was first published in 1967. He also assumes that Elvish song must be sung like Gregorian chants in an interview of the 1960s (cf. "The Man who understands Hobbits"; *L* no. 294).

The corresponding Gregorian chant takes place in the nocturns (Matins) of the *Holy Triduum* (Maundy Thursday, Good Friday, and Holy Saturday), which is part of the *Tenebræ*. The Council of Trent (1545-63) set that the recitative tone would be close to 6th psalm tone. This *tonus lamentationum* had been first published in 1582 in the *Directorium Chori* by Giovanni Domenico Guidetti. It is very close to psalmody, rather than the chant of the epistles or gospels. During the Middle Ages, there was a lot of *toni lamentationum* in the different traditions of the liturgical chant.[10] The simple melody of Guidetti had been

---

8   For analysis of the relation Tolkien/Swann, see Kobot, Phemister, Jorgensen, and Leonberger.
9   Scull and Hammond 1, 668. Part of the correspondence is at the Marion Wade Center (Tolkien letter collection, 19 items), as Archives of Donald Swann. Other archives are hold in Battersea (London).
10 Cf. Zapke 452; and Kendrick saying that "the overall structure of Matins and Lauds was roughly similar across the wide variety of late medieval practice" (2).

known since the end of 11th century.¹¹ The text of the *Lamentations of Jeremiah Prophet* is divided into lessons. Each one begins with a Hebrew letter as a mark. Tolkien sings the first word of *Namárië* (*Ai!*) in the melody used for the Hebrew letter in the *Lamentations of Jeremiah* during *Tenebræ*, but one can notice that both the inflection (*mediatio*) and ending (*terminatio*) are streamlined; without differentiation, founded on the mother tone in C with a *clivis* (while there's a melisma on the last two syllables in the melody of the *Liber usualis*). That is 6th mode (mother tone in C going up to E for recitation; or a mother tone in E, going to C for the ending and intonation).

Dies iræ

Tolkien also involved (but not in Middle-earth) Gregorian chant in another fictional work: *The Homecoming of Beorhtnoth*. The text was first published in 1953.¹² It is of course nonsense to say that it is properly Gregorian; there is no musical score with square notation on four lines, nor neumatic notation! In the text published in *Essays and Studies*, he concluded the second part with the *Dirige*. So we must have a look at that chant.

Tolkien partially recorded *The Homecoming of Beorhtnoth* before May 3rd, 1954 (published in 1992), and in his letter to Rayner Heppenstall of November 17th, 1954, he selected lines from *Dies iræ* to replace *Dirige* as the conclusion. In fact, in his record he sung both *Dies iræ* and *Dirige*. Rayner Heppenstall answered on November 22nd that different recordings of the *Dies iræ* were considered. On December 1st and 2nd, Tolkien replied that the selected lines of the *Dies iræ* "make sense, are apt, and preserve the rhyme-scheme. They are either recited in speaking voice or sung to simple tone or tune (which preserves the metre and emphases the rhyme)".¹³ Indeed, it was what he did in his own record, singing, speaking, and reciting on the simple tone (recitation chord of D, second mode). Here is the text Tolkien effectively sung (bold italics) and said (italics).¹⁴

---

11 Naples, BN, VII, Aa 3, following Stäblein col. 136. The manuscript is sometimes dated 12th century.
12 Scull and Hammond (1, 167) gave 1931 as the first date of existence of the text, but the Gordon-Tolkien collection in Leeds seems to have drafts of a dialogue of alliterative verse from the 1920s (*MS* 1952/2/1, 6 leaves).
13 Scull and Hammond 1, 469. Rayner Heppenstall doesn't seem to give further details about this project in his volumes of memoirs: *Four absentees* and *The Intellectual Part*.
14 We were unable to gain access to the archive of the BBC. We would have liked to know if the selected text of the *Dies iræ* is the same.

Dies iræ, dies illa, *Solvet sæclum in favílla,* *Teste David cum Sibýlla!*	Day of vengeance, ah, that day! When the world shall burn away, As David and the Sibyl say.
Quantus tremor est futúrus, *quando judex est ventúrus,* *cuncta stricte discussúrus!*	Ah, the trembling! ah, the fearing As the Judge to us is nearing, Our world in pieces strict to lay.
Tuba mirum spargens sonum *per sepúlcra regiónum,* *coget omnes ante thronum.*	Trumpets sprinkling awesome soundings In the graveyards and surroundings Will drive us all before the throne.
Mors stupébit et natúra, *cum resúrget creatúra,* *judicánti responsúra. (...)*	Death stands gaping, as does Nature; While arises every creature Facing the judge to atone.
Rex treméndæ majestátis, *qui salvándos salvas gratis,* *salva me, fons pietátis.*	Monarch of mighty majesty, Who frees the men who should be free, Save me, fountain of the pure!
Juste Judex ultiónis, *donum fac remissiónis* *ante diem ratiónis.*	O just judger of perdition, Give my soul gift of remission Before the issue of the World!
Ingemísco, tamquam reus, *culpa rubet vultus meus,* *supplicánti parce Deus. (...)*	I am groaning like one guilty; Redness now has overspilled me – Spare this kneeling man, O Lord!
Preces meæ non sunt dignæ, *sed tu bonus fac benígne,* *ne perénni cremer igne.*	All my prayers sound so lowly, But be kindly and be holy Lest in endless ash I burn!
Inter oves locum præsta, *et ab hædis me sequéstra,* *státuens in parte dextra.*	Put me with your shriven sheep, No company with goats I'll keep, Standing ever at your right hand.
Lacrymósa dies illa, *qua resúrget ex favílla* *judicándus homo reus.*	O that day of tears When arises from the ashes Man, accused, to be judged
Huic ergo parce, Deus. *Pie Jesu Dómine,* *dona ei réquiem. Amen.*	Therefore, spare him, O Lord O pious Lord Jesus Give him rest. Amen.

The *Dies iræ* is among the few sequences that the Council of Trent lets be sung. Frederick Raby, in his classic book reissued by Oxford University Press in 1953 (just before Tolkien recorded this piece), thought it was "the most majestic of medieval sequences. Perfect in form, and exhibiting complete mastery of the two-syllabed rime" (443). But if Tolkien is attentive to the rhyme, he is not to the two-syllabed rime: he didn't sing it as a sequence as such where the melody alternates after two tercets (otherwise he would have changed the melody with *Tuba…*). Tolkien is manifestly mindful of the rhyme!

Since Bartholomew of Pisa, it was long reputed to be a hymn by Thomas de Celano (see e.g. Warren), but this Franciscan friar was born two centuries after the battle of Maldon. This anachronism is quite surprising for a medievalist like Tolkien. But is it anachronism for certain? Tolkien cut the sequence, alternating speaking and singing. That's a kind of deconstruction, going back in a sense to the time of the elaboration of this sequence. We know quite little about liturgy in England in the 10th Century and about liturgy in Ely Abbey (see Pfaff 53-5, 186 sqq., Dumville 127-32). But we know that the origin of *Dies iræ, dies illa* can be found explicitly in canticles such as *Ad te Deum gloriose* (in existence in the 10th century) and from the *tropus Audi tellus, audi magni maris limbus* of the Reponsory *Libera me Domine* (around the year 1000[15]). After all, in 1931, Dom Mauro Inguanez discovered in Naples a manuscript of the third part from the 12th century without the *Lacrimosa* tercet (furthermore also in existence in the 12th century as a *tropus* of the *Libera me*)[16], only rejoining it in c. 1250. So it seems that Thomas de Celano only worked on previous material to give it the shape we know thereafter. Tolkien used the received text with *Lacrimosa*, but let's note he put it after a spoken stanza, which is a kind of cutting.

What about the music itself? "The author of the melody of *Dies iræ*, as well as the exact time of its composition remain unknown," said Robert Chase (509), and it may be that it was Adam of St. Victor in Paris (died around 1146). Tolkien indeed didn't sing the Gregorian melody as such but used the simple

---

15 See Payen 52. Some even say there are Hebrew and Byzantine antecedents for that hymn (see Werner, "Hebrew and Oriental Christian Metrical Hymns" 424, who mentions that the similarities are known as early as Armand Kaminka in 1906, who considered parallels with Aramean or Syriac penitential poems (cf. his *The Sacred Bridge* 252-5)), but the similarities occur where Tolkien cuts the text for the first time! Even if these studies were published in 1906 and 1950, Tolkien did not follow them!
16 See Ignuanez and Amelli (cf. Inguanez, *Revista liturgica*, 18, 1931, 277-82). Vellekoop confirms, on the basis of a French source of the 12th century, the existence of the text before Thomas de Celano. See more recently Chase 509.

tone. His goal here was not historical consistency nor musical performance or plausibility, but poetic effect for the metre and rhyme.

Dirige

Let's finish with the *Dirige*[17]. It is sung in the Roman Office of the Dead as the opening of the first nocturn of the Matins. Tolkien chooses only three verses (coming from Psalm 5.8-9) before the doxology. The first line comes indeed from Psalm 5.9. He seems to cut the first line, not retaining *Deus meus* in "*Dirige Domine Deus meus in conspectus viam meam*". Almost all manuscripts include *Deus meus*, but a single manuscript of the 13th century (Aachen, Domarchiv, D-AAm G 20) has the same lesson. Some think that the Office was introduced in England around 680 (see Ottosen 34). The basic structure of European treatment of the dead was in place by the 9th century, and the shape of the funeral evolved from that time due to the monks' habit (see Quivik 31-2), but the rite is still reputed to have not been unified until around 900 (see Thompson 63, and Wieck, "The Death desired"). The antiphon *Dirige* is attested in the 10th century (*Le Ponticifical romano-germanique du dixième siècle* 287). The Office of the Dead takes place in the so-called *Red Book of Darley*.[18] This text, interesting for its Tolkienian title (*Red Book*), has been given the date c. 1061 (see Gittos). The *Regularis Concordia* (code of monastic law produced in 970) shows that the Office of the Dead contained Matins, Lauds, and Vespers (also known as *Placebo*). The use of Sarum was followed in England, but here or there a monastery could have deviated from its use (see Schell 50-2). There's no printed material, even for the Missal, from Ely; manuscripts were sufficient before the Sarum book became paramount.[19] In the manuscript, the *Vetus Liber Archidiaconi Eliensis* (13th century) mentions the *Dirige* (*Vetus Liber Archidiaconi Eliensis* 4, 168, 200). Praying the Office *for* the Dead (as it was long said) was considered a secure way to reduce the purgatory[20] period. The Matins were recited from Breviary or chanted from Antiphonary by

---

17 Under the form *Dirge*, it sometimes refers to the whole Office of the Dead. This form was acclimated in English in the 14th century. See Koszul 103.
18 Cambridge, Corpus Christi College MS 442, p. 429-444. See Pfaff 94.
19 See Wordsworth and Littlehales 174. The Office of the Dead in the 1531 Sarum Breviary can be read in the edition *Breviarium ad usum insignis ecclesiæ Sarum*, ed. by Procter & Christopher Wordsworth, col. 273. Not surprisingly, the Matins begin with the *Dirige*.
20 The concept and name of Purgatory as a place is earlier that that of the state of purification, see Le Goff (book I, ch. 3.) who dates it from 1170. Augustine is considered the true father of Purgatory.

monks hired for that prayer (see Wieck, "Prayer for the People" 412). So when Tolkien chose the monks of Ely, he showed that he well knew the practice of the Middle Ages. He sung the *Dirige* in an archaic psalm tone, the final remaining on the recitation chord (D) with a characteristic melisma of the mother tone of D (D-D-D-D-C-D-E-E-D). Tolkien, just before and after singing the *Dirige* of his own, mumbles prayers (that's part of his scene play), and we still remain unable to clearly hear what he "said". Here is the text of the *Dirige*[21].

Dīrige, Domine, in cōnspectū tuō viam meam.	Ps. 5.9 O Lord, make your way straight before me.
Intrōībō in domum tuam: adōrābō ad templum sanctum tuum in timōre tuō.	Ps. 5.8 I will enter your house: I will bow down toward your holy temple in awe of you.
Domine, dēdūc mē in jūstitiā tuā: propter inimīcōs meōs	
dīrige in cōnspectū tuō viam meam.	Ps. 5.9 Lead me, O Lord, in your righteousness because of my enemies; make your way straight before me.
Glōria Patrī et Fīliō et Spīrituī Sanctō: sicut erat in prīncipiō et nunc et semper et in sæcula sæculōrum.	Doxology Glory to the Father, and to the Son, and to the Holy Ghost as it was in the beginning, is now, and ever shall be, world without end.
Dīrige, Domine, in cōnspectū tuō viam meam.	
(cf. HBBS, 142)	Ps. 5.9 O Lord, make your way straight before me.

Conclusions

We can suggest three conclusions.

1. Tolkien's first real encounter with Gregorian chant is in the Oratory of Birmingham in 1903/1904. The differences in sacred music between Gregorian chant and modern music were obvious at this turning point in the history of the Church. Tolkien loved the Latin language (he was first a student in Classics!) and was able to understand it. Singing in Latin was not a trouble for him.

2. The *Kyrie eleison* encapsulates Tolkienian thought for considerations of Mercy. The litany prayer offers a feeling of the transcendence of God contrasting with

---

21 Text with macrons marking etymological long vowels by Bertrand Bellet and Benjamin Babut <https://www.jrrvf.com/glaemscrafu/English/dirige.html>, accessed Feb 23rd, 2018.

our finitude. Furthermore, Tolkien translated it into Quenya; Elves also deserve Mercy! What about Estel for them?

3. Laments, in his mind, are usually the kinds of texts requiring the pattern of Gregorian chant. *Dirige, Dies iræ* (Office of the Dead), and the *Lamentation of Jeremiah Prophet* (*Tenebræ*) are all but accidental choices. Gregorian chant conveys the Christian spirituality of Death, an important matter for Tolkien.

Tolkien took patterns from Gregorian chant for his imaginary worlds. He never, as far as we know, used it for reading *Beowulf.* Studies for that point came about after his death (see for example Luecke, and Sato). No matter, he can now sing even better in thanksgiving, intercession, and praise: *Kyrie eleison*!

About the Authors

MICHAËL DEVAUX (Ph.D. in Metaphysics) teaches Philosophy of Education at the University of Caen Normandy (at Alençon). He has also lectured on Tolkien since 2010 in Paris (*Collège des Bernardins*). He is the academic editor of four books about Tolkien, and has published, for example, previously unknown texts about Elvish Reincarnation. He has lectured on Tolkien in France, England, Italy, Germany, and the Netherlands.

GUGLIELMO SPIRITO (Ph.D. in Theology) is a Conventual Franciscan friar (Minorit). He is professor at the Theological Institute of Assisi (ITA) since 1994. On J.R.R. Tolkien, he has published essays, articles, and books, including *Tra San Francesco e Tolkien* and *Lo Specchio di Galadriel* with Il Cerchio (2006, in Italian) and several papers with Walking Tree Publishers and *Hither Shore* (2008-2015, in English).

List of Abbreviations of Tolkien's Works

L	*The Letters of J.R.R. Tolkien*
LotR	*The Lord of the Rings*
S	*The Silmarillion*

Bibliography

AINSLIE, John R. "English Liturgical Music before Vatican II." *English Catholic Worship: Liturgical Renewal in England since 1900*. Eds. James Dunlop Crichton, H.E. Winstone, and John R. Ainslie. London: Geoffrey Chapman, 1979.

BELLASIS, Edward. *Cardinal Newman as a Musician*. London: Kegan Paul Trench, Trübner, 1892.

BLACKHAM, Robert S. *The J.R.R. Tolkien Miscellany*. Stroud: The History Press, 2012.

BLATCHLY, John, and Richard WILSON. *The Chapels and Music of Ipswhich School*. 23 p. http://www.ipswichschoolmuseumandarchives.co.uk.

Breviarium ad usum insignis ecclesiæ Sarum. Ed. Francis Procter and Christopher Wordsworth. Cambridge: Cambridge University Press, 1879, fasc. II.

CHASE, Robert. *Dies iræ. A Guide to Requiem Music*. Oxford: The Scarecrow Press, 2003.

CILLI, Oronzo. *Tolkien e l'Italia. Il mio viaggio in Italia. Diario inedito dell'agosto 1955*. Rimini: Il Cerchio, 2016.

COMBE, Pierre (Dom). *The Restoration of Gregorian Chant*. Trans. Theodore Marier and William Skinner. Washington, D.C.: The Catholic University of America Press, 2003.

CROUAN, Denis. *The History and the Future of the Roman Liturgy*. Trans. Michael Miller. San Francisco, CA: Ignatius Press, 2005.

DEVAUX, Michaël. *Le Gondole di Gondor: il viaggio di Tolkien a Venezia (1955)*. S.l.: Società Tolkieniana Italiana, n.d.

DROUT, Michael D.C. (ed.). *J.R.R. Tolkien Encyclopedia*. London: Routledge, 2007.

DUMVILLE, D. N. *Liturgy and the Ecclesiastical History of Late Anglo-Saxon England*. Woodbridge: Boydell & Brewer, 1992.

EDEN, Bradford Lee. "Gregorian Chant as Influence on Tolkien's Development of Lyric and Song." *Kalamazoo, 40th International Congress on Medieval Studies*, May 2005 (unpublished).

ELIOT, T.S. "Four Quartets." *The Complete Poems and Plays of T.S. Eliot*. London: Faber & Faber, 1969, 190.

FERRANDEZ BRU, José Manuel. *La Conexión Española de J.R.R. Tolkien "El Tío Curro"*. Astorga: CSED, 2013.

GITTOS, Helen. "Is there any evidence for the liturgy of parish churches in late Anglo-Saxon England? The Red Book of Darley and the status of Old English." *Pastoral Care in Late Anglo-Saxon England*. Ed. Francesca Tinti. Woodbridge: Boydell Press, 2005, 63-82.

HAMMOND, Wayne G. *J.R.R. Tolkien. A Descriptive Bibliography*. With the assistance of Douglas A. Anderson. Winchester: St Paul's Bibliographies, 1993.

HAYBURN, Robert F. *Papal Legislation on Sacred Music, 95 A.D. to 1977 A.D.* Collegeville, MN: The Liturgical Press, 1979.

HUMPHREYS, Maggie, and Robert EVANS (eds.). *Dictionary of Composers for Church in Great Britain and Ireland*. London: Mansell 1997.

HUTTON, Arthur Wollaston. "Personal reminiscences of Cardinal Newman." *The Expositor*, 4th series, 2.3 (1890): 223-40.

IGNUANEZ, Mauro, and Ambrogio AMELLI. "Il Dies iræ in un codice del secolo XII." *Miscellanea Cassinese* 11 (1931): 5-11.

SAINT JOHN PAUL II. *Apostolic Letter Orientale Lumen. The Light of the East*. Boston, MA: Pauline Books & Media, 1995.

JORGENSEN, Estelle R. "Myth, Song, and Music Education: The Case of Tolkien's *The Lord of the Rings* and Swann's *The Road Goes Ever On*." *The Journal of Aesthetic Education* 40.3 (2006): 1-21.

JUNGMANN, Joseph. *The Mass of the Roman Rite: its Origins and Development (Missarum Solemnia)*. Vol. I. New York City, NY: Benziger Brothers, 1950.

KENDRICK, Robert L. *Singing Jeremiah: Music and Meaning in Holy Week*. Bloomington, IN: Indiana University Press, 2014.

KENNEDY, Michael and Joyce. *The Oxford Dictionary of Music*. 6th ed. Ed. Tim Rutherford-Johnson. Oxford: Oxford University Press, 2013.

KOBOT, Joanna. "Dynamics in Correlation: Words and Music in a Song by J.R.R. Tolkien and D. Swann." *Inklings: Jahrbuch für Ästhetik* 5 (1987): 311-34.

KOSZUL, André. "Le latin dans l'anglais." *Bulletin de l'association Guillaume Budé* 1.3 (1956): 92-106.

LE GOFF, Jacques. *The Birth of Purgatory*. Trans. Arthur Goldhammer. Chicago, IL: University of Chicago Press, 1984.

LEONBERGER, Richard G. *A Swann's song in Middle-earth: an exploration of Donald Swann's* The Road Goes Ever On *and the development of a system of lyric diction for Tolkien's constructed, elvish languages*. Baton Rouge, LA: Louisiana State University, 2016.

LUECKE, Jane-Marie (OSSB). *Measuring Old English Rhythm. An Application of the Principles of Gregorian Chant Rhythm to the Meter of* Beowulf. Madison, WI: University of Wisconsin Press, 1978.

MIQUEL, Pierre. "Newman et Dom Guéranger.", *La Vie monastique selon saint Benoît*. Paris: Beauchesne, 1979, 286-92.

MITCHELL, W.H. "First fruits of the Gregorian Commission." *The Tablet* (74) 2 (1905).

Muir, Thomas Erskine. "Sacred Sound for a Holy Space: Dogma, Worship and Music at Solemn Mass during the Victorian Era, 1829-1903." *Music and Theology in Nineteenth Century Britain*. Ed. Martin Clarke. London and New York City, NY: Routledge, 2012, 37-60.

― *Roman Catholic Church Music in England, 1791–1914: A Handmaid of the Liturgy?* London: Routledge, 2008.

Murray, Paul. *In the Grip of Light. The Dark and Bright Journey of Christian Contemplation*. London: Bloomsbury, 2012.

Newman, Saint John Henry. *The Idea of a University*. Ed. Frank M. Turner. New Haven, CT and London: Yale University Press, 1996.

Nicholls, Guy. "The Contribution of the Oratories to the liturgical life of England." 1999. www.oratoriosanfilippo.org/conferenza-nicholls.pdf. 27 May 2017).

Ottosen, Knud. *The Responsories and Versicles of the Latin Office of the Dead*. Aarhus: Aarhus University Press, 1993.

Payen, Jean-Charles. "Le *Dies Iræ* dans la prédication de la mort et des fins dernières au Moyen Âge." *Romania* 86 (1965): 48-76.

Pfaff, Richard W. *The Liturgy in Medieval England: A History*. Cambridge: Cambridge University Press, 2009.

Pius X. "Motu proprio Tra le sollicitudini." *Acta Sanctæ Sedis* 36 (1903-4): 387-95. http://w2.vatican.va/content/pius-x/la/motu_proprio/documents/hf_p-x_motu-proprio_19031122_sollecitudini.html.

Pius XII. "Musicæ Sacræ Disciplina." *Discorsi e Radiomessaggi*, vol. 17: *Diciassettesimo anno di Pontificato, 2 marzo 1955–1o marzo 1956, Vatican: Tipografia Poliglotta Vaticana, 1965*, 571-88. http://w2.vatican.va/content/pius-xii/la/encyclicals/documents/hf_p-xii_enc_25121955_musicae-sacrae.html.

Phemister, William. "Fantasy Set to Music: Donald Swann, C.S. Lewis and J.R.R. Tolkien." *Seven: An Anglo-American Literary Review* 13 (1996): 64-82.

Le Pontifical romano-germanique du dixième siècle. Ed. Cyrille Vogel and Reinhard Elze. Vatican: Biblioteca Apostolica Vaticana, vol. I, 1963.

Quivik, Melinda A. *A Christian Funeral*. Minneapolis, MN: Augsburg Fortress, 2005.

Raby, Frederic J.E. *A History of Christian-Latin Poetry*. Oxford: Clarendon Press, (1927) 1953.

Reznikoff, Iégor. "La spirale ascendante et profonde du *Kyrie Eleison*." *La Transcendance, le corps et l'icône dans les fondements de l'art sacré et de la liturgie. Actes du colloque Nicée II, 787-1987, douze siècles d'images religieuses* (Paris, 1986). Paris: Le Cerf, 1987, 8-9.

Sato, Noboru. "*Beowulf* and Gregorian Chant." *Otsuka Review* 18 (1982): 85-100.

SCHELL, Sarah. *The Office of the Dead in England* [...] *c. 1250-c. 1500*. Edinburgh: University of St. Andrews, 2009.

SCULL Christina, and Wayne G. HAMMOND. *The J.R.R. Tolkien Companion and Guide*, vol. 1: *Chronology*; vol. 2: *Reader's Guide*, Revised and Expanded Edition. London: HarperCollins Publishers, 2017.

STÄBLEIN, Bruno. "Lamentatio." *Die Musik in Geschichte und Gegenwart*. Vol. 8. Ed. Friedrich Blume. London: Bärenreiter, 1960, 133-48.

SWANN, Donald. *Swann's Way: A Life in Song*. Ed. Lyn Smith. London: William Heinemann, 1991.

The Road Goes Ever On. 2nd ed. London: Allen & Unwin, 1968.

THOMPSON, Oscar (ed. in chief). *The International Cyclopedia of Music and Musicians*. Dodd: Mead, 1985.

THOMPSON, Victoria. *Dying and Death in Later Anglo-Saxon England*. Woodbridge: The Boydell Press, 2002.

TOLKIEN, J.R.R., *The Letters of J.R.R. Tolkien*. Ed. Humphrey Carpenter with the assistance of Christopher Tolkien. London: HarperCollins Publishers, 2000.

Litany of Loreto in "Words of Joy (Part Two)." Ed. Patrick Wynne, *Vinyar Tengwar* 44 (2002): 11-20.

The Lord of the Rings. 60th Anniversary edition. Eds. Wayne G. Hammond and Christina Scull. London: HarperCollins Publishers, 2014.

"The Man who understands Hobbits." *The Daily Telegraph Magazine*, 22 March 1968: 31-35 (Interview by Charlotte and Denis Plimmer).

The Silmarillion. London: HarperCollins Publishers, 1994.

"The Homecoming of Beorhtnoth, Beorhthelm's son." *Tree and Leaf*. London: HarperCollins Publishers, 2001, 121-150.

TOLKIEN, Priscilla. "Foreword." *A Tribute to J.R.R. Tolkien*. Ed. Rosemary Gray. Pretoria: University of South Africa, 1992, vii-x.

VANAUKEN, Sheldon. *A Severe Mercy*. New York City, NY: HarperCollins Publishers, 1977.

VELLEKOOP, Kees. *Dies irae dies illa. Studien zur Frühegeschichte einer Sequenz*. Bilthoven: Creighton, 1978.

Vetus Liber Archidiaconi Eliensis. Ed. C. L. Feltoe and Ellis H. Minns. Cambridge: Cambridge Antiquarian Society, 1917.

WARREN, Charles F.S. *The Authorship, text, and history of the hymn Dies Iræ*. London: Baker, 1902.

WASHINGTON, Henry. "The Oratory Musical Tradition." *The London Oratory Centenary, 1884-1984*. Eds. Michael Napier and Alastair Laing. London: Trefoil Books, 1984.

WENDLING, Woody and Susan. "A Speculative Meditation on Tolkien's Sources for the Character Gollum." *Inklings Forever* (vol. 8): *A Collection of Essays Presented at the 8th Frances White Ewbank Colloquium on C.S. Lewis and Friends*. Upland: Taylor University Press, 2012.

WENDLING, Woody. "The Quest for Pity and Mercy in Tolkien's Middle Earth." *Inklings Forever* (vol. 5): *A Collection of Essays Presented at the 5th Frances White Ewbank Colloquium on C.S. Lewis and Friends*. Upland: Taylor University Press, 2006.

WERNER, Eric. "Hebrew and Oriental Christian Metrical Hymns: A Comparison." *Hebrew Union College Annual* 23.2 (1950-1951): 97-432.

The Sacred Bridge. The Interdependence of Liturgy and Music in Synagogue and Church during the First Millenium. London: Dobson, 1959.

WIECK, Roger S. "Prayer for the People: The Book of Hours." *A History of Prayer: The First to the Fifteenth Century*. Ed. Roy Hammerling. Leiden: Brill 2008, 389-440.

"The Death desired: books of Hours and the Medieval Funeral." *Death and dying in the Middle Ages*. Eds. Edelgard E. DuBruck, and Barbara I. Gusick. New York City, NY: Lang, 1999, 431-76.

WILLIAMS, Benjamin, and Harold ANSTALL. *Orthodox Worship*. Minneapolis, MN: Light and Life Publishing Company, 1990.

WORDSWORTH, Christopher, and Henry LITTLEHALES. *The Old Services-Books of the English Church*. London: Methuen, 1904.

ZAPKE, Susana. *Hispania Vetus*. Bilbao: Fundación BBVA, 2007.

Nancy Martsch

Middle-earth Improv:
Song Writing and Improvisation in Tolkien's Works

Abstract

The Hobbit and *The Lord of the Rings* contain many poems said to have been read, recited, chanted or sung by the participants in the stories. This essay will focus on the improvisation of songs and the writing of words to tunes: first treating these stories as authentic fictional history, translated by J.R.R. Tolkien, to observe how the characters created their songs; and then treating the stories as feigned history written by J.R.R. Tolkien, to examine how Tolkien created the songs himself. We will also examine previously created poems interpolated into *The Lord of the Rings*, and songs which Tolkien created (and sang) elsewhere.

Introduction

[Sam] murmured old childish tunes out of the Shire, and snatches of Mr. Bilbo's rhymes that came into his mind like fleeting glimpses of the country of his home. And then suddenly new strength rose in him, and his voice rang out, while words of his own came unbidden to fit the simple tune. (*RK* 185)

Thus begins "In western lands", a song improvised by Sam in the orc tower. *The Hobbit* and *The Lord of the Rings* contain many poems, said to have been read, recited, chanted, or sung by the participants in the stories. When Bilbo transcribed the words to the dwarves' song at Bag-End, he remarked with regret, "this is like a fragment of their song, if it can be like their song without their music" (*H* 21). Unfortunately, the music has not come down to us, only the words. So, except for the two songs which Tolkien sang when he recorded selections from his works, we don't know what the music sounded like[1] (although many guesses have been made[2]). Therefore, this treatment of Middle-earth songs will focus on the words. In this discussion "song" will be used to mean words intended to be sung to a tune, and "sing", the articulation

---

1 Nor do we know if these were the actual Middle-earth melodies, or just real-world tunes which Tolkien found suitable.
2 See, for instance, *Music in Middle-earth*. Eds. Heidi Steimel and Friedhelm Schneidewind, Walking Tree Publishers, 2010.

of words to a melody. And, to avoid confusion, "compose" will refer the creation of the melody or tune, and "write" to the words. A musically talented person can create an entire song, both tune and words. A less talented individual can still create a song by writing words to an existing tune. And, especially when inspired or under duress, he may be able to improvise a song on the spot, either setting words to an existing tune or perhaps composing a simple tune as well. And finally, the words may be written first, then set to music or sung to a pre-existing tune. We will find examples of all of these in Tolkien's work.

This essay will examine song creation, primarily song *writing*, in the form of on-the-spot improvisation and writing words to existing tunes, in *The Hobbit* and *The Lord of the Rings*, and elsewhere. I will first treat *The Hobbit* and *The Lord of the Rings* as true history, translated from the Red Book of Westmarch by J.R.R. Tolkien, and then as feigned history, created by J.R.R. Tolkien; first to observe how Tolkien ascribed song-creation to his characters, and then to see how Tolkien created songs himself. And lastly, I will examine poems and songs previously created by Tolkien which he interpolated into *The Lord of the Rings*, and songs which he is known to have created (and sung) elsewhere.

The Hobbit and *The Lord of the Rings* as True History in the Literary World

First, let us examine the true history as presented in Tolkien's work. *The Hobbit* and *The Lord of the Rings* were excerpted and translated by the author from "The Downfall of the Lord of the Rings and the Return of the King" in *The Red Book of Westmarch*. Bilbo Baggins's memoir, "There and Back Again", became *The Hobbit*. Frodo Baggins's memoir, with additional material by Samwise Gamgee and others, became *The Lord of the Rings* (*RK* 307). Frodo took care to name the sources of the tunes, when he knew them (mostly Hobbit songs); Bilbo did not name the sources of the tunes that he reported, though guesses can be made. All of the peoples of Middle-earth, from elves to orcs (and maybe even trolls) seem to have been musical, capable of singing and of improvising songs. This is consistent with a society in which books are copied by hand (and thus rare), so knowledge is transmitted orally, often in the form of songs and rhymes.[3]

Let us begin with song improvisation, then consider song modification and writing words to existing tunes. There are three songs which are stated to have been improvised on the spot: Sam's song in the orc tower (cited above) and Bilbo's two songs taunting the spiders of Mirkwood. Sam and Bilbo each found himself in a tight spot and employed song to rescue his friends, one by accident, the other by intent. With Sam's effort, we get a glimpse into the process of song-creation, though we don't know if Sam composed the "simple tune" or not. Bilbo resorted to singing to lure the spiders away from the dwarves imprisoned in the spiders' webs. His first song, "Old fat spider spinning in a tree!" (*H* 138) resembles a schoolyard taunt, and may have been based on some such. But his second song, "Lazy Lob and crazy Cob" (*H* 139), seems too sophisticated to have been composed on the spot.[4] (The same observation applies to Aragorn and Legolas's Lament for Boromir, "Through Rohan over fen and field", *TT* 19-20.)[5] Might Bilbo have polished up his song when writing his memoirs?[6] Or even substituted a new poem? Interpolations can be found in *The Lord of the Rings*: two alliterative verses composed by Rohan's bards after the events described[7] were added to the text, perhaps when the manuscript was copied in Gondor. Frodo, inspired by the laments of the Lothlórien elves, also created a song (and tune?) to eulogize Gandalf ("When evening in the Shire was grey", *FR* 374-5); and Sam improvised an additional verse. And both King Théoden and Éomer spouted alliterative staves in the Battle of the Pelennor Fields, prob-

---

3 The ability of the peoples of Middle-earth to improvise songs and to write new words to existing songs is discussed extensively in Julian Eilmann's Ph.D. thesis, *J.R.R. Tolkien: Romanticist and Poet*, especially in chapters III.2 and III.4. That we both came to similar conclusions is a result of independent study, as neither was aware of the other's work. I am grateful to Dr. Eilmann for allowing me to read his thesis prior to publication.
4 "This little bit of verse is actually quite sophisticated in its metrics" (Rateliff, *Mr. Baggins* 299). Corey Olsen observes that "like the first song, Bilbo's second poetic effort also contains wordplay and double meanings that are quite clever" (163) without considering the poetic skill needed to make these up on the spot.
5 Eilmann makes a similar observation regarding these two songs (356, 417).
6 Or might the song have been polished by Tolkien the translator? All of the songs in *The Hobbit* and *The Lord of the Rings* are very regular in meter and rhyme, a characteristic of written (but not of oral) poetry. Songs from the oral tradition (such as folksongs) frequently have irregular lines, the meter being carried by the tune.
7 The ride of the Rohirrim ("From dark Dunharrow in the dim morning", *RK* 76-7) and the "song of the Mounds of Mundburg" ("We heard of the horns in the hills ringing", *RK* 124-5).

ably drawing on standard battle-cries and their bards' oral alliterative-verse histories (*RK* 112, 119, 122).

But so many of the songs in *The Hobbit* are direct comments on the action that one wonders if these people were either *very* good at song improvisation, or else they were inventing words to existing tunes.[8] In some cases internal evidence suggests the latter. The goblins' dreadful "Burn, burn tree and fern!" (*H* 95) is similar in meter to their march "Clap! Snap! the black crack!" (*H* 59), so it may have used the same tune. The two songs with which the Rivendell elves greeted their visitors, "O! What are you doing" (*H* 48-9) and "The dragon is withered" (*H* 249-50), are variations on the same song, both having the same meter and similar chorus. Perhaps this was a standard song which these elves used to greet and tease their visitors, while improvising comments on the visitors' actions and appearance. And the dwarves' song at Bag-End, "Chip the glasses and crack the plates!" (*H* 19-20) must have been a mighty act of improvisation, unless it was based on some other dwarf song which we don't know about. (Other dwarf songs in *The Hobbit* will be discussed later.)

Far fewer songs in *The Lord of the Rings* comment so directly upon the action. But (unlike in *The Hobbit*) there are instances of the singer modifying the words to the same song or poem to fit the circumstances: Bilbo's poem, "Roads go ever ever on", inspired by his return to Bag-End in *The Hobbit* (*H* 252-3), is recited several times in *The Lord of the Rings* by both Frodo and Bilbo, with appropriate variations in the words (*FR* 44, 82; *RK* 266). And Frodo is noted to have changed the words to Bilbo's old walking-song (*FR* 86-7; *RK* 308).[9] The elves' Hymn to Elbereth, sung English (Westron) and Sindarin ("A Elbereth Gilthoniel"), has differing sets of words, too, though these could be either modifications or just different verses (*FR* 88-9, 250; *TT* 339; *RK* 308). But the variations on "Roads" and the walking-song definitely can be considered forms of improvisation.

---

8 Literary studies name this process "contrafactum, i.e. the adaption of popular melodies for new lyrics, melodies, rhythms, the structure of stanzas and verses, possibly whole parts of the word material, especially its sound qualities, are kept in the process" (Eilmann 353).
9 "Presently [Sam] became aware that Frodo was singing softly to himself, singing the old walking-song, but the words were not quite the same. *Still round the corner there may wait*" (*RK* 308).

Did other songs make use of improvisation? Corey Olsen believes that the song sung by the Lake-men ("The King beneath the mountains", *H* 169) was "in fact a new song, inspired by the overheard snatches of the old songs" (187). Perhaps he was influenced by the comment that the Lake-people were soon singing new songs (predicting the dragon's death and coming prosperity) as well as the old ones (*H* 170). And Ben Koolen is of the opinion that Gimli, in *The Lord of the Rings*, "added a stanza to ["The Song of Durin"] and possibly adapted the original text to the actuality of the devastation he had seen [in Moria]" (82). Though neither interpretation is specified in the text.

As for writing new words to existing tunes, we have several good examples, especially in *The Lord of the Rings*. Both Bilbo and Sam are stated to have set new words to old tunes: Sam, his "Stone Troll" song (*FR* 219-20); Bilbo, his walking-song ("Upon the hearth the fire is red", *FR* 86-7) and his song "There is an inn" (*FR* 170-2).[10] Bilbo also wrote the narrative song "Eärendil was a mariner" (with a few additions by Aragorn), which he chanted in Rivendell to a tune not named (*FR* 246-9). Bilbo Baggins was a hobbit of great learning who translated songs from the elvish and wrote poetry; indeed, he was known in the Shire as a writer of verse and singer of songs (c.f. Sam's song in the orc tower, above). Though less widely recognized as such, Samwise Gamgee was also a songwriter and poet. But the finest example of writing words to an existing tune comes from the dwarves' song at Bag-End, which was the source for at least one, possibly two, others. As recounted in *The Hobbit*, at the start of their quest the dwarves sang their song of grim resolve: "Far over the misty mountains cold" (*H* 21-2). Probably this song had been created for their quest at an earlier time, but whether it was original or based on some pre-existing model we do not know. However, later in the Lonely Mountain, when the dwarves wanted to cheer up their leader Thorin, they serenaded him with "Under the Mountain dark and tall", which, as Bilbo reported, "was much like the song they had sung long before in Bilbo's little

---

10 Sam's "Stone Troll" song: "he began to sing to an old tune. *Troll sat alone on his seat of stone* [...] 'Where did you come by that, Sam?' asked Pippin. 'I've never heard those words before.' [...] 'It's out of his own head, of course,' said Frodo" (*FR* 219-20). Bilbo's walking-song: "Bilbo Baggins had made the words, to a tune that was as old as the hills, and taught it to Frodo" (*FR* 86). Frodo's song at the inn: "Then in desperation [Frodo] began a ridiculous song that Bilbo had been rather fond of (and indeed rather proud of, for he had made up the words himself). [...] *There is an inn, a merry old inn*" (*FR* 170).

hobbit-hole" (*H* 221-2). Since several of the verses are very similar, it may have been written to the same tune. And finally, in *The Lord of the Rings*, Merry and Pippin prepared a song to launch their adventure, which they sang at Crickhollow: "It was made on the model of the dwarf-song that started Bilbo on his adventure long ago, and went to the same tune: *Farewell we call to hearth and hall!*" (*FR* 116). Though it was lighter in tone, as befits hobbit sensibility. So, in *The Hobbit* and *The Lord of the Rings* we have examples of on-the-spot improvisation, modification of words to existing songs, writing new words to existing tunes, and song and poetry composition – all by ordinary folk, not by professional bards. All of the peoples of Middle-earth were musical, and all races sang and improvised songs.

The Hobbit and The Lord of the Rings as Feigned History Created by J.R.R. Tolkien

Now let us turn away from considering *The Hobbit* and *The Lord of the Rings* as true history, and instead consider them as feigned history – two novels which J.R.R. Tolkien created. Did the author derive any of the songs in his stories from real-world songs? We will first survey Tolkien's education as a poet and possible song sources, then examine the writing of *The Hobbit* and *The Lord of the Rings* to see how many of the songs might have been based on real-world songs. Lastly we will observe the poems which Tolkien interpolated into *The Lord of the Rings*, and then look at other, non-Middle-earth songs which Tolkien is known to have written and sung.

First, Tolkien's background. One could say that poetry was "in the air" during Tolkien's youth and young manhood. As a schoolboy, he was required to translate English poems into Latin poems (*L* 213; Turner 214-7), which gave him a solid foundation in poetic structure. Like many educated young men of his day, he read and wrote serious poetry, some of which displays the first glimmerings of what would later become his "Silmarillion" mythology, his *legendarium*. As both a university student and later as a professor, he studied the poetry of past ages, and wrote poetry in those styles: in the meter of the *Kalevala*, in Icelandic *fornyrðislag*, in the style of the Breton lay, in Old English alliterative verse. He wrote poetry in other languages, too: Gothic, Old and Middle English, and his invented elven tongues. And he translated medieval poetry into English poetry. So Tolkien certainly had expertise as a poet.

But (like today), music was also "in the air" in the early 20th century. Recordings and radio were still relatively new inventions, which would gain prominence as the century progressed. People enjoyed live music in the concert hall and elsewhere. And they made their own music: at church and at school, in amateur theatricals, and in the home. Tolkien's fiancée Edith Bratt was an accomplished pianist. The dwarves' impromptu concert at the beginning of *The Hobbit* is a parody of a musical salon (and informal music can also offer words and tunes for the would-be songwriter). So there was plenty of material available, both academic and popular, to provide sources for the songs in Tolkien's novels. But did Tolkien draw on these sources, or were all of his creations original? Did Tolkien write his songs to existing tunes?

Our evidence for songwriting derives from Tolkien's own words, the recollections of his friends, and from his recordings. Tolkien sang at mass and to his children.[11] He recorded excerpts from *The Hobbit*, *The Lord of the Rings*, and *The Adventures of Tom Bombadil*.[12] Most of the recorded poems and songs are read or declaimed. The Ents' Marching song ("We come, we come with roll of drum", *TT* 88-9) is half-sung, with variations in rhythm and pitch, but no tune. Only two, the "The Stone Troll" and "Namárië", are actually sung to a tune.

The Hobbit was the first of the Middle-earth novels to be published. It arose from a story which Tolkien created and read to his sons (Tolkien recorded a wonderfully dramatic reading of "Riddles in the Dark", but none of the songs). To the best of our knowledge, "virtually all of the poems in *The Hobbit* were apparently written in sequence with the manuscript of the book" (*Annotated Hobbit* 92). Though elements of *The Hobbit* may have developed orally prior to being written down. *The Hobbit* was not originally conceived as part of Tolkien's *legendarium*. Nor did he include different languages for the different

---

11 I asked Colin Havard, the son of Inkling Dr. Robert Havard, if he had any information about J.R.R. Tolkien singing during Inklings meetings, either while reading drafts from his *The Lord of the Rings* or elsewhere. Colin Havard replied, "I can only say I have no memory of hearing him sing except perhaps at Mass." And Michael Foster (who had forwarded my inquiry) added, "According to Simon Tolkien, JRRT did participate actively in the singing of the Mass" (NM to CH and MF, October 13, 2016).
12 First issued by Caedmon Records, now available as the *The J.R.R. Tolkien Audio Collection*. Tolkien also recorded "The Homecoming of Beorhtnoth" on his own tape recorder, and *sang* the chant of the monks of Ely at the end.

peoples, as he would later do in *The Lord of the Rings*. But he did distinguish among the different peoples through the poetic structure of their songs. Each group – the dwarves, Rivendell and Mirkwood elves, goblins, the hobbit Bilbo, the Lake-men – has its own preferred rhyme schemes and meter.[13] To give one example, the Rivendell elves are the only people whose songs consistently make use of feminine rhyme.

Christopher Tolkien remembers his father having sung the Hobbit songs during these readings.[14] But were these songs fully sung, like the "The Stone Troll", or perhaps half-sung, like the Ents' Marching Song?[15] Without recordings or references to specific tunes, we may never know.

The Hobbit novel was a success, so when Tolkien's publishers asked for a sequel, Tolkien began work on what would become *The Lord of the Rings*. After many false starts, the story grew, eventually becoming attached to the *legendarium*. Now Tolkien distinguished among the peoples of Middle-earth through their languages and styles of speech. The Rohirrim were given Old English names, their songs written in the meter of Old English alliterative verse. Hobbit songs were modeled after English folksongs. Songs in the elven languages were included, and fragments of other tongues. Many drafts have been preserved, so the process of song composition is visible.[16] Songs could be transferred from one character to another: thus Aragorn's Lament for Boromir was first written as "The Lament of *Denethor* for Boromir" (*TI* 384, emphasis added). Sam's song in the orc tower, said to have been improvised on the spot, was actually the product of much labor on Tolkien's part (*SD* 27-8). Occasionally a source can be recognized: for instance, Aragorn's song in Rohan, "Where now the horse and the rider?" (*TT* 112), is "an echo of the Old English poem known as The

---

13 For an excellent analysis of all *The Hobbit* poems, see Corey Olsen's *Exploring J.R.R Tolkien's The Hobbit*.
14 "Thus Christopher Tolkien recalls 'I have a faint dim feeling that for some of them, at any rate, like "far over the misty mountains", he used some sort of recitative' (CT to JDR, November 1993)" (Rateliff, *Mr. Baggins* 66). When, in preparation for this paper I asked Christopher Tolkien if his father sang the songs in *The Hobbit* (or any other songs), Christopher replied "my father did actually sing some of his songs: he didn't have a 'singing voice', but the tunes that he sang to were perfectly evident. I can't actually recall his singing songs from *The Hobbit* when I was a child […] but I think it a virtual certainty that he did so" (CT to NM, 16 October 2016).
15 "If the evidence of Tolkien's recordings […] may be trusted, more often Tolkien did not actually sing the pieces but used a sort of recitative" (Rateliff, *Mr. Baggins* 58).
16 The drafts comprise *The History of Middle-earth*, vols. 6-9: *The Return of the Shadow, The Treason of Isengard, The War of the Ring*, and *Sauron Defeated*.

Wanderer" (Hammond/Scull 399; *TI* 449). Readers will recognize "All that is gold does not glitter" in Bilbo's poetic description of Aragorn (*FR* 182, 260), or see a resemblance to the cadence of the Psalms in the Eagles' proclamation of the fall of the Dark Tower, "Sing now, ye people" (*RK* 241).[17] Scholars have found resemblances for certain songs in *The Hobbit*, too.

And, as we have seen, two songs were sung to tunes. These are Sam's "The Stone Troll", which is sung to the tune of the English folksong "The Fox Went Out on a Winter's Night".[18] And Galadriel's lament "Namárië" is sung to a little-known Gregorian chant from the Dominicans' Tenebrae service.[19] The words to "Namárië", created for *The Lord of the Rings*, might have been written with the Tenebrae chant in mind. The words to "The Stone Troll" are known to have been written much earlier, to the tune of "The Fox", and interpolated into *The Lord of the Rings*. But were any other songs in these novels written to specific tunes – or were they just literary poems masquerading as songs?

Poems and Songs Interpolated into *The Lord of the Rings*

Tolkien interpolated at least seven previously written poems into *The Lord of the Rings*, modifying them as necessary to fit the circumstances of Middle-earth. These are "Roads go ever ever on", from *The Hobbit* (discussed above); Sam's "The Stone Troll" and "Oliphaunt"; Bilbo's "There is an inn" and "Eärendil"; Aragorn's song about Lúthien; and the chapters about Tom Bombadil. The history of these poems is known, and can be studied. Perhaps these studies may shed some light on the way other songs were created for *The Hobbit* and *The Lord of the Rings*.

---

17 A useful list of the poems in *The Lord of the Rings* with a description of their meters can be found in Mary Quella Kelly's "The Poetry of Fantasy: Verse in *The Lord of the Rings*", in *Tolkien and the Critics*. Petra Zimmermann describes "The Function of Poems in Tolkien's *The Lord of the Rings*", in *Tolkien's Poetry*. Other studies can be found.
18 *Not* the same tune as "The Fox Went Out on a Winter's Night" recorded by Burl Ives, Peter, Paul and Mary, and others. The American version is different, as Douglas Anderson observes in *The Annotated Hobbit* (73).
19 "Tenebrae is a sung church service, consisting of selected psalms and biblical readings, celebrated nowadays only on Good Friday and Holy Saturday – but before the reform of the Second Vatican Council held also on Maundy Thursday. During the Offices of the Holy Week, of which Tenebrae are a part, the Dominicans traditionally sing the Lamentations of Jeremiah the Prophet, one of the biblical books. The melody set for these Lamentations was the melody of Galadriel's lament in Lórien" (Morawski 103).

Like *The Hobbit* novel, the poem "The Adventures of Tom Bombadil" arose from stories which Tolkien created for his children in the early 1930s, in this case inspired by a Tom Bombadil doll. The poem was published in the *Oxford Magazine*, 1934. When Tolkien began his "new Hobbit" story, this poem provided the characters, syntax, and even lines for what would become the Tom Bombadil chapters in *The Lord of the Rings*. Following the success of *The Lord of the Rings*, this poem, slightly modified, was published in a small book of poetry eponymously titled *The Adventures of Tom Bombadil* (*ATB* 123, 131-3; Hammond/Scull 124 ff).

Frodo's song at the Prancing Pony inn, "There is an inn", was written in 1919-20, and published as the poem "The Cat and the Fiddle, or A Nursery Rhyme Undone and Its Scandalous Secret Unlocked" in *Yorkshire Poetry*, Leeds, 1923. It purports to be the story behind the nursery rhyme "The Cat and the Fiddle". It's published (slightly revised) in *The Adventures of Tom Bombadil*, under the title "The Man in the Moon Stayed Up Too Late" (*ATB* 173; *Guide* 581; *RS* 145-7). The song Aragorn sings about Lúthien, "The leaves were long" (*FR* 204-5), originated in 1919-20 as the poem "Light as Leaf on Lindentree", very early in the creation of the *legendarium*. Revised in 1923 and 1924, it was inserted into Tolkien's "The Lay of the Children of Húrin", and published in *The Gryphon*, Leeds University, 1925 (*LB* 120-22; *RS* 180).

The hobbit poem "Oliphaunt" ("Grey as a mouse", *TT* 254-5), recited by Sam Gamgee on the border of Mordor, is subject to debate. Wayne G. Hammond and Christina Scull believe that "Oliphaunt" derived from Tolkien's humorous poem "Iumbo, or ye Kinde of ye Oliphaunt", a satire on medieval bestiary poems, published in "Adventures in Unnatural History and Medieval Metres, Being the Freaks of Fisiologus" in *Stapeldon Magazine*, Oxford, 1927 (*ATB* 215-6; Hammond/Scull 460; *Guide* 682-3; *L* 343). But John Rateliff, noting that the meter of "Oliphaunt" is quite different from "Iumbo", believes that this poem, which Tolkien sent in a 1944 letter to his son Christopher (*L* 77), was instead a new poem. He derives it from the style of the Old English *Exeter Book* riddles ("Inside Literature" 136, 147-8). If Rateliff is correct, then "Oliphaunt" was written for *The Lord of the Rings*, and is not an interpolated poem.

But Bilbo's "Eärendil was a mariner" is definitely an interpolated poem, with a long and complex history. "Eärendil" evolved through many iterations from Tolkien's poem "Errantry", probably written in the early 1930s, which he read to an undergraduate club. A later version was published in the *Oxford Magazine* in 1933, and both versions entered general circulation. Then composer Donald Swann set "Errantry" to music for his song cycle *The Road Goes Ever On* in 1967 (Hammond/Scull 210, 214; *L* 161-3; *TI* 85 ff).

About "Errantry", Tolkien wrote, "It is for one thing in a metre I invented (depending on trisyllabic assonances or near-assonances, which is so difficult that except in this one example I have never been able to use it again – it just blew out in a single impulse)" (*L* 162-3). And in a 1966 letter to Donald Swann,

> [it] was intended for *recitation* [emphasis added] with great variations of speed. [...] The "stanzas" as printed indicate the speed-groups. In general these were meant to begin at speed and slow down. [...] It was begun very many years ago, in an attempt to go on with the model that came unbidden into my mind: the first six lines, in which, I guess, *D'ye ken the rhyme to porringer* had a part. (*TI* 85)

But John Rateliff thinks that Chaucer's "Tale of Sir Topas" could also be a source ("Inside Literature" 136). And Dale Nelson, in his *Tolkien Encyclopedia* entry on "Literary Influences, Nineteenth and Twentieth Centuries", suggested that Gilbert and Sullivan's song "I am the very model of a modern major general" (from *The Pirates of Penzance*) was an "influence" for "Errantry" (cited by John R. Holmes (31), who analyzes "Errantry" with respect to this tune). However "Errantry" doesn't fit this tune very well, because "Major General" has four-line stanzas and the stanzas in "Errantry" vary. So, given that Tolkien *recites* "Errantry" on his recording, his descriptions and the poem's history, it is virtually certain that "Errantry" was not written to a tune. Indeed, none of these six interpolated poems appear to be based on tunes. They are all literary creations. But the seventh interpolated poem, Sam's "The Stone Troll", definitely *was* written to a tune. As were other songs not part of *The Hobbit* and *The Lord of the Rings*.

Songs Written (and Sung) by J.R.R. Tolkien

> Setting his own lyrics to traditional tunes was a favorite hobby of Tolkien's: *Songs for the Philologists* includes both funny jingles [...] and serious pieces [...]. (Rateliff, *Mr. Baggins* 57)

In the 1920s, two English professors at Leeds University, E.V. Gordon and J.R.R. Tolkien, set a number of songs to existing tunes for their students. These "Leeds Songs" circulated in mimeographed copies. Later, in 1935-6, a former student, A.H. Smith, now teaching at University College, London, had his students typeset some of these songs as a printing exercise. The resulting booklet, titled *Songs for the Philologists* (1936), contained thirty songs *with the names of their tunes*. Thirteen were by J.R.R. Tolkien: one in Gothic, six in Old English, and six in Modern English (*RS* 145).[20] Three were translations of modern English songs into Old English: "I Love Sixpence", "Who Killed Cock Robin?", and "The Mermaid".[21] Others were set to the tunes of "Twinkle, Twinkle, Little Star", "O'Reilly", "The Vicar of Bray", "Polly Put the Kettle On", and so on (*Guide* 967-8).

One 1926 song, "Pēro and Pōdex" ("Boot and Bottom") – titled "The Root of the Boot" in *Philologists*), was set to the tune of "The Fox Went Out on a Winter's Night". This is the song which became Sam's "The Stone Troll". And Tolkien *sings* it to the tune of "The Fox" on his recording (ibid. 981; *RS* 142-5). When writing *The Lord of the Rings* Tolkien pondered various places to insert this song into the narrative: to be sung by Bingo (later Frodo) at the Prancing Pony inn? by Bilbo at Rivendell? by Sam in the orc tower? before giving it to Sam beside the petrified trolls (*ATB* 198; *RS* 142, 144; *TI* 333).

Christopher Tolkien writes that "my father was extremely fond of this song, which went to the tune of *The fox went out on a winter's night*, and my delight in the line *If bonfire there be, 'tis underneath* [in 'The Root of the Boot'] is among my very early recollections" (*RS* 142). As "The Fox Went Out on a Winter's Night" exists in multiple versions and in multiple tunes, and dates back to the 15th century, it would have appealed to Tolkien professionally, too.

---

20 The complete list is in *The J.R.R. Tolkien Companion and Guide: Reader's Guide*, 968.
21 This is "The Mermaid" which begins with the lines "It was in the broad Atlantic/ 'mid the equinoctial gales." There are quite a few other songs with the same title.

Which again brings us back to the two songs in *The Lord of the Rings* which were sung to existing tunes, one written for the story, one created long before. It appears, therefore, that the majority of poems said to be "songs" in *The Hobbit* and *The Lord of the Rings* were actually literary creations, not written to tunes. For if others were written to specific tunes, we lack the evidence for them.

Were Other Songs Set to the Tune of "The Fox Went Out"?

As Tolkien was so fond of "The Fox Went Out on a Winter's Night", might he have written other songs to this tune? "The Fox" has stanzas of four lines each, the first three rhymed (a triplet), the fourth unrhymed and usually ending on a variation on "town-o". The chorus is formed by repeating "town-o" and the last two lines. "The Stone Troll" also has four-line stanzas, but Tolkien elaborated upon the rhyme scheme while retaining the same format for the chorus.

At least two of Tolkien's other poems follow this pattern: "The Lay of Beowulf" and "The Corrigan" II. Dimitria Fimi asserts that "The Lay of Beowulf" was "written to be sung to the tune of [...] 'The Fox'" (28). By 1926, Tolkien had written a prose translation of *Beowulf* for his students. At some point he also wrote two ballads, collectively titled "The Lay of Beowulf" (*Beowulf* 417ff). (The second version, "Beowulf and the Monsters", is merely an expansion of the first, "Beowulf and Grendel".) And he specified that "Beowulf" was "*intended to be sung*" (emphasis added). Christopher Tolkien recalls hearing his father *sing* "The Lay of Beowulf" in the early 1930s (*Beowulf* 416).[22] Unfortunately for us he does not name the tune. The meter is very similar to "The Stone Troll" and "The Fox Went Out" but lacks a written chorus of repeated lines. Every fourth line ends in "Heorot" (or in the expanded version, "Heorot", "Denmark", or "Beowulf").

Another poem, titled "The Corrigan" II in *The Lay of Aotrou and Itroun*, edited by Verlyn Flieger (47-52), also fits the format of "The Fox" and "Beowulf". In

---

22 "I have found no mention of these lays even of the slightest nature among my father's writings (apart from the name 'Beowulf' penciled on an early typewritten list of his poems), but the texts are preceded by a page on which he wrote in ink 'Stages in the accretion of new matter to The Lay of Beowulf'. [...] On this cover page there is also a penciled note 'Intended to be sung'. As mentioned in the Preface I remember his singing this ballad to me when I was seven or eight years old, in the early 1930s (but of course it may have been in existence years before that). I think it very probable that it was the first version, *Beowulf and Grendel*, that he sang" (Christopher Tolkien, in *Beowulf* 415-6).

1930 Tolkien wrote three poems based on two Breton songs in Vicomte Hersart de la Villemarqué's *Barzaz Breiz: Chants Populaires de la Bretagne*. Villemarqué *included the tunes*, so Edith Tolkien could have played them for her husband on the piano. The Breton song "Aotrou Nann Hag ar Gorrigan" was the source for two of Tolkien's poems, "The Lay of Aotrou and Itroun" and its predecessor "The Corrigan" II.[23] This Breton song has stanzas of rhymed couplets or triplets. Tolkien's "The Lay of Aotrou and Itroun" has stanzas of varying length, so (like "Errantry" and "Major General"), while it can be sung to the Breton tune, it doesn't fit very well. It is a literary lay.

But Tolkien's preliminary version, "The Corrigan" II, is singable. It has four-line stanzas consisting of a triplet plus unrhymed line, with the additional flourish that each pair of fourth lines rhyme: the same meter as "The Lay of Beowulf". And it can be sung to the tune of "The Fox". It can also be sung to the Breton tune, though not as well. Tolkien also rewrote a second Breton song, "Ar Bugel Laec'hiet", titled "The Corrigan" I (*Aotrou*-Flieger 33-7). The Breton song is in rhymed triplets, but Tolkien's version consists of four rhymed lines, three long and one short, so it cannot be sung to the Breton tune. Interestingly, with both "The Corrigan" I and "The Corrigan" II, although Tolkien had access to the original songs, he chose to set his versions to different verse forms. One of which was the same meter as "The Fox". But did Tolkien have the tune of "The Fox Went Out on a Winter's Night" in mind when writing "The Lay of Beowulf"? Or "The Corrigan" II? With "Beowulf", possibly. With "The Corrigan" II, we may never know.

Conclusion

Tolkien included many poems in *The Hobbit* and *The Lord of the Rings*, said to have been spoken, recited, chanted, or sung by the participants in the story. Members of all races sang and created songs, improvised songs on the spot, modified words, wrote new words to old tunes – all processes of song-creation which occur in our world. Even though Tolkien did write new words to existing

---

23   The words and tune to "Aotrou Nann Hag ar Gorrigan" are printed in *The Lay of Aotrou and Itroun* edited by Aleksandar Mikić (dual Serbian-English edition) (186-91). *Barzaz Breiz* can be accessed online.

tunes – and sing them! – it appears that, for the most part, he did not follow these processes when writing the songs in his novels. All but two of his songs seem to have been written as literary poems, ascribed to his characters as songs but not actually written with tunes in mind. So if we want to sing them it will be up to "other hands" to compose the music.

About the Author

NANCY MARTSCH has for many years been the Co-ordinator of the J.R.R. Tolkien Special Interest Group of American Mensa and editor of its newsletter *Beyond Bree*. She has presented at Tolkien Conferences and published essays on Tolkien's work. Contact: beyondbree@yahoo.com

List of Abbreviations of Tolkien's Works

ATB	*The Adventures of Tom Bombadil*
FR	*The Fellowship of the Ring*
H	*The Hobbit*
L	*The Letters of J.R.R. Tolkien*
LB	*Lays of Beleriand*
RK	*The Return of the King*
RS	*The Return of the Shadow*
SD	*Sauron Defeated*
TI	*The Treason of Isengard*
TT	*The Two Towers*

Bibliography

DE LA VILLEMARQUÉ, Vicomte Hersart. *Barzaz Breiz, Chants Populaires de la Bretagne*, 6th ed. Paris: Librairie Académique, Didier et Cie., 1867. https://babel.hathitrust.org/

EILMANN, Julian. *J.R.R. Tolkien. Romanticist and Poet*. Zurich and Jena: Walking Tree Publishers, 2017.

FIMI, Dimitra. "Tolkien and Folklore: *Sellic Spell* and *The Lay of Beowulf.*" *Mallorn, The Journal of the Tolkien Society* 55 (2014): 27-28.

HAMMOND, Wayne G. and Christina SCULL. *The Lord of the Rings: A Reader's Companion.* Boston, MA and New York City, NY: Houghton Mifflin, 2005.

HOLMES, John R. "'A Metre I Invented': Tolkien's Clues to Tempo in 'Errantry'." *Tolkien's Poetry.* Eds. Julian Eilmann and Allan Turner. Zurich and Jena: Walking Tree Publishers, 2013, 29-44.

KELLY, Mary Quella. "The Poetry of Fantasy: Verse in *The Lord of the Rings.*" *Tolkien and the Critics: Essays on J.R.R. Tolkien's The Lord of the Rings.* Eds. Neil D. Isascs and Rose A. Zimbardo. Notre Dame, IN and London: University of Notre Dame Press, 1968 and 1976, 170-200.

KOOLEN, Ben. "The Song of Durin." *Lembas Extra 2009: Tolkien in Poetry and Song.* Ed. Cécile van Zon. Tolkien Genootschap Unquendor, 2009, 74-85.

MORAWSKI, Marcin. "The Rivendell Hymnal and Tenebrae – Tolkien, Elves and the Roman Liturgy." Trans. Joanna Piech. *Aiglos Special Issue #2, A Selection of Tolkien Studies in Poland 2005-2011*, Summer 2012. Annual publication of the Tolkien Section of the Silesian Science-Fiction Club. Katowice: Śląski Klub Fantastyki, 103-9.

OLSEN, Corey. *Exploring J.R.R. Tolkien's The Hobbit.* Boston, MA and New York City, NY: Houghton Mifflin, 2012.

RATELIFF, John D. *The History of The Hobbit: Part One, Mr. Baggins and Part Two, Return to Bag-End.* Boston, MA and New York City, NY: Houghton Mifflin, 2007.

"Inside Literature: Tolkien's Explorations of Medieval Genres." *Tolkien in the New Century: Essays in Honor of Tom Shippey.* Eds. John Wm. Houghton, Janet Brennan Croft, Nancy Martsch, John D. Rateliff, and Robin Anne Reid. Jefferson, NC: McFarland, 2014, 133-152.

SCULL, Christina and Wayne G. HAMMOND. *The J.R.R. Tolkien Companion and Guide: Reader's Guide.* Boston, MA and New York City, NY: Houghton Mifflin, 2006.

STEIMEL, Heidi and Friedhelm SCHNEIDEWIND (eds.). *Music in Middle-earth.* Zurich and Jena: Walking Tree Publishers, 2010.

TOLKIEN, J.R.R. *The Adventures of Tom Bombadil.* Eds. Christina Scull and Wayne G. Hammond. London: HarperCollinsPublishers, 2014.

The Annotated Hobbit. Revised and Expanded Edition. Annotated by Douglas A. Anderson. Boston, MA and New York City, NY: Houghton Mifflin, 2002.

Beowulf: A Translation and Commentary, together with Sellic Spell. Ed. Christopher Tolkien. Boston, MA and New York City, NY: Houghton Mifflin, 2014.

The Hobbit. 50th Anniversary edition. London and Sydney: Unwin Hyman, 1987.

The Lay of Aotrou and Itroun. Ed. Aleksandar Mikić with the assistance of Elizabeth Currie. 2nd ed. Dual Serbian-English edition. Novi Sad: Snoviðenja, 2015.

The Lay of Aotrou and Itroun, together with The Corrigan Poems. Ed. Verlyn Flieger. London: HarperCollinsPublishers, 2016.

The Lays of Beleriand (*The History of Middle-earth* vol. 3). Ed. Christopher Tolkien. Boston, MA: Houghton Mifflin, 1985.

The Letters of J.R.R. Tolkien. Selected and edited by Humphrey Carpenter, with the assistance of Christopher Tolkien. Boston, MA: Houghton Mifflin, 1981.

The Lord of the Rings. Collector's Edition (one volume). (*The Fellowship of the Ring, The Two Towers, The Return of the King*). Boston, MA: Houghton Mifflin, 1987.

The Return of the Shadow (*The History of Middle-earth* vol. 6). Ed. Christopher Tolkien. Boston, MA: Houghton Mifflin, 1988.

Sauron Defeated (*The History of Middle-earth* vol. 9). Ed. Christopher Tolkien. London: HarperCollinsPublishers, 1992.

The Treason of Isengard (*The History of Middle-earth* vol. 7). Ed. Christopher Tolkien. Boston, MA: Houghton Mifflin, 1989.

TURNER, Allan. "Early Influences on Tolkien's Poetry." *Tolkien's Poetry.* Eds. Julian Eilmann and Allan Turner. Zurich and Jena: Walking Tree Publishers, 2013, 205-221.

ZIMMERMANN, Petra. "'The glimmer of limitless extensions in time and space': The Function of Poems in Tolkien's *The Lord of the Rings*." *Tolkien's Poetry.* Eds. Julian Eilmann and Allan Turner. Zurich and Jena: Walking Tree Publishers, 2013, 59-89.

Audio

TOLKIEN, J.R.R. and Christopher TOLKIEN. "J.R.R. Tolkien: The Homecoming of Beorhtnoth." Read by J.R.R. Tolkien and Christopher Tolkien. "Tolkien: The Centenary 1892-1992." "Presentation copy to commemorate the 100th Anniversary of the birth of J.R.R. Tolkien and the 1001st Anniversary of the battle of Maldon." George Allen and Unwin (Publishers) Ltd, 1975, [1992], cassette.

The J.R.R. Tolkien Audio Collection. Read by J.R.R. Tolkien and Christopher Tolkien. Harper Audio/ Caedmon, a division of HarperCollinsPublishers, 1975, 2001, 4 CDs.

Łukasz Neubauer

"What news from the North?": The Compositional Fabric, Intricate Imagery and Heroic Christian Character of the "Lament for Boromir"

Abstract

In its classical sense, an elegy is a commemorative poem or song which deals with someone's – usually, the hero's – demise. It may therefore focus upon a vast array of themes connected with death and dying, such as remembering the one(s) who have died or comforting those who have lost their dear one(s). Very often they invoke the name of the deceased (as in Walt Whitman's "O Captain, My Captain!"), imaginatively summoning the one(s) who will, unfortunately, no longer be able to respond at the earthly stage of their existence. Finally, they may also lament the passing of an old way of life (as in the so-called *ubi sunt* poems), which may often be seen in the poetic works of Anglo-Saxon provenance. Frequently submerged in sorrow, various characters in the works of J.R.R. Tolkien are not in the least different from their literary models of the past. Their reasons may vary, of course, and so may the actual modes of their expression. Nevertheless, they all have at least a few noteworthy things in common – to express their undying love and honour those who have come to pass from Middle-earth. The following paper seeks to examine the often complex nature of elegiac verses in *The Lord of the Rings* with a particular emphasis upon their compositional and performative dimensions, symbolism, heroic resonances and Christian implications in the "Lament for Boromir", a moving farewell song performed by Aragorn and Legolas in the wake of their companion's impressive, if hastily organised, boat-burial in the mould of ancient funerary rites for the heroic fallen.

Of all the numerous themes, motifs and images that recurrently come to the surface as highly essential, perhaps even fundamental, constituents of Tolkien's subcreated legendarium, those of death and, consequently, mortality (as well as immortality) often seem to be of prime significance. Indeed, as the author of *The Lord of the Rings* once said in the television documentary *Tolkien in Oxford* 1968),[1] "human stories are practically always about one thing, aren't they? Death. The inevitability of death" (Scull/Hammond, *Reader's*

---

[1] *Tolkien in Oxford*, originally aired on BBC2 on 30 March 1968, is a less-than-half-an-hour-long documentary that features recorded interviews with J.R.R. Tolkien. In it, the then-retired 76-year-old professor shares his views upon a variety of subjects including his works of fiction, languages and love of nature.

Guide 611). While his words might give the appearance of being something of an overstatement – after all there are countless narratives, literary as well as cinematic, which neither explicitly deal with, nor even subtly allude to the eschatological dimensions of human existence – it cannot be denied that there is a vast array of stories, from the Sumerian *Epic of Gilgamesh* (first half of the second millennium BC) to Kazuo Ishiguro's *Never Let Me Go* (2005)[2] and beyond, that focus almost exclusively, or, at least, predominantly, upon the theme of death, both approaching and concluded, natural and tragic, sought-for and undeserved[3].

Of course, for Tolkien, not only a devout Catholic, but also a veteran of the Great War, the themes of death are, as he himself says in a letter to Joanna de Bortadano (or, rather, its published draft), "much more permanent and difficult" (*L* 186). Hence, the actual foil against which the eschatological mode of his writings should be measured is not the amount of mounds and tombstones erected to enshrine the mortal frames of Thorin, Théoden and other heroes of the long-standing conflict with Sauron and his allies. Nor should it be limited to the heart-aching sorrow that follows the passing of Boromir or accompanies the partings at the Grey Havens whence, in due course, Middle-earth ships sail to the Undying Lands of Aman. Instead, as Christopher Garbowski maintains in the entry on "Death" in *J.R.R. Tolkien Encyclopedia*, the theme of mortality in *The Lord of the Rings* – and, one may also add, a great deal of his other writings – is something that "pervades the novel structurally" and is, in fact, "central to Tolkien's entire mythopoeic writing" (119).

Not surprisingly, both the death and the grief that comes with the passing of Tolkien's characters have been the subject of numerous academic studies. In addition to the aforesaid encyclopaedic entry by Christopher Garbowski, where the Polish-Canadian scholar outlines some of the most vital issues likely to be encountered by the readers of, in particular, *The Lord of the Rings* and

---

2 The narrative of the former centres mainly upon the hero's ultimately failed efforts to gain immortality. The latter is a dystopian novel in which human clones, bred solely for the purpose of providing their organs for the "real" people, dream of love and a longer life.
3 To this list one should also add the works that Tolkien personally loved, explored as a scholar and, last but not least, used as major sources of his literary inspiration including: *Beowulf*, *The Battle of Maldon*, *The Song of Roland* or *The Saga of the Vǫlsungs*. In many of them, the main character – respectively, Beowulf, Byrhtnoth, Roland and Sigurd – ultimately dies, leaving his people lordless and likely to be annihilated, enslaved or otherwise suppressed by the foreign enemies.

The Silmarillion (119-120), the theme of death has also been notably discussed at length by Christina Scull and Wayne G. Hammond in *The J.R.R. Tolkien Companion and Guide. Vol. 2 Reader's Guide* (604-614) and, a few years later, in the excellent book *The Broken Scythe: Death and Immortality in the Works of J.R.R. Tolkien* (2012), in which nine Italian scholars, including the editors Roberto Arduini and Claudio A. Testi, take a close look at such diverse yet mutually complementary subjects as eschatology, immortality, memory and, to a certain degree, even thanatology itself. Furthermore, all those who would wish to get acquainted with Tolkien's own understanding of death and its applicability in his fiction should also consult the writer's published correspondence, in particular his letters to Milton Waldman (*L* 131), Father Robert Murray SJ (156), Joanna de Bortadano (186), C. Ouboter, Voorhoeve en Dietrich (208) and Rhona Beare (211).[4]

Yet despite this noticeable flourishing of academic interest in Middle-earth mortality, there are still, it appears, certain gaps and potential challenges in the field of Tolkien studies with regard to the grief-stricken and often lyrically expressive reactions to the death of some of the most important figures in, particularly, though not exclusively, *The Lord of the Rings*. Some interesting thoughts upon the aftermath of the death of Denethor's elder son might be found in Lynn Forest-Hill's article "Boromir, Byrhtnoth, and Bayard: Finding a Language for Grief in J.R.R. Tolkien's *The Lord of the Rings*" (73-97). The songs which serve as formal farewells to Gandalf, Boromir or Théoden are also succinctly referred to in the critical works of, for instance, Verlyn Flieger (65-66) or Stuart Lee and Elizabeth Solopova (254-260).

Of all the lyrical passages in *The Lord of the Rings* that, in one way or another, articulate the characters' grief over the loss of their leader, friend or companion,[5] no doubt the most poignant ones are those whose chief focus lies upon the figures

---

4 The above list of publications, academic as well as epistemological, is, of course, far from being exhaustive. For a more comprehensive list, see section B of the bibliographic list provided at the end of Arduini and Testi's book (224-225). To this list of publications, one should also add Christopher Garbowski's recent article "Tolkien's Philosophy and Theology of Death" (125-144).
5 In some cases, two or three of these functions could obviously be combined.

of Gandalf (*LotR* 359-360), Boromir (417-418) and Théoden (843, 849, 976).[6] Since the scope of this publication does not allow for a more comprehensive analysis of each of them – let alone a study of the other verses whose thematic tone may, for the sake of terminological convenience, be described as elegiac[7] – it is, perhaps, best to consider only one, namely that in which Aragorn and Legolas bid their versified farewell to the son of Denethor. The said song, usually known as the "Lament for Boromir" (e.g. Flieger, *Interrupted* 65, "Poems" 528; Croft 53), is in many ways characteristic of Tolkien's lyrical style and provides a fine example of how the author managed to combine his enormous fondness for the old heroic lays, such as, obviously, *Beowulf* or *The Battle of Maldon*, with the often fundamentally different ethics of Christian living. Finally, it is also a captivating lyrical effort of the man whose literary career actually began with poetry and, perhaps to a certain degree, a moving reflection upon the passing of the heroic spirit in the age of increasingly mechanised warfare and senseless deaths of millions of young people.[8]

In the following study of the song which accompanies Boromir's departure for his ultimate journey, we shall therefore take a look at a variety of aspects – compositional, lexical as well as conceptual and aesthetic – that, in one way or another, pertain to the theme of death. From its metrical structure and mode of delivery, through the emotional appeal and resonance at the time of the hero's funeral, to the more functional connotations and various eschatological underpinnings of the lyrical efforts of both Aragorn and Legolas, we should see that the "Lament for Boromir" is not just a piece of poetic expression which, some readers may erroneously think, was intended to fill the narrative gaps

---

6 To these one may also add Bregalad's dirge for the trees cut down by the Orcs from Isengard (483-484). However, since his arboreal friends are not otherwise known to the reader, it is hard to sympathise with the lamenting Ent as much as one does with the mourners of Gandalf, Boromir or Théoden.

7 The semantic capacity of the term "elegiac" is quite flexible here. Much as in the extant corpus of Old English verse, the so-called elegiac elements in Tolkien's fiction could be of diverse nature, encompassing such themes as the loss of specific characters, meditation upon the inevitability of death and contemplation of the world's decay (e.g. the "Where now the horse and the rider?" song (*LotR* 508), which elaborates upon the *ubi sunt* motif, well known to the readers of *The Wanderer*). For more detailed analyses of the thematic scope in Old English elegies, see, for instance, Christine Fell's "Perceptions of Transience" (172-189) or the last chapter of Stanley B. Greenfield and Daniel G. Calder's *A New Critical History of Old English Literature* (280-302).

8 Himself a veteran of the Great War, Tolkien was obviously highly distressed over the new global conflict which began in 1939 with the German and Soviet invasions of Poland. He is believed to have written "The Departure of Boromir", the first chapter of Book III, in late 1941 or early 1942, when the Second World War was at full volume (Scull/Hammond, *Chronology* 251).

and, in some way, imitate the language and style of the old lays. Perhaps best seen in the broader light of particularly, but not exclusively, early medieval norms and values, it is a versified meditation upon the inevitable end of the Heroic Age, a pensive contemplation whose somewhat implied objective, as in the concluding passage of *Beowulf* (ll. 3110-3182), is to delineate the disastrous consequences of warfare and express uncertainty over one's fate after death. Last but not least, worth noting are also its various Christian underpinnings, in fact, not unlike the subtle allusions of the *Beowulf* poet, whose funerary depictions seem to have much to do, thematically as well as aesthetically, with that of Denethor's eldest son.

Typological Considerations

As has been observed, the so-called "Lament for Boromir" is a song in which Aragorn and Legolas bid emotional farewell to their fallen companion. Some scholars suggest that it was not, perhaps, initially meant to be put in the mouths of the two grief-stricken friends (Flieger 528). In its earliest known version, it is referred to as the "Song" or "Lament of Denethor for Boromir" (*TI*, 382), which seems to suggest that it may have been first intended to be performed by the Steward of Gondor, possibly at a later point of the narrative. If so, it could somewhat instinctively evoke in the more informed reader the still culturally-recognisable images of Priam's immeasurable grief over the mutilated body of Hector (likewise, his beloved first-born child) or, to those of the more northern literary interests, that of the tenth-century skald Egill Skallagrímsson lamenting the loss of his two sons, Gunnar and Bǫðvarr, in the heart-rendering poem known as *Sonatorrek* "The Loss of Sons" (*Egils saga*, ch. 78).

Christopher Tolkien appears to be rather sceptical on the matter of the song's performance, arguing that had his father originally meant it to be performed by Denethor, the "Lament for Boromir" would not, in its earliest known version, have appeared on the same page as the words of Trotter (later known as Aragorn) who, to make the matters more complicated, says "in a low voice" that soon "They shall look out from the white tower [i.e. the tower of Ecthelion where the Stewart of Gondor presides] and listen to the sea" (*TI* 382). It may be, however, that, singing their song, both Aragorn and Legolas merely assume the poetic persona of Denethor, thus imagining the father's anxiety and anticipating the Steward's ultimate grief over the loss of his beloved son and heir, a grief that they themselves doubtlessly share. This way or another, the sorrow is certainly immense and the reader's awareness of the fact that, at some point, the "Lament" may have been merely intended to be performed by the heartbroken father makes its words even more emotionally stirring.

In the published version, the words are, nevertheless, put in the mouths of Boromir's companions, members of the now broken Fellowship of the Ring. Being under the pressure of time, Aragorn, Gimli and Legolas decide not to bury the body of the fallen Gondorian, as would seem appropriate for a person of his rank and heroic record. On the other hand, they are decided not leave him in some hastily-erected mound which a group of passing Orcs could easily desecrate in their spiteful urge to destroy everything their opponents hold dear (Wainwright, 78). Instead, the three companions opt for a more practical, if – it seems at that point – just as ephemeral, boat burial that the readers of *Beowulf* should obviously recollect from the opening lines of the Old English poem (ll. 32-52).[9] While the practice itself is of evidently pre-Christian provenance, there is in it a noticeable hint of Christian hope, as the elven-boat in which Boromir's body is ultimately laid (amidst his most precious earthly possessions – the horn, the sword as well as the golden belt which he received in Lórien), is later believed, "in Gondor in after-days", to have ridden "the falls and the foaming pool, [...] down through Osgiliath, and past the many mouths of Anduin, out into the Great Sea at night under the stars" (*LotR* 417).[10]

Once Boromir is laid in the boat, his companions remain silent, perhaps in some unspoken prayer. Then, after his remark about the anxious people in the White

---

9   Interestingly enough, only two years before Tolkien wrote the first chapter of book III (late 1941 or early 1942), during the archaeological excavations at Sutton Hoo, the remains of an impressive Anglo-Saxon ship burial were discovered in the so-called Mound 2 (Carver 8-24). Tolkien, who is known to have subscribed to *Antiquity*, the academic journal published quarterly by the Cambridge University Press (Scull/Hammond, *Chronology* 820), would have surely read about the discovery in volume 14 (53) which came out in the March of 1940 and featured eight articles devoted to the Sutton Hoo excavations (6-87).

10 See the words of the *Beowulf* poet who, clearly winking at his Christian audience, claims that *men ne cunnon secgan to soðe, selerædende*, [...] *hwa þæm hlæste onfeng* (ll. 50-52) "men cannot say for certain who received that cargo [i.e. the body of Scyld Scefing, the legendary ancestor of the Skjǫldung family]".

Tower (here somewhat altered in comparison with the afore-quoted passage that appears in *The Treason of Isengard*), Aragorn begins to sing:

> Through Rohan over fen and field where the long grass grows
> The West Wind comes walking, and about the walls it goes.
> 'What news from the West, O wandering wind, do you bring to me tonight?
> Have you seen Boromir the Tall by moon or by starlight?'
> 'I saw him ride over seven streams, over waters wide and grey;
> I saw him walk in empty lands until he passed away
> Into the shadows of the North, I saw him then no more.
> The North Wind may have heard the horn of the son of Denethor.'
> 'O Boromir! From the high walls westward I looked afar,
> But you came not from the empty lands where no men are.' (ll. 1-10)

He is then joined by Legolas:

> From the mouths of the Sea the South Wind flies, from the sandhills and the stones;
> The wailing of the gulls it bears, and at the gate it moans.
> 'What news from the South, O sighing wind, do you bring to me at eve?
> Where now is Boromir the Fair? He tarries and I grieve.'
> 'Ask not of me where he doth dwell – so many bones there lie,
> On the white shores and the dark shores under the stormy sky,
> So many have passed down Anduin to find the flowing Sea.
> Ask of the North Wind news of them the North Wind sends to me!'
> 'O Boromir! Beyond the gate the seaward roads runs south,
> But you came not with the wailing gulls from the grey sea's mouth.' (ll. 11-20)

Finally, Aragorn sings again:

> From the Gate of the Kings the North Wind rides, and past the roaring falls;
> And clear and cold about the tower its loud horn calls.
> 'What news from the North, O mighty wind, do you bring to me today?
> What news of Boromir the Bold? For he is long away.'
> 'Beneath Amon Hen I heard his cry. There many foes he fought.
> His cloven shield, his broken sword, they to the water brought.
> His head so proud, his face so fair, his limbs they laid to rest;
> And Rauros, golden Rauros-falls, bore him upon its breast.'
> 'O Boromir! The Tower of Guard shall ever northward gaze,
> To Rauros, golden Rauros-falls, until the end of days.' (ll. 21-30)

Needless to say, the "Lament for Boromir" unavoidably evokes the sorrowful dirges sung in praise of the great heroes of, in particular, early medieval lore:

the Germanised Christ in *The Dream of the Rood*[11] and the mighty ruler of the Geats, the principal character in *Beowulf*, who in the end meets his destiny in the form of a dragon.[12] However, the correspondence could often be superficial. In the case of the former, we do not even know whether the *sorhleoð* (*The Dream of the Rood* l. 67) "dirge" (lit. "sorrow-song") would actually focus upon the ghastly reality of the Passion or whether it was also meant to praise the "heroic deeds" of the Saviour. In the latter, the contents of the song are merely alluded to, yet it is quite evident that apart from the death itself – and, of course, the growing anxiety over its geopolitical consequences – the main elegiac thread does indeed pertain to Beowulf's *eorlscipe* (*Beowulf*, l. 3173) "heroism" and *ellen-weorc* (l. 3173) "courageous deeds".

The overall tone of the "Lament for Boromir" is, as we shall see in the later part of this paper, slightly different. With its call-and-response rhythm and continuous flow of images whose lyrical spotlight is constantly upon the absent Gondorian, the song gradually reveals the increasing futility of the search for the son of Denethor. For this reason, it is perhaps fair to say that it has more in common with the so-called *ubi sunt* elegies, of which the Old English *Wanderer* is a perfect, albeit not the only, example.[13] As a matter of fact, much as its ninth- or tenth-century counterpart,[14] the "Lament for Boromir" neatly balances between the personal, and thus more emotional, and general (more conceptual, perhaps in some way even abstract) perspectives upon the loss of human life. In Tolkien's verse the equilibrium is evidently in favour of the former, subtly, it appears, alluding to the tragic circumstances of the brave

---

11 See *Ongunnon him þa sorhleoð galan earme on þa æfentide* (ll. 67-68) "Then they began to sing for Him [i.e. Christ] a dirge, sorrowful in the eventide".
12 Compare *Þa ymbe hlæw riodan, hildedeore æþelinga bearn, ealra twelfa, woldon care cwiðan, kyning mænan, wordgyd wrecan, ond ymb wer sprecan: eahtodan eorlscipe ond his ellen-weorc* (ll. 3169-3173) "Then rode around the barrow twelve warriors brave in battle, chieftains' sons, twelve in all; they wished to express their grief, mourn the loss of their king, sing a dirge and speak about the man: praise his heroism and his courageous deeds".
13 Naturally, the most easily discernible example of an *ubi sunt* elegy in *The Lord of the Rings* – in fact, in all the published works of Tolkien – is the song composed by "a forgotten poet long ago in Rohan" (*LotR* 508) which begins with a series of rhetorical questions mirroring those of *The Wanderer*. See Tolkien's "Where now the horse and the rider?" (ibid.) with *Hwær cwom mearg? Hwær cwom mago?* (l. 92) "Where is the horse gone? Where is the rider?" of the anonymous Anglo-Saxon poet.
14 For the dating of *The Wanderer* (and other Old English elegies), see, for instance, Anne L. Klinck's book *The Old English Elegies: A Critical Edition and Genre Study* (19-21).

Gondorian's moral collapse ("Boromir the Bold",[15] "His head so proud"[16]), though, at the same time, not disregarding the rather universal anxiety about the fleetingness of human existence ("empty lands where no men are", "many bones there lie").[17] Needless to add, such a skilful combination of highly emotive images would require a great deal of poetic inventiveness and, in particular, compositional dexterity on the part of the lyricist, which is where we shall now turn our attention.

Oral-Formulaic Roots and Performance

As has been observed, the (early) medieval stylisation of the "Lament for Boromir" pertains just as much to its thematic scope as it does to the compositional character of the song. In trying to make it fall in line with the old practices of oral versification and delivery, customary in, say, Anglo-Saxon England or Viking Ages Scandinavia, Tolkien appears to lay special emphasis upon the way in which the song is actually performed by Boromir's companions. Naturally, this comes to be reflected in a substantial number of features, including, it seems, the general improvisation-like character of Aragorn and Legolas's singing and their not infrequent employment of quasi-formulaic language (alliteration, parallelism, repetition etc.). We shall now consider each of them in turn.

That the "Lament for Boromir" is a thoroughly improvised song, orally composed and delivered at the time of the hastily arranged funeral is, of course, self-evident. Desperately pressed for time, neither Aragorn nor Legolas have enough time to actually stand and reflect upon the compositional features of their verse (and, least of all, to write it down). Instead, they seem to make apt use of some conventional themes and motifs which, poets or listeners, the inhabitants of Middle-earth – evidently far more orally-dependent than, for instance, twentieth- or twenty-first-century Europeans (Lichański 39) – should be instantly able to recognise and, in certain situations, perhaps even find a use

---

15 According to J.R. Clark Hall, the Old English adjective *beald* could cover a relatively wide range of meanings, from "brave", "confident" and "strong" to "presumptuous" and "impudent" (34).
16 Pride (or overconfidence) is, as we know, the very reason why Beowulf, Byrhtnoth and Roland, Boromir's early medieval models, come to lose their lives.
17 In this, the "Lament for Boromir" seems to emulate certain passages from *The Ruin*, an Old English poem of an evidently contemplative nature whose focus is not only upon the crumbling walls of a Roman city (perhaps Bath), but also the people who once used to live within them.

for in their own poetic compositions.[18] Obviously, unlike some of the Anglo-Saxon *scopas*, Norse *skáld* or Provençal *troubadours*, Aragorn and Legolas are not in the least inclined to even think of any form of financial or prestigious gain (nor is there any opportunity for that). In other words, their sudden urge to create could only come about as a result of a powerful emotional distress. Hence, with regard to its purpose of creation, their song should, above all, be analysed in view of the immense grief that they feel as a consequence of their companion's untimely death (additionally fuelled by the growing uncertainty over the whereabouts of the four hobbits).

It may, naturally, strike one as rather improbable that suddenly, in the midst of all woes, Boromir's companions should burst into a song whose metrical composition, lexical stratum, thematic integrity and elevation of tone evidently suggest that the author(s) of the song had a little bit of time (and peace of mind) to actually create it. It should not be forgotten, however, that we are, first and foremost, dealing with a work of literature which operates under somewhat different rules. After all, just as questionable in their authenticity are, for instance, the long (of up to twelve lines) alliterative speeches delivered by the combatants, English as well as Danish, in *The Battle of Maldon*. Indeed, certain artificiality of what the characters say (or sing), commonly referred to as diction, is a *signum specificum* of practically every literary creation, even the thoroughly realistic novels of Charles Dickens or Mark Twain.

As for this particular literary creation, namely the first chapter of book III of Tolkien's *The Lord of the Rings*, the time of its being written (early 1940s) obviously determined not only the song's language (slightly archaised – "you came not" (ll. 10 and 20), "he doth" (l. 15) etc. – though never beyond the understanding of the average reader), but also its metrical organisation (three equal-length stanzas of five rhyming couplets each (AA, BB, CC and so on) – "grows"/"goes" (ll. 1-2), "tonight"/"starlight" (ll. 3-4), "grey"/"away" (ll. 5-6) etc. – that would not seem out of place in, for instance, early- or mid-twentieth-century poetry). It is, however, interesting to note that its rhythmic structure is somewhat irregular, with a varied number of syllables per line (from thirteen to seventeen). It may

---

18 Whether they should also be able to do it depends on a number of factors, including the characters' literary skills and willingness to create.

be that this was actually intended to reflect the improvisational character of the song, yet it is just as probable that Tolkien's intention was that the "Lament for Boromir" should, at least in some way, reflect the alliterative metrics of Old English poetry, where the line could be of indeterminate length, provided that the number of strongly stressed syllables (the so-called "lifts") in each half-line should always be the same (two).[19]

Of course, the dirge performed by Aragorn and Legolas at Boromir's funeral is not, in the strict sense, a suitable example of alliterative verse. Most of its lines do indeed contain alliterating syllables, as in the song's second line ("The **West Wind** comes **walking**, and about the **walls** it goes"; my emphasis), yet their number is highly variable, ranging between two and four. In some cases, as in Aragorn's very first words, the line contains two pairs of alliterative syllables ("Through Rohan over **fen** and **field** where the long **grass grows**"; my emphasis). In some, there is no alliteration at all, as in the fourth line of the middle stanza sung by Legolas ("Where now is Boromir the Fair? He tarries and I grieve"). Hence, it is fair to say that the alliterating syllables are there merely for the sake of poetic stylisation, with absolutely no purpose but to make the song look more ancient – one may add, Old Germanic-like – and in this way further accentuate the quasi-medieval character of Boromir's funeral.

Quite the same thing may be said of the singers' regular employment of vastly repetitive language, which further adds to the song's formulaic-like diction. These repetitive elements are of various nature, sometimes replicating certain phrasal structures, as in the third stanza, when Aragorn, voicing the words of the North Wind, in a catalogue-like manner, gives a vivid portrayal of Boromir's body being placed in the boat ("His cloven shield, his broken sword, [...] His head so proud, his face so fair, his limbs they laid to rest"; ll. 26-27), and sometimes even entire passages, which, despite their not being identical, clearly communicate the same emotional intent, as is the case in, for instance, the second couplet of each stanza:

> 'What news from the West, O wandering wind, do you bring to me tonight?
> Have you seen Boromir the Tall by moon or by starlight? (ll. 3-4)

---

[19] For more information on the metrical peculiarities of Old English verse, see, for instance, Donald G. Scragg's paper "The Nature of Old English Verse" (55-70) or Jun Terasawa's book *Old English Metre: An Introduction*.

'What news from the South, O sighing wind, do you bring to me at eve?
Where now is Boromir the Fair? He tarries and I grieve. (ll. 13-14)

'What news from the North, O mighty wind, do you bring to me today?
What news of Boromir the Bold? For he is long away.' (ll. 23-24)

Such parallelic patterns are very common in the oral literary traditions, Germanic, Celtic, Hebrew or other. As has been indicated, Tolkien's use of quasi-formulaic language in the "Lament for Boromir", including the aforementioned parallels, epithets – "Boromir the Tall" (l. 4), "Boromir the Fair" (l. 14), "Boromir the Bold" (l. 24) – and a catalogue, might have been aimed, at least in some part, at recreating the sound and feel of ancient verse, giving it the impression of a genuine oral-formulaic composition.[20]

Yet another vital ingredient of the funeral scene, one which may go easily unnoticed, even though it is as much evocative of the song's oral character as any of the aforementioned components, is the way in which the "Lament for Boromir" is performed. As we have seen, the first to sing of the West Wind is Aragorn (ll. 1-10). He is then followed by Legolas chanting of the South Wind "from the mouths of the Sea" (ll. 11-20). It seems quite natural then to expect that the questioning of the East Wind should be left to their dwarfish companion. Gimli, however, bows out of it, claiming that, doubtlessly on account of some figurative associations with the land of Mordor, he "will say naught of it" (*LotR* 418). The final stanza, the one addressed to the North Wind, is therefore sung by Aragorn (ll. 21-30). As Karol Zieliński points out in his article dealing with the role and function of oral tradition in Tolkien's fiction, this practice of joining in the song was once very common amongst those peoples that were, for the most part, still at the pre-literate stage of their cultural development (156).[21] One may also assume, perhaps with a little bit of imaginative (and wishful) thinking, that the *word-gyd* (l. 3172) which is performed by the twelve *æþelinga bearn* (l. 3170) "chieftains' sons" at Beowulf's funeral and the *sorhleoð* (l. 67) intoned by the disciples in *The Dream of the Rood* are not some

---

20 There are numerous instances of such repetitive formulaic patterns in the extant corpus of early Germanic verse, many of them doubtlessly conceived at an earlier, in all likelihood oral, stage of the poems' existence. Some of them may be found in the eddic poems of gnomic content, such as *Hávamál* or *Vafþrúðnismál*. Notable, though far less evident examples can also be identified in Old English poetry, e.g. in *The Wanderer*.
21 There are, he says, numerous examples of that in the early Greek texts, for example in the *Iliad* (Zieliński 156).

premeditated dirges chanted in unison by the forlorn mourners. Despite being only imitative in its oral character, the "Lament for Boromir" is therefore a worthy continuator of the old practices of poetic composition, an inspiring monument to the elegiac heroic tradition of the Anglo-Saxon *scopas* and their counterparts in other parts of Europe and beyond.

Compositional Intricacies and Emotional Appeal

This sequential organisation of Aragorn's and Legolas's song is also worth examining with regard to the general mournful tone that pervades the "Lament for Boromir" and the narrative-like construction of each stanza. The pattern, which, as we have seen, has its roots in the oral-formulaic tradition, is invariable and consists of four clearly distinguishable phases, as in, for instance, the first part of the song:

1. introductory remarks about one of the three Winds (the Eastern Wind, as we know, is not to be spoken of):

> Through Rohan over fen and field where the long grass grows
> The West Wind comes walking, and about the walls it goes. (ll. 1-2)

2. inquiry about Boromir's whereabouts and fate (quite conceivably "voiced" by Denethor himself; see the use of personal pronouns "me" and "I", rather than "us" and "we", if the words were to come from the mouths of some indeterminate Gondorians):

> 'What news from the West, O wandering wind, do you bring to me tonight?
> Have you seen Boromir the Tall by moon or by starlight?' (ll. 3-4)

3. the Wind's reply, and a suggestion (in the first two stanzas) that the North Wind should be more knowledgeable in this matter:

> 'I saw him ride over seven streams, over waters wide and grey,
> I saw him walk in empty lands until he passed away
> Into the shadows of the North, I saw him then no more.
> The North Wind may have heard the horn of the son of Denethor.' (ll. 5-8)

4. apprehensive or, in the last stanza, unequivocally grievous comment about Boromir's lot (once more, this is very likely to be the "voice" of Denethor; see

the pronoun "I" and the mention of the Tower of Guard as a possible figurative representation of Boromir's father):

> 'O Boromir! From the high walls westward I looked afar,
> But you came not from the empty lands where no men are.' (ll. 9-10)

It is quite evident that the structure of each stanza and, by extension, the entire "Lament for Boromir" is meant to manifest the inquirers' mounting anxiety. Interestingly, however, despite the fact that Aragorn and Legolas, in the strictly poetic sense, seem to take up the personality of Denethor (or, what is less likely, the Gondorians in general), they actually speak mainly for themselves. Unlike the inhabitants of Minas Tirith, they know, of course, about Boromir's fate, yet it does not make the apprehensive inquires any less justified. Their questions are not factual, but rhetorical. In other words, they are perfectly aware of how and why the elder son of Denethor came to breathe his last breath,[22] but, in order to make Boromir's death less insufferable, they try to pursue the sorrow within their own hearts. Only then, when the grief is fully experienced, worked through and expressed, can there actually be any hope of its ever being healed.

The fact that the singers decide to take up the role of Boromir's father also demonstrates the level of their empathic abilities. By questioning the three Winds, Aragorn and Legolas prove that they truly understand the consequences of their companion's death, familial as well as political. As has been observed, the Tower of Guard (i.e. the city of Minas Tirith) that "shall ever northward gaze" (l. 29) could emblematise both Denethor (in its narrow reading), and the people of Gondor (in the broader, socio-political, sense). If the former were to be the case, Tolkien, himself the father of four – including three sons at that time in their early twenties (John and Michael) or late teens (Christopher) – would have doubtlessly empathise with the first anxious and then grieving Steward of Gondor.[23] If the latter, his recollections of the Great War, when many a young local lad had found his grave on the continent, would have been fresh enough

---

22 In addition, Aragorn – and, it seems, only Aragorn – is acquainted with the circumstances that led to the breaking of the Fellowship.
23 In the early stages of the Second World War, from November 1939 until May 1940, John (b. 1917) was a student of the Catholic Seminary (the Venerable English College) in Rome (Scull/Hammond, *Chronology* 233). Later, both Michael (b. 1920) and Christopher (b. 1924), were active soldiers on the fronts of the war, in France and Germany (Michael) as well as South Africa and England (Christopher). All of them managed to return unscathed, but it is very likely that their parents actually knew a number of families whose children were not as fortunate as the Tolkiens.

to keep in his mind the fact that in the years 1914-18 a significant portion of the generation born in the 1880s and 1890s came to be killed, shell-shocked or otherwise traumatised, all of which obviously affected the social fabric of early-twentieth-century Britain. This way or another, Tolkien's feelings for the incalculable victims of the two global conflicts and, analogically, those of Boromir's companions – as they express their compassion for Denethor (and, not improbably, all the Gondorians) – appear to be deep; sensitive, empathic and, most importantly, authentic.[24]

Another intriguing constituent of the "Lament for Boromir", one which evidently builds upon the *ubi sunt* – or, in this case, rather, *ubi est* – motif, is the song's increasing suspense (in the first two and, partly, in the last stanza) that culminates with the heart-breaking reply of the North Wind (second half of the third stanza). Both Aragorn and Legolas skilfully postpone the news of their companion's death, correctly assuming that for a man of his social status an immediate reply revealing Boromir's fate in a straight-forward manner would not create enough of the emotional momentum. Their lyrical effort thus breaks the grim news by degrees, projecting the contrived feeling of a fading, but not easily forlorn, hope reflected in the question-and-answer sequence of the first two stanzas. It is only in the last part of the "Lament" that the tragic fate of Denethor's son is finally revealed.

Worth noting here is, of course, the fact that, even though the West Wind clearly suggests that the question of Boromir's whereabouts should be directed to its Northern counterpart, Legolas, who sings the second stanza, chooses to sustain the tension by interrogating the South Wind. This does not only extend the song's length, but also, perhaps most importantly, imitates the fading, though still living, hopes of Denethor and/or the people of Gondor who, having not seen the Captain of the White Tower for months,[25] seem to be expecting the worst. One might even imagine him/them desperately, against all reason and

---

24 Despite Tolkien's claims that neither war "had any influence upon [...] the plot" of *The Lord of the Rings* (*L* 226), it appears that his masterpiece actually owes a great deal to the horrors of both conflicts and their aftermath. Various echoes of the World Wars may also be found in his other works, such as, for instance, the alliterative part of "The Homecoming of Beorhtnoth Beorhthelm's Son".

25 According to the chronology of the "Great Years" in Appendix B of *The Lord of the Rings*, Boromir sets out from Minas Tirith on 4 July 3018 (*LotR* 1091) and dies on 26 February 3019 (1092). This means that when they hear the sound of his horn (1092), the Gondorians have not seen their Captain for nearly eight months.

good sense, obviate what, in due course, cannot be avoided, search where, logically, no hope is to be found.²⁶

Whoever the lyrical inquirer happens to be, though, he/they must be aware of the fact that the first two replies actually disclose, albeit implicitly, certain vital clues concerning Boromir's fate. In the first stanza, the West Wind not only seems to allude to the Gondorian's demise by suggesting that "The North Wind may have heard the horn of the Son of Denethor" (l. 8),²⁷ but it also actually uses the wording that leaves very little to interpretation: "I saw him walk in empty lands until he **passed away** / Into the shadows of the North, **I saw him then no more**" (ll. 6-7; my emphasis).²⁸ Likewise, the South Wind, notwithstanding its evident lack of chance to have ever seen the south-faring Boromir, evades any form of direct answer and, instead, conjures up the images of "the white shores and the dark shores under the stormy sky" where "so many bones [...] lie" and "many have passed down Anduin to find the flowing Sea" (ll. 16-18).²⁹ Hence, it is as if the apparently ambiguous and indefinite words of the two Winds actually led to the emotional climax of the song, merely hinting on what is then so painfully confirmed by the North Wind in the last three couplets of the "Lament".

Symbolism of the Wind

Naturally, the symbolism behind the three (or, in fact, four) Winds is also important for our comprehension of the song's elegiac character and its numerous figurative components. After all, in various, not only Indo-European, cultures, the wind may signify a number of things: the flow of time, instability, unpredictability, restlessness etc. In the Book of Genesis, the very first movement detected "over the face of the waters" (1:2), is of the *ruach* (חוּר), which

---

26 It would be hard to imagine the Gondorians naïvely ignorant of the fact that Boromir, who went north to "Seek for the Sword that was broken: In Imladris [where] shall counsels be taken" (*LotR* 246), could not return from the south.
27 As we know, the last time the horn is wound, after which it is cloven in two and Boromir dies, its sound can be heard as far as Minas Tirith (*LotR* 666, 755, 1092).
28 Although the verb "to pass" may denote some form of physical movement, also in combination with the adverb "away", the expression "to pass away" almost invariably means "to die". The latter phrase from the first stanza of the "Lament for Boromir" needs, I think, no further explanation.
29 Compare Faramir's words, as he recounts the sequence of his precognitive dream: "I do not doubt that he is dead and has passed down the River to the Sea" (*LotR* 666).

may be translated as either "breath" or "wind", obviously denoting the "Spirit of God". In the New Testament Gospels and Acts, the analogical Greek term *pneuma* (πνεῦμα) is used to mean the Holy Spirit, the third hypostasis of the Trinity. Numerous divine – in this cases pre-Christian – associations could also be detected in other works of the European canon, as in, for instance, Homer's *Odyssey* (bk. V, ll. 295-96) or Hesiod's *Theogony* (ll. 379-80), where they are associated with, respectively, the sea god Poseidon and the divine pair of Astraeus and Eos.

The wind – not just the aforesaid four Winds – seems also an important, if somewhat overlooked, constituent in Tolkien's Middle-earth. One notable example of that is the heart-rending passage in which we see the coming of a Great Eagle to the people of Minas Tirith. Right after the ultimate fall of the Dark Lord, "a great wind rose and blew", as a result of which "the Shadow departed, and the Sun was unveiled [...], and in all the houses of the City men sang for the joy that welled up in their hearts from what source they could not tell" (*LotR* 963). These wondrous phenomena are then followed by the actual coming of the majestic bird that brings to the people of Minas Tirith "tidings beyond hope" (963), singing a psalm-like song whose principal focus is upon the end of the realm of Sauron and the eventual return of the King. Given the evident sublimity and biblical-like phrasing of the said passage, it is hard not to think of both the wind and the Eagle as some sort of a reimagining of the sudden appearance of the Holy Spirit in Luke 3:21-22 and Acts 2:2 (Neubauer 100).

There is, of course, not enough evidence to take it for granted that the three Winds in the "Lament for Boromir" (and the fourth one in the words of Gimli) should be more or less directly associated with the Great Eagles or, analogically, some vaguely delineated Tolkienian conception of the Holy Spirit. It is, however, not implausible that the much-knowing Winds do possess – within the realms of their territorially bound constituencies – certain unusual powers that enable them to not only see where Boromir has (or has not) fared, but also communicate their knowledge to the apprehensive inquirers. In this way, they are perhaps a bit like the Miltonian "Heav'nly Muse" (bk. I, l. 6), a Christian compromise between Urania, the Greek muse of astronomy, and the Holy Spirit that most modern readers doubtlessly think of, reading the opening lines of *Paradise Lost*.

If such indeed had been Tolkien's intent (conscious or not),[30] the Winds would attain an interesting dimension, namely that of knowledgeable, though not, as we have seen, omniscient, beings of quasi-divine, perhaps angel-like, awareness and capacities. Consequently, the interrogation, or, rather, invocation, would take the form of a prayer or, at least, some sort of (indirect) interaction with the One. Should we therefore assume that a prayer's primary objective is to communicate with God (rather than to strive to alter the circumstances of one's life, as some may erroneously deem), Aragorn and Legolas's song would also, regardless of its being a *bona fide* elegy, come to be poignant evidence of the singers' spiritual commitment to their companion, not merely grieving his untimely death and, as we shall soon see, praising his heroic deeds, but also, most importantly, caring for the soul – or its Middle-earth equivalent – of Denethor's son.

Another probable reading of the Winds' symbolic significance, not excluding, of course, the divine and Christian-inspired one, is that which is triggered by their physical properties, namely their apparent (but not actual) lack of any tangible form.[31] In other words, the invisible, albeit still detectable, Winds may easily be imagined as epitomising the physical absence of Boromir, emotionally unsettling, painful and resulting in an easily perceptible void, physical as well as psychological. The wind – in general, rather than any specific one of the four – thus blows and howls through the realm of Rohan (l. 1) and, most importantly, that of Gondor, where it goes "about the walls [of Minas Tirith]" (l. 2), moans "at the gate" (l. 12) and calls "about the tower" (l. 22),[32] each time bringing in, much as the Arnoldian "roar of pebbles" in the famous poem "Dover Beach" (ll. 9-10), "the eternal note of sadness" (l. 14).

Equally emblematic could be another possible, again biblical, interpretation of the role that the song's animistic addressees play in the "Lament for Boromir".

---

30 As we know from Tolkien's correspondence with his friend Robert Murray SJ, *The Lord of the Rings* is "a fundamentally religious and Catholic work; unconsciously so at first, but consciously in the revision" (*L* 142).
31 In reality, winds consist of numerous atmospheric gases of varied density. They are, nonetheless, practically invisible to the human eye.
32 What Aragorn seems to have in mind is almost certainly the White Tower (also known as the Tower of Ecthelion), where, as we have seen, Boromir's father usually presides. However, one cannot exclude the possibility that the "tower" in question may also stand for the city of Minas Tirith, which in Sindarin means the "Tower of the Guard", and so, in a sense, the whole realm of Gondor.

Just as the "four winds" in the Old Testament Books of Ezekiel (37:9), Daniel (7:2), Jeremiah (49:36) and Zechariah (2:6; 6:5) as well as the Gospel of Matthew (24:31) and the Book of Revelation (7:1), the Winds referred to by the three remaining members of the Fellowship after the sudden assault of Saruman's Orcs may simply refer to the four corners of the world, and so, in fact, everywhere, even the smallest nook and cranny of Tolkien's Middle-earth.[33] Yet even there, far in "the empty lands [of the West] where no men are" (l. 10), in "the sandhills and the stones" (l. 11) of the South, in the ghastly realms of the East, the son of Denethor is not to be found. Nor is he to be located anywhere in the North, as his mortal frame – at least in Aragorn's opinion – has already been claimed by "golden Rauros-falls" (l. 30). All things considered, wherever the apprehensive Gondorians may look for, they will never be able to find their Captain in the world of the living.

It seems, though, that if Boromir were ever to be found, he ought to be looked for beyond Middle-earth, in the lands "to the west of West, / where night is quiet / and sleep is rest" (*BLS* ll. 30-32), whither the White Ship with the Ring-bearers sails in the last chapter of *The Lord of the Rings*. The South Wind, which would obviously have to be aware of that, appears not to deny the possibility of the Gondorian's safe passage to the Blessed Realm. Perhaps amongst the many that, according to the South Wind, "have passed down Anduin to find the flowing Sea" (l. 17) is also the son of Denethor who, despite his erstwhile moral struggles and temporary collapse upon the slopes of Amon Hen, does, nevertheless, expiate his wrongdoings by protecting his two hobbit companions, Merry and Pippin, against the swarming hordes of Saruman's Orcs. More importantly still, driven by contrition, he confesses to Aragorn that he made an attempt to take the Ring from Frodo and in this way ultimately manages to clear his conscience, thus indubitably earning for himself – like the Penitent Thief in the Gospel of Luke (23:40-43) – a place in what we might perhaps refer to as the Tolkienian equivalent of Paradise.[34] There is, of course, a certain ambiguity in the words of the South Wind, as they are in effect uttered by Legolas who, unlike Aragorn, does not necessarily have to be aware of the very nature of Boromir's

---

[33] Most of the aforesaid biblical references to the "four winds", such as the "four winds of heaven" in Daniel 7:2 appear to be of even more universal nature, clearly alluding to all God's creation.

[34] See, however, Tolkien's declaration below that even in the Undying Lands men will never be immortal.

earlier confession. Nevertheless, the South Wind's subtle allusions to those who "have passed down Anduin to find the flowing Sea" (l. 17) and, at the same time, the fact that it does appear to know what happened to the son of Denethor – "Ask of the North Wind news of them the North Wind sends to me!" (l. 18) – make this salvific interpretation not utterly improbable.

Having looked at the "geographical" symbolism behind the South Wind, it is but a logical extension that we should turn to the figurative significance of its northern counterpart. It is, of course, self-evident that, having fared to Rivendell, the Captain of Gondor would have to head north. One must bear it in mind, though, that the symbolism of the North Wind may also have something to do with Tolkien's literary (and linguistic) preferences, namely his life-long fascination with the Northern European cultures. After all, if any cultural concept should fittingly describe the character of Boromir, it would evidently be the "northern heroic spirit" that the Oxford professor famously examines in "The Homecoming of Beorhtnoth Beorhthelm's Son" (13) or the "northern courage" he refers to in "Beowulf: The Monsters and the Critics" (20).[35] As a "northerner", the proud and sometimes impetuous son of Denethor would then symbolically join the vast legion of Northern – in the sense of non-Mediterranean – European heroes of, particularly, Germanic (e.g. Beowulf, Byrhtnoth, Sigurd, Roland),[36] but also Finnish (Kullervo) and Celtic (Cú Chulainn) provenance.

Heroic-Elegiac Resonances

This notion of Boromir's northern associations brings us again to the question of the song's typological affinities. As has been observed, the "Lament" is an elegiac type of work whose foremost emphasis is upon the death of the fallen hero and the mourning of those who happen to be present at his spur-of-the-moment boat burial. Much as the elegiac-like poems of the Anglo-Saxon canon, the song performed by Aragorn and Legolas pays much attention to the indisputable prowess of the one whose death is being grieved. As we shall see,

---

35 In both cases, what Tolkien has in mind is the excess of heroic pride which often leads to serious consequences, including the hero's ultimate demise.
36 Although *The Song of Roland* is an Old French poem, dating back to the late eleventh or early twelfth century, its title hero was in reality a Frankish, and thus Germanic, warrior whose name, in its earliest known form was Latinised in Einhard's *Vita Karoli Magni* as *Hroudlandus* (ch. 9).

all this is reflected in the third, "northern", part of the song, where Boromir's deeds are rather explicitly, though not with much specificity, referred to.

However, before we take a more comprehensive look at the heroic deeds that are ascribed to the son of Denethor in the third stanza of the "Lament", it might be worthwhile to consider Boromir's physical appearance, as it is almost invariably the distinctive feature of many an early medieval hero. Of course, the conciseness of the song does not allow for a more comprehensive portrayal of the fallen Captain of Gondor, yet both Aragorn and Legolas manage to interweave their verses with some graphic references to Boromir's looks. The first of them calls him "Boromir the Tall" (l. 4), which, in the strict literary sense, is practically a *sine qua non* for the most celebrated heroes of the past.[37] Of course, the son of Denethor is a descendant of the House of Húrin, a proud people who are known to be of high Númenórean blood,[38] yet his tall stature is so reminiscent of Beowulf,[39] Byrhtnoth,[40] Sigurd,[41] and Roland[42] that one just cannot help envisioning Boromir as a genuine hero of some early medieval poem, song or saga.

Analogically, the overall physical attractiveness, which naturally goes hand in hand with the past heroes' stature, is also accentuated in their "Lament" by both Legolas and Aragorn. The former refers to his fallen companion as "Boromir the Fair" (l. 14), the latter uses the same adjective as a complement to Boromir's face (l. 17). The hero's "cloven shield" and "broken sword" (l. 16), which are lain in the elven-boat with the mortal remains of Denethor's son – along with his hood and cloak, belt, helm, horn and the swords of his foes, which are only mentioned in the

---

[37] There are obviously a few notable exceptions to this, such as the Homeric Odysseus or Attila the Hun in Jordanes' *Getica*. However, almost as a rule, the majority of great heroes, ancient, medieval or other, are imagined as tall men of fairly broad build.

[38] The Númenóreans were not only long-lived, but also exceptionally tall.

[39] Upon seeing the Geatish warriors disembark from their ship, Beowulf amongst them, the watchman of the Spear-Danes excitedly exclaims, *Næfre ic maran geseah eorla ofer eorþan, ðonne is eower sum, secg on searwum* (*Beowulf*, ll. 247-250) "Never have I seen a greater earl on earth, that certain one amongst you, the man in armour".

[40] The ealdorman of Essex was, as the author of *Vita Sancti Oswaldi* informs us, *ipse statura procerus, eminens super ceteros* (fol. 18r) "tall in stature, eminent above others".

[41] According to the *Vǫlsunga saga, at um ath ferð ok voxt var engi hans maki* (ch. 13) "in his conduct and physical stature there was no one like him".

[42] Although he is never described as being exceptionally tall, one may rather safely assume that, when Grandoine recognises Charlemagne's nephew through his *fier visage* (*Chanson de Roland*, st. CXXIV, l. 1640) "fierce expression" and, most importantly, the *cors qu'il out gent* (1640) "noble stature", the anonymous poet almost certainly does not mean that Roland is short or of medium height.

main narrative (*LotR* 416-7) – complete the image of Boromir as a Beowulf-like figure, whose own pyre, as the poet tells us, was *helmum behongen, hildebordum, beorhtum byrnum, swa he bena wæs* (*Beowulf*, ll. 3139-40) "with helmets hang about, battle-shields, bight byrnies, as was his wish."[43]

Notwithstanding his stature and looks, a hero's real worth should, of course, first and foremost, be measured in his deeds of valour. Here again, Boromir's brief portrayal in his companions' "Lament" does not in the least deflect from the conventional depictions of various literary figures of great military renown. As the song gradualy reveals the tragic fate of Denethor's son, it also discloses, albeit vaguely and in a very indirect manner, certain particulars of his last heroic stand.

The first indication that something has indeed happened to the Captain of Gondor is the very sound of the North Wind – "From the Gate of the Kings the North Wind rides, and past the roaring falls, / And clear and cold about the tower its loud horn calls" (ll. 21-22) – which appears to echo the call of Boromir's own horn, whose blast "smote the hills and echoed in the hollows, rising in a mighty shout above the roaring of the falls" (*LotR* 413). While it does not automatically mean that the Gondorian is performing some incredible feats of arms, it does suggest that he is in great peril, the only explanation of which is that he is badly outnumbered by the swarming attackers (much as Byrhtnoth at Maldon or Roland at Roncevaux Pass).[44] In fact, these assumed anxieties are soon confirmed by the words of the North Wind, claiming that "Beneath Amon Hen [...] many foes he fought" (l. 25).

With the odds so evidently in his disfavour, Boromir is thus practically destined to be engaged in some extraordinary acts of heroism, particularly that the elder son of Denethor is certainly not a man who shys from military responsibility, such as, in this case, protecting the two hobbits whose cousin he has just so dishonourably wronged. This spontaneous urge to make immediate amends is doubtlessly reflected in Boromir's cry, heard by the North Wind "Beneath Amon Hen" (l. 25), particularly that it immediately precedes the information

---

43 That the affluent depictions of ship burials in *Beowulf* are not exaggerated one may see particularly in the British Museum, where the most significant of all Sutton Hoo findings (helmet, buckle, shield-fittings, shoulder-clasps, purse-lids etc.) are on display.
44 Unlike the latter, however, Boromir does not hesitate to call for the reinforcements.

that this is the very spot where the Gondorian happens to have faced so "many foes" (l. 25). At the same time, though, it cannot be ruled out that the said cry might just as well refer to Boromir's involuntary reaction to the enormous physical pain he must have been in, as he was being "pierced with many black-feathered arrows" (*LotR* 413). In fact, since the North Wind never explicitly refers to Boromir's demise – the information about his cry and the battle he fought against the "many foes" (l. 25) being directly followed by the particulars of his funeral (l. 26-8) – it seems like a fairly rational, if not the only plausible, explanation. Finally, it might also be that, in the often multi-semantic world of poetic discourse, the dramatic cry, that so startled the North Wind, could in effect refer to both sounds that, within a not-too-long stretch of time, came from the Gondorian's lips. His battle call, as he strove to defend the hobbits, and the somewhat later groan of agony, when he was being pierced by the lethal points of the Orcs' arrows, would thus figuratively merge into one continuous sound of anger and pain, so highly evocative of the final moments in the lives of many an early medieval hero, Beowulf, Byrhtnoth or Roland.

Christian Implications

This, for the most part, conventional image of Boromir as a Germanic-like hero of the early Middle Ages is, of course, detectible in his words and deeds, from the turbulent Council of Elrond, when the proud son of Denethor first comes onto stage, to the ultimately failed attempt to seize the Ring from Frodo upon the slopes of Amon Hen, where Boromir's fate is practically sealed. Evidently disposed to the rather universal heroic weakness of *hubris* – or what the *Maldon* poet refers to as *ofermod* "overconfidence"[45] – he seems doomed the very moment his initially polite suggestions turn into accusations and the accusations become threats. From there, it is but a short step to joining some of the greatest heroes of the past: Beowulf, Byrhtnoth and Roland, each of whom appears to have sought everlasting fame in the proverbial jaws of death, often as a more or less direct consequence of their recklessness or determined obstinacy.

---

45 In "The Homecoming of Beorhtnoth" Tolkien translates it as "overmastering pride" (13).

Interestingly though, despite the fact that they may well reproach their fallen companion for his evident contribution to the breaking of the Fellowship, Aragorn, Legolas and Gimli treat Boromir with utmost respect, both in their deeds (impressive, if, of course, hastily prepared, burial) and in their words (the heart-rending "Lament" they sing after the boat is set adrift). There are, it seems, two very reasonable explanations for that. First of all, much as is the case with his early medieval archetypes, whose great accomplishments are very often excessively eulogised in the complicated world of poetic imagination,[46] Boromir's moral collapse is simply "forgotten,"[47] deemed, no doubt, absolutely unsuitable for a farewell song dedicated to a great hero.

Most importantly, however, the son of Denethor seems finally exonerated by his companions upon the grounds of his principled conduct after the violent argument with Frodo. Having realised that the momentary madness has passed, Boromir makes a desperate attempt to atone for his misdemeanour and stake his life upon protecting Merry and Pippin, even against the odds that no single man, hero or not, could possibly overcome. More importantly still, before he dies, Boromir makes an unavoidably compressed but sincere confession to Aragorn, the confession which, in the strictly Christian sense, should definitely earn him a place in Heaven.

It appears that this very hope for Boromir's ultimate redemption – coupled, perhaps, with some sort of Middle-earth equivalents for resurrection and afterlife – could also be detected in the words of his companions, as they intone their mournful "Lament" for the stout-hearted Gondorian. This may be perceived particularly in the fact that Boromir's is actually a boat burial, rather than the customary inhumation, and the singers' careful choice of vocabulary, suggesting that the son of Denethor is there merely "to rest" (l. 28) "until the end of days" (l. 30).

---

46 Certain words of implicit criticism may, nevertheless, be detected in, for instance, *The Battle of Maldon*, where the poet reproaches Byrhtnoth for his *ofermod* (89) "overconfidence" or in *Beowulf*, where the deceased king of Geatland is described in the last verse of the poem as being *lofgeornost* (3182) "most eager for fame".

47 Besides, as has been observed, Legolas and Gimli may not be aware of what actually passed between Boromir and Frodo before the latter's sudden disappearance.

Being confronted with a suggestion that this evidently heathen tradition could, in effect, emblematise Boromir's ultimate ascension to Heaven – or whatever Christian analogy Tolkien appears to have had in mind – may seem rather confusing at first. However, in his subcreated world of hallowed wizards and eucatastrophic "beasts of battle,"[48] even such ostensibly un-Christian-like elements are very likely to find a proper place, particularly when their cultural roots lie in Anglo-Saxon England.[49] Hence, the "departure of Boromir", which is the title of the first chapter of the third book of *The Lord of the Rings*, does not, in all likelihood, denote merely the physical death of Denethor's son and the launching of the elven-boat in which his body is ultimately "laid to rest" (l. 27).

This implicit promise of an afterlife, once his mortal frame has "passed down Anduin to find the flowing Sea" (l. 17), rests upon the attractive, if somewhat risky, assumption that the so-called "Undying Lands" of Aman, the "Blessed Realm of Tolkien's mythology" (Scull/Hammond, *Reader's Guide* 41) constitute a Tolkienian equivalent of the Christian Paradise. The main drawback of this theory is that Tolkien himself denies any possibility of human immortality there. In fact, living in this little-changing land, surrounded by the creatures who do not reveal any traces of old age, man would become even more envious, continuously troubled by the growing discontent with his own manhood, hating those who happen to be more richly endowed (*MR* 428). In such a place, Tolkien maintains, "Man would not be blessed but accursed" (429).[50]

---

48 The so-called "beasts of battle" is a poetic trope commonly employed in Old English and, to a certain degree Old Norse, poetry. It pertains to the inauspicious trio of the eagle, the raven and the wolf which – in various numbers and combinations – may be see on and above the battlefields of early medieval Europe. Some of their most emblematic appearances are to be found in, for instance, the three Old English battle poems – *The Battle of Maldon*, *The Battle of Brunanburh* and *The Finnesburg Fragment*. In Tolkien's fiction, *The Hobbit* and *The Lord of the Rings*, the "beasts of battle" trope seems to have taken the form of the Great Eagles of the Misty Mountains, much altered in their overall character, yet, at the same time, so similar in their intimidating physical appearance and timing of arrival.
49 Hallowing pre-Christian customs is quite common in Old English poetry. An interesting example of that, in a corresponding context of funerary rites, may be found in *Beowulf*. As the hero's body is being consumed by the flames on top of a mighty pyre, we are informed that *heofon rece swealg* (3155) "heaven swallowed the smoke", an ambiguous comment, since the word *heofon* could mean both "sky" and "Heaven".
50 The other possibility is that the boat would somehow find its way to the Halls of Mandos, on the shores of Valinor, where the spirits of Men (as well as Elves) are said to go in order to await their respective fates.

We must not forget, though, that one-to-one correspondence with various elements of Christian theology – as well as many other issues of spiritual, cultural or historical significance – is not, as a rule, to be expected of the works penned by the author of *The Lord of the Rings*. Instead, we should try to find some signs of not-too-far-fetched applicability, bearing in mind the fact that his medieval sources of inspiration are often of equal, if not more, ambiguous character.[51] Hence, when the elven boat ultimately sets sail, replacing the firmness of the shore with the fluid, and thus far less tangible, waters of Anduin and, in the long run, the Great Sea, it is really hard not to think of Boromir as a man whose soul has recently been freed from the physical constraints of this world. In this, he is, perhaps, a bit like Simon, the mysterious teenage character in William Golding's *Lord of the Flies*, whose body ultimately floats away "towards the open sea" (190), surrounded by the visual aura of sanctity,[52] or William Blake, the main protagonist in Jim Jarmusch's film *Dead Man* (1995), who is actually on the verge of passing away when the canoe he is in sails off into the unknown.[53]

It is difficult to tell whether for the contemporary artists like Golding and Jarmusch the afore-described episodes should constitute some sort of a rite of passage to their equivalents of Heaven. It would be more difficult still, to think of Tolkien's characters – in particular, the Penitent-Thief-like ones, such as Boromir or Thorin – who should be so easily deprived of any chance for eternal life. This would be even more astonishing in the case of the former character, whose body comes to be so wondrously preserved when, three days after his heroic death, the undamaged eleven-boat appears to his younger brother. That it should happen on the third day could, of course, be seen as highly symbolic, although, unlike Frodo, Gandalf or Aragorn, the Captain of Gondor does not even appear to possess any Christ-like features. Instead,

---

51 Compare, for instance, the aforementioned passage from Beowulf, in which the body of Scyld Scefing is taken over the waves into the unknown whence it once came (ll. 32-52) and the oft-exploited image of King Arthur's departure for Avalon (as in Geoffrey of Monmouth's *Historia Regum Britanniae* and the subsequent Arthurian tales).
52 There is no possibility that Tolkien could have been in any way inspired by Golding's novel (or the other way round). *Lord of the Flies* came out on 17 September 1954, less than two months after the publication of *The Fellowship of the Ring* (29 July) and not long before *The Two Towers* first saw print (11 November).
53 Suggesting some possible sources of inspiration for the American director, Julian Rice, mentions the practices of ancient Polynesian peoples, of which the author of *The Lord of the Rings* may have been unaware, as well as the Norse traditions (91), whose funerary customs provided, of course, a fertile ground for Tolkien's imagination.

the miraculous preservation of his body, which would otherwise be likely to have fallen prey to the roaring Falls of Rauros, could, perhaps, call to mind the corporeal incorruptibility of some saints (e.g. Padre Pio, Mary of Jesus of Ágreda, Catherine Labouré) as a sign of their holiness. Naturally in the case of the saints of the Roman Catholic and the Eastern Orthodox Churches, the declaration of incorruptibility stems from their being in some way invulnerable to the usual process of bodily decay, while in Boromir's case it is the fact that the boat he is in does not capsize or is smashed to pieces in the falls but comes undamaged to the lower reaches of Anduin, where it is seen by Faramir. In both cases, however, that of the preservation of the body from decay and that of its not being in any way affected by the normally expected damage from external causes, the design could only come directly from God.

Hence, despite Aragorn's words that, from now on, the watchful Steward of Gondor (or his people) "shall ever northward gaze, / to Rauros, golden Rauros-falls" (ll. 29-30), there is, it seems, a certain feeling of anticipation that for Boromir death is not the end of all existence. In fact, certain textual clues appear to hint at the possibility of some sort of a resurrection for the son of Denethor, at least in some indefinite Middle-earthian sense of that word.

The first inkling that there might be something in stock for the fallen Gondorian is to be found in the words of the North Wind, claiming that, after the fight, Boromir's head, face and limbs were "laid to rest" (l. 27). While the verb "to rest" is now often used in connection with the deceased without any distinct resurrectional connotations, it should not be ignored that one of its possible meanings is "to come to a pause, stop being active for a period of time."[54] If such indeed be the case with Boromir's resting, it would naturally imply that the son of Denethor might one day rise from the dead to stand for the Final Judgement, or what Tolkien may have envisioned for his characters in Middle-earth.

Needless to say, the correctness of this particular reading of Aragorn's words depends exclusively upon our choice from the several possible definitions of the verb "to rest". It is far less ambiguous, however, to take into consideration the very last words of the song, namely the assertion that "The Tower of Guard

---

54 Such could also be the meaning of its Old English equivalent *restan*.

shall ever northward gaze, / To Rauros, golden Rauros-falls, **until the end of days**" (ll. 29-30; my emphasis). Here again, the temporal expression informing the reader/listener that the waiting for Boromir shall continue "until the end of days" could be variously understood, with or without any clear-cut eschatological connotations. Be that as it may, it cannot be ignored that it is with practically the same words – of course in translation – that the author of the Book of Daniel brings his prophecy to the conclusion: "go thou thy ways until the time appointed: and thou shalt rest, and stand in thy lot unto the end of the days" (12: 13).

The above is naturally a quotation from the Catholic Douay Version of the Bible that Tolkien is very likely to have owned (Walton 63). The exact wording may naturally differ, depending on the translation (e.g. "at the end of days" in King James Bible), yet the sense remains the same: "at the end of time, when the dead shall rise from their graves". Worth noting here is also the use of the verb "to rest", which in the Book of Daniel evidently carries the meaning of some temporal repose in the grave (as well as any other place of interment, inurnment etc.) until the ultimate resurrection of the bodies on the Day of Judgement.

Could it be, then, that the last few lines of the "Lament for Boromir" should, in effect, carry a somewhat veiled promise of the eternal reward in Heaven? It may, of course, be no more than our wishful thinking, yet it appears that there are at least a few interesting clues that, coupled with the intriguing choice of vocabulary ("rest", "until the end of days"), could indeed support this tantalising assumption. First of all, as has been observed, Boromir is a Penitent Thief type of a hero who manages to make a last-minute confession to the man who should soon be crowned king of Gondor.[55] Secondly, both the miraculous preservation of his body and, in due course, southern direction of the elven-boat's course clearly indicate that the Gondorian's ultimate vocation is not necessarily to be left in a grave until his mortal frame (or, in fact, his whole being) should turn to dust. Tolkien's admission that "*The Lord of the Rings* is of course a fundamentally religious and Catholic work; unconsciously so at first, but consciously in the revision" (*L* 142) does not add any certainty to the intriguing question of

---

55 What, after all, would be the point in Boromir's repentance, confession and heroic – also in the Christian sense – death in defence of his helpless companion from the Shire?

Boromir's resurrection.[56] However, it does provide us with a possible (and not at all improbable) interpretative framework of the last few lines of the "Lament" that Aragorn and Legolas sing, watching the boat depart, "waning to a dark spot against the golden light" (*LotR* 417).

Concluding Remarks

Grief is a natural feeling that needs to be properly experienced and expressed, otherwise it may easily become a crucial obstacle in trying to come to terms with the loss of a friend, a family member or a loved one. Furthermore, strictly determined burial rites and the ensuing period of mourning have also been traditionally required by the cultural standards of a given community since at least the early Antiquity.[57] The actual reasons for such intricate efforts may naturally vary, depending on the beliefs and values held by the people that partake in the mourning process. Nevertheless, what appears to break through all these *post mortem* practices is a genuine concern for those who have passed away, a profound reverence for the human body which, it must have dawned upon our ancestors at some point during the Palaeolithic,[58] is far more than just a heap of bones and rotting flesh. In fact, as the much later generations of humans ultimately came to discover, both the mortal frame and the soul that lives in it, are sacred, and so infinitely precious to their Maker, in whose image and likeness we are said to have been fashioned (Genesis 1:27).

No doubt, this same endorsement of the dignity of "human" existence might be found in the works of Tolkien,[59] particularly, but not exclusively, in *The Lord of the Rings*, where the long-standing conflict with Sauron regularly takes its gruesome toll upon the peoples of Middle-earth. Apart from the heart-stirring episodes in which some of the most significant (and likeable) characters come to breathe their last breath, often in the most heroic of fashions (Boromir,

---

56 But then, of course, why should it? The Lord, as we know, often works in mysterious ways.
57 See, for instance, Priam's grief over the loss of his son Hector and the funeral games organised by Achilles in honour of Patroclus in, respectively, books XXII/XXIV and XXIII of the *Iliad*. Worth noting is also Antigone's ethical consciousness in burying her brother Polynices, which the daughter of Oedipus decides to place above the strict orders of Creon.
58 The earliest evidence of deliberate human burials date back to the Middle Palaeolithic (Gamble 34-35).
59 In the case of Tolkien's fiction, the semantic coverage of the term "human" should, of course, be broadened to include the anthropomorphic races of the Elves, Dwarves, Hobbits etc.

Théoden), or are, at one point, very close to joining the ever-growing ranks of their distinguished ancestors (Faramir, Éowyn, Merry), perhaps the most striking passages are those in which the fallen ones are bid emotional farewell in the form of a song, usually composed upon the spot by their living companions.[60] It appears, however, that, when it comes to their overall emotional appeal and, perhaps most perceptibly, efficacious combination of the ancient heroic spirit with modern Christian ethics, none of them could equal the afore-examined "Lament for Boromir", whose complex lyrical fabric, as we have seen, distinctly touches upon so many issues that are known to have been dear to the writer's heart.

Finally, it must be pointed out that the mournful tones of the funeral songs which resonate within the vast realms of Middle-earth provide supporting evidence to what Tolkien claimed was the hub of well-nigh all human stories, namely, "the inevitability of death" (Scull/Hammond, *Reader's Guide* 611). In the case of Boromir's demise, this inevitability seems to be of double kind. First of all, it pertains to the general issue of human mortality, the fact that, whether they want it or not, men must eventually go the way of all flesh. Secondly, however, it accentuates the fundamental truth about all literary narratives where even a distinctly evil incident (such as the Gondorian's attempt to seize the Ring) might bring about the consequences whose impact upon the ensuing chain of events could really be assessed as being in due course positive (breaking of the Fellowship, Merry and Pippin's escape and rouse of the Ents, Saruman's defeat at Isengard etc.). Boromir's heroic death upon the slopes of Amon Hen is therefore all the more remarkable, as it not only brings to mind some of the most commendable performances of early medieval combatants, but also, as it turns out, leads to the consequences whose definitive effect is the destruction of the Ring. The former comes to be praised in the heart-rending "Lament" that Aragorn and Legolas sing in the first chapter of book III. The latter, however, turns out to be the major thread in what, with a little bit of imaginative thinking, could be described as Tolkien's song in prose, the great *chanson de geste* known in the Common Speech as *The Lord of the Rings*.

---

60 The exceptions here are, of course, the dirges sung in memory of Gandalf ("When evening in the Shire was grey; *LotR* 359-360), which is performed in Lórien a few days after the wizard's dramatic fall in Moria and the "Song of the Mounds of Mundburg" ("We heard of the horns in the hills ringing"; 849), which, we are told, was composed "long afterward [by] a maker in Rohan" (849).

About the Author

ŁUKASZ NEUBAUER received his PhD in English philology from the University of Łódź. He is a researcher and lecturer at the University of Koszalin, Poland, where he teaches courses on Tolkien, Old English literature and Arthurian romances. Apart from his publications dealing with various medieval as well as Christian influences and resonances in *The Lord of the Rings*, he has written papers on *The Battle of Maldon, Beowulf, Hêliand*, Icelandic sagas and the so-called "beasts of battle" trope in, particularly but not exclusively, Old Germanic poetry. He is also a member of the British branch of the International Arthurian Society and a conceptual coordinator of the annual Medieval Fantasy Symposium in Mielno-Unieście, Poland.

List of Abbreviations of Tolkien's Works

BLS   *Bilbo's Last Song.*

L   *The Letters of J.R.R. Tolkien*

LotR   *The Lord of the Rings*

MR   *Morgoth's Ring*

TI   *The Treason of Isengard*

Bibliography

ARDUINI, Roberto and Claudio A. TESTI (eds.). *The Broken Scythe: Death and Immortality in the Works of J.R.R. Tolkien*. Zurich and Jena: Walking Tree Publishers, 2012.

ARNOLD, Matthew. *Selected Poems*. London: Penguin Books, 1994.

BJARNI Einarsson (ed). *Egils Saga*. London: Viking Society for Northern Research, 2003.

BYRHTFERTH of Ramsey. *The Lives of St. Oswald and St. Ecgwine*. Ed. and trans. Michael Lapidge. Oxford: Oxford University Press, 2008.

CARROLL, Robert and Stephen PRICKETT (eds.). *The Bible: Authorized King James Version*. Oxford: Oxford University Press, 2008.

CARVER, Martin. *Sutton Hoo: Burial Ground of Kings?* London: British Museum Press, 2000.

CRAWFORD, Osbert, Guy STANHOPE and Roland AUSTIN (eds.). *Antiquity: A Quarterly Review of Archaeology* 14 (1940).

CROFT, Janet Brennan. *War and the Works of J.R.R. Tolkien*. Westport, CT and London: Praeger, 2004.

DICKINS, Bruce and Alan S.C. Ross (eds.). *The Dream of the Rood*. London: Methuen, 1951.

FELL, Christine. "Perceptions of Transience." *The Cambridge Companion to Old English Literature*. Eds. Malcolm Godden and Michael Lapidge. Cambridge: Cambridge University Press, 2002, 172-189.

EINHARD. *Vita Karoli Magni / Das Leben Karls des Großen*. Ed. and trans. Evelyn Scherabon Firchow. Stuttgart: Reclam, 2014.

FLIEGER, Verlyn. *Interrupted Music: The Making of Tolkien's Mythology*. Kent, OH and London: The Kent State University Press, 2005.

"Poems by Tolkien: The Lord of the Rings." *J.R.R. Tolkien Encyclopedia: Scholarship and Critical Assessment*. Ed. Michael D.C. Drout. New York City, NY and London: Routledge, 2007, 522-532.

FOREST-HILL, Lynn. "Boromir, Byrhtnoth, and Bayard: Finding a Language for Grief in J.R.R. Tolkien's *The Lord of the Rings*." *Tolkien Studies* 5 (2008): 73-97.

GAMBLE, Clive. "The Peopling of Europe, 700,000-40,000 Years before the Present." *The Oxford Illustrated History of Prehistoric Europe*. Ed. Barry Cunliffe. Oxford: Oxford University Press, 2001, 5-41.

GARBOWSKI, Christopher. "Death." *J.R.R. Tolkien Encyclopedia: Scholarship and Critical Assessment*. Ed. Michael D.C. Drout. New York City, NY and London: Routledge, 2007, 119-120.

"Tolkien's Philosophy and Theology of Death." *Tolkien and Philosophy*. Eds. Roberto Arduini and Claudio A. Testi. Zurich and Jena: Walking Tree Publishers, 2014, 125-144.

GOLDING, William. *Lord of the Flies*. London and Boston, MA: Faber and Faber. 1996.

GREENFIELD, Stanley B. and Daniel G. CALDER. *A New Critical History of Old English Literature*. New York City, NY: New York University Press, 1986.

GRIMSTAD, Kaaren (ed. and trans.). *Vǫlsunga Saga. The Saga of the Volsungs*. Saarbrücken: AQ-Verlag, 2005.

HALL, John Richard Clark. *A Concise Anglo-Saxon Dictionary*. Toronto, Buffalo, NY and London: Toronto University Press, 2000.

HAMMOND, Wayne G. and Christina SCULL. *The J.R.R. Tolkien Companion and Guide. Vol. 1. Chronology*. Boston, MA and New York City, NY: Houghton Mifflin, 2006.

The J.R.R. Tolkien Companion and Guide. Vol. 2. Reader's Guide. Boston and New York City, NY: Houghton Mifflin, 2006.

HESIOD. *Theogony and Works and Days.* Trans. Martin Litchfield West. Oxford: Oxford University Press, 2008.

The Holy Bible. Douay-Rheims Version. Charlotte, NC: Saint Benedict Press and TAN Books, 2000.

HOMER. *The Iliad.* Trans. Robert Fitzgerald. Oxford: Oxford University Press, 2008.

The Odyssey. Trans. Emile Victor Rieu. London: Penguin Classics, 2009.

JARMUSCH, Jim (dir.). *Dead Man.* DVD, 2015.

JONIN, Pierre (ed. and trans.). *La Chanson de Roland.* Paris: Gallimard, 1979.

KLINCK, Anne L. *The Old English Elegies: A Critical Edition and Genre Study.* Montreal and Kingston: McGill-Queen's University Press, 2001.

LEE, Stewart and Elizabeth SOLOPOVA. *The Keys of Middle-earth: Discovering Medieval Literature Through the Fiction of J.R.R. Tolkien.* New York City, NY: Palgrave Macmillan, 2015.

LESLIE, Roy Francis (ed.). *Three Old English Elegies: The Wife's Lament, The Husband's Message, The Ruin.* Manchester: Manchester University Press, 1966.

(ed). *The Wanderer.* Exeter: Exeter University Press, 1985.

LICHAŃSKI, Jakub Zdzisław. "Oralność i piśmienność – do zagłady Numenoru. Wizja literacka czy opis procesów kulturowych?" *Kultury oralne a mityczny świat J.R.R. Tolkiena i jego następców. Quaestiones Oralitatis* II.2 (2016): 27-43.

MILTON, John. *Paradise Lost.* London: Penguin Classics, 2014.

NEUBAUER, Łukasz. "The Eagle is not Coming: Some Remarks on the Absence of the News-Bearing Eagle in Peter Jackson's Adaptation of *The Lord of the Rings.*" *Fantastic Animals, Animals in the Fantastic. Fastitocalon* 6 (2016): 99-108.

RICE, Julian. *The Jarmusch Way: Spirituality and Imagination in Dead Man, Ghost Dog, and the Limits of Control.* Lanham: Scarecrow Press, 2012.

SCRAGG, Donald George (ed.). *The Battle of Maldon.* Manchester: Manchester University Press, 1981.

"The Nature of Old English Verse." *The Cambridge Companion to Old English Literature.* Eds. Malcolm Godden and Michael Lapidge. Cambridge: Cambridge University Press, 2002, 55-70.

SOPHOCLES. *Antigone.* Trans. Robert Fagles. London: Penguin Books, 2015.

TERASAWA, Jun. *Old English Metre: An Introduction*. Toronto, Buffalo, NY and London: University of Toronto Press, 2011.

TOLKIEN, John Ronald Reuel. "Beowulf: The Monsters and the Critics." *The Monsters and the Critics and Other Essays*. London: HarperCollins, 2006, 5-48.

Bilbo's Last Song. London, Sydney, Auckland, and Johannesburg: Hutchinson, 2002.

"The Homecoming of Beorhtnoth Beorhthelm's Son." *Essays and Studies by Members of the English Association* 6 (1953): 1-18.

Morgoth's Ring. London: HarperCollins, 2002.

The Letters of J.R.R. Tolkien. Ed. Humphrey Carpenter with the assistance of Christopher Tolkien. London: HarperCollins, 2006.

The Fellowship of the Ring. London: HarperCollins, 2005.

The Two Towers. London: HarperCollins, 2005.

The Return of the King. London: HarperCollins, 2005.

The Treason of Isengard. London: HarperCollins, 2002.

WAINWRIGHT, Edmund. *Tolkien's Mythology for England: A Middle-Earth Companion*. Frithgarth: Anglo-Saxon Books, 2004.

WALTON, Christina Ganong. "Bible." *J.R.R. Tolkien Encyclopedia: Scholarship and Critical Assessment*. Ed. Michael D.C. Drout. New York City, NY and London: Routledge, 2007, 62-64.

WRENN, Charles Leslie and Whitney French BOLTON (eds.). *Beowulf*. Exeter: University of Exeter Press, 1988.

ZIELIŃSKI, Karol. "W kwestii tradycji ustnej Hobbita i Władcy pierścieni." *Kultury oralne a mityczny świat J.R.R. Tolkiena i jego następców. Quaestiones Oralitatis* II.2 (2016): 147-176.

Jörg Fündling

"Go forth, for it is there!"
An Imperialist Battle Cry behind the Lament for Boromir?

Abstract

The first chapter of Book III of *The Lord of the Rings* includes a poem which, despite various similarities to songs and poems in that novel, surprises by its highly recursive and catalogue-like structure – even though this may almost seem a necessity, given that three of the winds that blow over Minas Tirith are questioned on the whereabouts of Boromir. But yet another reason consists in Tolkien's rather unlikely pattern for such a striking composition: in Rudyard Kipling's "The English Flag", first published 1891 as a call for toil and sacrifice in the service of the British Empire, lavishly equipped with evocative place names and the promise of mortal danger. By all probability Tolkien absorbed the technical brilliance and blatant patriotism of this pervasive piece of art in his early years. In the winter of 1941-2, when Britain's colonies in East Asia were falling to the Japanese in quick succession, he used the framework and, partly, the moods of the very first instance of Kipling's Imperialist verse for his own purpose. In Tolkien's poem the winds convey a message of death, uncertainty, and sorrowful memories; the events of the day may well have left their marks during the process.

1. A Poem unlike the Others

The first piece of lyric that meets the reader's eye in Book III of *The Lord of the Rings* stands out of the novel's many-shaded poetical landscape. In fact it is one of its kind among what we know of Tolkien's lyrics today. In terms of the narrative context the Lament is a spontaneous and, one might say, incidental song, an improvised eulogy and dirge sung by Aragorn after the boat carrying Boromir's body has vanished in the falls of Rauros. It develops into an antiphony as Legolas easily continues in the same metre and pattern. Aragorn brings it to a close with the third stanza while Gimli listens in silence. Effortless as the inhabitants of Middle-earth may express their feelings in poetic modes of language, there still is a marked role allocation between those three members of the Fellowship: The Dwarf – to suggest an explanation from inside the work – hails from another lyrical tradition than both his companions, Elf and Dúnadan, who tend to 'erupt' into verse at more than this one occasion.[1] Gimli has learned by heart his people's songs of the fallen glory of Khazad-dûm and knows how to recite them in an expressive and moving manner, but he is no impromptu poet.

Such a two-voice literary 'co-production' is the great exception among dozens of songs and poems which are mostly recited or sung by individuals or, sometimes, a chorus. But this does not yet sum up the singular status of the "Lament for Boromir". A very first glance on its three times ten verses shows how peculiar a mixture of rigid pattern, plainness, and flexibility they represent. The rhyming couplets follow a near-ubiquitous pattern of English folk ballad, the "ballad stanza", which Germans like to call *Chevy-Chase-Strophe* and modify into couples of alternate rhymes.[2] The poem's printed image tends to conceal the fact that each of Tolkien's lines contains a caesura which allows to split it into a longer and a shorter half verse – one tetrameter and one trimeter; furthermore, this break is quite prominent in almost every single line. There are no enjambments, still the author chose to use two lines, not four, per rhyming couplet – a telltale decision we shall return to.

Each line's backbone, therefore, is an iambic tetrameter followed by a trimeter after the caesura. Some lines present themselves without any modifications to this:

$$\cup — \cup — \cup — \cup — | \cup — \cup — \cup —$$

I saw him walk in empty lands, until he passed away (l. 6)

More often, though, Tolkien makes use of the ballad stanza's versatility, for the syllables without accent may be either doubled or suppressed. This allows Legolas to lend an almost dactylic spring to his opening line:

---

[1] General poetic giftedness: Eilmann 410 cf. 421: "wie leicht die Protagonisten in lyrisches Sprechen verfallen." One of his major examples for this is precisely the "Lament for Boromir" (423f.; 483f.). Aragorn (in *LotR* I.11) spontaneously translates and reshapes part of the Lay of Leithian (see Eilmann 402f.) and responds in verse to the sight of the White Mountains (III.2) while Legolas probably invents, not quotes, the song that expresses his longing for the Sea (VI.4).
[2] Cf. Best 91, "Chevy-Chase-Strophe"; Drabble 667, "Metre".

U U — UU —U — U —| U U —U — U —

From the mouths of the Sea the South Wind flies, from the sandhills and the stones;
(l. 11)

The converse effect appears in each stanza's second lines: they are slowed down by metrical devices in order to mark an incision; the line ends in a sequence of three stressed syllables (which, technically speaking, transforms the iambic trimeter into an epitrite).

U — U — U— U — |U — — —

And clear and loud about the tower its loud horn calls. (l. 22 cf. 2. 12)

Familiar formal devices, such as enjambments, are absent; the end of each line end is very marked, just the right thing for a text we must imagine as improvised and sung to a sad and solemn (ancient?) tune. So far the lyrics closely match their narrative setting and genesis, just as their syntax is simple, linear and paratactic. Ebba-Margareta von Freymann's German version splendidly renders the simplicity although her lines appear somewhat more regular than the original and show no retardation of speed – except one choice shift that omits the trimeter's upbeat and inserts three dactylic elements at once.

U —U U —U U —U—| — U —UU —

Wo blieb er, der Schöne? Um Boromir halt ich traurige Wacht. (l. 14)

Not only the metre conveys the impression of 'cantabile' lyrics the spontaneity of which is quite believable; Aragorn's first stanza also predetermines both the shape and the contents of the other two. Consequently, he and Legolas are able to 'fill up' about half of each stanza while only six of ten lines demand (or allow) additions of their own free choice.

The Lament as such is a questioning of the Four Winds by an anonymous watcher on the White Tower of Minas Tirith who looks out for Boromir in vain. We might identify him with Denethor waiting – how Tolkien himself originally seems to have done (*TI* 384) – but this is in no way cogent. Lines 1 and 2 of each stanza describe the arrival of the West, South or North Wind at the Guarded City, each time in a fixed pattern that includes one topographical marker (Rohan, the sea, the Argonath), the name of the wind in question and one characteristic of the landscape (grass, dunes, the Fall of Rauros) in the first line and an evocation of City and tower in the second. Now the lookout asks his question in the least changeable line of them all (set phrases in bold type):

What news from the South, O sighing **wind, do you bring to me** at eve? (l. 13)

Only the wind direction, the adjective describing the mood, and the daytime vary; it appears that the watchers have to wait several days, for one night (l. 3) and the next evening pass (13) until certainty is achieved at daytime (23). Each stanza's fourth line adds another question more to the point (and always at the same metric position) – whether there is news about Boromir ("the Tall", "the Fair", "the Bold") – so that the sense of painful uncertainty is enhanced.[3]

The next element, the answer of the wind in ll. 5-8, is the most variable part of each stanza. For the West Wind Aragorn decides on an "I saw …" phrase ending in a referral to the North Wind; this wind has much to tell but the very outcome is missing. The South Wind, voiced by Legolas, confesses itself simply overtaxed by the number of corpses washed down to the sea and unable to tell if Boromir is one of them; again l. 8 advises that the question be passed on to the North Wind. When it finally arrives it tells of the battle and burial – yet what is now to fill the eighth line? It turns out to be Rauros; the giant falls of Anduin devour the body or carry him on, depending on how l. 28 ("bore him upon his breast") is read at that point of the story. Thus the Great River may have become Boromir's tomb or, just as well, have transported the corpse away. This intended double meaning is prepared by the narrator when he introduces the tale of the boat having reached the Great Sea in a far more final undertone: "The River had taken Boromir" (III 1, 437). Aragorn's song subtly continues this motif but only Faramir's much later report will dissolve the ambiguity (IV 5, 692f., cf. 696).

---

3 It is no coincidence that Boromir's face is called "fair and pleasant" at the very moment when his craving for the Ring distorts it (II, 9, 419; twice called "smiling and kind", "kind and friendly" (417; 418)); Faramir will later add: "His face was more beautiful even than in life" (IV 5,696). Aragorn is most generous to credit his dead companion from the line of Mardil with Elendil's most famous epithet "the Tall" (II 2, 260; App. A I, 1072; but cf. Faramir, IV 5, 704: "Elendil the Fair"); this is subtle proof how thoroughly Elendil's heir has forgiven his weaker comrade-in-arms. Aragorn is taller than Boromir, by the way, as we learn at Redhorn Pass (II 2, 309). As for boldness, Faramir – the wiser man – expounds the ambiguity of the word: "Boromir the proud and fearless, often rash" (IV 5,698); after all, Faramir himself is "bold, more bold than many deem […] Less reckless and eager than Boromir, but no less resolute" (V 1, p. 797).

In lines 9 and 10 of each stanza the lookout has his final word, always beginning with an exclamation: "O Boromir!" His gaze follows the opposite course the winds had taken, back from the respective architectural details of Minas Tirith (the outer walls, the Great Gate, the Tower of Ecthelion) to the direction the wind came from – a very artistic trait, maybe almost too much so. The final lines twice deplore the continuing uncertainty, Boromir's absence, and again use a set formula ("But you came not"). The closing line of the song, when things have become all too certain, takes up the North Wind's 'last word' from l. 28 ("To Rauros, golden Rauros-falls") and promises the only thing that may still be achieved – eternal memory. The choice of words creates a glimpse of brightness, some element of comfort and beauty; it is certainly no coincidence that Faramir will see his brother surrounded, even washed around, by a faint shimmer of light (the boat is "almost filled with clear water, from which came the light; and lapped in the water a warrior lay asleep", IV 5, 692). One obviously thinks of the Galadhrim who built the boat and whose magic just *might* make the water shine; from a narrative and poetic point of view, though, it is no less likely that we see an afterglow of the golden late-afternoon light, given that its gleam in the mist above the falls is mentioned twice (II 1, 437).

The actual lament is written between the lines; it transpires in Gondor's yearning for his captain and heir apparent, in his honorific epithets, the urgent questions, the longingly spoken "O Boromir!". One single word of outspoken grief appears at the end of line 14, almost at the song's central axis: "he tarries and I grieve." Speedy as the writing of this poem has been – we shall return to this aspect – it shows nonetheless a great amount of art.

2. Related Types of Lyric in Tolkien's Oeuvre

All in all the Lament for Boromir stands out as an oddity among Tolkien's poems: well-crafted but to a degree folkloristic, quite rigid in its call-and-response structure. Moreover it surprises us as a song about valour that rather focuses on mourning, doom and death and only in its entirety adds up to a lament.

While the closest metric parallels in *The Lord of the Rings* are found at some distance from this song, they still occur in striking numbers. A few dozen pages before it Galadriel sings of her grief to be parted from Eldamar (II 8, 392f.), her seven rhyming couplets as flawlessly regular as we would expect from the Lady of Lórien. The voice therein coincides with the poet's and singer's own person who discloses, together with part of her story (and her power to make things from her imagination take shape in song), her fears and even a certain hopelessness.[4] This makes "Galadriel's Song of Eldamar" a beautiful example how poetry deepens the prose narrative and enters into a dialogue with it, now charged with tension, now full of resonance.[5]

Two further poems in ballad stanzas, again strictly observed in metrical terms, follow the Lament for Boromir at about the same distance by which it is preceded by Galadriel's song. Both appear in the Ent chapter "Treebeard" (III 4, 498f.; 505); strikingly both speak of longing and grief to which themes the first adds the notion of a long, and possibly futile, spell of waiting. Treebeard explicitly calls his "The Ent and the Ent-wife" (*When Spring unfolds the beechen leaf*; III 498f.) an improvised translation from Entish – such a hasty effort of the oldest of Ents to translate *ad hoc* from one foreign language into another can but amaze! It takes Treebeard's measured perspective to call the dialogue in verse between the separated lovers – each one has three times four lines (two lines corresponding to one ballad stanza) – with the Entwife's constant evasions from the Ent's wooing "lighthearted, quickworded, and soon over" (III 4, 499): before the two finally meet in ll. 25-6 they have missed each other for three seasons, each one obviously a stage of their long lives, all for the love of land and nature. It is the loss of those that eventually brings about the couple's freedom, dearly bought as it is, to meet again and to start anew in the West, "far away" (l. 26) just as a prophesy mentioned by Treebeard has it (III 4, 498:

---

4 Incidentally Galadriel may have answered Haldir's question if mallorn-trees grow beyond the Sea (II 6, 367). It is known that the seedlings for the vast groves of Númenor came from Eressëa (*UT* 2, I, p. 167f.). Yet if we choose to take the beginning of this song not symbolical or metaphorical (such as Scull and Hammond, *Companion* 311, 372 [I: 389]), the words "I sang of leaves, of leaves of gold, and leaves of gold there grew [...] And by the strand of Ilmarin there grew a golden Tree" (II 8, 392f.; l. 1. 4) allow for the interpretation that Galadriel played a role in the origin of the first mallorn which in this case should still grow in Aman outside Tirion. (Provided that the tree of *golden leaves* mentioned in l. 1 is not simply Laurelin – yet this Tree's peculiarity were golden *flowers*, not golden *leaves*. "Galadriel, like others of the Noldor, had been a pupil of Aulë and Yavanna in Valinor" (*UT* 2, IV, p. 235); this seems to speak in favour of such a reading.
5 See Eilmann 394-96; 398-427, a synthesis of many points on the question how strictly the lyric in *The Lord of the Rings* is bound to the novel and its plot (though written in order to strengthen autonomous readings in future reception; 497-500 on *The Hobbit*).

"But it is foreboded that that will only be when we have both lost all that we now have"). Cheerfulness sounds different, so does light-heartedness – except, possibly, in Entish – as hopeful as the ending may appear.

The same applies even more to the metric twin of this poem, Bregalad's lament for the trees he minded, now annihilated by Saruman's woodcutters ("Bregalad's Song" *O Orofarnë, Lassemista, Carnimirië!*; III 4, 505). In the manner of a line-long exclamation, the names of three trees specially beloved of the traumatized Ent frame the poem proper. The six lines in between are a good deal more complex, not least thanks to internal rhymes (as in l. 2: *O rowan fair, upon your hair how white the blossom lay!*) – the same complication as, for instance, in parts of Coleridge's "The Rime of the Ancient Mariner" (1798). Like Galadriel Bregalad, too, remembers lost and dearly loved beauty – only that in this case it is all about the beauty of shapely rowan-trees, an aspect that on first sight appears tragicomic but turns out to be moving enough.

Yet another instance of the ballad stanza is Legolas' Common Speech song of Nimrodel, said to come from Rivendell (II 6, 358f.). The seventh and final example is Sam's song in the Tower of Cirith Ungol, a document of defiance in the face of what may be inevitable death and a praise of the undiminished beauty of the world, especially the stars (VI1, 943). It emerges that this stanza and metre, whenever chosen, show a remarkably close link to a well-defined number of issues: sadness and grief, loss, yearning, and – a theme that steps back but is by no means absent in Boromir's case ("Boromir the fair") – beauty; to be more precise, lost and longed-for beauty.

Beyond the boundaries of the great novel analogous specimens are readily found; indeed they are in rich supply. Among Tolkien's published poetry the ballad stanza is used several times in *The Adventures of Tom Bombadil* of 1962 – No. 9 ("The Mewlips") and, even more, 13 ("The Shadow-Bride") strike a strict fifteen-syllable metre while more liberties occur in Nos. 6 ("The Man in the Moon Came Down Too Soon") and 8 ("Perry-the-Winkle"). No. 6 is well known to derive from a far older version, first published in *A Northern Venture* in 1923.[6] Yet this is not the oldest sample of that lyric form: the very oldest known poem

---

6 See *LT I* 204-206 with an early stage; Scull and Hammond, *Chronology* 121, June 1923.

related to Tolkien's legendarium, "The Voyage of Éarendel the Evening Star" (later called *Éalá Éarendel Engla Beorhtast*) of 1914, is in a modified ballad stanza with many iambs (∪ —) dissolved into anapaests (∪ ∪ —) at will.⁷ This makes that catchy but versatile poetic scheme a candidate for the most frequent type in the whole of Tolkien's still far too little explored lyrical work.⁸

The ballad stanza was therefore part of his literary creations from their early stage, although with a variety of themes which is – outside *The Lord of the Rings* – as manifold as the usage of the stanza in English literature in general. But the marked narrowing of its thematic field within the novel is more obvious, and more meaningful, than just the decision to typeset the stanzas in two lines instead of the usual four. In Tolkien's early poetry it is still fitting to convey lighter notes next to solemn ones. This changes, at the latest, with Galadriel's song. To our knowledge this text (*TI* 284), just as the published version of the Lament for Boromir, lacks a long and complex textual history which predates the novel itself – as was the case for, say, Frodo's song in Bree (I 9, 174-76; formerly part of the *Songs for the Philologists* as "The Cat and the Fiddle", cf. *RS* 144-47), the only cheery lyrical relation of the ballad-stanza group in *The Lord of the Rings*,⁹ let alone the "Song of Eärendil", offspring of a now famous metamorphosis beyond recognition from the 1933 "Errantry" (*RS* 412 n. 6; *TI* 84-105).

Thanks to Tolkien we know how very brief the road from concept to finished poem was in this case (*TI* 384 and 388 n. 7); its temporary title expressly assigned it to Denethor. "The song is, at any case, Denethor's Lament. The occurrence of "Trotter" here [= in the preceding sentences of the text, J. F.] suggests that it belongs to this time" (384). The preparatory sentences, still spoken by Aragorn

---

7 Cf. *LT II* 267-69; Scull and Hammond, *Chronology* 54, 24, September 1914; Garth 44-7; 52-3.
8 Unexploited riches: Eilmann 206, 387-393; useful list of known poems now in Scull and Hammond, *Companion*, 1504-1525 (by titles), 1525-1542 (by first lines).
9 Frodo's song "There is an inn, a merry old inn", untitled in Tolkien's own index in *The Lord of the Rings* but developed from "The Cat and the Fiddle", is a derivative of the ballad stanza: the third line is doubled, the rhyme scheme of the resulting five-line stanza changes to *abccb*. This remained a solitary decision; even the typography marks it as different from the classical stanzas of the seven other poems, printed in lengthy couplet lines. One would only expect borderline cases of this kind with such a flexible metre and scheme. Just another specimen is "The Last Ship", No. 16 in *ATB*. Here the suppression of upbeats, stressed lines and endings creates a peculiar oscillation between the ballad stanza and its relative, the *Vagantenstrophe*, a trochaic twin of the common metre, best known from medieval Latin (*Meum est propositum / in taberna mori* ...).

in the work as published, would evidently be pointless without the song, even though it was written on a separate sheet. During the very next chapter, III.2, *Trotter* (the predecessor of *Strider* as an 'everyday name' for the Ranger yet older than the concept of him as a Man and heir to kings) was systematically supplanted by *Aragorn* (*TI* 394). By a lucky coincidence, jottings on the verso of the draft version for *The Lord of the Rings* II.10-III.1 allow these chapters to be dated to the war winter of 1941/2 – I will return to that subject later.

Two interesting changes, though, were in fact made during the draft stage. In the beginning the structure of the stanzas was not so regular (only the last stanza ending on the "O Boromir!" couplet consisted of ten lines and the others of only eight) – and, which is important, the concept included the makings of a stanza on the East Wind (a fragment for ll. 1-2 in *TI* 384: arriving "past the Tower of the Moon", from the Shadow past Minas Ithil/Morgul). Still in the end only the well-known outcome remained: Gimli refuses to say something on this direction of bad omen, and Aragorn agrees with him – "In Minas Tirith they endure the East Wind, but they do not ask it for tidings" (*The Lord of the Rings* II 1, 438). As a matter of fact it did not make much sense that anyone in Minas Tirith should have expected news on Boromir from Mordor, of all places: a peculiarity one would like to explain – which may prove possible.

3. An Unexpected Parallel

In the poem's earliest stage, then, we are facing a call-and-response pattern that includes all four winds, not just those three that would presently remain; what is more, all four were connected by almost refrain-like verbal repetitions from the outset. This idea at least was no invention of Tolkien's – and we must inevitably take for granted that he, like his whole generation, knew the poem which had used it shortly before his birth. Rudyard Kipling's "The English Flag", reprinted countless times since its first publication on April 4, 1891, was its author's first foray into the region of imperialist poetry, a topic to which present-day memory, *Jungle Books* apart, connects its author almost automatically.[10]

---

10 I quote Kipling's text from Peter Keating (ed.), *Rudyard Kipling. Selected Poems*. London (Penguin) 1990, 35-38; notes 202f.

The occasion for Kipling's poetic intervention, made ready for press within a matter of days, was his anger at a newspaper item of March 27th, superficially a reflection on the displeasure of large parts of the Irish who felt that their status as part of Great Britain amounted to foreign domination. As if Kipling had wanted to prove the violent Cork demonstrations right, the title of his poem – although it sings the praise of the Union Jack, not of the St George's Cross – is not "The *British* Flag". In his eyes the flag-tearing incident at Cork was symptomatic for a general rejection of Britain, the Empire, and their greatness by too many British (in his words, "Irish liar" and "English coward" alike; l. 6). Only ignorance that verges on stupidity may excuse them, so Kipling confronts them with some patriotic-didactic poetry, brilliantly composed at that. On the face of it, the author completely withdraws from the text as early as in line 8 (of 68) – it is not his speech for the defence that is to teach what the flag is about, but he calls the powers of nature into the witness box: "Winds of the World, give answer!" are his very first words (l. 1), for only the worldwide Anglo-British presence and activity can explain the true sense of the Anglo-British flag – "what should they know of England who only England know?" (l. 2) Thus the poem unfolds into a lesson both on the biography of empire and on enthusiasm.

All four of the winds have their say, one pair of opposites and then another – North and South, East and West. Their shares are slightly unequal; while the North Wind's siblings are given 16 lines each it has to do with twelve. Unlike Tolkien did almost exactly half a century later, Kipling decides on an extremely fashionable verse of his age, a long line composed of two times three anapaests (∪ ∪ —) that may be replaced by iambs. Similarities to Tolkien begin with the obligatory middle caesura of this line, brought to the utmost of its potential by the masterful poems of A. C. Swinburne (no staunch imperialist he). For the anapaestic hexameter (plus its linking syllable) is almost never filled out to the maximum of 18+1 syllables; this is why it can approach from 'above' the 15-syllable iambic pattern that Tolkien uses, until both lines are hardly distinguishable:

∪ ∪ — ∪   — ∪— ∪ | ∪ ∪ — ∪ — ∪ —
And they see strange bows above them and the two go locked to death.
("The Flag of England", l. 60)

almost coincides with our earlier example by Tolkien:

∪ ∪ — ∪∪ —∪ — ∪ —| ∪ ∪ —∪ —∪ —

From the mouths of the Sea the South Wind flies, from the sandhills and the stones;
(l. 11)

This is not the end of the formal similarities. In fact, beyond the eight-line prologue that has no counterpart in Tolkien's Lament, the winds of Kipling partly also speak in fixed words and sentences – and they do it exactly where we would by now consider a repetition most likely: in a refrain-like manner at the end of their appearance. Just as Tolkien will do in his opening and closing lines, Kipling creates an 'insert here' exercise, only that his extends over two lines and applies an even larger part of predetermined vocabulary with a Biblical flavour[11] (marked again in bold type for our purpose):

> **What is the flag of England? Ye have but my** reefs **to dare,**
> **Ye have but my** seas to furrow. **Go forth, for it is there!** (l. 35f.)

On its way to these four couplets the long poem, at times forceful and then again almost playfully alliterative, employs recurrent enumerations that provide for a smooth transition to the 'present' part:

> The desert-dust hath dimmed it, the flying wild-ass knows,
> The scared white leopard winds it across the taintless snows. (l. 49f.)
>
> The dead dumb fog hath wrapped it – the frozen dews have kissed –
> The naked stars have seen it, a fellow-star in the mist. (l. 65f.)

As these samples show, all of the four speeches are teeming with markers of climate and local colour, place names and loanwords, so that an interlaced web of associations arises. The East Wind speaks of typhoons, lotus flowers, junks and cobras ("a hooded snake", 43), marks out the farthest boundary of the Far East (the Kuriles, 37) and names the great naval and commercial ports of Hong Kong (which is behind "Kowloon" and probably also "Praya", a local expression for harbour promenades, l. 40), Singapore ("your richest roadstead": l. 42) and Calcutta (on the "Hugli", l. 43).

---

11 To this *Ye* and *Go forth* corresponds *hath* for *has* elsewhere. These winds do not accidentally speak as if they were "the four spirits of the heavens, which *go forth* from standing before the Lord of all the earth" (*King James Version*, Zechariah 6,5).

It is not realistic to expect similarities of content between "The Flag of England" and a dirge for Boromir – yet it is possible to stand up even for that. Kipling's obvious main theme is the flag, flying and waving on all decent continents in every conceivable clime (and apparently never drooping in a calm, even in the tropics – this poem guarantees for it, full of wind as it is). But another motif, presented in an almost obtrusive way, runs parallel: the number of (English) lives that the presence of this flag has cost. To fill out the gaps in this army and to close ranks is, of course, the message of that peremptory "Go forth" – and there are many gaps to fill. The fishermen of the "nutshell navies" (l. 14) who have been feeding England for centuries "died, but the flag of England blew free ere their spirits passed" (l. 16). The South Wind meets other mariners "dying, adrift in a hopeless sea" (l. 31), and covers their bodies with the colours; every day at least one person of every age dies in the East "for England's sake [...]/ Because on the bones of the English the English flag is stayed" (l. 46; 48); the West Wind sinks the grain and cattle transports or sends them on a collision course in the fog (l. 56; 59f.). So all the seas are a battlefield on which the English fight for the continuing existence of their land and people, yet those who have died in that endless war make it a duty in its own right to follow their example – at least part of the way, though a hero's death is definitely part of the perspective. It should be stated that this warlike imagery is tempered with the promise of exotic sights and adventures, a persistent topic: in 1902 Kipling's *Just So Stories for Little Children* will advise his audience, even for a first reading, a comparison of the shipping news in *The Times* with the places in their parents' atlas "(and that is the finest picture-book in the world)".[12]

In itself it may not be a cogent parallel – but the middle part of the Lament for Boromir has no other theme but manifold death. The South Wind baulks at the demand to identify Boromir's body ever among the corpses from so many battles that have been washed ashore on both banks of the disputed Great River and along the seashores – it remains unsaid whether these are only the last months' fights or if the whole warlike history of Gondor is meant: "so many bones there lie / On the white shores and the dark shores under the stormy sky. / So many

---

12 In his annotation to the poem *China-going P & O.s...* after "The Crab that Played with the Sea" (a note often omitted in modern reprints such as the Macmillan Classics edition, London 2015, 163).

have passed down Anduin to find the flowing Sea. / Ask of the North Wind news of them the North Wind sends to me!" (ll. 15-18)

It goes without saying that Tolkien was familiar with the existence of *the* British writer of his youth; in fact, he "liked Kipling more than twentieth-century men of letters were supposed to", as John R. Holmes comments (27) – but it is highly probable that he knew far more of Kipling's works than research has so far been able to demonstrate. Dale Nelson suggested that the 1902 short story "Wireless" influenced "The Notion Club Papers" and pointed out that several themes and moods of special interest to Tolkien's legendarium are present in *Puck of Pook's Hill* (1906) at once, thereby putting fresh emphasis on Norman Talbot's hint (Talbot 97-8) that this part of Kipling's oeuvre constitutes "one of Tolkien's major influences" (Nelson 376). Christina Scull and John Hammond recognized the influence of one of Kipling's drawings for *Just So Stories* in Tolkien's early drawing *Eeriness* (1914) – and in a letter dating from 1915 Tolkien's correspondant and former teacher R. W. Reynolds thought to have detected the influence of Kipling's style in a series of poems.[13]

Moreover it is possible to add another specimen to the list of "quasi-Psalms of victory" after successful battles that Dale Nelson compiled from Henry Rider Haggard's *King Solomon's Mines* (1885) and the eagle's song in *The Lord of the Rings*. In the decades between them there is a poem in *The Jungle Book* with the less-than-laconic superscription "Mowgli's Song that he sang at the Council Rock when he danced on Shere Khan's hide"; again Kipling opts for a Biblical language, this time rather loaned from the Song of Songs and its exuberant call-and-response passages, but he changes the mood into an alternation of euphoria and the wistful melancholy of a youth who feels homeless.[14]

Tolkien's "Eagle's Song" is far more closely related to Haggard's Song of Ignosi, to be sure. Then again, both of the *Jungle Books* (1894-95) are, just like *Puck* and the *Just-So Stories*, episodic books in which stories and poems alternate – with each poem as an integral part that reinforces its preceding tale and hints

---

13 Traces of Kipling in "Eeriness": Hammond and Scull, *Artist* 43, Nr. 40; accepted by Garth 37. Letter from Reynolds: Hammond and Scull, *Chronology* 71 ad July 19, 1915 (with a brief regestum of the letter).
14 "Mowgli's Song that he sang at the Council Rock when he danced on Shere Khan's hide"; quoted from Kipling 65f.

at possible interpretations as to emotions or content. In the *Jungle Books* and *Puck* Kipling adds further poems as introductory mottos; each of them may play the role of a leitmotif or add to the atmosphere – a device their author had already made use of, without the final poems, in *Kim* (1901)[15]. This interrelation of prose and poetry is most exciting; admittedly, Tolkien always inserts his poems in mid-chapter and does not opt for positions at the beginning or end,[16] but the great variety of voices, metrics and lyrical moods, a common trait of both authors, deserves closer enquiry. To give but one example: *Puck*'s eponymous hero, "the oldest Old Thing in England", again and again intersperses his tales with verse or at least switches to metric or rhyming speech. This does indeed recall "die Mühelosigkeit, mit der die Bewohner Mittelerdes dazu fähig sind, im Handlungsvollzug – aus dem Stehgreif heraus – Verse zu dichten und ihre Lage auf diese Weise zu ästhetisieren und zu meistern." Tolkien's declared intention to have songs and poems treated as inseparable parts of his narrative – which is to say, impossible to skip without grave damage to the prose portions and general structure of the novel – points in the same direction. Beyond verbal parallels and motifs an intensified search for formal models and creative inspirations, to be undertaken in a more systematic way than hitherto, would be indicated.[17]

4. Marginalia from Contemporary History

But why should Tolkien have had recourse, consciously or not, to just this specific Kipling poem for just this stage and song of his emerging novel? After all *The Lord of the Rings* can hardly be considered an exercise in deliberate intertextuality. It would certainly be absurd to impose a mechanical explanation by force, like active browsing of Tolkien's shelves for some inspirational form or motif (just because it was poetry's turn again after a longish stretch of prose?) A less blunt assumption would be that Tolkien remembered the invocation of

---

15 Tolkien got hold of *Kim* for José and Ventura del Rio and their companion Eustaquio in Paris: Scull and Hammond, *Chronology* 45, August 20, 1913.
16 With the notable exception of the "Song of the Mounds of Mundburg" (*We heard of the horns in the hills ringing*) at the very end of *The Lord of the Rings* V.7.
17 Quotation: Eilmann 2016, 421. Cf. loc. cit. 389 for Tolkien's pertinent letter to his German translator Margaret Carroux of September 29, 1968 (excerpt in Scull and Hammond, *Chronology* 732-33) in which he states that poems and prose text are to be treated as inseparable.

the winds – effective poetry that it was, and larded with mnemonic aids on top – well enough to benefit from it in a rather indirect way; it would anyway have been highly uncharacteristic of his methods as we know them if he had written some pastiche or wrested-away replica of "The English Flag".

As for the time in question, we are in the happy and rare situation to have some – by all probability quite unintentional – hints by the author himself. Christopher Tolkien noted that the transitional chapters of Books 2 and 3 of *The Lord of the Rings* showed several jottings of daily news – "Chinese bombers", "North sea convoy", "Muar River", "Japanese attack in Malaya".[18] They almost add up to a timetable of disasters, for they represent major links in that chain of bad news which World War II had in store after Pearl Harbor and the brief elation at the shaping of the worldwide Great Alliance; bad news especially for the inhabitants of Great Britain, her dominions and colonies. As 1941 turned into 1942, the rapid Japanese onslaught wiped British presence in South and East Asia off the map. Hong Kong surrendered on December 25, 1941.[19] The invasion of Malaya was under way since December 8; bridgeheads at Kota Bharu and elsewhere quickly developed into an advance across the whole of the peninsula. Muar River, crossed by the Imperial Army on January 16, was the last promising line of defence on the mainland – and as most radio listeners and newspaper readers probably suspected, the battle for that position was a harbinger of great misfortune, namely the loss of all Malaya, only excepting the island fortress of Singapore, then thought indispensable (and impregnable). Heavy losses and the constant growth of Japanese superiority damaged British morale. Even Winston Churchill's post-war memoirs still draw a picture of significant gloom.[20] To crown it all, that very same January 16 saw the beginning of the invasion of Britain's Burmese colony from Thailand, now under Japanese occupation. If its first objective, the cutting of the Burma Road into Chinese Kunming, was achieved, the vital Western supplies to China's Kuomintang government and army might dry out; this actually happened on March 8. By the

---

18 *TI* 379 with 387 n.1. Brief orientation on the chronology of work on *The Lord of the Rings* chapters II.10-III.4 and the keywords "Muar River": Scull and Hammond, *Chronology*. 191.
19 See Churchill 562-566 on Hong Kong.
20 A highly critical overview of "this greatest debacle in British military history" is offered by Weinberg (350-353) who sometimes verges on an anti-British stance and tends to consider the US point of view the only valid one.

middle of May all Burma was overrun and the Japanese forces stood on the Indian frontier. The public was convinced that the loss of India was possible – which in its turn would even have allowed for a joining of hands between the Japanese and German armies through Central Asia or Iran.[21] The battle for Singapore ended as early as February 12 with the altogether unexpected loss of what had been deemed Britain's strongest position throughout the East.

The North Sea convoys, mentioned by Tolkien, and their cargo – Western war supplies for the Soviet Union – were a constant theme during the months of fighting in Malaya. Before and after the battle of the Muar, convoys PQ 7 (26. 12.-11./12. 1. 42), without loss of shipping, and PQ 8 (8.-17.1.42), with some losses, arrived at Murmansk – events that took ample space in the media. Since every American truck or tank for Stalin would be lost to the homeland's underequipped troops, British newspapers rarely failed to point out (as was correct) that Russia would not be able to withstand Hitler without support. As the convoy battles against the German navy and the Luftwaffe claimed a great many lives of (mainly British) sailors, their outcome was followed at home with attention and anxiety (cf. Woodman *passim*).

"Chinese bombers" is more ambiguous. Tolkien may either refer to news about Allied bomb raids in the Japanese-held areas of China (by the National Chinese Air Force and the Flying Tigers, piloted by American volunteers) or, which seems less likely, he notes Japanese attacks on unoccupied China (especially its provisional capital Chongqing), acts which were widely published and evoked respect and compassion for the suffering civilians. From the British point of view there were similar causes for concern as in Burma: if China fell the Japanese army would be released for assaults on India, Australia and in the worst case even the continental United States (a less realistic fear).

As brief as Tolkien's sparse notes are, they still mirror his worries about the war events concerning all those main powers of the Alliance under immediate threats: Britain in the first place, but also Republican China and even the USSR. Yet the tale they tell is mainly the ongoing or imminent collapse of

---

21 Burma: Weinberg 1995, 355-357; threat of India and its limits: 359-362.

British colonial rule in South East Asia which was growing into the risk to lose India and with it the keystone of the Empire. Only months ago such a scenario would have been unthinkable. Even non-racist contemporaries suffered at the same time from the shock of being defeated by a civilization without European origins – a shock that was to boost the South and South East Asian independence movements after 1945 and to speed up the process of decolonisation by years and possibly decades. This meant that at the turn of 1941/2 part of that British self-view with which Tolkien's generation and even that of his children had grown up evaporated within a matter of months.

5. From Paean to Swan Song

While Tolkien during the winter of 1941/2 followed reports on the hauling down of the British flag in places he – a child of the Colonial Age in the truest sense of the word – had known from childhood, it was not really far-fetched to think of *the* poet of the Empire and one of his most famous works. This association may easily be conceived of as one more step within a personal development spanning decades. The self-same youth who in his school days had witnessed debates on the Yellow Peril, entered the Cadet Corps and – even after some years had passed – thought of himself as a non-expansionist Nationalist,[22] nonetheless (as far as we know) passed up his chance to beat the poetic war drums as hundreds of young men, and thousands of their elders, did in 1914. He even proved enough of an independent mind to ask for an officer's patent not until his exams in June 1915, thereby postponing his entry of the Army –

---

22 Cf. the topic "That the awakening of the Yellow Races is a menace to the safety of Europe", accepted by a vast majority of the King Edward's School Debating Society in 1909; there is no mention of the usually genial and witty atmosphere in this case (Scull and Hammond, *Chronology*² 20 [December 17, 1909). Less relevant, if at all, is Tolkien's own speech against international arbitration to prevent wars (ibid. 22 [²26] ad November 18, 1910); as usual the proposition was exaggerated ("A System of Arbitration would be in every way preferable to War") and mainly meant to provoke a maximum of quick answers and clever rhetoric. Cf. also Tolkien's declaration to be a non-militarist nationalist, written to Christopher Wiseman (excerpts: ibid. 56-57 [²65-66] ad November 16, 1914; Garth (51) translates this into "cultural self-realisation, not power over others").

no small feat, given the amount of family pressure.[23] The eventual participant, and survivor, of that earlier war was all too familiar with the experience of a dissolving world, and from the *Lost Tales* onward this had left deep scars in Tolkien's works. There were more stages of this personal trajectory to undergo: "as I know nothing about British or American imperialism in the Far East that does not fill me with regret and disgust, I am afraid I am not even supported by a glimmer of patriotism in this remaining war", he wrote in mid-1945 to his son Christopher (*L* 115). He could hardly have been more explicit in his dismissal of the war aim to regain, and if possible keep, the Empire.[24]

Early literary influences, the events of the day and the demands – both structural and contentual – of a nascent novel coalesced without any special effort in this case. Amid the string of Tolkien's songs and poems that this time brought forth, most of them with death, uncertainty and sorrowful remembrance in the foreground, Kipling's fanfare from the heyday of imperialism set things going in an altogether unexpected direction. Tolkien went the way of creative acquisition and, simultaneously, change of purpose when he spun the older poem round one of its axes – namely, the question how high the cost of human lives may be. Kipling, whose son had not yet been declared missing in Belgium, had offhandedly approved of such a price if his vision of the Empire demanded it. Tolkien has his protagonists question the winds in a far more subdued voice and does not make them glorify, far less demand, anonymous crowds of victims. They who sing the Lament have lost one from their midst, and with the prospect of lasting memory of Boromir goes the prospect that this loss will never be compensated. As in many other cases the element of threat and uncertainty merges with two further keynotes prevalent throughout *The Lord of the Rings*: the sense of farewell and the desire for things unscathed or indestructible.

---

23 John Garth on the outbreak of hostilities: "Tolkien, it appears, kept off the bandwagon" (39). See also ibid. esp. 50, 69, 82, on Tolkien's later course of action and his hopes to be assigned to G. B. Smith's regiment or even battalion. Cf. Scull and Hammond, *Chronology* 54 [²60 and note p. 826] ad "Late September 1914": "he faces considerable family disapproval" (55) [²62] ad "Mid-October 1914-June 1915": "there is considerable public pressure on all young men to join up, and great disapproval of those who do not."
24 This is about the post-war situation Tolkien foresaw in the Pacific region.

About the Author

JÖRG FÜNDLING received his PhD in Ancient History from Bonn University, where he also read Latin and Ancillary Sciences of History, for a commentary on the Latin Life of the Roman emperor Hadrian. Apart from teaching Ancient History and Ecclesiastical History at RWTH Aachen University, he has done extensive work as an author and translator of biographies and historical monographs. His main fields of research include the history of Imperial Rome, the cultural history of Antiquity, and the reception of classical themes and motives.

List of Abbreviations of Tolkien's Works

ATB	*The Adventures of Tom Bombadil. Tales from the Perilous Realm*
L	*The Letters of J.R.R. Tolkien*
LotR	*The Lord of the Rings*
LR	*The Lost Road and Other Writings*
LT I	*The Book of Lost Tales, Part One*
LT II	*The Book of Lost Tales, Part Two*
RS	*The Return of the Shadow*
TI	*The Treason of Isengard*
UT	*Unfinished Tales of Númenor and Middle-earth*

Bibliography

BEST, Otto F. *Handbuch literarischer Fachbegriffe: Definitionen und Beispiele*. 2nd ed. Frankfurt am Main: S. Fischer, 1982.

CHURCHILL, Winston S. *The Second World War Vol. III: The Grand Alliance*. London: Cassell 1950; repr. Boston, MA: Houghton Mifflin, 1985.

DRABBLE, Margaret (ed.). *The Oxford Companion to English Literature*. 6th revised edition. Oxford: Oxford University Press, 2006.

EILMANN, Julian. *J.R.R. Tolkien. Romantiker und Lyriker*. Essen: Oldib, 2016.

HAMMOND, Wayne G. and Christina SCULL. *J.R.R. Tolkien. Artist and Illustrator*. Boston, MA and New York City, NY: Houghton Mifflin, 1995 (new ed. 2000).

HOLMES, John R. "Art and Illustrations by Tolkien." *J.R.R. Tolkien Encyclopedia. Scholarship and Critical Assessment.* Ed. Michael D. C. Drout. New York City, NY and Oxford: Routledge 2007 (repr. 2013), 27-32.

GARTH, John. "Artists and Illustratory Influence on Tolkien." *J.R.R. Tolkien Encyclopedia. Scholarship and Critical Assessment.* Ed. Michael D. C. Drout. New York City, NY and Oxford: Routledge 2007 (repr. 2013), 36-37.

KIPLING, Rudyard. *The Jungle Books.* Ed. W. W. Robson. (Oxford World's Classics.) Oxford: Oxford University Press, 1987. (pbk. edn. 2008).

NELSON, Dale. "Literary Influences, Nineteenth and Twentieth Centuries." *J.R.R. Tolkien Encyclopedia. Scholarship and Critical Assessment.* Ed. Michael D. C. Drout. New York City, NY and Oxford: Routledge 2007 (repr. 2013), 366-378.

SCULL, Christina, and Wayne G. HAMMOND. *The J.R.R. Tolkien Companion and Guide: Chronology.* Boston, MA and New York City, NY: HarperCollins, 2006. [Revised and expanded edition 2017. Page numbers in square brackets beginning with the numeral ² refer to the 2017 version.]

The Lord of the Rings. A Reader's Companion. London: HarperCollins, 2006. [Revised and expanded two-volume edition 2017. Page numbers in square brackets refer to this edition.]

TALBOT, Norman. "Where do Elves go to? Tolkien and a Fantasy Tradition." *Proceedings of the J.R.R. Tolkien Centenary Conference, Keble College, Oxford, 1992.* Ed. Patricia Reynolds and Glen H. GoodKnight (*Mythlore* 80 [1995] = *Mallorn* 33 [1995].) Milton Keynes and Altadena, CA: The Tolkien Society/ The Mythopoetic Press, 1995: 94-106. http://faculty.smu.edu/bwheeler/tolkien/online_reader/Talbot.pdf.

TOLKIEN, J.R.R. *The Adventures of Tom Bombadil. Tales from the Perilous Realm.* London: HarperCollins, 1998, 59-118.

The Letters of J.R.R. Tolkien. Ed. Humphrey Carpenter. London: HarperCollins, 2006.

The Lord of the Rings. London: Harper Collins, 1991.

The Book of Lost Tales I (The History of Middle-earth 1). Ed. Christopher Tolkien. London: Unwin Hyman, 1985 (repr. 1987).

The Book of Lost Tales II (The History of Middle-earth 2). Ed. Christopher Tolkien. London: Unwin Hyman, 1986 (repr. 1987).

The Return of the Shadow (The History of Middle-earth 6). Ed. Christopher Tolkien. London: HarperCollins, 1992.

The Treason of Isengard (The History of Middle-earth 7). Ed. Christopher Tolkien. London: HarperCollins, 1992.

Unfinished Tales of Númenor and Middle-Earth. Ed. Christopher Tolkien. London: Unwin Hyman, 1982 (repr. 1989).

WEINBERG, Gerhard L. *Eine Welt in Waffen. Die globale Geschichte des Zweiten Weltkriegs.* (orig. *A World at Arms.* New York City, NY 1994). Stuttgart: DVA, 1995.

WOODMAN, Richard. *The Arctic Convoys, 1941-1945.* London: Casemate, 1994.

The Power of Music

Elizabeth A. Whittingham

"A Matter of Song": The Power of Music and Song in Tolkien's Legendarium

Abstract

The Silmarillion uses music for some of the same purposes as *The Hobbit* and *The Lord of the Rings*, but the tales and histories of the legendarium go beyond the use of song in these works. *The Silmarillion* begins with the Great Music in the *Ainulindalë* through which the entire cosmos is created, and music's creative power is evident in other parts of the legendarium. Early in the *Quenta Silmarillion*, Fëanor suggests that being remembered in song will somehow justify what the Elves will suffer, a perspective that Manwë seems to corroborate. Song is even used in battle and as a means of leveling a fortress. These uses along with its creative ability are distinctly different from those in the popular works and indicate that music is the most powerful force in Tolkien's universe and essential to the beings of Middle-earth.

In *The Hobbit*, there are numerous songs: the Dwarves remember Smaug's attack on the Lonely Mountain and tease Bilbo as they clean up after dinner at Bag End; the Elves of Rivendell serenade Bilbo and his companions, and as the goblins march the same group underground to meet the Great Goblin, they crudely chant about their evil intentions; the people of Esgaroth set to music the prophecy of rivers running with gold, and upon his return home, Bilbo reflects upon his journey. In *The Lord of the Rings*, the songs only seem to multiply: besides the Hobbits' various songs for walking, reflecting, and bathing, Gildor and the Elves in the Shire woods praise Elbereth; Tom Bombadil uses song nearly as often as spoken words to convey his thoughts; Aragorn commemorates the deeds of Beren and Lúthien, and Legolas, Galadriel, and Treebeard put to music various laments, legends, and hymns. *The Silmarillion* uses music for some of the same purposes, but since the Hobbits are absent so are their folksy songs of home and hearth, and the tales and histories of the legendarium go beyond the use of song in the popular works, identifying music as essential to the beings of Middle-earth and as the most powerful force in Tolkien's universe.

It is not surprising that *The Silmarillion* puts great emphasis on the importance and value of music and song, but the text introduces new roles for music and indicates that it is central to the very existence of Arda and is far more powerful than the popular texts by Tolkien suggest. Early in Book 3, the *Quenta Silmarillion*, Fëanor responds to the Doom of the Noldor pronounced by Mandos, claiming, "the deeds that we shall do shall be the matter of song until the last days of Arda" (*S* 88). This declaration is made in such a way as to suggest that these songs will somehow make up for the "tears unnumbered" and the "echo of [...] lamentation" that will be theirs as "the Dispossessed" and as "houseless spirits" (*S* 88), which is the future foretold for them. That songs might have such power is an astonishing assertion, but it is confirmed by Manwë's response to Fëanor's defiance: "So shall it be! Dear-bought those songs shall be accounted, and yet shall be well-bought. For the price could be no other" (*S* 98). These comments leave the reader wondering what these songs might be and what value they hold. Furthermore, the published *Silmarillion* begins with the *Ainulindalë*, in which by the power of Eru the music of the Ainur brings the universe into existence, weaving music into the very fabric of the created world, and the tales that follow show other purposes for song not evident in *The Hobbit* or *The Lord of the Rings*.

Commemoration and Communion

Songs within a story may function in a variety of ways. Estelle Ruth Jorgensen's article on music in *The Lord of the Rings* mentions several purposes of song: to celebrate, encourage, mourn, remember [...] and protect" (7). She also suggests that music "is [...] powerful in altering emotional states" (3) and that in certain situations "[can] promote a unified grasp of human culture [and] the experience of wonder and awe" (16). Indeed, the songs provide insight into each of the cultures represented in the text. Jorgensen's examination of the songs in *The Lord of the Rings* reveals their ability to educate and inform about good and evil, freedom, choice, redemption, hope, and destiny (8-9). These purposes evoke corresponding responses from those who listen and learn from the songs they hear and sing. The various characters join together in celebration of victory and heroic deeds, are encouraged by such stories, remember and mourn past losses and sorrows, and are warned and protected by words of caution and prophecy.

Similar ideas are echoed in Amy M. Amendt-Raduege's article, "'Worthy of a Song': Memory, Mortality and Music." She discusses Anglo-Saxon heroic elegies, such as *Widsith* and *The Seafarer*, and their role in helping later generations to remember and commemorate, recognizing that doing so is valued universally: "remembering the names and deeds of those who died remains important, to us as to the Anglo-Saxons before us" (Amendt-Raduege 117). Examining the songs and stories in *The Lord of the Rings*, Amendt-Raduege asserts they "serve the trifold purpose of commemoration, consolation, and communion" (118). The singers extol the great deeds of their heroes and ancestors, recall their lost loved ones, and commiserate with others over defeat and death. The author points out Théoden's insight into the connection between song and "knowledge," that the loss of the former results in the loss of the latter (Amendt-Raduege 120). Correspondingly, it is Théoden who suggests to Aragorn that if their foray fails at Helm's Deep they may "make such an end as will be worth a song" (*TT* 527), indicating that there is intrinsic value in heroic deeds as well as in the songs that validate those acts. Amendt-Raduege also considers the connection that Sam makes between song and "communal memory" (121) when he speculates that Frodo and his journey might be remembered in song, as indeed they are by the minstrel of Gondor. The songs in *The Hobbit* and *The Lord of the Rings* naturally suit the character of each singer and often are a people's expression of its own identity. The qualities of song that these articles identify – remembrance, preservation of knowledge, commemoration, consolation, and communion – are likewise true of the songs of the legendarium.

The remembrance in the Third Age of great battles and heroic deeds and the commemoration of the legendary characters of the past – many of whom lived thousands of years earlier – are what create the depth of time in Tolkien's popular texts that the author referred to in his letter to Milton Waldman during the early 1950s. Tolkien refers to his tales "drawing splendor from the vast backcloths" (*L* 144), which in *The Lord of the Rings* is provided by the extensive history laid out in *The Silmarillion*, from before the creation of the universe though the Valian years and the Four Ages of Men. *The Lord of the Rings* is full of references to heroes such as Beren and Lúthien, Túrin and Húrin, Eärendil, Gil-galad, Elendil, and others whose stories are known only in part or, in some cases, not at all by the readers of the popular work. Remembrance of the past and the commemoration of the glorious victories enacted and the tragic defeats suffered by Elves and Men are depicted in songs that look backwards over the millennia of Arda's history.

Túrin Turambar and Songs of Remembrance

The longest of Tolkien's songs is *Narn i Hín Húrin*, the Tale of the Children of Húrin, which, like *The Lord of the Rings*, includes examples of songs used to commemorate great heroes. The story is referred to as the "Tale of Grief" because of the incredible loss and pain endured by this one family, in which the "most evil works of Morgoth" are disclosed (*S* 199), for Morgoth imprisons Húrin, cursing the warrior's family, and is held accountable for their dark doom. The story came to be the author's "great saga" (*WJ* ix) and became, as Christopher Tolkien claims, "the dominant and absorbing story of the end of the Elder Days" (*WJ* viii-ix). The story of Túrin, his sister Nienor, and the rest of their ill-fated family exists both as a prose tale in *The Silmarillion* and in verse form in *The Lays of Beleriand*. In "Of Túrin Turambar," in the *Quenta Silmarillion*, the grief-stricken hero sings a song for his friend, Beleg Cúthalion, whom Túrin, to his great sorrow, has accidentally slain. The song is called *Laer Cú Beleg*, the Song of the Great Bow (*S* 209). Despite the danger that enemies might overhear, Túrin sings loudly in praise of his friend, commemorating his remarkable deeds and his skills as a warrior.

In the verse work, *Narn i Hín Húrin*, found in *The Lays of Beleriand*, Túrin similarly sings for his companion the song, "The Bowman's Friendship." In a voice "strong and stern" (*LB* 64, line 1653), Túrin lifts "a song of sorrow and sad splendour / the dirge of Beleg's deathless glory" (*LB* 64, lines 1657-58). In this poetic version of Túrin's tale, which Tolkien wrote in alliterative verse, the hero is portrayed as a great musician: "in weaving song / he had a minstrel's mastery" (*LB* 355, lines 353-54). Unexpectedly, his song for Beleg is so powerful that the water and trees reply, and the rocks are filled with pity (*LB* 64, lines 1660-61). Though the statement may be metaphorical, it suggests that music has great power and may even evoke a response from inanimate objects – a reaction different from the examples of music in *The Lord of the Rings*. Furthermore, the poem itself identifies the song as one of remembrance, for it reports that in the hidden kingdom of Nargothrond, the song is sung long after. This example provides depth to the tales of the First Age by looking forward in time, the reverse of the process used in *The Lord of the Rings*. The reference to the song being sung for many years in the future is one that Tolkien uses repeatedly in *The Silmarillion* and the greater legendarium, suggesting that Elves and Men in centuries or even millennia to come will remember a particular event. Additionally, the text states that the song inspires the armed forces of Nargothrond in their war with Morgoth, another purpose of song.

During his time in Nargothrond, Túrin learns from the Elves and improves upon his skills as a musician: "cunning there added [...] in subtle mastery of song and music / and peerless poesy, to his proven lore / and wise woodcraft" (*LB* 75, lines 2122-25). The Elves of the hidden kingdom love him and compliment his abilities, and when it is time for stories to be told, "then they bade and begged him be blithe and sing / of deeds in Doriath in the dark forest" (*LB* 76, lines 2161-62). The role of minstrel does not appear in the prose version of Túrin's tale, but it is a significant quality of the hero in the narrative poem. The verse text contains many other references to singing that are absent from the prose version – often for entertainment or celebration. In Thingol's halls, the people gather for the express purpose of singing: "to raise awhile / the secret songs of the sons of Ing" (*LB* 17, lines 420-21), referring to the people of Ingwë, known as the Vanyar, or perhaps meaning all the Elves. They celebrate the beautiful "city of Tûn" in the Far West (*LB* 17, line 430), and remember their kin who fell in "the slaying at the Swanships' Haven" (*LB* 17, line 434). Other groups use music to entertain: the outlaws Túrin briefly joins who sing around the campfire (*LB* 31, lines 625-27) and the people of Nargothrond who welcome Gwindor home (*LB* 70, lines 1921-26). These uses are similar to many examples of music in *The Hobbit* and *The Lord of the Rings*.

In the prose text in *The Silmarillion*, one other song is associated with the tale of Túrin Turambar. At the end of the story, when Nienor has cast herself to her death and Túrin has begged the Black Sword likewise to take his life, Mablung and other Elves of Doriath, bury their one-time companion and sing "a lament for the Children of Húrin" (*S* 226). Besides this musical tribute, the Elves place a stone on the site with the names of the brother and sister and the epithet *Dagnir Glaurunga*, meaning Glaurung's Bane (*S* 226), so that until the changing of the land passersby will remember the great warrior who slew the malicious and evil dragon. When Túrin and Nienor's mother dies beside the stone, Húrin, their father, carves her name on the reverse. The narrator reports that Glirhuin, a musician of the Men of Brethil who is gifted with foresight, sings that the Stone of the Hapless will not fall or be despoiled (*S* 229-30), another reference to future remembrance. The text further claims that after the world is changed at the end of the First Age and the lands flooded, the stone remains there still. The sorrowful tale of the Children of Húrin is sung in remembrance of their remarkable deeds and profound suffering under the curse of Morgoth. Though the various examples of song in the tales about Húrin's family – both prose and verse – include songs that are sung to remember, celebrate, and commemorate as in Tolkien's more popular works, the evocation of a response from inanimate objects raises an additional impact of music.

Creation

The songs of the First Age, their words and context, reveal the power alluded to in the words of Fëanor and Manwë and the way in which these works function in Tolkien's world, with power that is greater than what is revealed in *The Hobbit* and *The Lord of the Rings*. The most significant musical piece is the *Ainulindalë*, which is preeminent both in its position at the beginning of the published *Silmarillion* as well as in its purpose and power in creating the universe. The twelve volumes of the History of Middle-earth series, which contain multiple versions of many of the tales and are the main source of much that comprises the legendarium, often provide greater detail about the events and characters in *The Silmarillion*. The first version of the creation story, *The Music of the Ainur*, written between late 1918 and early 1920 (*LT I* 45), establishes the idea that the divine music prefigures and – through the Secret Fire – creates the world, its inhabitants, and the events that unfold in the stories of Middle-earth. It is a universe that has been created by Ilúvatar, the Elvish name for Eru, the One, who exists before all else. The text affirms that Ilúvatar is sovereign: "no theme can be played save it come in the end of Ilúvatar's self, nor can any alter the music in Ilúvatar's despite" (*LT I* 55). Although Melko raises a theme of "discord and noise" (*LT I* 54) through which evil becomes part of the very fabric of the created world – "pain and misery [...] cruelty [...] death without hope" (*LT I* 55) – Ilúvatar proclaims that Melko's additions "make the theme more worth the hearing, Life more worth living" (*LT I* 55). Ilúvatar's sovereignty is confirmed both in these words and in the events that follow. The "world [...] and its history" (*LT I* 55) has its beginning in and is shaped by the Great Music, the themes that Ilúvatar declares and the Ainur perform.

The Music of the Ainur, written early in the nearly six decades during which Tolkien composed and revised his stories of Middle-earth, is also a blueprint for its author. Though Tolkien made many changes over the years, much of the tale and its main concepts remained the same, so he established for himself a design from which to work. As Verlyn Flieger notes, "this story [...] sets up the parameters for his Secondary World" (161). As Tolkien explains in his essay, "On Fairy-Stories," to be believable, to possess "the inner consistency of reality" (69), necessitates that the author exerts "labour and thought, and [...] demand[s] a special skill" (70). Though the Great Music is not restrictive, it does establish certain "parameters" for the World and for the author. In her article, "The Music and the Task: Fate and Free Will in Middle-earth," Flieger argues and clearly demonstrates that another one of these principles is the free will of Men: as stated in Tolkien's creation story, although the "Music of the Ainur [...] is as fate to all things else," Ilúvatar gives Men "free virtue whereby within the limits of the powers and substances and chances of the world they might fashion and design their life beyond even the original Music" (*LT I* 59). The creation of Tolkien's Secondary World through the Ainur's Great Music provides a foundation that requires in Middle-earth that Ilúvatar be sovereign, that evil be part of the nature of the created world itself, and that Men have free will. Examples of music possessing the *Ainulindalë's* ability to create are limited in *The Lord of the Rings* where only Bilbo's song in Rivendell's Hall of Fire seemingly causes images to appear to the audience. However, Julian Eilmann in *J.R.R. Tolkien – Poet and Romanticist* also notes that "The Tale of Aragorn and Arwen" in Appendix A refers to "the gift of the Elf-Minstrels, who can make the things of which they sing appear before the eyes of those that listen" (*RK* 1033). Although Aragorn thinks that Lúthien has appeared before him as he has sung, he soon discovers that the Elf maiden is Arwen

Undómiel, so though the reference confirms that some minstrels do possess such a creative ability, the hero has not actually caused the legendary character of the First Age to appear.

The *Ainulindalë*, being the first example of music in *The Silmarillion* and the first book of that five-book work, emphasizes the essential nature of music within Tolkien's world. The Great Music is at the center of the short book and is at the heart of the tale's power and splendor. Tolkien describes the music's variety and beauty: "like unto harps and lutes, and pipes and trumpets, and viols and organs, and like unto countless choirs singing with words" (*S* 15). This majestic music stands in clear contrast to Melkor's embellishments. When "the discord of Melkor" (*S* 16), is added, "it seemed [...] that there were two musics progressing at one time [...] The one was deep and wide and beautiful, but slow and blended with immeasurable sorrow [...] The other [...] was loud and vain, and endlessly repeated [...] a clamorous unison as of many trumpets braying upon a few notes" (*S* 16-17). Though Melkor possesses "the greatest gifts of power and knowledge" among the Ainur (*S* 16), he clearly cannot rival the authority and supremacy of Ilúvatar; however, from the diversity of the "two musics" comes all of Ëa, the universe, and the inhabited world of Middle-earth with its mountains, plains, and seas and with its numerous creatures and races.

Tolkien's demonstration of music's tremendous creative power has been discussed by many scholars. Robert A. Collins explains, "Tolkien approaches the essential nature of being in aesthetic terms, seeking the nature and purpose of creation not as physical or theological extrapolation, but as aesthetic process governed by formal principles" (257). Collins assigns to the *Ainulindalë* and its Great Music the highest purpose and the greatest power as Eru's creative agent. Jane Chance notes that the *Ainulindalë*'s "conclud[ing] with the words 'story and song,'" is most apt since "these tales celebrate the power of creation and goodness through the image of song, music, and its triumph over destruction and evil" (189). Although the creative power is Eru's, music is the medium that has the versatility and potency to be capable of being a vessel for the infinite variety and beauty of the created universe. The preeminence of song in Tolkien's world is evident in its primacy in *The Silmarillion* and in Tolkien's description, which shows its multiplicity and might.

In its opening passages, the *Ainulindalë* references another occasion for song: the Second Music. The text compares the Great Music of creation to the future music following the end of the world, claiming, "Never since have the Ainur made any music like to this music, though it has been said that a greater still shall be made [...] by the choirs of the Ainur and the Children of Ilúvatar after the end of days" (*S* 15). This Second Music will also have creative power and purpose since Ilúvatar's themes will "take Being in the moment of their utterance," for "Ilúvatar shall give to their thoughts the secret fire" (*S* 15-16). Before the universe and Middle-earth have been created, the text is describing the end of time and the new world that will follow. Furthermore, the new creation will not be flawed from its beginning, for the singers will "understand fully [Ilúvatar's] intent in their part" (*S* 16), and "the themes of Ilúvatar will be played aright" (*S* 15). Melkor's destructive pride and discordant arrogance will not introduce evil into the nature of this new world, which Tolkien refers to as New Arda and Arda Unmarred in his Notes to "Laws and Customs among the Eldar" (*MR* 251-52) or as Arda Remade in the "Athrabeth Finrod Ah Andreth" (*MR* 319-20). The Second Music will be greater than the original Music of the Ainur because it will create a New Arda that is whole and uncorrupted, a superior creation to Arda Marred, which has been stained by Melkor's evil that permeates every aspect of the original universe. Clearly, however, in both instances music is essential to the act of creation and, as becomes apparent in the tales that follow, permeates creation itself.

The *Ainulindalë* includes numerous references to music and its essential role in Tolkien's created world. After the completion of the Great Music, Ilúvatar provides the Ainur with a Vision of what was in the Music. The text states that they celebrated water above all other things, for "in water there lives yet the echo of the Music of the Ainur more than any substance else that is in this Earth" (*S* 19). The text projects that for this reason, Elves and Men are both drawn to the Sea's sounds even though they do not realize the reason. Ulmo, who is later known as the Lord of Waters, delights in what he sees in the Vision. In response, Ilúvatar demonstrates his sovereignty by explaining to Ulmo that Melkor's violence against creation, introducing into the Music freezing cold and unrestrained heat, has resulted in snow and frost, in clouds and mist (*S* 19). Ilúvatar points out to Ulmo that in the clouds, he is brought together with Manwë, Lord of the Breath of Arda, the airs above the Earth. Ulmo and Manwë are kindred spirits, so Ulmo rejoices and proclaims, "I will seek Manwë that he and I may make melodies forever to thy delight!" (*S* 19), by which action the Ainur's Music endures throughout time. Despite Melkor's efforts to destroy creation, Ilúvatar in his sovereignty has used Melkor's malicious deeds to create even greater beauty and splendor.

The Music of the Valar and Maiar

After Ilúvatar speaks and gives life to what the Ainur have sung, some of them enter into the World, and the greater spirits are known as the Valar and the lesser spirits as the Maiar. It is their purpose to accomplish the work needed to bring about what they had sung in the Great Music and seen in the Vision, and music continues to be fundamental to their existence. The *Valaquenta*, the second book of *The Silmarillion*, refers to "the trumpets of Manwë" (*S* 27), and to the mighty horn of Oromë, the hunter, which is called the Valaróma (*S* 29). Likewise, Ulmo "make[s] music upon his great horns, the Ulumúri" (*S* 27). Those beings who hear Ulmo's music yearn for the sea ever after. Indeed, it is the music of Ulmo's horns that awakens a yearning for the sea in the hearts of the Elves (*S* 57). In "The Coming of the Valar," the earliest form of the *Valaquenta*, the sprites and nightingales of Lórien fill his gardens with music (*LT I* 71). The youngest Vala, Amillo, who disappears from later versions of the tale, sings blissfully to the accompaniment of Salmar's stringed instruments (*LT I* 75). At the times of harvest, the inhabitants of Valinor gather together and express "their joy in music and song" (*S* 75). The Valar and Maiar, having participated in the Great Music, express themselves through music in the Undying Lands, for it is essential to the very nature of these divine beings.

When Melkor destroys the two lamps that light the world, as described in the *Quenta Silmarillion*, the Vala Yavanna uses song again to create. Yavanna prays over a grassy hillock; then, with all the Valar assembled around, "she sang a song of power, in which was set all her thought of things that grow in the earth" (*S* 38). As she sings, two green sprouts appear, grow into seedlings, flower, and develop into the Two Trees of Valinor, which light the surrounding lands. In the earliest version of the tale, "The Coming of the Valar," Vána sings a "song of spring" beside Yavanna, and Lórien's sprites play music close by them (*LT I* 71). Music again reveals its creative powers in a momentous way because the Two Trees are central to the entire legendarium: the Trees light the lands in the Far West, and when the Elves come to Valinor, Fëanor crafts the three Silmarils from the Tree's golden and silver lights. Varda, Queen of the Valar, blesses the Silmarils, and Mandos, the Doomsman of the Valar, prophesies about them.

The Silmarils become not only the focus of *The Silmarillion* but also of the entire history of the World. In pursuit of the Silmarils stolen by Melkor, Fëanor leads the Elves in rebellion out of Valinor and back to Middle-earth. The wars of the First Age continue largely because of the desire of Fëanor and his sons to recover the Silmarils. At the end of that Age, when the Valar intervene to rescue Elves and Men, the divine beings raise Eärendil in his boat, and he bears one of the Silmarils into the skies where the light of the Silmaril shines above Middle-earth. The star Eärendil is mentioned repeatedly in *The Lord of the Rings*, and its light is captured by Galadriel and contained in the star-glass that she gives Frodo, which is instrumental in the furtherance of his quest and the fall of Sauron. One prophecy of the Last Days claims that the three Silmarils will be recovered from earth, sea, and sky to light the World after the destruction of the Sun and Moon (*LR* 333). The Two Trees that Yavanna sings into existence contain a life and brilliance that cannot be entirely extinguished and are woven into the story of every Age.

The *Quenta Silmarillion* contains many other references to music. One of the pieces of music described early in the collection of tales is the *Nurtalë Valinóreva*, or the Hiding of Valinor, which is sung by the Valar as they enchant the seas to prevent the rebellious Elves from returning to the Undying Lands. The Powers form and place the Enchanted Isles and alter the character of the surrounding waters, "fill[ing] them with shadows and bewilderment" (*S* 102), intending that no being – Elf, Man, or Dwarf – will be able to successfully reach Valinor. The Valar's precautions are fully effective until the coming of the one whom the text refers to as "the mightiest mariner of song" (*S* 102). Like the Music of the Ainur, the *Nurtalë Valinóreva* is music that not only creates but also changes the nature of the World. The creative power of music and its crucial role in Tolkien's universe is evident throughout the legendarium.

The Children of Ilúvatar: Musicians by Nature

The Children of Ilúvatar show that they are truly the descendants of their creator because music is a part of who they are from the very beginning. When the Elves first awake, they recognize that being able to express themselves verbally makes them unique: "Themselves they named the Quendi, signifying those that speak with voices; for as yet they had met no other living things that spoke or sang" (S 49). The Valar know about the coming of the Children of Ilúvatar from the Great Music, for it is in a theme introduced by Ilúvatar, and they are eager for the awakening of the Elves, but they do not know when and where they will first appear. The Vala Oromë is the first to make contact, and his first awareness is when "in the quiet of the land under the stars he heard afar off many voices singing" (S 49). The possession of voices lead the Elves to want to sing, and it becomes an essential skill at which some of them excel.

All three kindreds of Elves – the Vanyar, Noldor, and Teleri – have some connection to music. The Vanyar, who are Manwë's favorite, "received song and music" directly from the Lord of the Valar (S 40). The Noldor are distinguished by being "renowned in song" (S 53) since they comprise most of the Elves who rebel and leave Valinor and become the primary warriors in the war against Morgoth. Furthermore, from among the sons of Fëanor comes Maglor, "the mighty singer" (S 60), who composes the lament about the Kinslaying at Alqualondë, entitled *Noldolantë*, the Fall of the Noldor (S 87). Maglor is held as one of the greatest of the Elvish minstrels, named as second only to Daeron of Doriath (S 183). Finally, the Teleri are taught much about "sea-lore and sea-music" by the Maia Ossë (S 58). They love the seas, so "their songs were filled with the sound of waves upon the shore" (S 58). The Elves are surrounded by music and revere the skilled musicians among them.

The Lays of Beleriand, the third book of the History of Middle-earth, contains the verse form of the *Lay of Leithian*, which provides numerous examples of the use of song by the Children of Ilúvatar. The lengthy poem – over 4200 lines of heroic couplets – is more detailed than the story in the published *Silmarillion*, but covers only a small portion of the tale. It portrays Dairon the minstrel as being the greatest of all the Elvish musicians: he "played with bewildering wizard's art / music for breaking of the heart" (LB 174, lines 499-500). Dairon loves

Lúthien, and before the coming of Beren, he would often play while Lúthien dances and sings. Besides Daeron and Maglor, the legendarium contains many other references to Elven minstrels and poets.

Though it is thousands of years later when Men appear – the Younger Children of Ilúvatar – they, too, are singers like their creator. Finrod Felagund is the first Elf to make contact with Men, and he becomes aware of their presence in the woods of Ossiriand when he hears singing. He is surprised because "the singers used a tongue that he had not heard before" (*S* 140). The narrator declares that "they sang because they were glad" (*S* 140), and Finrod watches them and wonders, for he has never seen such beings before. When they sleep, Finrod "took up a rude harp [...] and he played music upon it such as the ears of Men had not heard" (*S* 140). They are mesmerized by the wondrous music, and listen intently as he sings about creation "and the bliss of Aman beyond the shadows of the Sea" (*S* 141). Though they cannot fully understand his words, what is in his song, "came as clear visions before their eyes" (*S* 141). Finrod's singing creates marvelous images in the minds of his audience, and music becomes the medium that first establishes contact between the two peoples. Throughout the stories of Middle-earth, making music and expressing themselves in song is clearly essential to the very nature of the Children of Ilúvatar.

One unique example that appears in the prose tale "Of Beren and Lúthien" is a musical composition with actual words. Most of the songs in *The Silmarillion* are described, but unlike those in *The Hobbit* and *The Lord of the Rings*, no words are provided. When the brothers, Curufin and Celegorm, maliciously attack Beren and Lúthien, Beren cannot endure the thought that Lúthien may be put in danger again, so he returns to his quest without her (*S* 177-78). In his Song of Parting, Beren glorifies Lúthien's beauty and the wonder of her existence:

> Though all to ruin fell the world
> and were dissolved and backward hurled
> unmade into the old abyss,
> yet were its making good, for this –
> the dusk, the dawn, the earth, the sea –
> that Lúthien for a time should be. (*S* 178)

Beren both honors Lúthien and celebrates her life, and as Lúthien pursues Beren through the woods on Huan, she sings her response, before the two lovers continue on their quest together.

Tuor: Hero and Minstrel

Another of the great hero tales from the First Age, "Of Tuor and the Fall of Gondolin," portrays Tuor as a musician. The version of Tuor's story in *Unfinished Tales of Númenor and Middle-earth* states, "[Tuor] took up the harp which he bore ever with him, being skilled in playing upon its strings, and [...] he sang an elven-song of the North for the uplifting of hearts" (20), an example of Jorgensen's concept of music for encouragement. A few pages later, the same text depicts Tuor resting in the Echoing Mountains of Lammoth and playing his harp and singing. *The Fall of Gondolin*, included in *The Book of Lost Tales, Part Two*, is one of the earliest texts about Middle-earth composed by Tolkien, dating back to 1916-17 (*LT II* 146), making Tuor the first of the great heroes to be depicted. The text describes Tuor's "rugged harp of wood and the sinews of bears" (*LT II* 149), which he strums while sitting beside Lake Mithrim. The text states that, "hearing of the power of his rough songs," people came from the surrounding area to listen (*LT II* 149), depicting music as entertainment. As Tuor journeys, he carefully pays attention to the music of the water, singing and writing "new songs on his old harp," inspired by the sounds of flies, bees, beetles, and butterflies (*LT II* 154). Living in the wild alone, the hero learns music from the created world around him, for music is a part of the essential nature of Arda.

These specific depictions of Tuor as musician are absent from the version of the tale in the *Quenta Silmarillion*, but it references this older and more detailed account, which is a tale of remembrance and commemoration, relating the story of King Turgon's betrayal and the vicious attack by Morgoth's armies of dragons, Balrogs, and Orcs in which both the king and his magnificent kingdom fall, recalling "the deeds of desperate valour there done" (*S* 242). According to this early version of the tale, when Tuor eventually arrives at Gondolin, the inhabitants wonder at Tuor's height, his lance, and "his great harp" (*LT II* 159). Having lived alone in the wilderness for many years, Tuor is untrained and learns much from the Elves: "Musics most delicate he there heard [...] Many of these subtleties Tuor mastered and learned to entwine with his songs to the wonder and heart's joy of all who heard" (*LT II* 163). This ancient tale about Tuor in Gondolin and the City's destruction is referenced in *The Hobbit* when Elrond informs Gandalf and Thorin of the origin of the blades that they found in the troll's lair (49), but no mention is made of Elrond's relationship with the heroes of the past.

Even though more than six thousand years have passed since Gondolin's destruction, it is not surprising that the tale is still remembered in Rivendell since Tuor and Idril are Elrond's grandparents, and the Half-Elven is the great-grandson of King Turgon. The City is mentioned at least three times in *The Lord of the Rings*, once by Elrond, in Gimli's verses about Durin, and by Galadriel, who like Elrond lived during the events of the First Age. The events and heroes of the Elder Days are not forgotten many millennia later. With Eärendil being the only child of Tuor and Idril and also Elrond's father, it is understandable that Strider tells Bilbo that he has "cheek" to write a song about Eärendil in the house of Elrond (*FR* 231). The examples from Tolkien's more popular works confirm the fact that the events in Gondolin and the descendants of Tuor and Idril are remembered and still commemorated in song even in the Third Age.

After the City falls, the refugees are ambushed, and Glorfindel, Lord of the people of the Golden Flower, finds himself in fierce and desperate combat with a Balrog that ends in their mutual destruction. When the survivors' escape is accomplished, they have a feast in remembrance of Gondolin and all who have been lost: "for Glorfindel the beloved many were the songs they sang" (*S* 244). According to the *Book of Lost Tales, Part II*, "still do the Eldar say when they see good fighting at great odds of power against a fury of evil: 'Alas! 'Tis Glorfindel and the Balrog'" (194). Among some of the final words that Tolkien ever composed about Middle-earth are those that further indicate Glorfindel's significance in the tales of the Four Ages. In *Late Writings* in *The Peoples of Middle-earth*, Tolkien explains that after Glorfindel's death, the Elf rests in the Halls of Waiting until released by Mandos and that he is reincarnated and ultimately returns to Middle-earth (379-82). As a result, he resides at Rivendell in the Third Age and is the same Glorfindel who rescues Frodo and his companions as they are chased by the Nazgûl on their way to Rivendell. The songs about Glorfindel are among numerous songs of commemoration mentioned in the published *Silmarillion*.

Lúthien's Powerful Spell-Songs

The vital and potent role of music is stressed throughout *The Silmarillion*, and the great songs of the First Age tell "tales of sorrow and ruin" (*S* 162). In these stories, "joy" exists in the midst of "weeping" and there is a "light that endures" even "under the shadow of death" (*S* 162). These impressive claims about the ancient compositions appear at the beginning of the chapter that relates the tale of Beren and Lúthien, which the Elves count as the "most fair" (*S* 162). That song, called the *Lay of Leithian*, meaning "Release from Bondage" (*S* 162), may be found in a variety of versions throughout Tolkien's works. In *The Road to Middle-earth*, Tom Shippey claims that Tolkien developed "more than twelve versions of the story besides Chapter 19 of *The Silmarillion*, the only full rendering" (257). Although the lengthiest of the verse renditions is in *The Lays of Beleriand*, the entire tale is alone found in the *Quenta Silmarillion*'s prose account. Adopting Jorgensen's terms, this song of Beren and Lúthien's heroic deeds celebrates, mourns, and remembers. Furthermore, it is a tale that is full of music and that demonstrates the value and power of music in a wide variety of situations. Indeed, it is by Lúthien's song that the Elven princess and the Man, Beren, are initially brought together: "Keen, heart-piercing was her song as the song of the lark that rises from the gates of night and pours its voice among the dying stars, seeing the sun behind the walls of the world" (*S* 165). The very earth responds to her music as winter disappears and spring spreads across the land of Doriath. The creative potency of the Music of the Ainur seems to empower Lúthien's song – conceivably through the Maian blood of her mother, Melian.

Melian is a divine being, and Lúthien is the only Elf or human to be half Maian. Additionally, her father, Elu Thingol, is one of the four great Fathers of the Elves and one-time leader of all the Teleri. Along with this exceptional heritage, Melian may have taught her daughter and helped her to develop the abilities that are the gift of her bloodline, but whatever the cause, Lúthien is the most powerful singer in all the tales of Middle-earth. Throughout the *Lay of Leithian*, Lúthien uses song to achieve her purposes. To prevent Lúthien from following Beren on his quest, Thingol builds "an airy house" (*LB* 202, line 1373) in the branches of the Queen of Beech trees and sets guards below. Lúthien, determined to aid Beren in his mission, draws on her matchless talent, and "sang a song of growth and day [...] of night / and darkness without end [...] And all names of things / tallest and longest on earth she sings" (*LB* 205, lines 1481, 1483-84, 1486-87); Lúthien's song causes her hair to grow to her feet and then far longer yet. Her achievement seems like "magic," but as Eilmann points out, Tolkien rejects the use of that word as "a technique" that seeks the "domination of things and wills," suggesting in its place the use of the word "enchantment" (*OFS* 73). Rather than dominating, Lúthien seeks to sacrifice her own safety and draw on her power to aid Beren that they might together achieve Thingol's quest and ultimately his acceptance of their love.

Over the dark robe that Lúthien creates from her woven hair, she sings enchantments of "sleep and slumbering" (*LB* 206, line 1503) so that the robe is "drenched with drowsiness" (*LB* 207, line 1545), and thereby, she overcomes her guards and effects her escape. The text even asserts that Lúthien's robe is "enchanted with a mightier spell than Melian's raiment" (*LB* 207, lines 1546-47) that she wore when Thingol came upon her and was lost in her spell for what the *Quenta Silmarillion* declares was "long years," the two standing in the woods together without speaking (*S* 55). Since Melian is a divinity, a Maia, the suggestion that her daughter exceeds her enchantments claims inestimable power for the songs of Lúthien, which is confirmed in her later triumphs. Her song that causes Elven hair to grow to an unbelievable length again portrays creative power, in part perhaps attributable to Lúthien's divine blood. *The Lay of Leithian* celebrates her escape that she might rescue and be reunited with Beren and remembers the power and beauty of this incomparable singer. Moreover, Jorgensen's assertion that song may inform about "good," "evil," "choice," "freedom," "hope," and "destiny" (8-9) seems to catalog qualities that are all witnessed in this one work. The tale's length and the variety of adventures that the heroic couple experience provide a venue for songs of many purposes.

Battle and Ultimate Triumph

While containing numerous references to song, the tale "Of Beren and Luthien" includes three moments of music that stand out from all the others. The first of these scenes reveals what is perhaps the most startling use of music in the legendarium. Having accepted the challenging quest set by Lúthien's father, Beren obtains the aid of King Finrod Felagund, and the two warriors and their companions start out only to be captured by Sauron, Morgoth's evil lieutenant. Finrod and Sauron use song in a totally new and astonishing way – to battle each other: Sauron's "song" is one "of wizardry, / Of piercing, opening, of treachery" and Felagund "Sang in answer a song of staying, / Resisting, battling against power" (S 171). The excerpt of the verse rendition of the *Lay of Leithian* that appears in the *Quenta Silmarillion* tells of the great power of Finrod Felagund's song: "all the magic and might he brought / Of Elvenesse into his words" (S 171). Sauron, however, gains the upper hand, throwing Beren and Finrod into the dungeons of the fortress that Finrod himself had built and where Finrod is eventually slain.

Though defeated by Sauron's song, the eventual liberation of Beren is aided by another piece of music. Coming to rescue Beren, Lúthien's song, "that no walls of stone could hinder" (S 174), reaches him in the bowels of the earth and levels the fortress. Lúthien uses song to physically raze a stone citadel and leave it in complete ruins. Beren responds with a song he wrote "in praise of the Seven Stars, the Sickle of the Valar that Varda hung" (S 174). In these musical episodes, the *Lay of Leithian* first commemorates the potency of Finrod Felagund's song, then mourns the defeat of the two friends and their loss when confronted by the treachery of Sauron, and finally celebrates the reunion of Beren and Lúthien made possible by Lúthien's valor and the exceptional power of her song. Using song to battle against an enemy and destroy a fortress are uses of song that do not appear in either *The Hobbit* or *The Lord of the Rings*. These events show music as possessing a physical authority and command that is unparalleled in the heroes tales of Middle-earth and emphasizes the essential and powerful role that music holds in the legendarium.

The second of the momentous scenes in the *Lay of Leithian* is Lúthien's confrontation with Morgoth. When the couple enters Morgoth's hall, Lúthien proposes "to sing before him, after the manner of a minstrel" (*S* 180). Morgoth is conquered by his own desire for her: "suddenly she eluded his sight, and out of the shadows began a song of such surpassing loveliness, and of such blinding power, that he listened perforce; and a blindness came upon him, as his eyes roamed to and fro, seeking her" (*S* 180). Music is again being used as a weapon, disarming the Dark Lord and causing him to collapse before his throne. This feat is one of immeasurable power and authority. Morgoth has been confronted in battle by some of the greatest warriors of the First Age. Fingolfin, the High King of the Nolder in Beleriand, was previously one of the few to ever challenge Morgoth to single combat. Though Fingolfin wounds Morgoth repeatedly, the King, described as the "most proud and most valiant of the Elven-kings of old" (*S* 154), is slain. Nonetheless, Lúthien flattens Morgoth and leaves him lying helpless on the floor of his own stronghold. Furthermore, her song enchants everyone within hearing, causing them to sleep. As a result, Beren is able to recover a Silmaril, so they escape, though Beren loses his hand to Carcharoth, the Wolf of Angband. Morgoth, once considered the mightiest of the Ainur who sang the universe into being, is overthrown by the power of Lúthien's irresistible song, and the seemingly impossible quest set by King Thingol is achieved.

The third of the noteworthy scenes unfolds before the Valar. The events in the *Lay of Leithian* result in Beren's death, and Lúthien pursues Beren's spirit to the halls of Mandos, the Houses of the Dead. There, like Orpheus before Dis, Luthien sings to the Vala Namo: "The song of Lúthien before Mandos was the song most fair that ever in words was woven, and the song most sorrowful that ever the world shall hear" (*S* 186-87). The superlatives set this song in a place by itself above all the music of Elves, Men, and every other creature. Even the immortal gods revere it, for "unchanged, imperishable, it is sung still in Valinor [...] and listening the Valar are grieved" (*S* 187). Lúthien sings about the great suffering endured by the Children of Ilúvatar, by Elves and Men, and their profound distress. The power and efficacy of her song is foremost evident, however, in Mandos, the Doomsman of the Valar (*S* 28), who "was moved to pity, who never before was so moved, nor has been since" (*S* 187). Mandos, therefore, goes to Manwë on Lúthien's behalf, and the Lord of the Valar reveals the choices that by the will of Eru are offered to Beren and Luthien. Because Lúthien chooses to relinquish her immortality, Beren is allowed to return from death, and he and Lúthien are reunited for a brief time. The further fruit of Lúthien's song is manifest in their descendants in whom flows the blood of Elves, Men, and the divine Maiar. These descendants include great heroes and powerful women who, throughout the Four Ages of Men, are themselves remembered and celebrated in song. It is, however, the incredible potency of Lúthien's song that levels Sauron's fortress, temporarily overthrows Morgoth, and moves Mandos to pity – deeds that are beyond the abilities of other warriors and musicians.

The Sea Longing

From the earliest days of Arda, Ulmo's music awakens a desire for the sea in the hearts of the Children of Ilúvatar, and as stated in the *Ainulindalë*, the power of the Music of the Ainur is still evident in water. The Sea is both the barrier that keeps Elves and Men from the Undying Lands but also the only way by which they might ever reach the Far West, the deep desire of their hearts. Following the destruction of the lost City of Gondolin, as the refugees feast and remember their lost kingdom, Tuor composes for his son, Eärendil, an unnamed song about Ulmo, the Lord of Waters, coming to Nevrast, an event from early in Tuor's journeys. As a result of Tuor's song, "the sea longing woke in his heart, and in his son's also" (S 244). This particular piece of music, therefore, has long-reaching effects. Tuor's desire for the Sea results in his finally setting out with Idril and sailing into the West, looking for the Undying Lands. What happens to the couple is unknown, but the text states, "in after days it was sung that Tuor alone of Mortal Men was numbered among the elder race, and was joined with the Noldor, whom he loved; and his fate is sundered from the fate of Men" (S 246). Though this final note at the end of his tale is brief and merely stated as a possibility, it suggests a phenomenal occurrence, for Eru alone has the ability to change a being's very nature, and such a thing has only before happened with Lúthien whose transformation was the opposite of what is believed happened to Tuor. The occurrence, however, seems to be remembered solely because it is chronicled in song.

The consequence of the sea-longing awakening in Eärendil is even more significant and brings about inestimable good, for Eärendil eventually becomes "the mightiest mariner of song" (*S* 102), whose coming was foretold by the narrator of the *Quenta Silmarillion*. Eärendil alone passes the Enchanted Isles and through the Shadowy Seas to intercede with the Valar on the behalf of all peoples suffering under Morgoth Bauglir. Afterwards was written *The Lay of Eärendil*, which recounts "his adventures in the deep and in lands untrodden" (*S* 246). The Valar do respond to Eärendil's petition and make war on Morgoth, the violence of which changes the face of the Earth, covering all of Beleriand under the Sea. Eärendil is long remembered, for even in the last days of the Third Age, the time recounted in *The Lord of the Rings*, his name is repeatedly spoken and his story sung – both in reference to the hero and to his existence as a star in the heavens. In fact, having recounted the tale of how the Silmaril came to Eärendil and the light of the star to Frodo's star-glass, Sam declares to Frodo, "we're in the same tale still!" (*TT* 697). Indeed, the help and forgiveness achieved by Eärendil not only results in Morgoth's defeat but in the Elves being allowed to return to Valinor, including Galadriel and Elrond who eventually travel there with Bilbo and Frodo. Those who sing *The Lay of Eärendil* and all the other songs mentioned in the legendarium are warned and protected by words of caution and prophecy. They sing in celebration of victory and heroic deeds, are encouraged by such stories, and remember and mourn past losses and sorrows.

In conclusion, though similar purposes are also served by many of the songs in *The Hobbit* and *The Lord of the Rings*, the songs of the legendarium differ from those of the other works in two significant ways. In the First Age, both Elves and Maiar, such as Sauron, battle with song – opposing, holding, breaking, and conquering their enemies in combat – demonstrating the might of music over both the mental and the physical. Furthermore, song is the medium by which all things are created, initially in the *Ainulindalë* and then later by the Valar and even Lúthien, the daughter of a Maia. In these cases, true virtue, inconceivable power, and exquisite beauty are evident. The claim made by Fëanor in *The Silmarillion* that these "dear-bought" songs might ultimately offset the Doom of the Noldor becomes credible, for by them the deeds and names of great heroes are remembered; tales of good over evil, of hope and of redemption, are celebrated; towers are thrown down; mountains are raised up; and the stars are set in the deeps of space. Music is not simply important in

Tolkien's world, but it is part of the world's essence and the nature of created and divine beings alike. Without exception, song is the most powerful force in the universe for destruction, creation, and renewal.

About the Author

ELIZABETH A. WHITTINGHAM teaches English at the College at Brockport State University of New York and at Monroe Community College in Rochester, New York. Her 2008 book, *The Evolution of Tolkien's Mythology: A Study of the History of Middle-earth* (McFarland), examines nearly six decades of Tolkien's writings. She has been published in *A Companion to J.R.R. Tolkien*, a part of the Blackwell Companions to Literature and Culture Series (Wiley Blackwell, 2014); the 2006 *Tolkien Encyclopedia* (Routledge); *The Mythic Fantasy of Robert Holdstock* (McFarland, 2011); and in various journals. In 2009, she was a guest lecturer at the NEH Tolkien Institute. She has presented at various conferences, most frequently at the International Conference on the Fantastic in the Arts.

List of Abbreviations of Tolkien's Works

FR	*The Fellowship of the Ring.*
H	*The Hobbit*
LB	*The Lays of Beleriand*
LR	*The Lost Road and Other Writings*
LT I	*The Book of Lost Tales, Part One*
LT II	*The Book of Lost Tales, Part Two*
MR	*Morgoth's Ring*
OFS	"On Fairy-Stories"
PME	*The Peoples of Middle-earth*
S	*The Silmarillion*
TT	*The Two Towers*
UT	*Unfinished Tales of Númenor and Middle-earth*
WJ	*The War of the Jewel*

Bibliography

AMENDT-RADUEGE, Amy M. "'Worthy of a Song': Memory, Mortality and Music." *Middle-earth Minstrel: Essays on Music in Tolkien*. Ed. Bradford Lee Eden. Jefferson, NC: McFarland, 2010, 114-25.

CHANCE, Jane. *Tolkien's Art: A Mythology for England*. Rev. ed. Lexington, KT: University Press of Kentucky, 2001.

COLLINS, Robert A. "'Ainulindalë': Tolkien's Commitment to an Aesthetic Ontology." *Journal of the Fantastic in the Arts* 11 (2000): 257-65.

FLIEGER, Verlyn. "The Music and the Task: Fate and Free Will in Middle-earth." *Tolkien Studies* 6 (2009): 151-81.

JORGENSEN, Estelle Ruth. "Myth, Song, and Music Education: The Case of Tolkien's *The Lord of the Rings* and Swann's *The Road Goes Ever On*." *Journal of Aesthetic Education* 40.3 (2006): 1-21.

SHIPPEY, Tom. *The Road to Middle-earth*. Rev. and expanded ed. Boston, MA: Houghton Mifflin, 2003.

TOLKIEN, J.R.R. *The Book of Lost Tales, Part One*. (The History of Middle-earth 1). Ed. Christopher Tolkien. London: George Allen and Unwin, 1983; Boston, MA: Houghton Mifflin, 1984.

The Book of Lost Tales, Part Two. (The History of Middle-earth 2). Ed. Christopher Tolkien. London: George Allen and Unwin; Boston, MA: Houghton Mifflin, 1984.

The Fellowship of the Ring. Vol. 1 of *The Lord of the Rings*. 2nd ed. Boston, MA: Houghton Mifflin, 1966.

The Hobbit. London: George Allen and Unwin, 1937; 2nd ed, London: George Allen and Unwin, 1951; Boston, MA: Houghton Mifflin, 1966.

The Lays of Beleriand. (The History of Middle-earth 3). Ed. Christopher Tolkien. London: HarperCollins, 1992.

The Lost Road and Other Writings. (The History of Middle-earth 5). Ed. Christopher Tolkien. London: Unwin Hyman; Boston, MA: Houghton Mifflin, 1987.

Morgoth's Ring. (The History of Middle-earth 10). Ed. Christopher Tolkien. London: HarperCollins; Boston, MA: Houghton Mifflin, 1993.

"On Fairy-Stories." *Tolkien Reader*. New York City, NY: Ballantine, 1966, 33-99.

The Peoples of Middle-earth. (The History of Middle-earth 12). Ed. Christopher Tolkien. London: HarperCollins; Boston, MA: Houghton Mifflin, 1996.

The Silmarillion. Ed. Christopher Tolkien. London: George Allen and Unwin; Boston, MA: Houghton Mifflin, 1977.

The Two Towers. Vol. 2 of *The Lord of the Rings.* 2nd ed. Boston, MA: Houghton Mifflin, 1966.

Unfinished Tales of Númenor and Middle-earth. Ed. Christopher Tolkien. London: George Allen and Unwin; Boston, MA: Houghton Mifflin, 1980.

The War of the Jewels. (The History of Middle-earth 11). Ed. Christopher Tolkien. London: HarperCollins; Boston, MA: Houghton Mifflin, 1994.

Bradford Lee Eden

"The Scholar as Minstrel": Word-music and Sound-words in Tolkien's "New Works"

Abstract

This chapter builds upon previous papers and book chapters by the author related to Tolkien's use of musical allusion in his works, as well as his roots in language and sound that are now supported by a number of "new" works that have been published in recent years, specifically *The Story of Kullervo, Beowulf: A Translation and Commentary, The Lay of Aotrou & Itroun, The Legend of Sigurd & Gudrún, The Fall of Arthur,* and *A Secret Vice.* Tolkien's earliest experiments and writings in his mythology show an intense interest in the use and power of music as a creational and thematic expression. The publication of these "new" works provide further evidence that Tolkien definitively favored a strong relationship between music and language, specifically using terms like sound-words, word-music, sound symbolism, and sound aesthetics.

Introducion

In my book *Middle-earth Minstrel: Essays on Music in Tolkien*, I mention coming across Tolkien's drafts in the Bodleian Library of a lecture he did titled "The Tradition of Versification in Old English, with special reference to the Battle of Maldon and its alliteration." Tolkien indicated that the Battle of Maldon poet was a kind of "minstrel turned scholar," documenting in hasty metre the events that transpired during this event for his medieval audience, yet in effect becoming an historical observer for those of us reading the surviving manuscripts. I wanted to title my book at that time *The Scholar Turned Minstrel: Tolkien and Musical Allusion in his Writings* based on this fact, but McFarland Publishing wanted something a little more direct and eye-catching so that the public would buy the book.

A number of 'new' critical editions of Tolkien's works have appeared posthumously in recent years (see Table I). The chronology of these writings within Tolkien's oeuvre have provided more direct evidence regarding connections Tolkien made and saw between language, sound, and music than previously recorded. I have written about some of these connections related to his earliest stories in his legendarium, as well as his roots with his Victorian and Edwardian counterparts (cf. Eden: "Strains"). Now with these new editions revealing even more on Tolkien's thoughts regarding sound symbolism, phonetic symbolism, and what he terms *word-music*, it is obvious that Tolkien truly thought of language not just as communication but as art, and that, in his mind, his invented languages and those like Finnish and Welsh for which he had an affinity could be referred to in terms of music terminology and allusion.[1]

The Story of Kullervo and *A Secret Vice* contain the majority of direct connections on these topics, and in a sense frame both early and mid-career thoughts by Tolkien on these concepts. Each of these publications will be discussed in the order of their supposed creation/writing.

Table I. Chronology of Tolkien "new works"

Date of composition	Title	Date of publication
1910s-	*The Children of Hurin* (various versions, various decades)	2007
1912-16	*The Story of Kullervo*	2015
1926	*Beowulf: a translation and commentary*	2014
1930	*The Lay of Aotrou & Itroun*	2016
Early 1930s?	"The Lay of Beowulf" (in *Beowulf: a translation and commentary*)	2014
Early 1930s	*The Legend of Sigurd & Gudrún* (includes "Lay of the Völsungs," "Lay of Gudrún," "Prophecy of the Sibyl," and fragments of a heroic poem of Attila in Old English).	2009
Early 1930s	*The Fall of Arthur*	2013
1931	*A Secret Vice* (lecture)	2016
Early 1940s	"Sellic Spell" (in *Beowulf: a translation and commentary*)	2014

---

1 *The Children of Húrin* tale will not be discussed, as the main plot and characters are so involved in the doom that is placed upon them that musical allusion is rarely if ever encountered except for passing references to minstrels and their laments within the text. *Sellic Spell* also contains little in terms of musical allusion.

The Story of Kullervo (1912-16)

As indicated in Verlyn Flieger's excellent edition of this manuscript,[2] Tolkien first read the 1907 English translation of *Kalevala* in 1911 at the age of nineteen (*K* xi). When he went up to Oxford that fall, he immediately borrowed C.N.E. Eliot's *Finnish Grammar* from the Exeter College Library in order to attempt to read the Finnish original (which he records as an unsuccessful attempt). Tolkien was drawn to the main character of Kullervo, whose tragic story inspired him to write his own version of this tragedy between 1912-16 (*K* xiii). He was especially drawn to the songs of the Kalevala, so different from the rest of the European myth corpus with their pagan flavor and uniqueness. He even gave two presentations on *Kalevala* in November 1914 and February 1915, as evidenced by two versions also provided and edited by Flieger (*K* 63-131). The importance of the *Kalevala* on the writing of *The Story of Kullervo* is seen as a preliminary foundation of Tolkien's *Children of Húrin* story along with its tragic hero, Turin Turambar. As Flieger indicates, "without The Story of Kullervo there would be no Turin" (*K* xvii). Flieger also mentions Tolkien's fascination with Vainamoinen, one of the 'big three' heroes of *Kalevala*, whose singing is magical and who appears to be a model for Kullervo, who also uses magical singing and instrumental playing (cow-bone pipe) (*K* 49-50).

If we look at the draft of *The Story of Kullervo* we see Tolkien's use of music, both as language and as magic, similar to what he experienced in his reading of the *Kalevala*. The first time the reader experiences this is with the "Song of Sakehonto in the woodland," split into two sections to mirror Kullervo's/Sakehonto's splitting of logs in the forest, and set in the so-called *Kalevala* metre (*K* 13-14, 55). The understanding is that this poetry is both sung and spoken (similar to speech-song), and that both the words and the music together carry magic and power. Other sing-song/Sprechstimme magic occurs when Kullervo/Sari sings answers to his mother's and sibling's pleas for patience (*K* 16-19), the long prayer/song of Asemo's wife (*K* 21-27), and the reference in the text when Kullervo sings the wolves into cattle and the bears into oxen and then leading them back to Asemo's wife while playing the cow-bone pipe made from the leg

---

[2] Tolkien, J.R.R. *The Story of Kullervo* (hereafter *K*). Edited by Verlyn Flieger. London: HarperCollins, 2015.

of Urula the old cow (a reference to the Pied Piper myth?) (*K* 29-30). Indeed, one can feel the power of magic in the opening line of the prayer of Asemo's wife (which closely follows Runo 32 of *Kalevala*):

> Guard my kine O gracious Ilu
> From the perils of the pathway
> That they come not into danger
> Nor may fall on evil fortune
> If my herdsman is an ill one
> Make the willow then a neatherd
> Let the alder watch the cattle
> And the mountain ash protect them
> Let the cherry lead them homeward
> In the milktime in the even. (*K* 22, 57-58)

"...from the singer's hot imagination of the moment"

Flieger discusses the references to magic in *Kalevala* in her Notes and Commentary, indicating that remnants of primitive shamanism and shamanic practices are usually performed through singing (*K* 49). In looking at Tolkien's discovery and fascination with the *Kalevala*, and hence his attempt to replicate its magic in *The Story of Kullervo*, his comments as a young scholar on the interconnections between music, poetry, and magic in Finnish society are enlightening. One has to also remember that it was at this time that Tolkien was just beginning to write down early myths and stories of his own legendarium, many of them inspired by his reading of the *Kalevala*.

In the manuscript and typewritten drafts of his 1914/1915 student presentation titled "On 'The Kalevala' or Land of Heroes," (*K* 67-125) Tolkien elaborates on why *Kalevala* has made such an impression on him. Interspersed among these early musings by the young Tolkien on the power that this myth has had on him, and in his attempts to convey that magic to his listeners, we get the first glimpses of Tolkien's connections between language, music, and myth. I have already discussed the importance of musical allusion as a conscious and subconscious element in Tolkien's early mythological writings,[3] so this even earlier evidence supports the fact that Tolkien felt a very strong musical power within the constructs of myth and language. One has only to mention the numerous times that he places music and language together in his drafts of his *Kalevala* presentation:

> [...] so much so that the music of language is apt to be expended automatically and leave no excess with which to heighten the emotion of a lyric passage. (*K* 77)

> The remarkable and delightful thing for us, however, is that these "songs of bygone ages" have somehow been preserved without being tinkered with. (*K* 110)

> Indeed it suffers like many languages of its type from an excess of euphony; so much so that the **music of the language** (bold italics are mine) is liable to be expended automatically, and leave over no excess [...] Where vowel-harmony and the assimilation and softening of consonants is an integral part of ordinary grammar and of everyday speech there is much less chance for sudden unexpected sweetnesses. (*K* 115)

> If, however, pathos or not, you are bored by the interminable sing-song character of this metre, it is well to remember again that these are only, as it were, accidentally written things – they are in essence song-songs, sing-songs chanted to the monotonous repetition of a phrase thrummed on the harp while the singers swayed backwards and forwards in time [...] So opens the Kalevala, and there are many other references to the rhythmic swaying of the monotonous chanters: ***I wish I had ever heard them with my own ears, but I have not*** (bold italics are mine). (*K* 118-119)

Tolkien especially mentions and quotes from the Origin of Beer song in *Kalevala*, making the comment that the Finnish minstrel would be "cracking up at his own profession" through this song, much better than any English or French minstrel.

The influence of *Kalevala* on Tolkien's imagination has been known for some time, but this edition of the *Story of Kullervo* itself, along with the transcription of his manuscript and typewritten drafts of his 1914/1915 presentations

---

3 First in "The 'music of the spheres': relationships between Tolkien's Silmarillion and medieval cosmological and religious theory" (2003); then in "Strains of Elvish songs and voices: Victorian medievalism, music, and Tolkien" (2010); and finally in "Tolkien and music" in *A Companion to J.R.R. Tolkien*, ed. Stuart Lee (Wiley Blackwell, 2014), 501-13. See bibliography at the end of article for full references.

on *Kalevala*, now provide earlier evidence of this myth's effect on Tolkien's development of his legendarium, especially in relation to the character of Turin Turambur and *Children of Húrin*. Flieger neatly summarizes the quandary of the *Kalevala*'s discovery on Tolkien's priorities: what with "teaching himself Finnish albeit unsuccessfully, drafting the *Story of Kullervo*, and inventing the Qenya language, he almost lost his scholarship to Oxford" (*K* 138).

Beowulf: a Translation and Commentary (1926)

Tolkien's translation of *Beowulf* (hereafter *B*) into modern English prose was published by Christopher Tolkien in 2014, along with commentary and including "Sellic Spell" (early 1940s) and "The Lay of Beowulf" (early 1930s?). In describing his father's attempt to make a translation of *Beowulf* "as close as he could to the exact meaning in detail of the Old English poem, far closer than could be attained by translation into 'alliterative verse', but nonetheless with some suggestion of the rhythm of the original," Christopher says that "this rhythm, so to call it, can be perceived throughout. It is a quality of the prose, by no means inviting analysis, but sufficiently pervasive to give a marked and characteristic tone to the whole work" (*B* 8-10). As is well known, this poem was recited and sung as part of the repertoire of an Anglo-Saxon scop, and thus its original presentation would have involved music using voice, instrument, or both. Tolkien provides detailed examination of this rhythm in his "Prefatory remarks on prose translation of 'Beowulf'", especially the section "On Metre".[4] Some discussion of *Beowulf*'s performance as well as other Old English poems is provided by Christopher in the Commentary section (*B* 344-48). Indeed, "The Lay of Beowulf" included at the end of this volume is a version of *Beowulf* in the form of a ballad written about the same time period. It mentions that Tolkien wrote on the cover page 'Intended to be sung', and the memory of its sung performance by his father when Christopher was seven or eight years old is a distinct recollection from his childhood (*B* xiii, 416).

---

4 *Beowulf and the Finnesburg fragment* (George Allen & Unwin, 1940), ix-xliii.

The Lay of Aotrou & Itroun (1930)

This story with its manuscript versions (hereafter *LAI*), edited by Verlyn Flieger with a note on the text by Christopher Tolkien, was published in 2016. It is apparent from the manuscripts that Tolkien stopped at Canto X of "The Lay of Leithian" in 1930 to write both this piece as well as the many stories contained in *The Legend of Sigurd & Gudrún* (*LAI* xi). Besides the fact that Tolkien often indicated sung tales and stories by the term *lay*, he also would include numerous references within his tales of singing, music, harping, horns, and bells (the latter having a special connotation in Breton folklore and religion). To provide some examples:

> [...] as still the Briton harpers tell.
> [...] there minstrels sang [...]
> [...] in fire and song yet men rejoice [...]
> A song now falls from windows high [...]
> [...] singing to her babes lullay [...]
> [...] horns were wound [...]
> [...] as his horn winds in Broceliande.
> [...] the sound of bells along the air [...]
> [...] the Corrigan now shrunk and old was sitting singing [...]
> She heard no horn[...] she heard the bells that slowly tolled [...]
> There was singing slow at dead of night[...] rang the sacring knell [...] heard a single bell [...]

In the two "Corrigan" poems written as drafts to *LAI*, it is interesting that there are no musical references in the first version, but the second draft contains quite a few:

> There is a song from windows high, why do they sing?
> [...] His horn faintly yonder [...]
> [...] singing a secret litany [...]
> [...] In the old moon singing...And in my ears a singing...In the tower slow bells shake [...] Why are the white priests chanting low [...]
> [...] I heard bells ring [...] Priests chanting a litany [...] There sang a fay in Brittany. (*LAI* 49-52)

In the various fragments, manuscript drafts, and typescript leading up to the final version, a few more musical allusions were considered but eventually deleted:

> [...] like music slow in deeps apart [...]
> [...] the sound of bells along the air/that mingles with the sound of seas [...]
> [...] a Corrigan was singing in a dell [...]
> [...] He woke at eve, and murmured: 'ringing/of bells within my ears, and singing,/a singing is beneath the moon [...] (*LAI* 65-83)

The Legend of Sigurd & Gudrún (early 1930s?)

These "new lays" were also undertaken after the "Lay of Leithian" was abandoned near the end of 1931 (*LSG* 5). They were published by Christopher Tolkien, along with various other related writings by his father, in 2009. These lays were inspired by the Volsung and Nibelung legends, which survived in Old Norse. In his discussion of the verse-form of the poems, Christopher details the three metres as found in the Eddaic poems, and that his father's purpose was to present these legends in a metrical format (*LSG* 45-50). Documentation of musical allusion in these lays is provided below.

> **"The New Lay of the Volsungs"**
> A seer long silent/her song upraised –
> The horn of Heimdal/I hear ringing [...]
> The guests were many/grim their singing [...]
> Birds sang blithely/o'er board and hearth [...]
> Birds sang blissful/over boards laden [...]
> Moon was shining/men were singing [...] Volsung vanished/voices chanted [...]
> In songs he heard/of sweetest maiden [...]
> High sang the horns/helms were gleaming [...]
> The sword of Sigmund/sang before him [...] the sword of Grimnir/singing splintered [...]
> Men sing of serpents/ceaseless guarding [...]
> [...] they flickered with flame,/as it flashed singing [...]
> Birds in the branches/blithe were singing [...]
> [...] in Gjuki's house/glad the singing.
> There Gunnar grasped/his golden harp/while songs he sang/silence fell there.
> Then Sigurd seized/the sounding harp [...]
> [...] song fell silent/and Sigurd ended.
> [...] horns were sounded/home rode Sigurd.
> Sigurd sat silent/the singing heard not [...] then sat unsmiling/the singing heard not.
> In Gjuki's house/glad the singing...harp-strings were plucked/by hands of cunning [...]
> Clamour rose again/clear the singing- [...]
> When Heimdall's horn/is heard ringing [...]
> (Excerpts from *LSG* 59-180)

> **"The New Lay of Gudrún"**
> [...] Our horns shall be heard/Hunland rousing [...]
> In the hoar forest/horns they sounded [...]
> Horns they sounded/hall-walls echoed [...]
> [...] Now songs let us sing/of our sires of yore. Of the Goths' glory/

Gunnar sang there [...]
A harp she sent him/his hands seized it/strong he smote it/strings were ringing. Wondering heard men/words of triumph/song up-soaring/ from the serpent's pit."
There slowly swayed they/slumber whelmed them/as Gunnar sang/of Gunnar's pride.
[...] of Odin sang he/Odin's chosen [...]
[...] Huns still heard him/his harp thrilling/and doom of Hunland/ dreadly chanting [...] harp fell silent/and heart was still.
Lift up your hearts/lords and maidens/for the song of sorrow/that was sung of old. (Excerpts from *LSG* 253-308)

"Old English poem of Attila"
[...] but Guthhere wrathful-hearted struck/the harp in his hiding-place. Rang, resounded/string against finger. His voice came/clear as a war-cry through the grey rock/in rage against his enemies [...]
(*LSG* 376)

The Fall of Arthur (early 1930s)

This unfinished poem of Tolkien's, long known from Humphrey Carpenter's biography, was published by Christopher Tolkien in 2013 (hereafter *FoA*). Christopher indicates that it was probably composed between 1930-34, after the Norse poems (*The Legend of Sigurd and Gudrún*) had been written. Again Tolkien is experimenting with metre, rhythm, and alliteration in this story, which appears to have been the last of a number of writings after "The Lay of Leithian" had been set aside in 1931. Musical allusion runs throughout this story as well:

[...] As a glad trumpet/his voice was ringing [...]
[...] they heard a horn/in the hills trembling [...]
[...] The horns of the wind/were its mort blowing [...]
[...] Blaring of trumpets [...]
[...] trumpet sounding/he would sail overseas [...]
[...] No horn he blew, no host gathered [...]
[...] Alone standing/with the flame of morn in his face burning/ the surge
he felt of song forgotten/in his heart moving as a harp-music./
There Lancelot, low and softly/to himself singing [...]
[...] Far over the sea faintly sounding/trumpets heard they [...]
[...] Wild were the trumpets/Beacons were blazing [...]
Then Gawain sounded his glad trumpet [...]

[...] the clear ringing/of bells to hear...trumpets sounding [...]
[...] bells were silent, blades were ringing [...] (*FoA* 17-57)

At the end of this book, Christopher has given an Appendix titled "Old English Verse," which provides some extracts from a BBC interview on January 14, 1938 with his father on that topic. The subject "is very different in scope and manner though belonging to the same period as the *Prefatory Remarks* (to the new edition of *Beowulf* by J.R. Clark Hall in 1940)" (*FoA* 223-31). It is worth mentioning some of the Tolkien's comments from this interview, as they show the influence of his *Secret Vice* lecture from 1931 along with his "On Metre" section from the 1940 edition of *Beowulf*. After reading the concluding lines from *The Battle of Brunanburh* and its English translation, Tolkien states: "So sang a court poet 1000 years ago – 1006 this autumn to be precise: commemorating the great Battle of Brunanburh, AD 937" (*FoA* 225). Tolkien indicates that this metre was used for "a great body of oral verse dealing with ancient days in the northern lands known to minstrels in England" (*FoA* 227). In discussing the way in which the Old English poems were delivered, Tolkien states that the word for 'warrior'/'war-smith' was used as both a kenning and "at the same time to give a sound-picture and an eye-picture of battle" (*FoA* 230). Finally, Tolkien ends his lecture by saying "The language of our forefathers, especially in verse, was slow, not very nimble, but very sonorous..." (*FoA* 231).

A Secret Vice (1931)

At the same time as many of the above poems and stories were being composed, Tolkien gave a lecture on November 29, 1931 titled *A Secret Vice* (hereafter *SV*), which was published as a critical edition in 2016. We see the maturity and indeed what I would call the synonymous use and understanding for Tolkien of both language and musical terminology as he describes to his listeners the effect that language invention has on his conscious and subconscious imagination. As the editors so aptly state, just as "On Fairy-stories" is Tolkien's 'manifesto' on the art of writing, so *SV* is Tolkien's 'manifesto' on the parallel and coeval art of language invention (*SV* ix). *SV* was written at the height of the international vogue for international auxiliary language creation, research and theoretical work on sound symbolism, and Modernist experimentation with language (*SV* viii). In their Introduction, the editors provide a succinct summary of Tolkien's interest in languages and language creation in the context of early twentieth-century developments in this area. Many of his created languages (Animalic, Nevbosh, Naffarin, Qenya, Gnomish, Quenya, Noldorin, and Sindarin) are mentioned. *SV* includes a critical edition of Tolkien's lecture given to members of the Johnson Society of Pembroke College on November 29, 1931, along with a critical edition of "Essay on Phonetic Symbolism," which the editors assume was a rough draft first idea for the *SV* lecture focused on phonetic symbolism, which appears to have been abandoned when the more personal topic of language invention was chosen. Both the lecture and the essay provide new proof of Tolkien's thoughts on the interconnections between language, sound, music, and myth.

The *SV* Manuscript

Very early in his lecture, Tolkien describes in detail how he came across someone by happenstance during training exercises before his military orders to France, taking almost two pages to describe an encounter with this "little man… composing a language, a personal system and symphony that no one else was to study or to hear" (*SV* 6-7). Tolkien commented extensively in the conclusion to *SV* about the relationships between language and music, weaving through a number of descriptions that almost sound more like a musician speaking than a linguist:

> It is an attenuated emotion, but may be very piercing – this construction of sounds to give pleasure. The human phonetic system is a small-ranged instrument (compared to music as it has now become); yet it is an instrument, and a delicate one. (*SV* 32)

The editors comment in their Introduction that "Tolkien progressed swiftly from invented languages as communication to invented languages as art… The latter corresponds to the notion of 'sound symbolism,' the idea that there is a direct relationship between the sounds making up a word and its meaning" (*SV*, li). Tolkien corroborates this assessment on p. 33 of his lecture (pauses indicate places where I have clipped portions within the paragraph):

> The word-music [...] So little do we ponder word-form and sound-music [...] the poet has struck an air which illuminates the line like a sound of music half-attended to may deepen the significance of some unrelated things thought or read, while the music ran [...] in a living language this is all the more poignant [...] and at the same time sing carelessly [...] when even Homer could pervert a word to suit sound-music [...] Kalevala [...] phonetic trills [...] mere notes in a phonetic tune struck to harmonize with penkerelle, or tuimenia which do "mean" something. (*SV* 33)

Tolkien's examples of his own Qenya poetry are used as illustrations of this sound-music. For instance, in the *Narqelion* poem which is used in Tolkien's draft of the lecture but never incorporated, the phonetic makeup of the Qenya words clearly show that Tolkien was attempting to create a link between sound aesthetics and semantics (SV 95). The sound-music is also apparent in the *Earendel* and the *Earendel at the Helm* poetry which was actually incorporated into the lecture:

> this boat hummed like a harp-string
> Chanting wild songs/Taut ropes like harps tingling/
> From far shores a faint singing. (*SV* 30-31)

I have discussed in a previous article how the Victorian poets such as Alfred Tennyson, Algernon Charles Swineburne, and William Morris exhibited a similar use of sound-music and musical allusion in their pseudo-medieval poetry and prose, and Tolkien being a product of his time and era would have known and read these writings, even if he did not overly like them.[5] This historical overlay and combination of Victorian medievalism, musico-literary symbolism, and fiction writing, along with the *Kalevala* mythology and the musicality of the Welsh and Finnish languages, provided many of the ingredients for Tolkien's Cauldron of Story and one could even say his Harp of Sound Symbolism as he began to experiment in the creation of his legendarium. The editors of *A Secret Vice* point out this specific quote by Tolkien from the lecture: the highest standard of language creation was to attempt to fulfil "the instinct for 'linguistic invention' - the fitting of notion to oral symbol, and *pleasure in contemplating the new relation established*" (*SV* xv, 15-16).

As the editors indicate in their Coda, Tolkien enumerates on what he considers the four key elements of invented languages: 1) the creation of word forms

---

5 See footnote 2.

that sound aesthetically pleasing, 2) a sense of fitness between word form and meaning, 3) the construction of an elaborate grammar, and 4) an interlacing with myth, story-telling, and secondary world building (*SV* 132-33). The first two specifically relate to the importance and interrelationship in Tolkien's linguistic and imaginative worlds of music and words.

"Essay on Phonetic Symbolism"

Tolkien's Essay on Phonetic Symbolism on pp. 63-80 of *SV* brings out the interrelationship of language and music even more, and it is a new piece of primary source evidence for Tolkien linguists and scholars. In the fragmented and extensive manuscripts to this abandoned prequel to the *SV* lecture, Tolkien clearly links language invention to music:

> [...] certain subordinated parts of the distinctive music. But unfair to call it a mere 'metrical' experiment. One might call music a mere "accompaniment." We can pass to "pure sound" only by writing "articulate sounds" in measure – but sounds which have no 'meaning." The music is their "voice" – like a little tune on a whistle without accompaniment of voice or other instrument [...] (*SV* 92)

> Speech sounds are productive of "pleasure" which juxtaposes a total effect of sequences – similar probably (if different) to musical pleasure – air, melody. Not pleasurable merely or at all because of musical tone; but because of individual beauty or merely of contrast – yet total of human phonemes limited. (*SV* 99)

Conclusion

In the end, as I have demonstrated in my previous scholarship and as Verlyn Flieger has mentioned many times in her publications, Tolkien was definitely a "composer of words." I think that he would have found this an apt description of himself, along with "a medieval bard out of his time." With the imminent publication of *Beren and Lúthien* in the near future,[6] these "new" primary source contributions to Tolkien research will definitely have a dramatic impact on future discussions and scholarship related to Tolkien's conscious or subconscious approach to his secret vice of what I would term "musico-language invention."

---

6 Beren and Lúthien was published in 2017, but the discussion of this important primary source could not be included in this chapter.

About the Author

BRADFORD LEE EDEN is Dean of Library Services at Valparaiso University. He has a masters and Ph.D. degrees in musicology, as well as an MS in library science. His recent books include *Middle-earth Minstrel: Essays on Music in Tolkien* (McFarland, 2010); *The Associate University Librarian Handbook: A Resource Guide* (Scarecrow Press, 2012); *Leadership in Academic Libraries: Connecting Theory to Practice* (Scarecrow Press, 2014), *The Hobbit and Tolkien's Mythology: Essays on Revisions and Influences* (McFarland, 2014), and the ten-volume series *Creating the 21st-century Academic Library* (Rowman & Littlefield, 2015-17). He is the founder and editor of the *Journal of Tolkien Research* (http://scholar.valpo.edu/journaloftolkienresearch).

List of Abbreviations of Tolkien's Works

B	*Beowulf: A Translation and Commentary together with Sellic Spell*
FoA	*The Fall of Arthur*
K	*The Story of Kullervo*
LAI	*The Lay of Aotrou and Itroun together with The Corrigan poems*
LSG	*The Legend of Sigurd and Gudrún*
SV	*A Secret Vice: Tolkien on Invented Languages*

Bibliography

EDEN, Bradford Lee. "Strains of Elvish songs and voices: Victorian medievalism, music, and Tolkien." *Middle-earth Minstrel: Essays on Music in Tolkien*. Ed. Bradford Lee Eden. Jefferson, NC: McFarland, 2010, 85-101.

— "The 'music of the spheres': relationships between Tolkien's *Silmarillion* and medieval cosmological and religious theory." *Tolkien the Medievalist*. Ed. Jane Chance. New York City, NY: Routledge, 2003, 183-93.

— "Tolkien and Music." *A Companion to J.R.R. Tolkien*. Ed. Stuart Lee. Oxford: Wiley Blackwell, 2014, 501-13.

TOLKIEN, J.R.R. *Beowulf: A Translation and Commentary together with Sellic Spell*. Ed. Christopher Tolkien. Boston, MA: Houghton Mifflin, 2014.

— *The Fall of Arthur*. Ed. Christopher Tolkien. Boston, MA: Houghton Mifflin Harcourt, 2013.

— *The Lay of Aotrou and Itroun together with The Corrigan poems*. Ed. Verlyn Flieger. London: HarperCollins, 2016.

— *The Legend of Sigurd and Gudrún*. Ed. Christopher Tolkien. Boston, MA: Houghton Mifflin, 2009.

— *A Secret Vice: Tolkien on Invented Languages*. Eds. Dimitra Fimi and Andrew Higgins. London: HarperCollins, 2016.

— *The Story of Kullervo*. Ed. Verlyn Flieger. London: HarperCollins, 2015.

Lynn Forest-Hill

Tolkien's Minstrelsy: The Performance of History and Authority

Abstract

The Lord of the Rings reflects medieval minstrelsy primarily in the recollection of culturally significant history for the purposes of entertainment or solace. This paper considers the functions of the many instances of 'informal', or non-professional minstrelsy in the story. It highlights the essential importance of the informal oral dissemination of history in Middle-earth for racial and social integration. As historical recollection in *The Lord of the Rings* necessarily and predominantly references *The Silmarillion*, the paper argues that Tolkien historicises the relationship between oral and textual versification in ways that challenge notions of textual authority and status, and that he thereby claims the absolute authority of the creative process by smuggling into print versions of *Silmarillion* material which are the subjects of informal minstrelsy.

Tolkien's depiction of minstrelsy in *The Lord of the Rings* necessarily takes the form of the poems that are performed orally by characters within the story, but not all the forms of poetry found there can be considered to represent acts of minstrelsy, so I begin with a series of definitions based on theories of minstrelsy in the medieval primary world in order to distinguish the forms and functions which are most significant to its representation in *The Lord of the Rings*. John Southworth's key distinction in his analysis of medieval minstrels is payment.[1] No performer in *The Lord of the Rings* is shown being paid for his (or her) performance although professional minstrels are briefly mentioned. The place of minstrels in the culture of Rohan is shown by Théoden's comment to Merry, "if the battle were before my gates, maybe your deeds would be remembered by the minstrels" (*LotR* 786). Of these, the 'maker in Rohan', is not named (*LotR* 831), but can hardly be Gleowine, because this official minstrel composed nothing else after his elegy for Théoden (*LotR* 954). Another minstrel recites the names of the Lords of the Mark. The minstrel on the field of Cormallen is, like those

---

1 John Southworth notes that medieval minstrels were "*professionals* in the simple sense that they depended for their livelihood […] on their professional skills." But he also notes the use of "minstrel" as a catch-all term used to translate a variety of Latin terms for diverse entertainers (4).

in Rohan, noticed only briefly but, like them, would be a servant of the ruling hierarchy receiving payment of some kind from them.²

Tolkien's depictions of minstrelsy in *The Lord of the Rings* do not deal with other traditional images of professional minstrels. The itinerant minstrel who made a living performing in taverns and at fairs is not included. Tolkien touches only in the most oblique way on the historical function of minstrels employed in noble households and whose travels were an informal means of asserting lordly influence and establishing reciprocal relationships by means of entertainment.³ Nor are his depictions of minstrelsy obviously influenced by either the goliardic songs of the wandering scholars of the twelfth century (*Songs of the Wandering Scholars* 292ff), or the courtly love songs of the aristocratic troubadours of the thirteenth.

Because minstrelsy in *The Lord of the Rings* does not entirely conform to that recorded in the medieval primary world, I focus here on acts of informal minstrelsy rather than the work of the briefly-mentioned professionals. The very brevity of those references suggests Tolkien's intentional differentiation of his depictions from professional minstrelsy, with its implications of social stratification. In his depictions, however, he reflects many aspects of medieval minstrelsy whose highest-status function had been from earliest times to recount stories of putatively historical heroism suited to the interests of aristocratic audiences and which were, nevertheless, popular at all levels of society.⁴

In the high Middle Ages these stories took the form of *chansons de geste* – tales of the deeds of noble men. Under their influence, infused with an imperfect understanding of classical epic, and with Celtic influences and supernatural elements derived from Breton *lais*, the romance form evolved, characteristically identifying its heroes with specific, known, geographical locations. All these forms were cast in verse, initially to aid the minstrels' memories for oral performance. More complex versification would later be accommodated in

---

2 Southworth notes the ultimate derivation of the term minstrel from Latin (*ministrellus*) (3). For a more detailed analysis of the shift of meaning in the vernacular from "servant" to "minstrel", see Page (176).
3 A shadowy allusion to this might be understood in Frodo's performance at Bree, where his song provides a link between the societies of the Shire and Bree.
4 For an insightful critique of the historical dimension of medieval storytelling genres see Green, *The Beginnings of Medieval Romance*.

textual forms which derived from, or pretended to be, oral performances, only giving way to prose long after minstrelsy began to be written down. During the intervening period written works that may never have been given oral performance continued the tradition of presentation in verse form (Reichl, *Medieval Oral Literature* 20),[5] and continued to be designated as romances. In both oral and textual forms, therefore, verse was the accepted framework for the artistic recollection and repetition of history, as well as myth, and legend.[6]

Despite its novelistic form, the prosimetric structure of *The Lord of the Rings* includes the versification expected of accounts of heroic deeds as it exploits medieval minstrelsy's primary functions: the provision of entertainment and the recollection of history. Performances of informal minstrelsy extend these functions into the theoretical dimension as Tolkien considers the effects of minstrelsy and the processes of dissemination it enables, although these operate at times on different planes: that which is interior to the story, and that which is exterior.

Informal Minstrelsy

I take as the basic requirement for a performance of informal minstrelsy a poem that is presented in the text as if a character not designated as a minstrel voluntarily sings, chants or recites it in the presence of one or more auditors. These performances most frequently take as their subject the recollection of culturally significant historical content, usually for the purposes of entertainment or solace. Racial and social integration become a by-product of the resulting dissemination through interaction between performers and auditors. These are not, however, straightforward representations of oral performance, because through them Tolkien shifts from story to theory as he reflects upon the development of textualisation,[7] with its implications of status and authority,[8] based upon,

---

5 Some MSS present a carefully structured written text in which the representation of oral performance is a stylistic decision (Jacobs 294-301).
6 On the association of minstrels with the performance of romances and chansons de geste see Southworth, *Medieval Minstrels* 87; Page, *Owl and Nightingale* 69-73; Baldwin, *Masters, Princes and Merchants*, vol. I, 203-4; Putter, "Middle English Romance and the Oral Tradition" 340-41. All these works discuss the relationship between minstrels, their performance milieu and textuality.
7 Reichl, "Plotting the Map of Medieval Oral Literature" 20. Reichl defines the emergence of "fictitious orality" in texts.
8 Machan, "Editing, Orality, and Late Middle English Texts" 242-43.

and consciously echoing oral minstrelsy, in a process of 'cross-fertilisation'. The topic is extensive, so I focus primarily on a cluster of poems which illustrate these issues. With one exception, I exclude communal performances such as hymns, elegies, marching songs, walking songs, and bath-songs in which characters of the same race and status participate together. Likewise, I omit Tom Bombadil's solo performances; and prophetic and mnemonic rhymes. My focus on informal minstrelsy and the recollection of history also necessarily distinguishes this mode from specifically text-based history such as the archives of Minas Tirith which, being restricted, become forgotten. As at Minas Tirith so too with Elrond's 'books of lore': the transmission of information in both instances depends on access as well as literacy, thus implying the essential importance of the social recollection of history in Middle-earth via minstrelsy rather than via hoarded texts.

On the theoretical plane, informal minstrelsy within *The Lord of the Rings* explores in fictional form the dynamic between orality and textuality as media for the recording of history, and their relationship to matters of social, linguistic, and cultural status. The process of exploration enables Tolkien's assertion of his own creative authority as he uses acts of informal minstrelsy to smuggle into print adapted fragments of some of the most long-lasting stories from the (putatively) unpublishable *Silmarillion* material.[9] This can be seen additionally as Tolkien's questioning of textual authority, through fiction, as he engages with minstrelsy at yet another level, through his adaptations of his early *Silmarillion* material, in ways that challenge notions of textual authority in favour of the absolute authority of the creative process.

Forms and Functions of Minstrelsy

Because depictions of minstrelsy in *The Lord of the Rings* depend entirely on textual presentation in poetic form they necessarily lack the musical element that was a characteristic part of minstrel performances in the medieval primary world. Only by narratorial references to the mode of performance is the reader

---

9 Tolkien's attempts in 1937 to publish the original Silmarillion material, including a version of the Lúthien and Beren story in medieval verse form, were unsuccessful (*LB* 364-5). He was still trying to get it published during the writing of *The Lord of the Rings* (*L* 137).

alerted to the musical dimension of the informal performances of poems. The harp, quintessential instrument of minstrels in the primary world, is rarely mention in *The Lord of the Rings* and associated then only with the highest status.[10] None of the Fellowship takes any instrument into the wild. However, we are told, for example, that Aragorn chants when he performs for the hobbits and later, when he recalls the *ubi sunt* verses of Rohan.[11] We learn that Sam sings his song of the Troll; that Gimli chants "in a deep voice" when performing the metrical version of the history of Moria for Sam (*LotR* 307); and that Legolas sings of Nimrodel (*LotR* 331-2). These descriptions give some indication of the 'aesthetics of the voice', which would be supported by, and support, the aesthetics of each poetic form;[12] but as Carol Braun Pasternack has pointed out, textual representation cannot entirely capture the range of vocal and facial expressions that would accompany performance.[13]

Narration can more easily suggest the range of audience responses prompted by performance, and the reader is given details such as those of Frodo's informal performance at Bree, where noisy acclaim and audience participation greet his lively rendering of the "Man in the Moon": "There was loud and long applause [...] 'Let's have it again, master!'[...] [M]any of them joined in" (*LotR* 156-7). Frodo's encore, complete with capering, is that of a *jongleur*, a minstrel who entertained with lively and acrobatic gestures as well as with songs and stories; and in an echo of the moral uncertainty surrounding such performers in the Middle Ages, it not only denotes Frodo's naïve folly, but has potentially dangerous consequences.[14] Later, on Weathertop, no such moral implication arises as "the hobbits moved and stretched" (*LotR* 190), expressing the extent to which that audience was absorbed in the power of the story and its teller's performance, as Aragorn, like Sam before him, and Bilbo later, performs as a *gestour* – a teller of *chansons de geste*. To these responses may be added individual

---

10 On the relationship between song and instrumental music in Elvish society, see Steimel, "Bring out the Instruments: Instrumental Music in Middle-earth" (102), who associates harps with high status.
11 These instances of chanting are differentiated from the singing of the elegies for Boromir (*LotR* 407-8).
12 Boutet, "The Chanson de Geste and Orality" (363).
13 See Pasternack, "Introduction" 3. Tolkien briefly addresses the matter of vocal expression in front of the Doors to Moria when Gandalf speaks spells in various tones, but this is not minstrelsy (*LotR* 299).
14 Southworth notes the acrobatic accomplishments of *jongleurs* as part of their performance (*Medieval Minstrels* 8). On theological concerns about the moral status of *jongleurs*, see Baldwin, *Masters, Princes and Merchants*, vol. I, 198.

comments. Pippin's anxious reaction to Sam's selective omission of the end of the "Fall of Gil-galad": "Going to Mordor![...] I hope it won't come to that!" (*LotR* 182), shows he knows the significance of the name. By comparison, Sam's "'I like that", and desire to learn Gimli's Song of Durin (*LotR* 309), bears out his enthusiasm for remote or 'exotic' history, and confirms the cultural detachment prompting his selective response to "Gil-galad". Although the narration of minstrelsy has its limitations, it nevertheless serves to evoke a deeper understanding of characters, their relationships and emotions. In addition, these performances recall the cultural history of their origins, but Pippin's and Sam's reactions show that in the process of dissemination that history becomes subject to adaptation in ways that alter its essential significance.

Frodo's performance at Bree offers one simple version of the theme of dissemination which Tolkien continually explores through informal minstrelsy. Sam's performance of the excerpt from Bilbo's translation of the "Fall of Gil-galad" takes up this theme in its more serious relationship to history, while infusing it with considerations of status. Both versions introduce the reader to the one episode in the history of the highest-status and most ancient confrontation with evil in Middle-earth and it is significant that Bilbo sets out to transpose what he knows of that most authoritative history into a more accessible but essentially different form, which then becomes available to an entirely new audience or readership. We may note that he does not translate from Quenya – the Elvish equivalent of Latin,[15] but from Sindarin, which derives from Quenya as French derives ultimately from Latin. Nevertheless, translation by a hobbit from Elvish into the vernacular Common Speech establishes access to and participation in the authoritative history of Middle-earth. Sam's performance is therefore politically inflected, firstly because it is the translator and/or minstrel who "determines whose stories will be told" (Amendt-Raduege 115), and secondly because his selection only reiterates part of a story that was pivotal in the history of Middle-earth and in the personal history of Aragorn, the king-in-waiting. As adaptation evolves alongside the new linguistic form, the hobbits intervene in the iconic history of the Last Alliance and the resulting selectivity inevitably loses something of the tale's original social meaning and personal impact.

---

15 *The Lord of the Rings* Appendix F, "Of the Elves" 1101.

In Bilbo's hands the story of Gil-galad becomes textualised and translated from the highest-status language in Middle-earth into the vernacular, a move that inevitably engages with the politics of language. Examples from the medieval primary world illuminate the significance of this shift in language and form. Tim Machan has observed of the Middle English period that Latin was the language of tradition, authority and power (230-31), and that "as a work in the vernacular, any Middle English text necessarily lacked the lexical and thematic prestige associated with a text produced by an *auctor* in the language of *auctoritas*" (234). The medieval English linguistic environment was, however, characterised by a hierarchy of languages of which Latin was the most prestigious, (Norman) French was the language of the ruling elite, and the vernacular was considered lexically impoverished.[16] Thus the intermediate form – the language of the elite, itself derived from and bearing the grammatical markers of Latin, carried its own dominant status in comparison to the vernacular. Aragorn's response to Sam's assertion that Bilbo *wrote* the poem is to explain that it was not Bilbo's creation but his translation (*LotR* 181). In medieval terms Aragorn challenges the status of Bilbo as *auctor*, and thus the *auctoritas* of his translation from Sindarin into the Common Speech, the vernacular of Middle-earth.[17] However, in a letter Tolkien noted the effect of translation and dissemination when he wrote that "'legends' depend on the language to which they belong; but a living language depends equally on the 'legends' it conveys" (*L* 231).

The connection between translation and dissemination in the primary world is picked up by Sarah Foot who notes King Ælfred's "conscious effort to shape an English imagination by disseminating beyond the court his ideas about the nature of Englishness and his fictive interpretation of history, and his use of the vernacular in order that his ideas might be most accessible" (56); while Elizabeth Dearnley has noted the influence of Latin textual tradition on subsequent vernacular writers (21). These observations then illuminate the way translation into the vernacular Common Speech from the prestigious Sindarin may borrow authority and scope from the original but, while inevitably disseminating aspects of the culture from which the translation takes place, that

---

16 On the status of the early English vernacular, see Wogan-Browne, Watson, Taylor and Evans (eds.). *The Idea of the Vernacular* 260. See also Treharne, *Living through Conquest* 128.
17 On medieval sensitivity to the role of *auctor* and *auctoritas* when creating translations from Latin into the vernacular, see Dearnely, *Translators and their Prologues* 25-6.

translation is also an assertion of a new cultural politics which "suggests a great deal of confidence in the [vernacular] language" (53), echoing Ælfred's insistence on creating a shared national and cultural identity among a wider audience through the medium of the vernacular (Dearneley 45), and testifying to Tolkien's understanding of the value to a "living language", a vernacular, of translated material that extends its cultural richness (ibid. 9).

Aragorn's "Song of Beren and Lúthien" is a further acknowledgement of the process of adaptation that is inherent in the transmission of stories whether by oral or by textual means. As it illuminates another episode in Elvish history, it continues the theme of dissemination, but directs attention to other aspects of minstrelsy, including the association with status. Within the *legendarium*, the origins of the story of Beren and Lúthien connote its high cultural status, a status which Aragorn strives to maintain in his own 'translation' of the original *ann-thenneth* form. This is itself a further expression of status through the very fact of its difficulty.[18] As Tom Shippey notes, Aragorn performs his song "with a certain reluctance, explaining [...] 'this is a rough echo of it'" (146). This may suggest that Bilbo is more gifted than Aragorn at translating Elvish poetry, or that the original of "Gil-galad" was less technically difficult, but these instances of translation align with Tolkien's assertion that *The Lord of the Rings* is a 'prehistory' of the primary world.[19] He notes in a letter that "English cannot have been the language of any people [in the Third Age]. What I have in fact done, is to equate the Westron or widespread Common Speech of the Third Age with English" (*L* 175). As they describe processes in the transmission of ancient history from the elite Elvish language into the vernacular, and between the oral medium of minstrelsy and the textual, Bilbo's and Aragorn's translations not only project the enriching of the vernacular but imply that the consequences of these acts of dissemination result in the text before the reader.

Minstrelsy and its Effects

Both the minstrelsy of Aragorn and that of Sam reflect the special license given by the twelfth-century English theologian Thomas of Chobham when he per-

---

18 Martin, "Music, Myth, and Literary Depth in the 'Land Ohne Musik'" 142.
19 Tolkien refers to *The Lord of the Rings* as a "fiction of long ago" (*L* 250), and also of a "forgotten epoch" (*L* 86).

ceived the benefit of minstrels who "sing of the deeds of princes and other useful things [...] to give comfort against [...] sadness, weariness [...] or against bodily infirmities" (Broomfield 292). A similar benefit was noticed by Thomas's tutor, Peter the Chanter who, while condemning many kinds of minstrels, accepted those who "sing of exploits to give relaxation and perhaps to give instruction" (Dugauquier 22). These examples may illuminate Tolkien's understanding of medieval religious attitudes to minstrel performances; they certainly reveal the extent to which his depictions of informal minstrelsy echo the morally acceptable forms and functions of medieval minstrelsy. Significantly, they also legitimate his own production of stories that entertain and in the process may offer the consolation of Christian ethical subtexts as heroic adventure shades into *psychomachia* in *The Lord of the Rings*.

When Sam acts as a minstrel for his companions, in addition to his recollection of high-status heroic deeds in "Gil-galad", his singing exemplifies some of these licensed functions and circumstances of minstrelsy. At their most basic his songs merely entertain through novelty and simple artistry, like his performance of "Oliphaunt" in Ithilien; but his "Rhyme of the Troll", inspired by Frodo's family history, serves as a diversion to cheer through humour and shared knowledge. In so doing, it deflects the atmosphere of threat briefly regenerated by the encounter with the petrified troll, but this lively composition of Sam's has a further beneficial effect because it has the power to degrade the growing influence on Frodo of the wound from the Morgul blade. The power of minstrelsy among the hobbits is therefore a challenge to the presumed greater power of evil, even though it does not have the overt status and authority of the earlier Elvish hymn to Elbereth which drove off the imminent danger of a Black Rider.

Aragorn's performance of the "Song of Beren and Lúthien" has no such occult effect but adds new dimensions to his character. At the time of his performance he is still identifiable to the hobbits and to readers only as a Ranger, but he 'chants' the Song to comfort the anxious hobbits. That the grim-faced Ranger Chieftain and king-in-waiting acts as a minstrel may seem a strange subversion of his identity, even though his knowledge of Elvish history and prosody suggest he is cultured. However, the motif of a disguised king performing as a minstrel appears in both quasi-historical and supernatural forms in the primary world. In

Beowulf the aged King Hroðgar narrates many tales, including histories of his people, although he has a *scop* in his hall (Klaeber ll.2105, 496). In the twelfth century the chronicler William of Malmesbury described how King Ælfred entered a Viking camp disguised as a minstrel (Frank 156).[20] Minstrelsy as a disguise appears two centuries later in *Sir Orfeo*, where the king performs in the guise of a poor minstrel in order to save his wife from the vicious king of the fairies (Sands, *Sir Orfeo* ll.38-1447). The differences between these kingly acts of minstrelsy are illustrative: while Hroðgar demonstrates he is learned in lore, the story of Ælfred (whether truth or fiction) shows his resourcefulness and skill, but Sir Orfeo's actions illustrate his humility and devotion. In Aragorn's case his performance establishes new dimensions to his character showing him to be sensitive to the hobbits' fears, and resourceful and modest enough to entertain them, simultaneously thereby displaying his access to knowledge that positions him within the hierarchy of Elvish culture, as he reveals when he asserts that only Elrond knows the tale as it should be told (*LotR* 187).

The use of minstrelsy to define qualities of kingship based on cultural accomplishment and personal sensibility was, then, a storytelling device well-known to Tolkien from his work on *Beowulf* as much as on *Sir Orfeo*, and Aragorn's performance, far from subverting his status, begins the process of asserting his suitability for kingship through his care for others, later to be demonstrated more dramatically when he sends the Dúnedain to comfort the captives on the black ships, and assigns the defence of Cair Andros to men daunted by the power of Mordor. Lynn Staley has noted that themes associated with minstrelsy include "harmony [and] sensual pleasure" (317). While Aragorn's minstrelsy is to him a recollection of part of the tale of his most ancient lineage, equally importantly, his performance serves as a symbol and metaphor for the kingly quality of creating harmony, here linked to an acknowledgement of the need for diversion through the aesthetics of culture. Aragorn's minstrelsy may therefore be read as an expression of his kingly qualities grounded on cultural accomplishment, no less than on martial prowess.

---

20 Roberta Frank notes that William of Malmsebury briefly recorded Ælfred's minstrelsy, but gives more details regarding that of the Viking Anlaf, whose act of minstrelsy is analogous to that of Pippin in Minas Tirith. Anlaf disguises himself as a minstrel in order to spy out the Anglo-Saxon camp and sings in the presence of King Æthelstan during a feast before battle (Frank, "The Search for the Anglo-Saxon Oral Poet" 156). In *The Lord of the Rings* Denethor commands Pippin to sing. He later accuses Gandalf of introducing the hobbit to spy on him (*LotR* 835).

The wider consequences of this kingly minstrelsy are illuminated by Christopher Page who has discussed the relationship between music and the emergent State. He writes that in the thirteenth century scholars set out "to classify musical forms, both sacred and secular [...] and to show how they contribute to the stability of the *civitas*" (171).[21] Aragorn's metrical performance of history not only signifies his ability to bring harmony, but further symbolises his potential to bring the kind of order that defines musical structure to the re-establishment of the *civitas* (the State) of the two kingdoms. This symbolism may then be extended to the performances of historical material by Gimli in Moria and Legolas at the Falls of Nimrodel, which equally illuminate their suitability for the roles they would play in restoring order and stability to their respective lands after Sauron's defeat. That Bilbo and Sam also sing elvish history aligns the hobbits with the political hierarchies upon which order and stability will be founded, and which will in turn guarantee the order and stability of the Shire.[22]

Minstrelsy, Form, and Text

The Hall of Fire at Rivendell is the highest-status location for the most authoritative minstrelsy west of the Mountains, as the Elves there sing songs commemorating their most ancient history, without apparently devolving this to designated minstrels. Bilbo's chanting of his version of the Eärendil story within that environment of communal equality is treated indulgently by Elrond and his household, perhaps because they recognise that this is an act of gratitude by Bilbo for the honour bestowed on him by their hospitality. While the household acknowledges his right to repay it in this way, his adaption of a story that for Elrond, grandson of Eärendil, is a part of his personal history, draws Aragorn's

---

21 See also Page's translation: "We call that kind of cantus a *chanson de geste* in which the deeds of heroes and the works of ancient fathers are recounted, such as [...] the battles and adversities which the men of ancient times suffered[...]. This kind of music should be laid on for [...] working citizens and for those of middle station when they rest from their usual toil, so that, having heard the miseries and calamities of others, they may more easily bear their own and so that anyone may undertake his own labour with more alacrity. Therefore this kind of *cantus* has the power to preserve the whole city." (Page, "Johannes de Grocheio on secular music" 22-23.

22 Sarah Foot has observed that "racial differences were generally considered less relevant in the formation of concepts of nationhood in the middle ages than cultural qualities such as customs, language and law" (53).

comment on the impertinence inherent in the hobbit's performance (*LotR* 231). However, Thomas A. DuBois's observation that "the poetics of medieval orality did not simply clothe events in an outward form suited to easy recall; rather, the events were often reshaped substantively into aesthetically effective and satisfying forms" (221), illuminates the issue of literary decorum raised by Lindir's critique of Bilbo's performance. This is registered as a matter of racial difference when the Elf remarks on the difficulty of distinguishing Bilbo's work from Aragorn's intervention, saying "It is not easy for us to tell the difference between two mortals" (*LotR* 230).

It appears that elvish ideas of effective oral aesthetics do not align with those of mortals. Tom Shippey has nevertheless proposed that "there is an elvish streak [...] in the poetry of *The Lord of the Rings*, defining this as 'barely unprecedented intricacies of line and stanza'" (173). He goes on to observe that "the elvish idea of poetry comes through an unexpected subtlety" (175). In the medieval primary world, verse forms initially used to aid minstrels' memories became more complex in texts derived from, or pretending to be, oral performances. Therefore, when Shippey goes further and suggests that the late fourteenth-century poem, *Pearl*, provides the basis for the complexity of elvish-influenced poetry generally (176), citing Bilbo's and Aragorn's adaptations among his examples (175), he positions these in terms of learned *textual* composition, not the orality that characterises performances of adapted historical commemoration in, what are for Elrond, Aragorn, and elvish society in the Third Age, *chansons de geste*.

The aesthetics of the complex metre of Bilbo's rendering of "Eärendil" that appear to fit Shippey's assessment, and might be thought to follow naturally as elvish history is picked up and rewritten by the hobbit, are further problematised in the Preface to *The Adventures of Tom Bombadil* which was first published 1962. In his discussion of the origins of the Rivendell "Eärendil", Tolkien subverts the notion of a natural decorum between topic and form when he stated that the complexity of the metre used in "the Rivendell version" is "found transformed and applied *somewhat incongruously*, to the High Elvish and Numenorean legends of Eärendil. Probably because Bilbo invented its metrical devices and was proud of them" (*ATB* 31, my emphasis).[23] This playfully defines *a lack of*

---

23 See also J.R.R. Tolkien, *The Treason of Isengard* (95).

decorum viewed from within the *legendarium*. Bilbo's version of "Eärendil" therefore illustrates an instance of tension between adaptation and aesthetics, at the level of attempted decorum. Moreover, when Aragorn explains that he finds it difficult, for all his exposure to elvish culture, to replicate the original *ann-thennath* form in his "Song of Beren and Lúthien" (*LotR* 189), it is clear that the version he performs has also lost something of the aesthetic of the original. Similarly, Sam's "Gil-galad", another extract of elvish history, has taken on an aesthetic form suited to dissemination in new contexts. In all instances, as the adapted oral forms clearly lose elements conveyed by the aesthetics of their originals — within the story — readers are constrained in their appreciation of these adapted acts of minstrelsy by what they *see*.

Tolkien's fellow-Inkling, Owen Barfield, notes that in the primary world there can be a considerable difference between poetry composed for oral presentation and that composed with "architectural" complexity to engage the eye as much as the ear (90-92). In his textual presentation of informal minstrelsy, Tolkien certainly exploits familiar visual aesthetics associated with complex verse form. He does not limit himself to replicating rhyme or stanza forms, such as the tetrameter couplets or tail-rhyme that were characteristic of the verses created by medieval minstrels for oral, or putatively oral, performance. The forms he chooses to indicate acts of minstrelsy more frequently satisfy the modern reader's aesthetic pre-conceptions and expectations of 'poetry', although these may be subverted by the topic or the social status of the speaker, adding significant subtexts to a 'performance'.[24] The forms Tolkien chooses nevertheless reference the tradition in which poetry has always played a part in the recording and commemoration of history through the filter of aesthetic presentation, whether orally performed or recorded in text.

Minstrelsy and History

Both informal and professional minstrelsy within *The Lord of the Rings* present primarily oral recollections of history, and indeed the significance of the professional minstrels when they appear is that they show the process of of-

---

24 Katherine O'Brien O'Keefe has noted that "literacy becomes a process of spatialising the once-exclusively temporal" O'Brien O'Keefe, *Visible Song* (4).

ficial commemoration in action. In the story Tolkien fictionalises the process by which minstrelsy disseminated the highest-status history to bourgeois and artisan audiences via individual acts of textualising and translation, while maintaining the authority conferred by oral presentation.[25] Peter Wilkin has examined the relationship between elvish history and poetry in terms of the longing of exiles (49). Thus Sam's version of "Gil-galad" and Bilbo's "Eärendil" must be understood to rupture "that consensus that would supply traditional coherency" to elvish history,[26] as the hobbits appropriate it in adaptations of their own making and inflected with their own preferences. Even though the forms and content of these (and even Aragorn's) adaptations may echo those of the Elves' originals, the implicit elvish nostalgia and sense of communal displacement cannot apply in the same way to the versions of those histories created and recited by the hobbits, who may be influenced by elvish culture, but are not of it. The effect of appropriation applies similarly to Sam's desire to learn "Durin's Day" as all instances of the transmission, translation, and reconfiguring of songs of history necessarily alter the scope of their original signifying potential.

The effect of this runs counter to Tolkien's 'internal' time-line of *The Lord of the Rings* from the myths of the Simarillion to the 'history' of the Third Age (*L* 207), as hobbit appropriation of elvish history may be understood as one stage in what John D. Niles describes as the myth-making impulse behind such primary world poetry as *The Battle of Maldon* (448; 459). This impulse to commemorate in aesthetic form, rather than in chronicles or annals, results in a reconfiguring of immediate historical meaning within the traditions and conventions of heroic legends, and the historical event commemorated becomes mythicised through its adapted aesthetic representation.[27] Barfield has observed that "myths still live on a ghostly life as fables after they have died as real meaning" (144), that "these fables are like corpses which, fortunately

---

25 Citing the German heroic tradition of the thirteenth century, D.H. Green writes that "for those who transmitted these largely oral works, as well as for their recipients, heroic literature was the main vehicle for knowledge of the past and as such reliable and beyond questioning" (137).
26 I borrow this phrase from a discussion of Chaucer by John Miles Foley and Peter Ramey, "Oral Theory and Medieval Literature" (88).
27 D.H. Green remarks that "the presence of a contrived symmetry, for example, in a narrative suggests that history is subordinated to the demands of fiction and that we are dealing with an 'artistic control' of signification" (93). The imposition of poetic structure and aesthetic devices therefore reshapes signification more overtly.

for us, remain visible after their living content has departed out of them", and that "mythology is the ghost of concrete meaning" (83-4), further illuminating this process. The effect of the dissemination of history within *The Lord of the Rings* is to reshape its meaning in the process of rewriting it. That effect is borne out by Tom Shippey's comment on Bilbo's "Eärendil" that "what the song means and what story lies behind it are typically not explained in *The Lord of the Rings*, but remain in suggestiveness until *The Silmarillion*" (145). It is a feature of minstrelsy within *The Lord of the Rings* that elvish history from the unpublished *Silmarillion* undergoes dissemination in adaptations that are in the process of losing their original meaning, thereby becoming mythicised in a different way to their new audiences. Minstrelsy is thus privileged as a 'frame-breaking' device linking history and myth on both planes.

Minstrelsy, Textuality, and *The Silmarillion*

The relationship between history and minstrelsy exists on many levels in Tolkien's work and underpins his treatment of many of its characteristic themes. From an historical perspective, for example, Tolkien's interest in minstrelsy originates very early with his creation of Tinfang Warble in 1914. The development of this creature of Faerie, named variously a "leprawn" and a "fay", is recorded in *The Book of Lost Tales* (*LT* 107). Other Silmarillion material, as it existed at the time of the creation of *The Lord of the Rings*, illuminates the extent of Tolkien's interest in minstrelsy and its relationship to textuality and dissemination.

In the early "Appendix on Runes" in *The Treason of Isengard* Tolkien describes ancient modes of cultural transmission in an account of the way writing was first employed to record the songs of Dairon/Daeron the minstrel of Doriath, whose minstrelsy was set down by Rúmil in the original elvish runes. This script, originally devised for inscriptions, (*TI* 453) was given the name "alphabet of Dairon" due to "the preservation in [it] of *some fragments* of the songs of Dairon, the ill-fated minstrel" (*TI* 454, my emphasis). Tolkien goes on to describe the loss of other texts east of the Sea in the destruction of Númenor, so that the transmission of ancient minstrelsy and the culture it preserves, are projected as a matter of chance survival when confined to texts.

When Tolkien pushed the origins of Daeron's runes back into the remote history of Middle-earth, he opened a mythic perspective on the relationship between minstrelsy in its oral and textual forms. However, Christopher Tolkien has urged comparison between his father's early description of the association between minstrelsy and writing in "The Appendix on Runes", and the later Appendix E (II) in *The Lord of the Rings*, which reconstructs Daeron as both minstrel and 'loremaster' of King Thingol,[28] emphasising the connection between minstrelsy and history. Tolkien had, then, a view of minstrelsy as more than a form of oral entertainment, diversion, or consolation, suggesting in his own historical developments a sense of its fundamental function in the asserting of social and cultural identities through the preservation and transmission of historical information not only within, but between races and cultures.[29]

In a further process of transmission, the original dissemination of the elvish runic system among Dwarves survived, though heavily adapted, in Moria,[30] but not for its original use. In their adapted form, 'Daeron's runes' in the Third Age had become a medium by which another race chronicled its recent history in prose as the Book of Mazarbul records the ill-fated resettlement of Moria. However, the most ancient history of Moria is recalled by Gimli in the "Song of Durin", which he performs for Sam. Tom Shippey observes that this song is "dwarvishly plain and active" (147), and indeed the form is predominantly made up of simple tetrameter couplets with few rhetorical flourishes apart from examples of repetition and alliteration such as "He named the nameless hills and dells", and the recollection of how "harpers harped" (*LotR* 308). These nevertheless shed light on Dwarvish aesthetic appreciation (at least in translation). In spite of the literacy witnessed by the Book of Mazarbul, here reserved for practical, territorial records, and the tomb inscription, the aesthetics of orality preserve the most ancient commemoration.

Tolkien's referencing of major elements of the history of the First Age in *The Lord of the Rings* under the aegis of minstrelsy illustrates the extent to which he is alert to the historical simultaneity of oral and textual modes. This becomes

---

28 The same combination refers to one of the minstrels of Rohan (*LotR* 955).
29 John D. Niles has written that oral narrative is "the chief basis of culture itself" (Niles, *Homo Narrans* 2).
30 The writing in the book found in the Chamber of Mazarbul is described as a specifically Dwarvish adaptation of the Certhas Daeron (*LotR* Appendix E "The Cirth" 1097-98).

explicit when he depicts the relationship between Bilbo's written translation of the "Lay of Gil-galad", and Sam's recitation, but takes on a further dimension in Sam's assumption that he and Frodo will be commemorated in writing as well as orally. On the pass of Cirith Ungol Sam refers to their tale being read from a book at home (*LotR* 697). The creation of this book illuminates Tolkien's interest in the transition of historically significant events from orality to textuality, depicting that transition taking place via a text that will later be read aloud.[31] The relative dominance of orality or textuality is certainly governed in Middle-earth by racial preference for an aesthetics of presentation, thus textuality and the reading of history are associated with the domestic environment of at least some hobbits, although textuality is more often associated with loss, as even Sam's reference to closing the book shows how censorship by the audience, their exercising of choice, may contribute to altering the extent of what is actually disseminated.[32]

A different set of contexts come into play, however, after the Ring has been destroyed, when Sam refers to the possibility that they will hear told the tale of "Nine-fingered Frodo [...] And then everyone will hush" (*LotR* 929). On the field of Cormallen, one of the professional minstrels does indeed beg leave "to sing [...] of Frodo of the Nine Fingers" (*LotR* 933). This commemorative performance by a servant of the Gondorian hierarchy is infused with ideological status. As the story plots not just the transmission of history but the way its signification alters in the process of adaptation to its expected format in specific cultures, it poses the domesticity of textual recollection in hobbit society against Elvish, Dwarvish, Gondorian, and Rohirric cultures which all prioritise oral commemoration of great deeds in the equivalent of *chansons de geste*.

Minstrelsy in Middle-earth is never, then, associated with itinerants. In *The Lord of the Rings* it is performed by those who travel, but for some purpose other than providing entertainment and is associated less with popular entertainment and more closely with the relationship between the preservation

---

31 That many medieval texts were originally "written to be heard" is asserted by A.N. Doane (Doane and Pasternack xii). Nicholas Howe has also noted that medieval reading could be a spoken act performed within a "textual community'" (Howe 2).
32 Howe further observes in relation to reading that "reading and interpreting has the social effect of creating a community" and that "a community depends upon but also in turn creates 'general agreement on the meaning of a text'" (3).

and transmission of history, which connotes status, and takes both oral and textual forms. The oral culture of all the races that make up the Fellowship is a matter in which all levels of the social hierarchy may participate, and is the medium by which the unifying power of shared values is preserved, recalled, and disseminated. In addition, Tolkien uses the motif of participation to define characters whose minstrelsy, far from demeaning them, defines their power, authority, or status, through their knowledge of the histories that underpin the highest-status societies. But he takes the notion of minstrelsy within *The Lord of the Rings* a stage further than the potential meshing of cultures, when he acknowledges that as part of the creative process, a desire to exert power may move outwards from authorial control over the creation of a text. He wrote in *On Fairy-Stories* "when we can take green from grass, blue from heaven, and red from blood, we have already an enchanter's power – upon one plane; and the desire to wield that power in the world external to our minds awakes" (*OFS* 122). Christine Chism has remarked on the "the longing for power expressed in this statement" (68). Tolkien satisfies that longing when minstrelsy within *The Lord of the Rings* enables him to tell significant parts of the Silmarillion mythology that had long been deemed unpublishable in its own right, thereby asserting a subversive authorial control over the scope of his storytelling.

Minstrelsy and Authorial Control

Even as it provides cultural points of contact among the different peoples of Middle-earth,[33] oral performance in *The Lord of the Rings* opens up history to diminishing significance through continual adaptation.[34] In this diminishment it echoes the image of the 'fading time' of the Elves with whom the highest-status history originates in Tolkien's wider view of his *legendarium*, but this view also clearly reflects issues and ideas concerning minstrelsy in the primary world. Although minstrelsy in Middle-earth does not conform in all respects to definitions of minstrelsy in the medieval primary world, in one respect it is exactly the same – it is characterised on both the interior and exterior planes by

---

33 Julian Eilmann has also noted the importance of song as a vector for cultural contact between different races in *J.R.R. Tolkien: Romanticist and Poet*, Walking Tree Publishers: Zurich and Jena, 2017 (353).
34 Verlyn Flieger has discussed diminution as thematic to Tolkien's wider mythology, and diminishment may be included in this theme (Flieger 62).

what Paul Zumthor calls *mouvance* (textual mobility). He regards the textual mobility characteristic of medieval literature as the result of its origin in oral culture (71), and notes the kinds of alterations that *mouvance* encapsulates – from simple scribal error to wholesale adaptation. Following Zumthor, the "instability of medieval works in the vernacular" has been asserted by Bernard Cerquiglini (34). Both Zumthor and Cerquiglini see textual mobility as intrinsic to societies in which orality and textuality co-exist. Refining these ideas, Derek Pearsall has written that "the surviving manuscripts of a poem [...] make it clear that each act of copying was to a large extent an act of recomposition, and not an episode in a process of decomposition from an ideal form" ("Text and Textual Criticism" 126-7). Of the manuscripts of *Sir Orfeo* specifically he notes, however, that they "are not examples of the beauties of *variance* so enthusiastically celebrated by Cerquiligni, or of the need to view all the witnesses to the text of a popular romance as examples of recomposition equally or necessarily worthy of attention" ("Madness in Sir Orfeo" 52). However, although variant forms may not all be equally polished or appealing Zumthor maintains that variation is "pas [...] une «faute» mais [...] une régénération rendue possible par la mobilité textuelle" (72). John Dagenais has taken the problem of variant forms a stage further in his critique of the practice of textual editing that

> works back from the manuscript texts to some originary authentic text (of which the various manuscript witnesses are but debasements). [He continues:] the very work of textual criticism involves the creation of a hierarchy which inevitably situates the manuscripts and their readings in an inferior and negative position vis-à-vis a generally absent 'archetype' or 'original' (248-9).

In the primary world the marginal status of minstrels and their association with vernacular storytelling has been judged to have been one determining factor behind the phenomenon of medieval *mouvance*, whether perceived as oral or textual in origin.[35] Tolkien's informal minstrels are, though, with the debatable exceptions of the hobbits, all high-status characters who use the vernacular of Middle-earth for their performances. Bartłomiej Błaszkiewicz comments on poetic creativity in the Shire, referring to the existence of a "small group of the elite" whose contact with Elves ensures that "literacy combines with sufficient erudition and refinement" (37-8). However, those hobbits make entertaining

---

35 Southworth remarks that "it is not just that the status of the minstrel was low [...] the minstrel was worse off than a serf [...] the minstrel had no place [in the medieval hierarchy] at all" (Southworth 4).

songs such as "The Man in the Moon" and perform their own history, as in Sam's "Troll Song", alongside their appropriation of the highest-status history for transmission in the vernacular via translation and recomposition. So, minstrelsy in *The Lord of the Rings* is not limited to the replication of high-status topics or aesthetics, and whatever its particular focus, the oral and textual forms associated with it remain subject to *mouvance* through the process of the transmission both within the story, and beyond its borders, in ways that illuminate Tolkien's almost obsessive recomposing as a challenge to the critical notion of textual hierarchy and authenticity.

Deanna Delmar Evans notes that Tolkien revised the title and form of his poem the "Lay of Leithian" many times (79), and proposes the influence of *Sir Orfeo* on this version of the Beren story, although she does not notice the omissions and alterations that differentiate the three manuscript versions of the medieval poem.[36] These were features of medieval textual tradition with which Tolkien was very familiar, not only from his work on *Sir Orfeo* but from his work on the many variant textual forms of *Ancrene Wisse* (*L* 114).[37] As Bella Millett has noted with reference to this instructional work:

> There is no doubt that the textual history of *Ancrene Wisse* reflects in its own way the effects of mouvance [... It] was continuously reworked, over a period of nearly three centuries, by a succession of adaptors, translators and [...] participatory scribes. (13)

Tolkien, the early editor of *Sir Orfeo*, replicates throughout his own creative work patterns of loss and adaptation that he would have encountered during his editorial work, and that were characteristic of medieval textual *mouvance*. This can be traced within *The Lord of the Rings* as he defines the means by which stories are disseminated and altered in their forms and significance, but it appears most prominently in the Silmarillion material and in its relationship to the later story. Throughout his work on the *legendarium* Tolkien develops examples of *mouvance*, as distinct from simple revisions, in which chronology alone defines textual hierarchy so that performances of informal minstrelsy in *The Lord of the Rings* may appear as authoritative versions of Silmarillion

---

36 J.A. Burrow, ed., *English Verse* (4). The Auchinleck *Orfeo* lacks its original prologue but its editor in 1954, A.J. Bliss, gave it the prologue used to introduce two other later mss. of the poem, and *Lay le Freine*, in all of which the story that follows it is described as a *lai* (Sands 233).
37 This letter dates from 1945. Carpenter notes that *Ancrene Wisse* was only finished in 1962 (*L* 441).

stories, when they are, in fact, only variant forms, and all are associated with assertions of authority in various ways.

Minstrelsy is, then, profoundly implicated in *mouvance* throughout Tolkien's work. When Bilbo selects from and conveys the high-status elvish history of Gil-galad into the vernacular through translation, his choice of what and how to translate asserts his authority over its mode of presentation in a new context. The authority of that text then becomes unstable as the story passes into oral form when Sam selects from the translation only what pleases him, but both hobbits assert their authority over an original history that is not their own. Similarly, Bilbo's "Eärendil" song in Rivendell, like Aragorn's brief version of "Beren and Lúthien" display degrees of *mouvance* that assert authority not only through the display of knowledge of high-status history, but through the process of adaptation into the Middle-earth vernacular – the Common Speech.

The significance of the related elements of *mouvance* – textuality, recomposition, and authority, may be extended further. When Sam remarks on the Pass of Cirith Ungol that he and Frodo are in the same story as Beren and Eärendil (*LotR* 696-97), this is only true of the versions delineated in *The Lord of the Rings*, which are the latest versions of episodes and characters that Tolkien has derived from the ongoing Silmarillion material.[38] His treatment of his work replicates the complexity and paradoxes of the transmission of (hi)story via the conventions of minstrelsy – oral and textual – as he continually adapts his own texts. The historical elements of both the entire *The Lord of the Rings* and many of the inserted poems are unequivocally the latest, but not necessarily the last, developments of stories that Tolkien had been creating as part of his *legendarium* from its earliest inception. He also recomposes forms and themes deriving from his earlier poetry,[39] so that when these developments appear in *The Lord of the Rings* they are not simply part of the fiction, but genuine 'witnesses', variants of existing texts transposed into the textual representation of oral performance, which are not limited by their fictional context. Tolkien's treatment of the relationship between minstrelsy, history, and authority then

---

[38] Tolkien refers explicitly to *The Silmarillion* as the book upon which he based *The Lord of the Rings* (*L* 31).
[39] Sam's Troll Song began as "Pero and Podex" before becoming "The Root of the Boot" and then "The Troll Song". On the poem's development see Scull and Hammond (*ATB* 193-200).

opposes any straightforward view of these 'witnesses' by filtering in the intervention of various cultures, the processes of choice and translation, and a consequent diminishment of the full force of history, although its authority may be appropriated through transmission. The continual process of creativity is not, then, a matter of preferred versions, but of alternative developments and 'variations on a theme' analogous to musical composition.

Within the putative chronology of *The Lord of the Rings* vis-à-vis the primary world, when Frodo performs at Bree, Tolkien posits the diminution of a song from entertainment for adults in the Third Age to a nursery rhyme ('Hey diddle diddle') for infants in the modern age.[40] But similar intentional *mouvance*, without implications of diminishment, is clearly a feature of his larger creative methodology demonstrated by the variant forms of *legendarium* stories, and the new versions of old poems, such as the sequential rewriting of "Pero & Podex" (Sam's "Troll Song"), and "Errantry", which becomes Bilbo's "Eärendil". In addition, all these examples align with Tolkien's theory of 'sub-creation',[41] as he expresses it in "Mythopoeia" and asserts again in one of his later letters: "sub-creation" was a tribute to "the infinity of [God's] potential variety" (*L* 186). However, in Tolkien's creative methodology they serve to declare the absolute authority of the author and define his relationship to his creativity.[42] Although he appears to engage in an almost obsessive process of serial revision, what we see when we review the scope of his work is that whether by rewriting nursery rhymes and the circumstances in which his reader would expect to see them, or through the many recompositions of the great Beren and Lúthien story and its modes of presentation, what is certain is that Tolkien deliberately engaged in the process of *mouvance* in an assertion of his authority over his creative ideas.

That non-preferential recomposing was part of Tolkien's creative method is demonstrated by Christopher Tolkien, who shows in *The Lays of Beleriand* how his father created and retained many versions of the Beren and Lúthien

---

40 Apart from the many versions of "The Man in the Moon", there are other instances when Tolkien recasts nursery rhymes, such as the line from "Bye Baby Bunting" in which a "rabbit skin to wrap a Baby Bunting in" becomes a "hobbit-skin to wrap an elven princeling in" (*LotR* 327).
41 Christopher Tolkien traces the complex history of the "Errantry" poem and its "Rivendell version", including his father's creation of an alliterative form, as well as the designation of an "'A.V.' ('Authorised Version')" and an "'R.V.' ('Revised Version')" (*TI* 90-105).
42 Darielle Richards describes Tolkien's theory of sub-creation as part of a wider temporal process, itself redolent of dissemination (Richards 63).

story from its earliest recorded incarnations, continually reworking its essential elements (*LB* 150-3); altering the race to which Beren belongs; changing the relationship between Daeron and Lúthien; altering the minstrel's role and influence; even changing the spelling of his name,[43] as well as the title and the genre to which the story was assigned;[44] and he still deferred any possibility of a final authoritative version beyond Aragorn's assertion that none but Elrond in the Third Age "remember it aright as it was told of old" (*LotR* 187). As Christopher Tolkien observes, even "when *The Lord of the Rings* was finished [my father] turned to the [*Lay of Leithian*] and recast the first two cantos and a good part of the third, and small portions of some others" (*LB* 151). Although some revisions to the story had been prompted by C.S. Lewis's critique of the early work in 1929-30, as Tolkien's statements on sub-creation show, the variant forms of his works should not necessarily be taken to imply his dissatisfaction with his efforts at any stage. Nor should the variants be disregarded in a search for some definitive version of the story, nor should one be preferred over any other, as Tolkien shows by his post-publication versions of *The Lay of Leithian* and his fifteen versions of "Bilbo's Song at Rivendell" (*TI* 90). The form any poem or *legendarium* story takes in *The Lord of the Rings* becomes simply specific to that context.

The Lord of the Rings itself exemplifies *mouvance* as it gathers together tropes, motifs, and other conventions associated with medieval minstrelsy. Its rich literary texture is based around plot, character types, structural and didactic conventions familiar to any medieval minstrel's audience. The quest, interlacing of plot strands, authorial prologue and comments, are all structural conventions belonging to medieval romances, as are the thematic motifs of the displaced hero (Aragorn), the wooing lady (Éowyn), and the supportive guide and mentor (Gandalf), while the Christian or moral subtext which emerges in discrete episodes has echoes in, for example, the romance of *Sir Bevis of Hampton*.[45] The

---

43 For a convenient summary see Eden, "Strains of Elvish Song and Voices: Victorian Medievalism, Music, and Tolkien", (96).
44 Tolkien gives the earliest A version dated 1925 the unwieldy title: *The Gest of Beren son of Barahir and Luthien the Fay called Tinuviel the Nightingale or the Lay of Leithian* (*LB* 150-53). Since "Gest" and "Lay" derive from separate medieval genres of oral storytelling and each defines a different set of generic conventions, Tolkien perhaps intentionally implies the instability of the form in which the story is presented.
45 See Forest-Hill, "Fantasy Elements in Medieval Romance".

matter of translation may also be revisited in this context because medieval works associated with minstrels were frequently translated from French into English.[46] Within the framework of *The Lord of the Rings*, it is the Red Book of Westmarch that has been translated into the book in front of the reader as textual *mouvance* comes to the fore through the very strategies Tolkien uses to create its historical depth by smuggling in Silmarillion stories. In the face of his publisher's resistance, Tolkien recast the forms and content of those stories to suit the circumstances of informal minstrelsy in *The Lord of the Rings* and the readership he knew he had to satisfy, but through those variations and under the fiction of oral performance he maintained and extended his authority over the texts he created.

The "Appendix on Runes" shows that at an early stage in his development of his *legendarium* Tolkien gave extended thought to the matter of the transition of culturally significant material from oral to textual forms in the context of minstrelsy, and Eden has noted another early witness to Tolkien's consideration of transition in the context of historical commemoration. In a number of drafts of a lecture on the Old English poem *The Battle of Maldon*, Tolkien suggests that it was created by a "minstrel turned scholar".[47] The relationship between orality and textuality is not, then, simply a fictionalised detail in either *The Lord of the Rings*, or the *legendarium*, but one which reverberates between his primary-world scholarship and his sub-created world. Eden goes on to propose that Tolkien himself could be construed as a "scholar turned Minstrel".[48] This may be justified, trivially perhaps, because, with *The Lord of the Rings*, Tolkien is being paid to create a work that reiterates many of the tropes and motifs that had traditionally made up the matter of the heroic romances disseminated far and wide by medieval minstrels. Furthermore, A.C. Spearing comments on Chaucer, noting the renowned medieval poet's "role as deferential entertainer, his audience's humble servant" (23), highlighting the conjunction of minstrelsy, humility and erudition that in part characterises Aragorn, but also, in part,

---

46 For example: *Sir Orfeo* may have had a French (Breton) source. *Sir Bevis of Hampton* certainly began as an Anglo-Norman tale and was translated into Middle English by the end of the fourteenth century.
47 Eden quotes from Bodleian Tolkien MSS Box A 30/2 (Eden 3).
48 Ibid. However, Roberta Frank has noted William of Malmsbury's account of Abbott Aldhelm, founder of Shaftesbury Abbey performing as a minstrel "who used to sing to crowds to persuade them to go to church", and she remarks on the image of a "named sophisticated scholar singing to and serving unlettered countrymen" (Frank 156).

defines Tolkien's relationship to his work and his readers. But Tolkien, like Chaucer, may be seen to exploit the paradoxical freedom of a minstrel to adapt old and familiar material and insert allusions to matters of didactic import in the process of creating something new to please others (*L* 189). And because minstrelsy could be a narrative posture in medieval manuscripts which relied on an audience's familiarity with the versification that characterised the work of the medieval minstrels, Tolkien's role as minstrel is by no means compromised by the genre in which he writes. It is simply the form of narrative most familiar to his readers. Thus, *The Lord of the Rings*, in its entirety may be considered as an act of minstrelsy that has taken on the generic form expected by the society for which it is intended.

Tolkien declared that in his *legendarium* he was writing a "mythology for England" (*L* 144, 231). The performance of minstrelsy in *The Lord of the Rings*, with its implicit engagement with history, authority, and intertextuality on the exterior plane, traces intermediary stages in the process of cultural development that were impelled by minstrelsy in the primary world. Its depictions of informal minstrelsy echo many of the conditions in which vernacular English developed and changed its status, including different forms of *mouvance*. Bilbo's translation of "Gil-galad" is one instance of the process in progress. By tracing instances of translation, transmission, and dissemination, what Tolkien creatively imagines are the first stages in the 'vernacularisation' of the history and culture upon which his mythology for England was founded, and upon which later literature would notionally depend. His is not, of course, an intrinsically political intention outside of his creative vision, but within the story it has cultural significance as, through Bilbo's translation, and Sam's performance, he reiterates the trajectory by which the English vernacular gained status against the authority of Latin and Norman French by means of translation. The Middle English poems Tolkien edited and translated, *Sir Gawain and the Green Knight* and *Sir Orfeo*, while pretending to have oral origins, had been created under the influence of French chivalric ideals and French (Breton) poetic form and content. In terms of the fourteenth-century politics of language, their original adaptations are an assertion of authority intended to remind their audiences and readers that vernacular English was in fact capable of appropriating material and poetic forms that had connotations of high culture. The matter of the politics of language and its manifestation via *mouvance* that was intrinsic to Middle English romances was, then, implicitly part of Tolkien's intellectual landscape when he came to write his own medieval romance (*L* 103).

In *The Lord of the Rings* Tolkien creates that romance, and it is as a fundamental element in a late manifestation of that genre that we should understand his depiction of minstrelsy in the story. He alludes there to many earlier, ancient instances of minstrelsy from within the *legendarium* to create a sense of historical depth, but the earliness of his work on Daeron's runes, its length and later revisions, indicate the seriousness with which he originally regarded this theoretical matter even though it is only alluded to briefly in the later work. The role of minstrelsy as entertainment and as commemoration of history defines societies with special relationships to the oral presentation of knowledge in *The Lord of the Rings*, but through the device of Daeron's runes Tolkien projects the dissemination of textuality, while through the relationship between Bilbo's translation and Sam's song he appears to acknowledge that "there is in fact no clear point of transition from a non-literate to a literate society",[49] and that as in the Middle Ages, "orality and literacy [...] merged and supported each other".[50] Nevertheless, by imagining the transmission and recording of elvish history in the vernacular via informal minstrelsy, Tolkien delineates the role of minstrelsy in the dissemination and development of literacy and the culture it inscribes. In *The Lord of the Rings*, therefore, minstrelsy serves as the nexus at which Tolkien draws together the processes begun in his mythology to illustrate the essential role of minstrelsy in the development of textual culture and the enabling of the dissemination of cultural history, which has the effect of integrating races through the recognition of shared values. However, by adopting as part of his creative methodology the *mouvance* associated with minstrelsy and justified by his theory of sub-creation, Tolkien governs the dissemination of his own mythology and thereby asserts the absolute authority of his creativity.

---

49 Stock, *Implications of Literacy* 9.
50 Wolf, "Medieval Heroic Traditions and their Transitions from Orality to Literacy" 67.

About the Author

LYNN FOREST-HILL taught medieval and early modern literature and drama at the University of Southampton before leaving to concentrate on writing. She has published articles on Shakespeare as well as those relating to Tolkien studies. Her most recent research is in the area of medieval romance. She was for ten years the Education Officer of the Tolkien Society and remains a Fellow of the Centre for Medieval and Renaissance Culture at the University of Southampton.

List of Abbreviations of Tolkien's Works

ATB   *The Adventures of Tom Bombadil and other verses*
L   *The Letters of J.R.R. Tolkien*
LB   *The Lays of Beleriand*
LotR *The Lord of the Rings*
LT   *The Book of Lost Tales*
TI   *The Treason of Isengard*

Bibliography

AMENDT-RADUEGE, Amy. "'Worthy of a Song': Memory, Mortality and Music." *Middle-earth Minstrel*. Ed. Bradford Lee Eden. Jefferson, NC: McFarland, 2010, 114-125.

BALDWIN, John W. *Masters, Princes and Merchants*. 2 vols. Princeton, NJ: Princeton UP, 1970.

BARFIELD, Owen. *Poetic Diction: A Study in Meaning*. London: Faber and Faber, 1927.

BŁASZKIEWICZ, Bartłomiej. "Orality and Literacy in Middle-earth." *O What a Tangled Web: Tolkien and Medieval Literature, A View from Poland*. Ed. Barbara Kowalik. Zurich and Jena: Walking Tree Publishers, 2013, 29-45.

BOUTET, Dominique. "The Chanson de Geste and Orality." *Medieval Oral Literature*. Ed. Karl Reichl. Berlin/Boston, MA: Walter de Gruyter, 2016, 353-69.

BROOMFIELD, F. (ed.). *Thomae de Chobham Summa Confessorum*. Louvain: Éditions Nauwelaerts: Paris: Béatrice-Nauwelaerts, 1968.

BURROW, J.A. (ed.). *English Verse 1300-1500*. Vol. 1. London: Longmans, 1977.

CARPENTER, Humphrey (ed.). *The Letters of J.R.R. Tolkien*, with the assistance of Christopher Tolkien. London: HarperCollins, 1995.

CHISM, Christine. "Middle-earth, the Middle Ages, and the Aryan Nation: Myth and History in World War II." *Tolkien the Medievalist*. Ed. Jane Chance. London: Routledge, 2003, 63-92.

CERQUIGLINI, Bernard. *In Praise of the Variant*. Trans. Betsy Wing. Baltimore, ML: Johns Hopkins University Press, 1999.

DAGENAIS, John. "That Bothersome Residue: Towards a Theory of the Physical Text." *Vox Intexta: Orality and Textuality in the Middle Ages*. Eds. A.N. Doane, and Carol Braun Pasternack. Madison, WI and London: University of Wisconsin Press, 1991, 246-262.

DOANE, A.N., and Carol BRAUN PASTERNACK (eds.). *Vox Intexta: Orality and Textuality in the Middle Ages*. Madison, WI and London: University of Wisconsin Press, 1991.

DEARNELY, Elizabeth. *Translators and their Prologues in Medieval England*. Cambridge: D.S. Brewer, 2016.

DUBOIS, Thomas A. "Oral Poetics: The Linguistics and Stylistics of Orality." *Medieval Oral Literature*. Ed. Karl Reichl. Berlin and Boston, MA: Walter de Gruyter, 2016, 203-224.

DUGAUQUIER, J.-A. (ed.). *Pierre le Chantre Summa de sacramentis*. III, 2a. Louvain, 1954-67.

EDEN, Bradford Lee. "Strains of Elvish Song and Voices: Victorian Medievalism, Music, and Tolkien." *Middle-earth Minstrel*. Ed. Bradford Lee Eden. Jefferson, NC: McFarland, 2010, 85-101.

EILMANN, Julian. *J.R.R. Tolkien: Romanticist and Poet*. Walking Tree Publishers: Zurich and Jena, 2017.

EVANS, Deanna Delmar. "Tolkien's Unfinished 'Lay of Luthien' and the Middle English Sir Orfeo." *Middle-earth Minstrel*. Ed. Bradford Lee Eden. Jefferson, NC: McFarland, 2010, 75-84.

FLIEGER, Verlyn. *Splintered Light: Logos and Language in Tolkien's World*. Kent, OH: Kent State University Press, 2002.

FOLEY, John Miles and Peter RAMEY. "Oral Theory and Medieval Literature." *Medieval Oral Literature*. Ed. Karl Reichl. Berlin and Boston, MA: Walter de Gruyter, 2016, 71-102.

FOOT, Sarah. "The Making of Angelcynn: English Identity before the Norman Conquest." *Old English Literature*. Ed. R.M Liuzza. New Haven, CT and London: Yale University Press, 2002, 51-78.

FOREST-HILL, Lynn. "Fantasy Elements in Medieval Romance: History or Imagination?" *Yearbook of Eastern European Studies* 6 (2016): 61-77.

FRANK, Roberta. "The Search for the Anglo-Saxon Poet." *Textual and Material Culture in Anglo-Saxon England: Thomas Northcote Toller and the Toller Memorial lectures.* Ed. D.G. Scragg. Cambridge: D.S. Brewer, 2003, 137-60.

GREEN, D.H. *The Beginnings of Medieval Romance: Fact and Fiction 1150-1220.* Cambridge: Cambridge University Press, 2002.

HOWE, Nicholas. "Cultural Construction of Reading". *Old English Literature.* Ed. R.M Liuzza. New Haven, CT and London: Yale University Press, 2002, 1-22.

JACOBS, Nicholas. "*Sir Degarré, Lay le Freine, Beves of Hamtoun* and the 'Auchinleck bookshop'." *Notes and Queries,* 29 (1982): 294-301.

KLAEBER, Fr. (ed.). *Beowulf and the Fight at Finnsburg.* 3rd ed. Boston: D.C. Heath, 1922.

MACHAN, Tim William. "Editing, Orality, and Late Middle English Texts." *Vox Intexta: Orality and Textuality in the Middle Ages.* Eds. A.N. Doane and Carol Braun Pasternack. Madison, WI and London: University of Wisconsin Press, 1991, 229-245.

MARTIN, Gregory. "Music, Myth, and Literary Depth in the 'Land Ohne Musik'." *Music in Middle-earth.* Eds. Heidi Steimel and Friedhelm Schneidewind. Zurich and Jena: Walking Tree Publishers, 2010, 127-148.

MILLETT, Bella. "Mouvance and the Medieval Author." *Late Medieval Religious Texts and their Transmission: Essays in Honour of A.I. Doyle.* Ed. A.J. Minnis. Cambridge: Boydell and Brewer, 1994, 9-20.

NILES, John D. *Homo Narrans: The Poetics and Anthropology of Oral Literature.* Philadelphia, PA: University of Philadelphia Press, 1999.

"Maldon and Mythopoesis." *Old English Literature.* Ed. R.M Liuzza. New Haven, CT and London: Yale University Press, 2002, 445-74.

O'BRIEN O'KEEFE, Katherine. *Visible Song: Transitional Literacy in Old English Verse.* Cambridge: Cambridge University Press, 1990.

PAGE, Christopher. *The Owl and the Nightingale: musical life and ideas in France 1100-1300.* Berkeley, CA and Los Angeles, CA: University of California Press. 1989.

"Johannes de Grocheio on secular music: a corrected text and a new translation." *Plainsong and Medieval Musik* 2, 1 (1993): 17-41.

PASTERNACK, Carol Braun. "Introduction." *Vox Intexta: Orality and Textuality in the Middle Ages.* Eds. A.N. Doane and Carol Braun Pasternack. Madison, WI and London: University of Wisconsin Press, 1991, 3-4.

PEARSALL, Derek. "Text, Textual Criticism, and Fifteenth-Century Manuscript Production." *Fifteenth Century Studies*. Ed. Robert F. Yeager. Hamden: Archon, 1984, 121-36.

"Madness in Sir Orfeo." *Romance Reading on the Book: Essays on medieval narrative presented to Maldwyn Mills*. Eds. Jennifer Fellows, Rosalind Field, Gillian Rogers, and Judith Weiss. Cardiff: University of Wales Press, 1996, 51-63.

PUTTER, Ad. "Middle English Romance and the Oral Tradition." *Medieval Oral Literature*. Ed. Karl Reichl. Berlin and Boston, MA: Walter de Gruyter, 2016, 335-351.

REICHL, Karl (ed.). *Medieval Oral Literature*. Berlin and Boston, MA: Walter de Gruyter, 2016.

"Plotting the Map of Medieval Oral Literature." *Medieval Oral Literature*. Ed. Karl Reichl. Berlin and Boston, MA: Walter de Gruyter, 2016, 3-71.

RICHARDS, Darielle. "J.R.R. Tolkien: A Fortunate Rhythm." *Middle-earth Minstrel*. Ed. Bradford Lee Eden. Jefferson, NC: McFarland, 2010, 61-74.

SANDS, Donald B. (ed.). *Middle English Verse Romances*. Exeter: University of Exeter Press, 1986.

SHIPPEY, Tom. *The Road to Middle-earth*. Boston, MA: HarperCollins, 2005.

SOUTHWORTH, John. *The English Medieval Minstrel*. Woodbridge: The Boydell Press, 1989.

SPEARING, A.C. *Medieval to Renaissance in English Poetry*. Chicago, IL: University of Chicago Press, 1985.

STALEY, Lynn. *Languages of Power in the Age of Richard II*. University Park, PA: Penn State University Press, 2005.

STEIMEL, Heidi. "Bring out the Instruments: Instrumental Music in Middle-earth." *Music in Middle-earth*. Eds. Heidi Steimel and Friedhelm Schneidewind. Zurich and Jena: Walking Tree Publishers, 2010, 93-120.

STOCK, Brian. *The Implications of Literacy: Written Language and Models of Interpretation in the Eleventh and Twelfth Centuries*. Princeton, NJ.: Princeton University Press, 1983.

SWEET, Henry (ed.). *King Alfred's West-Saxon Version of Gregory's Pastoral Care*, EETS, O.S. 45, 50. London: N. Trübner, 1871.

TOLKIEN, J.R.R. *Bodleian Tolkien MSS Box A 30/2*.

The Book of Lost Tales (The History of Middle-earth 1). Ed. Christopher Tolkien. London: George Allen and Unwin, 1983.

The Lays of Beleriand. Ed. Christopher Tolkien. London: Allen and Unwin, 1985.

The Lord of the Rings. London: HarperCollins, 1995.

The Treason of Isengard (The History of Middle-earth 2). Ed. Christopher Tolkien. London: HarperCollins, 2001.

The Monsters and the Critics and Other Essays. Ed. Christopher Tolkien. London: HarperCollins, 2006.

The Adventures of Tom Bombadil and other verses. Eds. Christina Scull and Wayne G. Hammond. London: HarperCollins, 2014.

TREHARNE, Elaine. *Living through Conquest: The Politics of Early English*. Oxford: Oxford University Press, 2012.

WADDELL, Helen. *Songs of the Wandering Scholars*. Ed. Felicitas Corrigan O.S.B. London: The Folio Society, 1982.

WILKIN, Peter. "æfre me strongode longað: songs of Exile in the Mortal Realms." *Middle-earth Minstrel*. Ed. Bradford Lee Eden. Jefferson, NC: McFarland, 2010, 47-60.

WOGAN-BROWNE, Jocelyn, Nicholas WATSON, Andrew TAYLOR and Ruth EVANS (eds.). *The Idea of the Vernacular: an Anthology of Middle English Literary Theory 1280-1520*. Exeter: University of Exeter Press, 1999.

WOLF, Alois. "Medieval Heroic Traditions and their Transitions from Orality to Literacy". *Vox Intexta: Orality and Textuality in the Middle Ages*. Eds. A.N. Doane and Carol Braun Pasternack. Madison, WI and London: University of Wisconsin Press, 1991, 67-88.

ZUMTHOR, Paul. *Essai de poétique medieval*. Paris: Seuil, 1972.

Maureen F. Mann

Musicality in Tolkien's Prose

> It has always been with me: the sensibility to linguistic pattern which affects me emotionally like colour or music. (*L* no. 163, 212)

Abstract

Using statements from *A Secret Vice*, the "Essay on Phonetic Symbolism", and Tolkien's *Letters*, this paper examines Tolkien's prose style in light of his own comments about the significance of phonetics and the role of sound in communicating meaning, as well as the role of mellifluous expressions to enhance or help formulate the comprehension of meaning. The methodology applies historical interrogation and textual analysis using traditional rhetorical devices from public speaking (such as anaphora, epistrophe, symploce, word schemes, and schemes of arrangement for grammar) to identify rhythmic emphasis and sound repetition which create musicality. It focusses almost exclusively on works published in Tolkien's lifetime with some comparison to *The Book of Lost Tales*. It also examines the various narrative situations which show musicality.

It would be remiss in a book about music and Middle-earth if there were no discussion of music and language in Middle-earth, not elvish languages nor even lyrical and poetic language, but English prose, the linguistic matter usually thought of as "prosaic". The recent publication of the scholarly edition of *A Secret Vice* with the previously unpublished "Essay on Phonetic Symbolism" and the new editions of *The Children of Húrin*, *The Story of Kullervo*, and *Beren and Lúthien* should remind readers of some of the expectations and values Tolkien held about the significance of sound and beauty in language. In place of his term "phonaesthetic pleasure" (*L* no. 144, 176) this paper uses the word "musicality", in keeping with the theme of this book. The paper examines various stylistic traits in Tolkien's prose (not all of Middle-earth) from the claims he made for the important effects of the sound of language, as well as other claims about the aesthetics of language. As Ursula Le Guin has said,

> Like Charles Dickens and Virginia Wolf, Tolkien must have heard what he wrote. The narrative prose of such novelists is like poetry in that it wants the living voice to speak it, to find its full beauty and power, its subtle music, its rhythmic vitality (LeGuin 102).

There is both rhyme and reason behind the very popular habit of Tolkien's readers to gather and read aloud his prose.

Tolkien's theorising about the significance of sound and beauty in language is found in several sources. The most extensive is the essay dedicated to his invented languages, originally presented as a lecture, "A Secret Vice". Other sources include the lecture "English and Welsh" where he extends his thoughts about beauty in language to real world languages, and his "Valedictory Address" where he railed against ears deaf to the tone of language in academic study. Tolkien writes about the topic in several letters as well. His "Essay on Phonetic Symbolism" explores the linguistic topic of the relationship of sound and meaning. Tolkien's theorising was first brought together in Ross Smith's *Inside Language* and then given a comprehensive interrogation in Dimitra Fimi's *Tolkien, Race, and Cultural History*, with the sixth chapter devoted to "Linguistic Aesthetic: Sounds, Meaning and the Pursuit of Beauty". Smith points out that Tolkien's interest lay with "phonosemantics", the relationship between sound and meaning (R. Smith 51), an interest that put Tolkien outside mainstream, orthodox linguistics, and "phonetic fitness", the relationship between sound and pleasure (57). Fimi's analysis of Tolkien's theorising identifies a number of ideas related to Tolkien's term "phonaesthetic pleasure". Firstly, Tolkien's "underlying principle [. . .] that language is not just a utilitarian tool for communication, but also a potential form of artistic creation" (Fimi 77). Secondly, that the beauty lies "primarily in the sound of language" (ibid.). Thirdly, that beauty can be experienced when we disassociate the "word form from its meaning" (ibid.). A final source of beauty arises when the word seems to fit it meaning – "when a word sounds right for what it signifies" (78). Because these claims appeared in *A Secret Vice* where Tolkien was speaking of invented language, readers have largely considered them in terms of his elvish languages. However, readers also familiar with Tolkien's claim about the beauty of Welsh,[1] Finnish,[2] and Gothic,[3] as well as Tolkien's claim that English is a desiccated language,[4] might perceive how Tolkien's use of English reflects his theorising. This paper examines these claims of phonaesthetics, as well as a thematic comment or two, as they apply to his prose.

Tolkien identified sound as the most significant quality in response to language. Some of his most strenuous defences of the significance of sound, as exemplified by the study of philology, came in his "Valedictory Address", when he obviously felt free to state his opinion about the culture war of his time, lang versus lit. In defense of philology, he wrote:

> If it seems too much concerned with "sounds", with the audible structure of words, it shares this interest with the poets. [...] Which is nearer akin to a poem, its metre or the paper on which it is written? Which will bring more to life poetry, rhetoric, dramatic speech, or even plain prose: some knowledge of the language, even of the pronunciation, of its period, or the typographical details of its printed form? (VA 234, 235 *passim*).

He concludes his tirade by acknowledging those students of philology for whom the Old English *drēam* – the "sound of their glad voices and the music of their feasts" (VA 240) is not lost. In his essay "English and Welsh" Tolkien also iterated the importance of sound and sound patterns:

> The basic pleasure in the phonetic elements of a language and in the style of their patterns, and then in the higher dimension, pleasure in the association of these word-forms with meanings, is of fundamental importance. This pleasure is distinct from the practical knowledge of a language, and not the same as an analytical understanding of its structure. It is simpler, deeper-rooted, and yet more immediate than the enjoyment of literature. Though it may be allied to some of the elements in the appreciation of verse, it does not need any poets, other than the nameless artists who composed the language. (EW 190)

---

1 The Welsh names on a coal truck fascinated him as a child, while learning some Welsh as an undergraduate provided "an abiding linguistic-aesthetic satisfaction" (*L* no. 163, 213).
2 "It was like discovering a complete wine-cellar filled with bottles of an amazing wine of a kind and flavour never tasted before. It quite intoxicated me" (*L* no. 163, 214).
3 "I was fascinated by Gothic in itself: a beautiful language, which reached the eminence of liturgical use" (*L* no. 272, 357).
4 "But even say in English (a fairly extreme example of a largely desiccated language) it [phonetic symbolism] remains operative as a disturbing factor in the way of the smooth course of bold semantic and phonetic inheritance" (EPS 68).

Tolkien used this aesthetic sense when he evaluated invented languages—it was his reason for preferring Esperanto to other Invented Languages.[5] Yet Tolkien also warned about an "excess of euphony" in his essay "On the Kalevala or Land of Heroes" where he used a metaphor of music to suggest how relative effects of sounds can best be used:

> In fact [Finnish] suffers like many lang[uages]of its type from an excess of euphony: so much so that the music of language is apt to be expended automatically and leave no excess with which to heighten the emotion of a lyric passage. Where vowel harmony and the softening of cons[onants] is an integral part of <u>ordinary speech</u>, there is less chance for sudden unexpected sweetness. (*SK* 76-77. Bracketed elements from editor)

Tolkien does in fact use such linguistic aesthetics to heighten emotion in his prose. Especially in "On Translating Beowulf" he insisted upon the significance of sound: "Translation of the individual simple words means, or should mean, more than just indicating the general scope of their sense: for instance, contenting oneself with 'shield' alone to render Old English *bord, lind, rand* and *scyld*. The variation, the *sound* of different words, is a feature of the style that should to some degree be represented" (OTB 56). Tolkien also emphasised that alliteration "depends not on *letters* but on *sounds*" and is in fact "head-rhyme" (OTB 66). As Christopher Tolkien states, his father himself "achieved great mastery" in using the Old English verse metre in modern English, in several forms.[6] As we shall see, Tolkien's hand was also highly skilled in using alliteration in modern English prose.

Written at the same time as "A Secret Vice", the "Essay on Phonetic Symbolism" addresses different topics. Two points are germane to the argument here, his comments on onomatopoeia and his statement about phonetic symbolism. Both relate to the importance of sound. The first Tolkien says is an imitation of sound while the latter reflects a symbolic relationship between the phoneme and the meaning, the relationship between the two being when onomatopoeia is "removed a stage further from its purely 'echoic' basis, and can become one of the sources

---

5 "N**, for instance, is ingenious, and easier than Esperanto, but hideous – 'factory product' is written all over it, or rather, 'made of spare parts' – and it has no gleam of the individuality, coherence, and beauty, which appear in the great natural idioms, and which do appear to a considerable degree (probably as high a degree as is possible in an artificial idiom) in Esperanto – a proof of the genius of the original author" (Quoted by Smith and Wynne, 41).
6 "The Evolution of the Great Tales", *CH* 269.

of a 'linguistic feeling'" (EPS 64). Both reflect aspects of language development "before the waning of phonetic attention" (EPS 66). Clearly Tolkien employed onomatopoeia; nor did he hesitate to use the "rudest form" of sound imitation.[7] There's a "hard rat-tat" from Gandalf on Bilbo's beautiful green door (*H* 22). The names of the ravens in *The Hobbit*, Carc and Roac, are obvious examples, ravens being noted for their harsh, croaking call (Fimi, EPS 76). Bilbo tries to determine the nature of the underground water he has found after losing the dwarves while escaping the goblins: "when he listened hard, drops drip-drip-dripping" (*H* 93). Or the name of the wretched Gollum, "And when he said *Gollum* he made a horrible swallowing noise in his throat" (*H* 95). The use of "clippety-clippety-clip [...] clippety-clip" to announce the coming of Glorfindel's horse is another (*LotR* 204). The nightly noises which bother Pippin as he tries to sleep in Bombadil's house are "*tip-tap, squeak*" and "*creak, creak, creak*" (*LotR* 125). Such imitative sound-words are italicised in the text, just as the poems and songs are. The name Rauros for the Falls of the River Anduin is onomatopoeic; Tolkien wrote it means "roar rain" but the sound is clearly signified also."[8] *Roverandom*, Tolkien's fanciful retelling of the Man in the Moon nursery rhyme,[9] incorporates a gleeful riot of sound designed to send children giggling. There is cacophony in the skies above the Isle of Dog, "yaps and yelps, and yammers and yowls, growling and grizzling, whickering and whining, snickering and snarling, mumping and moaning, and the most enormous baying, like a giant bloodhound in the backyard of an ogre" (*R* 21). Goblins in *The Hobbit* produce similar sound patterns, "The yells and yammering, croaking, jibbering and jabbering, howls, growls and curses; shrieking and skriking, that followed were beyond description" (*H* 86).

For Tolkien, phonetic symbolism is a refinement of onomatopoeia where there is "a readiness to associate notions with sound-groups [...] the idea or belief or fact that certain combinations of sounds are more fitted to express certain no-

---

[7] Steven Walker discusses the "penetrating onomatopoeia" of Tolkien's prose (133) but he does not relate his findings to Tolkien's theorising about phonaesthetics and when he claims the name *Lalaith* is onomatopoeic with "laughter" he is not using the meaning Tolkien suggests in EPS, for the name imitates the English lexeme but not the sounds of laughter itself. In fact, it comes from the Sindarin river name Nen Lalaith, "water of laughter". The name more precisely falls under the category of sound symbolism or "phonosemantics" (R. Smith 57).
[8] Or" Rush-rain", *TI* 285. Tolkien also referred to words in Quenya "in which r had some phonetic or onomatopoeic significance [...] cf Rauros(se) 'roaring rain' – a name of a large, loud waterfall." QP, PE 19, 99.
[9] For the significance of nursery rhyme in Tolkien, see Mann, 9-36.

tions than to express others [...] [with] sound groups having certain phonetic elements" (EPS 64-65). The Buckland call to arms suggests that the phoneme /f/ might signify words related to fighting, a "sound cluster" (Fimi, fn 21, EPS 75). Freddy Bolger raises the alarm against the Black Riders in Crickhollow with "AWAKE! FEAR! FIRE! FOES! AWAKE" (*LotR* 172, capitals in text) and the same alarm is raised, called "the Horn-cry of Buckland" in "The Scouring of the Shire" (*LotR* 984, also with capitals).[10] Something similar might be happening with the battle cry in *Children of Húrin*, "Lacho calad! Drago morn! Flame Light! Flee Night!", at least in the English translation of the elvish even though the cry uses /fl/ rather than /f/. *The Hobbit* is replete with such sound groups, particularly in Gollum's speech: "'Curse us and crush us'" (*H* 106); "'nassty nosey thing'" (*H* 110); "'creepsy and tricksy'" (*H* 110); "'Bless us and splash us, my preciouss!'" (*H* 95); the Great Goblin also cries "'Slash them! Beat them! Bite them! Gnash them!'" (*H* 85); the narrator himself uses the habit: "they were all grabbed and carried through the crack, before you could say *tinder and flint*" (*H* 80); he describes the goblins who come out hunting for Bilbo as "hooting and hallooing, and hunting among the trees" (*H* 116); and then, "Out jumped the goblins, big goblins, great ugly-looking goblins, lots of goblins, before you could say *rocks and blocks*" (*H* 80). Such phonetic fitness Tolkien suggests "is mostly a product of the association of all words of similar form and similar sound" (EPS 69).[11]

There is one last feature of Tolkien's theorising that reiterates the pleasure of the "word form itself, even unassociated with notion" (ie, meaning) (*ASV* 16-17). In concluding *A Secret Vice*, Tolkien remarks upon our habitual failure to recognise phonetic music:

> In poetry (of our day – when the use of significant language is so habitual that the word-form is seldom consciously marked, and the associated notions have it almost all their own way) it is the interplay and pattern of the notions adhering to each word that is uppermost. The word-music, according to the nature of the tongue and the skill or ear (conscious or artless) of the poet, runs on heard, but seldom coming to awareness. At rare moments we pause to wonder

---

10 If Tolkien did relate the phoneme /f/ with this notion, it might explain his choice of names for Finwe and Feanor, as well as for the unfortunate half-brothers Findis, Fingolfin, and Finarfin.
11 See Tolkien's view of sound symbolism in his review of a Bloomfield article: "Lautsymbolik comes in for scorn [...]. The grouping of words which is here offered both in rhyming and in alliterative series (*flame, flare, flash, &c; flash, splash, &c*) brings out many interesting points of word-formation." Quoted by Fimi, "Introduction" *ASV*, lvi.

why a line or couplet produces an effect beyond its significance; we call it the 'authentic magic' of the poet, or some such meaningless expression. So little do we ponder word-form and sound-music, beyond a few hasty observations of its crudest manifestations in rhyme and alliteration, that we are unaware often that the answer is simply that by luck or skill the poet has struck out an air which illuminates the lines like a sound of music half-attended to may deepen the significance of some unrelated thing thought or read, while the music ran. (*ASV* 32-33)

Perhaps Tolkien's notion of musicality took a cue from the word *usswiggwan* in his beloved Gothic, which Tolkien said did not carry the original meaning of "gather" which *lisan, las,* and *galisans* had, nor the sense of "read" from the Latin *lego,* but meant "'recite' (sing out)" (*L* no. 272, 356). It is well to recall that Tolkien created a mythology in which music preceded language. As Anthony Wood has observed, "When Ilúvatar's cry of 'Ea!' initiates the process of creation, imagery which was previously contained within the aesthetic form of music has now found conscious expression in the form of words."[12] Perhaps it is not surprising that musicality flows in Tolkien's prose, where the notion of "word-form" and "sound-music" is so important.

Where to begin? With a study of texts which demonstrate both the possibilities and the difficulties of stylistic analysis of Tolkien's prose, the various versions of the Túrin Turambar story. The versions of this story range from the recent edition of *The Children of Húrin* edited by Christopher Tolkien (2007) to the earlier versions in *Book of Lost Tales* (1919), *The Silmarillion* (1977), and *Unfinished Tales* (1980). Tolkien first wrote the story of Túrin Turambar in prose, then turned his hand to the alliterative verse form of Old English poetry (early 1920s), and ultimately returned to prose versions. The final version, written c.1950-51 and published in 2007, has been called by Christopher Tolkien the "chief narrative fiction of Middle-earth after the conclusion of *The Lord of the Rings*" (*CH* 281). I'd like to provide excerpts from this final version to demonstrate the kind of cadences and alliterations Tolkien was capable of in modern English prose, albeit he clearly was aiming for a style which suggested heroic times, without being specifically archaic.[13] The risk of such excerpts, as Tolkien observed about another matter, is that of taking a small piece out of

---

12 Wood claims, "while the world is actualised by a word, the cosmology is shaped by music. Indeed, it can be argued that music is the primal language of the world" (Wood 98).
13 Allan Turner investigates archaic style in *The Lord of the Rings* as linguistic register, 393-396.

context.[14] The prose passages chosen here demonstrate strongly the qualities of cadence, rhythm, alliteration, assonance, and repetition that produce the melodious quality.

> There they wandered in great hardship among the hills beneath the sheer walls of the Crissaegrim, until they were bewildered in the deceits of that land and knew not the way to go or to return. (*CH* 35)

> But the wiser were uneasy still, fearing that Maedros revealed his growing strength too soon, and that Morgoth would be given time enough to take counsel against him. "Ever will some new evil be hatched in Angband beyond the guess of Elves and Men," they said. (*CH* 38)

> But Túrin delighted most in Sador's tales, for he had been a young man in the days of the Bragollach, and loved now to dwell upon the short days of his manhood before his maiming. (*CH* 41)

> For a long while the life of the outlaws went well to their liking. (*CH* 136)

> Then the warriors of Nargothrond went forth, and tall and terrible on the day looked Túrin, and the heart of the host was uplifted as he rode on the right hand of Orodreth. (*CH* 176)

> At length as Húrin stood there silent she cast back her tattered hood and lifted up her face slowly, haggard and hungry as a long-hunted wolf. Grey she was, sharp-nosed with broken teeth, and with a lean hand she clawed at the cloak upon her breast. (*CH* 258)

> Now even as Níniel fled away, Túrin stirred [...] (*CH* 248)

> Now the power and malice of Glaurung grew apace, and he waxed fat, and he gathered Orcs to him, and ruled as a dragon-king, and all the realm of Nargothrond that had been was laid under him. (*CH* 221)

> Thingol was heavy-hearted, for it seemed to him that the mood of Morwen was fey; and he asked Melian whether she would not restrain her by her power. (*CH* 200)

> At last worn by haste and the long road (for forty leagues and more had he journeyed without rest) he came with the first ice of winter to the pools of Ivrin, where before he had been healed. But they were now only a frozen mire, and he could drink there no more. (*CH* 182)

---

14 Granted Tolkien was speaking of Medieval Welsh. "The pleasure is not solely concerned with any word, any 'sound-pattern+meaning', by itself, but with its fitness also to the whole style. Even single notes of a large music may please in their place, but one cannot illustrate this pleasure (not even to those who have once heard the music) by repeating them in isolation. It is true that language differs from any 'large music' in that its whole is never heard, or at any rate is not heard through in a single period of concentration, but is apprehended from excerpts and examples" (EW 192-193).

> Beleg sought among the dead for Túrin to bury him; but he could not discover his body. (*CH* 151)
>
> Many songs are yet sung and many tales are yet told by the Elves of the Nirnaeth Arnoediad, The Battle of Unnumbered Tears, in which Fingon fell and the flower of the Eldar withered. If all were now retold a man's life would not suffice for the hearing. Here then shall be recounted only those deeds which bear upon the fate of the House of Hador and the children of Húrin the Steadfast. [...] Having gathered at length all the strength that he could Maedros approached a day, the morning of Midsummer. (*CH* 52)

Several of these passages introduce chapters, but not all. Dialogue also demonstrates these linguistic features. Their qualities are more apparent seen beside the other versions of this last quotation, the opening to The Battle of Unnumbered Tears, (although, because the narratives differ so much, the comparison is not exact). The first is from *The Silmarillion*; the second, *Unfinished Tales*.

> At length Maedhros, having gathered all the strength that he could of Elves and Men and Dwarves, resolved to assault Angband from east and west; and he purposed to march with banners displayed in open force over Anfauglith. [...]
>
> On the appointed day, on the morning of Midsummer, the trumpets of the Eldar greeted the rising of the sun and in the east was raised the standard of the sons of Feanor, and in the west the standard of Fingon, High King of the Noldor. [...] Then in the plain of Anfauglith, on the fourth day of the war, there began Nirnaeth Arnoediad Unnumbered Tears, for no song or tale can contain all its grief. (*S* 224-227 *passim*)
>
> Many songs are sung and many tales are told by the Elves of the Nirnaeth Arnoediad, the Battle of Unnumbered Tears, in which Fingon fell and the flower of the Eldar withered. If all were retold a man's life would not suffice for the hearing; but now is to be told only of what befell Húrin son of Galdor, Lord of Dor-lómin, when beside the stream of Rivil he was taken at last alive by the command of Morgoth, and carried off to Angband.
>
> Húrin was brought before Morgoth, for Morgoth knew by his arts and his spies that Húrin had the friendship of the King of Gondolin; and he sought to daunt him with his eyes. (*UT* 86)

The forerunner of this tale, "Turambar and the Foalókë," differs greatly, with archaic verb forms and where even the name of the great battle was not yet decided; Tolkien uses "Battle of Lamentation", "Unnumbered Tears" and "Uncounted Tears" within the space of fourteen pages (*LT* II, 70, 73, 83). In "The Evolution of the Great Tales" and "The Composition of the Text", Christopher Tolkien provides an explanation of the "formidable complex of manuscripts" concerning the development of Túrin's tale (*CH* 283). What has bearing on this analysis of style is the nature of the succinct synopsis "Sketch of the Mythology" and its development into the *Quenta Noldorinwa*, which Christopher says his father viewed "very much as a *summarising* work" (*CH* 274), that is, a condensing of events and character rather than a creative or aesthetic storytelling narrative.[15] Very clearly, Christopher Tokien's intent in the initial editing of the manuscripts for *The Silmarillion* was to follow the development of action and character rather than to give a fully styled account, a fact which makes questionable any discussion of musicality in it.

On the other hand, it appears that in the 1952 version of Húrin's tale Tolkien worked to establish a style fitting to the tenor of the tale, a style which in some ways echoes qualities of the Old English alliterative verse he wrote in the early 1920s (*CH* 269), qualities which have been identified as belonging to Old English prose as well, particularly as they highlight sound. Janet Bately has described these traits:

> The ornaments of style used by Anglo-Saxon prose writers were many, a significant proportion of them involving patterns of sound. Of these the favourite seems to have been alliteration, while verbal parallelisms, such as the repetition of a word-stem or word-ending and the use of balanced phrases or clauses, are also commonplace features, along with the use of word-pairs that are either synonymous or closely related in meaning. (83-84)

She finds the fullest exploitation of patterns of sound in "the later works of Ælfric and in Wulfstan's writings, which make extensive use of what is often known as rhythmical prose" (84). There are not many published statements from Tolkien about sound patterns in Old English prose although there are many unpublished manuscripts of his lecture notes in Marquette University (Honegger 29) which might contain relevant comments. However, in a 1923 review of an edition of the alliterative prose homily *Hali Maidenhad*, ("In her maiden bliss") Tolkien provided these observations on the 'vehicle', that is, the prose style which harkens back to Old English.

> The vehicle is a rhythmic and highly alliterated prose that has tempted editors of other pieces to see in it a loose verse-form, but which defies such analysis

---

15 As Christopher Tolkien says, "there are brought to light passages of close descriptions or dramatic immediacy that are lost in the summary, condensed manner characteristic of so much Silmarillion narrative writing" (*BL* 13).

> as much as does the rhythmic, alliterative, and highly finished prose of late Old English. In the rhythm and beat of it when read aloud, in its declamatory rhetoric, and in the general character and idiom of its speech, it is apparent that the early Western prose of this type is in the main derived from that Old English tradition, and through it connected with the tradition of Old English alliterative verse, and with the survival of alliterative verse into Middle English in the West [...]. This language was in its day no mere archaic survival of a dying tradition, but was in the closest touch with the living colloquial speech, [...] (Review)

At the very least, this review suggests Tolkien's great interest in the cadences and rhythms that are possible in English prose and which he was to use to great effect in his own writing.

Túrin's tragic tale is not the only story which Tolkien wrote in both alliterative verse and alliterative prose; he did so also for the Beren and Lúthien tale as well.[16] The habit he perhaps learned from studying and teaching *Beowulf*, for which he wrote translations that alliterated in both verse and prose. Christopher Tolkien compares excerpts in both of lines 210-216 of the Old English poem describing the voyage to Denmark. He offers this comparison specifically to show how his father wanted to provide "some suggestions of the rhythm of the original", with the further claim, "I have found nowhere among his papers any reference to the rhythmical aspect of his prose translation of *Beowulf*, nor indeed to any other aspect, but it seems to me that he designedly wrote quite largely in rhythms founded on 'common and compact prose-patterns of ordinary language'" (*B* 8). Here is the passage in modern English prose:

> Time passed on. Afloat upon the waves was the boat beneath the cliffs. Eagerly the warriors mounted the prow, and the streaming seas swirled upon the sand. Men-at arms bore to the bosom of the ship their bright harness, their cunning

---

16 In Beren and Lúthien Christopher claims that when Tolkien returned to the tale after the publication of *The Lord of the Rings* he worked on the verse form (cf. *BL* 257). However, Nelson Goring has noted this comment from Christopher in *The Lost Road*: "At the time when he turned again to the Lay of Leithien [...] he embarked also once more on a prose 'saga' of Beren and Lúthien. This is a substantial text, though the story goes no further than the betrayal by Dairon to Thingol of Beren's presence in Doriath, and it is so closely based on the rewritten form of the Lay as to read in places almost as a prose paraphrase of the verse. It [...] was not known to me when The Silmarillion was prepared for publication. (*The Lost Road, HoMe* V, 295)" (Goring). This prose version is not included in the recent edition of *Beren and Lúthien*; having never been published, it cannot be compared with the prose style of the contemporaneous *The Children of Húrin*. What is also intriguing for this study of musicality is that Christopher Tolkien remembers his father reciting the tale to him, "speaking it without any writing, in the early 1930s" (*BL* 17).

gear of war; they then, men on a glad voyage, thrust her forth with her well-joined timbers. (*CH* 10)

Of the passage, Christopher specifically claims, "this rhythm, so to call it, can be perceived throughout. It is a quality of the prose, by no means inviting analysis, but sufficiently persuasive to give a marked and characteristic tone to the whole work" (*B* 10). This paper argues that not only can Tolkien's theorising about language be found in his prose, both fiction and non-fiction, but also that his profound experience of Old English finds its way into his writing style. His words about its verse can, I suggest, apply also to its prose, words which also highlight the significance of sound and musicality: "And therein lies the unrecapturable magic of ancient English verse [...], filled with the beauty and mortality of the world, [...] aroused by brief phrases, light touches, short words resounding like harp-strings sharply plucked" (OTB 60).

Now to turn to the text which probably demonstrates the greatest range of styles that Tolkien would employ, *The Lord of the Rings*. Its length prohibits comprehensive treatment so discussion reflects observations on individual passages.[17] Tolkien highlighted aesthetics in a letter about *The Lord of the Rings* to his American publishers, in a retrospective statement (June 1955). His comment has often been taken to refer mainly to the elvish languages, but the precise phrasing of his statement suggests a wider net: "there is a great deal of linguistic matter (other than actually 'elvish' names and words) included or mythologically expressed in the book. It is to me, anyway, largely an essay in 'linguistic aesthetic' as I sometimes say to people who ask me 'what is it all about?'" (*L* no. 165, 220). There is one character in *The Lord of the Rings* who is famously (or perhaps infamously) known for linguistic aesthetics, Tom Bombadil. Ursula LeGuin has written an insightful essay exploring rhythmic patterns in the chapter "Fog on the Barrow Downs" as well as in Tom's speech. Most pertinent is her observation that Tom speaks metrically: "His name is a drumbeat, and his metre is made up of free, galloping dactyls and trochees with tremendous forward impetus" (102).[18] She does not find this metrical feature

---

17 In order to observe the limitation on word count, discussion is largely limited to lexemes, cadences, and rhythm and so extensive discussion of how syntax contributes to musicality is omitted.
18 Verlyn Flieger has related Tom's "rhythmic, chanted speech" to the *Kalevala* (SK 141) while Tom Shippey claims Bombadil "does not yet seem to have discovered, or sunk into, prose" (Shippey, *Road* 107).

in dialogue anywhere else in the book, although she says Théoden drops into iambs occasionally (103). Yet it is not only Tom's dialogue that falls into cadences. The prose style of the opening and concluding sentences of the chapter is also marked with mellifluous sound patterns and cadence, more subtly of course than Tom's, as is the opening to "In the House of Tom Bombadil" and much of the narrative of that chapter, as well as Frodo's pique about Tom's play with the ring.[19] At their first dinner, the hobbits "became suddenly aware that they were signing merrily, as if it was easier and more natural than talking" (*LotR* 123). Tom's and Goldberry's enchanting influence on the hobbits–and on readers–derives not just from what they say and do, but from the narrative style which represents them.

Sweetness of euphony is a major characteristic in the presentation of Faramir and Ithilien. The chapter "Of Herbs and Rabbits" shows its calming, soothing effect in the choice of phonemes, in assonance, in rhyme, and in alliteration. The chapter begins with the sentence: "For the few hours of daylight that were left, they rested, shifting into the shade as the sun moved, until at last the shadow of the western rim of their dell grew long, and darkness filled all the hollow" (*LotR* 634). The initial sentences of the subsequent paragraphs show similar traits as do other sentences in the paragraphs:

> The dusk was deep when at length they set out, creeping over the westward rim of the dell, and fading like ghosts into the broken country on the borders of the road [and] for many miles the red eye seemed to stare at them as they fled, stumbling through a barren stony country [...] with hearts strangely lightened they now rested again, but not for long. (*LotR* 634)

The sentence culminating the paragraph which identifies the new terrain echoes with alliteration in a nostalgic summation of the landscape: "Ithilien, the garden of Gondor now desolate kept still a dishevelled dryad loveliness" (*LotR* 636). The paragraph following is replete with doublets and triplets, assonance, alliteration, and rhyme: "tamarisk and pungent terebinth", "walls were already starred with saxifrages and stonecrop," "Primeroles and anemones were awake in the filbert-brakes" (*LotR* 636). No dialogue interrupts this melodious description.

---

19 "He was perhaps a trifle annoyed with Tom for seeming to make so light of what even Gandalf thought so perilously important. He waited for an opportunity [...]" (*LotR* 131).

These episodes come from the parts of *The Lord of the Rings* that we might expect would reflect Tolkien's idea about the heightened effect of sound. However, phonaesthetics are also found in other events of significant emotion to the story. The passage at Weathertop, when Frodo and Aragorn spy the Black Riders, employs alliteration to suggest danger, although it lacks the syntactic complexities and density of the Ithilien passage. This time, Tolkien chose harsh consonants rather than soft ones.

> Slowly they crawled up to the edge of the ring again and peered through a cleft between two jagged stones. The light was no longer bright, for the clear morning had faded, and clouds creeping out of the East had now overtaken the sun, as it began to go down. They could all see the black specks, but neither Frodo nor Merry could make out their shapes, for certain; yet something told that there, far below, were Black Riders assembling on the Road beyond the foot of the hill. (*LotR* 184)

Some of the succeeding paragraphs do not demonstrate such style but others do. Strider's words about defense against the Black Riders show assonance and repetition: "'Let us take this wood that is set ready for the fire as a sign. There is little shelter or defence here, but fire shall serve for both. Sauron can put fire to his evil uses, as he can all things, but these Riders do not love it, and fear those who wield it. Fire is our friend in the wilderness'" (*LotR* 185). The paragraph describing the fire and the surrounding lands also is stylistically marked, as are, slightly, the paragraphs which lead up to Strider's chanting of the tale of Tinúviel, in verse with some lines echoing the metre of Old English poetry (*LotR* 187). The attack of the Black Riders, however, uses balanced parallelism in syntax with inversion: "In their white faces burned keen and merciless eyes; under their mantles were long grey robes; upon their grey hairs were helms of silver; in their haggard hands were swords of steel" (*LotR* 191); Frodo feels "a pain like a dart of poisoned ice pierce his left shoulder. Even as he swooned he caught, as through a swirling mist, a glimpse of Strider leaping out of the darkness" (*LotR* 191).

Yet narrative description in the ensuing flight to the Ford of Bruinen in the next chapter generally lacks phonaesthetics. The long days of heavy marching and toil are described using language consistent with the narrative style of contemporary novels. However, alliteration, adverbial inversion, and rhyme increase with the arrival of Glorfindel the elf: "Suddenly into view below came a white horse, gleaming in the shadows, running swiftly. In the dusk its headstall flickered and flashed, as if it were studded with gems like living stars. The rider's cloak streamed behind him, and his hood was thrown back" (*LotR* 204). To Frodo, the Black Riders "seemed to sit upon their great steeds like threatening statues"; in response to Glorfindel's elvish command, "at once the white horse sprang away and sped like the wind"; "fear now filled all Frodo's mind"; and the waters of the Bruinen "foamed about his feet" (208). The repetition of the /f/ phoneme could again suggest Tolkien's use of sound symbolism. And then the attack culminates, and Book I concludes, with the eucatastrophic effect of Elrond's spell delivered with several alliterations, repetition, adverbial fronting, and embedded subordination:

> At that moment there came a roaring and a rushing: a noise of loud waters rolling many stones. Dimly Frodo saw the river below him rise, and down along its course there came a plumed cavalry of waves. White flames seemed to Frodo to flicker on their crests and he half fancied he saw amid the water white riders upon white horses with frothing manes. The three Riders that were still in the midst of the Ford were overwhelmed: *they* disappeared buried suddenly under angry foam. Those that were behind him drew back in dismay. (*LotR* 209)

Despite these examples, heightened stylistic marking is not pervasive in *The Fellowship of the Ring*. There is nothing in Bilbo's birthday party except the lexical statements of jocularity; Gandalf's fireworks are described without sound effects; even some of the early appearances of the Black Riders are described without heightened phonetic effect, although the attack on Crickhollow certainly is, in addition to the resounding call to arms in Buckland which repeats the phoneme /f/ (*LotR* 172-3). Gandalf's aphorisms to Frodo, which are probably some of the best remembered lines in the novel, are marked by their pithy syntax, lexical repetition, alliteration, and possibly sound symbolism.[20] The attraction of rhyme, metre and specific sound is enacted by the hobbits themselves in the many songs they "hum softly" or sing rather than expressed in the prose. Phonaesthetics in fact is not significantly used until Tom Bombadil appears with his "Hey dol! merry dol! ring a dong dillo!" verse (*LotR* 116), which

---

20 "'So do I,' said Gandalf, 'and so do all who live to see such times. But that is not for them to decide. All we have to decide is what to do with the time that is given us'" (*LotR* 50). And "'Deserves it! I daresay he does. Many that live deserve death. And some that die deserve life. Can you give it to them? Then do not be too eager to deal out death in judgement.'" (*LotR* 58). The sound emphasis here is the voiced dental plosive /d/.

highlights sound rather than rational meaning; for the first time in Book I, it could be said that the prose itself is highly stylistically marked. To bring into prominence the significance of sound could indeed be another purpose of Tom Bombadil. An hypothesis might be that Tolkien in *The Lord of the Rings* was taking his readers on a philological journey back to a time when language was heard differently from the analytical approach of the modern era.

Phonaesthetic pleasure is not the only aspect of Tolkien's theorising that can be found in *The Lord of the Rings*. Ross has argued that Tolkien's naming patterns–Withywindle, Tom Bombadil, Denethor for example–show phonosemantics (Ross 57).[21] In addition to names, word fitness is probably also strongly shown in the orcish attack on the Fellowship in Khazad-dûm where Tolkien reiterates the sound relationship between "doom" and the "boom" of the orcish battle drums, almost an enactment of the movement from onomatopoeia to sound symbolism.[22] As Thomas Honegger has pointed out, "the English word 'doom' with its dark long vowel, final nasal sound and its connotations of judgment and catastrophe may serve as an example" of how the "sound form of a word and the way it expresses the semantic content in a suitable and fitting manner" are related (31). At least part of passage deserves quotation here. It is replete with alliteration:

> Gandalf had hardly spoken these words, when there came a great noise: a rolling *Boom* that seemed to come from depths far below, and to tremble in the stone and their feet. They sprang towards the door in alarm. *Doom, doom* it rolled again, as if huge hands were turning the very caverns of Moria into a vast drum. Then there came an echoing blast: a great horn was blown in the hall, and answering horns and harsh cries were heard further off. There was hurrying sound of many feet. [...] *Doom, doom* came the drum beat and the walls shook. [...] *Doom, boom, doom* went the drums in the deep. (*LotR* 315)

Something of the same long drawn out quality of the vowel and sound fitness also influences Entish not only in the Ents' battle song but throughout Treebeard's speech. The "dark long vowel" is perhaps fitting, with its echoic relationship to doom, for a species that will die out if it fails to find the entwives.

---

21 The names "Rover" and "Roverandom" are other prime examples as well; cf. *R* 26, 28.
22 In discussing a Dutch translation Tolkien says doom has "become a word loaded with senses of death; finality; fate [...] The use in the text as a word descriptive of sound [...] associated with *boom* is of course primarily descriptive of sound but is [...] to recall the noun *doom* with its sense of disaster" (Hammond & Scull 768-9). Tolkien's concept of translation is similar to George Steiner's, "meaning can never be wholly separated from expressive form" (Steiner 240).

There is one last feature of Tolkien's theorising prominent in *The Lord of the Rings*, that of the ability of sound to give pleasure or heightened effect even when unassociated with meaning. Several important scenes show the characters being moved by sound irrespective of meaning. One of the earliest is the hobbits' meeting with Gildor Inglorion and the High Elves when they are trying to evade the Black Riders. "Yet the sound blending with the melody seemed to shape itself in their thoughts into words which they only partly understood" (78). The House of Tom Bombadil provides the hobbits with another experience of words which have an affect outside of their meaning (see Mann 30-32). And after Tom has rescued the hobbits from a Barrow-wight, when Tom explains about the treasures he has taken from the barrow, "the hobbits did not understand his words, but as he spoke they had a vision as it were of a great expanse of years behind them" (*LotR* 142). In Rivendell, at the Hall of Fire, Frodo listens to "the interwoven words in elven-tongues, even though he understood them little [...] Almost it seemed that the words took shape, and visons of far lands and bright things that he had never yet imagined opened out before him" (*LotR* 227). Yet there is another event, not associated with elves, that even more than these shows Tolkien's linguistic theorising: Sam's battle with Shelob, where sound literally shapes Sam's thoughts.

The two chapters, "Shelob's Lair" and "The Choices of Master Samwise", show a high degree of linguistic marking, both syntactically and phonetically. The first chapter opens with a highly rhythmic clause, "It may indeed have been daytime now [...]" (*LotR* 701) but that cadence is not maintained. Yet soon the sentences in the description of Shelob forgo the more common paratactic style in favour of complex syntax. Many sentences are left branched, with adverbials, prepositional phrases, and subordinate clauses preceding the subject and verb. "There agelong she had dwelt, an evil thing in spider-form"; "How Shelob came there, flying from ruin, no tale tells, for out of the Dark Years few tales have come"; "Far and wide her lesser broods, bastards of the miserable mates, her own offspring, that she slew, spread from glen to glen" (*LotR* 707). The description includes multiple uses of alliteration: "But other potencies there are in Middle-earth, powers of night, and they are old and strong" (*LotR* 704); "weaving webs of shadows"; "her evil will walked through all the ways of [Gollum's] weariness" (*LotR* 707), and we are told that Shelob and Sauron "both lived, delighting in their own devices" (*LotR* 708). Frodo and Sam lose any sense of time walking further into the tunnel and that effect seems mimicked by a style which extends syntactically and becomes more ornate in its ascription of wickedness.[23] Reminded by Sam of Galadriel's phial, Frodo cries out in an elvish phrase and "knew not what he had spoken for it seemed that another voice spoke through his, clear, untroubled by the foul air of the pit" (704). And in the succeeding chapter, Sam also speaks out in elvish,[24] and "his tongue was loosed and his voice cried in a language which he did not know", the Elvish hymn to Varda (*LotR* 713).[25] (The two recite different languages, Sindarin and Quenya.)[26] The words without meaning provide Sam with strength and fortitude and he begins his final assault on Shelob. The assonance and alliteration become extremely dense:

> As if his indomitable spirit had set its [the phial] potency in motion, the glass blazed suddenly like a white torch in his hand. It flamed like a star that leaping from the firmament sears the dark air with intolerable light. No such terror out of heaven had ever burned in Shelob's face before. The beams of it entered into her wounded head and scored it with unbearable pain, and the dreadful infection of light spread from eye to eye. She fell back beating the air with her forelegs, her sight blasted by inner lightnings, her mind in agony. Then turning her maimed head away, she rolled aside and began to crawl, claw by claw, towards the opening in the dark cliff behind. [...]
>
> Shelob was gone; and whether she lay long in her lair, nursing her malice and her misery, and in slow years of darkness healed herself from within, rebuilding her clustered eyes, until with hunger like death she spun once more her dreadful snares in the glens of the Mountains of Shadow, this tale does not tell. (*LotR* 713)

The passages on Shelob rival the descriptions of Ithilien with evidence of phonaesthetics. "Linguistic aesthetics" is not always about the sweetness of euphony.

---

23 George Steiner suggests that metrical speech and "syncopated prose" "punctuate our sensations of time-flow" (130).
24 See the discussion on light and the name Elbereth and the two elvish languages in Flieger, *Light* 88-94.
25 Tolkien says of Sam's invocation, "Though it is, of course, in the style and metre of the hymn-fragment, I think it is composed or inspired for his particular situation" (*L* no. 211, 278).
26 Tolkien's discussion of these lines reminds us that there is a middle 'vehicle' of language between prose and poetry, chant; he refers to the invocations as both chant and hymn. Cf. Tolkien, "Notes" 66.

The Hobbit and *Roverandom* are not often considered together, even though they were written during the same stage of Tolkien's life, perhaps because of the long span of time which separates their publication.[27] Yet as the examples in the discussion on sound symbolism show, they share several traits in phonaesthetics. They are books for ears which take a delight in the sounds of words.[28] As the narrator says of Bilbo's long hello to Gandalf, "You will notice already that Mr. Baggins was not quite so prosy as he liked to believe" (*H* 16-7). The same could be said of his story and certainly of the fairy-dog's story.

Similarly to *The Lord of the Rings*, *The Hobbit* moves slowly into phonaesthetics; however, it lacks the broad range of registers that the sequel shows, and does not move into the registers of romance that Turner finds in the sequel (Turner 400). Instead, it appears that Tolkien was pursing an interest in using sounds and "word patterns" to mark dangerous situations and villains that stir the blood. It is worth noting that the dwarves' singing is what moves Bilbo's mind and heart to awake "something Tookish" inside him (*H* 28). There are many examples of what might be incidental alliteration and assonance: "They were on ponies, and each pony was slung about with all kinds of baggages, packages, parcels, and paraphernalia" (*H* 46); "Bother burgling and everything to do with it! I wish I was at home in my nice hole by the fire, with the kettle just beginning to sing!" (*H* 47-48); "Bilbo never forgot the way they slithered and slipped in the dusk down the steep zig-zag path into the secret valley of Rivendell" (*H* 66); "Wind got up, and willows along its banks bent and sighed" (*H* 48).

Gollum's speech regularly displays sibilants: "'Is it nice, my preciouss? Is it juicy? Is it scrumptiously crunchable?'" (*H* 100). "'Shake him. Wake him'" say the wood-elves about Galion (*H* 222). Yet in keeping with Tolkien's claim about the value of the relative effect of euphony, the occurrences of musicality increase as the adventures intensify. The goblins are introduced in a paragraph with a high number of doublets and triplets and long lists, so there is a cumulative effect in the naming of their wickednesses (*H* 83-84). The first description of

---

27 Tom Shippey, "Introduction" xiv: "Like all Tolkien's stories, [*Roverandom*] grew in the telling, being written down, with several of Tolkien's own illustrations, probably around Christmas 1927, and reaching final shape at about the same time as *The Hobbit*, in 1936."
28 See Tolkien's comment in EPS: "I think [sound symbolism] exists and existed, and was once stronger – or rather in languages as the rational and analytic gradually gains upper hand (and the notion gets more separated from the symbol) it is weakened" (EPS 68).

Gollum alliterates: "Deep down here by the dark water lived old Gollum, a small slimy creature. I don't know where he came from, nor who, or what he was. He was Gollum – as dark as darkness" (*H* 94). Tolkien again uses parataxis to describe the stultifying effect of Mirkwood on the dwarves and Bilbo (*H* 175). Lake-town is a town of Men, "who still dared to dwell here under the shadow of the distant dragon-mountain" (*H* 234). The narrator tells us that the Master of Lake-town operated by "giving his mind to trade and tolls, to cargoes and gold, to which habit he owned his position"; he's not a man given to joining his people in singing the King beneath the Mountain song, but this effect of the arrival of the dwarves demonstrates the story's movement into more stirring action (*H* 240). As might be anticipated, Thorin's speech to the Master of Lake-town is full of alliteration and it is what stirs up the memories of the old songs in the people: "'It is true that we were wrongfully waylaid by the Elvenking and imprisoned without cause as we journeyed back to our own land,' answered Thorin. 'But lock nor bar may hinder the homecoming spoken of old. Nor is this town in the Wood-elves' realm'" (*H* 240). Leading up to the "Desolation of the Dragon", even the geographical names alliterate (although not all):

> In two days going they rowed right up the Long Lake and passed out into the River Running, and now they could all see the Lonely Mountain towering grim and tall before them. The stream was strong and their going was slow. (*H* 246)
>
> There was no laughter or song or sound of harps, and the pride and hopes which had stirred in their hearts at the singing of old songs by the lake died away to a plodding gloom. (*H* 247)

Surely "plodding gloom" is sound fitness at work.

These examples, among others, are scattered over the first 250 pages of *The Hobbit*. As the story nears its climax, the linguistic marking becomes more pronounced and common. For instance, when Smaug addresses Bilbo, he speaks with rhyme, alliteration, and repetition, but his words are printed as prose: "'I kill where I wish and none dare resist. I laid low the warriors of old and their like is not in the world today. Then I was but young and tender. Now I am old and strong, strong, strong, Thief in the Shadows!'" (*H* 273-74).

Chapter 14 is dense with musicality. The opening lines to "Fire and Water", which sees the death of the dragon, could be scanned metrically as poetry (*H* 296). The alarm of trumpets is "suddenly sounded" (*H* 297); preparations for defense are described with alliteration and repetition (*H* 298); Bard the saviour is "grim-voiced and grim-faced" but was accused of "prophesying floods and poisoned fish" (*H* 300). The demise of the dragon abounds with alliteration.

> The great bow twanged. The black arrow sped straight from the string, straight for the hollow by the left breast where the foreleg was flung wide. In it smote and vanished, barb, shaft and feather, so fierce was its flight. With a shriek that deafened men, felled trees and split stone, Smaug shot spouting into the air, turned over and crashed down from on high in ruin. Full on the town he fell. (*H* 301)

Note again the use of the phoneme /f/ with fighting. The nasty political wrangling of the townspeople with the Mayor over Bard is of course anything but heroic, and so given without linguistic marking until Bard speaks up, "Why waste words and wrath on those unhappy creatures? Doubtless they perished first in the fire" (*H* 304). And Bard's actions are alliterated: "he had a hard task to govern the people and direct the preparation for their protection and housing. Probably most of them would have perished in the winter that hurried after autumn, if help had not been to hand" (*H* 305).

Yet, interestingly, the subsequent chapters, even that of the Battle of Five Armies, do not show such density of phonaesthetics. There is some, mainly to highlight the valiant deeds of the heroes. The beginning of the battle is marked by cadence: "So began a battle that none had expected; and it was called the Battle of the Five Armies" (*H* 337). The tide turns with the coming of the Goblins: "Still more suddenly a darkness came on with dreadful swiftness! A black cloud hurried over the sky. Winter thunder on a wild wind rolled roaring up and rumbled in the Mountain, and lightning lit its peak. And beneath the thunder another blackness could be seen whirling forward" (*H* 336). Beorn's contribution to the battle rings with repetition: "Swiftly he returned and his wrath was redoubled, so that nothing could withstand him, and no weapon seemed to bite upon him. He scattered the bodyguard, and pulled down Bolg himself and crushed him. Then dismay fell on the goblins and they fled in all directions" (*H* 348). Thorin's deathbed apology to Bilbo achieves its dignity through mild alliteration: "'Farewell, good thief,' he said. 'I go now to the halls of waiting to sit beside my fathers, until the world is renewed. Since I leave now all gold and silver, and go where it is of little worth, I wish to part in friendship from you, and I would take back my words and deeds at the Gate'" (*H* 346). But largely the chapters after the demise of the dragon do not reflect a high degree of linguistic aesthetics, not pleasure, not sound fitness, not sound symbolism. The choice of words and style in fact reflect denouement – or perhaps a reflective focus on the quiet courage of the good thief.

Roverandom shows greater sound symbolism than Bilbo's story, perhaps because it retains so much of the nursery tale and particularly an oral story. In addition to the onomatopoeic parts named above there are expressions such as "tiny tot" (*R* 250) or Rover the moon-dog's "Rat and rabbit it! And we seem to have missed our way altogether, too. Bat and bother it! Let's find a hole to creep in!" (*R* 34). Psamathos rants: "'Done by a seaweed wizard, blister and wart him!' he swore. 'done by Persian plum-picker, pot and jam him'" (*R* 61). And Artaxerxes "will never go back to Persia, or even Pershore" (*R* 55) and the old Greek gods of the sea, "Proteus, Poseidon, Triton, Neptune and all that lot, they've all turned into minnow or mussels long ago" (*R* 55). The name of the wizard Psamatos Psamathides provides much opportunity for humorously educating children about the silent spelling of "ps": "The oldest of all the sand-sorcerers lived in that cove, *Psamathists* as the sea-people call them in the splashing language. Psamathos Psamathides was this one's name, or so he said, and a great fuss he made about the proper pronunciation" (*R* 12).

For comic effect, Tolkien repeats the linguistic play, when Roverandom must address the wizard who has put the curse on him: "Poor Rover was spluttering because he was trying to get in a very polite "'Mr. P-samathos'. Eventually he did. 'P-P-Please, Mr. P-P-P-samathos,' he said, most touchingly. 'P-Please p-pardon me'" (*R* 60). The phonaesthetics is closely connoted with statements about the 'queer' nature of lands frequented by the fairy people. "They visited the valley of the white moon-gnomes (moonums, for short) that ride about on rabbits, and make pancakes out of snowflakes" (*R* 53). In these two books, begun as oral stories for children, Tolkien plays with sound fitness, onomatopoeia, alliteration, for comic effect. Perhaps Tolkien felt that growing up followed the same pattern of loss of sound appreciation that he believed happens with the historical development of language. Or perhaps originally he was simply stimulating his children's delight in the sounds of language – and his own. Yet linguistic aesthetics also play a part in some of Tolkien's most important prose:

> I propose to speak about fairy-tales, thought I am aware that this is a rash adventure. Faerie is a perilous land, and in it are pitfalls for the unwary and dungeons for the overbold [...] In that realm a man may, perhaps, count himself fortunate to have wandered, but its very richness and strangeness tie the tongue of a traveller who would report them. (*TOFS* 27)

With these cadences and alliterations and assonances, Tolkien begins *On Fairy-stories*. Linguistic marking is not something highly present in this essay, but it does distinguish some of his most memorable lines:

> Fantasy remains a human right: we make in our measure in our derivative mode, because we are made, and not only made, but made in the image and likeness of a Maker. (*TOFS* 66)

In this sentence, Tolkien made one of his best-known statements about fantasy. I would hazard a guess that the statement has reverberated as much for its style as for its notion. Tolkien did not limit his use of musicality to his fiction, but used it, if sparingly, to illumine some of his most significant statements about fantasy. Here is his defense of the human desire for a sub-creative art: "In this world, it is for men unsatisfiable and imperishable. Uncorrupted, it does not seek delusion, nor bewitchment and domination; it seeks shared enrichment, partners in making and delight, not slaves" (*TOFS* 64). And here is his culminating statement on eucatastrophe: "Far more powerful and poignant is the effect in a serious tale of Faerie. In such stories when the sudden 'turn' comes we get a piercing glimpse of joy, and heart's desire, that for a moment passes outside the frame, rends indeed the very web of story, and lets a gleam come through" (*TOFS* 76). Even in his prose, Tolkien was "combining nouns and redistributing adjectives" (*TOFS* 64). Perhaps because this essay began its life as a lecture, it owes something in particular to the habit of rhythm which Christopher Tolkien called a "marked and characteristic tone" in Tolkien's prose translation of "Beowulf", a habit found commonly in much of Tolkien's writing (*B* 10).

My intention was not to argue for a "Ronald the Rhymer"[29] but to show that, as Julian Eilmann has argued about Tolkien, "a song sleeps in all things abounding" (182) and that includes Tolkien's prose. Tolkien applied much of his theorising about language in his own writing, theorising which placed significant emphasis on sound and the effects of word patterns. He relied not only on his knowledge of philology but also on his knowledge of phonetics in his writing. As he claimed in *A Secret Vice*, "the human phonetic system is a small-ranged instrument (compared with music as it has now become); yet it is an instrument and a delicate one" (32). No wonder that at one point Tolkien thought of writing an epilogue to *The Lord of the Rings* which would have had Sam reading aloud the Red Book to his children (Hammond & Scull 487). He settled for Frodo prophesying that Sam "will read things out of the Red Book" (*LotR* 1006).

About the Author

MAUREEN F. MANN holds a PhD in English literature from the University of Toronto and taught at Wilfred Laurier University, York University, and the University of Toronto before retiring. Her research included Victorian, 18th Century, and Canadian literature, with other interests in stylistics and communication, medieval literature, and fantasy. She is co-editor of *Laughter in Middle-earth: Humour in and around the Works of Tolkien*, to which she also contributed an article on Nonsense in Tolkien.

List of Abbreviations

ASV	*A Secret Vice*
B	*Beowulf*
BL	*Beren and Lúthien*
CH	*The Children of Húrin*
EPS	"Essay on Phonetic Symbolism"
EW	"English and Welsh"
H	*The Hobbit*

---

29 Tolkien mentions Thomas the Rhymer in *TOFS* 31, a legendary Scotsman who was carried off by a Queen of Fairy and given the choice "to carpe or to harpe" (to write poetry or music) as a gift upon leaving her. See James A.H. Murray's edition of the extant writings of Thomas of Erceldoune.

L   *The Letters of J.R.R. Tolkien*
LotR   *The Lord of the Rings*
LT II   *The Book of Lost Tales II*
OTB   "On Translating Beowulf"
PE   *Parma Eldalamberon*
QP   "Quenya Phonology"
R   "Roverandom"
Review   A review of *Hali Meidenhad*, first published in the *TLS* of April 26, 1923.
SG   *The Legend of Sigurd & Gudrun*
SK   *The Story of Kullervo*
TI   *Treason of Isengard*
UT   *Unfinished Tales*
VA   "Valedictory Address"

Bibliography

BATELY, Janet. "The nature of Old English prose." *The Cambridge Companion to Old English Literature*. Eds. Malcolm Godden & Michael Lapidge. 1st ed. Cambridge: Cambridge University Press, 1991, 71-87.

EILMANN, Julian. "Sleeps a Song in Things Abounding: J.R.R. Tolkien and the German Romantic Tradition." *Music in Middle-earth*. Eds. Heidi Steimel and Friedhelm Schneidewind. Zurich and Jena: Walking Tree Publishers, 2010, 167-184.

FIMI, Dimitra. *Tolkien, Race and Cultural History: From Fairies to Hobbits*. Basingstoke, Hampshire: Palgrave MacMillan, 2010.

FLIEGER, Verlyn. *Green Suns and Faerie: Essays on J.R.R. Tolkien*. Kent, OH: Kent State University Press, 2012.

Splintered Light: Logos and Language in Tolkien's World. 2nd ed. Kent, OH and London: Kent State University Press, 2002.

GORING, Nelson. "I haven't seen too many reactions to Beren and Lúthien on this page so far." *Public Internet Communication*. 6:45 pm EDT, June 28, 2017. Tolkien Society Facebook page. http://bit.ly/2x8bpUj.

HAMMOND, Wayne C. and Christina SCULL. *The Lord of the Rings: A Reader's Companion.* London: HarperCollins, 2014.

HONEGGER, Thomas. "Academic Writings." *A Companion to J.R.R. Tolkien.* Ed. Stuart Lee. Oxford: Wiley Blackwell, 2014, 27-40.

LE GUIN, Ursula K. "Rhythmic Pattern in *The Lord of the Rings*." *Meditations on Middle-earth.* Ed. Karen Haber. New York City, NY: St. Martins, 2001, 101-116.

MANN, Maureen F. "'Certainly not our sense': Tolkien and Nonsense." *Laughter in Middle-earth: Humour in and around the Works of J.R.R. Tolkien.* Eds. Thomas Honegger and Maureen F. Mann. Zurich and Jena: Walking Tree Publishers, 2016, 9-36.

MURRAY, James A.H (ed.). *The Romances and Prophecies of Thomas of Erceldoune.* Early English Text Society, 1875. http://bit.ly/2wzGi6b.

SHIPPEY, Tom. *The Road to Middle-earth.* Revised and expanded edition. Boston, MA: Houghton Mifflin, 2003.

"Introduction." *Tales From the Perilous Realm.* London: HarperCollins, 2008, ix-xxviii.

SMITH, Arden R. and Patrick H. WYNNE. "Tolkien and Esperanto." *Seven: An Anglo-American Literary Review* 17 (2000): 27-46.

SMITH, Ross. *Inside Language: Linguistic and Aesthetic Theory in Tolkien.* 1st ed. Zurich and Jena: Walking Tree Publishers, 2011.

STEINER, George. *After Babel: Aspects of Language and Translation.* London: Oxford University Press, 1976.

TOLKIEN, J.R.R. "A review by J.R.R. Tolkien of *Hali Meidenhad: An alliterative prose homily of the thirteenth century.* Ed. F. J. Furnivall and O. Cockayne, first published in the TLS of April 26, 1923." *Times Literary Supplement.* From the Archives. June 28, 2017. http://bit.ly/2wjJHXb.

A Secret Vice. Eds. Dimitra Fimi and Andrew Higgins. London: HarperCollins, 2016.

Beowulf: A Translation and Commentary. Ed. Christopher Tolkien. London: HarperCollins, 2014.

"Beowulf: The Monsters and the Critics." *The Monsters and the Critics and Other Essays.* Ed. Christopher Tolkien. London: HarperCollins, 2006, 5-49.

Beren and Lúthien. Ed. Christopher Tolkien. London: HarperCollins, 2017.

"English and Welsh." *The Monsters and the Critics and Other Essays.* Ed. Christopher Tolkien. London: HarperCollins, 2006, 162-197.

"Essay on Phonetic Symbolism." *A Secret Vice*. Eds. Dimitra Fimi and Andrew Higgins. London: HarperCollins, 2016, 63-80.

"Notes and Translations." *The Road Goes Ever On*. J.R.R. Tolkien and Donald Swann. 2nd ed. London: HarperCollins, 2002, 66-75.

"On Translating Beowulf." *The Monsters and the Critics and Other Essays*. Ed. Christopher Tolkien. London: HarperCollins, 2006, 49-71.

"Quenya Phonology." Ed. Christopher Gilson. *Parma Eldalamberon* 19 (2010): 68-107.

"Roverandom." *Tales from the Perilous Realm*. London: HarperCollins, 2008, 1-97.

The Book of Lost Tales II. Ed. Christopher Tolkien. London: HarperCollins, 2002.

The Hobbit or There and Back Again. London: HarperCollins, 1998.

The Legend of Sigurd & Gudrun. Ed. Christopher Tolkien. London: HarperCollins, 2010.

The Letters of J.R.R. Tolkien. Ed. Humphrey Carpenter. London: HarperCollins, 2006.

The Lord of the Rings. London: HarperCollins, 1995.

The Silmarillion. Ed. Christopher Tolkien. London: HarperCollins, 1999.

The Story of Kullervo. Ed. Verlyn Flieger. London: HarperCollins, 2015.

Tolkien On Fairy-stories: Expanded Edition with Commentary and Notes. Eds. Verlyn Flieger and Douglas A. Anderson. London: HarperCollins, 2014.

Treason of Isengard. Ed. Christopher Tolkien. London: HarperCollins, 2002.

Unfinished Tales of Numenor and Middle-earth. Ed. Christopher Tolkien. London: HarperCollins, 1998.

"Valedictory Address." *The Monsters and the Critics and Other Essays*. Ed. Christopher Tolkien. London: HarperCollins, 2006, 224-240.

TURNER, Allan. "Style and Intertexual Echoes." *A Companion to J.R.R. Tolkien*. Ed. Stuart Lee. Oxford: Wiley Blackwell, 27-40.

WALKER, Steve. *The Power of Tolkien's Prose*. Basingstoke: Palgrave Macmillan, 2009.

WOOD, Anthony. *Melancholia, mourning and the Quest for renewal in the legendarium of J.R.R. Tolkien*. PhD Dissertation. University of Essex, September 2013.

Petra Zimmermann

"A deep silence fell": Silence and the Presentation of 'Voices' in Tolkien

> "When there is nothing to hear, so much starts to sound. Silence is not the absence of sound but the beginning of listening." (Voegelin 83)

Abstract

In Tolkien's work, silence has a role in two contexts: on the one hand as silence experienced in nature in landscape descriptions, and on the other hand in the field of (musical) presentations of poems. For Tolkien silence (almost) always serves as a background for the sounding of multifarious 'voices' – either of voices from nature or of voices from the characters of the novels who recite a poem or sing a song. The following essay explores how these 'voices' are presented against the background of silence and how Tolkien achieves to hook the reader into the narrative world through the interaction of silence and voices.

Silence is a precious jewel in our time – and it is one that J.R.R. Tolkien had also to strive for, who often complained about the noise caused by cars (see *L* 77, 165, 235, 345). In everyday life, as in music, silence is regarded as the apparent absence of sounds and noise – 'apparent' because complete silence is only possible "in a completely soundproof physical test lab" (Finscher 99). Accordingly, a definition of silence is as follows: "Silence is what we call the acoustic space of quiet, hardly noticeable sounds [...]" (Seidel 1759). Outside of laboratory situations sounds and noises cannot be avoided: "Silence sounds. It is full of quiet noises, tunes, rhythms in the exterior world and from our inside" (Finscher 99).

1 Silence and Voices in Nature

Landscapes of Silence

In Tolkien's novels *The Hobbit* and *The Lord of the Rings* silence is an important part of the landscape descriptions. We encounter it almost everywhere, e.g. in the Dark Forest, in the Old Forest, in Moria, Lothlórien or on the way to Mordor. Often it accompanies darkness and gloom, for example in the forest at the foot of the Misty Mountains ("and all the while the forest-gloom got heavier and the forest-silence deeper", *H* 100) or in the dark passages of Moria ("they heard nothing at all", *LotR* I 406). Landscapes, where there is silence, have got something barren, lifeless, like the Bree-land or Emyn Muil ("in the silence of that barren country", *LotR* II 262) or the surroundings of Mount Doom in Mordor ("like a dead land, silent, shadow-folded", *LotR* III 268). Often silence is connected to coldness, as in the Weather Hills: With the closing in of the "cold evening" "an empty silence" sets in (*LotR* I 247). It is a quiet environment, hostile to life, where breathing is hard, e.g. in Cirith Ungol ("Here the air was still, stagnant, heavy, and sound fell dead", *LotR* II 410), but also in the Old Forest ("The air seemed heavy", *LotR* I 156) and in Fangorn ("queer stifling feeling", *LotR* II 74). Landscapes of silence are characterized by quiet 'inhabitants' that nevertheless mean mischief, the trees: "The forest was grim and silent" (H 153) or "the ill will of the wood pressing on them. So silent was it [...]" (*LotR* I 156).

Silence is not only connoted in a negative way because of the landscape in which it is embedded but also through adjectives connected to it: Silence is "empty" (*LotR* I 247), "dead" (*LotR* I 371), "black" (*LotR* II 280) or "dreadful" (*LotR* III 67). So it is not surprising that from silence comes a feeling of horror and immediately impending danger. In Hollin, Aragorn interprets the absence of sounds as a sign of danger ("'But I have a sense of watchfulness, and of fear'", *LotR* I 371), and in the silence of Moria Frodo feels that "dread came over him" (*LotR* I 414). Even in Lothlórien it creates "the feeling of immediate danger" (*LotR* I 447). And on the Paths of the Dead there is "an utter silence more dreadful than the whispers before" (*LotR* III 67). Silence creates an almost unbearable tension, like the lull before the storm: in this way Mordor is characterized as a quiet land "waiting for some dreadful stroke" (*LotR* III 268).

This kind of silence which is "uncanny and terrible when it is put like pressure on the ear" (Wetz 277), is very difficult to bear. As a result the characters in the novels are repeatedly trying to break the silence. The silence experienced as menacing in the Old Forest weighs so heavily on them that they feel provoked to spontaneous vocal utterances: "Pippin suddenly felt that he could not bear it any longer, and without warning let out a shout. 'Oi! Oi!' he cried" (*LotR* I 155). A little while later Frodo tries to sing an encouraging song, however, he fails when he tries to break the silence: "*Fail* – even as he said the word his voice faded into silence" (*LotR* I 156). Silence cannot be dominated, because it seems to embrace its own will: "the silence seemed to dislike being broken", says a telling passage in *The Hobbit* (62).

So silence is not really "dead" because it can be felt ("Then the silence grew until even Sam felt it", *LotR* I 371; "a silence that could be felt", *LotR* II 313) and it can be perceived through its impact. That silence is by no means "dead" will become clear in the following paragraph: "A few melancholy birds were piping and wailing, until the round red sun sank slowly into the western shadows; then an empty silence fell. The Hobbits thought of the soft light of sunset glancing through the cheerful windows of Bag End far away" (*LotR* I 247). Here the "empty silence" creates a gap which the characters fill with a vision of the distant Shire: The silence is 'animated' by images from within.[1]

The Sounds of the Call of Nature

A vitalization of silence happens especially through separate sounds of nature that are raised against the background of silence. When the term 'silence' is mentioned in *The Hobbit* or *The Lord of the Rings* it is – in accordance with the above-mentioned definition of silence – hardly ever complete soundlessness. Even when "absolute stillness" (*LotR* II 389) is specifically mentioned, it is described in the same breath as being broken by sound: "broken only now and again by the faint rumbling [...]". "Silence sounds" (Finscher 99). Paradoxically, it creates space for the sounds of manifold noise from the external world or

---

[1] This is also made clear in the following passage: "Sam was silent, deep in his memories" (*LotR* III 374).

from within (see appendix 1): the flutter of a bat (*H* 76), spiders talking to each other (*H* 152f.), falling drops of water (*LotR* I 155) or the own heartbeat (*LotR* I 194). Silence creates the condition for perceiving all the subtle sounds from the exterior and interior noises that are usually not noticed: "Then the silence grew until even Sam felt it. The breathing of the sleepers could be plainly heard. The swish of the pony's tail and the occasional movements of his feet became loud noises. Sam could hear his own joints creaking, if he stirred. Dead silence was around him [...]" (*LotR* I 371).

The exterior noise of nature, sounding against this background of silence, is often described as "voices". In *The Hobbit* the voices of animals can often be heard in the silence (e.g. the spiders, as mentioned above), in *The Lord of the Rings* other natural phenomena receive a voice, too: trees, leaves, the wind – and frequently the water. The river Nimrodel in Lothlórien, the river Isen or the stream in Mordor, Morgulduin, they all have a "voice" which sets itself apart from silence:

- "*At length a silence fell,* and they heard the music of the waterfall running sweetly in the shadows. Almost Frodo fancied that he could hear *a voice* singing [...]. 'Do you hear *the voice* of Nimrodel?' asked Legolas" (*LotR* I 440).
- "[...] but they saw and *heard no other strange thing,* save one: the *voice* of the river [Isen]" (*LotR* II 196).
- "Frodo could hear its [Morgulduin's] stony *voice* coming up *through the silence*" (*LotR* II 383, my emphasis).

When the word "voice" is not explicitly mentioned, 'human' manners of articulation such as whispering, laughing, murmuring, sighing, hissing, etc. are attributed to the natural phenomena:

- "all the trees were *whispering* to each other, passing news and plots along in an unintelligible language" (*LotR* I 153f.)
- "the leaves rustled and *whispered,* but with a sound now of faint and far-off *laughter*" (*LotR* I 163)
- "The water began to *murmur*" (*LotR* I 168).
- "nothing but the wind *sighing* over the edges of the stones – yet even that reminded them of breath softly *hissing* through sharp teeth" (*LotR* II 262)
- "hearing nothing but the wind *hissing*" (*LotR* II 301, my emphasis)

The sounds of nature are also connected to musical means of expression: The trees flutter "as of a song half whispered" (*LotR* I 161f.), Old Man Willow sings ("'Hark at it singing about sleep now!'", *LotR* I 162), as does the wind ("the wind sang loudly in his ears", *LotR* III 15). The river Nimrodel causes "the music of the waterfall" (*LotR* I 440), and the "Seven Rivers of Ossir" sound like "music in the Summer" (*LotR* II 84). All these 'voices' and anthropomorphisms create an animation of nature, which even encompasses the physically inanimate natural phenomena as well as the silence: "This is a vociferous world, a world of such vigorous communing among its beings that even the inanimate is involved, and every object in Middle-earth proves at least potentially capable of communication" (Walker 45).

"On the edge of hearing": 'Guided Listening' and Heightened Cognitive Ability

The apparent contradiction of silence and the sound of voices can be resolved when we recognize silence as the precondition of listening closely. It is the silence which draws the attention to the perception of acoustic stimulants, as described in the following passage: "A deep silence fell. One by one the others fell asleep. Frodo was on guard. [...] He listened. All his mind was given to listening and nothing else for two slow hours; but he heard no sound [...]" (*LotR* I 413f.).[2] This concentration ("All his mind was given to listening and nothing else") is typical for an enhanced alertness which is provoked by silence: "The quietness enhances my perception; I take notice of every whisper, hum and buzz" (Voegelin 85). The concentration on acoustic stimulants is increased when at the same time eyesight takes a back seat.[3] This happens in Lothlórien, for example, when the characters walk through the forest blindfolded and are temporarily deprived of their sight: "Being deprived of sight, Frodo found his hearing and other senses sharpened. [...] He could hear many different notes in the rustle of the leaves overhead, the river murmuring away on his right, and the thin clear voices of birds in the sky" (*LotR* I 453).

---

[2] A nice example of focussed listening is Donald Swann's setting of "I sit beside the fire and think" in which a caesura between the lines "I listen for returning feet" and "and voices at the door" causes silence.

[3] "'All ears' are we only when we are not 'all eye'. Only to whom the eye closes, the ear will open" (Utz 7).

We are going to have a closer look at a passage of *The Lord of the Rings* (chapter *The Old Forest*) to see how the characters of the novel are 'taught' to listen in the silence and are drawn into the world of sound by fading out their sight:

> There now seemed hardly a sound in the air. The flies had stopped buzzing. Only a gentle noise on the edge of hearing, a soft fluttering as of a song half whispered, seemed to stir in the boughs above. [...] They looked up at the grey and yellow leaves, moving softly against the light, and singing. They shut their eyes, and then it seemed that they could almost hear words, cool words, saying something about water and sleep. They gave themselves up to the spell and fell fast asleep [...] (*LotR* I 161f.).

There is silence in the Old Forest which, barely beneath the threshold of hearing, is broken by a quiet sound, a flapping, which is akin to a 'song'. Not until the Hobbits close their eyes and neutralize their sight, does the "song half whispered" turns into audible words which have a magic effect. The Hobbits cannot defy the (sleeping) spell ("gave themselves up to the spell") and fall asleep. The silence and the hardly audible noise mean that the characters 'prick up their ears' and listen carefully. The whole setting is characterized by a high sense of uncertainty. We find the words "it seemed" three times. There is "hardly" any noise, the song is "half" whispered, the Hobbits can "almost" understand the words which mention "something" about water and sleep. These phenomena which are characterized by uncertainties lead to constant scrutinizing: Is there any sound at all, is a song really raised and if yes, what is the text? All these uncertainties require a more and more intensive listening so that the mind is completely focused on the acoustic impressions and the hypnotizing effects of the things heard can evolve.[4]

How can we explain the power exerted by sounds and noises over the listeners? Unlike "vision, [which] by its very nature assumes a distance from the object" (Voegelin xi), the listener is part of the world of sounds. He is not able to evade even if he would prefer 'not to listen': "in listening I am in sound, there can be no gap between the heard and hearing [...]" (ibid. 5). This creates "complicity and commitment" (ibid. xv) on the part of the listener who is directly immersing into the world of sound.

---

4 Concerning the song caused by the 'sleeping spell' in Tolkien see also Eilmann 462.

Immersion of the Reader into the World of Sound

According to Walker the fictional characters' process of listening is also spread to the reader who imagines mentally what the characters hear in the novel: "Everywhere we hear with the Hobbits 'the noise of water and the wail of wind and the crack of stone'" (45). Walker's theory implies that the reader has to accomplish the step from the visual perception of the letters while reading to the imagination of the auditive stimulus. There is a neurological basis in our brain that this really happens during the reading process. An experiment concerning the so-called quiet reading has revealed "how the brain simulates aspects of the situations being described by the words on the page" (Petkov/Belin 2013). Petkov and Belin examined which cerebral areas become active while reading passages with direct speech, e.g. statements of fictional characters in inverted commas. Here "voice-sensitive brain regions" are activated which usually only take an active part when we hear real voices. This proves that our brain is able to simulate sounds set into writing and indicated as sounds (here by inverted commas) as real aural impressions – the reader hears inwardly what is written on paper. The text just serves him as a "guiding 'script' that provides the raw material for what will appear on the mental 'screen' and serves to trigger aesthetic illusion" (Wolf 146). The aesthetic distance which still persists between the reading subject and the text while reading ('seeing') the text is suspended through the mental hearing: When the reader hears inwardly what the characters of the novel hear and the listener becomes a part of the surrounding world of sounds, the logical conclusion is that also Tolkien's reader becomes immersed into the (sound-)world of Middle-earth and becomes a part of this narrative world. The mental hearing caused by the interaction of silence and sounds is, consequently, a means to provide the 'immersion' into the story which Tolkien had in mind while writing *The Lord of the Rings*: "'I wanted people simply to get inside this story and take it (in a sense) as actual history'" (Carpenter 198f.).[5]

---

5 Also see the discussion of 'Secondary Belief' in *On Fairy-Stories* (TL 49ff.).

2 Silence and Voices at Song Recitals

Embedding of Recitals of Poems

Silence is not only a topic in connection with nature scenes, it also surrounds the (musical) recital of many of the poems included in *The Lord of the Rings* (see appendix 2).[6] While leaving the Shire, Frodo, for example, pauses silently before he recites the poem "The Road goes ever on and on" ("Frodo was silent", *LotR* I 107). Also in the Old Forest his song "O! Wanderers in the shadowed land" arises from silence ("So silent was it [...], *LotR* I 156) and fades back into it ("his voice faded into silence"). Before Aragorn strikes the "Song of Beren and Lúthien" on Weathertop, "he was silent for some time" (*LotR* I 257), and at the end of the singing he briefly lapses into silence again: "Strider sighed and paused" (*LotR* I 259). Aragorn, Legolas and Gimli silently gaze after the boat with Boromir's corpse ("For a while the three companions remained silent", *LotR* II 17), before Aragorn starts the "Lament for Boromir". Treebeard is silent, too, before and after reciting his song "In the willow-meads of Tasarinan" (*LotR* II 84f.). And in the Orc-tower Sam's Song contrasts strongly with the eerie silence: "It was quiet, horribly quiet" (*LotR* III 220).

Here we recognize the same pattern as in the descriptions of the landscape: The 'voice' (reciting a poem or a song) contrasts against the background of silence or falls back into the silence. Here silence is also used to turn the attention to the sounding voice. However, the voices are no longer merely *described* but are allowed space for a lyric-musical interlude in which the full poem or song is recited.

Thus silence before and/or after the insertion of the poem represents a pause – for the reciting person or his surroundings – before the change of genre takes place, from the prose of the novel to the lyricism of the poem. This shift of genres is accompanied by a different manner of articulation which, for example, is indicated clearly at Aragorn's sung recital of the "Song of Beren and Lúthien" where it is stated: "[he] paused before he *spoke* again" (my emphasis).

---

6 There is no connection between recitals of poems and songs and silence in *The Hobbit*.

The shift of genres also indicates a different "construction of 'reality'" (Beil 13), that is to say a shifting from the "empirical code" of prose, where an event is (re-)narrated, to the "imaginary code" of poetry that "[transcends] everyday speech, the contingency of empiricism and [creates] the 'impression of a closed and self-consistent world'" (Beil 35). According to Beil, this implies a "presentness" of the poem (392) which interrupts the chronological-linear narrative flow for a moment. Silence introduces this transition into the timelessness of the poem in a coherent way because in the silence the linearity of time seems to be abrogated: "Total presentness is the principle of its perception" (Seidel 1764).

The passage in which, before and/or after the recital of a poem, there is complete silence or hush is just one part of a multi-layered network of information surrounding the recital of verse and which is called a "semantic co-text" elsewhere (see Zimmermann 60). Information about the kind of recital, the authorship, the tradition of poetry, or the effect on the listeners all contribute to the visualisation of the scene and draw the attention of the reader to participate in the listening: "The songs [in this case the recitals of Songs in Goethe's *Wilhelm Meister*, P.Z.] virtually ask for *listening* to a voice and not 'just' spelling them out as versified texts" (Beil 321). This results in a 'manual for listeners' for the reader who can experience inwardly the sequence and the effect of the performance, and even takes the part of the singer himself:

> Instead of just inspiring the imagination, this presentation tempts the readers to leave the narrow area of fiction and to read so carefully as if they could hear, murmuring the words themselves, the sound of this *voice* and each word it recites. […] Suddenly it is us who speak, who take the singer's part, and his voice becomes our voice (Beil 391f.).

Thus, we find the 'guided listening' here, too, which enables the readers to become immersed into the narrative world by the shift of silence and voices and many other 'aural clues'.

The voice in the recitation clue 'chant' and silence

We are going to have a closer look at the presentation of the voice against the background of silence by taking the examples of three songs which, according to their semantic surroundings, have the recitation clue 'chant'.

1 Aragorn on Weathertop (*LotR* I 257ff.)

"He was silent for some time, and then he began not to speak but to chant softly: *The leaves were long, the grass was green* [...]. Strider sighed and paused before he spoke again."

2 Gimli in Moria (*LotR* I 411f.)

"He rose and standing in the dark he began to chant in a deep voice, while the echoes ran away into the roof. *The World was young, the mountains green* [...]. 'I like that!' said Sam 'I should like to learn it. *In Moria, in Khazad-dûm!* But it makes the darkness seem heavier, thinking of all those lamps. Are there piles of jewels and gold lying about here still?' Gimli was silent. Having sung his song he would say no more."

3 Treebeard in Fangorn (*LotR* II 84f.)

"Treebeard fell silent, striding along, and yet making hardly a sound with his great feet. Then he began to hum again, and passed into a murmuring chant. Gradually the hobbits became aware that he was chanting to them: *In the willow-meads of Tasarinan* [...]. He ended, and strode on silently, and in all the wood, as far as ear could reach, there was not a sound."

The poems sprinkled through *The Lord of the Rings* are sometimes recited but most of them are sung or – as in these three examples – recited in a kind of sing-song ('chant'). All three examples give the impression that the word 'chant' was not chosen accidentally but that the narrator puts a certain effort into it, taking the word centre stage to make the reader aware of it. In example 1 he puts an emphasis on 'chant' by isolating it from mere reciting ("not to speak").

In example 2 'chant' is emphasized by information about the pitch ("in a deep voice") and the spreading of sound ("the echoes ran away into the roof"). Eventually, in example 3 'chant' appears twice, first as a noun ("a murmuring chant"), and then as a verb ("he was chanting"). It seems as if the narrator is pointing directly to this word.

What does 'to chant' mean? There is the following definition in Merriam-Webster: "to sing words and especially religious prayers by using a small number of musical notes that are repeated many times". In addition to that, as an intransitive verb 'chant' means "to celebrate or praise in song or chant"[7] (ibid.). Two aspects of 'chant' seem to be especially important: On the one hand there is an emphasis on melodic simplicity ("small number of musical notes") and repetition ("repeated many times") which make 'chant' seem to be something in between singing and a heightened form of speech. On the other hand 'chant' has a religious context ("especially religious prayers"): A 'sacred' text is intonated for the purpose of praise.[8]

An example of the use of the noun 'chant' is the Gregorian Chant, a monophonic Latin chant where the words of the Bible are intonated as a part of the Christian mass and take a special effect: "Through the Gregorian modulations, he [man] discovers a privileged space where his being momentarily can rest, aloof from the daily trials. To tell the truth, Gregorian chant gives a glimpse of paradise to those who wish it" (Tomatis, *Pourquoi Mozart*, quoted in Bourmaud). As a regular churchgoer Tolkien was acquainted with Gregorian Chant and could experience its effect himself: "To Tolkien, a conservative Catholic, Gregorian chant would have been the music of *holiness* and closeness to God" (Bratman 143, my emphasis).[9] Tolkien obviously uses the term 'chant' with deliberation because what they sing about is 'sacred' to each of the three characters:[10] They all have a strong inner relationship with the contents of their poems. Aragorn makes recourse to his own love story with the elf Arwen by means of telling the

---

[7] These shades of meaning result from the etymology of the term 'chant', which derives from the old French 'chanter'. 'Chanter' encompasses apart from 'sing' also 'celebrate' (see *Online Etymology Dictionary*).
[8] See also the definition at Wiktionary: "To sing or intone sacred text."
[9] In this context Bratman points to the 1952 tape recordings in which Tolkien recited his poem "Namárië" in the style of a Gregorian chant (see 143).
[10] The acoustic in example 2 is characterized by high ceilings which reminds of the acoustics in churches.

story of Beren and Lúthien. His strong emotional involvement while chanting the poem and the following narration is revealed by his "strange eager face": "His eyes shone, and his voice was rich and deep" (*LotR* I 260). Gimli's inner relationship to the text of the song is obvious because it is about the former splendor of Moria at the time of his ancestors. Finally, Treebeard praises bygone days when he wandered in the lost 'paradise' of Tasarinan in the First Age.

In all passages there is the contrast between a reality perceived as depressing and a bygone, lost world touched – as in the above quotation about Gregorian chant – with the juxtaposition of "daily trials" and "glimpse of paradise". Aragorn chooses the poem at the request of Sam who wants to escape the darkness of the night: "'I would dearly like to hear more about Elves; the dark seems to press round so close" (*LotR* I 257). Aragorn clearly couches the intended effect in terms of his chant: "it may lift up your hearts" (ibid.) – an effect which subsides in the same moment that Aragorn finishes his chant: "Frodo felt a cold dread creeping over his heart, now that Strider was no longer speaking" (*LotR* I 260). Gimli's chanting of the *Song of Durin* is a reply to Sam's dismissive verdict of Moria as "darksome holes" (*LotR* I 411): "'This is the great realm and city of the Dwarrowdelf. And of old it was not darksome, but full of light and splendor [...]'" (ibid.). Treebeard's song, a praise of the "broad days" (*LotR* II 84), can be regarded as an antithesis to the degenerated condition of Fangorn Forest, about which the Hobbits are told by Treebeard (see *LotR* II 82f.).

All three lyrical interpolations transcend reality in the sense of the "imaginary code" (Beil 35, see above) and create a 'Secondary World' (within the secondary world of Middle-earth created by Tolkien) which enables the fictional characters to escape this reality for a moment. According to *On Fairy-Stories*, a secondary world is evoked by enchantment: "Enchantment produces a Secondary World into which both designer and spectator can enter [...]" (TL 54). The word 'enchantment' is etymologically connected to 'chant',[11] so that it is not completely unreasonable that the recitation clue 'chant' has a share in creating the 'enchantment' which is necessary for the creation of the secondary world. The enchantment has an effect not only on the singers

---

11 The old French term 'chanter' from which developed the English 'chant' is based on the Latin 'cantare' which also forms the etymological basis for 'enchantment' (see Online Etymology Dictionary).

but also on the listeners and even – as in example 3 – on the surroundings: the whole forest is silent.

In this context it figures prominently that the presentation of the poem is a *performance* for an audience. In example 1 the presentation takes place at the request of the 'audience' (the Hobbits), in example 2 the singer assumes a pose ("He rose") and in example 3 it is explicitly stated that "he was chanting to them [Merry and Pippin]". Here the author makes use of silence again because in all three examples the singers fall quiet after the performance, both before *and* after in examples 1 and 3. This shift of silence and voices reproduces a ritual that is usual at performances in front of an audience (as in a concert hall). The performer and the listener put themselves in the right mood for the presentation, and after the performance they let the things heard continue to have an effect in silence: "Before the music starts, musicians and listeners take the inward turn for a long moment, and after it has ended they allow the music some time to pass into silence" (Seidel 1760).

What happens in the silence when performer and listener "take the inward turn for a long moment"? At the beginning of this essay we noted that silence leaves space for developing inner images. What can happen within the listener during the silence between the musical performances will be demonstrated with the following passage (see also Eilmann 431):

> After they had eaten, Goldberry sang many songs for them, songs that began merrily in the hills and fell softly down into silence; and in the silences they saw in their minds pools and waters wider than any they had known, and looking into them they saw the sky below them and the stars like jewels in the depths (*LotR* I 182).

The silence creates space which the fictional characters fill with images that transcend ("wider than any they had known") or even invert reality ("the sky below them"): The phases of silence let them immerse themselves into a 'secondary world'. Also in the three passages mentioned above silence serves to attune to the imagined 'secondary world' or facilitate its further development. The contrast between 'secondary world' and reality is especially revealed in example 2 when Sam's attempt to create a connection to reality ("'Are there piles of jewels and gold lying about here still?'") is answered by silence: Gimli has been drawn into the secondary world from which he will not be 'startled out' until later (see *LotR* I 413).

What does this imply for the readers? Due to the 'guided listening' they not only become a part of the sound-world of Middle-earth but the fictional characters also show them how to succeed in filling 'space' and imagine a secondary world: "it is deliberately insufficient to realize Middle-earth without active imaginative involvement of the reader" (Walker 112). Here the text of the novel has a similar function to the score of a piece of music, that only makes sense when the sound is realized: "From the point of the reader, [...] the text is like a musical score waiting to be performed. [...] In the case of texts, the process of actualization involves not only the process of 'filling in the blanks' [...] but also simulating in imagination the depicted scenes, characters, and events [...]" (Ryan 45). In the same way as the 'silent reading' of music "constitutes an inner listening that transforms signs into sound" (Dahlhaus 23), the 'silent reading' of the novel serves the readers as a guide for the 'inner listening' and 'inner seeing' and enables them to be drawn into the world of Middle-earth. All the senses are "bodily inside" (TL 54) and we are not mere "spectators" (TL 54) and listeners but through "active imaginative involvement" secondary creators, too: "Tolkien's style is at every level from word choice to narrative pattern an open invitation to subcreation" (Walker 172).

About the Author

PETRA ZIMMERMANN, Dr. phil., studied Musicology, German Philology, History and German as a Foreign Language in Cologne and Berlin. After teaching German at Polish and Chinese universities for several years, she worked as a lecturer and deputy head of the language centre at TU Clausthal between 2007 and 2016. In addition, she acts as a translator for Chinese medicine textbooks. Since 2008 various teaching activities in the field of musicology and intercultural communication. She has published several articles on Tolkien, e.g. in *Tolkien's Poetry*, focussing on different aspects of *The Lord of the Rings* and its drafts printed in *The History of Middle-earth*.

List of Abbreviations of Tolkien's Works

H	*The Hobbit*
L	*The Letters of J.R.R. Tolkien*
LotR	*The Lord of the Rings*
TL	*Tree and Leaf. Smith of Wootton Major. The Homecoming of Beorhtnoth*

Bibliography

BEIL, Ulrich Johannes. *Die hybride Gattung. Poesie und Prosa im europäischen Roman von Heliodor bis Goethe.* Würzburg: Königshausen & Neumann, 2010.

BRATMAN, David. "Liquid Tolkien: Music, Tolkien, Middle-earth, and More Music." *Middle-earth Minstrel. Essays on Music in Tolkien.* Ed. Eden, Bradford Lee. Jefferson, NC andLondon: Mc-Farland & Company 2010, 140–170.

BOURMAUD, Fr. Dominique: "Doctor Mozart and Gregorian Chant." *The Angelus* (2010). https://www.olrl.org/misc/mozart.shtml. 25 March 2017.

CARPENTER, Humphrey. *J.R.R. Tolkien. A Biography.* London: Unwin Paperbacks, 1977.

"Chant." *Merriam-Webster Dictionary.* https://www.merriam-webster.com/dictionary/chant. 25 March 2017.

"Chant." *Online Etymology Dictionary.* http://www.etymonline.com/index.php?term=chant. 25 March 2017.

"Chant." Wiktionary. https://en.wiktionary.org/wiki/chant. 25 March 2017.

DAHLHAUS, Carl. *Musikästhetik.* 3rd ed. Köln: Musikverlag Hans Gerig, 1976.

EILMANN, Julian. *J.R.R. Tolkien. Romantiker und Lyriker.* Essen: Oldib-Verlag, 2016.

FINSCHER, Ludwig. "Stille in der Musik." *Festschrift Walter Wiora zum 90. Geburtstag.* Ed. Christoph-Hellmut Mahling. Tutzing: Schneider, 1997, 99–112.

PETKOV, Christopher I. and Pascal BELIN. "Silent Reading: Does the Brain 'Hear' Both Speech and Voices?" *Current Biology* 23/4 (2013): 155–156. http://www.cell.com/current-biology/fulltext/S0960-9822(13)00005-5. 25 March 2017.

RYAN, Marie-Laure. *Narrative as Virtual Reality. Immersion and Interactivity in Literature and Electronic Media.* Baltimore, MD and London: Johns Hopkins University Press, 2001.

Seidel, Wilhelm. "Stille." *Die Musik in Geschichte und Gegenwart*. Sachteil. vol. 8.2., revised ed. Kassel: Bärenreiter, 1998, col. 1759–1765.

Tolkien, J.R.R. *The Hobbit*. London: Unwin Paperbacks, 1979.

The Letters of J.R.R. Tolkien. Selected and edited by Humphrey Carpenter, with the assistance of Christopher Tolkien. London: HarperCollins, 1995.

The Lord of the Rings. Vol. I–III: *The Fellowship of the Ring, The Two Towers, The Return of the King*. 3rd ed. London: Unwin Paperbacks, 1979.

Tree and Leaf. Smith of Wootton Major. The Homecoming of Beorhtnoth. London: Unwin Paperbacks, 1975.

Utz, Peter. *Das Auge und das Ohr im Text. Literarische Sinneswahrnehmung in der Goethezeit*. München: Fink, 1990.

Voegelin, Salomé. *Listening to Noise and Silence. Towards a Philosophy of Sound Art*. New York City, NY and London: Continuum, 2010.

Walker, Steve. *The Power of Tolkien's Prose. Middle-Earth's Magical Style*. New York City, NY: Palgrave Macmillan, 2009.

Wetz, Franz Josef. *Die Magie der Musik. Warum uns Töne trösten*. Stuttgart: Klett-Cotta, 2004.

Wolf, Werner. "Illusion (Aesthetic)." *Handbook of Narratology*. Ed. Peter Hühn. Berlin: de Gruyter, 2014, 144–159.

Zimmermann, Petra: "'The glimmer of limitless extensions in time and space': The Function of Poems in Tolkien's *The Lord of the Rings*." *Tolkien's Poetry*. Eds. Julian Eilmann & Allan Turner. Zurich and Jena: Walking Tree Publishers, 2013, 59–89.

Appendix 1: Examples of silence and sounds in descriptions of landscapes

passage in text	place	silence	sound
H 76	Misty Mountains	and still he heard no sound of anything …	… except the occasional whirr of a bat by his ears
H 100f.	Forest at the foot of the Misty Mountains	so quiet …	… that he could hear the dwarves' breathing like a loud noise
H 153	Dark Forest	in the silence and stillness of the wood …	… he realized that these loathsome creatures were speaking one to another
LotR I 155	Old Forest	There was no sound, …	… except an occasional drip of moisture
LotR I 156	Old Forest	So silent was it …	… that the fall of the ponies' hoofs […] seemed to thud in their ears
LotR I 194	the ancient Barrow	There was a sudden deep silence, …	… in which Frodo could hear his heart beating
LotR I 371	Hollin	Then the silence grew until even Sam felt it.	The breathing of the sleepers could be plainly heard.
LotR I 406	Moria	There was no sound …	… but the sound of their own feet
LotR I 406	Moria	they heard nothing at all, …	… unless it were occasionally a faint trickle and drip of unseen water
LotR I 440	At the river Nimrodel	At length a silence fell, …	… and they heard the music of the waterfall
LotR I 447	Lothlórien	There were no more sounds.	he could hear stealthy movements at the tree's foot far below

LotR II 33	Rohan	There was a silence in the empty fields, …	… and Gimli could hear the air moving in the grass
LotR II 262	Emyn Muil	Sometimes in the silence of that barren country …	… they fancied that they heard faint sounds behind them
LotR II 301	The Dead Marshes	they walked in silence with bowed heads, seeing nothing, and hearing nothing …	… but the wind hissing in their ears
LotR II 382f.	At the Cross-roads	and all about them was silence; silent woods; the silence seemed deeper	Frodo could hear its stony voice coming up through the silence
LotR III 69	Paths of the Dead	No other sound they heard	he cried in a great voice
LotR III 197	At the Black Gate	There was a long silence	the silence was broken suddenly. There came a long rolling of great drums
LotR III 246f.	Mordor	All now seemed dry and silent	he caught the sound of trickling
LotR III 248	Mordor	when suddenly in the stillness of the night …	… they heard the sound that all along they had secretly dreaded: the noise of marching feet

Appendix 2: Embedding of poetry and songs in passages of silence

passage in text	silence before	poem/song	silence after
LotR I 59		*The Road goes ever on and on*	He paused, silent for a moment.

LotR I 107	Frodo was silent. [...] Suddenly he spoke, aloud but as if to himself, saying slowly:	*The Road goes ever on and on*	
LotR I 156	So silent was it [...]	*O! Wanderers in the shadowed land*	*Fail* – even as he said the word his voice faded into silence.
LotR I 167		*Hop along, my little friends*	After that the hobbits heard no more.
LotR I 174		*And that proved well for you*	He fell silent again [...]
LotR I 194		*Ho! Tom Bombadil, Tom Bombadillo!*	There was a sudden deep silence [...]
LotR I 257	He was silent for some time [...]	*The leaves were long, the grass was green*	Strider sighed and paused before he spoke again.
LotR I 411ff.		*The World was young, the mountains green*	[...] Gimli was silent. Having sung his song he would say no more.
LotR II 17	For a while the three companions remained silent [...]	*Through Rohan over fen and field*	
LotR II 84f.	Treebeard fell silent, striding along, and yet making hardly a sound with his great feet.	*In the willow-meads of Tasarinan*	He ended, and strode on silently, and in all the wood, as far as ear could reach, there was not a sound.
LotR III 220f.	It was quiet, horribly quiet.	*In western lands beneath the Sun*	'Beyond all towers strong and high,' he began again, and then he stopped short. [...] But now he could hear nothing.
LotR III 375	Sam was silent [...]	*Still round the corner there may wait*	
LotR III 376		*A! Elbereth Gilthoniel!*	Frodo and Sam halted and sat silent in the soft shadows [...]

Music of Different Texts and Characters

Renée Vink

Dance and Song: "The Lay of Leithian" between "The Tale of Tinúviel" and "Of Beren and Lúthien"

Abstract

Beren and Lúthien: from "ballet" to "opera". This is a tale rich with music and song, from Daeron's "music from a pipe unseen" to Lúthien's song before the inexorable Mandos. However, though music was always present in this core story of *The Silmarillion*, it was not always the predominant art form. This paper shows how, over the years, Tolkien turned it from a story dominated by dance into one in which music and song gradually began to take over until only one dancing scene remained. But it was the most important one, and the most personal to Tolkien himself.'

In a world created through music, like Tolkien's Arda, frequent references to music in general and song in particular, do not come as a great surprise. Among the characteristics of his major opus, *The Lord of the Rings*, the many and various songs stand out. All sentient races sing at some point, including the Eagles, and even the Orcs are caught singing. Tolkien's works have inspired a great many individual songs, but also several complete operas and operatic cycles, in classical style and otherwise, (Bratman, *MeM* 161). Among the more popular subjects is the story of Beren and Lúthien. This is sung in part by Aragorn in Chapter XI of *The Fellowship of the Ring*, first told in full in *The Silmarillion* and also found in several different versions and stages of completion throughout *The History of Middle-earth*. The most notable version is the long, unfinished poem "The Lay of Leithian" published in *The Lays of Beleriand* (*LB*), and partly republished in the recent volume *Beren and Lúthien*. While the "Narn I Hîn Húrin", the tale of the hapless Túrin Turambar and his sister Nienor, can be said to be Tolkien's Middle-earth version of a classical tragedy, the tale of Beren and Lúthien is undoubtedly the most operatic of his stories.

The first complete, though brief opera about these two was composed by Paul Corfield Godfrey from the UK during the 1980s. It was partly inspired by a draft libretto of Denis Bridoux, discovered by the composer while he was working on a text of his own. It forms part of an electronic music cycle based on *The Silmarillion* and was not meant to be staged.¹ In the early 1990s the professional American tenor, Adam Klein, embarked on his opera *Leithian*, a concert version of which was performed in 2006 and 2007 in New York City.² This opera has 17 vocal parts (!) and was written with a full symphonic orchestra in mind, plus an organ and a choir (Kasimierczak 72-3). Both these works are composed in the classical tradition. Rather different is the album *The Lay of Leithian* of the Italian group Ainur (2009). This is a rock opera based on Tolkien's tale, performed by a group of 25 singers and instrumentalists;³ whether it has ever been performed on stage is unknown to me.

In addition, there are other compositions covering the full story of Beren and Lúthien, like the "Elven Oratory" *The Lay of Leithian* by the Russian group Lind Erebros,⁴ and the Lay-based album *Of Lúthien and Beren* by the Australian composer Michael Horsphol.⁵ But these have few lyrics or are entirely non-vocal, and certainly do not qualify as operas. The number of standalone pieces based on episodes of the story, with or without lyrics is still greater. As "The Lay of Leithian" is not exactly mainstream Tolkien fare, this is quite remarkable.

A reason for this could be that, whereas music and song mostly have an ornamental function in widely read and hugely popular texts like *The Hobbit* and *The Lord of the Rings*, in the legend of Beren and Lúthien they permeate the story to a much greater degree than is the case elsewhere, and achieve more (despite the singing of Bombadil, or the battle hymn of the Ents). In addition, they often move the intrigue forward. Most of the songs could be cut from the Ring epic – and have been so in the film version – without detracting too much from the story that is being told. In the case of Beren and Lúthien this is simply impossible.

In an article in a Polish online art journal, Katarzyna Klag discussed the role of music in Tolkien's life along with the story's biographical elements, its

---

1 https://sites.google.com/site/paulcorfieldgodfrey/beren-and-luthien (accessed 19-1-2017).
2 A recording of these performances, held at St. Michael's Episcopal Church, NYC, as well as the full libretto, can be found here: http://www.thehalloffire.net/forum/viewtopic.php?t=553 (accessed 19-1-2017). The quality of the recording is suboptimal, though.
3 https://it.wikipedia.org/wiki/Lay_of_Leithian (accessed 27-1-2017), in Italian. A sample of the music can be found here: https://www.youtube.com/watch?v=p7JOtwDwrL.
4 https://www.youtube.com/watch?v=XsBNyiVyIb0 (accessed 19-1-2017).
5 http://mp3red.su/30187059/michael-horsphol-luthien-and-beren-defeat-morgoth.html (accessed 19-1-2017).

pivotal importance in the Legendarium, and the musical aspects of the 19th *Silmarilion* chapter, "Of Beren and Lúthien". Among other things she points at the remarkable number of characters who engage in some form of music, either in the narrative itself, or in descriptions of previous events (Klag 15-19). These are the two protagonists, Daeron, Finrod, Sauron and Melian. Klag also calls attention to the power of music and song, especially Lúthien's song, whose power increases as the story progresses (16).

Though aware of its existence, Klag does not discuss "The Lay of Leithian" separately. Early on in her article she writes: "At the beginning of the chapter 'Of Beren and Lúthien', it is stated that this story itself gave rise to a song called 'Lay of Leithian'" (14). A bit further on she calls it "a tale which became a song" (14-5). This is not entirely correct. What is stated in the first paragraph of the chapter in question is: "Of their lives was made the Lay of Leithian, Release from Bondage, which is the longest save one of the songs concerning the world of old" (*S* 162). Klag's phrasing suggests that a story telling the legend of Beren and Lúthien preceded the Lay. However, the statement in *The Silmarillion* rather suggests that the Lay *was* the account of their lives in poetic form, or in the form of a song (the word "lay" is either derived from Old and Middle High-German *leich*, meaning something played, "a melody or a song" (OED, lay n. 4), or from Irish *laid*, also meaning "song" (Zipes 62).

This may look like splitting hairs, but I hope to show it is not. The Lay is not based on an earlier story with mostly the same content. It is, in fact, the earliest version of what would later become Chapter 19 of *The Silmarillion*. Tolkien's first 'instalment' of this story, "The Tale of Tinúviel" in *The Book of Lost Tales 2* (3-68) contains the seeds of the later legend of Beren and Lúthien, but it is by no means the same narrative. Beren, for instance, is not a mortal but an Elf of a different kindred. His beloved does not yet bear the name Lúthien. The character of Dairon (later spelled Daeron) is her brother instead of her unsuccessful suitor, and Sauron – or Thû, as he is called in the Lay – is a large, evil feline called Tevildo in the Tale. But there is another, more significant difference.

To support my further argument, I shall present the results of a minor piece of quantitative research I carried out on three of Tolkien's texts telling the story of Beren and Lúthien. In reverse chronological order these are 1) the final and best-known version: the account in the 1977 *Silmarillion*; 2) "The Lay of Leithian", the poetic version in *The Lays of Beleriand*; 3) "The Tale of Tinúviel" in *The Book of Lost Tales 2*.

My research involved counting words, terms and phrases having to do with music in a wider sense. Included were:

- the names of song birds and their sounds: nightingale, lark; trilling, warbling, shrilled
- the names of musical instruments and sounds associated with them: trumpets, bells, harps, a flute, horns, viols; playing (of music), fluting, piping, drumming, ringing, blowing, knelled; words like voice (if raised in song) and lament (if melodious, and not just complaining with words), and related words like singing, chanting, choirs, croons.
- musicians: minstrels
- technical terms: notes, musical themes
- instances in which a word that does not by definition have a musical connotation was combined with some form of music, such as "listening to a song".[6]

I decided furthermore that it might also be a good idea to count all the times the word "dance" (both the nominal and verbal forms) occurred, mostly because dance is closely associated with music, especially in the scene of Beren's first sighting of Lúthien in the Forest of Neldoreth. This turned out to be a momentous decision, as will become clear later.

The three texts are not of equal length. "Of Beren and Lúthien" is 25 pages long and the first version of "The Tale of Tinúviel" 38 pages. But "The Lay of Leithian" counts over one hundred pages. Now the verses of the Lay only take up about three fifths of prose, but even with 60+ pages this version is longer than the Tinúviel text, and more than twice as long as the *Silmarillion* chapter. In addition, the last part of the Lay (covered by about four pages in *The Silmarillion*) was never written. This needs to be taken into consideration when looking at the results.

---

6 This list is not complete; hopefully the reader will take me on my word if I promise that I did not count any wolf howling, though I was tempted to do so. Also, I can't guarantee the count is exact: all these music words and terms were hand-counted, so I may have overlooked a couple.

Those results are interesting, to say the least. As might be expected, the Lay contains almost three times as many music-related words as the *Silmarillion* chapter. But it contains about four times as many music words as the Tale, which turns out to be considerably more than one would expect. However, the most striking difference lies in the frequency in which words for song and dance are used in these three texts.

In "The Lay of Leithian" the noun *song*, together with various declension forms of the verb to *sing*, is by far the most frequent musical term. The same applies to "Of Beren and Luthien". In comparison, there are far fewer dance terms in the Lay; there the ratio song: dance is about 4:1. One would expect this ratio to be approximately the same in "Of Beren and Lúthien", but surprisingly, given the iconic character of the dancing scenes in the legend, in this late text the ratio song: dance is only about 16:1! In fact, words for dance occur only twice in the entire *Silmarillion* chapter, both in the episode where Beren watches Lúthien dancing in the forest to the music of Daeron's pipe, follows her and later sees her dance again. All other references to dancing have disappeared, including the passage in the Lay in which Beren and Lúthien dance together (*LB* 185).

Before going on, I shall briefly dwell on this discrepancy, which is mostly caused by the fact that in the *Silmarillion* any references to Lúthien dancing before Morgoth have vanished: there, she only sings. At least, it is hard to read phrases like "suddenly she eluded his sight" (*S* 180) and "Lúthien catching up her winged robe [the bat-fell of Thuringwethil] sprang into the air, and her voice came dropping down like rain" (*S* 181) as references to dance.

The absence of any dance terms in this scene in the *Silmarillion* chapter is interesting. The commentary to Canto XIII makes us none the wiser; it briefly refers to this chapter (*LB* 306), but without mentioning Lúthien's dance. In the "Quenta Noldorinwa", chronologically the version of the legend following the Lay and published in *The Shaping of Middle-earth* (*SME*), she still both dances and sings in Angband (*SM* 112). Nor does Christopher Tolkien refer to her dance in his list of alterations made by Tolkien sr. to the "Quenta Noldorinwa", published in *The Lost Road* (298-302). He does admit that the list is not exhaustive (302), but it seems rather unlikely that a change like this would have been glossed over.[7] In the recently published volume *Beren and Lúthien*, where he presents the evolution of the story from *Lost Tales* onwards, the commentary contains no specific reference to Lúthien dancing before Morgoth's throne either.

Commenting on "A Passage from the Sketch of the Mythology", Christopher states that "there have been great changes in the legend" (that is, since "The Tale of Tinúviel"), but he only mentions Thû, and Beren's new identity as a mortal Man (*BL* 91, 31). So, the decision to remove Lúthien's dance from the Angband episode came late in the development of the story. As I hope to show, it was the logical next step after the Lay.

Now in the Lay words like "song" and "singing" occur eighty-five times, against nineteen dance words, a ratio of more than 4:1. As the poem was never finished, song words are underrepresented here: Lúthien's plea before Mandos is missing from the Lay. In "Of Beren and Lúthien" the Mandos episode has five song words. Extrapolating, the Lay could have had between ten and fifteen of them, in which case the ratio song: dance for this text would be about 5:1.

But in fact, it is not necessary to add the Mandos episode to the count for the Lay. In "The Tale of Tinúviel", things are different anyway. In this text, I counted thirty-three dance words against twenty-one song words. So, dancing occurs more frequently than singing in this first version of the story; it is the dominating "music term" here. As might be expected, most of the dancing is done by Tinúviel. But her mother, here named Wendelin or Gwendeling, is renowned both for her singing and her dancing (*LT II*, 8), unlike Melian in *The Silmarillion*. Tinúviel is introduced as a dancer (10), and at some point, Beren even asks her to teach him how to dance. Her answer is typical for the atmosphere of the Tale: "'[I]f thou wouldst dance, follow me,' said the maiden, and she danced before Beren away, [...] and ever and anon she would look back and laugh at him stumbling after, saying 'Dance, Beren dance! as they dance beyond the Bitter Hills!'" (*LT II*, 12)

In the Tale, Tinúviel dances both Karkaras (the evil wolf Carcharoth's equally unpleasant predecessor) and then Morgoth to sleep; in the case of the latter

---

7 The "Later Quenta Silmarillion" in *WJ* (*HoMe* 11), does not contain a version of the episode in Angband and has therefore been omitted from this discussion.

the dance is enhanced by a song. In Canto XII of the Lay, however, she commands the wolf to sleep without singing or dancing (*LB* 291), and in Canto XIII she first puts all movement in Angband to a halt through the power of her song alone (298), before finally dancing and singing before Morgoth and his minions:

> [...] And her wings she caught
> then deftly up, and swift as thought
> slipped from his grasp, and wheeling round,
> fluttering before his eyes, she wound
> a mazy-wingéd dance, and sped
> about his iron crowned head.
> Suddenly her song began anew;
> and soft came dropping like a dew
> down from on high in that domed hall
> her voice bewildering, magical,
> and grew to silver-murmuring streams
> pale falling in dark pools in dreams.
>
> She let her flying raiment sweep,
> enmeshed with woven spells of sleep,
> as round the dark void she ranged and reeled.
> From wall to wall she turned and wheeled
> in dance such as never Elf nor fay
> before devised, nor since that day;
> than swallow swifter, than flittermouse
> in dying light round darkened house
> more silken-soft, more strange and fair
> than sylphine maidens of the Air
> whose wings in Varda's heavenly hall
> in rhythmic movement beat and fall.
> (*LB*, Canto XIII 4056-4079)

As a result, every living thing present, including Beren, falls into a deep sleep. Morgoth is the last to succumb, but not even he can resist Lúthien's magic. The text indicates she is fluttering around in mid-air using the bat wings she appropriated from Thuringwethil. Nonetheless the description obviously refers to a dance: this word is used twice, and as her movements are being compared to rhythmic wing-beating, they have to be rhythmic as well. The dance references that were cut from the *Silmarillion* chapter are still present here.

In all, and put a little frivolously, the Tale is more of a ballet, in the sense of a story using dance (usually to music, though in the Tale this is not always the case). The Lay on the other hand is more of an opera, a theatrical drama set to music, featuring some dancing but a great deal more singing,[8] with the *Silmarillion* chapter as its retelling in musical prose, in which the role of dancing has been reduced even further. This important shift, which took place at an early stage in the legend of Beren and Lúthien, has hitherto been overlooked. The brother-turned-secret-admirer, the Elf-turned-mortal and the cat-turned-Maia have drawn more attention, as characters are wont to do. (And the shift from Elf to Mortal was, of course, a very important one.)

So, between the Tale and the Lay, the role that singing plays in the story increased markedly. The Tinúviel of *Lost Tales* is first and foremost a marvellous magical dancer; though the Lay's Lúthien Tinúviel remains a great dancer, her greatest power lies in her song.

Now it is well-known that the character of Lúthien Tinúviel was inspired by Tolkien's wife Edith Bratt. During a walk in the woods at Roos in Yorkshire in 1917 she danced for him, and the scene in which Beren first comes upon Lúthien dancing in Doriath is largely based on this biographic event. In a letter to Christopher written after Edith's death in 1971, Tolkien stated that "in those days her hair was raven, her skin clear, her eyes brighter than you have seen them, and she could sing – and *dance*" (L 420; italics by Tolkien). From this, it should be clear that it was above all Edith's dancing that had made an indelible impression upon her husband. Therefore, it does not come as a great surprise that dancing plays such an important role in the first version of the story based on this episode: this was a young Tolkien's tribute to his beloved.

In the introduction, "The Tale of Tinúviel" is said to have been written in 1917 (*LT II*, 3) – that is, shortly after the event, when the image of Edith's dancing was fresh in Tolkien's mind. "The Lay of Leithian" dates from a later period: 1925-1931. So, between 1917 and the second half of the 1920s, the centre of artistic and musical gravity in the story, so to speak, shifted from dance to song. A shift that did not merely result in the use of far more music words, but also to more episodes featuring some form of music, from three in the Tale to ten in the Lay, and to more different singers and musicians as well. The Tale has only three, the Lay twice that number, not counting birdsong. Not even that of

---

8 The form operas generally took until far into the 19th century, before Wagner introduced the music drama, banishing the ballet.

Melian's nightingales: their role remains the same in both versions. Generally, birdsong is of no significance to the plot, though it does serve to boost the musical quality of the story. Something that happens much more often in the Lay than in the Tale, one might add.

The Tale has three musicians: Tinúviel's mother Wendelin or Gwendeling, her brother Dairon, and Tinúviel. Of these, only the latter sings in the story proper; her mother's singing is told, not heard, while Dairon is a piper and does not sing at all. In the Lay, this still applies to Daeron, but Lúthien's mother Melian sings 'on stage' now (*LB*, Canto XIII 172). Felagund and Thû sing, and so does Beren, while (Lúthien) Tinúviel sings more often than she does in *The Silmarillion*, and much more often than in the Tale. There, she does so merely when she causes her hair to grow to escape from her tree prison, and later before Morgoth. In the Lay she is found singing happily in the forest of Neldoreth and singing sadly besides the river Esgalduin. She sings to rescue Beren from Thû's dungeons. She heals him with a staunching song after the fight with Curufin and Celegorm, and again while nursing him after Carcharoth has bitten his hand off. As the Lay never reaches this episode, I did not take her song before Mandos into consideration, though it would probably be justifiable to do so. All other versions of the story have this episode; undoubtedly Tolkien intended to end the Lay with it as well.

The number of "singing moments" in the Tale is limited to three: Tinwelint (>Thingol) hearing the music of Gwendeling's (>Melian's) nightingales (here I did take birdsong into consideration), Tinúviel singing to make her hair grow, and then again while dancing for Morgoth. In the Lay we have all the additional times Lúthien raises her voice in song (see the list given in the previous paragraph), the singing contest between Felagund and Thû, Beren's desperate song in the dungeon and the one he sings after he has left Lúthien behind for her own good – or thinks he has.

In one case, the significance of music in the Lay lies in its absence rather than its presence. The moment Beren has left to fulfil his promise to her father, Lúthien ceases to sing (*LB*, Canto IV, 1186). The music stops – a sad and ominous silence before a storm of events, somewhat reminiscent of the silence in Valinor after Ungoliant has swallowed the light of the Two Trees.

The question is: what may have caused this shift in emphasis, this movement away from physical self-expression towards the combination of words and music generally known as "song"? One explanation could be that Tolkien began to consider the Tale too whimsical in tone for a story ultimately about death and – qualified – resurrection. We are given several possible endings; in the most elaborate of these, both the Elvish protagonists die but are allowed to return from Mandos as mortals, who "oftentimes were [...] seen dancing magic dances down the hills, and their name became heard far and wide" (*LT* II, 40). To many, the thought of seeing two mortals dance magically out of a tale that is bittersweet rather than happy, may seem a bit odd.[9] Compare this ending to the conclusion of Aragorn's song in *The Lord of the Rings*, where the two lovers "passed away in the forest singing sorrowless" (*FR* I, Ch. 11). Song seems a more suitable note to end the story on – although knowing Aragorn's song beforehand may have led this reader to entertain preconceived notions regarding the proper ending. There is no telling how exactly the Lay was to end, but if the "Quenta Noldorinwa", which follows the Lay and was written for the most part in 1930 (*SM* 76), is any indication, Beren and Lúthien would not have been seen dancing away over the hills.

Leaving aside the (again, speculative) possibility that everyday married life with its many down-to-earth concerns may have dampened the dancing mood of Roos, there is yet another explanation for the increased preponderance of song over dance in the Lay. In 1917, Tolkien's mythology was still in its very early stages, but the years from 1918-1920 saw the genesis of a very important new element, one that would lend structure to Tolkien's future Legendarium: *the Music of the Ainur*.

It is in this new element in the mythology that we encounter the birth of the idea that Arda was conceived through music. Unlike the Tale of Tinúviel, the first version of the "Music of the Ainur" in *The Book of Lost Tales 1* (*LT I*, 52-63) does not differ fundamentally from the later "Ainulindalë" as published in the 1977 *Silmarillion*; it sprang more or less fully orchestrated from the mythmaker's head. The second version in *The Lost Road* (155-166) was already renamed

---

9 Not to mention that it's peculiar to see two mortals dance *magic* dances – unless this is supposed to be metaphorical magic.

Ainulindale, which is the Quenya term for "the music of the Ainur"; Quenya *lindalë*, "music", stems from the root *LIN2* meaning "sing" (*LR* 369, *S* 361).

In his introduction to this second version Tolkien's son writes that his father followed the *Music of the Ainur* "fairly closely, though rephrasing it at every point" (*LR* 155). Later, the wording of the Ainulindalë in *LR* "became the vehicle of massive rewriting many years later" (156), but this need not concern us here. The rewrites postdate the Lay and chiefly involve changes to Tolkien's cosmology (ibid.). They are of no significance for this article, which is not about the "Ainulindalë" and focuses chiefly on the influence it had on the story discussed here.

What *is* significant, is that the concept of music underlying the existence of Arda, of the world itself, had now set "the tone for all that [was] to follow", to use the words of Verlyn Flieger (2005, 140). Which meant that music also had to become somehow instrumental to the story of Beren and Lúthien, to the shaping of its structure and texture. This demanded not merely a rewrite or rephrasing, but a thorough reconceptualising. The toning down of the dance motif that dominated the Tale, making it secondary to the music, was among the results. In two steps – from the Tale to the Lay and other writings from this period, and from there to the final text published in *The Silmarillion* – most of the references to dancing were cut from the story. In the end, only the iconic image of Beren watching Lúthien dance in the forest of Neldoreth with the eyes of a lover remained, becoming all the stronger for it. The disappearance of Lúthien's dance in Angband constitutes a logical conclusion of the legend's textual history.[10]

A fair number of Tolkien scholars have discussed the Music of the Ainur and its role and meaning in Tolkien's Legendarium, but few make a direct connection between his musical creation account and the role and power of song in

---

10 We do not necessarily have to assume that the idea of Lúthien (who probably always evoked his wife Edith) dancing before Morgoth's lewd eyes, over the years became less and less attractive to Tolkien. However, it could be the case: as dancing is a more physical act than singing, it also has stronger sexual connotations, which was probably more than acceptable while it was Beren who was watching, but less so when it was Morgoth. On the other hand, in the Lay Lúthien is dancing in the air in semi-darkness using a pair of bat wings, which is not exactly a description evoking Salomé dancing before King Herod. The cover of the Blind Guardian album *Nightfall in Middle-earth* does not seem to get it quite right.

the story of Beren and Lúthien. Among the most recent are Jensen (2010) and Coutras (2016).[11] They both use the final versions of the Ainulindale and the chapter about Beren and Lúthien in the 1977 *Silmarillion*. It will be interesting to see to what they have found, and whether their findings regarding the Silmarillion chapter also apply to the Lay.

Jensen dwells only briefly on the connection in his article "Dissonance in the Divine Theme". He compares the music of Lúthien to that of Ilúvatar himself: "Luthien uses musical themes, weaving them sorrowfully yet triumphantly together, as Ilúvatar weaves his theme with Melkor's dissonance to make a triumphant world" (Jensen 108). As a summary, this is somewhat sketchy, to put it mildly. It also leaves the impression that Lúthien remains fully in charge of her own fate, the way Ilúvatar remains in charge of the creation of Arda, which is obviously not the case. She is unable to influence the outcome of Mandos' intercession, for instance.

However, Jensen is not entirely wrong when he sees a parallel between Ilúvatar and Lúthien. This parallel becomes even stronger when the version of the creation account from *LT* 1 is brought into play: there we are told that Ilúvatar "sang into being the Ainur first" (52).[12] In the "Ainulindale" the Ainur are the offspring of his thought, and instead of singing he proposes a theme to them. But Ilúvatar remains the "prime musician"; as Devaux writes: "The music of the Ainur comes from Ilúvatar, not only the theme of the music [...] but also the faculty of musicianship" (94). The Ainur then "fashion" Ilúvatar's theme into music with voices "like unto instruments and choirs" – Tolkien takes care to tell us that their singing is not to be taken literally (*S* 15).

---

11 Slack makes the connection, too, when she comments on Lúthien's song releasing the bonds of winter and bringing about spring: "Lúthien's voice calls forth things in the physical world, because her voice and presence are manifestations of the first voice that called forth the whole of creation" (Slack 70). But this reference to the Music of the Ainur is indirect and implicit, and the wording is imprecise in view of what Tolkien really wrote. Elsewhere Slack compares Beren's oath to avenge his father to the "Valar singing Middle-earth into being", because "there, also, words fashioned the course of the future" (ibid. 67). Again, the wording is imprecise and Slack disregards the musical component of the song of the Ainur.

12 Thoughts of a parallel between Ilúvatar and Tinúviel the Dancer may evoke associations with the "Lord of the Dance" (the hymn, that is - https://www.youtube.com/watch?v=PEAIJV6CmtA -, not the Irish dance company): "I danced in the morning when the world was begun" etc. But the text dates from in 1963 and any connections with Tolkien do not reside in the Legendarium. He might have approved, though. Incidentally, the song is not Irish: the melody is American and the lyrics were written by an Englishman.

One of these Ainur is Melian, Lúthien's mother, whose musical aspect is embodied in her nightingales. In the Tale, this mother was "a fay, a daughter of the gods" (*LT II*, 10); it was only later that she became a spirit from the Timeless Halls beyond Eä before descending to Arda as a Maia and taking a body. This also affected the status of her daughter, who was born half Elf, half Maia. As Coutras writes: "As an incarnate being, Lúthien exists and lives within the Great Music; yet, as one of 'divine race', she herself has the potential to participate in the Music. As such, she weaves her own song into themes of creation and into the eternal themes of Ilúvatar" (115).

As shown before, Lúthien is the character who sings most in the story. Some of her songs are merely mentioned, some are described, like the one she sings before Mandos at the end of chapter 19 of the *Silmarillion* (*S* 187). "Her song becomes 'unchanged' and 'imperishable', suggesting its eternal quality" (Coutras 115). Especially "imperishable" is a significant term in the context of Tolkien's mythology. Only one other thing in it is called imperishable, to wit the Secret Fire burning at the heart of the World, the Flame Imperishable with which Ilúvatar "kindled" the Ainur in the beginning (*S* 15). This suggests a direct link between Lúthien's song before Mandos and the great Music of the Ainur in which her mother participated. "Her song draws upon the eternal, for she herself is descended from Melian, who once dwelt in the 'Timeless Halls'", writes Coutras (109). She even goes as far as calling Lúthien a "god", be it in quotation marks (116).

It could be argued that Coutras is overstretching her point here. When Carcharoth denies Beren and Lúthien entry into Angband, Tolkien writes that "suddenly some power, descended from of old from divine race, possessed Lúthien" (*S* 180), suggesting that she does not always and not by definition dispose of such powers. Therefore, we should be careful which of her deeds and feats we ascribe to her semi-divine origins. It may seem hard to believe that Lúthien could, for instance, have "released the bonds of winter" so that "frozen waters spoke, and flowers sprang from the cold earth where her feet passed" (*S* 165), if she had not been the daughter a Maia. But in *FotR*, Galadriel claims to have done a similar thing: "I sang of leaves, of leaves of gold, and leaves of gold there grew: / of wind I sang, a wind there came and in the branches blew" (*FR* II, Ch 8). Galadriel is not semi-divine, only a very powerful Elda, but apparently no less capable of influencing nature and the elements with her song than Lúthien is.

Nor should we forget her brother, Finrod, another great singer: he can hold his own against Sauron for quite a while, only succumbing in the end because, like all the Noldor who left Valinor against the counsel and wishes of the Valar, he is under the Curse of Mandos (*S* 88, 171). As an eternal spirit from before the creation of Eä, Sauron was by definition more powerful than Finrod, of course. He is a fallen Maia, a moral stain that most likely affects his powers: he is unable to overcome Huan the Hound (*S* 175), who possibly is a Maia himself (*MR* 410). But Finrod is a fallen Elda. If he had been unaffected by the Curse of Mandos, the odds might have been more even, so to speak, though even so it is dubious whether Finrod would have been victorious.[13]

In *The Silmarillion*, for instance in Ch. 5 of the "Quenta" ("Of Eldamar and the Princes of the Eldalië", *S* 57-62) we are told that the Valar became the instructors of the Eldar in the Blessed Realm. It is possible that Elves like Galadriel and Finrod learned their singing skills there, before the Noldor returned to Middle-earth. In the case of Galadriel, who dwelled in Doriath during most of the First Age, it is possible she was instructed by Melian the Maia, a singer herself. That Lúthien learned a great deal from her mother, seems obvious. In any case, the Elves probably had had a natural talent for developing song magic, enhanced by the teaching of the Ainur.

To return to Lúthien's song before Mandos: The Lay does not cover this episode, while Tolkien only introduced both the Flame Imperishable and the Maiar to his Legendarium after the publication of *The Lord of the Rings*. However, Melian, in the Tale described as a fay and a daughter of the gods, has already acquired the epithet "divine" in the Lay (*LB*, Canto III, l. 455), while her daughter is "half Elven-fair and half divine" (ibid., 493, 174). This seems a considerable step up from the Tale, where Tinúviel was simply identified as an Elf (e.g. *LT II*, 25, 33). How far up, compared to the version in the *Silmarillion*? The Mandos episode, absent from the Lay, cannot help us here.

---

13 Regarding the power of (Elvish) song, see also Eilmann, 448-465.

The passage where Lúthien's song turns winter into spring is more enlightening. The Tale does not contain anything of the kind, but in the lay "snowdrops spring beneath her feet" and a frozen brook thaws after she has passed (*LB*, Canto III, l. 701-704). There is no suggestion, however, that it is her singing that causes this. When she finally does sing, winter is already dying; she dances "until the dawn of spring", yet the bonds that break when she chants "some wild magic thing" are not those of winter but the bonds that hold Beren enthralled (ibid., 717-722). In other words, the ingredients are all present, but they have not yet quite fallen into place.

The episode best comparable to the plea before Mandos is the one where Lúthien influences another of the Ainur with her song, the scene before Morgoth's throne.[14] In "Of Beren and Lúthien" the song she sings there is "of such surpassing loveliness, and of such blinding power", that he [Morgoth] listened perforce' (*S* 180). In Coutras' view "songs of power draw their potency from the Great Music that frames the structure of reality. Lúthien's song draws upon that same timeless reality; its 'profound and dark'[15] quality corresponds to the 'Outer Void', which lay beyond creation and time" (109).

What do the earlier texts have? In the Tale, Tinúviel dances for Melko, meanwhile singing a song from the gardens of Lórien that her mother, the fay, taught her. Her voice is described as "low and wonderful", and very beautiful.

> The voices of nightingales were in it, and many subtle odours seemed to fill the air of that noisome place [...], and Ainu Melko for all his power and majesty succumbed to the magic of that Elf-maid, and indeed even the eyelids of Lórien had grown heavy had he been there to see. (*LT II*, 33)

Tolkien does not explain how the magic of the "Elf-maid" Tinúviel can have had power over two divine spirits, one of them not morally inferior to her at all. Also, the idea that Lórien would have become sleepy seems incompatible with the tone and general drift of the later versions, where the Valar are rarely described in such anthropomorphic terms. If her mother's song

---

14 Lúthien's songs of power on the bridge to Sauron's isle (*LB* Canto IX, 251-2; *S* 174) are another example. But the differences between the Tale and all later versions are huge here, and Sauron is a lesser Ainu.
15 *S* 181, in Coutras' book provided in an end note. It is actually Lúthien's voice, not her song, that is described as "profound and dark" in this scene, but I do not think this undermines Coutras' interpretation.

contributes to the effect of Tinúviel's magic, as seems to be the case, it is in a rather instrumental way, more like an acquired trick than an example of the power of her singing.

Much of the corresponding passage in the Lay has already been quoted earlier, but I will repeat the relevant lines here: "Soft came dropping like a dew / down from on high in that domed hall / her voice bewildering, magical / and grew to silver-murmuring streams / pale falling in dark pools in dreams" (*LB*, Canto XIII, l. 4063-67). Bewildering magic, instead of surpassing loveliness and blinding power. Softness, instead of a force to which Morgoth cannot shut his ears. The word "dark" is there, but not as a quality of Lúthien's voice. It appears that Tolkien has not yet quite found his own voice (and no, this is not just because of the 'rhyme' hall – magical); in the Lay we are still in a fairy-tale, not in a legend aspiring to myth, though the shape of things to come is already visible.

Concluding, it can be said that the legend of Beren and Lúthien Tinuviel, as published in *The Silmarillion*, was informed and transformed in stages by the story of the Music of the Ainur. Over the years, it turned from a somewhat whimsical fairy tale featuring dance and song into a mythical opera composed of poetic and musical words and images, instead of music notes. The Ainulindale, the great chorus of the divine spirits before Ilúvatar the Creator, manifests itself in Tolkien's work first and foremost, and increasingly so, in the powerful and magical singing of Lúthien Tinuviel, the semi-divine maiden whose mother was one of the Ainur. From a dancer and sometimes a singer in "The Tale of Tinúviel", Lúthien became a singer and dancer in "The Lay of Leithian". Finally, she became the true representative and, in a way, the embodiment of all that is beautiful, pure and powerful in the Great Music of creation, briefly as a dancer – Tolkien's tribute to his wife dancing for him among the hemlock flowers lasted to the end – but more emphatically and richly, as a singer of the Great Song.

About the Author

RENÉE VINK studied Scandinavian languages and German in Leiden and Gothenburg. She has translated several texts by Tolkien into Dutch, among them his *Beowulf*, *Beren and Lúthien*, *The Fall of Gondolin*, and the poetry in *The Legend of Sigurd and Gudrún*. Also, she is a co-founder of Unquendor, the Dutch Tolkien Society, and has authored a number of papers on Tolkien for journals like *Tolkien Studies*, *Hither Shore* and *Lembas Extra*. In 2012 her monograph *Wagner & Tolkien: Mythmakers* appeared. In the past Renée was active as an author of medieval mystery stories (in Dutch).

List of Abbreviations of Tolkien's Works

L	*The Letters of J.R.R. Tolkien*
LB	*The Lays of Beleriand*
LotR	*The Lord of the Rings*
LR	*The Lost Road*
LT I	*The Book of Lost Tales 1*
LT II	*The Book of Lost Tales 2*
MR	*Morgoth's Ring*
S	*The Silmarillion*
SME	*The Shaping of Middle-earth*

Bibliography

AGAN, Cami D. "Lúthien Tinúviel and Bodily Desire in the Lay of Leithian." *Perilous and Fair. Women in the Works and Life of J.R.R. Tolkien*. Eds. Janet Brennan Croft and Leslie A. Donovan. Altadena, CA: Mythopoeic Press, 2015, 168-188.

BRATMAN, David. "Liquid Tolkien: Music, Middle-earth and More Music." *Middle-earth Minstrel*. Ed. Bradford Lee Eden. Jefferson NC: McFarland, 2010, 140-170.

COUTRAS, Lisa. *Tolkien's Theology of Beauty*. London: Palgrave Macmillan, 2016.

DEVAUX, Michaël. "The origins of the Ainulindalë." *The Silmarillion. Thirty Years On*. Ed. Allan Turner. Zurich and Berne: Walking Tree Publishers, 2007, 81-110.

EILMANN, Julian. *J.R.R. Tolkien, Romantiker und Lyriker.* Essen: Oldib Verlag, 2016.

FLIEGER, Verlyn. *Interrupted Music. The Making of Tolkien's Mythology.* Kent, OH and London: The Kent State University Press, 2005.

JENSEN, Keith W. "Dissonance in the Divine Theme: The Issue of Free Will in Tolkien's Silmarillion." *Middle-earth Minstrel.* Ed. Bradford Lee Eden. Jefferson, NC: McFarland, 2010, 102-113.

KASIMIERCZAK, Karolina Agata. "Unfolding Tolkien's Linguistic Symphony." *Arda Philology* 2. Ed. Beregond Anders Stenström. Proceeding of the Second International Conference on J.R.R. Tolkien's Invented Languages, Omentielva Tatya, Antwerp, 2007, 56-79.

KLAG, Katarzyna Wiktoria. "The Power of Music in the Tale of Beren and Luthien by J.R.R. Tolkien." *Analyses, Rereadings, Theories* 2 (2014): 13-20. Online version: https://analysesrereadingstheories.files.wordpress.com/2015/01/art_journal_3_music_transformations_metamorphoses.pdf (accessed 23-2-2017).

SLACK, Anna. "Moving Mandos: The Dynamics of Subcreation in 'Of Beren and Lúthien'." *The Silmarillion. Thirty Years On.* Ed. Allan Turner. Zurich and Berne: Walking Tree Publishers, 2007, 59-80.

The Oxford English Dictionary. 2nd ed. 1989. OED Online. Oxford University Press. 21 April 2010.

TOLKIEN, J.R.R. *The Lord of the Rings.* London: George Allen & Unwin, 1954. 1955.

The Silmarillion. Ed. Christopher Tolkien. London: George Allen & Unwin. 1977.

The Letters of J.R.R. Tolkien. Ed. Humphrey Carpenter, London: George Allen & Unwin, 1981.

The Book of Lost Tales 1 (The History of Middle-earth 1). Ed. Christopher Tolkien. London: George Allen & Unwin, 1983.

The Book of Lost Tales 2 (The History of Middle-earth 2). Ed. Christopher Tolkien. London: George Allen & Unwin, 1984.

The Lays of Beleriand (The History of Middle-earth 3). Ed. Christopher Tolkien. London: George Allen & Unwin, 1985.

The Shaping of Middle-earth (The History of Middle-earth 4). Ed. Christopher Tolkien. London: George Allen & Unwin, 1986.

The Lost Road (The History of Middle-earth 5). Ed. Christopher Tolkien. London: Unwin Hyman, 1987.

Morgoth's Ring (The History of Middle-earth 10). Ed. Christopher Tolkien. London: HarperCollins, 1990.

The History of Middle-earth Index. (The History of Middle-earth 13). Ed. Christopher Tolkien. London: HarperCollins, 2002.

Beren and Lúthien. Ed. Christopher Tolkien. London: HarperCollins, 2017.

ZIPES, Jack. *The Oxford Companion to Fairy Tales*. Oxford: Oxford University Press, 2009.

Jennifer Rogers

Music and the Outcast: Songs of the Wanderer in Tolkien's Time-Travel Fragments

Abstract

Tolkien's time-travel fragments, *The Lost Road* (*LR*) and *The Notion Club Papers* (*NCP*), contain a number of songs which seem disconnected from the two texts' main narratives. However, an ethnomusicological review of these songs shows how the music in *LR* and *NCP* discuss some of the stories' central themes: mortality and belonging. By studying these songs and their singers in cultural context, it will be argued that Tolkien uses music to draw a clear picture of the singers' personal and communal identities as they explore ideas of mortality within the texts. The same ethnomusicological approach used to study the songs of *LR* and *NCP* will then be applied to current primary world songs in order to argue for the characteristic ability of music to discuss questions of mortality while defining the personal and communal identities inherent to those questions.

1 Introduction: Scope of Study

The wanderer is a central figure in the works of J.R.R. Tolkien. To list Tolkien's outcasts and wanderers from Túrin to Bilbo to Niggle would require a paper of its own, and the study of these characters has already generated many papers more. On the other hand, community ranks thematically high in Tolkien's writings as well. *The Hobbit* and *The Lord of the Rings* are soaked in alliances, fellowships, and home-comings which cross cultures, languages, and space. Many of Tolkien's works end in restored or newfound relationship, such as Niggle and Parish's growing friendship towards the end of their story. In reflection of this trend, one has only to peruse an index of recent Tolkien scholarship to note that collaboration and community are at the front of the field.

Despite the direction towards outcasts and camaraderie in much of Tolkien criticism, the wandering and communal characters of Tolkien's time-travel fragments, *The Lost Road* (*LR*) and *The Notion Club Papers* (*NCP*), receive only passing attention from Tolkien scholars. Were it not for the desperately fragmented nature of *LR* and *NCP*, this silence would be unwarranted. In *LR*, a widowed father and son travel back to the lost island of Númenor through dreams and language. In *NCP*, an orphaned philologist discovers Númenor with a little help from his literary friends. Perhaps no two works by Tolkien have such a high concentration of misfits and, reciprocally, such a heavy emphasis on relationship as do these novels. Professors, orphans, widowers, philologists, and poets comprise their character lists. Each protagonist brings his own form of wandering isolation to the stories, whether familial or creative or scholarly, and yet in each fragment the characters belong to strong sub-communities, whether through a strong father-son or close friendship bond. What exists of the two stories are long and deep conversations between the characters, conversations that bring out the unique strengths and fears of every individual, and the personal choices to face those fears and strengths alongside someone else. This tension between isolation and community pervades the texts.

So does music. In fact, one could argue that music bridges the gap between the outcast and society as much as does any other device Tolkien uses in these stories. A basic plot summary of each fragment is that certain protagonists receive flashes of poetry in old languages which set them on time-travel journeys into the past. Notes Tolkien left for these stories' continuation indicate he intended song to play a key role in these novels, particularly the Song of Ælfwine. Yet other songs fill the pages of his time-travel stories, too, songs already incorporated into the completed sections he left his readers. In *LR*, two lines of Fíriel's hymn make it into the written text while the full version is provided in Tolkien's notes. This hymn moves quickly through cosmology, eschatology, and ontology though it is sung by a minor character with little introduction and no further narrative. Arry Lowdham's drinking songs sound even more anomalous, yet they prove insightful to the movements of *NCP* and help overcome the anomalous character of Lowdham himself and the messages he brings to his literary club. These snatches of song seem irrelevant at first – it is tempting to think the narratives could move along just as well without them. However, this paper argues that the seemingly superfluous music of both Arry and Fíriel strikes the central theme of Tolkien's time-travel stories by defining the relationship of the mortal outcast to his or her community and universe.

The boundary-crossing nature of music is not unique to Tolkien's time-travel texts. In *The Lord of the Rings*, outbursts of song frequently differentiate an individual from the crowd while welcoming outsiders into that individual's community. Gimli's "Song of Durin" informs an ignorant Sam about the culture of the Dwarrowdelf while pinpointing Gimli as in some way belonging to that culture (*LotR* 307-309). In like manner, Legolas's "Song of Nimrodel" connects him to the Elves of Lothlórien apart from the rest of the Fellowship while giving the Fellowship a taste of the culture into which they are about to enter (330-332). Thus, Tolkien often uses song to draw cultural and spatial lines, which lines the music then enables readers and characters to cross. Tolkien's music is at once isolating and collective. To readers of *The Silmarillion* this comes as no surprise, for in it music is the creative and communal force of Tolkien's secondary cosmology. The musical themes sung by Ilúvatar spring from his mind, are added to by the Valar, and then fragment into the actual existence of the universe (*S* 15). Music in Middle-earth has been used to contrast individuals and create community since Ilúvatar first sang at the beginning of time.

The study of music in Tolkien's time-travel fragments would therefore benefit from an approach that appreciates the importance of culture and boundary within the musical field. Ethnomusicology offers just such an approach. In his introduction to *How Musical Is Man?*, ethnomusicologist John Blacking states that "*all* music is folk music, in the sense that music cannot be transmitted or have meaning without associations between people" (x). This link between the relationships of people to their music becomes the foundation for the rest of his study of the Venda people in South Africa. Blacking's premise is that "music is a product of the behavior of human groups, whether formal or informal: it is humanly organised sound" (10). Ethnomusicologists since have recalled Blacking's words to reinforce the profoundly cultural nature of music. Bruno Nettl expands this ethnomusicological idea of music as "humanly organised sound" in *Theory and Method in Ethnomusicology* when he says, "Perhaps the most important task which ethnomusicology has set itself is the study and discovery of the role which music plays in each of man's cultures past and present, and the knowledge of what music means to man" (224). Both authors, like Tolkien, realise music is closely tied to the idea of what it means to be a person within society so that the study of music gives us knowledge of society.

This last concept signals another reason why ethnomusicology is an ideal approach to Tolkien's time-travel songs: ethnomusicology is highly philological. In fact, in *Theory and Method*, Nettl notes that one of the founders of ethnomusicology, A.J. Ellis, was a philologist and that the earlier name for ethnomusicology was comparative musicology, echoing comparative philology and its mechanism of discovery through collation and divergence among languages and cultures (15, 8). Nettl believes that "especially in studying the relationship of the words and music of songs are these two disciplines [ethnomusicology and linguistics] in close alliance" (5). Since Tolkien's works are rooted in philology and since most of what we have left of the music of Middle-earth are its lyrics, the songs in *LR* and *NCP* would benefit from an ethnomusicological approach. The present paper is therefore a preliminary application of ethnomusicology to Fíriel's hymn and Arry's drinking songs as they relate to the larger topics of mortality and belonging which appear in the texts. First, the paper examines the singers themselves, since ethnomusicologically their individuality and culture will affect their music, and then the songs themselves will be considered in light of the texts' themes of mortality and belonging. The paper here focuses on the way music interacts with the boundaries of individuality in society and the search for meaning, or, on music and the outcast. Finally, the paper will conclude with a brief overview of music with similar themes in the contemporary primary world to consider the musical reality of wandering all around us. Since, ethnomusicology begins and ends with people, there this study will begin and end as well.

2 The Singers: Fíriel and Arry

The first person to sing an overtly melodic song in Tolkien's time-travel fragments is Fíriel in *LR*. Both singer and song abruptly enter the narrative and leave as quickly as they came. From the text, readers know that Fíriel's father, Orontor, sailed from Númenor and is never expected to return, leaving Elendil, friend of Orontor and main character of the story, in some sort of care-taking role towards the abandoned girl. Readers learn that Fíriel sings so well her melody quiets even the nightingale, an iconic figure of spell-like vocal beauty in Tolkien's works and a reference to Lúthien Tinuviel, the first elven maid to choose a mortal life. Finally, the brief introduction makes clear that Fíriel has undergone an underground upbringing. Her hymn comes to Elendil "far off and strange as some melody in archaic speech sung sadly in a forgotten twilight in the beginning of man's journey in the world" while it speaks openly of Ilúvatar, an unacceptable God in Fíriel's Sauron-ruled society, and of a gift beyond the sun, an unacceptable eschatology in her society's quest for immortality on individual and cosmological levels (*LR* 69). All Tolkien writes of Fíriel, then, communicates that she is abandoned and ideologically alienated – an outcast in every way.

Although Fíriel receives basic attention at best in *LR*, the name Fíriel makes several minor appearances in Tolkien's legendarium, and each appearance gathered together creates a consistent image. To begin where Tolkien usually did, with philology, Fíriel means "mortal woman" or Everywoman (Shippey 281). Going by her name, which in Tolkien is usually a good idea, Fíriel finds her identity in her mortality. This picture holds true as we pursue her name in other works. For one, Finwë's first wife Míriel is re-named Fíriel upon her death – the first willing death of the Eldar to occur in the Undying Lands (see *MR* 205-270). Another Fíriel is wed to the last king of the North-kingdom, Arvedui; this Fíriel lives to see the death of her father, brothers, and husband while she presumably remains to raise a son in the line of Isildur (*LotR* 1017-18, 1024-26). Even Lúthien, the Elven woman famed for choosing mortality, is according to Tolkien's vast appendices associated with Fíriel (*LR* 382). Death clearly surrounds both name and character – mortal, of the earth, Fíriel.

There is one more Fíriel in Tolkien's legendarium who solidifies this individual as a picture of mortality. She appears in Tolkien's two versions of the Fíriel poem, the first "Firiel" and the second "The Last Ship". In both tellings, Elves beckon the human Fíriel at dawn to depart on a swan-ship to Elvenhome, away from "Middle-earth" and "mortal lands" where "grass fades and leaves fall, / and sun and moon wither" (*ATB* 112). In both tellings, Fíriel watches the Elven ship glide away before returning to her daily, mortal life. Though the plot-line remains the same, these two renditions of "Fíriel" strike very different tones. In the first poem, Fíriel remains behind by choice: "her heart misgave and shrank" before she "walked back from the river […] earth's fair daughter" (261). She dons a green and white dress after leaving her vision of Faërie with the night and returns to mortality's mix of realities: "brooms, dusters, mats to beat" and "voices loud and merry"; the poem famously ends on the cheerful note of "please, pass the honey!" (ibid.). Here, mortality is paradoxically a life to be embraced and daily lived, with future possibilities, as hopeful as they are, unknown. Opportunity abounds in a life that will die. Not so in "The Last Ship," where the white and green dress of Faërie is exchanged for an earthly brown gown and honey is replaced by mortal waters and fading songs. Two extra stanzas indicate the Elves calling Fíriel sailed the last ship to tread mortal waters; the last seat it contained would forever remain empty due to Fíriel's choice to stay. And this choice in the second version can hardly be so called since Fíriel dares a first step toward the ship but is held back because "deep in clay her feet sank" (113). The earth physically prevents her from joining the last ship so that regret rather than hope fills the poem (see Shippey 282). This tension between hope and regret, each compounded by fear, is the mortality complex faced by Fíriel in *LR* as she sings her song.

This mortality complex appears not just in her identity but also in her context. Fíriel's hymn is textually surrounded by history, cosmology, eschatology, religion, and social warfare as it interrupts an important conversation between Elendil and his son Herendil about death. The conversation quickly becomes a debate, for in Fíriel's world there are two factions fighting about the nature of death: the mainstream Númenoreans, who under Sauron hate death and wish to fight the Lords of the West in order to make the sun live forever and life never die, versus the secret Faithful, who believe "[death] is a gift from the One" – a gift so great that "even the Lords of the West shall envy" men their fate (*LR* 72). In Elendil's words, a cultural battle rages over whether the shadow of Númenor is death itself or "the fear of Death," a life-changing distinction for father and son between embracing mortality and the hope it offers for something beyond this world or living everyday in dread of death as the end of all things (75). The battle is so fierce that the people's "old songs are forgotten or altered" along with their old language, Eressëan (75). The people of Númenor are fighting with separate histories, separate cosmologies, separate languages, and separate songs. And in the middle of this struggle about mortality and belonging, Fíriel's hymn is heard.

Though it may seem difficult to rival Fíriel's identity, society, and song, Alwin Arundel (Arry) Lowdham of *The Notion Club Papers* rises to the occasion.

This time-travel fragment is closely connected to *LR* in subject, the drowning of Númenor, and in themes, mortality and belonging. However, unlike *LR*, *NCP* anchors its narrative primarily in the modern world with a few of its protagonists sometimes thrown into the past in dreams through language. One of these characters is Arry Lowdham, whose importance is seen in Part Two's title, "The Strange Case of Arundel Lowdham" (*SD* 146). Readers first learn that Arry is a Comparative Philologist, a lecturer of Anglo-Saxon and Icelandic, and an infrequent writer of verse. Put another way, his chief interest is words – their history, their story, their meaning. As Part One progresses, Arry emerges as a boisterous and people-oriented individual, whose hearty drinking involves his many friends and open home (233). But Arry's jocularity only complements his philological quest for meaning: his teasing often accompanies wordplay, revealing an acute perception of both character and language. This combination soon pushes the story into its themes of mortality and belonging.

According to Christopher Tolkien, this push occurred first in his father's mind between writing Parts One and Two of *NCP* when Tolkien got the idea to "do the Atlantis story" (282). Tolkien revises Arry from an amusing aside to the story's main show by establishing his name as "Arry" rather than "Harry", changing his stated interest from "18th century monarchs" to Comparative Philology, and writing into Part One hints of a connection between Arry and an island downfallen (281-82). Interestingly, Tolkien retains the character's uniquely sociable habits and traits. In other words, Tolkien retroactively constructs (retcons) Harry Loudham, jocular commentator, into Arry Lowdham, communal philologist and time-traveller.

Just as Fíriel and her hymn are tied to larger themes in Tolkien's legendarium, so do the three steps of Tolkien's retconning tie Arry and his drinking songs to themes that reach even deeper into Tolkien's world of Middle-earth than those of the "mortal woman" herself. The first step, turning Arry into a philologist, links Arry to both mortality and belonging since comparative philology is by nature cross-cultural and, at least in Tolkien's mind, inextricable from the question of mortality. As Tom Shippey writes in *The Road to Middle-earth*, "It is clear that Tolkien's major theme [...] was Death [...]. And Tolkien saw this theme not only in fiction or in dream, but also in history and archeology"

(301). In *LR*, Tolkien through Oswin Errol notes that philology and archeology are cooperative in "going back [...] within the limits prescribed to us mortals" by reliving world history so far as serious study allows (*LR* 44). Arry becoming a philologist is Arry becoming a traveller into the world's past and what it means to die. "Alwin Arundel," the second retconning act, likewise links Arry to belonging and mortality since the name puts him in the line of Ælfwine, Tolkien's ever-present "elf-friend" character who according to Verlyn Flieger in an essay in *Tolkien's Legendarium* is "the connector or mediator between the 'real' or natural world and the world of Faërie – the supernatural world of myth and the imagination" (185). "Alwin" means "elf-friend" while "Arundel" is a modernisation of Eärendel, the first mortal in Tolkien's mythology to step foot on Valinor and plead with the Lords of the West to save Elves and Men from Morgoth. Just by his name, Arry (Alwin Arundel) is associated with death and bridges the borders of belonging. That Tolkien thirdly fastened Arry's story to the downfall of Númenor only reinforces the thematic developments of the first two changes in Arry's character, for Númenor is Tolkien's basic story of human mortality and Arry must use philology to reach that long-forgotten isle. Finally, Part Two reveals that Arry, like Fíriel, is an orphan. His father Edwin has mimicked Orontor and Eärendel by sailing away in search of Western lands. In every way, then, Tolkien has crafted Arry Lowdham into the perfect Ælfwine: mortal, social, and a wanderer.

But in ethnomusicology it is not enough to view the singer alone, for as Blacking states, music is "concerned with communication and relationships between people" (12). How, then, does Arry interact with his society? In a way, Arry's cultural context resembles that of Fíriel in that he belongs to two opposing communities at once. The first is his modern world, which according to the text has just experienced the Six Years' War, or the Second World War, and is doing everything it can to avoid death, just like the Númenoreans in *LR* (*SD* 157). Similar to the growing use of machines in Númenorean culture (*LR* 74), Arry's world attempts to fight death and time through technological progress, a reality encapsulated in the Club's Part One conversation about time-travel machines. In it, Guildford argues against travel mechanisms that do not appreciate man's growing understanding of the universe: "A gravitation-insulator won't do. Gravity can't be treated like that. It's fundamental. It's a statement by the Universe of where you are in the Universe, and the Universe can't be tricked by a surname with *ite* stuck on the end, nor by any such abracadabra" (*SD* 166). In other words, humans even in their stories should not be so hubristic to think they can control the basic forces of the universe through wordplay. Note that Guildford unconsciously realises the power of time-machines lies not so much in their physical but philological attributes. Arry astutely responds that "people of this blessed century think primarily of travelling and speed, not of destination, or settling. It's better to travel 'scientifically', in fact, than to get anywhere" (166-167). Arry's first culture believes more in prolonging the journey than reaching its end, an ontological statement as good as any Fíriel would have encountered in Númenor.

The second community our extroverted wanderer engages with is his Notion Club, analogous to the circle of the Faithful found in *LR*. In opposition to the hatred and fear of the Six Years' War and the increasing mechanisation of the modern world, this band of brothers are bound by a joint love of words, a love so cross-cultural that even Germanic languages are welcome. As Guildford's comment makes plain, along with the rest of Part One, the Club believes not just in the fellowship but in the power of words against all technological odds, much like the Faithful believe in the fellowship and power of Ilúvatar against all the odds of Sauron's lies. Clearly, a cultural struggle exists in Arry's college rooms as much as it rages in Fíriel's chamber, and this cultural war at the level of mortality and belonging is the vital premise for an ethnomusicological approach to the songs of these two individuals.

3 The Songs: A Hymn and Three Drinking Songs

In Fíriel's case, the cultural conflict regarding mortality and belonging is overtly religious. Do men belong to this world or is the gift of Ilúvatar a means to a destiny beyond the sun? Is Ilúvatar good? Is he real? These are all fundamentally religious questions in the secondary world of Middle-earth, and so Fíriel responds to this conflict with a hymn, a melodic address to a divine being, or religion done musically. Such a move makes ethnomusicological sense, for Karen Ralls-MacLeod states that in Celtic tradition, to which Tolkien adheres in his time-travel narratives, "music is seen as a universal 'connector' to the Otherworld" (15). Fíriel shows great cultural and personal awareness when she chooses a hymn to engage with her context. Even outside Celtic or Northern or Númenorean contexts, many ethnomusicologists believe the highest criteria for musical performance and interpretation is in some way spiritual (Yakupov 21; see Blacking 28). Culturally, Fíriel's hymn brings readers straight to mortality through religious and Otherworld connections. However, in ethnomusicology "any assessment of human musicality must account for processes that are extramusical," including the place and time of musical creativity, performance, and reception (Blacking 89). Since readers only have literary cues to work with in analyses of Tolkien's time-travel music, this paper limits itself to noting the form of the songs and the physical position of the singers. In this case, Fíriel sings her hymn during twilight, at the top of a high tower, through a window sill – close to the edge in every direction (*LR* 62-63). Ralls-MacLeod's study shows that such a stance is highly "liminal," a boundary space between this world and the Otherworld in which humans can meet the Otherworld without being permanently absorbed into it (180). Thus, Fíriel's liminal position reflects the religious form of her song, each of which points to mortal interaction with an immortal Other and so culturally cues her hymn's deeply mortal content.

For Fíriel's hymn asks the central question of *LR*: "What will the Father, O Father, give me in that day beyond the end when my Sun faileth?" (69). It is Fíriel's question, Elendil's question, and the question of Númenoreans in general. She begins with cosmological and historical statements: "the Father made the world for Elves and Mortals, and he gave it into the hands of the Lords"; "to all they gave in measure the gifts of Ilúvatar"; and her "heart resteth not here for ever; for here is ending [...] but yet it will not be enough, not enough" (79-80). The hymn is thus a gesture of ideological solidarity with the Faithful as well as a personal question pushed into longing. These functions of Fíriel's hymn support Thomas A. DuBois's claim in *Lyric, Meaning, and Audience in the Oral Tradition of Northern Europe* that "performed to proclaim publicly a shared understanding of the cosmos and the sacred, hymns can also serve as sources of personal comfort or reassurance in times of trial" (99). Fíriel with her hymn is drawing personal and societal lines, lines that are a necessary part of the process to discovering the nature of her and her universe's mortality.

Tolkien's hint of what her hymn sounded like – far off, strange, sadly sung in a forgotten twilight at the beginning of man's journey – relates that even what readers know of the tone supports themes of unfulfilled quests about mortality (*LR* 69). According to Blacking, this tonal agreement is not a coincidence, for "the decisive style-forming factor in any attempt to express feeling in music must be its social content" and to understand songs one must look "to the social situations in which they are applied and to which they refer" (73). Questions of belonging and mortality are both presented in Fíriel's hymn and weaved together into a journey setting, because by the hymn's end the quest for meaning has only begun.

Although Fíriel's hymn clearly links to textual themes and her cultural context, it also sheds light on her identity as a mortal wanderer. The song puts her in the role of a journeyer, and this transition must be considered fundamental since it turns Fíriel, the outcast wanderer, into a pilgrim. First, the hymn establishes her individuality, stating beliefs and taking on the personal pronoun to inquire into Fíriel's personal destiny. This step coincides with musical anthropology, for John Kaemmer notes that "meaning is found when humans relate something in their current experience with previous experiences stored in their memories. Thus, most meanings are personal and based on a form of association" (109). At the same time, Fíriel's individualising process requires her to establish a connection with the community, as seen in the initial instructional section of the hymn which communicates to whomever hears the personal beliefs that distinguish her from most Númenoreans. Most importantly, by realising and addressing the state of her society, and by identifying herself with a subgroup of that society – the Faithful – Fíriel is actually making a statement about herself and her connection to ultimate meaning: Ilúvatar himself. The last, central question includes a sudden brief switch from third to second person in reference to Ilúvatar, reinforcing that Fíriel's cosmology, history, religion, and identity reach the heights of the One. DuBois again points out how this makes sense in light of his cultural study: "In the invocation, the temporal and spatial limitations of the world disappear: the singer-speaker is placed at the very site of sacred events, allowed to share in their core human emotions" (141). So, through music, Fíriel reaches a space where she is at once most cosmologically connected and most herself. Though the nature of her ultimate destiny cannot be determined, her hymn grants her the vast and specific meaning of what it means to be mortal every day until there are no days left: she must pilgrim towards what cannot die.

Ethnomusicologically speaking, the hymn remains consistent in form, position, tone, and content to link Fíriel to the true nature of her mortal identity, namely, that she must seek something beyond the sun at Ilúvatar's hand. Through this hymn, Fíriel also builds and crosses societal boundaries, which furthers her pilgrimage by casting her out from mainstream Númenor and identifying her with the Faithful. Though a seemingly insignificant aside in what would have been a massive time-travel work, Fíriel's hymn states the central wanderer's theme of the whole multi-millennial story in what is so simple as a paragraph of song.

Arry Lowdham's drinking songs are naturally less religious in nature than Fíriel's, but just as Arry and Fíriel share similar identities, so their songs point to similar themes. In communicating these themes, Tolkien remains consistent with his narrative premise that languages and other anthropological features are "echoes coming through" of a deeper – a Númenorean – past (*LR* 43). In Fíriel's song, readers find explicit references to mortality and belonging contained in the frankly religious form of a hymn; she is, after all, living in the midst of Númenor's struggle over death. Arry's songs, on the other hand, sung millennia later in a language far removed from Fíriel's Eressëan, reflect the distant, fragmentary nature of their message by couching said message in an equally diffuse form: not one hymn but three drinking songs, sung twice during Club meetings and once in a letter to the Notion Club. Although none of the songs are complete and, apart from one, are to this author unidentifiable, pieced together they give readers a surprisingly clear picture of Arry's wandering quest into mortality.

The three melodic fragments of *The Notion Club Papers* are not only more diluted in content than Fíriel's hymn but also more communal. The form of Arry's music – drinking songs reminiscent of medieval and folk verse – highlights community through the space in which it occurs traditionally in history and actually in the text: with friends. Additionally, Inskip et al. reference David Brackett's *Interpreting Popular Music* to note that "folk music has an unknown composer, is evolving, and is by and for the community," so that the largely untraceable medieval folk element of Arry's drinking songs only heightens the social aspect of his "musical events" (12-13; see Kaemmer 36).

Arry's stance while singing goes further to connect the melodies to his identity by at once reinforcing and problematising the level of community in Arry's music. He sings every song surrounded by friends and in all instances the songs are directed to them. His first song, which we will refer to as "Briny Notion", appears towards the beginning of Part Two when he enters a Club meeting with the song already underway; the singing does not stop throughout the evening. The second song, a recasting of the introduction to Havelok the Dane, is addressed to Frankley in another meeting to poke fun at his French heritage and affinities in contrast to the Anglo-Saxon roots that Arry values. The third piece, the beer song, comes in written form while Arry and Jeremy are trekking the coast in an attempt to receive more Númenorean flashes of pictures and poetry. In every case, the social nature of the song is compounded by an increasing distance on Arry's part. First, during "Briny Notion", Arry is "restless, and would not sit down" (*SD* 224). Then the Havelok revision draws Frankley and Arry together in an Anglo-Norman song by highlighting the antipathies between the English and French. Finally, the beer song serves as a farewell notice to the rest of the Club – Arry and Jeremy are jaunting to "happy haunts where the beer flows wild and free" (254). A tension between individuality and community hence arises in the case of Arry just as it did in the case of Fíriel. His songs' communal form highlights Arry's increasing distance just as the personal form of the hymn highlights Fíriel's growing community with the Faithful. So too, while the unoriginality of Fíriel's hymn ties her to the Faithful, the originality of Arry's first song unties him from the camaraderie of the Club. Blacking would not be surprised by this tension of creativity and community:

> Although human creativity may appear to be the result of individual effort, it is in fact a collective effort that is expressed in the behavior of individuals. Originality may be an expression of innate exploratory behaviour with the accumulated materials of a cultural tradition; and the ability to synthesise [...] may express the comprehensive cognitive organisation that is generated by experience of the relationships that exist between social groups who use and develop the techniques of tradition. (106)

Arry belongs to just such a social group and, for all his conviviality, expresses innate exploratory behaviour through his languages and lyrics. Arry's musical progression, then, outlines his personal progression: he is diving deeper and deeper into the Númenorean world, or, is transforming his outcast nature into one of a pilgrim.

Connecting recurring music to textual themes fits an ethnomusicological approach. DuBois's study reveals that in Northern epics, "such lyric 'interludes' embody and ennoble the associated narrative's characters. The narrative in turn supplies the interpretive framework within which to appreciate the broad themes, oblique references, and small details of the lyrics" (38). In other words, Arry's songs link him to Anglo-Norman romantic tradition through Havelok and to the common man through his beer song, while the narrative questions raised in *NCP* feed the strange lyrics of "Briny Notion." It is worth quoting the lyrics as given in full here:

> *I've got a very Briny Notion*
> *To drink myself to sleep.*
> *Bring me my bowl, my magic potion!*
> *Tonight I'm diving deep.*
> *down! down! down!*
> *Down where the dream-fish go.* (SD 224)

The song sounds like nonsense apart from its literary and communal context. At face value, the song sings of drunken stupors and magic tripping – on potions, on dreams, perhaps on hallucinogenic fish. In context, the nature of the "trip" is clear as the song heralds a reality of which not even Arry is yet aware: he will travel to Númenor before his story's end. Arry's "Notion" connects him to the Club and its topics, which of late have proven full of the briny seas of Atlantis and the history-centred dream-travel routes used to get there. Unclear in the song, however, is the reason Arry subconsciously wants to reach Númenor, and this uncertainty causes unsettlement: "the song was not well received, least of all by Ramer" – Ramer, who alone is equipped as a philologist and dream-traveller to understand just what Arry's drinking song really means.

The uncertainty of Arry's quest echoes the uncertainty in the closing lines of Fíriel's hymn: what awaits man, if anything, beyond the sun? Arry's last drinking song strangely solidifies the true nature of his wandering with Fíriel's wondering, for this beer song is a shanty of escape, away from papers and colleges and electric lights to "happy, happy haunts" (254). The point of the song, of course, is not to say that the chief end of man is to drink beer in meadows hidden from stacks of ungraded papers, but that Arry, like Fíriel, is looking for paradise, and the first step to reach that nameless land is through Númenor, back to where Fíriel is, cosmologically, communally, and individually. This journey toward a universal paradise also brings Arry closer to his personal past as he seeks the West like his long-lost father did. So while Fíriel's musical quest for paradise takes her from isolation to community, Arry's musical quest takes him from communal to individual understanding.

That Tolkien encapsulates the longing themes of paradise in music stays true to Celtic Otherworld perceptions of music and an ethnomusicological view of the roles music plays in society. Thus, an ethnomusicological study of the songs in Tolkien's time-travel fragments brings readers to the point of the narratives: man as an individual within community is mortal and as such must find a way to escape. Although the themes of mortality and belonging remain the same across cultures, individual stories will differ. Fíriel's musical story brings her from a mortal outcast to a pilgrim alongside other pilgrims whose destination remains to be understood. Arry's musical progression turns his linguistic wandering into a physical journey towards his past and the world's history. From what Tolkien managed to write, readers know that in Tolkien's mind both an individual commitment to seeking paradise and a strong community with which to do the seeking are necessary to this pilgrimage of escape. But neither *LR* nor *NCP* were ever completed, so the full answer for successfully and finally going where the dream-fish go or reaching the place beyond the sun can never be found within his time-travel texts. This is just as well, for it reflects the known yet unknown ideas of history and eternity within the texts' songs. Like the first "Fíriel" poem stresses, the quest of mortals can only be carried out everyday.

4 The Singing Never Stops: Music for Modern Wanderers

The everydayness of this mortal quest for paradise can also be observed in our primary contemporary world where, as in Tolkien's, it crosses musical genres and communities. A brief review of three songs belonging to three different musical spaces in modern Anglo-American culture shows all too glaringly that Tolkien's search for some sort of paradise still pervades man's mind, regardless of background. The review accepts the same limitations required to review Fíriel's hymn and Arry's drinking songs in order to stay consistent with the paper's general study.

The first song belongs to a small subgroup of modern Anglo-American music: the contemporary spiritual folk ballad. To present a current sample of this ever-evolving group of songs, the paper turns to "Far Kingdom" by The Gray Havens, one of the many American religious bands continuing the modern folk revival and a return to lyrics based on literary tradition. The song comes from their arguably most mythically influenced album, *Fire and Stone*, which relies heavily on the voyaging theme found in works from *The Odyssey* to Lewis's *Narnia* stories. The literary nature of the album complements an ethnomusicological approach since *Fire and Stone* through those references builds on the cultural traditions of its context, much like Fíriel's hymn reveals a strong cultural interaction (see Nettl, *Study* 242). With that foundation, the Gray Havens musically draws attention to the universal wandering, mortal nature of Everyman and Everywoman. The album closes with "Far Kingdom," whose last verse epitomises the mortality and belonging themes of Tolkien's time-travel fragments through the spiritual pilgrimage theme of the album:

> There is a far, far kingdom
> There at the end of the sea
> Where they know my name
> And until that far, far kingdom
> Calls me home
> Oh, my soul, I will wait ("10. Far Kingdom")

Like Fíriel, a sense of current lack of belonging is countered with an ultimate sense of belonging to a kingdom whose nature is yet unknown but must be sought daily. In this song and Fíriel's hymn, mortality and eternity reign in the present. The second verse of "Far Kingdom" states that though the final destination is unknown "still there is more gladness / longing for the sight / than to behold or be filled, by anything," which echoes Fíriel's perilous decision to identity with the Faithful and Ilúvatar in order to find her very personal inheritance. In Fíriel's mind and in that of The Gray Havens, the personal journey and public identification are worth the risk because each together acknowledge the question of mortality by offering to it answers and hope. Thus, the Eressëan hymn and modern spiritual folk ballad share one message: the mortal quest of mankind creates individuality within community and causes wanderers to be intentional pilgrims everyday because the gift beyond the sun is worth it.

Not surprising from an ethnomusicological perspective, the "Far Kingdom" performance video reflects the song's message, just like Fíriel's stance while singing reinforces her lyrics. In the video, the performers sit in a staggered line. This stance is an interesting blend of the traditional, horizontally linear position that highlights pop's performing individuals, and the common folk setup of a close semicircle that highlights folk's communal spirit. It is another example of the way "Far Kingdom" builds on its musical culture(s). The Gray Havens' staggered line also gives viewers the ability to see all performers in one forward glance and makes the performers seem to be sitting in a cluster while still emphasising their individuality in the progression. Performers toward the back of the line can see performers ahead of them, while the nearest performer to the camera looks straight ahead, presumably to the "Far Kingdom". Simultaneously, their seated position reveals a certain degree of rest in the song despite the longing themes of the lyrics, which corresponds to Firiel's forward-looking stillness at her window and contrasts Arry's restlessness as he strides across the Club meeting singing "Briny Notion". Not just lyrically but in a positional sense, the song communicates its paradoxical message of longing and hope, present and future, individuality and community, the outcast and the Far Kingdom.

If the first song fits rather neatly with Firiel's hymn, the second song serves as a helpful backdrop to Arry's Briny Notion. Like Arry's drinking song, Iron Maiden's "Ghost of the Navigator" strikes a strong seafaring tone full of questions about mortality and belonging. The song springs from the metal community, which is defined by its hardcore metallic and rhythmic sound but shares a similarity with folk in offering a dynamic community alternative to the pop sphere. As its name suggests, "Ghost of the Navigator" describes in pictorial flashes the singer-sailor's "final journey": "On the bow I stand, west is where I go" (Iron Maiden, "Ghost"). "West" culturally cues final bliss while the sirens in the song recall everyman's odyssey towards home. Through references known to their communities, both this and Arry's songs communicate a quest for paradise. And though there are stated directions in "Briny Notion" and "Ghost" – down and west – the same sense of uncertainty pervades the journey in "Ghost" that was observed in Arry's tune: throughout the song, the "Navigator's son" must face "skeletons accusing" and grapple with the idea that he is "chasing rainbows" (ibid.). The song ends with, "Where I go I do not know [...] Dreams they come and go [...] Nothing's real until you feel" (ibid.). The emphasis on uncertainty is appropriate to metal since the genre specialises in exploring the darker struggles of humanity in a subtly spiritual context, much like the scientific time-travel romances of Tolkien's day focus on humanity's unstable ontology in utopian and dystopian contexts (see Hjelm, et al., 14). However, against this uncertainty there stands a cry to "take [the singer's] heart and set it free" much like Arry feels confident he and Jeremy through their linguistic dream-travel will find the "happy, happy haunts" of his final beer song. Apparently, both Arry and Iron Maiden have encountered the doubts and hopes of the journey to paradise. This mortal quest is compounded in the Iron Maiden song by increasing isolation within community, another parallel to Arry's case. The singer's father is acknowledged but absent while the appearance of skeletons implies that the singer at once belongs to a larger community of travelers but must abandon them to continue the journey. "Ghost" is Arry's story put in metal terms, though lyrically it leaves listeners in stronger doubt and isolation than Arry's song cycle does, reflecting the conflictive mood appropriate to its genre.

It is in the spatial aspect of "Ghost of the Navigator" that the communal reality of the song comes to life, mirroring the complex isolating and socialising nature of Arry's journey to Númenor. Deena Weinstein in her essay "Communities of Metal" defines the ideal metal community as one that has "shared values, mutual identification, interaction, solidarity, and boundaries," turning a heavy metal concert experience into a powerful expression of community (11). The performance video of "Ghost" displays the metal – and Tolkienian – tension between isolation and community when the song's isolating lyrics are performed on stage. Band members initially line up across the stage, visually emphasising individuality, but as the song progresses performers move towards each other while the singer concentrates on a physical dialogue with the audience through intense histrionics, communicating the social possibilities of the individualising lyrics. Arry's restless walking and dialogue with his own "band members," the Notion Club, as he starts to sing and unfold his past to explain the Númenorean journey he feels compelled to take mirrors the movements of Iron Maiden as they sing about the Ghost of the Navigator and his own journey to the west. In both cases, the Tolkienian tension of individuality and community is underscored through the spacing of the seafarer's story to paradise. Whether in Middle-earth, an Oxford meeting room, or a metal concert, the ideas of mortality and belonging are aptly addressed through music in physical community.

It is easy to set aside wandering songs as belonging strictly to musical subcultures, but this review's last song takes readers to a band at the centre of current Anglo-American pop: Coldplay. Their hit song "Paradise" stays true to its name, telling the story of "a girl [who] expected the world / but it flew away from her reach / so she ran away in her sleep and dreamed of paradise" (Coldplay, "Paradise"). This song could have been sung about either Arry or Firiel, emphasising as it does the basic idea of searching for paradise. The song musically focuses on the concept and word of "para-para-paradise" for most of its 4 minutes and 38 seconds but the simplicity of its lyrics ethnomusicologically fits its pop genre. As the Inskip et al. study shows, since pop music by definition runs on commercial success, it must appeal to an audience that spans cultures and narrative traditions, thereby creating and allowing for a wide variety of interpretations in musical communication feedback (23-24). Rather than the overtly religious references in "Far Kingdom" and the classical seafaring references of "Ghost of the Navigator", "Paradise" limits itself to universal images of storms and the rising sun. Lyrically this means the song is too general to provide answers about the quest for paradise besides that it is a personal process in a big world and ends in something good. The universal nature of the song defaces the community in which the quest takes place and obscures the identity of the individual who faces it. However, what the song's universality loses in specificity, it gains in applicability. It is unmistakable that whether one identifies with Arry or Firiel or the Venda tribe, one must take a personal journey to find "Paradise."

Coldplay's music video positionally adheres to the idea of a profoundly individual quest to reach paradise, while additionally stressing the need for belonging noted throughout this ethnomusicological study. Like Arry and Firiel, the main singer is an outcast, shown by his "elephant in the room" costume, trapped in a cage. Also like Arry and Firiel, the outcast elephant has to break free from his mainstream community to make a solitary journey to his version of paradise. The scenes of the elephant holding cardboard signs reading "para-para-paradise" immediately communicate to an Anglo-American audience the idea of a homeless wanderer writing out what he or she needs most. Finally, like Arry and Firiel, the music video concludes that paradise must involve community or relationship, for the song ends with the elephant band being reunited in their natural African habitat. Whether approached lyrically or positionally, Coldplay's "Paradise" sings in highly distilled form the same story of the wanderer that inspired Tolkien all his life, showing that themes of mortality and belonging are still relevant even in modern pop culture.

5 Conclusion: Escape and Its Sound

And so, from buried hymns of the Secondary World to the songs streaming on mobile devices in the Primary one, music can be a powerful tool for defining individuality, community, and a longing for something beyond the everyday sun. Reviewing the songs of Tolkien's time-travel fragments through an ethnomusicological lens reveals that Tolkien believed music is integrated into public expression of personal conviction and exploration; reviewing similar songs in the modern world reveals that Tolkien was right to believe so. What is more, an ethnomusicological approach to primary and secondary-world songs shows that music plays a central role in expressing a universal sense of wandering and need for escape, that noble escape of the prisoner from his cell (see *OFS* 169). In each of the songs reviewed, music has the ability to lyrically and positionally communicate a dissatisfaction with the everyday while establishing individual purpose and relational solidarity to respond to that longing. The art of recognising this longing is perhaps the greatest strength of Tolkien and of music, and it is the point of this study that Tolkien's themes of mortality and belonging and music's ways of expressing them are best kept together. Referencing Gustav Mahler, Blacking identifies why music and Middle-earth belong together: "Music can create a world of virtual time [and] may lead to 'the other world' – the world in which things are no longer subject to time and space" (51). This is the world Tolkien wrote about and filled with wanderers seeking, and perhaps finding, consolation, and it is the world that music is uniquely equipped to bring us to: paradise.

About the Author

JENNIFER ROGERS (née RAIMUNDO) lives near Washington, D.C., where she studies medieval literature and the works of J.R.R. Tolkien. Jenn is currently writing her thesis on Tolkien's time-travel fragments while working administratively at Signum University. In her free time, Jenn likes to explore the scattered villages and beautiful hikes that Virginia has to offer.

List of Abbreviations

ATB	*The Adventures of Tom Bombadil*
LotR	*The Lord of the Rings*
LR	*The Lost Road and Other Writings*
MR	*Morgoth's Ring*
OFS	"On Fairy-Stories."
S	*The Silmarillion*
SD	*Sauron Defeated*

Bibliography

BLACKING, John. *How Musical Is Man?* Seattle, WA: University of Washington Press, 1973.

COLDPLAY. "Coldplay – Paradise (Official Video)." Youtube, Coldplay Official. www.youtube.com/watch?v=1G4isv_Fylg. 18 October 2011.

"Paradise." http://www.coldplay.com/recordings/mylo_xyloto/paradise/.

DUBOIS, Thomas. *Lyric, Meaning, and Audience in the Oral Tradition of Northern Europe*. Notre Dame, IN: University of Notre Dame Press, 2006.

FLIEGER, Verlyn. *A Question of Time: J. R. R. Tolkien's Road to Faërie*. Kent, OH: Kent State University Press, 1997.

"The Footsteps of Ælfwine." *Tolkien's Legendarium*. Ed. Verlyn Flieger and Carl Hostetter. Westport, CT: Greenwood Press, 2000, 183-198.

THE GRAY HAVENS. "The Gray Havens – Far Kingdom." Youtube, GrayHavensMusic. 11 Sept. 2014. www.youtube.com watch?v=19RghmEGw8E.

"10. Far Kingdom." The Gray Havens Music, 21 July 2016. http://www.thegrayhavensmusic.com/blog/2016/7/21/10-far-kingdom.

HJELM, Titus, et al. "Heavy Metal as Controversy and Counterculture." *Popular Music History* 6.1-2, (2011): 5-18.

INSKIP, C., et al. "Meaning, Communication, Music: Towards a Revised Communication Model." *Journal of Documentation*, 64.5 (2008): 687-706.

IRON MAIDEN. "Iron Maiden – Ghost of the Navigator (Rock in Rio)." Youtube, zajacmp3. 16 Sept 2007. www.youtube.com/watch?v=nJL-ELn3Jwc.

"Iron Maiden – Ghost of the Navigator Lyrics." AZ Lyrics. https://www.azlyrics.com/lyrics/ironmaiden/ghostofthenavigator.html.

KAEMMER, John. *Music in Human Life: Anthropological Perspectives on Music*. Austin, TX: University of Texas Press, 1993.

NETTL, Bruno. *The Study of Ethnomusicology: Thirty-Three Discussions*. Champaign, IL: University of Illinois Press, 2015.

Theory and Method in Ethnomusicology. New York City, NY: The Free Press of Glencoe, Collier-Macmillan Limited, 1964.

RALLS-MACLEOD, Karen. *Music and the Celtic Otherworld: From Ireland to Iona*. Edinburgh: Edinburgh University Press, 2000.

Shippey, Tom. *The Road to Middle-earth: Revised and Expanded Edition*. New York City, NY: Houghton Mifflin Company, 2003.

Tolkien, J.R.R. *The Adventures of Tom Bombadil*. 1962. Ed. Christina Scull and Wayne Hammond. London: HarperCollins, 2014.

"On Fairy-Stories." 1964. *Poems and Stories*. New York City, NY: Houghton Mifflin, 1994, 113-192.

The Lord of the Rings. New York City, NY: Houghton Mifflin, 1955.

The Lost Road and Other Writings. Ed. Christopher Tolkien. New York City, NY: Random House, 1987.

Morgoth's Ring. Ed. Christopher Tolkien. New York City, NY: Houghton Mifflin, 1993.

The Silmarillion. Ed. Christopher Tolkien. 2nd ed. New York City, NY: Houghton Mifflin, 2001.

Sauron Defeated. Ed. Christopher Tolkien. London: HarperCollins, 2002.

Weinstein, Deena. "Communities of Metal: Ideal, Diminished and Imaginary." *Heavy Metal Music and the Communal Experience*. Ed. Nelson Varas-Díaz and Niall Scott. London: Lexington Books, 2016, 3-22.

Yakupov, Alexander. *The Theory of Musical Communication*. Newcastle upon Tyne: Cambridge Scholars Publishing, 2016.

Angela P. Nicholas

Aragorn, Music and the "Divine Plan"

Abstract

The following paper examines the different aspects of music (vocal and instrumental) and verse in relation to the life and character of Aragorn, considering him as a musician and poet in his own right, as someone who understands and appreciates music and poetry, and as the subject of songs and verses. Particular attention is paid to his circumstances and emotions, thus gaining psychological insight into the nature of his struggles and hardship. Overall the discussion is set within the context of the significance of music in Aragorn's Maian/Elven ancestry and background, and in his role in Tolkien's legendarium.

During recent years I have spent a considerable amount of time studying Aragorn, looking at his life, character, importance, struggles and qualities, as well as his ancestry, the prophecies relating to him, and his relationships with his contemporaries in Middle-earth. However, although aware of him as a singer, reciter and poet, and as someone who generally appreciates music, I have not yet looked at this aspect of him in detail. This omission will now be addressed by considering the following topics:

1) Music in the blood: Aragorn's ancestry and background
2) Aragorn: musician and poet
3) Aragorn: connoisseur of music
4) Aragorn as the inspiration for songs and verses
5) Aragorn and the "Divine Plan" (*L* 194)

1 Music in the Blood: Aragorn's Ancestry and Background

Although Aragorn was born right at the end of the Third Age his line can be traced back:

- Through the Third Age via the Chieftains of the Dúnedain and the Kings of Arnor and Gondor.
- Through the Second Age via the royal lines of Númenor to the island's first King, Elros, the brother of Elrond.
- Finally through the First Age until we arrive at the Maia/Elf union of Melian and Thingol, the parents of Lúthien Tinúviel.

Let us look at what *The Silmarillion* has to say about the Maiar in general, and about Aragorn's Maian fore-mother in particular:

> With the Valar came other spirits whose being also began before the World, of the same order as the Valar but of less degree. (S 21)

> Melian was a Maia, of the race of the Valar. She dwelt in the gardens of [the Vala] Lórien, and among all his people there were none more beautiful than Melian, nor more wise, *nor more skilled in songs of enchantment*. (S 54; emphasis added)

> She was akin before the World was made to Yavanna herself [...]. (ibid.)

> Of her there came among both Elves and Men a strain of the Ainur who were with Ilúvatar before Eä. (S 55)

Thus it can be seen that Aragorn's ancestry went back to a being who would have taken part in the Ainulindalë, the original music at the creation of the world. Lúthien too, being half Maia, was outstandingly gifted musically, being able to render Morgoth senseless (S 212-3), and stir Mandos to pity (S 220) with her singing.

In addition, a more detailed look at Aragorn's pedigree (Nicholas 8, 412) shows him to be descended from all the three Houses of the Elves (Vanyar, Noldor and Teleri/Sindar) and from the three Houses of the Edain (those of Bëor, the Haladin and Hador). The link to music can be seen here too. When the Vala Oromë first came across the newly-created Elves they were singing (S 46). Likewise the Elf Finrod Felagund first became aware of Bëor's people when he heard them singing (S 162-3). Realising that the voices were not those of Elves, Dwarves or Orcs he watched them, unseen, until they fell asleep around their campfire, at which point he picked up Bëor's harp and started singing himself. As the Men woke "each thought that he was *in some fair dream*" and the things that Finrod sang about "came as *clear visions before their eyes*" (S 163; emphasis added – see Chapter 2 in this paper). These first, musical encounters stirred feelings of love for the new beings in both Oromë and Finrod.

During the Third Age Elrond became deeply involved in protecting his long-dead brother's descendants, especially after the demise of the North Kingdom of Arnor when it became crucial that the survival of the royal line of Isildur remained a closely-guarded secret. In Third Age 2933, on the death of the fifteenth Chieftain of the Dúnedain (Arathorn II), Elrond took in the new Chieftain, the two-year-old Aragorn II, his great(x62)-nephew, and reared him in Rivendell as his foster-son, keeping his true name and identity a secret from him until he reached the age of twenty. By this arrangement Aragorn also gained two foster-brothers, namely the Half-elven sons of Elrond – Elladan and Elrohir – who would be companions not only in his early years but throughout his struggle for the kingship. Thus, apart from the presence of his mother, Gilraen, who accompanied him to Rivendell, Aragorn's childhood was spent in a completely Elvish environment. However it is worth noting that Gilraen too had Maia and Elf ancestry through her father who was descended from a junior branch of Isildur's line. In fact in an earlier version of her story (*PME* 263) her mother also had royal blood in her veins.

Evenings in the Hall of Fire with the emphasis on song must have been an intrinsic part of Aragorn's life in infancy, childhood and adolescence. Frodo's experience of this music, described in *The Lord of the Rings* gives some idea of the intensity of it:

> The beauty of the melodies and of the interwoven words in elven-tongues [...] held him in a spell [...] *Almost it seemed that the words took shape, and visions of far lands and bright things that he had never yet imagined opened out before him*; and the firelit hall became like a golden mist above seas of foam that sighed upon the margins of the world. *Then the enchantment became more and more dreamlike, until he felt that an endless river of swelling gold and silver was flowing over him* [...] it became part of the throbbing air about him and it drenched and drowned him. (*LotR* 233; emphasis added – see Chapter 2 in this paper).

After Aragorn left Rivendell to take up his role as Chieftain of the Dúnedain he became a close friend of Gandalf who, as the Maia Olórin, would also have been present at the original music. He too had lived in the garden of Lórien while in Valinor and would undoubtedly have encountered Melian and her singing. There are indeed instances of Gandalf himself singing, notably about

Galadriel in Théoden's hall in answer to Wormtongue's slur on her (*LotR* 514), and on the ride to Minas Tirith with Pippin when the Hobbit hears him "singing softly to himself, murmuring brief snatches of rhyme in many tongues " (*LotR* 597) prior to a rendering, in Common Speech, of a song describing the White Tree and the Palantíri being brought to Middle-earth – objects of crucial significance to Aragorn, especially as, at this point in the story, he has just taken possession of the Orthanc Stone. Thus it is clear that music was an inherent and fundamental part of Aragorn's life and being, through his ancestry, through his upbringing and through those close to him in adulthood.

2 Aragorn: Musician and Poet

I will now examine the episodes in *The Lord of the Rings* which depict Aragorn as a musician, analysing the context and emotions involved where appropriate. Aragorn's life prior to the events related in *The Lord of the Rings* is recorded in an Appendix entitled *Here follows a part of the Tale of Aragorn and Arwen* (*LotR* 1057-63), and it is here that we first meet him, in Rivendell. He is twenty years old and Elrond has just revealed his true identity to him, telling him that he is the Heir of Isildur and the Chieftain of the Dúnedain, and presenting him with some of his family heirlooms: the Shards of Narsil and the Ring of Barahir. He is now walking in the woods at sunset and – as with the first encounters with his distant ancestors described earlier – he is singing, rejoicing in his newly-discovered lineage and status, and expressing his excitement through music. Suddenly he notices a beautiful maiden close by, walking on the grass under some birch trees. He has been singing about Lúthien Tinúviel "And behold! there Lúthien walked before his eyes in Rivendell" (*LotR* 1058). This maiden is actually Elrond's daughter Arwen, newly returned to her father's home after a lengthy sojourn in Lothlórien with her maternal grandparents Galadriel and Celeborn. However Aragorn thinks he is seeing Lúthien herself, though he is not sure whether this is because he is dreaming, or because he has suddenly acquired the Elvish gift of seeing images of the things he has been singing about. Referring back to Chapter 1 in this paper, and the effect of Elvish music on Bëor's people and on Frodo, it is easy to see, from the passages I have emphasised, why the young Aragorn became confused – even to the point of putting himself in Beren's place and calling out "Tinúviel, Tinúviel!" (ibid.). This first encounter with him is a momentous occasion, doubly so with hindsight, as we know what the future holds for him and Arwen, and we understand the similarity of their story to that of Lúthien and Beren. Note that Aragorn is the one singing when he and Arwen first meet. This is the opposite of Beren's and Lúthien's first meeting when it is Lúthien who sings, as well as enchanting Beren with her dancing (S 193).

In the main narrative of *The Lord of the Rings* there are many more examples of Aragorn's musicianship. The first of these occurs when he and the Hobbits are preparing to spend the night on Weathertop, knowing that some of the Nazgûl are not far away. In order to try and calm his companions' fears Aragorn tells them stories of Elves and Men in earlier ages, culminating in a return to the lay of Lúthien and Beren. He tells of their first meeting, in verse form, chanting rather than speaking. Afterwards he recounts the rest of their story while the Hobbits note the effect on him as he becomes totally enwrapped in the tale. They "watched his strange eager face, dimly lit in the red glow of the wood-fire. His eyes shone, and his voice was rich and deep" (*LotR* 194).

With hindsight it is very clear why this particular tale affects him thus and why he chooses this moment to tell it. He has now been betrothed to the maiden he met in the birch woods at Rivendell for nearly forty years and we are told that during his absences, "from afar she [Arwen] watched over him in thought" (*LotR* 1061). Aragorn is currently in much need of her thoughts. He is under no illusions about the threat of the Nazgûl, as witnessed by his words to the Hobbits in the Prancing Pony earlier: "'They are terrible!'" (*LotR* 165) while "his face was drawn as if with pain, and his hands clutched the arms of his chair" (ibid.). This clearly implies previous personal experience of these creatures, who have recently inflicted terror and death on some of his Rangers at Sarn Ford and are now about to make an attempt to seize the Ring from Frodo. Aragorn also assumes that they are responsible for Gandalf's unexplained disappearance leaving him with the responsibility for protecting the Hobbits. His absorption in the tale which is so significant for him and his betrothed, enables him to feel closer to her and fully experience the spiritual protection she can give him.

When introducing the story to his companions Aragorn tells them: "it is a long tale of which the end is not known; and there are none now, except Elrond, that remember it aright as it was told of old. It is a fair tale, though it is sad, [...] and yet it may lift up your hearts" (*LotR* 191). When he finishes he explains: "from her [Lúthien] the lineage of the Elf-lords of old descended among Men. There live still those of whom Lúthien was the foremother, and it is said her line shall never fail" (*LotR* 194). The tale is long because it started in the very distant past with Lúthien and Beren, and is still continuing in the present through their descendants: Elrond and his children, and Aragorn himself. The future is unknown because it depends on the outcome of the war with Sauron. If Sauron is victorious Aragorn will lose Arwen to the Undying Lands. If Sauron is defeated and Aragorn regains his kingdoms he and Arwen will be able to marry, but she will become mortal and thus parted for ever from her father and the rest of the Elves who will suffer the grief of losing *her* as well as Lúthien. Although there will be sadness whatever the outcome, the belief that Lúthien's line shall never fail is also a cause for hope – for Aragorn, and for Elrond too who comes to realise that the loss of his daughter is the price he has to pay for Sauron to be defeated: "Maybe, it has been appointed so, that by my loss the kingship of men may be restored" (*LotR* 1061). As Aragorn knows, the Hobbits are also being drawn into this continuing story, with their involvement in the defeat of Morgoth's greatest servant. During the journey through Cirith Ungol Sam will come to realise that the Phial of Galadriel contains the light from Eärendil's Silmaril and that he and Frodo are in the same tale as Lúthien and Beren (*LotR* 712).

After Frodo has been wounded by the Lord of the Nazgûl Aragorn shows that he has the ability to use music as a spell by singing "a slow song in a strange tongue" (*LotR* 198) over the Morgul knife responsible, before infusing athelas leaves to bathe the wound. This method of healing, by singing combined with application of a herb, reveals another link with Lúthien who healed a wounded Beren in a similar manner. (*LB* 266; *Lay of Leithian* lines 3118-3128). The skill is inherited from his Maian/Elven forebears.

During the time on Weathertop it becomes clear to the Hobbits that Aragorn knows *all* the old tales and lays, not just that of Lúthien and Beren and it may be that a secondary reason for telling them is to educate the Hobbits about the history of Middle-earth given the relevance of some of the events to their current predicament. His reference to the alliance of Elendil and Gil-galad at the end of the Second Age prompts a question from Merry concerning the identity of the latter, which is followed by Sam's recital of some verses about the Elf-king learnt from Bilbo. Shortly afterwards Merry returns to the subject and Aragorn confirms that he knows the full lay of Gil-galad adding "so also does Frodo, *for it concerns us closely*" (*LotR* 191; emphasis added). Both he and the Hobbits – Frodo in particular – are in their present situation due to the failure of Isildur to destroy the One Ring after Sauron was brought down by Gil-galad and Elendil. Their danger is emphasised by Aragorn's abrupt end to the discussion when Frodo is on the point of referring to Mordor by name.

Aragorn's knowledge is further demonstrated during the stay in Rivendell when Bilbo seeks his help with writing a song about Eärendil, clearly recognising him as a fellow song-writer. Aragorn's contribution is to insist that there should be a reference to a green stone on Eärendil's breast. This lay too is relevant to Aragorn's own story as the green stone is the Elessar, originally made for Eärendil's mother Idril. The Elessar presented to Aragorn in Lothlórien by Galadriel (either the same jewel or a later copy[1]) gives him the name he has been prophesied to bear as king.

The next example occurs in very different circumstances, namely after the death of Boromir. To understand the significance of this event from Aragorn's point of view we need to consider what the previous six months have meant for him.

- Due to the disappearance of Gandalf just prior to Frodo's departure from the Shire he has taken it on himself to guide Frodo to the safety of Rivendell, a journey which has involved coming into contact with the One Ring for the first time and fighting off Nazgûl.
- More recently Gandalf – with whom he has been close friends for over sixty years – has apparently fallen to his death in Moria, again leaving him to take up the leadership.
- Knowing that he now has a duty to Frodo (in addition to his original – and only – purpose of accompanying Boromir to Gondor) he is tormented by

---

1 Tolkien wrote two different versions of its history (*UT* 321-6).

indecision as to what he and the Fellowship should do once they reach the point when they have to choose between going west to Minas Tirith or east to Mordor.
- On reaching Parth Galen the company becomes separated, and because Aragorn spends time climbing up to the look-out seat on Amon Hen, hoping to see something to guide him in his uncertainty, he is too far away to be able to help Boromir when he is attacked by Orcs. In fact Aragorn does not actually kill any of the Orcs who attack the Fellowship at this point.

When he finds Boromir fatally wounded at Parth Galen Aragorn is alone with the dying man. Boromir confesses that he tried to take the Ring from Frodo, apologising and pointing out that he has paid for what he did. His last words are an exhortation to Aragorn to go to Minas Tirith since he himself has failed. Aragorn takes his hand and kisses his brow with the words: "You have *conquered*. Few have gained such a *victory*. Be at peace! Minas Tirith shall not fall!" (*LotR* 414; emphasis added). Boromir's victory is over the lure of the Ring as well as over the Orcs. He now understands that he would not have been able to wield it for the good. When Legolas and Gimli reappear they find Aragorn weeping over Boromir who is now dead.

Boromir's river "burial" – chosen due to lack of time for a full burial or the building of a cairn – is followed by an impromptu lament sung by Aragorn and Legolas. As well as enabling the three companions to express their grief, the song commemorates Boromir's long solitary journey to Rivendell to unravel the verse from the dream, and his last battle at Parth Galen against the Orcs. The questioning of the three winds as to his whereabouts illustrates the growing anxiety and ensuing grief of those in Gondor, particularly Denethor, and Faramir who had had multiple occurrences of the dream and had wanted to go on the journey himself. There is also emphasis on Boromir's beauty, reflecting the efforts of his friends who array him in the boat with his weapons beside him, combing his hair, folding the Elf cloak as a pillow, and fastening the Lothlórien belt around his waist.

I will now look at this episode more specifically from Aragorn's viewpoint. The river funeral is *his* idea because of his belief that the Anduin will ensure that Boromir's bones are not dishonoured. He initiates the lament and contributes two verses of it, as opposed to the one verse sung by Legolas. He has additional memories relating to Gondor from his days as "Thorongil", favoured by the Steward Ecthelion, arousing the jealousy of Denethor, and perhaps encountering Boromir as a young child.[2] The episode also illustrates Aragorn's empathetic and compassionate attitude to Boromir. As well as recognising his victory over the Orcs, he respects him for his confession and his courage in admitting that he had been wrong about the Ring. Aragorn understands the lure of the Ring and grieves that someone of Boromir's calibre succumbed to it. Also from his own experiences in the Prancing Pony and on Weathertop he appreciates the shock Boromir felt on seeing the Ring in action. However there is no hint of any of this in the lament because he is protecting the dead man's reputation: "The last words of Boromir he long kept secret" (*LotR* 419).[3] Forest-Hill states:

> In the aftermath of Gandalf's death, Aragorn's grief is alluded to, but never freely expressed and until the completion of Boromir's funeral rites he often seems unable to act decisively or confidently. After Boromir's 'Departure', he becomes more positive in his decision-making, as though the expression of this grief purges an unresolved grief for Gandalf and restores his confidence. (86)

Although I believe that Aragorn does not fully regain his confidence until after his actual reunion with Gandalf, he certainly does become more decisive after Boromir's funeral as if his tears and the singing of the lament provide some relief from the prolonged stress and uncertainty which have been plaguing him.[4]

Aragorn, Legolas and Gimli now set off in pursuit of the Orcs who have captured Merry and Pippin. As day dawns on the first day of the chase Aragorn looks south and sees the mountains of Gondor, their snowy peaks "flushed with the rose of morning" (*LotR* 422). He spontaneously cries out "Gondor! Gondor! Would that I looked on you again in happier hour! Not yet does my road lie southward to your bright streams" (ibid.), before launching into a

---

2 Boromir was born in TA 2978. Aragorn's service to Ecthelion under the incognito of "Thorongil" ended c. 2980 (*LotR* 1090).
3 After the reunion with Aragorn, Legolas and Gimli, Gandalf comes to realise what Boromir has done: "You have not said all that you know or guess, Aragorn my friend […] Poor Boromir! […] Galadriel told me that he was in peril" (*LotR* 496). It is not made clear whether Legolas and Gimli pick up his meaning at this point.
4 He has had little respite since the disappearance of Gandalf in the summer of 3018. For example, while the Hobbits rest in Rivendell for two months he spends most of that time scouring the surrounding lands for signs of the Nazgûl.

verse extolling the silver tree and white towers of Gondor and describing the crown and throne he is striving to obtain (*LotR* 423). It is not clear whether he is reciting or singing at this point, but there is an especial poignancy in his words because he has actually given up on his original plan of going straight to Gondor, first with the intention of accompanying Frodo to Mordor now Gandalf is no longer with them, and then, when that is taken out of his hands, to try and rescue the two youngest Hobbits from the Orcs. He is basically sacrificing his own desires, namely saving Minas Tirith and regaining his kingship, thereby being allowed to marry Arwen. The effort required to put duty first is illustrated by the following passage: "'Now let us go!' he said, drawing his eyes away from the South, and looking out west and north to the way that he must tread" (*LotR* 423).

Although the pursuit of the Orcs proves fruitless it does result in a reunion with the resurrected Gandalf and a journey with him to Rohan. As the four of them gaze at the two lines of burial mounds where Théoden's ancestors rest Aragorn observes that to the Rohirrim, the beginning of their kingdom five hundred years ago "is but a memory of song, and the years before are lost in the mist of time. Now they call this land their home, their own, and their speech is sundered from their northern kin" (*LotR* 507). Then he softly chants a song mourning Eorl the Young, the charismatic first King. It is in the language of Rohan, and Legolas and Gimli do not understand it, but they still listen intently, "for there was a strong music in it." (*LotR* 508). Aragorn then repeats it, translated into the Common Speech. As a young man he spent time in Rohan serving under Théoden's father Thengel (who is now lying in the seventh mound on the left), hence his knowledge of the language and songs and of the events which brought about the kingdom's existence and close alliance with Gondor. The song is given an extra poignancy by the fact that the alliance now appears to be under threat, with Théoden's corruption by Saruman and rumours of Rohan's horses being supplied to Sauron. There is also a sadness in Aragorn's statement that the Rohirrim no longer know their northern history prior to the ride of Eorl, or the language they spoke in those days, the implication being that he knows this history and language himself and perhaps grieves at such ignorance. As with the Hobbits on Weathertop, Aragorn is shown to be teaching Legolas and Gimli something of the history of Middle-earth through song.

Earlier on I referred to Bilbo's recognition of Aragorn's musicianship. Sam too appreciates this quality in him. When Frodo, Faramir and Sam are sitting in Henneth Annûn talking after dinner the conversation turns to the Fellowship's visit to Lothlórien and Sam exclaims:

> "The Lady of Lórien! Galadriel! You should see her, indeed you should, sir. [...] I'm not much good at poetry – not at making it: a bit of a comic rhyme, perhaps, now and again, you know, but not real poetry – so I can't tell you what I mean. *It ought to be sung. You'd have to get Strider, Aragorn that is,* or old Mr. Bilbo, *for that*." (*LotR* 679-80; emphasis added)

It is clear that Aragorn's musical speciality is singing/chanting/reciting. References to musical instruments in connection with him are few, but nevertheless significant, and occur towards the end of *The Lord of the Rings*. There are two examples relating to horns: the "great horn" (*LotR* 782) blown by Halbarad as the Grey Company set out from Helm's Deep for the Paths of the Dead, and the silver horn blown by Aragorn himself to actually summon the Dead Men of Dunharrow. These horns mark the end of Aragorn's incognito. Up until now he has been at great pains to keep his identity as Isildur's heir a secret from Sauron, hence the *lack* of horns to announce himself. This makes an interesting contrast with the Rohirrim who use their horns readily, and with Boromir who is keen to announce his presence with his horn even when it might be better not to do so.[5] However the situation in *The Lord of the Rings* Chapter 5.2 is that Aragorn has just revealed himself to Sauron in the Palantír of Orthanc and has decided to make the journey through the Paths of the Dead. The Grey Company, sent by Galadriel, have travelled from the North to accompany him, asking openly for "Aragorn son of Arathorn" (*LotR* 774). He tells Théoden, "We must ride our own road, and no longer in secret. For me the time of stealth has passed." (*LotR* 779). It is essential that the Dead know that he is Isildur's Heir. When Halbarad blows his horn "the blast of it echoed in Helm's Deep: and with that they leapt away, riding down the Coomb like thunder, while all the men that were left on Dike or Burg stared in amaze" (*LotR* 782). The silver horn with which Aragorn summons the Dead at the Stone of Erech is given to him by Elrohir who has presumably brought it from Rivendell for this purpose.

---

5 When the Fellowship leave Rivendell he is reprimanded by Elrond for sounding his horn, when they are supposed to be setting off in secret. In contrast Aragorn is wearing simple, camouflaging Ranger clothing and does not blow a horn.

Assuming that this is the same horn used by Isildur at the original summoning of the Men of Dunharrow approximately three thousand years earlier, then it is of great historical significance.

Later on, as described by Steimel, trumpets will be blown to mark the progress of Aragorn's army on its journey to the Black Gate, accompanied by announcements from the heralds: "He also had trumpeters who blew fanfares in the lands through which his army passed on the way to the final stand at the Black Gate. This preceded the announcement of his rulership over the conquered country. Trumpets were then blown at the Black Gate, demanding the capitulation of the foe" (98). This is a further indication that secrecy is now a thing of the past. On a similar theme Hardgrave, writing on bell-ringing in *The Lord of the Rings*, lists all the examples where bells are used (15-16), four of which relate to Aragorn and occur in the year Third Age 3019. These will now be looked at in detail, in date order, showing how the bells too play their part in announcing the end of Aragorn's incognito:

March 8th: "Lights went out in house and hamlet as they came, and doors were shut, and folk that were afield cried in terror and ran wild like hunted deer. Ever there rose the same cry in the gathering night: 'The King of the Dead! The King of the Dead is come upon us!' *Bells were ringing far below, and all men fled before the face of Aragorn*" (*LotR* 789; emphasis added). Aragorn, the Grey Company and the Dead Men of Dunharrow have emerged from the Paths of the Dead and are riding at break-neck speed through the Morthond Vale to the Stone of Erech. The fear engendered by the Dead is further emphasised in the following quotations:

> The Paths of the Dead!" said Théoden and trembled [...] and it seemed to Merry that the faces of the Riders that sat within hearing turned pale at the words. (*LotR* 779)

> The terror of the Sleepless Dead lies about the Hill of Erech. (*LotR* 782)

> Folk say that Dead Men out of the Dark Years [...] suffer no living man to come to their hidden halls; but at whiles they may themselves be seen passing out of the door like shadows and down the stony road. Then the people of Harrowdale shut fast their doors and shroud their windows and are afraid. But the Dead come seldom forth and only at times of great unquiet and coming death. (*LotR* 797)

Such a time has come as the Dead have recently been seen gathering. Thus the spontaneous and panic-stricken ringing of the bells expresses an overwhelming terror at the appearance of the ghostly army and its dauntless leader. Aragorn, the Dúnedain and the Dead all appear as similar grey figures, leading to uncertainty as to who is who. Aragorn's identity at this point is that of "King of the Dead".

March 15th: "And some without order, for none could be found to command them in the City, *ran to the bells and tolled the alarm*; and some blew the trumpets sounding the retreat" (*LotR* 846; emphasis added). This refers to the appearance of the black ships at the Battle of the Pelennor Fields. They are assumed to contain the Corsairs of Umbar, hence the raising of the alarm, followed by the sounding of the retreat. In this case the enemy is actually a human one, and one with which Gondor has long been familiar. Aragorn himself, under the incognito of "Thorongil", has fought a naval battle against them within the last forty years. Warnings have been received of their approach so their arrival at the Harlond is not unexpected. Thus the main purpose of the bells would be to warn of their actual approach, with the retreat being sounded as resignation and despair set in, with defeat being seen as inevitable. A significant aspect of this incident is the lack of organisation within Minas Tirith, which is not surprising given that Denethor is now dead and Gandalf's main concern is for the condition of Faramir and others who are near death. Thus the ringing of the bells and the sounding of the trumpets are due to people acting on their own initiative as they see fit.

March 15th: "Thus came Aragorn son of Arathorn, Elessar, Isildur's heir, out of the Paths of the Dead, borne upon a wind from the Sea to the kingdom of Gondor; and the mirth of the Rohirrim was a torrent of laughter and a flashing of swords, and the joy and wonder of the City was *a music of trumpets and a ringing of bells*" (*LotR* 847; emphasis added). In contrast this example of bell-ringing relates to the same scene only minutes later, when it becomes clear that the fleet is actually being led by Aragorn – now revealed as the returning King. A thousand years have passed since the death of King Eärnur and the idea of a returning king is perhaps seen as an impossible dream to many in Gondor. In addition the Rohirrim, who of course know Aragorn's identity, believe that he has met his death in the Paths of the Dead. Thus there must have been an initial sense of disbelief, prior to realisation of the truth as Arwen's battle-standard is unfurled displaying the emblems of Elendil, Isildur and Anárion. The spontaneous sounding of the bells and trumpets indicate unrestrained delight and perhaps the dawning of hope that Sauron could actually be defeated.

May 1st: "And when the sun rose in the clear morning above the mountains in the East, upon which shadows lay no more, *then all the bells rang* and all the banners broke and flowed in the wind; and upon the White Tower of the citadel the standard of the Stewards, bright argent like snow in the sun, bearing no charge nor device, was raised over Gondor for the last time" (*LotR* 965-6; emphasis added). Nearly two months later Aragorn's coronation is about to take place with the bells being part of a well-planned, well-rehearsed celebration.

When Frodo and Sam are honoured on the Field of Cormallen after the destruction of the One Ring, horns and trumpets are played while the crowd shout their praises. This is followed by a minstrel singing "Frodo of the Nine Fingers and the Ring of Doom" (*LotR* 953-4). Aragorn has already demonstrated his recognition of the Hobbits' ordeal and achievements as indicated by his words to Sam, "It is a long way, is it not, from Bree, where you did not like the look of me? A long way for us all, but yours has been the darkest road" (*LotR* 954), and by his act of kneeling before them and sitting them on his throne. In addition he will have learnt much of their sufferings during the long-drawn-out process of healing them.[6] On returning to the Shire Frodo (and later Sam) will write his own account of the War of the Ring in the Red Book, thus providing a written record for posterity. "Frodo of the Nine Fingers and the Ring of Doom" will ensure that their heroism is also preserved in song.

3 Aragorn: Connoisseur of Music

As well as being a singer and a composer of songs Aragorn displays appreciation and knowledge of music, both technically and from the viewpoint of its history. This is partly due to his ancestry and upbringing – he must have learnt much from Elrond and Gandalf for example. However another very significant factor

---

6 Cf. the healing of Faramir when Aragorn shows an acute awareness of his patient's encounters with the Black Breath and the grief caused by his father's treatment.

is the great journeys he has made, incognito, prior to the events in *The Lord of the Rings*. The purpose of these was to prepare for kingship by uncovering the plots and devices of Sauron and his servants, and by getting to know the different peoples of Middle-earth, both those who would be his subjects or allies if he were to become king, and those who supported Sauron. This includes acquainting himself with their history, lore and culture. Trautman, in his MA thesis on the function of verse in *The Lord of the Rings*, states:

> Tolkien uses the poetry Aragorn recites to suggest his fitness for the throne he is to ascend to. By the diversity of the poetic material Aragorn knows Tolkien shows that he is well-educated in the history of the lands he will rule, and familiar with the cultures of the various sections of his realm. Aragorn's verses also show him to be a civilized, cultured person with admirable qualities which contribute to the air of regality seen in him even before his crowning. (56-7)

The best way to illustrate this aspect of Aragorn and music is to go back to the song about Eorl the Young (*LotR* 508). From his time in Rohan as a young man Aragorn knows the language of the Rohirrim, he appreciates their culture and music, and he is able to translate the song into Common Speech in a way that keeps the feel of the original. He also knows that the words were first spoken by a forgotten poet in praise of Eorl and that the song is still sung in the evenings. In addition he understands how the Rohirrim celebrate their fallen heroes by singing – rather than writing – about them. A good example of this is when Théoden announces that he is ready to ride to battle even if it leads to his death. Aragorn declares: "Then even the defeat of Rohan will be glorious in song" (*LotR* 518). Just under two weeks later Théoden is killed at the Battle of the Pelennor Fields helping to achieve a victory for Gondor. "Long afterward" (*LotR* 849) a poet of Rohan does indeed sing a lament mourning those who fell that day, not only the Rohirrim but those from the southern parts of Gondor as well. When hearing that song Aragorn may well have reflected on the omission of the name of his valiant kinsman Halbarad, (leader of the Grey Company, and standard-bearer) who also died in the battle. Being of the Northern Dúnedain he was unknown in the south.

In addition to Rohan, Aragorn's travels must also have involved going through Dunland, and we know that he has journeyed "far into the East and deep into the South" (*LotR* 1060) learning the lore of the peoples he encounters. Thus he probably knows Dunlending, Easterling and Haradrim songs as well. The same could also apply to Orc songs as he tells Éomer that "there are few among mortal Men who know more of Orcs" (*LotR* 433) than he does. Since a high proportion of his travelling has been done alone, much of his Orc know-how would have come from secret observation as opposed to actually fighting the creatures. Orcs of Mordor sometimes used Black Speech, the language of the Ring verse recited by Gandalf at the Council of Elrond. There is no indication of Aragorn's personal reaction to this but the episode should perhaps be viewed in the context of Isildur's failure to destroy the Ring and his own recent experiences of coming into contact with the Ring for the first time and witnessing its effect on Frodo.

In the scene at the Prancing Pony Inn it is clear that the inhabitants of Bree like songs, as one of the Bree-hobbits asks Frodo to sing and the cry is then taken up, "sing us something that we haven't heard before!" (*LotR* 158). As a long-standing patron of the inn Aragorn is no doubt familiar with most of the usual offerings. Also, according to Barliman Butterbur, he "can tell a rare tale when he has the mind" (*LotR* 156), which could involve him doing some singing or reciting himself. Whatever the case though, I think we can safely assume that Frodo's song on this particular evening does not meet with Aragorn's approval! Joking aside, the disappearing incident must have been deeply disturbing to him. A further example of a Hobbit song occurs during the journey to Rivendell when Aragorn and the Hobbits encounter the stone Trolls (*LotR* 206-7) and decide to stop there for a break. This is a welcome respite after the horrors of the attack on Weathertop and the subsequent struggle to avoid their pursuers. Frodo is feeling slightly better as the sun is warm and he is cheered by the reminders of Bilbo's successful journey. As the company joke about the bird's nest behind the ear of one of the Trolls and eat their mid-day meal under the legs of another the camaraderie in the group – Aragorn included – is very evident. This is reinforced by Sam singing his Troll song which is relevant to their situation but light-hearted. It also comes under the category of "something that we haven't heard before" and shows Sam in a new light.

A further respite takes place after the loss of Gandalf in Moria (*LotR* 339-41) when the Fellowship rest by the River Nimrodel and Legolas sings of the Silvan Elf after whom the river is named. However, looking back again to Frodo's experiences in the Hall of Fire in Rivendell, it occurs to me that there may be more to this incident than a brief rest stop. Although the Company are well away from Moria and have reached the eves of Lothlórien, it is now dark and thus they are still in grave danger from pursuing Orcs. Aragorn knows they can go no further that night and his plan is therefore to turn aside from the path after a short distance and try to find a safe hiding-place among the trees. Before this can happen they reach the Nimrodel where they stop *next* to the path. They now bathe their feet in the river, sit down and have something to eat, then listen to Legolas telling tales of Lothlórien which he has learnt in his own land of Mirkwood. There is then a silence during which Frodo fancies that he can hear actual singing mingling with the sound of the water. It is this which prompts Legolas's song of the Elf Nimrodel. When he has sung all that he can remember he relates the rest of Nimrodel's story as well as getting involved in a discussion with Gimli concerning the awakening of evil in Moria. It is actually Gimli who eventually alerts them to their present danger by suggesting that it might be safer to be up in the trees (like the Elves of Lothlórien), prompting Aragorn to observe: "We have sat here beside the road already longer than was wise" (*LotR* 341). The implication seems to be that the combined enchantment of Nimrodel's river and the song of Legolas has made the Company oblivious to their danger, *even Aragorn who, not long before, was expressing the urgent need to get off the path and seek concealment.*

Aragorn would certainly have appreciated the music which was performed at his coronation supplied by harpists from Dol Amroth, viol and flute players and singers from the vales of Lebennin (*LotR* 965, 968). From the technical point of view Aragorn displays an awareness of metres – such as the "an thennath" mode used in the Tale of Tinúviel (*LotR* 193).[7] Though it is difficult to render the tale in Common Speech he still manages to produce an acceptable interpretation of it. He also knows that the poem about Gil-galad recited by Sam on the approach to Weathertop was "part of the lay that is called 'The Fall of Gil-galad', which is in an ancient tongue" (*LotR* 186), going on to observe that Bilbo must have translated it.

---

7 Hammond and Scull (174-5) refer to the suggestion by Wynne and Hostetter (114) that "an thennath" means "long-shorts" or "longs and shorts", perhaps describing syllables of contrasting lengths.

4 Aragorn as the Inspiration for Songs and Verses

As well as singing and writing songs and poems Aragorn is also someone who has inspired them and will continue to do so, some eulogistic, some prophetic, some with both characteristics. "The Riddle of Strider", incorporated in Gandalf's letter which Frodo receives in Bree and quoted indignantly in Aragorn's defence by Bilbo at the Council of Elrond, is a song about him written by Bilbo himself. As well as praising his friend, Bilbo includes references to prophecies relating to him:

> From the ashes a fire shall be woken,
> A light from the shadows shall spring;
> Renewed shall be blade that was broken,
> The crownless again shall be King. (*LotR* 170, 247)

The verse from the dreams of Faramir and Boromir, also quoted at the Council of Elrond, contains the prophetic advice to "Seek for the Sword that was broken" pointing out that "Isildur's Bane shall waken" (*LotR* 246) – the finding of the One Ring being the signal for Elendil's sword to be reforged. When Éomer learns of Aragorn's great pursuit of the Orcs with Legolas and Gimli he declares "Strider is too poor a name [...] Wingfoot I name you. *This deed of the three friends should be sung in many a hall*." (*LotR* 436; emphasis added). This is a great compliment as the Rohirrim are not a literate people, instead using song to commemorate their heroes.

Aragorn's journey through the Paths of the Dead is the subject of prophetic verses, starting with Galadriel's message to him delivered by Gandalf on their reunion in Fangorn:

> Where now are the Dúnedain, Elessar, Elessar?
> Why do thy kinsfolk wander afar?
> Near is the hour when the Lost should come forth,
> And the Grey Company ride from the North.
> But dark is the path appointed for thee:
> The Dead watch the road that leads to the Sea. (*LotR* 503)

There is no further explanation at this point, nor any reaction from Aragorn, but Legolas, who has also received a message from Galadriel, seems to think he speaks for both of them in his comment: "Dark are her words, and little do they mean to those that receive them" (*LotR* 503). The first actual reference to the "Paths of the Dead" does not occur until the arrival of Aragorn's kinsmen in Rohan, when Elrohir gives him a message from Elrond reminding him: "If thou art in haste, remember the Paths of the Dead" (*LotR* 775), to which Aragorn replies, "great indeed will be my haste ere I take that road" (ibid.). This conversation shows that he is clearly aware of the Paths and the horrors associated with them. On realising that it is in fact necessary for him to take that route he enlightens Legolas and Gimli about the journey by quoting the alliterative verse prophecy made by Malbeth the Seer during the reign of Arvedui, the last king of the North Kingdom:

> Over the land there lies a long shadow,
> westward reaching wings of darkness.
> The Tower trembles; to the tombs of kings
> doom approaches. The Dead awaken;
> for the hour is come for the oathbreakers:
> at the Stone of Erech they shall stand again
> and hear there a horn in the hills ringing.
> Whose shall the horn be? Who shall call them
> from the grey twilight, the forgotten people?
> The heir of him to whom the oath they swore.
> From the North shall he come, need shall drive him:
> he shall pass the Door to the Paths of the Dead. (*LotR* 781)

Aragorn then explains that the oath in question was sworn to Isildur by the Men of the (White) Mountains who subsequently refused his summons to fight and were cursed by him as a result. However Isildur foresaw that they would be given another chance to fulfil the oath. This prediction was made over three thousand years previously at the end of the Second Age, and merely stated that the second summons would take place after "years uncounted" (*LotR* 782). Malbeth's verse, dating from the late 1900s of the Third Age, gives more detail, clearly specifying Aragorn's situation: namely the location for the summons, the heir of Isildur summoning the Dead with a horn, his origins in the North and the desperate need which obliges him to choose such a route. The rather cryptic verse of Galadriel now makes more sense. She knows that the journey through the Paths of the Dead is appointed to Aragorn and she will organise the summons of Aragorn's northern kinsmen (the Grey Company) to come to his aid. Aragorn himself will tell Éowyn, "I go on a path appointed" (*LotR* 783).

These two verses, along with the supplementary information provided, show the history and significance of the journey through the Paths of the Dead and its relevance to Aragorn, starting with Isildur's prediction, followed by the detailed prophecy of Malbeth, and then finally the messages from Galadriel and Elrond indicating that the time has come to summon the Dead again and give them the chance to fulfil their oath. As well as being prophetic, Malbeth's verse also acts as a piece of advice for the conduct of this second summoning, not only for Aragorn, but also for Elrond who ensures that Elrohir takes the silver horn to Aragorn and for Arwen who entrusts to Halbarad the battle-standard which she has made. The standard and the horn are both used as identification of Isildur's heir when Aragorn summons the Dead.

On a different subject is the rhyme quoted by the herb-master in the Houses of Healing:

> When the black breath blows
> and death's shadow grows
> and all lights pass,
> come athelas! come athelas!
> Life to the dying,
> In the king's hand lying! (*LotR* 865)

He refers to this as one of the "rhymes of old days which women such as our good Ioreth still repeat without understanding", and as "a doggrel [...] garbled in the memory of old wives" (ibid.). Ioreth has in fact already recognised the link between the kings and healing: "Would that there were kings in Gondor, as there were once upon a time, they say! For it is said in old lore: *The hands of the king are the hands of a healer*. And so the rightful king could ever be known" (*LotR* 860; emphasis added). The herb-master's quotation completes the process initiated by Ioreth's linking of the kingship with healing by introducing the virtue of athelas into the equation. Both of their contributions are taken seriously by Gandalf who ensures that some leaves of the vital herb are located. It is Aragorn's tireless night of healing, rather than victory in battle, which first leads to him being recognised as king in Gondor. This episode brings to mind Celeborn's advice to Boromir prior to the departure of the Fellowship from Lothlórien: "do not despise the lore that has come down from distant years; for oft it may chance that old wives keep in memory word of things that once were needful for the wise to know" (*LotR* 374).

Following the destruction of the Ring an Eagle flies westwards urging the people to sing because Sauron is no more and the King is victorious. It then prophesies that:

> your King shall come again,
> and he shall dwell among you
> *all the days of your life.*
> And the Tree that was withered shall be renewed,
> and he shall plant it in the high places,
> and the City shall be blessed. (*LotR* 963; emphasis added)

The third line of this verse, by the word "your" (as opposed to "his") appears to foresee Aragorn's long life. As he will reign for a hundred and twenty years he will actually outlive all those alive in Gondor at the time of his accession. In fact he himself predicts the same thing as shown by his words to Gandalf on Mount Mindolluin: "But I shall die. For I am a mortal man, and though being what I am and of the race of the West unmingled, I shall have life far longer than other men, yet that is but a little while; and when those who are now in the wombs of women are born and have grown old, I too shall grow old" (*LotR* 971).

Interestingly Tom Bombadil also has a role in prophesying the return of the King, though for once he seems to be talking rather than singing. While accompanying the Hobbits to the East Road following the incident on the Barrow Downs, he tells them some of the history of the Dúnedain and the old North Kingdom of Arnor: "Few now remember them, yet still some go wandering, sons of forgotten kings walking in loneliness, guarding from evil things folk that are heedless" (*LotR* 146). The Hobbits do not understand his words, but "they had a vision as it were of a great expanse of years behind them, like a vast shadowy plain over which there strode shapes of Men, tall and grim with bright swords, *and last came one with a star on his brow.*" (ibid.; emphasis added). The star is the Elendilmir, which the Kings of Arnor wore instead of a crown. This is not the place to discuss the identity of Tom Bombadil – Vala, Maia, Ilúvatar himself, or none of these – but we do know that he has been in existence since the beginning of the world: "Tom was here before the river and the trees; Tom remembers the first raindrop and the first acorn" (*LotR* 131). Also it is apparent that Aragorn knows him – quite well too if his familiar reference to him as "old Bombadil" (*LotR* 163) is anything to go by. After Frodo's meeting with Gildor

Inglorion during his flight from the Shire, a network of communication comes into operation – consisting of Tom (and Goldberry), Farmer Maggot, Gildor and Aragorn – via which information is exchanged about the whereabouts of Frodo and the Nazgûl. I have already argued that Bombadil actively helps to bring about the meeting between Aragorn and Frodo (Nicholas 387-9). Thus there is a further potential connection between Aragorn and a participant in the original music, and one to whom music is his way of communicating.

An early version of *The Lord of the Rings* App A.I.v refers to songs which will be written in future years recalling Aragorn's deeds in Third Age 3018-19: "Thus the War of the Ring began; and the shards of the sword of Elendil were forged anew, and Aragorn Arathorn's son arose and fulfilled his part, and his *valour and wisdom* were revealed to Men. *Songs were made after in Gondor and Arnor concerning his deeds in that time which long were remembered*" (*PME* 266; emphasis added). As well as the obvious subject of Aragorn's achievements in battle, these songs could also be assumed to recognise his healing skills, his courage in challenging Sauron in the Orthanc Stone in order to turn his attention away from Frodo, the journey through the Paths of the Dead, and the compassionate wisdom displayed in the dismissal of the faint-hearted at the Black Gate in a manner which enabled them to keep their self-respect.

After Aragorn's coronation Arwen's banner is unfurled on the topmost tower of the Citadel and "the reign of King Elessar began, *of which many songs have told*" (*LotR* 968; emphasis added). Thus Aragorn's deeds as king will also be immortalised in song, for example the peace treaties he makes in the immediate aftermath of the War of the Ring and, over the years, the renewal of the glory and beauty of his kingdoms, making them places of welcome for all races: Hobbits, Elves, and Dwarves as well as Men. In addition there are battles still to be fought, with Éomer at his side, for "the King of the West had many enemies to subdue before the White Tree could grow in peace [...] and beyond the Sea of Rhûn and on the fields of the South the thunder of the cavalry of the Mark was heard, and the White Horse upon Green flew in many winds until Éomer grew old" (*LotR* 1071).

I finish this section by looking at a short verse spoken by Aragorn's mother Gilraen in *Part of the Tale of Aragorn and Arwen*. It is eleven years prior to the events of *The Lord of the Rings* and Aragorn is taking his leave after paying her a visit. She tells him: "This is our last parting, Estel, my son. I am aged by care, even as one of lesser Men; and now that it draws near I cannot face the darkness of our time that gathers on Middle-earth. I shall leave it soon" (*LotR* 1061). When Aragorn tries to comfort her by encouraging her to believe that there will be a light beyond the darkness she answers with the following "linnod":

> "Ónen i-Estel Edain, ú chebin estel anim"
> [Translation: "I gave Hope to the Dúnedain, I have kept no hope for my self"] (ibid.)

"Estel" meaning "Hope" was the name given to Aragorn in his childhood to keep his identity secret and to emphasise the hope he represented, as prophesied by Gilraen's own mother, Ivorwen, prior to the marriage between her daughter and Arathorn: "If these two wed now, hope may be born for our people [...]" (*LotR* 1057). Regarding the word "linnod", Hammond and Scull (700) refer to the suggestion by Wynne and Hostetter (131-2) that it was derived from the Sindarin words "linn" meaning "song" or "chant" and "od" meaning "seven". The two halves of this piece of verse each contain seven syllables. A study by Straubhaar (237-40) of Gilraen's linnod identifies parallels for this type of verse from Old Norse poetry, giving examples of "kvidhlingar" (defined as "shorter epigrams, typically uttered under some emotional pressure") which have a strict number of syllables, use alliteration, and consist of a brief, emotional speech by a woman to a kinsman who is leaving her. Gilraen's grief at this final parting from her son is exacerbated by the fact that she has seen very little of him since his childhood. After his departure from Rivendell as a twenty-year-old "she seldom saw her son again, for he spent many years in far countries" (*LotR* 1061). Aragorn's own grief as he goes away "heavy of heart" (ibid.) is no doubt intensified by guilt at not visiting her more frequently, unavoidable though that was.

So far I have covered four of my five topics. To summarise these:

1) Aragorn is descended from the union of a Maia and an Elf. He has been brought up by Elves in an Elvish refuge. One of his closest friends in adulthood is a Maia. As a result music must be an essential and fundamental aspect of his psyche.

2) He uses music: to express emotion – joy, excitement, grief, yearning, nostalgia, to calm, to allay fear, to relax, to heal, to praise, to mourn and respect the dead, to tell the stories, lore and history of Middle-earth.[8]

3) He has a general knowledge of music, technically and culturally, through his upbringing and education and through his travels. He understands different metres and languages and has some ability as a translator of songs, preserving the feel/mood of the original.

4) He is the subject of songs, both prophetic and eulogistic.

5 Aragorn and the "Divine Plan"

For the fifth topic in this paper, I return to our first encounter with Aragorn as the excited twenty-year-old, newly aware of his true identity, singing about Beren and Lúthien in the birch-woods of Rivendell at the very moment when Arwen has returned from a lengthy sojourn in Lothlórien. Twenty-nine years later, while journeying near the borders of Lothlórien – when Arwen just happens to be there again – he is "admitted to the hidden land by the Lady Galadriel" (*LotR* 1060). Arwen sees him "walking towards her under the trees" (ibid.), whereupon "her choice was made and her doom appointed" (ibid.). Note the similarity to Lúthien's doom coming upon her when seeing Beren in the enchanted forest in the protected kingdom of Doriath. As Aragorn sings on Weathertop, "doom fell on Tinúviel" (*LotR* 192).

Events in *The Silmarillion* help us to understand Galadriel's role here. The Elfking Thingol is determined that no Man will enter Doriath while his realm lasts. The young Galadriel is living there at the time under the tutelage of Melian who tells her "one of Men, even of Bëor's house, shall indeed come, and the Girdle of Melian shall not restrain him, for doom greater than my power shall send him" (*S* 167). Two ages later these words must have been in Galadriel's mind when she allowed Aragorn into Lothlórien. Melian's speech continued thus: "And the songs that shall spring from that coming shall endure when all

---

8 Contrast this with Boromir who was uninterested in lore except for tales of old battles (*LotR* 1056), and with Éowyn who, until she fell in love with Faramir, only enjoyed "the songs of slaying" (*LotR* 965).

Middle-earth is changed" (ibid.). Two ages later Aragorn sings some of these songs – in Rivendell and on Weathertop.

There is a clearly defined plan here. These events cannot be due to mere chance. Aragorn is linked to the original music by his Maian and Elvish ancestry, and also, of course, so is Arwen who, being Half-elven and only five generations in descent from Melian and Thingol, possesses these characteristics to an even greater degree. When we finally see them together as husband and wife and King and Queen they are sitting by the fountain in the citadel of Minas Tirith and Arwen is singing a "song of Valinor, while the [White] Tree grew and blossomed" (*LotR* 974). The implication here seems to be that her song is encouraging the Tree to grow, thereby strengthening not only the Tree, but the kingship itself.[9] This power of Arwen's fits in with her close descent from Melian, and with Melian's kinship with the Vala Yavanna who created the original Two Trees of Valinor by singing. Another source is indicated in the song of Galadriel (her maternal grandmother): "I sang of leaves, of leaves of gold, and leaves of gold there grew" (*LotR* 372). Aragorn's and Arwen's gifts will be inherited by their children thus strengthening the line of the kings in the Fourth Age.

In *Athrabeth Finrod ah Andreth*, Tolkien states: "Thus from the union of Lúthien and Beren [...] the infusion of a 'divine' and an Elvish strain into Mankind was to be brought about, providing a *link* between Mankind and the Elder World, after the establishment of the Dominion of Men." (*MR* 340; *Athrabeth* Author's Note 3; emphasis added). By the end of the First Age this link is centred on Elrond and Elros [Arwen's father and uncle, and Aragorn's great(x62)-uncle and great(x61)-grandfather]: "And from these brethren alone has come among Men the blood of the Firstborn and a strain of the spirits divine that were before Arda" (*S* 306). Finally, in a draft letter to Peter Hastings, Tolkien writes of "a *Divine Plan* for the ennoblement of the Human Race, from the beginning destined to replace the Elves" (*L* 194; emphasis added). Aragorn's and Arwen's story is the final stage of this "Divine Plan" as laid out in the original music.

---

9 Towards the end of the Second Age Tar-Palantir, the very foresighted penultimate King of Númenor, prophesied that if the line of the White Tree failed the line of the Kings would also perish.

About the Author

ANGELA NICHOLAS graduated in Latin at London University (Royal Holloway College) in 1971 and also has post-graduate qualifications in Librarianship and Information Technology. She is now retired after a career first in higher education as a librarian and then in local government as an IT specialist. Her interest in Tolkien's works began in the early 1970s then, after lying dormant for some years, was reawakened on the release of Peter Jackson's films in 2001-3. Dissatisfied with the film version of Aragorn she embarked on a detailed study of the character as portrayed by Tolkien resulting in the publication of *Aragorn: J.R.R. Tolkien's Undervalued Hero* in 2012. She is a member of the Tolkien Society and of the Southampton UK Tolkien Reading Group and has contributed several articles to the Tolkien Society publication *Amon Hen*.

List of Abbreviations of Tolkien's Works

L	*The Letters of J.R.R. Tolkien*
LB	*The Lays of Beleriand*
LotR	*The Lord of the Rings*
MR	*Morgoth's Ring*
PME	*The Peoples of Middle-earth*
S	*The Silmarillion*
UT	*Unfinished Tales of Númenor and Middle-earth*

Bibliography

FOREST-HILL, Lynn. "Boromir, Byrhtnoth, and Bayard: Finding a language for grief in J.R.R. Tolkien's *The Lord of the Rings*." *Tolkien Studies* 5 (2008): 73-97.

HAMMOND, Wayne G. and Christina SCULL. *The Lord of the Rings: A Reader's Companion*. London: HarperCollins, 2005.

HARDGRAVE, Martin. "Bells and Bell-ringing in Middle-earth." *Mallorn* 31 (1994): 15-19.

NICHOLAS, Angela. *Aragorn: J.R.R. Tolkien's Undervalued Hero*. 2nd ed. Edinburgh: Luna Press, 2017.

STEIMEL, Heidi. "Bring Out the Instruments." *Music in Middle-earth*. Eds. Heidi Steimel and Friedhelm Schneidewind. Zurich and Jena: Walking Tree Publishers, 2010, 91-105.

STRAUBHAAR, Sandra Ballif. "Gilraen's Linnod: Function, Genre, Prototypes." *Tolkien Studies* 2 (2005): 235-244.

TOLKIEN, J.R.R. *The Lays of Beleriand*. (The History of Middle-earth 3). Ed. Christopher Tolkien. London: HarperCollins, 2002.

The Letters of J.R.R. Tolkien. Selected and edited by Humphrey Carpenter with the assistance of Christopher Tolkien. London: HarperCollins, 1995.

The Lord of the Rings. London: HarperCollins, 2007. Based on the 50th Anniversary edition 2004.

Morgoth's Ring. (The History of Middle-earth 10). Ed. Christopher Tolkien. London: HarperCollins, 2002.

The Peoples of Middle-earth. (The History of Middle-earth 12). Ed. Christopher Tolkien. London: HarperCollins, 2002.

The Silmarillion. Ed. Christopher Tolkien. London: HarperCollins, 1999.

Unfinished Tales of Númenor and Middle-earth. Ed. Christopher Tolkien. London: HarperCollins, 1998.

TRAUTMAN, David. *The Function of Verse in J.R.R. Tolkien's Lord of the Rings*. MA Thesis, Lehigh University, Department of English, 1980.

WYNNE, Patrick and Carl F. HOSTETTER. "Three Elvish Verse Modes." *Tolkien's Legendarium: Essays on The History of Middle-earth*. Eds. Verlyn Flieger and Carl F. Hostetter. Westport, CT: Greenwood Press, 2000, 113-139.

Sabine Frambach

"Where you hear song, you may rest at ease": The Music of the Evil Ones in Middle-earth[1]

Abstract

This paper draws our attention to the dichotomy of evil characters in Middle-earth and music. While music and song are mostly associated with positive aspects like joy and artistry, Frambach explains what kind of instruments are preferred by evil beings and how creatures like orcs make use of music in their own wicked way.

Preface

Where you hear song, you may rest at ease,
Without fearing a country's beliefs;
Where you hear song there will be no thieves,
evil people have no melodies.[2]

Is it true what the German poet Johann Gottfried Seume (1763-1810) states in his famous song? Do villains have no songs? Do they not play any instruments? Do they never hum or whistle and are they really lacking musical talent? What about the villains Tolkien put to paper? Who are they, what makes them the evil beings they are? And, most importantly, what does their music sound like?

---

1 Many thanks to Hans Renske for translating this paper.
2 "Wo man singet, da lass dich ruhig nieder, / ohne Furcht was man im Lande glaubt; / wo man singet, wird kein Mensch beraubt, / böse Menschen haben keine Lieder". This is the popular version of Johann Gottfried Seumes original poem "Die Gesänge" (1804): „Wo man singet, lass dich ruhig nieder,/ Ohne Furcht, was man im Lande glaubt; / Wo man singet, wird kein Mensch beraubt; / Bösewichter haben keine Lieder." (https://de.wikipedia.org/wiki/Johann_Gottfried_Seume; last visited 8.8.19)

Evil? An Attempt at a Definition

In her book Eichmann in Jerusalem Hannah Arendt reports "on the horrible banality of Evil" (371). It is called banal because the people doing evil things could not simply be included in the category of villains. These "killers were no mean villains; they also were not born sadists or otherwise perverted." She appropriately assesses: "They were regular people" (194). Regular people doing evil things. This is how it relates to Evil, it is part of their world and can therefore never be completely destroyed. Every single one of us has both good and bad inside. There also is a villain inside all of us. But what kind? Psychology knows various kinds of villains. The narcissists are vain and self-centred. The god lending them his name is in love with his own reflection. He tries to look for the stage, for the big entrance and for the admiration of others (cf. Zimbardo 608). They appear to be void of empathy and totally egocentric. They are usually cognitively capable of understanding other people's feelings, but have no compassion and are unable to feel guilt (609). Power-hungry people, who only strive to gain their own advantages, are excellent manipulators and can ingratiate themselves cunningly, if it serves their purpose. In reference to an Italian statesman we refer to power-hungry people as Machiavellists. These are occasionally joined by another kind of villain, the sadist. The sadist enjoys putting other people down or likes to torture them (612).

What all these villains have in common, is that they possess a tendency towards destructivity; they destroy and kill, rather than building up. Aggression, paired with the intent to do damage, shows malicious tendencies, whether it is a child destroying other children's sandcastles, or someone blowing up a high-rise with a bomb. This tendency is also present in all people, but its manifestation differs from person to person. Freud captured these negative desires in the term Aggression drive (cf. Mietzel 297-299). Evil acts aggressively towards everything else, such as things, plants, animals, other people and against society. We feel that aggressive and destructive behaviour only is evil, when it stems from selfish and egotistical motives. We would not believe a policeman who hurts a fugitive who is running away, or an explosives expert who blows up a ramshackle bridge, to be evil. Though they act aggressively and destructively, they do so for the good of the community. Anti-social behaviour, therefore, includes "all kinds of behaviour, which grossly disregards the interests of other people, or of the community, because of egoistical reasons" (Zimbardo 702).

Besides, successful villains fascinate other people. Their conduct can be charming, witty and impressive. They can mesmerise other people and exercise a huge influence on them. Hitler enticed entire masses of people with his conduct, and Jack the Ripper, the serial killer, is more interesting to people than his victims have ever been. This fascination with Evil does not stop at Middle-earth. Colin Manlove concludes: "Sauron is fascinating. He mesmerises people and he is meant to also mesmerise the reader" (118). Compared to these larger than life villains without remorse or compassion, the evil infantry appears to be of little interest. They often do not act out of their own free will; they merely execute orders or go with the flow. Acting evil requires that the person doing so still has his or her own free will. In short, the evil characters show the following characteristics: they are vain, self-loving and without compassion. They are power-hungry, manipulative, sadistic and fascinating… Which of Tolkien's villains fit this description? Are they evil by nature?

Evil in Middle-earth

At first sight, Middle-earth seems to be like a fairy tale environment. Good and Evil can be distinguished clearly and with little difficulty. Therefore the literary critic Edmund Wilson concludes that "what we are served here, is a simple confrontation […] between powers of Evil and powers of Good" (54) and, therefore, he refers to *The Lord of the Rings* as a "fairy tale novel" (52). Yet, upon closer examination, we are unable to effortlessly sort Tolkien's characters only into Good and Evil. Evil is part of the world, it consists of the drive for power. This aim for all-encompassing power can even originate from the initial wish to accomplish Good. In Tolkien's world the antagonist or enemy "always strives for pure domination, which is why he is Lord of magic and machinery; yet the problem is that this terrible Evil can grow out of a seemingly good root, i.e. the wish to be of use to the world and others" (30). Thus, in *The Lord of the Rings*, Tolkien shows how absolute power in the hands of a single person never leads to Good. So Gandalf shies away from the Ring, and Galadriel senses what might happen to her if she were to accept the Ring: "In place of the Dark Lord you will set up a Queen. And I shall not be dark, but beautiful and terrible as the Morning and the night!" (*LotR* I 381)

Evil, therefore, exists in this world; there is not a single evil one, there is not only black and white. It is more that Tolkien allows good characters to possibly be corrupted by power and greed; he allows them to succumb and fail. Bilbo has a hard time giving up the Ring, as "there was an angry light in his eyes. His kindly face grew hard" (*LotR* I 42), Boromir wants to accept the Ring to save Gondor, the wise sorcerer Saruman becomes power-hungry. "Saruman begrudged them that, for his pride and desire of mastery was grown great" (*S* 361).

Absolute power, symbolised by the One Ring, shows the effect it has and triggers evil thoughts. Tolkien writes: "And so big was the greed the Ring evoked in a person, that anyone who used the Ring was overcome by it; it exceeded any willpower" (quoted in Pesch 41). In Middle-earth, Evil also is nothing special, and everyone must deal with it. Tolkien presents it as part of the world. His villains are fallen figures, who succumb to Evil. The first case of a power-hungry creature who follows Evil can be found at the beginning of *The Silmarillion*.

Melkor and the False Tones

Eru created the Ainur and taught them a powerful melody. Among the Ainur was Melkor, abundantly gifted with power and knowledge. His behaviour is reminiscent of that of the angel Lucifer; Melkor, the creative spirit, looks for the everlasting flame. He was unhappy with the void and challenged the god.

> But as the theme progressed, it came into the heart of Melkor to interweave matters of his own imagining that were not in accord with the theme of Ilúvatar; for he sought therein to increase the power and glory of the part assigned to himself. [...] Some of these thoughts he now wove into his music. (*S* 4)

He did not wish to conform, he did not just want to play his part in the Ainur's music, but he wanted to create his own tones and be louder than the others. Melkor displays a hunger for power (machiavellistic behaviour) and wants to be at the forefront (narcissistic behaviour). Instead of harmony, because of his individual actions he generates disharmony. His song fights Ilúvatar's. Melkor's motivation is not the music, but proof of power. He wants to be admired "and he wished himself to have subjects and servants, and to be called Lord, and to be a master over other wills" (*S* 8). As all he does is generate volume and power, Melkor's song "was loud, and vain, and endlessly repeated: and it had little harmony, but rather a clamorous unison as of many trumpets braying upon a few notes" (*S* 5). His song aims to destroy the other song. The attempt to be louder, more important and more powerful, to raise himself above the community, is a defiant insubordination against Eru. So it had to be even more shocking to learn that this part of the music (and therefore also Good and Bad) also originates from Ilúvatar. It is part of the whole. Melkor, the Disturber, "shall prove but mine instrument" (*S* 6), Ilúvatar explains. Melkor's false tones belong to this world, just like Evil does. They are part of the music, without the ability to permanently change the tune. With this song, his rampage in this world starts. He does not only show a high degree of destructiveness musically; "they built lands and Melkor destroyed them; valleys they delved and Melkor raised them up; mountains they carved and Melkor threw them down; seas they hollowed and Melkor spilled them" (*S* 12). Whatever he cannot have for himself, no one should own. What others erect, is not to remain. His aggression drive is huge. Only once does he create anything: a corrupted people.

Orcs and their Music

Unlike the dazzling and powerful evildoer Melkor, the Orcs are more like foot soldiers. "Quendi who came into the hands of Melkor […] were put there in prison, and by slow arts of cruelty were corrupted and enslaved; and thus did Melkor breed the hideous race of the Orcs" (*S* 47). These broken, corrupted creatures are to play a clear executive part only; their potential for development is minimal. They are aggressive, greedy, without empathy and antisocial. They obey and hardly have their own free will and are thus useful and dependent minions to Sauron. They act on order. Through obedience and fright, they remain attached to their creator; they "hated everything beautiful and loved to kill and destroy" (Foster 388). What about their musical abilities? In *The Hobbit* we encounter singing Orcs, but their song is described as croaking and the songs are accentuated by the pounding of their feet. The song's function quickly becomes clear: it is a mocking song, a song that is meant to generate fear, to humiliate their opponent:

> The goblins began to sing, or croak, keeping time with the flap of their flat feet on the stone, and shaking their prisoners as well.
>
> Clap! Snap! the black crack!
> Grip, grab! Pinch, nab!
> And down, down to Goblin-town
> You go, my lad! (*H* 67-8)

Their songs sound "truly terrifying" (*H* 68) and represent a mockery of beautifully sounding songs: "The general meaning of the song was only too plain; for now the goblins took out whips and whipped them with a swish, smack!, and set them running as fast as they could in front of them" (*H* 68) The evil song is meant to intimidate, its rhythm makes the prisoners move. Such mocking songs are no longer found in *The Lord of the Rings*; the Orcs sing "with harsh voices" (*LotR* III 97), but no lyrics are mentioned. But now they do have instruments with them: horns, gongs and drums. "Sam heard a hoarse singing, blaring of horns and banging of gongs" (*LotR* II 351-2). As broken as the character has become, so has their music degenerated. The singing is missing or consists of a croaking, instruments are replaced by shields and whips, or feet. When instruments are used, they are instruments with a signalling effect. The music the degenerated Orcs make is primitive, practical and raw. Where the instruments are from remains unclear. It is conceivable that they scavenged them. They are not inept, but the drive to build their own instruments is supposedly not within them. In *The Hobbit* they are described as follows: "They make no beautiful things" (*H* 69). And an instrument certainly is an object of beauty.

The Instruments of the Villains

Melkor apparently does not own an instrument; he creates disharmony and chaotic tones without using an instrument. Tolkien, however, does compare Melkor's tones with the sound of many trumpets. It sounds as "a clamorous unison as of many trumpets braying upon a few notes" (*S* 5). The other villains also use no instrument; except for the Orcs, no instruments are found neither with Sauron nor with Saruman. An instrument assumes that one might use it to make music with it. Tolkien reduces the evil characters all the time to only using trumpets, which already were mentioned as comparison for Melkor, and drums, horns and gongs.

In Moria the fellowship reads in the Book of Mazarbul about "drums, drums in the deep" (*LotR* I 336) that were to be heard. Whilst looking for the captured Frodo, Sam heard "a hoarse singing, blaring of horns and banging of gongs, a hideous clamour" (*LotR* II 351-2). During the siege of Gondor the drums "rolled and rattled" (*LotR* III 102), and at the black gate "came a long rolling of great drums like thunder in the mountains, and then a braying of horns that shook the very stones and stunned men's ears" (*LotR* III 164). These instruments all have in common that they function as a signal and are often used to be sounded shortly and loud. They announce something or attract attention. This is how Sauron's warriors use their horns "in signal long arranged" (*LotR* III 167). The drum is often used in its capacity as a rhythm instrument during battles. It dictates the marching rhythm: "The music, shattering horns, drum rolls, drew us in" (Weißauer 44) it is written about a battle in World War II. In *The Lord of the Rings* drums are also mentioned frequently when there is marching going on or a battle starts: "Drums rolled and fires leaped up. The great doors of the Black Gate swung back wide. Out of it streamed a great host" (*LotR* III 167). By means of music as a stylistic device, Tolkien shows the aggressive focus of the villains. His evil characters know songs, but they are mocking songs. They know instruments, but only to provide a rhythm to an attack with, to set in motion, for instilling fear. The instruments the evil creatures use, are used appropriately to march, to send signals or to intimidate the enemy with. This is all about functional music.

Functional and Dysfunctional Music

What would a world be without its music? Sam prophecies a dark future, if Evil gains the upper hand. "How Samwise fell in the High Pass and made a wall of bodies round his master. No, no song. Of course not, for the Ring'll be found, and there'll be no more songs" (*LotR* II 345). I cannot formulate it any clearer than Sam did. Melkor's interfering tones, the Orcs with their mocking songs, the hoarse songs, the pounding of the drums, they all are no songs. Sam has beautiful songs in mind. Songs that elate the heart.

Music is heard for many reasons. In Tolkien's world it also has many functions: Songs tell stories, just like the minstrels once did. They underscore an undertaking in the form of a work song, or the dwarves doing the dishes: "Clap the glasses and crack the plates! / Blunt the knives and bend the forks!" (*H* 23) Songs accompany a funeral service, or sound as a battle hymn, to motivate one's own troops with or to frighten the opponent. These songs we can consider to be functional music; the music serves a particular purpose. In contrast, there is music, that comes from the heart, that has no purpose, dysfunctional music, which is only heard for the sake of it being music. Like when characters hum or sing only to themselves, and the song comes from their feelings. Tom Bombadil sings his song this way, while jumping through the Old Forest: He "was singing a song; a deep glad voice was singing carelessly and happily" (*LotR* I 130).

When we look at the villains, it is apparent that they use pretty much only functional music. Melkor aims to disturb their music and to increase his own power. His song "essayed to drown the other music by violence of his voice" (*S* 5). He uses music as a demonstration of power. Among the Orcs we find the mocking songs and the frightening music which accompanies a fight. It could be imagined that they are using work songs, which move the work or provide it with a rhythm to follow:

> He could hear the goblins beginning a horrible song:
> Fifteen birds in five fir trees
> their feathers were fanned in a fiery breeze!
> But, funny little birds, they had no wings!
> O what shall we do with the funny little things?
> Roast 'em alive or stew 'em in a pot;
> fry them, boil them and eat them hot? (*H* 107)

The evil characters' songs are limited to functional music. Music is used purposefully, to demonstrate power, to generate fear, and to mock opponents with. Only one supposedly evil creature dances to the beat of a different drummer here.

Gollum's Song

In *The Lord of the Rings*, we encounter a creature that supposedly should be considered to be evil, as it is full of greed, calculating and prepared to hurt other creatures. The creature did succumb to power and Evil and became a murderer out of greed, "because the gold looked so bright and beautiful" (*LotR* I 62). His desire to have the Ring became so overpowering, that he delivered Frodo to Shelob. He would sacrifice Frodo sociopathically and without compassion, just to get "the Precious, a reward for poor Sméagol who brings nice food" (*LotR* II 333). At the same time, Gollum demonstrates the ability to smooth-talk his way towards his goal. And this creature sings a song just to himself, a dysfunctional song, out of joy, and enjoys it, even.

> He seemed greatly delighted to feel the water, and chuckled to himself, sometimes even croaking in a sort of song.
>
> *The cold hard lands*
> *they bites our hands,*
> *they gnaws our feet.*
> *The rocks and stones*
> *are like old bones*
> *all bare of meat.*
> *But stream and pool*
> *is wet and cool:*
> *so nice for feet!*
> *And now we wish—* (*LotR* II 227)

What brings Gollum to sing this song? To sing it out of elation, and just to himself? At this moment Gollum's forgotten facet emerges. He appears to be only superficially evil; Gollum, corrupted by the Ring, becomes a killer, yet he does contain Good within himself, still. Because of this reason he cannot sing a song, but merely croak it, and still sing it for fun, to himself only: "There was a little corner of his mind that was still his own, and light came through it, as through a chink in the dark: light out of the past" (*LotR* I 64). Tolkien again demonstrates at this moment, that creatures are not evil right from the start, but that they are ruined by Evil; they could not resist the greed and the power. For this moment, Gollum once again is part of the foot soldiers, singing a song free of worry. The lyrics are like a riddle, thematically connecting him to the rounds of riddles he and Bilbo engaged in. Gollum interrupts it, only to croak: "Baggins guessed it" (*LotR* II 227-8), before continuing the song. Gollum happily sings a riddle song, while splashing around through the water. Even then, his song is not beautiful; he also croaks it, and does not sing it. Evil within him has gone too far already; just like Melkor's tones and the Orcs' voices he sounds disturbing and disharmonic. As an ambivalent character he sings a happy song, but with a croaking voice. But a different villain displays such a talent in singing, that he even wins a song contest.

Sauron's Victory

"Among those of his [Melkor's] servants that have names the greatest was that spirit whom the Eldar called Sauron or Gorthaur the Cruel" (S 23). He becomes more powerful while at the same time he becomes more aggressive, he acts "misshaping what he touched" (S 181). He is a shapeshifter and is therefore capable of deceiving his surroundings. He is a "master of shadows and of phantoms" (S 181), he is very influential and has a manipulative ability. In particular "flattery sweet of honey was ever on his tongue" (S 325). He invokes fascination and can captivate many creatures this way. "And he was crafty, well skilled to gain what he would by subtlety when force might not avail" (S 324).

Sauron thus meets the criteria of the gruelling sadist, the power-hungry machiavellist, and the sociopath without compassion. Sauron's pride makes him narcissistically strive, "to make him master of all things in Middle-earth" (S 346). Sauron is the perfect villain. Tolkien managed to let this antagonist below Melkor develop into a multifaceted creep, who eventually surpasses his one-time lord.

As the ideal villain he should barely use music. When he does use it, it should be for his own means and when he sings, he should be croaking. Instead, Sauron manages to defeat an elf in a song contest: "Thus befell the contest of Sauron and Felagund which is renowned. For Felagund strove with Sauron in songs of power, and the power of the King was very great; but Sauron had the mastery, as is told in the Lay of Leithian" (S 200). How could he pull that off? Felagund, the elf king, sings so beautifully during his first encounter with the sleeping Bëor and his companions that each of them "thought that he was in some fair dream, until he saw that his fellows were awake also beside him;

but they did not speak or stir while Felagund still played, because of the beauty of the music and the wonder of the song" (*S* 163).

This is the elf with the beautiful voice that Sauron competes against and beats in the singing contest. This can only be explained by assuming that he also uses his manipulative abilities while singing. It means he can flatter while singing. He sings so brilliantly that he even takes down a great singer. Apparently, this song does not only contain music. He sang "a song of wizardry" (*S* 200). In the song, powers beyond the singing performance unfold. The song is bewitched, Sauron uses witchcraft, and by doing so he demonstrates his power. The battle in the song flows back and forth. Finrod puts "all the magic and might he brought / Of Elvenesse into his words" (*S* 200-1), only to give up, because of the powerful images that Sauron conjures up through his singing. It is a victory of power and of Evil, but it is not a victory of the most beautiful singing.

> The wolf howls. The ravens flee.
> The ice mutters in the mouths of the Sea.
> The captives sad in Angband mourn.
> Thunder rumbles, the fires burn –
> And Finrod fell before the throne. (*S* 201)

In Conclusion

The villains in Tolkien's world know music, and they definitely sing, even though usually they sing for a particular purpose. They almost exclusively use functional music. They do not sing beautifully, but when sorcery and power are involved, they are able to sing powerfully. They do not sing for fun, unless for a moment they remember what and who they once were. They use few instruments only, which predominantly have a signalling effect, or provide a rhythm. The villains of Middle-earth do have music, but we should beware of their songs. Modifying Seume's poem ("evil people have no melodies") we could therefore conclude:

> Where someone croaks, you may not rest at ease,
> The song consists of fear and mocking and scorn,
> Sauron's witch songs may seem like a disease,
> Melkor's anger leaves every note quite torn.[3]

---

3 "Wo einer krächzt, da lasse dich nicht nieder, / das Lied besteht aus Furcht und Spott und Hohn, / mächtig wirken Saurons Hexenlieder, / Melkors Wut erklingt in jedem Ton." (Sabine Frambach)

About the Author

SABINE FRAMBACH (*1975) studied social education in Nijmegen and adult education in Kaiserslautern and now lives with her husband in Mönchengladbach, Germany.

List of Abbreviations of Tolkien's Works

H	The Hobbit
LotR	The Lord of the Rings
S	The Silmarillion

Bibliography

ARENDT, Hannah. *Eichmann in Jerusalem. Ein Bericht über die Banalität des Bösen.* 14th ed. Munich andBerlin: Piper Press, 2017.

DORGELÈS, Roland. "Die hölzernen Kreuze." *Soldatengeist.* Ed. Ludwig Weißauer. Berlin: Nibelungen Press, 1941, 44-46.

FOSTER, Robert. *The Complete Guide to Middle-earth.* 2nd ed. New York City, NY: Ballantine, 1979.

MANLOVE, Colin. "Der Herr der Ringe." *J.R.R. Tolkien – der Mythenschöpfer.* Ed. Helmut W. Pesch. Meitingen: Corian Press Wimmer, 1984, 91-121.

MIETZEL, Gerd. *Wege in die Psychologie.* 9th ed. Stuttgart: Klett-Cotta, 1998.

TOLKIEN, John Ronald Reuel: *The Hobbit.* London: Allan & Unwin, 1979.

The Lord of the Rings. Collector's Edition. 2nd ed. Boston, MA: Houghton Mifflin, 1987.

The Silmarillion. Ed. Christopher Tolkien. London: HarperCollins, 1999.

WILSON, Edmund. "Die bösen, bösen Orks." *J.R.R. Tolkien – der Mythenschöpfer.* Ed. Helmut W. Pesch. Meitingen: Corian Press Wimmer, 1984, 51-56.

ZIMBARDO, Philip G. and Richard J. GERRIG. *Psychologie.* 7th ed. Berlin and Heidelberg: Springer Press, 1999.

INSTRUMENTS IN MIDDLE-EARTH

Heidi Steimel

An Orchestra in Middle-earth

Abstract

Tolkien's Middle-earth has inspired many musicians to compositions, both vocal and instrumental. This paper introduces readers to the following classical orchestral works:

The Hobbit by Carey Blyton
Symphony Nr. 1, "The Lord of the Rings" by Johan de Meij
The Dreams of Gandalf by Aulis Sallinen
Middle Earth by Craig H. Russell
Quendi, Valaquenta I, Eldarinwe Lirí, Eärendil, the Mariner, and *Telperion and Laurelin*, all by Martin Romberg

Heidi Steimel examines the effect orchestral music has in evoking emotions and bringing its listeners into Middle-earth. After all, these compositions come from outside the secondary world and do not intend to sound as if they were authentically played within the context of the story. They are therefore different from music composed for Tolkien's poems and add variety to the mix of folk music, heavy metal, and film soundtracks which are popularly heard by Middle-earth fans. Music that has been composed for concert audiences may even help raise awareness of the depth of Tolkien's literary legacy and attract new readers.

"As an author I am honoured to hear that I have inspired a composer," Tolkien wrote in 1964 (*L* 350). Since then his books, especially those concerning Middle-earth, the secondary world he created, have been the inspiration for a great variety of musical works. Many are vocal, either settings for his poems and songs, or with original lyrics about his world.

One of the foremost authorities on Tolkien-related music, Chris Seeman, has counted thousands of artists who have set Tolkien's words to music, written new lyrics based on Tolkien's stories, and created instrumental, orchestral, and choral compositions using his works as a foundation or point of departure. (Scull/Hammond, *Guide* 620)

The style of these compositions includes such variations as medieval, folk, classical, and heavy metal. Some would be appropriate in Middle-earth, some not – unless the rock music would be ascribed to Melkor's and Sauron's followers.

Music that is used within the context of a story can be called "diegetic"[1] and judged not only on its own merit but also by its appropriateness within the secondary world setting.

Symphonic, orchestral works have no counterpart in Middle-earth and can therefore be considered "non-diegetic". They express the thoughts, impressions and emotions of the composer who is inspired by Tolkien's works. "Instrumental music can try to tell a story in music, like a tone poem of the kind perfected by Richard Strauss; it can be a character portrait; or it can be more amorphous and atmospheric" (Bratman 153). Of the music composed for instrumental performance, Howard Shore's film scores for Peter Jackson's movies are the most widely known works and have found their way into concert repertoire.

I would like to introduce the readers of this book to those symphonic compositions which have not only been written, but also made known through public performances and recordings.[2] For the most part, they are commercially available and thus accessible to all who are interested. The majority of them were composed before *The Lord of the Rings* and *Hobbit* movies were released and have therefore not been influenced by those.

Tolkien loved classical music and was married to a trained pianist. Though he did not himself play an instrument, he enjoyed concerts and operas. Unfortunately, he was not able within his lifetime to hear most of the compositions his work inspired – it would have been interesting to find out what he thought of them!

Where I have found information on the composers' intentions I have taken them into consideration in my discussion. Aside from that, the interpretation is entirely my own and every reader and listener is of course welcome to form a personal opinion that differs from mine. My introductions are just that – an attempt to crack the shell of works that may be hitherto unknown in order to reveal what is inside, to tempt the reader's appetite for more.

---

[1] This term, normally used in the context of filmmaking and playwriting, is here applied to differentiate the various types of music inspired by a literary work.
[2] I am aware that there are other works of which I have heard, but they have not been available to me at this time for evaluation.

The Hobbit Overture: Carey Blyton

"You certainly have my permission to compose any work that you wished based on 'The Hobbit'" (*L* 350). This letter, which also includes the quote at the beginning of this essay, was written by Tolkien to Carey Blyton in 1964. The composer had asked for permission to write a Hobbit overture. Many Tolkien fans have read this missive in *The Letters of J.R.R. Tolkien* without realising that the overture was actually composed.

Carey Blyton, nephew to the well-known author of children's books Enid Blyton, was born in 1932 and began his musical career relatively late. He began playing the piano out of boredom during an illness at the age of 16. After finishing his education he composed for movies, television, and radio – among others for the Dr Who series. He "was primarily a miniaturist, composing mainly songs, chamber music and short orchestral scores" (Blyton).

The Hobbit, a concert overture for orchestra (Opus 52a), was composed in 1967 and is, to my knowledge, the earliest classical orchestral work that was inspired by Tolkien's books. It is very short – only approximately five minutes long! It has the charm of a miniature and a style that is accessible to an audience that does not normally listen to classical music. Tolkien must have had some apprehension that the unknown piece could be too modern or abstract for his taste and hoped "that I might perhaps find the result intelligible to me, or feel that it was akin to my own inspiration" (*L* 350). There is no record that he was ever able to hear the composition, but I cannot help thinking that he would indeed have liked it.

The overture begins with a short French horn solo that is reminiscent of the fanfare theme of the classic Star Trek television series – the first three notes form the exact same melody! The following theme is cheerful and dance-like without being folksy. It suits Bilbo, the hero of the story, well. Further characters are introduced with short melodies. Appropriately, the harp is assigned to the Dwarven king Thorin, who plays the instrument in the book.

Gollum's theme is played by two instruments, oboe and bassoon, which join in a creepy duet, illustrating the character's split personality. A big jump in the storyline brings the music to the Lonely Mountain, with the Dwarven treasure. A chorale-like passage makes this audible. Suddenly Smaug's theme interrupts, followed by a plucked string which indicates the bow shot which killed the dragon. Descending notes show his fall. The Battle of the Five Armies is omitted, and the piece closes with repetitions of the various themes for the return journey home.

Though we do not know if Tolkien ever heard a performance of this composition, he apparently received a manuscript of it, which he lent to Joy Hill in 1967 (Scull/Hammond, *Chronology* 713). Carey Blyton was also mentioned as one of the guests who were invited to the reception when Donald Swann's *The Road Goes Ever On* was released (ibid. 721). The overture was played and recorded by the Royal Ballet Sinfonia, conducted by Gavin Sutherland. In my opinion this work embodies the spirit of the book which inspired it very well – it is entertaining, light-hearted, and humorous. That makes it accessible to both adults and children. Indeed, the only complaint might be that which Tolkien himself mentioned in writing about *The Lord of the Rings*: "too short"! (*LotR* xxv)

The Lord of the Rings, Symphony No. 1: Johan de Meij

The best-known symphonic work that was inspired by Tolkien's Middle-earth is the *Symphony No. 1, The Lord of the Rings*, written by Dutch composer and conductor Johan de Meij in 1984-88. The piece won the prestigious Sudler Composition Prize, beginning de Meij's successful career which continues to this day. He is sought after internationally as a guest conductor and lecturer. The symphony was composed for concert band, which gives it a unique sound. It has since been orchestrated for full orchestra by Henk de Vlieger. Bratman comments, "Although de Meij is Dutch, his music is very much in the tradition and style of popular British concert band and symphonic music by composers like Gustav Holst and Malcolm Arnold" (162). Its five movements are very vivid and different from one another.

"Gandalf" is the first movement – the wizard is introduced with fanfares, indicating the importance of his part in the story. A majestic theme follows, only to be replaced by a fast, restless passage, which brings his ride on Shadowfax to life. Then a chorale-like melody shows his lofty, angelic nature as a Maia before the movement ends with fanfares.

The second movement, "Lothlorien", paints a landscape with music. The songs of birds can be heard in the Elven woods as well as deep sounds for the mighty trees. Both the beauty and the dangerous, mysterious nature of the forest are depicted. A dance-like passage shows the gracefulness of Galadriel, then the music becomes threatening. A look in the Mirror has made the enemy visible.

Without a break, the music segues into the third movement, "Gollum". Now the sound is less harmonious, even discordant. The creature is characterized as fearful and aggressive, slinking, and crazed. An uneven, limping rhythm shows the unbalanced nature of both body and soul, and the music sounds almost like that of a circus. The listener may well have the eerie feeling of encountering an evil clown. The dramatic end to Gollum's life in the fire of Mount Doom can be heard at the end of the movement.

"Journey in the Dark" is the fourth movement. It tells the story of the Fellowship's journey through the underground realm of Moria. Deep tones and percussive beats bring the footsteps in the dark to life, at first slow and laborious, then when danger appears, fast and hectic. A rustling sound, like fire, introduces the Balrog. Then a death-knell rings for the fallen Gandalf. His theme from the first movement is repeated and develops into a dirge.

The final movement is cheerful. "Hobbits" takes up several of the previous themes and combines them. First we hear the fanfares from the opening movement, then a cheerful folk dance. However, the music shows that the Hobbits are not just funny, but have an important task to fulfill in Middle-earth. The melody becomes a hymn. Once more we hear Gandalf's theme, then the fanfare, but this seemingly dramatic finale is not yet the end. Calmly, peacefully, and with a bittersweet mood the piece ends, like Tolkien's story does, with the Ringbearers' last journey to the Grey Havens.

It is the contrast of the movements that make this symphony so interesting, some depicting characters, some landscapes, and others events. Listeners who may not otherwise enjoy classical music will still find this work very accessible. In addition to the afore-mentioned orchestration it has also been arranged for youth and school orchestra or band. It has become a popular, frequently played piece and there are several recordings. My personal preference is the original instrumentation for concert band. The composer himself was the musical advisor for the recording by the Dutch Royal Military Band, conducted by Pierre Kuijpers.

The Dreams of Gandalf, Symphony No. 7, op. 71: Aulis Sallinen

The Finnish composer Aulis Sallinen, one of the most important modern classical musicians of his country, is well-known internationally. David Bratman calls him "perhaps the world's leading living symphonist" (161). In addition to numerous works for orchestra and chamber music he has composed several operas. Sallinen's *Symphony No. 7, op. 71* is called "The Dreams of Gandalf". It was composed in 1995-96 and consists of a single movement which lasts 25 minutes.

The symphony begins with a drum beat and a fanfare-like sequence of five notes: G-A-D-A-F. These spell the name of Gandalf in musical form, at least as far as possible – there are of course no notes with the letters "N" and "L".[3] This theme is used later on in the piece as well.

Dramatic passages and quiet, even playful ones alternate, and some scale-like melodies seem to indicate the movement of journeys. Often the notes make up a tapestry of sound, followed by wind instruments and drum cadences. Melodies are interwoven, some of them quotes from older sources – medieval Finnish songs and French pieces. One that I recognized was the melody used for the traditional English Christmas carol "Good King Wenceslas". The symphony closes with a gradual diminuendo, a fading that could indicate Gandalf's final journey into the West.

---

[3] I am indebted to Bratman for this information, (162) which would not have been available to me without access to the score. There is a long musical tradition of spelling names, including those of composers, with notes of the scale. B-A-C-H is one example, which works in the German notation system, since B indicates B-flat and H is used for B-natural.

As the title of this work suggests, this piece does not necessarily tell a specific story, but rather reflects impressions and emotions. The composer himself says, "The symphony does not actually depict the events in the novel; rather it is a musical expression of the literary atmosphere and poetry" (14). The themes are partially taken from a previously planned composition, a *The Lord of the Rings* ballet, which was never completed.

This symphony is not easy listening for fans of popular classical music. It is a work which contains modern harmonies and dissonances and may require some familiarisation. Of its structure Martin Anderson says: "The work progresses not in wide symphonic spans but in a patchwork of differing moods and colours derived from its balletic origins" (14).

One especially interesting aspect concerning this composition is that it was written by a Finnish composer who was inspired by Tolkien, just as the author himself was inspired by Finnish mythology. Another work by Sallinen strengthens this connection – he composed the opera *Kullervo*, drawing on the legend of the tragic hero of the Finnish national epic *Kalevala*, who was the inspiration for Tolkien's character Turin in the Silmarillion. Sallinen was closely involved in the production of the recording of this symphony by the Staatsphilharmonie Rheinland-Pfalz, conducted by Ari Rasilainen, in 2002.

Middle Earth: Craig Russell

The American composer Craig H. Russell, who lives, composes, and teaches in California, wrote the suite *Middle Earth* in 1995 as a commission for the San Luis Obispo Youth Symphony. At the time, he was reading *The Hobbit* and *The Lord of the Rings* with his young family and decided that Tolkien's tales should provide the inspiration for the piece. The suite was finished within three days! The composer says that he deliberately tried to keep it short and, wherever possible, make it funny or clever (2). The individual movements are more characterisations than narratives, with sounds that make the various characters audible. The musical style is very much in the modern American tradition and shows similarity to the compositions of Aaron Copland. Originally the work had seven movements; two years later Russell re-orchestrated the suite and added two movements. The entire work has a total length of only 12 ½ minutes and is based on *The Lord of the Rings*.

"Frodo Leaves the Shire" is the first movement. It begins with a rhythmic basis; the composer superimposes a quiet melody above that. But the rhythm dominates, becomes more insistent, until it is clear that the protagonist must become active. The movement ends with the harmonies of open violin strings, which reminds me of the tuning of instruments at the beginning of a concert – appropriate for the start of the adventure.

In the second movement, "Gimli, the Dwarf" is characterised with an Irish dance. It would be interesting to find out why Russell chose to depict the dwarf as lively and folksy – perhaps he was remembering the unexpected party at the beginning of *The Hobbit*.

For "Galadriel and Her Elven Mirror" the composer chose a soft, romantic melody in ¾ time, a gentle waltz that sounds wistful, almost a love song.

"Gollum", the next movement, is very short – only half a minute! The string basses play deep notes in what the composer calls "'gulps'… creating a swallowing sound" (2). Tolkien described Gollum's voice in similar terms.

The fifth movement, "Gandalf: The White Rider", sounds almost like an early American hymn. That could indicate the Maia's origin as an angelic being. Interestingly, the composer divided the piece into two halves – the second one repeats the first, only upside down and backwards (2). Perhaps that is meant to depict the two halves of the wizard's life, first as Gandalf the Grey, then as the resurrected Gandalf the White.

"Shelob's Lair" begins with a wandering melody line, first alone, then joined by an increasing number of voices. This reminds me of the growing structure of a spider's web. Further sounds are eerie and otherworldly, with rustling and clicking noises.

In the seventh movement, "Orcs and Ring Wraiths" are characterised by strong, marching rhythms. Those are joined by clashing dissonances and wild sounds, some of which are produced by maltreating the piano with tennis balls! Ugly creatures are depicted by unpleasant music, which becomes increasingly chaotic and ends with the echo of marching feet.

"Strider and the Crowning of Aragorn" is by far the longest movement in the suite – 3 ½ minutes. This indicates that the composer considers Aragorn to be a very important character in the story. Short pieces of melodies show us glimpses of Strider, still hidden. The music increases in momentum, the melody becomes stronger, more distinctive, pronounced and active, played by the trumpet. The rhythms indicate adventures and journeys. Then the melody is interrupted, returning as a fanfare. Both melody and rhythm are majestic – the king is crowned.

The final movement, "Frodo and Company Return", repeats the beginning theme of the first movement and adds parts of the melodic themes of Gimli, Galadriel, and Gandalf. The various characters return to their homes. A brief closing chord sounds like a period ending the story. The beginning and ending of the suite are "there and back again".

This very entertaining musical work, with its light-hearted, witty miniatures, is sure to capture the attention of interested listeners, both adults and children. It was recorded by the San Luis Obispo Symphony, conducted by Michael Nowak.

Quendi; Valaquenta I; Eldarinwe Líri; Eärendil, the Mariner; Telperion and Laurelin: Martin Romberg

The previous works I have considered are single Tolkien-inspired pieces by different composers. Now I would like to introduce a young composer who has written several works based on Middle-earth.[4] Martin Romberg was born in Norway, studied music in Vienna, and now lives and works in France. Myths and fantasy tales are frequently his inspiration for compositions. Tolkien is especially important to him, and the *Silmarillion* is his major focus.

Quendi is a symphonic poem for orchestra, composed in 2008. It is a delightful work that displays some of the cheerful, light-hearted character of Tolkien's

---

4 For the sake of completeness I have included those works by Romberg which are Tolkien-inspired even if they are not orchestral.

Elves. The musical style is influenced by Impressionism, and the various tone colours of the instruments give the melodies charm and wit. The atmosphere is dreamy, allowing listeners to decide whether they are imagining a story, various characters, or general impressions – or all of these. No official recording has been released so far, but the piece, performed by the Orchestre National de Montpellier under Robert Tuohy, can be heard on YouTube.

Valaquenta is a collection of seven pieces for solo piano, one for each of the masculine Valar. The pieces reflect each person's character.

- "Manwe" is majestic, with powerful chords and deep bass notes, fitting for the King of the Valar.
- "Ulmo" has lively, flowing, sparkling sounds that are well suited to his element, water.
- "Aule" is surprisingly delicate, focusing on the smith's creative side rather than on his strength.
- "Orome" does not include obvious hunting references such as horns, but rather much movement by the use of arpeggios, which could refer to horse riding. The quieter passages could be a reflection of his role as "Lord of the Forests".
- "Mandos'" piece sounds much like a funeral march, a dark melody with deep chords that show us the keeper of the Houses of the Dead.
- "Lorien", the master of dreams and visions, is characterised by dreamy passages that sound like they come from afar.
- "Tulkas'" music is fast and powerful, like the strong hero who is faster on foot than any other creature.

Of this work Romberg says that he tried "to create a musical language that corresponds to the noble and mythic atmosphere of the text […] to tell a story with great respect for the simple, but with aspirations towards those large structures in which we have real time to reflect upon and integrate the emotional message of the drama" (Romberg). Pianist Aimo Pagin plays these challenging pieces with unhurried dignity and simplicity, contributing with his style toward that objective.

Eldarinwe Líri is a composition for girls' choir with soloists and harp accompaniment. It is based on five of Tolkien's Elvish language poems.

- "A Elbereth Gilthoniel", Tolkien's hymn to Varda, the goddess of the stars, appears in various versions in *The Lord of the Rings* and is one of the author's best-known songs. The language is Sindarin. (*LotR* 309, 1345)
- "Oilima Markirya" – This less-known poem is Tolkien's longest text in Quenya. The title translates as "The Lost Ark"; it is found in the essay "A Secret Vice" in *The Monsters and the Critics*, including Tolkien's own translation. (*MC* 213-215)
- "Nieninque" – This poem and its translation are also included in "A Secret Vice". (*MC* 215-216)
- "Firiel's Song" is not based on the well-known Firiel poem of the Tom Bombadil cycle but on one in Quenya from "The Lost Road", Volume 5 of *The History of Middle-earth*. (*LR* 63, 72)
- "Namarie" is the well-known farewell song sung by Galadriel in *The Lord of the Rings*. The book version is Tolkien's translation; the Quenya original can be found in Swann's *The Road Goes Ever On*. (66)

Martin Romberg dug deep to find the lyrics he wanted to set to music. The musical style of these pieces shows both modern and medieval influences, producing an otherworldly atmosphere which is appropriate for the non-human Elvish race. The lovely, unobtrusive harp accompaniment adds to it, especially since harps were the most important instruments of the Elves in Middle-earth. The haunting melodies for soloists and choir and the unusual harmonies sound different to Western listeners than the accustomed classical tradition.

Though a commercial recording is not yet available, a beautiful performance of this work in 2010 by Trio Medieval, The Norwegian Girls' Choir, and Johannes Wiik and Ellen Sejersted Bödtker (Harps), conducted by Benedikte Kruse, can be heard on YouTube.

Eärendil, the Mariner is a piece for solo piano, composed in 2013, that was commissioned by pianist Alexandra Silocea. She recorded it along with other pieces on the theme of water. The proximity of Romberg's composition to those of Debussy and Ravel clearly shows the influence of Impressionism on this piece. It is easy to hear the sparkling, flowing, and bubbling sound of water in the music. My impression is that it is more atmospheric than narrative, though elements of the story of the legendary sailor of Tolkien's world can be detected in swaying ship's movement, for example. Silocea plays the technically ambitious piece with wonderful clarity and effortlessness.

Telperion and Laurelin are Tolkien's mythological trees which gave the world light before they were destroyed. Romberg's symphonic poem reflects the dramatic aspects of the tale rather than being a programmatic retelling. It begins quietly, like first rays of light shining, then broadens to full brightness. Sparkling sounds are repeated throughout the piece, emphasising the theme of light. At the end, it fades away. The greater range of instrumental sounds, compared to his earlier orchestral works, shows Romberg's development as a composer. The style of his music has changed somewhat, sounding more modern in its harmonies and melodies, though the influence of Impressionism can still be heard.

This work, first performed publicly in 2013, has not yet been released as a recording, but is available on YouTube. It was performed by Orchestra Régional Avignon Provence, directed by Samuel Jean. Romberg plans to compose more pieces inspired by Middle-earth, which gives both Tolkien fans and fans of classical music something to anticipate.

How have these classical orchestral works contributed to Tolkien's world? They evoke emotions and express their creators' impressions of his mythology. They encourage listeners to use their own imagination to interpret their message and to broaden their horizons by discovering various styles. This "serious" music, which was composed for concert audiences, may even help to raise awareness of the depth of Tolkien's literary legacy, thereby making a new group of readers curious about the books and introducing them to the wonderful world of Middle-earth.

About the Author

HEIDI STEIMEL was born and educated in the U.S.A. and holds a Bachelor of Music from Grace University, Omaha, Nebraska. She now lives in Germany, where she has served as a church musician, piano teacher, translator and interpreter. She is a member of the German Tolkien Society, has lectured at the German Tolkien Seminar, and co-edited *Music in Middle-earth* as well as contributing to several other publications.

List of Abbreviations of Tolkien's Works

L   *The Letters of J.R.R. Tolkien*

LotR   *The Lord of the Rings*

LR   *The Lost Road and Other Writings.*

MC   *The Monsters and the Critics and Other Essays*

Bibliography

ANDERSON, Martin. Liner notes for CD *Aulis Sallinen, Symphonies 1 & 7*. Georgsmarienhütte: Classic Production Osnabrück, 2003.

BLYTON, Carey. Home Page. http://www.careyblyton.com/??=Biography. 25 May 2017.

BRATMAN, David. "Liquid Tolkien: Music, Tolkien, Middle-earth, and More Music." *Middle-earth Minstrel*. Ed. Bradford Lee Eden. Jefferson, NC: McFarland and Company, 2010, 140-170.

ROMBERG, Martin. Liner notes for CD "Valaquenta". *Valaquenta, Tableaux Fantastiques*. Aimo Pagin: Lawo Classics, 2011.

RUSSELL, Craig. Liner notes for CD *Rhapsody for Horn and Orchestra, Middle Earth, Gate City*. San Luis Obispo: Naxos, 2000.

SALLINEN, Aulis. Liner notes for CD *Aulis Sallinen, Symphonies 1 & 7*. Georgsmarienhütte: Classic Production Osnabrück, 2003.

SCULL, Christina, and Wayne G. HAMMOND. *The J.R.R. Tolkien Companion and Guide*. 2 vols.: *Reader's Guide, Chronology*. London: HarperCollins, 2006.

SEEMAN, Chris. The Tolkien Music List. http://www.tolkien-music.com/. 25 May 2017.

SWANN, Donald. *The Road Goes Ever On*. London: HarperCollins, 2002.

"Symphony No. 1 'The Lord of the Rings'." Wikipedia. https://en.wikipedia.org/wiki/Symphony_No._1_%22The_Lord_of_the_Rings%22. 25 May 2017.

TOLKIEN, John Ronald Reuel. *The Hobbit*. London: HarperCollins, 2006.

The Letters of J.R.R. Tolkien. Ed. Humphrey Carpenter, with the assistance of Christopher Tolkien, London: HarperCollins, 1995.

The Lord of the Rings. London: HarperCollins, 2007.

The Lost Road and Other Writings (The History of Middle-earth 5). Ed. Christopher Tolkien. London: HarperCollins, 2002.

The Monsters and the Critics and Other Essays. London: HarperCollins, 1997.

The Silmarillion. London: HarperCollins, 1999.

Discography

BLYTON, Carey. "The Hobbit." *British Light Overtures*, Royal Ballet Sinfonia/Gavin Sutherland. London: Sanctuary Classics, 2003.

DE MEIJ, Johan. "Symphony Nr. 1 '*The Lord of the Rings*'." *The Lord of the Rings*, The Royal Military Band/Pierre Kuijpers. The Hague: KMK & Ottavo Recordings, 1989.

ROMBERG, Martin. "Eärendil, the Mariner." *Sound Waves*, Alexandra Silocea. UK: Avie Records, 2013.

"Eldarinwe Líri." Trio Medieval / The Norwegian Girls' Choir/Johannes Wiik/Ellen Sejersted Bödtker/Benedikte Kruse. https://www.youtube.com/playlist?list=PLHHAVvTA_vRx9DqmDULP_SzUYHs2qSJhT.

"Quendi." Orchestre National de Montpellier/Robert Tuohy. https://www.youtube.com/watch?v=T75cZKkjvt4 and https://www.youtube.com/watch?v=rNlxr9JyF1c.

"Telperion and Laurelin." Orchestra Régional Avignon Provence/Samuel Jean. https://www.youtube.com/watch?v=B4hfXcXMwPs.

"Valaquenta." *Valaquenta, Tableaux Fantastiques*, Aimo Pagin. Lawo Classics, 2011.

RUSSELL, Craig. "Middle Earth." *Rhapsody for Horn and Orchestra, Middle Earth*, Gate City, San Luis Obispo Symphony/Michael Nowak/Richard Todd. San Luis Obispo: Naxos, 2000.

SALLINEN, Aulis. "Symphony No 7 op. 71, 'The Dreams of Gandalf'." *Symphonies 1 & 7*. Staatsphilharmonie Rheinland-Pfalz/Ari Rasilainen. Georgsmarienhütte: Classic Production Osnabrück, 2003.

John Holmes

Nis me ti hearpun hygi:
Harping on One String in Middle-earth

Abstract

The harp is a metonym for poetry in many cultures, and Tolkien's Middle-earth is no exception. But an inventory of references to harps throughout Tolkien's works reveals a preponderance of elegiac sentiment connected with the harp. In a passage from the Old English *Seafarer*, recollected in a dream by a character in Tolkien's *Notion Club papers* (*nis me ti hearpun hygi*, "for no harp have I heart"), the harp in the poem becomes an emblem of ancient music, and ancient language itself, calling to the modern mind in an inexplicable way. That ancient music provides the "Door to Other Time" Tolkien found in Fairy Story – as does language itself. A study of an Old English translation of Psalm 137 ("By the Waters of Babylon") suggests that the harp already had such associations in Judeo-Christian tradition. Tolkien's philological comments on the word "harp" in an (undated) lecture to the Lincoln Musical Society illuminate the role of the harp image in Tolkien's creative imagination.

One of the reasons that sane people everywhere like to avoid the highly educated is the unfortunate tendency of people with expertise in one narrow area to talk as if their competence spilled over into all other areas. Anyone who spends any time at all in the academic world knows at least one Ph.D. in Art History who regularly discourses on plasma physics and corporate finance, and has a strong opinion on every medical or legal issue that arises in conversation. Another way this species of academic intrudes where he doesn't belong is in using his own special discipline to explain every other. I lose my patience when that Art History guy explains that the way a navigator triangulates a position by sighting two landmarks is essentially identical to the dual horizon-point composition technique of the *mannerismo* painters of the sixteenth century.

I'd like to think I'm not that kind of academic, but like most of us, I'm afraid I recall too many social gatherings at which I sounded exactly like "that guy." I'd like to think that the phenomenon of the clueless academic who doesn't know when to shut up is limited to the lesser lights in each discipline. I like to think that the truly gifted intellect achieves excellence in one field because of a Socratic humility before the truth that would not allow for speaking more than one knows. That may be but a vain hope, but what record there is of the academic life of J.R.R. Tolkien suggests that he was an academic of the latter, virtuous type. Tolkien had a preeminence in philology that scarcely knew a parallel. Yet he did not presume authority even in areas reasonably related to his field, such as paleography and archaeology, though he would speak of such things when necessary. And when he did apply the tools with which he *did* have facility – such as when archaeologists excavating at Lydney Park in Gloucestershire asked him his opinion on the name *Nodens* appearing on an inscription – his philological investigations really did illuminate the archaeology.

Something similar happened when Tolkien was asked to address the Lincoln Musical Society. He professed a deep admiration for, but scant knowledge of, music. As David Bratman has pointed out, Tolkien's assertion of ignorance in musical matters was exaggerated, a characteristic modesty when stepping outside his academic jurisdiction: Tolkien was in fact as well versed in music as most Englishmen of his generation and education (40-41). Nevertheless, the one area in which he did have profound knowledge – the history of words – could yield up some secrets about the harp and its role in the songs of Middle-earth.

J.R.R. Tolkien's adaptation of the harp as metonymic for ancient poetry is not his invention: the harp was emblematic for the Psalms in the Old Testament, for lyric poetry among the ancient Greeks (who after all called such verse "lyric" because it was sung to the lyre), and appears anywhere poetry is mentioned in Old English writing. As Norbert Maier has pointed out in his study "The Harp in Middle-earth," the harp and the lyre are not the same instrument (108). But our comments here will have little to do with the physical structure of the instrument: this essay explores the *idea* of the harp in the emotional experience of the people of Middle-earth. There is a clear implication in many of Tolkien's references to the harp in his fiction – and more so in his poetry – that the music of the harp is the voice of sorrow. Just as Tolkien argued for elegy rather than epic as the genre of *Beowulf*, there is an elegiac mood to a majority of the passages in Tolkien's writing in which the harp is mentioned.

This essay will canvas the references to harps in the writings of J.R.R. Tolkien in an effort to demonstrate and comment on the note of elegy and even lamentation in various passages. Since Tolkien's first approach to all questions was philological, the essay closes with a look at Tolkien's comments on the word "harp" and its associations in Old English poetry, first in his unpublished lecture to the Lincoln Musical Society, and then in his 4 May 1958 letter to Fr. Robert Murray, S.J. Even when the sound of harp strings is the sound of merriment, the elegiac mood is not far away if the merriment is intended as an antidote or mask for sorrow. In an 8 January 1944 letter to his son Christopher – in a dark time near the end of the Second World War – Tolkien recommends the music of the Catholic psalms known as the "praises" – particularly "the Gloria Patri, the Gloria in Excelsis, the Laudate Dominum; the Laudate Pueri Dominum (of which I am specially fond), one of the Sunday psalms; and the Magnificat; also the Litany of Loretto (with the prayer Sub tuum præsidium)" (*L* 66).

The effect of these songs in banishing melancholy Tolkien underscores by quoting *Maxims I* from the Old English *Exeter Book*:

> Longað þonne þy læs þe him con léoþa worn,
> Oþþe mid hondum con hearpan grétan;
> Hafaþ him his glíwes giefe, þe him God sealde. (*L* 66)

Tolkien offers his own translation: "Less doth yearning trouble him who knoweth many songs, or with his hands can touch the harp: his possession is his gift of "glee" (= music and/or verse) which God gave him" (ibid.). And then Tolkien commented to his son: "How these old words smite one out of the dark antiquity! 'Longað'! All down the ages men (of our kind, most awarely) have felt it: not necessarily caused by sorrow, or the hard world, but sharpened by it" (ibid.).

The role of suffering in the enjoyment of beauty is central to Tolkien's aesthetic, but difficult to grasp, and easy to mistake for pessimism or morbidity. It is present even when the harp seems to represent "glee" in the modern sense of "delight, pleasure" (though its original sense was "song," Old English *gleow*), as invariably the bright images in songs of glory contrast current darkness. The emotional resonances to the sound of the harp in Tolkien's writing are complex: it is elegiac, sounding the note of exile, even when seeming most light; it evokes memories of ancient times with the same mingled sorrow and joy; it echoes the work of creation, which in Tolkien's mythology was effected through song; it evokes the mythic phenomenon of "true language," in which words spoken in a language foreign to the speaker is nevertheless intuitively understood (*glossolalia* or *xenoglossy*) – all of this is emblematized in the harp, as evidenced in the following brief canvas of various Tolkien writings.

The Harp in *The Silmarillion* and Related Myths

Tolkien's earliest reference to the harp – earliest not in the time of composition but in the timeline of his legendarium – connects it with the creation of the world through song in *Ainulindalë*. We are told that the voices of the Ainur are "like unto harps and lutes" – though an entire orchestra of ancient instruments is mentioned, "pipes and trumpets, and viols and organs, and like unto countless choirs singing with words" (S 15). The second appearance of the harp in The Silmarillion may be the most memorable: Fingon's rescue of Maedhros from his captivity by the evil Melkor (S 110). The emotional subtlety of the scene embedded in the bare-bones style of *The Silmarillion* (the narrative economy more typical of mythographies than fiction) illustrates the principle, articulated above, of the overwhelming presence of sorrow even in seemingly happy songs. As archetypal as the rescue of Maedhros is, Tolkien's fellow students of Northern heroic literature would recognize resonances of the story of the Völsung hero Gunnar among the Huns.

As Tolkien insisted in his essay *On Fairy Stories*, the differences in supposed narrative doublets (different versions of the "same" motif) can be more pertinent than folkloric similarities. The rescue of Maedhros invokes Tolkien's notion of *eucatastrophe*, the unexpected happy ending snatched from the jaws of death. The snake pit episode as Tolkien treats it in *The Legend of Sigurd and Gudrún* is decidedly tragic (or more precisely, in Tolkien's terms, *cacocatastrophic*),[1] and does end in Gunnar's death. Yet it shines with the Northern pagan "closest approach" to *eucatastrophe*, which is the expression of "Northern Courage," defined by Tolkien as "the doctrine of uttermost endurance in the service of indomitable will" (*HBBS* 21). The heart leaps up at Gunnar's heroic defiance, even if – perhaps even more so if – it knows that Gunnar will die.

In place of Fingon's song stirring the captive Maedhros, Gudrún sends the harp into the pit where her brother Gunnar faces his final foe, an "ancient adder" (*SG* 299). Tolkien prepares the reader for this dramatic climax by establishing Gunnar's harping earlier in the poem (Stanza 13) as particularly spellbinding.

> There Gunnar grasped
> his golden harp;
> while songs he sang
> silence fell there.
> (*SG* 131)

Much later, when the harp follows Gunnar into the pit, we have expectations of its power in Gunnar's hands to move hearts.

> A harp she sent him,
> his hands seized it,
> strong he smote it;
> strings were ringing.
> Wondering heard men
> words of strength,
> song up-soaring
> from the serpents' pit.
> (*SG* 298)

Far from hanging his harp on a willow, Gunnar's harping in the face of adversity is a call of hope to his fellows, and the sound of doom to his Hunnish captors.

---

[1] Tolkien's invention of this term, which occurs in a 7-8 November 1944 letter to Christopher Tolkien (*L* 102), was made inevitable and necessary by his earlier invention of *eucatastrophe*. The latter word appears to most Tolkien readers as an oxymoron, but it is not. *Eucatastrophe*, while a neologism, is a necessary one, and precisely the right word. Modern speakers of English hear the word "catastrophe" as a negative term, but in its earliest, technical meaning it was not. The prefix *kata-* indeed means "down," but Aristotle's meaning of the word *katastrophe* – "the line of a tragedy in which the hero's fall is inevitable" – is not *necessarily* (though most often is in practice) an "unhappy ending." In early English usage, "catastrophe" was a neutral term meaning "the turning point of a drama." Since it is theoretically possible for a given "catastrophe" to be a good thing to most of the characters in a story, Tolkien needed a word for a "good" catastrophe. But coining *eucatastrophe* inevitably suggested its opposite, a "bad" catastrophe – *cacocatastrophe*.

> A huge adder
> hideous gleaming
> from stony hiding
> was stealing slow.
> Huns still heard him
> his harp thrilling,
> and doom of Hunland
> dreadly chanting.
> (*SG* 299)

Tolkien's control of point of view in this scene places the reader in the same vantage point as Gudrún and the Völsungs: as long as they hear Gunnar's harp they know he still lives. Conversely, the quelling of the harp marks his death.

> An ancient adder
> evil-swollen,
> to breast it bent
> and bitter stung him.
> Loud cried Gunnar
> life forsaking;
> harp fell silent,
> and heart was still.
> (*SG* 299)

Just as Gunnar's fate resonates with Maedhros', no reader reasonably familiar with the Judeo-Christian tradition can mistake the overtones of Psalm 136 (137 in later numbering; "By the waters of Babylon") in the Rescue of Maedhros (*Silmarillion* chapter 13). In the Psalm, too, the singer (possibly Jeremiah) laments the captivity of his entire race after Jerusalem fell to the Babylonian Empire in 607 BCE. The lyric compression of the Psalm is a model for Tolkien's: the taunting Babylonian captors urge the Hebrew slaves to sing their happy songs from pre-conquest times, and the slaves refuse. It is no accident that the American musical genre of the Blues was born partly in African-American spirituals that saw in the Psalms of the Babylonian Captivity a reflection of their own suffering.

The Blues would not have been the context most ready to Tolkien's imagination for the rescue of Maedhros via harp, however. The conquest foremost in the heart of an Anglo-Saxonist might be neither the Babylonian Captivity nor American slavery, but the Norman Conquest of Anglo-Saxon England. In his academic life Tolkien struggled to maintain the *hearpan sweg / swutol sang scopes* ("sound of the harp / and the clear singing of the minstrel," *Beowulf* 89-90; *Beowulf Translation* 15) in English verse, potentially dampened by a Romance prosody that became dominant by the 16th century. Yet the native harp was not, Tolkien felt, hopelessly irretrievable. It survived the Gallic "captivity." Tolkien must have known the so-called *Eadwine Psalter* (Trinity College, Cambridge MS R.17.1), which documents the survival of English letters in the first full century after the Norman ascendency. Its probable date of composition is 1155-1160, just short of a century after the Battle of Hastings. The leaf on which Psalm 136 opens (folio 243 verso) captures, in both the text and the illumination, the emotional and historical subtlety by which the harp points simultaneously to the joys before and sorrows after 607 BCE (for Jeremiah) or 1066 CE (for the Master Scribe Eadwine).

The illumination, copied from the Utrecht Psalter but more detailed and richly colored, could be accused of a naïve literalism in illustrating Psalm 136/137, but I find it an insightful choice of images from the psalm. They key verse for the student of the harp is the second: "there on the willows we hung our harps," with the full context of the abandonment of song in the third: "for there our captors asked us for songs, our tormentors demanded songs of joy."[2] The illumination is largely composed of the "backstory" of the Babylonian captivity: in a series of sequential images (creators of graphic novels could learn a great deal about sequential storytelling by studying medieval art) we see the unarmed citizens (of Jerusalem) exhorting God (a hand in a cloud) while spear-wielding armies (the Babylonians) threaten. Then we see the spearmen threatening a besieged group cowering behind a gated wall. Then we see the gate opened. Finally the spearmen enter the gate and stab several Jerusalemites. Across the bottom of the illumination runs the *flumina Babilonis*, the "rivers of Babylon" and there, sure enough, are the harps of the captive Jews, each of slightly different construction, hanging on stylized trees. And the captives are indeed seated by the river and appear to be weeping, or at least mournful.

The positive note for the Anglo-Saxon viewing this Psalter in "Norman" England is in the second column of text from the margin (second from the left on *recto*, second from the right on *verso*), in which a translation in late Old

---

2   https://www.biblegateway.com/passage/?search=Psalm%20137;&version=NIV

English appears as an interlinear gloss. The Anglo-Norman that appears in the column closest to the margin might have been the language of the lawyers and the dukes, but Old English was still hanging on. The Latin versions in each column differed also, which bears implications for our harp: the so-called "Hebrew" version, Jerome's Latin translation from the Hebrew Bible, appears with the Norman gloss and the "Roman" (a Gallic Latin translation from the Hebrew Bible, corrected by Jerome) sports the Old English. Consequently, the "harp," which appears rightly enough as *cithara* in the Norman column, is more vaguely *organa* ("musical instruments") in the English column, vaguer yet in the Old English (*swegas*, "songs"), a hypostatic image – attractive as a translation because the word for willow in the Eadwine Psalter is not the Old English cognate *welig*, but a synonym, *salig* (modern English sallow; the Latin genus for willows is *salix*), which alliterates with *swegas*. In the 13th-century Great Canterbury Psalter (sometimes called "Paris Psalter," MS Paris, BN lat. 8824), the alliterative verse translation of this Psalm renders the harp also as *organan*, and preserves the *s*-alliteration:

> On salig we sarige swiðe gelome
> ure organan up ahengan.
> (lines 4-5)

The next appearance of the harp in *The Silmarillion*, in Chapter 17, plays on a variation of the "longing" Tolkien conflated with harping in the letter quoted above. The longing to return to a pre-conquest Jerusalem that permeated the "Songs of Zion" in Psalm 136/137 may sustain the exile in times of suffering, as Tolkien's letter suggested, but it also sets up a contrast between then and now which may prove for some unbearable. The exiles from Jerusalem after all hung up their harps, "forgetting" song, though the speaker of the Psalm exhorts himself never to do so: "If I forget thee, O Jerusalem, let my right hand forget her cunning" reads the King James version of verse 5. The word "cunning" (Hebrew *khawshab*) preserves the connection between the harp and the memories of Zion: the skill and knowledge that must not leave the right hand is its (or "her") ability to pluck the old joys out of the harp, joys that are now alloyed with sorrows by contrast to the present moment. Tolkien uses the same word (cunning), and the locus in the hand, for the harper's skill in *The Legend of Sigurd and Gudrún*:

> Morning woke with mirth,
> merry came evening;
> harp-strings were plucked
> by hands with cunning.
> (*SG* 143)

Sometimes, of course, the harp is abandoned because it is too painful. Tolkien encountered that motif, the harpist renouncing the harp for grief, in the fourteenth-century lay *Sir Orfeo*, on which he worked closely in preparing his first academic publication, his glossary to Kenneth Sisam's *Fourteenth-Century Reader* (1922), and which he edited for the use of his naval cadets at Oxford between January 1943 and March 1944 (Tolkien, *Sir Orfeo* 85). In that lay, it is the loss of his wife to Faerie that causes Orfeo to hang up his harp – not specifically on a willow, but in a hollow tree: "His harpe, whereon was al his gle, / He hidde in an holwe tre" (ibid. 96, lines 267-268). This passage, one of 28 instances of various forms of the word "harp" in the text as edited by Tolkien (*harpe*, 11x; *harped*, 2; *harpere*, 1; *harpes*, 1, *harping*, 7; *harpour*, 4; *harpours*, 2) finds the word *glee* already incorporating the later meaning of "happiness"; it is here something of a pun on the earlier meaning of "music."

In his expansion of the Húrin story from *The Silmarillion*, Tolkien describes Húrin's rejection of the harp after an excess of sorrow: "But Húrin mourned openly, and he took up his harp and would make a song of lamentation; but he could not, and he broke his harp" (Tolkien, *Children of Húrin* 40). In his earlier poetic version in alliterative measure, it is Húrin's story itself that puts a mournful note in Elvish harps:

> Lo! Hear what Elves with ancient harps [...]
> [...] sing still in sorrow of the son of Húrin,
> how his webs of doom were woven dark
> with Niniel's sorrow: names most mournful.
> (*LB*, lines 9, 12-14)

The role of song in opening "a door to other time," as Tolkien claimed for Fairy Story (*OFS* 48) is in Tolkien's legendarium mediated to humans by the mentoring of elves – which brings us to the harping in Chapter 17 of the *Silmarillion*. In the first interaction between elves and men in Middle-earth, the Noldorin King Finrod steals into the camp of Bëor where the human king and his men sleep, picks up Bëor's "rude harp" and plays "music [...] such as the ears of Men had not heard" (S 140). Moreover,

> wisdom was in the words of the Elven-king, and the hearts grew wiser that hearkened to him; for the things of which he sang, of the making of Arda, and the bliss of Aman beyond the shadows of the Sea, came as clear vision before their eyes, and his Elvish speech was interpreted in each mind according to its measure. (S 140-141)

This seeming Pentecostal invocation of "speaking in tongues" (*glōssais lalein*, Acts 2:4) is in Tolkien's fiction a consistent experience of non-elvish peoples encountering the gift of song, and part of the meaning of the harp seems to lie in the ability of music to do what "true language" is mythically supposed to do: hearken back to the moment of creation (through music, as we saw in the *Ainulindalë*), so that comprehension is not limited to current associations with the sounds of language. Sam and Frodo encounter elvish music in precisely that way in *The Lord of the Rings*.[3]

In his essay "English and Welsh" Tolkien describes the sounds of Welsh working in just such a way on the ears of many an Englishman to whom a language that preceded the Angles and Saxons in the British Isles stirs semi-conscious memories. And in putting into words the nearly-ineffable experience, the auditory image of the harp comes naturally: "For many of us it rings a bell, or rather it stirs deep harp-strings in our linguistic nature" (*MC*, 194). In reflecting on "invented" language in his essay "A Secret Vice," Tolkien alluded to the power of invented language to effect that stirring, once again invoking the image of the harp in a quotation from one of his early Eärendil poems – in Elvish, with this translation: "Taut ropes like harps tingling, / From far shores a faint singing" (*MC* 217).

---

3 See in particular Frodo's hearing of a song about Eärendil in the first chapter of Book II (*LotR* 233): "At first the beauty of the melodies and of the interwoven words in elven-tongues, even though he understood them little, held him in a spell" and his hearing of Galadriel's farewell song in Chapter 8 of the same book: "But now she sang in the ancient tongue of the Elves beyond the Sea, and he did not understand the words [..] Yet as is the way with Elvish words, they remained graven in his memory, and long afterwards he interpreted them [..]" (377).

The Harp in Tolkien's View of *Beowulf* and other Old English Poems

Tolkien imagines the Old English people of the "*Beowulf*-moment," the era in which the poem was composed, to apprehend harping similarly to the elvish view presented in Chapter 17 of *The Silmarillion*. The earliest recorded Old English verse (Caedmon's Hymn, which Tolkien considered contemporary with *Beowulf*) struck the ears of its listeners, in Bede's famous telling of the story, as transcendent notes from the music of creation. In his lectures to Oxford undergraduates required to read Bede's account in *Sweet's Anglo-Saxon Reader*, Tolkien imagined the Abbess Hild's (perhaps unintended) fusion of Germanic and Judeo-Christian antiquity in the harping at her abbey: "the minstrelsy and harping song in the ancient Northern measure which went on at feasts in the evening among the lay folk of her great household" (Tolkien MS A29a, fol. 82).

That this fusion of Christian and Northern pagan minstrelsy made *Beowulf* possible is a point on which Tolkien was adamant, particularly in opposition to a strain of literary history that clings to Alcuin's famous anathematizing of the pagan harp in his letter to Bishop Speratus of Lindisfarne: *Quid Hinieldus cum Christo?*, "What has [the pagan hero] Ingeld to do with Christ?" The modernist mind tends to hear in Alcuin (or, for the Anglo-Saxonist, *Eolhwin*, "Elk-friend") the voice of the whole of medieval Christendom. Tolkien reminds us, however, that the voices in the refectory singing heroic lays were themselves learned monks, perhaps a majority silent only because of the whims of time:

> But this is also evidence that in England even those trained and professed in religion could, whatever high authority felt, find room for both, and could preserve ancient heroic tradition. It might certainly be regarded by most then (as still) *indecens* (inappropriate) that the harpist should usurp the place of the lector in the refectory, but it was not necessarily improper that the same minds should contain the old histories and the faith. This was evidently a prevalent feeling. "The house is wide and has many rooms." To such a time and temper <u>Beowulf</u> belongs. (*B&C* 123-124)

When Tolkien attempted to recreate that "time and temper" creatively in two versions of a *Lay of Beowulf*, the harp in both versions is expressly tied to the mead hall Heorot. In each version the harp appears in the first stanza and the last, the first celebrating "the twanging harps of Heorot" (*Beowulf* 417, 420), and the last sighing "hushed were the harps of Heorot" (419, 425). In between the joy of the first stanza and the forgone harps of the last lies the suffering of the Grendelian Captivity – and even in opening harps we hear the curse of Grendel, who hates them because they reflect God's creation and glory.

The very confluence of Judeo-Christian creation hymns and the pagan story of Beowulf is itself a tribute to the "time and temper" of the *Beowulf*-poet, as Tolkien reminds us in his celebrated Golancz lecture, and is a means of answering the charge of "anachronism" so often leveled at the interface of Christian and pagan in the poem. "So excellent is this choice," Tolkien asserts, "as the theme of the harp that maddened Grendel lurking joyless in the dark without that it matters little whether this is anachronistic or not" (*BMC* 26). Tolkien's footnote to this passage disarms even those who would insist that anachronism matters a great deal by pointing out that ancient creation hymns of both Northern and Greco-Roman paganism resemble the Judeo-Christian stuff that informs both Caedmon's Hymn and Tolkien's *Ainulindalë*. The sound of the harp, by infusing the glory of creation, becomes the auditory analogue of the light of creation. It is that light that creatures of darkness like Grendel (and Gollum and Sauron) hate, and from Heorot spills both light and sound, synaesthetically united, so that Grendel's reaction to the revelry is not the justifiable pique of a sensitive soul with noisy neighbors. In the penultimate paragraph of his most famous lecture Tolkien points to the poet's reference to light that begins the Grendel passage (though he quotes a later line, 311). "A light starts – *lixte se leoma ofer landa fela* – and there is a sound of music; but the outer darkness and its hostile offspring lie ever in wait for the torches to fail and the voices to cease. Grendel is maddened by the sound of harps" (*MC* 33).

A study of the whole passage reveals the merger of light and music. The music that tortures Grendel is specifically a song of God's creation in joy, a joy and light contrapuntally divorced from the monster:

>   [...]   þær wæs hearpan sweg,
>   swutol sang scopes.   Sægde se þe cuþe
>   frumsceaft fira   feorran reccan,
>   cwæð þæt se ælmihtiga   eorðan worhte,
>   wlitebeorhtne wang,   swa wæter bebugeð,
>   gesette sigehreþig   sunnan ond monan
>   leoman to leohte   landbuendum

ond gefrætwade   foldan sceatas
leomum ond leafum,   lif eac gesceop
cynna gehwylcum   þara ðe cwice hwyrfaþ
(lines 89-98)

Tolkien's translation:

> There was the sound of harp and the clear singing of the minstrel; there spake he that had knowledge to unfold from far-off days the first beginning of men, telling how the Almighty wrought that earth, a vale of bright loveliness that the waters encircle; how triumphant He set the radiance of the sun and moon as a light for the dwellers in the lands, and adorned the regions of the world with boughs and with leaves, life too he devised for every kind that moves and lives. (Tolkien, *Beowulf Translation*, 15-16)

The potential of human music to hearken back to that primordial elvish music is perhaps not always achieved, but it kindles (or perhaps smolders in) the imagination of later generations of scops and would-be scops such as Tolkien's Torhthelm ("Totta") in *The Homecoming of Beorhtnoth, Beorhthelm's Son*, himself the son of a harper. For his companion, the older Tídwald ("Tída") the harp only carries the sorrows it sings of: "The world wept then, as it weeps today: / you can hear the tears through the harp's / twanging" (*HBBC* 10). As Totta and Tída archetypally present two contrasting views on heroism (the elusive *ofermod* of *The Battle of Maldon*), they also stand on two sides of the ubiquitous harp.

Although he is not an altogether sympathetic character – his predilection for the ancient songs, as well as his youthful inexperience, blind him from certain realities – Totta shows us some of the same qualities Tolkien intuited in the *Beowulf* poet. The composer, Tolkien tells us, was "a learned man, writing of old times, who looking back on the heroism and sorrow feels in them something permanent and something symbolical" (*BMC* 26). Totta, like the *Beowulf* poet, simply knew more of the heroic material that was fast fading: he was a type familiar to Romanticism, particularly to the Romantic project of attempting to recover a native literary past. Tolkien's academic field, comparative philology, was as much a product of that Romantic recovery as was Grimm's *Fairy Tales* or Child's *Ballads*; the icon the "last minstrel" still trained in the heroic tradition is best known from Sir Walter Scott's *Lay of the Last Minstrel* (1805). Scott was imagining a minstrel of the Scottish border as late as the 16th century, since Scots-English balladry maintained much of the "lost" folk material Tolkien once dreamed of recovering for England. But Tolkien, not only in his *Beowulf* lecture and *The Homecoming of Beorhtnoth*, but also in his early poem "The Bidding of the Minstrel" (1915), imagined a last minstrel centuries earlier. The minstrel's harp becomes an emblem of a vain attempt to recover memories of a fast-dying light:

> Who now can tell, and what harp can accompany
> With melodies strange enough, rich enough tunes . . .
> The song I can sing is but shreds one remembers
> Of golden imaginings fashioned in sleep.
> A whispered tale told by the withering embers
> Of old things far off that but few hearts keep .
> (*LT* II, lines 25-26, 33-36, p. 275)

The minstrel's lament was real and heartfelt for Tolkien, for the song that the unnamed listeners urge the minstrel to recall was the tale of Eärendil. Tolkien as he wrote this song was attempting to reconstruct the tale from the single word *Earendel* in a seemingly unrelated Christian lyric. The story was tantalizingly just beyond reach – but like the fruit Tantalus longed for it was right there, visible, but just out of grasp. It's enough to make you want to hang your harp on a willow.

The sentiment is felt by the scop of *The Seafarer* as well, and in Tolkien's *Notion Club Papers* the semi-autobiographical character Alwin Arundel Lowdham recounts a dream in which he hears ancient music that, upon waking, he recognizes as a passage from *The Seafarer* – yet in a strange dialectical form different from the poem that survives in the tenth-century *Exeter Book MS*. The differences in the word forms are not synchronic, however – another dialect from the same time – but diachronic – marking the words in Lowdham's dreams an "impossible" transmission from earlier time, that Lowdham can somehow understand – the same sort of xenoglossy as Finrod's harping in *The Silmarillion*, and what Elvish harping seems to represent to the mortal races in Middle-earth. Lowdham's memories of the primeval form of the *Seafarer* lines provide the title for this essay: *nis me te hearpun hygi*, "I have no heart for the harp" – the sentiment of the Babylonian captivity (and of Orfeo and of Húrin).

> Nis me ti hearpun hygi ni ti bringthegi
> ni ti wíbae wyn ni ti weoruldi hyct
> ni ymb oowict ellaes nebnae ymb ýtha giwalc.

In Tolkien's (or, in the story, Lowdham's) translation:

> For no harp have I heart, no hand for gold,
> in no wife delight, in the world no hope:
> one wish only, for the waves' tumult.
> (*SD* 243-244)

Even that most celebrated legendarium of England on which Tolkien touched only briefly, and never published in his lifetime – the Arthurian mythos – imaged the call of the former glory of Camelot, even as Arthur falls, as the sound of a distant harp.

> the surge he felt of song forgotten
> in his heart moving as a harp-music.
> (*FOA* 43, lines 212-213)

The Harp in *The Hobbit*

Harps in *The Hobbit* represent the simplest version of the bittersweet image established in the discussion above: the merriment and entertainment, but carrying with it the sufferings of the people in the own songs of their own Zion. In the case of the dwarves, their Zion was the ancestral home of Khazad-Dûm (not named in *The Hobbit*), now usurped by the dragon Smaug. In their dwarvish strain of "dragon sickness" their "yearning" is as much for treasure as for their home, and the idea of the harp is bound up in both.

While the "Unexpected Party" in the opening chapter of *The Hobbit* ended with a complete dwarvish orchestra of flutes, fiddles, drum, clarinets, and viols, the Dwarf King Under the Mountain, Thorin, led the ensemble with a harp. When the lyrics began with "Far over the misty mountains cold," the lost treasures of the dwarves include the harp: "Goblets they carved there for themselves / And harps of gold; where no man delves". And the song ends by weighing harps equally with gold as the treasure to be wrested from the worm: "We must away, ere break of day, / To win our harps and gold from him!" (*H* 23) In a less happy time (for the dwarves), in Mirkwood in Chapter 8, the elvish revelry that always eludes Thorin and Company is livened by the harp. "The elvish folk were passing bowls from hand to hand and across the fires, and some were harping and many were singing" (*H* 165).

In the same fashion, the prophetic (or hopeful) songs about the return of the King Under the Mountain in Chapter 10, harp and song share the billing with gold in heralding the event.

> His crown shall be upholden,
> His harp shall be restrung,
> His halls shall echo golden
> To songs of yore re-sung.
> (*H* 210)

And the singing of these hopeful songs, of course, had "the music of harps and of fiddles mixed up with it" (*H* 211). In the following chapter, the quelling of that joy is marked by the *absence* of harping: "It was a weary journey, and a quiet and stealthy one. There was no laughter or song or sound of harps, and the pride and hopes which had stirred in their hearts at the singing of old songs by the lake died away to a plodding gloom" (*H* 215-216). When they actually make it into the cave in Chapter 13, the dwarves can expel the dread and gloom only by their presence in the dragon hoard of harps: "Fili and Kili were almost in merry mood, and finding still hanging there many golden harps strung with silver they took them and struck them; and being magical (and also untouched by the dragon, who had small interests in music) they were still in tune" (*H* 251). When the dwarves darken the mood with their jealous siege in the build-up to the Battle of the Five Armies (Chapter 15), the ugliness of the "dragon-sickness" or gold-lust is lifted momentarily for Bilbo as he catches the sound of harping from the Elves' camp: "There was the sound, too, of elven-harps and of sweet music; and as it echoed up towards them it seemed that the chill of the air was warmed, and they caught faintly the fragrance of woodland flowers blossoming in spring" (*H* 273). The dwarves answer with their own harps, repeating the prophetic songs that had brought them back to their hoard.

> On silver necklaces they strung
> The light of stars, on crowns they hung
> The dragon-fire, from twisted wire
> The melody of harps they wrung
> (*H* 274)

And so we finish *The Hobbit* with, we might say, a meta-harping, the dwarves harping and singing about harping and singing. And if their detractors are tempted to see in dwarvish love of gold only what we might call materialism, the equation here of "the melody of harps" with silver and "the light of stars" suggests that such a base motive may be alloyed with something more transcendent – a love of beauty.

The Harp in *The Lord of the Rings*

The first reference to a harp in *The Lord of the Rings* comes, fittingly, from Samwise Gamgee. Something of the yearning for lost minstrelsy that we saw in "Totta" from *The Homecoming of Beorhtnoth* shows in Sam's echoing of the old songs he learned from Frodo, and ultimately from the elves: "Gil-galad was an Elven-king. / Of him the harpers sadly sing" (*LotR* 185). Later in Rivendell Frodo hears Bilbo sing a song of Eärendil, in which the litanies of wonders given to the pilot who sails the light of the Silmarils into the sky include harps:

> He tarried there from errantry,
> and melodies they taught to him,
> and sages old him marvels told,
> and harps of gold they brought to him
> (*LotR* 235)

When it's Gimli's turn to sing of dwarvish harps, the sound of the harp, as in *Beowulf* and Bede's story of Caedmon – as well as, we have observed, Tolkien's *Ainulindalë* – turns the mind back to creation. For the dwarves, creation was an "awakening," since their creator Aulë formed them prematurely and agreed they should sleep until the children of Ilúvatar arose. Gimli's song of the "awakening" of the primordial dwarf Durin, then, celebrates their first activity: mining, smithying – and harping.

> Unwearied then were Durin's folk
> Beneath the mountains music woke:
> The harpers harped, the minstrels sang,
> And at the gates the trumpets rang
> (*LotR* 316)

The prospect of Sauron's growing power in the era in which *The Lord of the Rings* takes place threatens a global captivity that again calls Psalm 136/137 to mind, offering another nuance to the motif of the captive Hebrew minstrels hanging their harps on willows. The simplest way to read the silencing of harps in the Third Age is the elegiac sense of loss: the joyous music of the past is too painful now. But in the shadow of war that grows throughout Tolkien's novel, eschewing the harp has another meaning: harping comes to represent a leisure activity, and studying war has banished such luxuries. While the Fellowship are balking at the requirement of blindfolds to enter Lothlorien, Haldir excuses the necessity to Legolas by blaming the times. "We live now upon an island amid many perils, and our hands are more often upon the bowstring than upon the harp" (*LotR* 348). Nevertheless, Haldir's queen, Galadriel, does not scruple to bear a harp to the borders of Laurien to sing a farewell to the Company of the Ring (*LotR* 372).

For the Riders of Rohan, who of all the peoples of Middle-earth most closely parallel Anglo-Saxon culture (and language), the elegiac note I have asserted to be the essence of the harp in Tolkien's writing takes the form of the Medieval *ubi sunt* trope, the lament for all that is gone. Tolkien's readers familiar with Old English literature have recognized the Rohirric song of lament in "The King of the Golden Hall" chapter as the ubi sunt section of the Old English poem now known as *The Wanderer* (lines 93 and following). But Tolkien cements the link between the harp and lamentation by increasing the concreteness of the image of the joys that are missed. *The Wanderer* speaks in abstract terms as "Where are the revels in the hall?" (*Hwær sindon seledreamas*, line 93), while Tolkien concretizes it as "Where is the hand on the harpstring, and the red fire glowing?" (*LotR* 508).

The hand on the harpstring is conspicuous by its absence in the Muster of Rohan (Book V, Chapter 3), and the narrator noticing the absence points to the irony of the songless gathering of horsemen itself being the occasion of song in the future. I have suggested above, reflecting on *Silmarillion* Chapter 17, that the harp imitates Fairy Story by acting as a "door on Other Time," and we have looked at examples of the harp calling up time past. But here we catch a glimpse of the other end of the process: future minstrels harping about the present moment. The harp is fundamentally bound in the nature of time: "And so without horn or harp or music of men's voices the great ride into the East began with which the songs of Rohan were busy for many long lives of men thereafter" (*LotR* 803).

Music's orientation toward the future rather than the past of creation may be a clue to the metaphysical significance of music in the abstract, particularized in the harp. The reason that music can reach into the past and point to the future is that, as an emblem of the transcendent, it places our temporal consciousness in touch with the eternal. The power of poetry and song (emblematized in the harp) to touch eternity was the source of the medieval tradition – which as early as the Pseudo-Dionysius (5th-6th century) was recognized as metaphoric – of angels playing harps,[4] and Tolkien follows a similar logic in the apocalyptic final couplets of his philosophical poem "Mythopoeia":

> Be sure they still will make, not being dead,
> and poets shall have flames upon their head,
> and harps whereon their faultless fingers fall:
> there each shall choose for ever from the All.
> (My 89)

Because our temporal minds cannot fully comprehend eternity, we apprehend the music that speaks of it in a paradoxical way – in temporal terms both past and future; in emotional terms both sadness and joy. Tolkien attempted, within the limits of, in his words "clumsy language," to explain in a wartime letter to his youngest son Christopher (7-8 November 1944) the "essential emotion" produced by *eucatastrophe*: "Christian joy which produces tears because it is qualitatively so like sorrow, because it comes from those places where Joy and Sorrow are at one, reconciled, as selfishness and altruism are lost in Love" (*L* 100).

With all of the "ironic" harping we have heard – joy mixed with sorrow – it is perhaps refreshing to hear *The Lord of the Rings* end with three unambiguously joyous harpings. When Sam awakes in the Field of Cormallen after the fall of Sauron, he stumbles over a number of metaphors for his joy, including "trumpets and harps and all the songs I have ever heard" (*LotR* 952). In the following chapter harpers from Dol Amrath celebrate the coronation the returned King, and the final chapter Elrond bears a harp as the last of the elves pass from Middle-earth at the Gray Havens.

---

4 See C.S. Lewis, *The Discarded Image*, 71. Lewis does not mention harps in particular, but comments on all of the physical elements of the medieval concept of angels in general.

That passing into an eternal realm had long been a part of Tolkien's myth. His early poem "The Last Ship," collected in his 1962 volume *Tom Bombadil and Other Poems*, marks the passing of the last elves into the west in this way.

> Flutes there were, and harps were wrung,
> and there was sound of singing,
> like wind-voices keen and young
> and far bells ringing. [...]
> With harp in hand they sang their song
> to the slow oars swinging:
> 'Green is the land, the leaves are long,
> and the birds are singing
> (lines 29-32, 41-44, p. 249)

Even the joy passing to a better realm entails a sadness for the long-lived elves, and sadness mingled with joy is distilled in the harp.

Harping on Philology

If this study seems by now an obsessive-compulsive catalogue of every iteration of the word *harp* in Tolkien's writings, the reader should be assured that (1) scrutiny of a single word is, if tedious, at least an imitation of Tolkien's method, and (2) there are after all one or two iterations of *harp* intentionally omitted. There is a modern English idiom for such a monomania. The idiom is "harping on one word." (More on that phrase in a moment.) But a study of the importance of the harp in Tolkien's writing would not be complete with just a litany of the word's appearances. To be true to Tolkien's philological method, we must at least glance at the nature of the word itself, its form and syntax.

Norbert Maier's illuminating study of the Harp in Middle-earth, already mentioned, offers an intriguing possibility in the etymology of the elvish word for harp. Maier's first observation is that there *is* no attested word for harp in the oldest Elvish languages, High-Elvish and Sindarin. But the science of comparative philology as perfected in the nineteenth century allows Tolkien to reconstruct one for his own invented languages. The first root Maier pointed to in his analysis brings us to the later (16th century) semantic drift of the English word suggested by the opening of this section, and the title of this essay: "harping on" in the sense of "insisting monotonously in an irritating way" (attested from 1562). Maier's summary of Tolkien's analysis is worth repeating:

> The first we find in connection with the hypothetical root "BOR" in Quenya the syllable "voro" is established as meaning: "always", "continuously". This is used as a prefix, for example, in *vorogandele* – "always playing the same thing with the harp" as a synonym for "continuous repetitions". (108)

In his invented language, then, Tolkien is reproducing a semantic shift that occurred in early modern English. The road from the original sense of the verb *to harp* (Old English weak verb *hearpian*) to the idiom *to harp on* does not require much excavation: the full original phrase must have been "harping on one string." That phrase does not appear in so many words before the sixteenth century, though it is implicit in this stanza from Chaucer's *Troilus and Criseyde* (1380's):

> For though the beste harpour upon lyve
> Wolde on the beste souned joly harpe
> That evere was, with alle his fyngres fyve,
> Touche ay o streng, or ay o werbul harpe,
> Were his nayles poynted nevere so sharpe,
> It sholde maken every wight to dulle,
> To here his glee, and of his strokes fulle.
> (II. 1030-1036)

In essence: "Even the best harper playing the finest harp would still make dull music if he harped always ("ay") on one string" (Benson 503). And, like so many poetic dicta, the idea can be found in Horace's *Ars Poetica* (19 BCE): "et Citharoedus / ridetur, chorda qui semper oberrat eadem," – "and the harper / may be laughed at, who always wanders over the same string" (355-356).

But where does the word *harp* come from? What does a philological examination of the word tell us about, first, the *idea* behind the word, and second, the ancient *instrument* behind the word? Tolkien's answer in his lecture to the Lincoln Musical Society revealed his status as that rare scholar described in the opening of this essay, reluctant to discourse on matters foreign to his field, but allowing his expertise in that realm to enrich another discipline. So even though he would have been familiar with the excavation of a lyre at Sutton Hoo (1939), Tolkien ventured no archaeological or musicological opinion on the instrument, but shared what could be learned from philology.

"I don't know much about *harps*," Tolkien began modestly, but then asserted two solid facts: "(1) it is an instrument of this *name* that is constantly associated with Old English poetry, and (2) the *name* at least is Germanic, beyond doubt" (Tolkien A 30/1 folio 96). A century of (mostly) German scholarship that refined the comparative method of cognates provided Tolkien's confidence here: tracing the regular consonant changes in Indo-European languages allows the philologist to determine roughly where and when words are borrowed, and the direction of the borrowing. Tolkien does not give the detailed argument for the professional certainty that *harp* is Germanic, but it would be more or less as follows.

The pattern of consonant changes popularly known as "Grimm's Law" would call for the initial *h* in *harp* to appear as *k* in non-Germanic Indo-European languages (e.g. Latin *cordis* → English *heart*), and the *p* in *harp* as *b* (Lat. *baculumn* → English *peg*). In the vowels, a consistent alternation of *o* and *a* distinguishes Germanic words (*okta* → *aht*, "eight"). Thus we would expect cognates with *harp* in Slavic, Celtic, Hellenic, or other IE families other than Germanic to look something like *korb. But what do we find? In Russian, *harp* is *arfa*; in Irish, *harp*; Greek, *arpa*; French, *harpe*. So the word (if not the instrument) must have been come from the Germanic languages – or as Tolkien put it, "when the name appears elsewhere (as in the Romance languages) it is borrowed from the North Southwards: not the reverse" (Tolkien A 30/1 folio 96).

Yet what if the expected cognate *korb does appear in non-Germanic IE languages, but with a changed meaning that obscures its connection? In a 1958 letter to Fr. Robert Murray, S.J. Tolkien discusses just such a semantic shift.

> The formal equivalent (the only known one) of our *harp* is Latin *corbis*. (The Romance *arpa* etc. are borrowed from Germanic.) But the poor philologist will have to call on some archaeological expert before he can decide whether any relationship between "harps" and "baskets" is possible – supposing Gmc. *harpō* always meant "harp" or *corbi-s* always meant "wicker basket"! *corbīta* means a fat-bellied ship. (*L* 270)

The context of Tolkien's entire letter helps us expand Tolkien's meaning: he had been discussing the limits of etymological investigation in general. Tolkien's appeal to the archaeologist here – another example of his professional modesty – is a warning not to assume that the cognate implies a physical similarity between baskets and harps. The warrant for such caution explains his final sentence: the proof that *corb-* may not always have meant "basket" in Latin is that the diminutive *corbīta* is a kind of ship (the word is ancestor to the French *corvette*).

Philology, however, is not just etymology and cognate studies. With a word that is so vital to poetry as *harp* – as Tolkien observed to the Lincoln Musical Society, *harp* is a metaphor for poetry in Old English – the image can be expressed in other words. The most characteristic form of metaphor in Old English poetry, the kenning, supplies us a number of expressions for "harp," as Tolkien indicates in his 1940 essay "On Translating *Beowulf.*" Tolkien looks at two kennings for *harp* in *Beowulf, gleo-beam* (2263) and *gomen-wudu* (1065), but urges caution in translating them. He warns of the "etymological fallacy" in the temptation to translate the first directly as "glee-beam," because both words in the compound have changed in meaning (glee = music → happiness; beam = tree, wood → plank).

If the musings of the philologist seem far removed from the poetic imagination that finds in the harp a "door to Other Time," Tolkien's conclusion to the first section of his translation essay reveals that he saw etymology as performing the same task, as Emerson observed in his 1844 essay, "The Poet": "Language is fossil poetry" (13). Hearing the earliest forms of our words is in fact like listening to a harp, he asserts metaphorically.

And therein lies the unrecapturable magic of ancient English verse for those who have ears to hear: profound feeling, and poignant vision, filled with the beauty and mortality of the world, are around by brief phrases, light touches, short words resounding like harp-strings sharply plucked (MC 60-61).

Even in this generalizing assessment of poetry, Tolkien cannot help but see in it "the beauty and mortality of the world."

Summary; One Final Note

The harp for Tolkien is a temporal object that mediates eternity. In its music joy is inextricable from sadness, because all beauty is transcendent, and the transcendent realm (paradise, in Judeo-Christian thought, but also to a degree *fairie* in the "lost" native tradition of England) reconciles oppositions. Hebrew and classical analogues for the harp image are helpful, but the word *harp* itself suggests Germanic origins. The music of the harp provides the "Door to Other Time" Tolkien found in Fairy Story – but so does language itself.

One of Tolkien's last explorations of the realm of *Fairy* in fiction, in the final decade of his life, was the story *Smith of Wootton Major* (1967). In the mundane world of Wootton Major, the only character who had been to *Fairy* was the baker's apprentice Alf (whose very name marks him as Elvish). When the apprentice himself became Master Baker, he trained his own apprentice in the mysteries and magic of the art of baking.

    The apprentice's name? Harper.[5]

---

[5] After 8,000 words harping on one string, the reader will be grateful for the moral restraint that prevented the author from observing that *Smith of Wootton Major* was published by HarperCollins.

About the Author

JOHN R. HOLMES has been teaching English literature (including Tolkien) at Franciscan University of Steubenville (Ohio) since 1985, and has authored some two dozen articles on Tolkien (including a chapter in Walking Tree's 2013 volume *Tolkien's Poetry*). A reader on the editorial board for the online *Journal of Tolkien Research*, Holmes is currently working on a book-length study of Tolkien's verse, and a shorter work on Tolkien's unpublished history of the Lord's Prayer. He and his wife Von write and direct musical comedies for community theater in Ohio.

List of Abbreviations of Tolkien's Works

BMC	*Beowulf: The Monsters and the Critics*
B&C	*Beowulf and the Critics*
FOA	*The Fall of Arthur*
H	*The Hobbit*
HBBC	"The Homecoming of Beorhtnoth Beorhthelm's Son."
L	*The Letters of J.R.R. Tolkien*
LB	*The Lays of Beleriand*
LotR	*The Lord of the Rings*
LT II	*The Book of Lost Tales, Part Two*
MC	*The Monsters and the Critics and Other Essays*
My	"Mythopoeia"
S	*The Silmarillion*
SG	*The Legend of Sigurd and Gudrún*

Bibliography

BENSON, Larry (ed.). *The Riverside Chaucer*, 3rd ed. Boston, MA: Houghton Mifflin, 1987.

BRATMAN, David. "Liquid Tolkien: Music, Tolkien, Middle-earth, and More Music." *Middle-earth Minstrel: Essays on Music in Tolkien*. Ed. Brad Eden. Jefferson, NC: McFarland & Company, 2010.

EMERSON, Ralph Waldo. *The Collected Works of Ralph Waldo Emerson*. Vol. 3: *Essays, Second Series*. Cambridge, MA: Harvard University Press, 1971.

GIBSON, Margaret, T. A. HESLOP, and Richard W. PFAFF (eds.). *The Eadwine Psalter: Text, Image, and Monastic Culture in Twelfth-Century Canterbury*. State College, PA: Penn State University Press, 1992.

LEWIS, C.S. *The Discarded Image*. Cambridge: Cambridge University Press, 1964.

MAIER, Norbert. "The Harp in Middle Earth." *Music in Middle-earth*. Ed. Heidi Steimel and Friedhelm Schneidewind. Zurich and Jena: Walking Tree Publishers, 2010, 107-124.

TOLKIEN, J.R.R. *Beowulf: A Translation and Commentary, together with Sellic Spell*. Ed. Christopher Tolkien. Boston, MA: Houghton Mifflin Harcourt, 2014.

Beowulf and the Critics. Ed. Michael D.C. Drout. Medieval and Renaissance Texts and Studies 248. Tempe, AZ: Arizona Center for Medieval and Renaissance Studies, 2002.

Beowulf: The Monsters and the Critics. London: Humphrey Milford, 1937.

The Book of Lost Tales, Part Two (The History of Middle-earth 2). Ed. Christopher Tolkien. London: George Allen & Unwin, 1983; Boston, MA: Houghton Mifflin, 1984.

The Children of Húrin. London: HarperCollins; Boston, MA: Houghton Mifflin, 2007.

The Fall of Arthur. Ed. Christopher Tolkien. London: HarperCollins, 2013.

The Hobbit. 50th Anniversary edition. Boston, MA: Houghton Mifflin, 1987.

"The Homecoming of Beorhtnoth Beorhthelm's Son." *The Tolkien Reader*. New York City, NY: Ballantine, 1966, 3-27.

The Legend of Sigurd and Gudrún. Ed. Christopher Tolkien. Boston, MA: Houghton Mifflin/London: HarperCollins, 2009.

The Letters of J.R.R. Tolkien. Ed. Humphrey Carpenter, with the assistance of Christopher Tolkien. London: George Allen & Unwin; Boston, MA: Houghton Mifflin, 1981.

The Lord of the Rings. 50th Anniversary edition. Boston, MA: Houghton Mifflin, 2004.

The Monsters and the Critics and Other Essays. London: George Allen & Unwin, 1983; Boston, MA: Houghton Mifflin, 1984.

"Mythopoeia". First published in *Tree and Leaf.* Second edition. London: Unwin Hyman, 1988; Boston, MA: Houghton Mifflin, 1989.

"On Fairy-Stories." *Essays Presented to Charles Williams.* Eds. Verlyn Flieger and Douglas A. Anderson. London: HarperCollins, 2008. London: Oxford University Press, 1947. Printed in revised version in *Tree and Leaf.* London: Unwin Books, 1964; cited here from *Tolkien on Fairy Stories.*

The Silmarillion. Ed. Christopher Tolkien. London: George Allen & Unwin; Boston, MA: Houghton Mifflin, 1977.

"*Sir Orfeo*: A Middle English Version." Ed. with Introduction and Notes by Carl F. Hostetter. *Tolkien Studies* 1 (2004): 85-123.

The Tolkien Reader. New York City, NY: Ballantine Books, 1966.

Allan Turner

The Horns of Elfland

Abstract

Perhaps the most iconic line of English poetry to evoke the world of the imagination just on the edge of consciousness is "The horns of Elfland faintly blowing" from "The Princess" by Tennyson. Music as a liminal area between the real and the imagined is a topos that figures in other works of fantasy, such as Lord Dunsany's *The King of Elfland's Daughter*, which refers back directly to Tennyson. In Tolkien the Elves in particular are associated with songs that operate more on the unconscious mind than the conscious. However, the essay that Tolkien wrote on his own *Smith of Wootton Major*, which has been little regarded by criticism so far, gives the alert reader a clue that access to the world of Faerie depends on the willingness of mortals to make music of their own that can resonate in harmony with the immortal tones. Echoes of this can be found in *The Lord of the Rings*, most obviously in the last chapter, where Frodo's variation on the walking song that sees him moving beyond the everyday paths into the unknown is immediately taken up by the Elves in their more elevated hymn to Elbereth. This echoes an idea found in medieval and renaissance Christian thought, that earthly music forms a link to the harmony of heaven, as formulated by Milton in his poem "At a Solemn Music".

As Tolkien did not quite say in his essay *On Fairy-stories*, fantasy is about the encounter between rational human beings and the marvellous world of their imagination. In fact he preferred to use metaphorical language: "the *aventures* of men in the Perilous Realm or upon its shadowy marches" (*TOFS* 32). He was probably wise to do that, since "Faërie cannot be caught in a net of words" (ibid.), so that only poetic images can capture the sensation. One of the most frequently cited of these poetic images is Tennyson's line, "the horns of Elfland faintly blowing" (292), which conjures up a mysterious call somewhere on the edge of perception. It is not surprising that this line is well known, or at least was well known to an older generation of poetry readers, since it has appeared in a number of anthologies, among them Quiller Couch's *Oxford Book of English Verse*, which according to Paul Fussell (157 and *passim*) was a favourite with Tolkien's contemporaries fighting in the First World War. However, there are two things about it that are rather more surprising. One is the use of the then rare word elfland, for which the *Oxford English Dictionary* has no citation between the *Catholicon Anglicum* glossary of 1483 and the present poem. However, Tennyson could well have come across it in an instance missed by the *OED*, the old ballad "Thomas the Rhymer", published by Sir Walter Scott in his *Minstrelsy of the Scottish Border* of 1802-3, which is the poem quoted by Tolkien near the beginning of *On Fairy-stories* (29), where he attempts to define the genre:

> That is the road to fair Elfland,
> Where thou and I this night maun gae.

The second surprise is that Tennyson should have mentioned Elfland at all, since he was not a writer of fantasy and the poem from which the line is taken is really concerned with purely human events and aspirations. It is worth looking at the words in their original context:

> The splendour falls on castle walls
>   And snowy summits old in story:
> The long light shakes across the lakes,
>   And the wild cataract leaps in glory.
> Blow, bugle, blow, set the wild echoes flying,
> Blow, bugle; answer, echoes, dying, dying, dying.
>
> O hark, O hear! how thin and clear,
>   And thinner, clearer, farther going!
> O sweet and far from cliff and scar
>   The horns of Elfland faintly blowing!
> Blow, let us hear the purple glens replying:
> Blow, bugle; answer, echoes, dying, dying, dying.
>
> O love, they die in yon rich sky,
>   They faint on hill or field or river:
> Our echoes roll from soul to soul,
>   And grow for ever and for ever.
> Blow, bugle, blow, set the wild echoes flying,
> And answer, echoes, answer, dying, dying, dying.

The kernel of the setting in the first two stanzas is sunset at a real castle, believed to have been inspired by the poet's visit to Killarney in Ireland (Batchelor 152) with the bugle signalling the end of the day for the garrison. In the third stanza the echo is revealed as a symbol of the love between two people. However, the literary effect lies in the way that the poetic description lets the reality melt into a scene as if from an old story, which is why the faint echoes of the bugle come to be metamorphosed into "horns of Elfland". The internal rhyme and the repetition of words depicting the dying echoes turn the whole piece into pure sound, which was set to music by Benjamin Britten in his *Serenade for Tenor, Horn and Strings*. The musical sounds of the poem combined with the imagery form, as it were, a liminal zone between reality and the world of the imagination.[1]

If Tennyson's musical echoes do not announce any actual Faërie, those of Lord Dunsany certainly do, since *The King of Elfland's Daughter* owes at least a part of its inspiration to that line of verse. Similar to Tolkien's *Smith of Wootton Major*, Dunsany's fantasy story presents a Perilous Realm that is physically close to the everyday world and can be entered from there, at least by certain privileged individuals at certain times, while the plot is concerned with a situation in which the relationship between mortals and immortals becomes unbalanced. However, unlike the people of Wootton Major, who in their prosperity have lost interest in the wondrous (see below), Dunsany's villagers have become bored with their humdrum existence and demand some magic, which is why their lord sends his son to Elfland to gain the hand of the king's daughter, Lirazel, and bring her back with him. Following a topos known from folk tales, the soulless immortal is unable to adapt to the restrictions of mortal, Christian existence, so that finally under the influence of her father's magic she secretly returns to Elfland. The rest of the story is about the quest of Alveric, her husband, to find a way back to Elfland in order to regain her. Their son Orion also yearns for his mother, and here the boy has an advantage, since being half immortal,

---

1 In fact, the situation is more complex, since these three stanzas form one of several lyrical interludes in a much longer narrative poem, *The Princess*, which has as its subject the position of women in society and the possibility of their pursuing a higher education. This work is half serious, half comic, half modern, half medievalising, but it certainly has no connection with the fantastic in the conventional sense. It appears that Tennyson took fright at the idea of offending his readers, for whom women's education was a highly controversial topic, and used as many distancing devices as possible, of which the lyrical interludes, most of them added later, were a part. They have appeared so often in anthologies divorced from their original context that it is perhaps not surprising that many readers do not realise that the "horns of Elfland" are (perhaps) only a simile, although the poem leaves it deliberately ambiguous. For a more detailed examination of *The Princess* and the circumstances of its composition, see Batchelor 138-148.

he can hear the distant horns at sunset that signal the presence of what lies beyond the border that is now hidden:

> [...] rank on rank of the elfin horns blowing far away eastwards in the chill of the coming dusk, very far and faint, like reveillé heard in dreams. From beyond the woods they sounded, all those ringing horns, from beyond the downs, far over the furthest curve of them; and he knew them for the silver horns of Elfland. (93)

At this point the connection with Tennyson is made completely explicit, since the narrator exceptionally steps completely outside the story with a subtly disingenuous metatextual comment:

> And how the horns of Elfland blew over the barrier of twilight, to be heard by any ear in the fields we know, I cannot understand; yet Tennyson speaks of them as heard "faintly blowing" even in these fields of ours, and I believe that by accepting all that the poets say while duly inspired our errors will be fewest. So, though Science may deny or confirm it, Tennyson's line shall guide me here. (93)

When the King of Elfland finally pronounces the spell that brings Alveric's village within his borders and allows the family to be reunited, it is accomplished by making Elfland slowly spread over the mortal fields, and that too is announced by music. The words of the spell are "like the notes of a band of violins, all played by masters chosen from many ages, hidden on midsummer's midnight in a wood" (223). Alveric and his companions perceive it approaching as "the soft sound of very old songs" (230), while others hear "old music and lost voices" (235) or "all the old songs lost from the nurseries of the Earth" (238), as the ravages of time are obliterated by "the wild glad song of birds from a hundred arbours" (239). Music, and particularly music that is perceived only indirectly, once again creates a liminal area between the real and the unreal, but this time one that is specifically adapted to the genre of fantasy.

Tolkien certainly knew Tennyson's line, since he alludes to it in *On Fairy-stories*, where he notes that the topos that one must keep one's promises is "one of the notes of the horns of Elfland, and not a dim note" (*TOFS* 74), while one of his letters contains a reference to characters from another of Dunsany's stories (*L* 375fn.). However, there is no evidence of any direct influence from either of these sources.[2] Nevertheless it seems possible that he might have applied, consciously or unconsciously, the same technique of using music to break down the barriers of reality and allow the creation of a bridge between the two modes of perception. In the following I will examine to what extent Tolkien used music not as performance, however moving (the dwarves at Bag End), nor as a spell (the song of Lúthien before Morgoth), nor as a cosmogonic myth (the Music of the Ainur), but as a marker of the liminal zone between the everyday and the wonderful.[3]

At first sight the evidence appears slim. There are plenty of horns at significant moments, but they do not really announce the proximity of Faërie. The horns of Boromir and Merry certainly set the wild echoes flying, but their unusual powers are grounded in ancient legend (Boromir's from "the wild kine of Araw" (*LotR* 755), Merry's from the hoard of Scatha the Worm (*LotR* 978)) and do not foreshadow any supernatural intervention: quite the opposite. Similarly, the horns of the Rohirrim on the Pelennor Fields produce a moment of breath-catching eucatastrophe, but they are nevertheless entirely real. Perhaps the closest example in *The Hobbit* is "the dim blowing of horns in the wood and the sound as of dogs baying far off" (*H* 156f.). However, mysterious though this is, we learn later that it is a real hunt of the Wood-elves, so less supernatural than the passage in *Sir Orfeo*, which served as a model, where at least the hunter is the king of Faërie and the quarry are unreal-seeming deer that are never caught.

Better examples are to be found in *The Book of Lost Tales*, the horn of Oromë guiding the Solosimpi to the coast, and more especially the conches of Ulmo, which captivate the mind of Tuor even before the Vala appears to him:

> Then coming along the river he sate among the reeds at twilight and played upon his thing of shells; and it was night to those places where Tuor tarried. And Tuor hearkened and was stricken dumb. There he stood knee-deep in the grass and heard no more the hum of insects, nor the murmur of the river borders, [...] but he heard the sound of waves and the wail of sea-birds, and his soul leapt for rocky places and the ledges that reek of fish, for the splash

---

[2] Dale J. Nelson suggests the possible influence of a short story by Dunsany on Tolkien's poem "The Mewlips", but the evidence is tenuous.
[3] For the wider musical symbolism in Tolkien's legendarium and the influence on it of Victorian poetry, see Bradford Lee Eden's article "Strains of Elvish Song and Voices: Victorian Medievalism, Music, and Tolkien".

of the diving cormorant and those places where the sea bores into the black cliffs and yells aloud. (*LT II* 155)

Unfortunately both of these evocative details were lost in later, less fairytale-like versions of the 'Silmarillion'.

A more promising approach is through song, particularly that of the elves, who in the Middle-earth of the Third Age represent the non-mundane. In both *The Hobbit* and *The Lord of the Rings* their presence is announced for the first time by their singing, in the first case with light-hearted nonsense and in the second with "a sound like mingled song and laughter" (*LotR* 78) which soon turns into a hymn to Elbereth in Elvish. This music is clearly something special since it conveys its meaning to the listening hobbits in some mystical way: "Yet the sound blending with the melody seemed to shape itself in their thought into words which they only partly understood" (79). The same effect is achieved by Galadriel's song of farewell, in Quenya, which Frodo does not understand well: "Yet as is the way of Elvish words, they remained graven in his memory, and long afterwards he interpreted them, as well as he could" (377). The most striking description of the effect of Elvish music is where Frodo listens to the singing in the house of Elrond:

> At first the beauty of the melodies and of the interwoven words in elven-tongues, even though he understood them little, held him in a spell, as soon as he began to attend to them. Almost it seemed that the words took shape, and visions of far lands and bright things that he had never yet imagined opened out before him; and the firelit hall became like a golden mist above seas of foam that sighed upon the margins of the world. (233)

All these songs sing of things that lie outside the everyday world; they mediate the mythology that forms the background to the main narrative, both for the mortal characters in the fiction and for the reader.

However, for mediation to take place, a way must be found for both sides to come closer to one another. Tennyson's lyrical voice needs to distance himself from the real castle in order to perceive the echoes of the bugle as echoes of the imagination. Orion would not hear the horns of Elfland if it were not for his elvish blood. In *The Lord of the Rings* it is less easy to see the process at work because the background stories that structure the narrative are myths and history at the same time; the Evening Star whose light reveals the ring on Galadriel's finger is both a star and the guardian spirit Eärendil. The significance of the liminal zone may be seen more easily in *Smith of Wootton Major*, in which, as mentioned above, Faery[4] is depicted as being physically close to at least a part of the everyday world, so that the relationship between the two is more directly thematised. In the narrative, the only music of Faery that is heard in the outside world is the lily bells that Smith brings back as a present for his grandson: "At the sweet sound the candles flickered and then for a moment shone with a white light" (50). However, when Smith first becomes aware of his special gift as the star is fixed to his forehead, that is also accompanied by sounds that reveal the beyond:

> Then the dawn came, and far away he heard the dawn-song of the birds beginning, growing as it came towards him, until it rushed over him, filling all the land round the house, and passed on like a wave of music into the West, as the sun rose above the rim of the world.
>
> "It reminds me of Faery," he heard himself say; "but in Faery the people sing too." Then he began to sing, high and clear, in strange words that he seemed to know by heart [...] (19f.)

The old Master Cook also starts to sing when he returns from Faery with Alf, so clearly there is some mutual influence at work here. Can it be that the liminal zone is announced by music on the earthly side too?

The key lies in Tolkien's essay, "Smith of Wootton Major", which was first published in Verlyn Flieger's edition of the short story and has so far received very little critical notice. The purpose of its composition is not clear, but it appears to be a memorandum to himself providing a more detailed history of the characters and events to make clearer the motivation, most of which is omitted in the story because it is written in the style of a fairy tale, in which things just happen without explanation, rather than a novel. To this extent it is analogous to the Appendices in *The Lord of the Rings*, which elaborate on events seen in the main narrative only from the limited point of view of the hobbits, although unlike them it is written from outside the text world and was clearly not meant for publication. More importantly, it attempts to explain the relationship in the

---

4 In *Smith* Tolkien prefers the spelling Faery, so I use it when referring specifically to that work.

story between the human characters and the nearby Faery: the inhabitants of Wootton Major have grown too prosperous and worldly to care for the world of the imagination, so that the king of Faery takes pity and devises a plan to save them from their own short-sightedness. There is no longer any occupation for the creative people: "Such folk as the Sedgers (the tale-tellers), the musicians: Pipers, Harpers, Crowthers, Fidlers and Horners and the Sangsters", as well as the craftsmen (92f.). This is a society where family names (and it is worth noting that all of these are genuine English names) denote their occupation; Sangster means a singer and a Crowther is a player on the ancient Welsh *crwth*; cf. Flieger's note of pp. 145-6. The old Master Cook's mother, for example, is a Piper, so that he has an affinity for Faery and can bring Alf back with him; and Alf's apprentice is called Harper, which suggests that he is a more suitable person than most to learn from the king of Faery. This essay also gives a more precise explanation of the concept of Faërie/Faery than any that is to be found in *On Fairy-stories*:

> Faery represents at its weakest a breaking out (at least in mind) from the iron ring of the familiar [...]. More strongly it represents love: that is, a love and respect for all things, "inanimate" and "animate", an unpossessive love of them as "other". [...] Faery might be said indeed to represent Imagination (without definition because taking in all the definitions of this word): esthetic: exploratory and receptive; and artistic; inventive, dynamic, (sub)creative. [...] this "Faery" is as necessary for the health and complete functioning of the Human as is sunlight for physical life[.] (*SWM* 101)

So music as a creative skill can form a powerful bridge to the world of the imagination. Even though the hobbit songs in *The Lord of the Rings* are simple and rustic (although less so than perhaps they seem), they prepare Frodo to be receptive to the higher art of the Elves, just as the fairy doll in *Smith* is a prefiguring of the Queen of Faery: "For some the only glimpse. For some the awakening" (*SWM* 38). When Frodo rides out with Sam for the last time, their journey re-traces the one they had made at the beginning of the story, but this time Frodo's old walking song, transformed by the effect of his experiences in a much wider world, is answered immediately by the Elves' hymn to Elbereth; the music forms a direct bridge from the lesser to the greater.

The idea of music as a link between the human and the superhuman is of course not unique to Tolkien; in fact it is widespread in Christian contexts.

Milton, for example, in his poem "At a Solemn Music"[5] sees earthly music as an echo of the harmony before the fall of mankind which will ultimately be restored:

> And the Cherubic host in thousand quires
> Touch their immortal harps of golden wires,
> With those just Spirits that wear victorious palms
> Hymns devout and holy psalms
> Singing everlastingly:
> That we on earth, with undiscording voice
> May rightly answer that melodious noise[.]

Or indeed in the popular Christmas carol "It came upon the midnight clear", which ends by imagining the coming of an age of gold,

> When peace shall over all the earth
> Its ancient splendours fling,
> And the whole world give back the song
> Which now the angels sing.[6]

This idea may have its archetype in the singing of the angels at the birth of Jesus in Bethlehem, which for Christians is a symbol of heaven descending to earth.[7] Within Tolkien's own mythology it is tempting to extend the argument to claim that the musical encounters between Men (or hobbits) and Elves are an echo of the great Music of the Ainur, which one day will be restored to its full harmony. However, it would be unfortunate if in that abstraction was lost the uniqueness of the "horns of Elfland", which come unexpectedly to those whose ears are attuned to them and are, like eucatastrophe itself, "a sudden and miraculous grace: never to be counted on to recur" (*TOFS* 75).

About the Author

ALLAN TURNER has master's degrees in medieval studies and general linguistics, as well as a doctorate in translation studies. He recently retired from his position as Lecturer in English at the Friedrich-Schiller University Jena, but is still active in research. His main interests within Tolkien studies lie in the fields of stylistics and translation.

---

5 This poem was set to music for choir and orchestra as *Blest Pair of Sirens* by the British composer Hubert Parry (1848-1918).
6 Complete words available at https://en.wikipedia.org/wiki/It_Came_Upon_the_Midnight_Clear
7 The Bible does not mention singing, but that is how it is almost invariably represented in both popular and "high" art.

List of Abbreviations of Tolkien's Works

H	*The Hobbit*
L	*The Letters of J.R.R. Tolkien*
LotR	*The Lord of the Rings*
LT II	*The Book of Lost Tales Part II*
TOFS	*Tolkien on Fairy-Stories*
SWM	*Smith of Wootton Major*

Bibliography

BATCHELOR, John. *Tennyson*. London: Chatto & Windus, 2012.

DUNSANY, Edward John Moreton Drax Plunkett, Lord. *The King of Elfland's Daughter*. London: Gollancz, 2001. First published 1924.

EDEN, Bradford Lee. "Strains of Elvish Song and Voices: Victorian Medievalism, Music, and Tolkien." *Music in Middle-earth*. Eds. Heidi Steimel and Friedhelm Schneidewind. Zurich and Jena: Walking Tree Publishers, 2010, 149-165.

FUSSELL, Paul. *The Great War and Modern Memory*. Oxford: Oxford University Press, 1975.

MILTON, John. "At a Solemn Music." *The Golden Treasury*. Ed. Francis Turner Palgrave. Harmondsworth: Penguin, 1994, 122-123.

NELSON, Dale J. "Possible Echoes of Blackwood and Dunsany in Tolkien's Fantasy." *Tolkien Studies* I (2004): 177-181.

SCOTT, Walter. *Minstrelsy of the Scottish Border*. 3 vols. London: Longman and Rees, 1802-3. http://bit.ly/2zoGmVb.

TENNYSON, Alfred. *The Poetical Works of Lord Tennyson*. London and Glasgow: Collins, n.d.

TOLKIEN, John Ronald Reuel. *The Book of Lost Tales Part II*. Ed. Christopher Tolkien. London: George Allen & Unwin, 1984.

On Fairy-stories. Eds. Verlyn Flieger and Douglas A. Anderson. London: HarperCollins, 2008.

The Hobbit. London: HarperCollins, 1998.

The Letters of J.R.R. Tolkien. Ed. Humphrey Carpenter. London: Allen & Unwin, 1981.

The Lord of the Rings. 50th Anniversary edition. London: HarperCollins, 2005.

Smith of Wootton Major. London: George Allen & Unwin, 1967. Extended edition prepared by Verlyn Flieger. London: HarperCollins, 2005.

Rainer Groß

Portatives in Middle-earth: A Speculative Approach to Organ Instruments in Tolkien's Work

Abstract

The following article is a speculative study on organ building in Middle-earth, which – although there is no explicit mention of it – could have taken place there. A specific kind of small organ, so called 'portative organ' or 'organetto', is described in different examples by its medieval design and its possible appearance in Middle-earth.

In many of the cinematic interpretations of Tolkien's fantasy worlds music or musical instruments only feature tangentially. At most, around elves some harps can be seen, and distant songs may drift down from the treetops. Humans and dwarves use horns as signals in battle. Music seems distant to Middle-earth. Is this really the case however? Of course not. Tolkien's texts are teeming with songs and hymns, which serve important roles in a myriad of situations.

The dwarves especially are described as a highly musical people. Answering Bilbo's question at the start of *The Hobbit* whether the dwarves will stay for dinner Thorin replies: "Of course! And after. We shan't get through the business till late, and we must have some fine music first. Now to clear up!" (*H* 11). After this the dwarves sing as they get to work. Not only can they sing however, they also have a large variety of different musical instruments with them:

> "Now for some music!" said Thorin. "Bring out the instruments!" Kili and Fili rushed for their bags and brought back little fiddles; Dori, Nori, and Ori brought out flutes from somewhere inside their coats; Bombur produced a drum from the hall; Bifur and Bofur went out too, and came back with clarinets that they had left among the walking-sticks. Dwalin and Balin said: "Excuse me, I left mine in the porch!"
>
> "Just bring mine in with you!" said Thorin. They came back with viols as big as themselves, and with Thorin's harp wrapped in a green cloth. It was a beautiful golden harp, and when Thorin struck it the music began all at once, so sudden and sweet that Bilbo forgot everything else, and was swept away

into dark lands under strange moons, far over The Water and very far from his hobbit-hole under The Hill. (*H* 13)

The throaty voices of the dwarves receive a lot of description as well as the priced treasures they were able to fashion out of all kinds of material through their excellent craftsmanship. After fleeing the mountain, the dwarves made their living in many different places as competent craftsmen and artful smiths. Where musicality and craftmanship met, the creation of musical instruments cannot be far. For me as an organ builder the question arises: How might the organ instruments of Middle-earth have looked like? What did they sound like? Were they big or small?

Was their appearance possibly like the Hydraulos or Hydraulis of antiquity, whose invention is attributed to the Greek engineer Ktesibios in the third century BC (cf. Jakob 11)? Ktesibios used an Aulos, a double reed instrument which was very popular at the time, for sound generation and placed multiple Auloi, each only delivering their base tone, arrayed on top of an air tank in which displaced water acted to maintain and normalize the pressure. A manual was used to turn the air-flow to specific Auloi on and off. This should suffice as far as the basic principles of this ingenious inventor are concerned, who incidentally also invented moving figures, piston pumps and water features.[1]

Image 1: Portative from the Saint Bartholomew Altarpiece, Cologne 1490/1495

---

1 Jakob. 11. Here it is also reported that Ktesibios was the son of a barber.

In Greece, organ music was greatly respected and played a major part in the public interest. There existed, for example, public organ competitions followed by award ceremonies (ibid. 12). Emperor Nero introduced an organ type with multiple stops into Rome in AD 67, making the organ well known in Rome

Image 2: Christ surrounded by angels, Hans Memling (1433-1494)

as well (ibid. 13). A century later, small oil lamps were produced in the shape of organs, an indicator of the special position organs held in the public consciousness.[2]

Many emperors of the later Roman empire played the organ themselves or were at the least infatuated with organ music. Out of the convention to play the organ during the entry and exit of the emperor grew the special position of the organ as an instrument of cult and ceremony. In the Western Roman Empire the knowledge of organ construction and organ music was lost in the chaos of the Migration Period. In the court of Byzantium, organ music continued to be

---

2 Reichloing 2001.

Image 3: Angel with portative, Stefan Lochne, apr. 1448

cultivated. It was only when Pepin the Short (AD 714-768) received an organ as a gift from emperor Constantine V. (AD 741-775) (ibid. 52) that the art of organ music in the Occident, after being completely forgotten for centuries, could be reignited.

Through its unique position as an instrument of imperial representation the organ acquired its place in church service. In this way, an instrument of representation for the emperor became an instrument of the religious ceremony. The first cathedral organs are mentioned around the year 1000 in Augsburg, Reims, and Winchester

(ibid. 53-55). Several centuries later, smaller organs called positive organs[3] are used in churches. These were not installed permanently but could be moved like furniture to different places depending on needs.

Apart from this, there have always existed so called portatives (from lat. portare: to carry) as miniature organs that could be held and played by a single musician using their arms or knees. Sadly, no originals of this miniature version of an organ, which was very popular in the Middle-Ages

Image 4: Angel with portative, choir of Cologne Cathedral, approx. 1270, coloring approx. 1840

---

[3] From lat. *ponere*: to put, to place.

and antiquity, remain. Portatives were used in ensembles but also as a solo instrument. Unfortunately, no original portatives survive. From depictions, sculptures etc. (Images 1 to 5) we can roughly deduce the following (without claiming complete accuracy):

Portatives were equipped with metal flue pipes (Image 1).

Like recorders, these flue pipes generate sound by blowing a stream of air over a sharp edge.

Image 5: Portative, Spain, 12th cent.

The dark color that is often used to depict the pipes in painting could be an indicator of an alloy with a high lead content.

Reed pipes, meaning pipes in which vibrating strips of metal generate the sound, or flue pipes made from wood are never depicted. They nonetheless may have existed; organ builders have always been inventive. The number of pipes varied from about 8 to 16 (Image 3), up to 30 in the case of very large instruments. At that point a certain limit in size existed. Larger instruments could not have been carried by a single person and would thus not have been portatives anymore.

The pipes were usually arrayed in one or two rows; larger instruments could even have three or four rows. Normally, the largest pipe was on the left with the others sorted by pitch towards the right. Some depictions however show an ordering right to left, largest to smallest, although it is difficult to determine whether this is because of simple ignorance on the part of the painter or because these descriptions are accurate. Portatives with a miter-shaped ordering, with the larges pipe in the middle, can also be found. At times, singular larger pipes were bundled into groups and encased in special sections of the housing (Image 4). Using them as drone pipes comes to mind naturally, which would accurately represent their use in practice at that time.

A housing in the strictest sense did not exist. The pipes stood arrayed on top of the wind chest, held in place by a simple wooden rod. The bellows were affixed to the back and built into a cohesive unit with the wind chest and the manual. The manuals consisted in part of buttons and in part keys of varying shapes: straight, rounded, curved, in varying colorings (i.e. wood types) for upper and lower manuals or uniformly colored. Early instruments likely used diatonic scales, with semitones only being added later (first F# and B_b), leading up to the fully chromatic manuals in later centuries.

The bellow was located at the back, at times also below or next to the wind chest. Some bellows were attached hanging vertically (Image 2) or lay horizontally to the side (Image 5).

Early instruments still used simple "Froschmaulbälge" (can be translated as wedge bellows or cuneiform bellows) with leather or fur pieces that were attached between the two boards of the bellows without a specific structure. In later periods we find cuneiform bellows with fold boards connected by leather hinges, as they are common in most types of organ construction. In most depictions we see a single hand operated bellows being used with one hand as the other is playing on the keyboard. Occasionally only the thumb is used to exert force on the upper board, sometimes using a leather strip, while the other finger is working the bellows against it. If one supposes there to have been two "wind systems" (a single hand-operated bellows or one using a magazine, meaning another bellow working in contrary motion) then there must have existed two fundamentally different forms of portative play: a single bellows requires pausing and phrasing. A portative musician would have to be careful and efficient in their air use. This moves them closer to the realm of singers and flutists, with all the options of modulation by varying air pressure this entails. The combination of a bellows and a magazine on the other hand allows for continuous play. This is especially useful in music that makes use of burden but simultaneously gives up on much of the direct control over wind, since the second bellows normalizes the air pressure. The depictions at least allow for the possibility that both types of wind systems existed simultaneously. As an example of contemporary constructions, here is a picture of three portatives from my workshop.

Image 6: Three portatives from my workshop: on the left oak and metal pipes, in the middle one with wooden pipes, on the right cedar and metal pipes

Let us, after this basic look at portative construction, make some space for imagination. How could portatives have looked like in Middle-earth?

The Elves are known for their elegant physique and graceful movements. We can picture their houses and furniture with delicate, sophisticated designs and an almost floral aesthetic. Delicate Elf-fingers would certainly be very adept at handling slim keys. The proportions would lend themselves to a vertical construction. The sleek cases would have to be drilled multiples times to enhance the lightness of the construction. For wood types, lighter or brighter woods would need to be considered, for example maple or cedar, maybe even elm. A possible design can be seen on the next page (Image 7).

The dwarves live in underground cities and are used to working with iron and stone. Their hands and fingers are tough and strong making them efficient craftsmen who build their musical instruments accordingly. The keys would have to be broader und topped with a more robust type of wood, maybe a burr veneer. For wood they would certainly prefer sturdy oak wood. Metal fittings on the sides and edges could protect the instruments during transport in the

tunnels and caves. The bellows likely would have been made in the way of the bellows found in their smithies, from cow leather, fitted with nails and iron hinges. For the pipes, silver is often used, which the dwarves would have easy access to through their activities as miners. Maybe a dwarven portative would look like this (Image 8):

Image 7: Elven portative

The hobbits use portatives with finely carved wooden cheeks. Because of the soft sound they would likely prefer wooden pipes over metal ones. The smaller scale of the construction would necessitate a higher pitch, making the instrument well suited for melodies and embellished high parts. To play and dance at the same time the Hobbits like to use a strap to sling the instrument over their shoulder. A pipe holder to help in the case impromptu singing performances is just as popular as a variety of secret compartments for tobacco bags and matches. Here is a possible design (Image 9, opposite page):

Image 8: Dwarvish portative

That would conclude my thought experiments regarding "portatives in Middle-earth". It remains a topic of discussion which allows for many subtle variations and offers a wide playing field for our imagination. I welcome you to play along in thought or on any instrument.

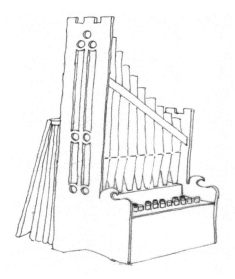

Image 9: Hobbit portative

About the author

RAINER GROSS is an organist and church musician who lives and works in Armsheim, Germany. In his workshop he creates individually designed portative organs based on historic descriptions, as well as freely developed instruments, being used in medieval and folk music. Contact: mail@knieorgel.de

Bibliography

Image Sources

Image 1: Anonymous."Portativ Bartholomäusaltar." Köln, 2006. Wikimedia Commons: https://commons.wikimedia.org/wiki/File:Portativ.png (Accessed 19/03/2019).

Image 2: Anonymous. "Music Making Angels" by Hans Memling. Antwerp, 2017. Wikimedia Commons: https://upload.wikimedia.org/wikipedia/commons/d/d8/Hans_Memling_-_Music-Making_Angels_-_KMSKA_780.jpg (Accessed 19/03/2019).

Image 3: Anonymous. "Engel mit Portativ." Orgellexikon: http://orgellexikon.gally.ch/navigation/geschichte/orgeln/portativ2.jpg (Accessed 19/03/2019).

Image 4: Anonymous. "Engel mit Portativ, Kölner Dom." Köln. Klais: https://klais.de/_klais/bilder/zz_bis_8_2017/kirchen/Koeln_Dom_Engel_3.jpg (Accessed 19/03/2019).

Image 5: Anonymous. "Cantigas." Portativo: http://www.portativo.it/foto/cantigas.jpg (Accessed 19/03/2019).

Image 6: Rainer Groß. "Three Portatives" (private). Arnsheim, 2018.

Images 7-9: Rainer Groß. "Elven Portative", "Dwarvish Portative", and "Hobbit Portative" (private). Arnsheim, 2018.

Print Sources

FINSCHNER, Ludwig (ed.). *Die Musik in Geschichte und Gegenwart. Sonderband Orgel*. Weimar: Metzler, 2001.

JAKOB, Friedrich. *Die Orgel*. Bern: Hallwag Verlag, 1976.

REICHLING, Alfred (ed.). *MGG Prisma: Orgel*. Ulm 2001, 50.

TOLKIEN, J.R.R. *The Hobbit*. New York City, NY: Ballantine Books, 1982.

Music beyond Tolkien

Anja Müller

The Lords of the Rings: Wagner's *Ring* and Tolkien's "Faërie"

Abstract

This essay attempts to assess correspondences between Richard Wagner's *Der Ring des Nibelungen* and J.R.R. Tolkien's *The Lord of the Rings* with respect to contents and conceptualization. A first part examines the analogies and differences that can be traced between the two eponymous rings of power in the tetralogy and the trilogy. A second section reads Wagner's *Oper und Drama* together with Tolkien's "On Fairy-Stories", exploring the question in how far Wagner's idea of a music drama as Gesamtkunstwerk actually approaches the genre of "fantasy drama" which Tolkien believed to be impossible. Employing an intertextual approach, the discussion seeks to eschew speculations concerning possible motivations for the investigated rela-tionships and refrains from evaluating one of the two works over the other.

The following essay attempts to assess correspondences and differences between Richard Wagner's *Der Ring des Nibelungen* and J.R.R. Tolkien's *The Lord of the Rings* with respect to contents and conceptualization. When pursuing such an endeavor, one cannot, of course, bypass Tolkien's reported denial and annoyance when it came to alleged analogies between his own work and Wagner's *Ring*. Tolkien was highly critical of Wagner's usage of Nordic mythology. "Both rings were round, and there the resemblance ceases", was, therefore, his reported answer to the question of possible relationships between the two "Rings" (Carpenter 270).[1] Since I am rather interested in conceptual and structural similarities than intended borrowings or conscious influence, I side with several scholars who argue that, despite this authorial verdict, one can nevertheless discover similarities and parallels between Wagner's *Ring* and Tolkien's *The Lord of the Rings*. K.C. Fraser, for example, perceives various comparable plot elements and concludes: "the two rings had more in common than being round" (13). John Ellison doubts whether Wagner directly influenced

---

1 So Tolkien's reaction to a remark by Ake Ohlmarks, the Swedish translator of *The Lord of the Rings*, that Tolkien's Ring to some extent resembled Wagner's.

Tolkien, yet he claims conceptual analogies in the ways both artists created their mythological worlds (Ellison 1998, 35). To date, probably the most comprehensive assessments of the relationship between Tolkien's and Wagner's Rings are two monographs published in 2012, by Christopher MacLachlan (*Tolkien and Wagner: The Ring and Der Ring*) and Renée Vink (*Wagner and Tolkien: Mythmakers*) respectively. Since both volumes contain thorough discussions of the state of the art in research on the topic, I shall refrain from repeating what they have already compiled so expertly. Whereas MacLachlan diligently scrutinizes parallels in content, plot and, especially, character, Vink also considers structures, concepts and technicalities of the myth making process in Wagner's and Tolkien's works. Pondering questions of influence and intentionality and sometimes enquiring into Tolkien's possible reasons and motivations, both monographs follow an author-centered approach. Thus, Vink frequently makes conjectures about what Tolkien may have thought or intended (for example, concerning his usage of motifs from the *Puss-in-Boots* fairy tale; 140), whereas MacLachlan refers back to Harold Bloom's psychological explanation for intertextual relationships: "Though there are some good reasons for being defensive about an association with Wagner, it is still possible there are also bad reasons, and in Tolkien's case one might be a state of denial born of the anxiety of influence" (184).[2]

My own essay is based on a talk given at a conference in 2006, and afterwards published in the journal *Musicorum* (2006/2007), hence at a time when a considerable number of the sources MacLachlan and, especially, Vink are quoting, had not been published yet. Nevertheless, I would argue that most of my findings have rather been corroborated than refuted by the later studies. I should perhaps emphasize, however, that my essay is neither interested in Tolkien's intentions or motivations, nor does it look for evidence of conscious influence. Instead, my investigation is informed by the theoretical framework of intertextuality and adaptation studies, which follow the premise that a) any text is basically an echo chamber, or an intricate network of allusions and references to previous texts and that b) the relationship between pretexts (or sources, as one calls them in influence studies) and texts that allude to those pretexts or

---

[2] The term and concept of the "anxiety of influence", at least, derive from Harold Bloom's eponymous study, even if MacLachlan does not reference this theoretical source in his bibliography.

adapt them, is not hierarchical, but each text is to be regarded and interpreted in its own right. In view of this presupposition, the question whether Tolkien's *The Lord of the Rings* would be downgraded – for whatever reasons – by owing any legacy to Wagner's *Ring des Nibelungen*, is entirely irrelevant for me. Both rings were round, and both Rings are equal in merit, as it were.

Having, hopefully, clarified this, my essay will follow the general pattern of previous studies on the relationship between Wagner and Tolkien as it discusses, in a first section, some of the similarities between *Der Ring des Nibelungen* and *The Lord of the Rings* on the level of contents, focusing in particular on a comparison of the two powerful rings. The second part will examine the conceptualization of both works as mythopoetic creations. For this purpose, I intend to read Wagner's theoretical observations, as stated in his *Oper* und *Drama*, together with Tolkien's article "On Fairy-Stories", which is based on a lecture held at the University of St. Andrews in 1939, and which I take to be an essential key to Tolkien's understanding of "Fantasy". For my argument, Tolkien's assertion in "On Fairy-Stories", that Fantasy and drama are eventually incompatible, is of chief interest. Contrary to Tolkien's statements uttered in that essay, I wish to explore the question whether Wagner's concepts of music drama and *Gesamtkunstwerk*, as exemplified in *Der Ring des Nibelungen*, do not, in fact, correspond or at least come very close to the Fantasy drama, whose existence Tolkien so vehemently repudiates.[3]

Unlike Robert Hall, who finds a likeness in the general structure of both works, I do not think that the structure of Wagner's tetralogy, consisting of one preliminary evening and three evenings, can be simply equated with Tolkien's *The Lord of the Rings* plus *The Hobbit* as a prelude. Although *Das Rheingold* and *Die Walküre* had their individual premieres at Munich in 1869 and 1870 (both ordained by King Ludwig II, to Wagner's great dismay), Wagner's four music dramas form a coherent musical and textual unit and were conceived

---

3 Whereas MacLachlan does not include Wagner's theoretical writings in his monograph, Renée Vink devotes a chapter to this topic ("Chapter 8, A World too Much? Fantasy versus (Stage) Drama"; 135-152). This chapter frequently refers to my findings and finally arrives at the same conclusions, although Vink otherwise seems to dismiss my earlier essay in her state-of-the-art section as basically uninformed (43-35; the majority of her arguments, however, seem to be based either on misprisions – e.g. her mistaken assertion that I would affirm Tolkien's statement – misunderstandings – e.g. of my statement that the wish for power in *The Lord of the Rings* is isolated, curtailed renditions of my arguments or the claim to know the ultimate meaning of Tolkien's or Wagner's texts and music).

by him as such from the beginning.[4] Modern performance practice may deviate from that concept with individual stagings of *Das Rheingold*, *Die Walküre*, *Siegfried* or *Götterdämmerung*, which are often due to the simple fact that not all opera houses can fulfil the necessary requirements for staging an entire *Ring*. Similarly, Tolkien also wanted that his readers regard *The Fellowship of the Ring*, *The Two Towers* and *The Return of the King* as three respective volumes of one single novel; therefore he rejected the term "trilogy" for *The Lord of the Rings*. With Peter Jackson's movie adaptation, however, the perception and reception of the work has somewhat changed: The movies were and, usually, are presented individually, often with a considerable interval between the respective presentations.[5] As a consequence, audiences and readers have taken to call *The Lord of the Rings* a "trilogy" despite Tolkien's dislike of the term. Moreover, Tolkien's *Hobbit*, written as a children's book, differs greatly from the trilogy in style and tone and needed later adjustments, for example, to bring the significance of Gollum's, respectively Bilbo's, ring into accordance with the concept of the One Ring presented in the three volumes of *The Lord of the Rings*. Other plot elements that are frequently discussed in critical literature thus seem to me more convincing parallels – one may think of the significant swords, the retreat of the immortals or parallels between characters such as Wotan and Gandalf. Since the scope of this essay does not allow me to explore the entire range of these parallels (and since other critics, most notably MacLachlan have already charted that territory in sufficient detail), I shall content myself with examining the eponymous Ring of the Nibelungs versus the One Ring from *The Lord of the Rings*.

In the context of Germanic and Nordic culture, rings had important symbolic functions within interpersonal relationships. They could serve as presents, signs of welcome or belonging. Wagner and Tolkien both seem to conceive of their rings as perversions of these traditional symbolic meanings, as both Alberich's ring and the One Ring mainly function as instruments of oppression and ultimately disrupt interpersonal relationships. Tolkien's One Ring may grant

---

4 In a letter to Franz Liszt, dated 20 November 1851, Wagner presents to the German composer the full outline and concept of his tetralogy – a project he had been planning on since 1848 (Kurt Pahlen includes a lengthy quote from that letter in his chapter on the history of *Das Rheingold*; see *Rheingold*, 204-205).
5 Exceptions are special triple bills in cinemas or private consecutive 'binge' screenings of all three movies for and by fans.

longevity (Gandalf hints at this regarding Bilbo), yet among its unpleasant side effects are also absolute isolation, physical decline and psychological degeneration, as is most impressively illustrated in the fate of Gollum.[6]

Such consuming powers do not inhere the two significant rings of Germanic mythology that may have served as models for Wagner and Tolkien. Draupnir, Odin's magic ring, was said to be forged by a dwarf (cf. Alberich) and to bring forth eight new rings each night (cf. the One Ring, which had been forged together with 18 other rings), yet it was also a symbol of prosperity, affluence and fecundity – the stark opposite to Wagner's and Tolkien's rings. Draupnir's end, however, (Odin throws it into Baldur's funeral pyre) is again strongly reminiscent of the 'fiery' ending of our two rings – Brünnhilde's pyre and Mount Doom. The second mythological ring of significance, which may have been a model to Wagner and Tolkien, was wrested from the dwarf Andvari by Odin, Loki and Hönir. The three latters had killed Otr and are then ordered to cover Otr's corpse entirely with gold. For this purpose, they steal this gold from Andvari, who even has to relinquish his ring to cover the last bit of Otr's dead body. Andvari thereupon curses the ring, which from now on will cost its owner his life.

Wagner's genuine contribution in this context was to couple the ring with the idea of power; the idea that the ring gives his owner power over the world cannot be found in Germanic or Nordic myths. In the *Nibelungenlied*, there is a rod with a similar effect, but this item is never used. K.C. Fraser sees in this coincidence proof of Wagner's influence on Tolkien and even goes as far as to claim that the title of Tolkien's trilogy was gleaned from Alberich's exclamation: "Zittre und zage, gezähmtes Heer: rasch gehorcht des Ringes Herrn!" (*Rheingold*, scene 3, 95). Without subscribing to such theories of influence, I want to focus in the following paragraphs on the two rings and ask how they are related to power in the two works. Where do the rings come from? Who

---

6 "Gollum used to wear it at first, till it tired him; and then he kept it in a pouch next his skin, till it galled him; and now usually he hid it in a hole in the rock on his island, and was always going back to look at it. And still sometimes he put it on, when he could not bear to be parted from it any longer, or when he was very, very, hungry, and tired of fish. Then he would creep along dark passages looking for stray goblins; […] for he would be safe. Oh yes, quite safe. No one would see him, no one would notice him, till he had his fingers on their throat" (*H* 85).

are their owners? What do they signify? How does the power connected with them manifest itself; and what are the consequences of that manifestation?

As far as origins are concerned, the Ring of the Nibelung is originally part of the Rhinegold, enlightening the depths of the Rhine with its shimmer and thus delighting the Rhine Daughters. Since "der Wassertiefe wonniger Stern", is beauty without a purpose, the material from which the Ring of the Nibelung is forged, is pure and innocent. Evil connotations come into play in the moment when unformed, disinterested, natural beauty is forced into a form and thus functionalized into a powerful instrument to subject the world.[7] This deformation of nature is only possible for someone who concedes to a deformation of his own person. Renouncing love, which the father of the Rhine Daughters had supposed to be an essential need of all beings, Alberich becomes the Lord of the Ring of the Nibelung – a monster exchanging love for lust and power. Eventually, when being forced to relinquish the Ring to Wotan and Loge, he will subject the Ring to a double curse: "Wie durch Fluch er mir geriet, verflucht sei dieser Ring!" (*Rheingold*, scene 4, 121). In the further course of the tetralogy, the ring will be owned by several further characters, each change of proprietor being connected with a violent act as it were.

Tolkien's One Ring, on the other hand, is presented as a powerful instrument of Evil from the very beginning. *The Silmarillion* (S 346-348) relates how Sauron deceives the Elves into allowing him to use his arts to aid them enrich Middle-earth. Helping the Elves to forge rings of power, he secretly forges the One Ring for himself, endowing it with the power to bind all other rings and their bearers.[8] Sauron does not need to renounce anything for this – he is evil. The same applies to the One Ring, which is intrinsically linked with Sauron, because, contrary to Wagner, Tolkien does not present his readers with an explicit prehistory of the original material from which the ring is forged. The One Ring makes its appearance as Sauron's creation; its material seems to be immaterial to its significance. Consequently, only Sauron is the Lord and owner

---

[7] Since Renée Vink also contends: "It is the Rhinegold that is pure and innocent, not the ring. Even the desire to forge it is evil, as it causes one to forswear love" (44), her verdict that my assessment is debatable (ibid.) appears inconclusive to me.
[8] It is worth noting that Sauron fails in binding the Elves, because they discard their rings. The Dwarves merely become greedy for treasure. Only the Humans can eventually be fully possessed by its power.

of this ring; all the others are called ringbearers.[9] Disinterested beauty can be found in Middle-earth in the art of the Elves, who endeavor to create beautiful things without a particular purpose. With Sauron's ring, the desire for power counterbalances this desire for beauty. Whereas Wagner's ring is thus explicitly presented as an object of fallen Nature, but originally as little evil as Alberich himself, the One Ring is introduced as something essentially linked to Evil. Its capacity to change its bearers or to guide them even makes it appear to be an individual being with its own will.

As deformed Nature in the hands of a monster, the Ring of the Nibelung is a powerful instrument, yet it achieves its truly destructive power only through Alberich's second curse, which infects it with an unquenchable desire: "Wer ihn besitzt, den sehre die Sorge, und wer ihn nicht hat, den nage der Neid" (*Rheingold*, scene 4, 121). The curse causes hatred and disquietude between human beings – the logical consequence and culmination of the renunciation of love of its first owner, who passes on with interest the first curse that struck him when he had forged the ring. As for the effects of the second curse on the ring's subsequent owners, one can say that Wotan, the second owner, briefly plays with the thought to keep the ring for himself to rule wisely, i.e. to use its power positively. Yet at this moment of the drama, Wagner has already introduced Wotan as someone who is not qualified for this noble project, since he has already sinned on his way to power, cutting his spear of contracts from Yggdrasil's trunk. This violation of nature correlates with that of Alberich, albeit with the difference that Wotan is unable to renounce love (which means that he would never have been able to forge the ring himself). The scene between Wotan and Brünnhilde in the second act of *Die Walküre* beautifully illustrates how Wotan is torn between the power of love and the power of power – the two contradictory forces in Wagner's *Ring*. These two forces ensnare the Wagnerian characters and they are only distinguished by the fact that the power of love can also be liberating if it redeems the lovers, transferring them to another world. Contrary to Alberich, Wotan does not become monstrous despite all his flaws, because the power of love is stronger in him than the power of power. Although presenting himself as an unfree person at the end of *Die Walküre*,

---

9 Gollum's degeneracy reveals itself, among other things, through his belief to be the owner of the One Ring – by which he, albeit unconsciously, presents himself as intrinsically evil.

he is still freer than Alberich; therefore he is even ready to relinquish the Ring when Erda asks him to do so.

The second owner of the Ring, the giant Fafner, is entirely devoid of this freedom. Having killed his brother, the Ring becomes for Fafner the paralytic power of dead property. Transmogrified into a dragon through the camouflage helmet, he becomes a monster, too, regaining his true appearance only in his death.

The subtlest effect of the ring is revealed in the relationship between Siegfried and Brünnhilde. As Siegfried takes possession of the Ring, the Ring initially seems to be returned to its original purpose, since the hero only acquires it as a 'trifle', even though the Bird had sung of the ring's power. And in the loneliness of Brünnhilde's rock, living only for themselves and their love, Siegfried and Brünnhilde appear to dam the curse for a certain period, covering it with their love. Yet this appearance is treacherous. In fact, the ring makes Siegfried's heroic deeds cause his downfall, because it becomes for Siegfried a token reminding him of his actions. Having grown up as an orphan, he needs these memories to gain self-assurance, and as such a token of remembrance he also offers the Ring to Brünnhilde when he leaves her to perform new deeds (thus consolidating his identity). In *Götterdämmerung*, the Ring tragically retains this significance for Siegfried even when Siegfried's memory is wiped out by the draught of oblivion. Having defeated Brünnhilde in the guise of Gunther, Siegfried takes the Ring as a sign of his victory. Talking to the Rhinedaughters, Siegfried emphasizes again and again the Ring's value to him, which ultimately also reflects his own personal value. This self-value becomes his doom, when he ignores the Rinedaughters' advice, because he considers it to be a warning and hence a threat to his self-assurance. The ring thus effects a subtle care of the self in Siegfried, a care of his own identity and personal memory, which finally makes Siegfried vulnerable. Even though he willy-nilly never uses the Ring as such, this proud self-sufficiency eventually leads to his death.

The Ring has a similarly tragic effect on Brünnhilde, who receives it first as a token of love. After Siegfried's departure, however, the ring immediately begins to corrupt the power of love as Brünnhilde's love becomes possessive and blind for others' needs (see the scene with Waltraute). This perversion of the power of love corresponds with the shift in the Ring's significance from a token of love into a *corpus delicti* of Siegfried's infidelity. Only after losing the ring, the sober recognition of the deceit inflicted on her and the enlightening conversation with the Rhinedaughters, can Brünnhilde become the redeemer who returns the Ring to the Rhinedaughters, whom she asks to finally complete the Ring's purification from its curse.[10]

Comparing the Ring of the Nibelung with Tolkien's One Ring one can instantly discern similar effects of the object on its bearers. The Ring's effect on Gollum is like that on Fafner – the Ring becomes Gollum's "Precious", for which he kills his brother Déagol, and he also retreats into a cave to possess the Ring for himself alone. Possession of the One Ring becomes essential to him, and for this he accepts his degeneration from the Hobbit Sméagol into the creature Gollum.

The next Ringbearer, Bilbo Baggins, finds the Ring by chance and merely sees in him a magical object, which makes its bearer invisible. Later, he also notices the Ring's life-extending function (which strongly contrasts to the life-shortening effect of the Ring of the Nibelung) – and the strange coincidence that it seems to be difficult to part from the Ring. In *The Lord of the Rings*, invisibility, at first sight only a magic effect, is gradually revealed as an expression of power, because the ringbearer's alleged invisibility in fact transports him into an intermediate world of sorts where he is exposed to Sauron's powerful eye. The invisibility caused by the One Ring is thus diametrically opposed to the invisibility caused by the camouflage helmet in Wagner's Ring, which gives power to its owner, who can use this invisibility to establish an illusion of ubiquity to oppress others. In Tolkien's novels, the alleged invisibility in fact makes the ringbearer even more visible, delivering him to Sauron. Both Wagner

---

10 Renée Vink apparently believes that the curse can only be removed from the Ring of the Nibelung if the ring's form is dissolved. Accordingly, she reads Brünnhilde's appeal to the Rhinedaughters – "Das Feuer, das mich verbrennt / rein'ge vom Fluch den Ring! / Ihr in der Flut löset ihn auf, / und lauter bewahrt das lichte Gold, / das euch zum Unheil geraubt" (*Götterdämmerung*, Act III, scene 4, 201) – as an order to dissolve the ring in the flood, referring "ihn" to "den Ring" and understanding "das lichte Gold" literally, that is, as the material gold from which the Ring once was forged (44-45). My own reading, in contrast, refers "ihn" to "Fluch" – a doubled command for purification, using the rhetorical device of repetition typical of Germanic poetry – and perceives "das lichte Gold" metonymically for the Ring that is to be purified by fire and water, yet not necessarily dissolved (how could it, technically, be dissolved in water, by water creatures?). Wagner's text implies and allows both readings, and so does his music which underlines Brünnhilde's lines with a transition from the "Rheingold"-leitmotif to the „Ring"-leitmotif and, later, accompanies the Rhinedaughters' play with the Ring with a pure rendition of their chant, as it had been presented in *Das Rheingold*.

and Tolkien have in common a play with visibility and invisibility during the establishment of a reign of terror; to the effect that, in both their works, the invisibility effect connected with the ring only serves the purpose of the ring's owners, but not necessarily that of their bearers.

In Middle-earth, the wish for power, represented in the One Ring, is isolated and unconditional, because it is not tied to a previous rejection of something else. The oppositional forces led into the field against it are seemingly powerless virtues such as sympathy, pity, friendship, freedom, faith or courage. In Tolkien's trilogy, power seems to be a disinterested force of its own. One tries to achieve power for power's sake – not as compensation for something else -, and it is precisely in this desire that evil is situated. The question, therefore, is not "Power or Love?" but "Power or no Power?" The various 'sinfalls' in Wagner and Tolkien differ analogously: whereas Wagner's trilogy contains two Falls – Alberich's renunciation of love and Wotan's will to power through contracts – the sinfalls in Tolkien's Middle-earth are always motivated by a desire for absolute power.[11]

All these characteristic features of Wagner's and Tolkien's rings also determine their respective ends and the modes of redemption from their curses. As already mentioned above, Wagner's Ring can recover its innocence by being returned to the Rhinedaughters' disinterested play. Thus, the Ring of the Nibelung pursues a path from the Fall to Redemption, because it is eventually not tied to its crafty creator but to its material origin, namely the Rhinegold. The One Ring, on the other hand, is intrinsically bound to its creator and owner and thus appears to carry the power of evil in itself. Its curse can only be broken by destroying the One Ring. Unlike the Ring of the Nibelung, redemption or a return of the Ring to an original, innocent state is impossible for the One Ring.

"Both rings were round, and there the resemblance ceased" – As far as the essential characters of both rings are concerned, Tolkien's assertion indeed appears to be justified, since Wagner and Tolkien obviously conceptualize the

---

11 Indebted to the writings of Michel Foucault, I understand power as a highly complex structural phenomenon of various shapes that affects relationships between and among individuals and groups in different ways. It includes, of course, the aspects of dominion or oppression (including slavery).

imminent power of their respective rings differently. Accordingly, somebody who is interested in influence studies could well argue that their works are independent creations, the correspondences of which can be explained either by sheer coincidence or, rather, by the fact that they are both adaptations using the same sources. An intertextual perspective, in turn, would point out the different transformations of common elements, always insisting that neither of the works is better or worse in using common material in its idiosyncratic way. Proceeding from these premises, the following section of this essay will add a further aspect, as I shall explore in how far convergences and divergences between Tolkien's and Wagner's works may be recognized on a theoretical level, namely in the conceptualization of "fantasy" on the one hand and "Gesamtkunstwerk" on the other. In this respect, I shall enquire whether Tolkien's explicit distinction of his own work from Wagner's indeed derives from the two authors' different aesthetic agendas. For this purpose, I shall read Tolkien's essay "On Fairy-Stories" alongside Wagner's treatise *Oper und Drama* pondering on the question if Wagner's idea of musical drama is essentially different from, or if it can, perhaps, be considered a realization of the fantasy drama which Tolkien so vigorously denies and rejects.

To understand Tolkien's essay, it is important to know what Tolkien means when he speaks of a "Faërie Story". For Tolkien, the term "faërie story" does not say anything about the figures in the story; it rather defines its location and origin: a faërie story tells about Faërie, the realm of the Elves. Elves, in turn, are immortal, powerful, awe-inspiring beings of light, who are experts in all different arts and crafts, but who only practice these arts and crafts only for beauty's sake. According to Tolkien, Faërie can be perceived by human beings, but it cannot be fully described in words.

The origin of stories is secondary to Tolkien, who is rather interested in the function and process of mythopoiesis. For Tolkien, myth is first and foremost the creation of a secondary world. Two moments are central to this process: the creator, i.e. the mythopoet who becomes a "sub-creator" through his creation, and language as the creative instrument through which a secondary world is built by linking already existing words and new creations into ever new combinations.

If one compares this to Wagner's remarks on the artist and on his own work, one can find that Wagner refers to his tetralogy from the very beginning as 'his myth' ("mein Mythos"; see Schnädelbach 145) and thus presents his *Ring* as a 'synthetic artistic myth' (so Schnädelbach 150). The affinity between Wagner's work and Tolkien's Faërie Story consists in this character of a synthetic artistic myth, because Wagner's *Ring* acquires the character of a sub-creation precisely as a piece of art, the product of a creator who works something new out of mythological material. When Tolkien emphasizes the creation of myths, always relegating it to a sub-creator, he draws on the romantic concept of the artist, which resembles the artist in Wagner, who "mit klarem Auge ersehen kann, wie sie [die Erscheinungen] der Sehnsucht sich zeigen" and who "vermag […] eine noch ungestaltete Welt im voraus gestaltet zu sehen, eine noch ungewordene aus der Kraft seines Werdeverlangens im voraus zu genießen" (Wagner, *Oper* 344).

Nevertheless, there are (gradual) differences: whereas Tolkien very consciously speaks of a "sub-creator", thus granting God full prominence as the first and true creator, Wagner conceives of his myth-creating artist as a godlike character. The transition from an artistic myth to a religion of art founded by the artist, which Tolkien's term "sub-creator" clearly excludes, is seamlessly possible in Wagner's concept. Moreover, both Tolkien and Wagner accentuate the relevance of language for the creative process, yet Tolkien sees the power of language rooted in the relationship between words and things, whereas Wagner finds it in sound, because he does not separate sound language and word language. In *Oper und Drama*, Wagner uses a conceit of begetting and giving birth for the process of artistic creation, according to which a male principle – word language – is as necessary as a female principle – sound language and music. Word language, which is so central to the philologist Tolkien, is, in Wagner's opinion, apparently incapable of autopoietic creation.

For Tolkien, the most important criterion of a sub-creation is its inner consistency, which convinces the reader of the truth of the secondary world, even if it differs significantly from the world of the readers, which Tolkien calls "primary world": "To make a Secondary World inside which the green sun will be credible, commanding Secondary Belief, […] will certainly demand a special skill, a kind of elvish craft. […] But when they are attempted and in any degree accomplished, then we have a rare achievement of Art: indeed narrative art, story-making in its primary and most potent mode" (*OFS* 140). The term "Secondary Belief" is important insofar as the reader must think the story and the world to be true, and this not simply because of a "willing suspension of disbelief". In other words, the sub-creation is not to be supposed to be merely an as-if world but reality.

The four major characteristic features of such a successful Faërie Story are Fantasy, Recovery, Escape and Consolation. For one thing, Tolkien extends the term "imagination", which ever since Romanticism had been restricted to the creative act as such, by reactivating the original meaning of the term, i.e. the perception of images without an external referent ("fancy"); this perception, so Tolkien, is only a gradually different form of making images. He then distinguishes the result of imaginative creation – the sub-creation – and its medium – art. Tolkien uses the term Fantasy for a form of art that produces secondary worlds springing from imagination. Fantasy is the supreme art form, because it is more difficult to create a consistent world that differs substantially from the primary world than to represent the primary world mimetically. Being a natural human activity, Fantasy is additionally said to be connected with the search for truth. Fantasy and reason are therefore no opposites, but Fantasy does not allow itself to be enslaved by reason. In all this, Tolkien does not go as far as to claim that Fantasy enables one to see things as they really are; he is more careful, saying that it makes one see things as they are supposed to be seen. In this context, the otherness of the secondary world functions like an alienation effect, elevating everyday objects (e.g. Pegasus ennobles all horses). Thus, Fantasy makes it possible to evaluate and discover the primary (= "Recovery"). Correspondingly, Tolkien rejects reproaches of escapism, contending that escape may as well be something very desirable – especially for those who find themselves enclosed in a prison. To Tolkien, the disenchanted modern world is such a prison from which one must escape through enchantment. The last feature, "Consolation", addresses what Tolkien defines with the term eucatastrophe as the goal of every good story: the spiritual joy in face of an unexpected, wonderful turning point towards a happy ending. Fantasy is said to offer hope and a clear view of a hidden (good) truth. In the epilogue to his essay, Tolkien finally exemplifies that all these characteristics can be found in the Gospel of Jesus Christ, which is to him the greatest Faërie Story of all.

All these characteristics offer themselves to comparisons with Wagner. Even if the creation of a secondary world is not central to Wagner, the human desire for truth and (self)recognition as the most prominent urge for artistic creation are very much so (see also Wagner, *Oper* 143). Similar to Tolkien, Wagner's poet achieves this aim through the alterity of his representation, which "an sich allerdings *ungewöhnlich* und *wunderhaft* erscheint, seine *Ungewöhnlichkeit* und *Wunderhaftigkeit* aber in sich verschließt, und vom Beschauer keineswegs als Wunder aufgefasst, sondern als verständliche Darstellung der Wirklichkeit begriffen wird" (197; emphasis in the original).

However, Tolkien's conservative critique of modernism without a doubt establishes a different context for the recovery of our world through a secondary one than Wagner's concept. Indeed, critics have discerned in Tolkien's four characteristics of the Faërie Story very significant differences to Wagner. Tolkien's conservative critique of modernism may be juxtaposed with Wagner's orientation towards the future. Nevertheless, one ought to consider that both Tolkien and Wagner attacked the outcomes of industrialization and mechanization; in Wagner's case, one may think of his critique of the stage machinery of contemporary opera (notwithstanding that his own productions at Bayreuth included quite intricate technical devices, such as the legendary swimming contraptions of the Rhinedaughters). Further on, Tolkien's idea of a eucatastrophe is sometimes contrasted with the apocalyptic ending of Wagner's *Ring* – a contrast to which I cannot fully subscribe because the fall of Walhalla simultaneously means "Erlösung für Gott und Welt" (which is by the way the result of a rather surprising reaction of Brünnhilde), and the final scene hints at a new era. The idea of redemption, central to all of Wagner's music dramas, constitutes a thoroughly eucatastrophical element, which may not always be presented on stage but is always hinted at in the music.

One difference doubtlessly exists between Tolkien's central concept of Fantasy and Wagner's theories. Before I come to this, however, I want to point at a passage in which Tolkien directly seems to allude to Wagner to differentiate his own work from that of the German artist. The remark that Fantasy can also be abused if man creates a sub-creation to his own praise, can easily be read as a lash at the religion of art that had emerged from Wagner's artistic myth and the ideological abuse of which was plainly before Tolkien's eyes in 1939, as a corrupted and degenerated "Fantasy".

Another slight occurs in a longer section of the article, when Tolkien presents the story as the sole genre adequate to Fantasy (*OFS* 140-142). For Tolkien, Fantasy is only possible in narrative art, oral or written; he utterly rejects visual representations.[12] For this reason, he also thinks dramatic performances to be incompatible with Fantasy: "Drama is naturally hostile to Fantasy" (*OFS* 140). One may be reminded of Thomas Mann's or G.B. Shaw's descriptions of performances of Wagner operas, when reading Tolkien's remarks that the characters' presence on stage inevitably counters the effect of fantasy, that it even ridicules the secondary world, because it can never be adequately represented with visual means. Even the most sophisticated stage machinery cannot replace the magic of the secondary world. Dramatic fantasy, therefore, can produce a willing suspension of disbelief at most. In other words: drama can only degrade or dissolve fantasy.

Since Tolkien's definition of Fantasy in "On Fairy-Stories" is largely worked out in distinction to other works of the period (e.g. Lewis Carroll's *Alice* books), I would argue that Tolkien's radical verdict against dramatic Fantasy – together with the reproach of abuse mentioned above – is (also) uttered with respect to Wagner's *Ring*. And maybe his reaction is so vehement precisely because one can indeed regard Wagner's *Ring* (maybe also his other music dramas)[13] as Fantasy dramas. I would like to elaborate on this thought in the remaining paragraphs of this article.

In his criticism of contemporary opera in the vein of Meyerbeer, Wagner speaks out against the use of stage machinery as destructive to fantasy. In contemporary opera, things "sollte[n] in materiellster Realität wirklich vorgeführt werden, um eine phantastische Wirkung so ohne alle Mitwirkung der Phantasie selbst hervorzubringen" (Wagner, *Oper* 92). Against this technique, Wagner

---

12 Although Tolkien did produce illustrations to his novels, these visualizations are rather manifest imaginations, inspired by the narrative sub-creation, than sub-creations in their own right.
13 Ellison does this, for example, with regard to *Die Meistersinger von Nürnberg*.

posits Shakespearean drama and its conditions of performance, which greatly appealed to the audience's imagination.[14] Wagner perceives in this necessity to complete an only rudimentarily represented scene on stage with the help of fantasy a more consummate performance than in any realistic representation of details (Wagner, *Oper* 131). The stage directions to Wagner's *Ring* correspond to this idea, because their exact realization on stage is eventually impossible, and most likely has never been intended to be fully put into practice[15]. Wagner's stage directions should therefore rather be seen in the tradition of Romantic drama, where stage directions and stage decor are no basis for mimetic representation but a space for imagination (see Weber 75). Tolkien's criticism is thus based on his generalization of an illusionist-realistic practice of performance, which encompasses the possibilities and the character of dramatic performance only very insufficiently. In contrast to this, the *Ring* envisages a version of the dramatic that liberates imagination instead of narrowing it by showing 'realistic' images.

Moreover, Wagner's music dramas can hardly be said to focus their performance merely on individual characters. The narrative element, which is so cherished by Tolkien, has a central function in Wagner's operas, interrupting the action again and again to establish coherence through narrations. In these moments the focus of attention is directed away from the narrating figure to the narration itself, except when stage directors feel the urge to adapt the performance on stage to the concentration span of generations grown up with MTV or Twitter with the help of projections or added actions on stage. These narrative interruptions may well be compared to those which Tolkien employs in his *The Lord of the Rings*.

Third, the idea of a festival comes very close to a thorough Faerian-drama experience as demanded by Tolkien. During the Bayreuth festival, the audience is transported to a secondary world of sorts. Wagner's music dramas become plays within the play as it were, because the proceedings of the festival include the works performed on stage as well as the opera house and the numerous rituals performed by the audience during the festival. In this context, one may

---

14 Think, for instance, of the Chorus in *Henry V*, which asks the audience to imagine spectacular scene changes.
15 A good example is the stage direction for the duel in the second act of *Die Walküre*.

also think of the covered orchestra pit, which makes the music that is played only heard and not seen, so that its imaginary power can unfold the better.

Speaking of music as an important element of imagination I have approached the major problem of Tolkien's rejection of a Fantasy-drama: the supremacy of the word. Tolkien may be a true philologist, but in view of his exclusive concentration on language and word art, one may also call him a logocentric. In contrast, Wagner does not separate word art and sound art, because "drama" is to him more than a literary genre, it always also includes the practice of performance. Unlike Tolkien, Wagner does not focus on the media of representation but on the sensual perception of representation and performance. For him, perception and creation are inextricably interlaced; the audience is therefore always engaged in imaginary processes and thus fantasy is activated. The channels of perception of this process are reason, feeling and the eye. Word language is the 'organ of reason' ("Organ des Verstandes") and sound language the 'organ of feeling' ("Organ des Gefühls"; see Wagner, *Oper* 290), which can represent the unnamable that cannot be grasped by reason. Visual representation is another means of representing the unnamable to the eye. Wagner's emphasis on the sensual quality of theatrical performances aims at a balance of information between the eye, feeling and reason; only in their interplay a perfect representation is possible. To all this corresponds Wagner's idea of fantasy as a mediating instrument of recognition that is always conceived of as a visual instrument, connected to processes of imagination[16] (cf. Wagner, *Oper* 142). Hence, Wagner's elaborations contain statements on imagination that come closer to the original meaning of this term, as postulated by Tolkien, than Tolkien's own term of 'Fantasy', because by restricting Fantasy to an exclusively verbal art Tolkien disconnects this verbal Fantasy from genuinely visual imagination. Founded on a unit of imagination and fantasy, visual representation, as it is envisaged in Wagner's

---

16 "Die natürliche Dichtungsgabe ist die Fähigkeit, die seinen Sinnen von außen sich kundgebenden Erscheinungen zu einem inneren Bilde von innen sich zu verdichten; die künstlerische, dieses Bild nach außen wieder mitzuteilen. [...] In diesem Maße vermag aber die Tätigkeit des Gehirns die ihm zugeführten, nun von ihrer Naturwirklichkeit losgelösten Erscheinungen zu den umfassendsten neuen Bildern zu gestalten, wie sie aus dem doppelten Bemühen, sie zu sichten oder im Zusammenhange sich vorzuführen, entstehen, und diese Tätigkeit des Gehirns nennen wir Phantasie. Das unbewußte Streben der Phantasie geht nun dahin, des wirklichen Maßes der Erscheinungen inne zu werden, und dies treibt sie zur Mitteilung ihres Bildes wieder nach außen, indem sie ihr Bild, um es der Wirklichkeit zu vergleichen, dieser gewissermaßen anzupassen sucht." (Wagner, *Oper* 142).

idea of dramatic performance, can have as much creative power as language. Given these presuppositions, Fantasy-drama becomes possible.

These last remarks lead me to the question of genre and medium. I have demonstrated that Tolkien conceives of mythopoetic creation chiefly in linguistic terms, whereas Wagner's idea of music drama as *Gesamtkunstwerk* offers a basis that allows us to regard Wagner's *Ring* as a Fantasy-drama. It is interesting to note that the question whether Fantasy-drama is possible can be raised once more today – and this in particular view of Tolkien's own work, and of the various medial forms in which *The Lord of the Rings* has meanwhile appeared. In how far are role plays, for example, variants of a Fantasy-drama that absorb their participants into a secondary world? In how far have Peter Jackson's two movie trilogies on *The Lord of the Rings* and *The Hobbit* established a new form of Fantasy-drama, a new visual iconography for fantasy on screen? Asking this question, I think in particular of one article, published in *The New Yorker* in 2003, in which the author finds resemblances between the musical score to Jackson's movies and the music to Wagner's *Ring* and uses this impression to develop his further argument, perceiving Jackson's movies as a Wagnerian *Gesamtkunstwerk*. Although the arguments are sometimes farfetched, the article nevertheless contains some interesting thoughts. For the author of the article, accustomed to and schooled by the medium of digital movies of the twenty-first century, the question whether a visual representation, in our context film, necessarily destroys illusion, does not occur. Quite on the contrary, he contends that the opposite is the case, and that the same holds true for opera performances, because both media capture and absorb their audiences into their worlds so much that the audience positively accepts their inherent rules. "You don't ask whether an elf could kill an oliphaunt, or even what an oliphaunt is; you go along with the premise. It is the same in opera" (Ross, 165).

The problem is thus one of genre, medium and representation: Tolkien perceives in visual representations an immediacy that does not exist, thus succumbing to the illusions brought forth by realism in painting and stage performance. Both Wagner's music drama and film, on the other hand, have always already played with this illusion; they have created visual secondary worlds engaging the audience and thus can be considered secondary worlds of the same rank as Tolkien's Faërie-Stories. With respect to film, these remarks particularly apply to the age of digitalization, which makes it possible to create fantastic animated figures populating secondary worlds that are coherent in themselves. Similarly, Wagnerian music drama as *Gesamtkunstwerk* neither destroys imagination nor Fantasy but rather enriches it. In a time that is increasingly dominated by multimedia forms of representation, the *Gesamtkunstwerk* offers itself as an adequate medium that can make us acquainted with other worlds. This can entail that, today, we may receive and perceive Wagner's tetralogy through Tolkien's trilogy – or vice versa. It is this mutual reception of Wagner's *Ring* and Tolkien's *The Lord of the Rings* as cultural events, each one influencing one's perspective of the other work respectively, which not only makes it possible to scrutinize both *Rings* together, but even makes it necessary.

About the Author

ANJA MÜLLER is Full Professor of English Literature and Cultural Studies at the University of Siegen. Her research interests and numerous publications range from eighteenth-century literature and culture to contemporary drama, intertextuality and adaptation, (historical) childhood studies, children's literature, and popular neomedievalist fantasy cultures. Publications include *Fashioning Childhood in Eighteenth-Century England: Age and Identity* (ed., Ashgate 2006), *Framing Childhood in Eighteenth-Century English Periodicals and Satirical Prints, 1689-1789* (Ashgate 2009, ChLA Honor Book), *Childhood in the Renaissance, Adapting Canonical Texts in Children's Literature* (ed., Bloomsbury 2013) and *Canon Constitution and Canon Change in Children's Literature* (co-ed., Routledge, 2017). Together with Bettina Kümmerling-Meibauer and Astrid Surmatz, she is also editing the series "Studies in European Children's Literature" with Universitätsverlag Winter.

List of Abbreviations of Tolkien's Works

H	*The Hobbit*
LotR	*The Lord of the Rings*
OFS	"On Fairy-Stories"
S	*The Silmarillion*

Bibliography

BIRZER, Bradley J. "'Both rings were round, and there the resemblance ceases': Tolkien, Wagner, Nationalism, and Modernity." Lecture held at the ISI Conference on "Modernists and Mist Dwellers" at the Seattle Opera House in Seattle, Washington, 3.8.2001. www.isi.org/lectures/text/pdf/birzer.pdf.

CARPENTER, Humphrey. *J.R.R. Tolkien: A Biography*. London: Allen & Unwin, 1977.

ELLISON, John A. "Tolkien's Shire and Wagner's Nuremberg: A Comparison." *Mallorn: The Journal of the Tolkien Society* 22 (1985): 13-16.

"Tolkien's World and Wagner's: The Music of Language and the Language of Music." *Mallorn: The Journal of the Tolkien Society* 36 (1998): 35-42.

FRASER, K.C. "Whose Ring Is It Anyway?" *Mallorn: The Journal of the Tolkien Society* 25 (1988): 12-14.

HALL, Robert A. "Tolkien's Hobbit Tetralogy as 'Anti-Nibelungen'." *Western Humanities Review* 32 (1978): 351-359.

MACLACHLAN, Christopher. *Tolkien and Wagner: The Ring and Der Ring*. Zurich and Jena: Walking Tree Publishers, 2012.

Ross, Alex. "The Ring and the Rings: Wagner vs. Tolkien." *The New Yorker* 79.40 (2003): 161-165.

SCHNÄDELBACH, Herbert. "'Ring' und Mythos." *In den Trümmern der eignen Welt: Richard Wagners ‚Der Ring des Nibelungen'*. Ed. Udo Bermbach. Berlin: Reimer, 1989, 145-162.

TOLKIEN, John Ronald Reuel. "On Fairy-Stories." *The Monsters and the Critics and Other Essays*. Ed. Christopher Tolkien. Boston, MA: Houghton Mifflin, 1984, 109-161.

The Hobbit. London: Grafton, 1991.

The Lord of the Rings. London: Grafton, 1992.

The Silmarillion. London: HarperCollins, 1994.

VINK, Renée. *Wagner and Tolkien: Mythmakers*. Zurich and Jena: Walking Tree Publishers, 2012.

WAGNER, Richard. *Oper und Drama*. Ed. Felix Groß. Berlin: Deutsche Bibliothek Verlagsgesellschaft, n.d. (1851).

Das Rheingold (1869). Ed. Kurt Pahlen. München: Goldmann, 1982.

Die Walküre (1870). Ed. Kurt Pahlen. München: Goldmann, 1982.

Siegfried (1876). Ed. Kurt Pahlen. München: Goldmann, 1982.

Götterdämmerung (1876). Ed. Kurt Pahlen. München: Goldmann, 1982.

WEBER, Elisabeth. *Die Phantasiebühne der Romantiker: Über das Verhältnis von Theater und Drama um 1800.* Dissertation Berlin, 1969.

Patrick Schmitz

"True Music in the Words": A Comparative Analysis of the Function of Music in Tolkien's *The Lord of the Rings* and Rothfuss' *Kingkiller Chronicles*

Abstract

This essay analyses different facets of music in Tolkien's *The Lord of the Rings* and Rothfuss' *The Kingkiller Chronicles*. In particular, it examines which function and effect the inclusion of music, music-related imagery and connected phenomena fulfils within the works of both authors. In doing so, similarities and differences between Tolkien's seminal work and the ground-breaking piece of new fantasy literature shall be revealed.

Most recently, Julian Eilmann's comprehensive work about Tolkien's use of lyrics within his oeuvre suggested the prominent role of poems and music in many secondary worlds of fantasy literature. Diana Wynne Jones has in turn already mentioned the importance (179) and "enormous power" (238f) of music in fantasy literature in her humoristic *Tough Guide to Fantasyland*. In addition, she also underlined that music serves to transport knowledge within the respective world and thus plays a role in keeping and passing on said lore (233f). Therefore, music indeed plays a major role as part of the cultural realm (Wolf 35) of a secondary world. Taking these aspects into consideration, this paper – based on Eilmann's analysis of music in *The Lord of the Rings* – is meant to present the function and effect of music and other connected phenomena (e.g. musical instruments). However, Eilmann's results will be compared to observations from one of the currently most influential works of high fantasy, Patrick Rothfuss' *Kingkiller Chronicles*. Ursula K. le Guin adequately wrote that the latter work, in which the readership accompanies the young, passionate musician Kvothe, conveys "true music in the words" (Rothfuss, *Name* Backcover). In the course of this paper, Eilmann's seminal findings about the role of music in Tolkien's *The Lord of the Rings* are to be presented first. In the following step, the basic functions of music as well as music-related imagery and comparative constructions in Rothfuss' work will be examined.

In his work, Eilmann emphasizes the importance and text-inherent function (cf. 389) of Tolkien's lyrics multiple times. In doing so, he follows the view of the author himself. According to Tolkien, the significance of song and music is not to be underestimated (cf. ibid.). Both are an essential part of the enchantment (405) of his readership. Because of this, it is not astonishing that music not only plays an important role within Tolkien's creation myth but also – together with his poetry – in Middle-earth. Kokot stresses that the "uniqueness and beauty" (194) of this world can indeed only be expressed by dint of poetry and music (cf. ibid.). The large number of poems and songs within *The Lord of the Rings*, 84 in total (Eilmann 390f), underlines this claim. Appropriately, creating poems and songs always seems to be effortlessly successful in Arda (410). The impression that music and poetry are an essential part of the world and its inhabitants cannot be denied. As it seems, some things in Middle-earth can be expressed via poetry and singing only (398). Even battle-tested warriors such as Éomer succeed in speaking in verse when facing the death of a beloved king and surrounded by battle and danger (410). Almost every character seems to be a poet and singer at the same time. So clearly, poetry and music are a substantial part of *The Lord of the Rings*.

What functions and characteristics can now be defined for music within this secondary world? Eilmann distinguishes between various and at times intertwined roles, the most essential of which are presented in the following. The first, basic position taken by music is the differentiation of literary worldbuilding through music (cf. Kokot 193). Musical pieces such as Bilbo and Aragorn's *Song of Eärendil* (*LotR* 233-6) or – to a certain degree – Gandalf's *Song of Lórien* (514) create a historical-mythological effect of depth (cf. Eilmann 398). Generally, it should be mentioned that Elvish songs in particular cover "past achievements" (Kelly 184). Eilmann states that, because of this, not only protagonists, but also readers gather knowledge about the depth of the secondary world by means of an oral tradition (399). Thus, songs help in preserving the fictional past (cf. Kokot 193f) and refer to the "vast backcloths" (Drout 4) of the world. Moreover, there are also songs within *The Lord of the Rings* that feature certain types of instructions or guidelines, a fact which again underlines the importance of an oral tradition of knowledge (cf. Eilmann 399). This is, for instance, the case with the lines from *When the*

Black Breath Blows (*LotR* 865). That information about the curative effect of Athelas is lyrically preserved, stresses the importance of songs and poems in preserving lore in a quasi-medieval world (cf. Eilmann 399).

Kelly's point that poetry and music are used to exert influence on the "remoteness and unreality" (172) must however be modified in this respect. Songs and poetry indeed play a stronger role in the daily-life of most of the readers' Primary World, but Tolkien puts his secondary world close to the customs of a pretechnological or medieval one. Hence the term 'temporal remoteness' would be more fitting, while one must cast doubts on the 'unreality'. In this respect Tolkien's own term strangeness (cf. MC 139) plays a certain role. The example of the lines about Athelas reveals that poetry is not used to deceive listeners (and readers) or to spread false information (cf. Eilmann 402). Similar things could be said about poems such as *All that Is Gold Does not Glitter* (*LotR* 170). Besides these functions of poetry, which can entail an "enrichment of the listener's knowledge about the world" (Kokot 192), the role of folk poetry and songs has to be emphasized (cf. Eilmann 416). This form of poetry is characterized by its simplicity, the underlying humor as well as its memorability and triviality (ibid.). Eilmann also mentions the age, anonymity of the author, flexibility of lyrics and presentation as well as the enjoyment of the folk song (ibid.). Especially the songs of the hobbits with their "effusion of joy and good cheer" (Kelly 175) largely fall into this category. Just think of Bilbo's numerous songs, such as the *Bath Song* (*LotR* 101) sung by Pippin or Frodo's performance of *The Man in the Moon Stayed up too Late* (159-160). All of these pieces of music are characterized by a strong connection to "amusement, leisure and entertainment" (Kokot 195). Further, these songs not only stress the hobbits' love for music (cf. Kelly 173), but also the necessity of the songs given their relevance for and influence on the mood and emotional situation of the protagonists (172).

The latter aspect, the physical, spiritual, and psychological refreshment of a listener via music, can be observed in several situations in Tolkien's books (cf. Eilmann 420). This becomes particularly obvious when Sam invokes the help of Elbereth with *A Elbereth Gilthoniel* (*LotR* 729f) in Shelob's Lair in order to become rejuvenated and encouraged. This performative power of song as well as its apparent influence on character and audience become obvious in this context, too (cf. Eilmann 406).

Closely related to this is also the aforementioned enchantment of both readership and characters. This is likewise made obvious by *A Elbereth Gilthoniel* (*LotR* 238) in Rivendell. The song leaves Frodo "enchanted" (ibid.), as the hobbit listens to "sweet syllables [and] clear jewels of blended words and melody" (ibid.). This effect of enchantment is also apparent in the case of Goldberry's singing, which enchants the hobbits including Frodo and even makes them sing along (123f).

A similar, almost magical effect is to be ascribed to the invocation-songs. These songs are for instance part of Tom Bombadil's background. The hobbits are capable of summoning Tom by dint of songs (cf. Kelly 181) in dangerous situations. Lines such as "come, Tom Bombadil, for our need is near us" (*LotR* 142) make this function clear to the readership. The summoned Tom, otherwise known for his "lighthearted nonsense" (Kelly 179), drives the barrow-wights away by using his very own songs. He uses such words as "get out, out old Wight" (*LotR* 142). Therefore, it can be determined that music and poetry such as Theoden's *Arise now* (838) or the Ents' *To Isengard* (485) do not only serve as a call to arms but as an actual weapon in battle (cf. Eilmann 450).

In conclusion, it can be said that music plays a central role and fulfils various functions in Tolkien's work. There is the deepening of a historical background, tradition, entertainment, enchantment, refreshment, and a call to arms as well as an actual weapon in a fight. In the next step, these results will be compared to the role and function of music in Patrick Rothfuss' *Kingkiller Chronicles*.

In Rothfuss' books, we accompany Kvothe, who grows up in a troupe of Edema Ruh. After his parents and all the members of this troupe are killed, Kvothe vows to kill their murderers, the Chandrian. The protagonist's childhood suggests to the reader a certain significance of music, since it is both part of the daily life within the secondary world (cf. Rothfuss, *Fear* 146) – comparable to Tolkien's approach – as well as an essential component of the main protagonist, Kvothe. This is made obvious by his relationship to music in general and to his lute in particular. He stresses, for instance, that music is "the glue that held [him] together" (Rothfuss, *Name* 255). Furthermore, he states that he learned to sing (i.e. to hum) before he was able to speak (cf. Rothfuss, *Fear* 82). He defines himself not simply as Kvothe but as "Kvothe the musician" (711) – most notably, when he faces the loss of his self when being attacked by Felurian.

His connection to music is further emphasised by its very absence in the frame narration. In these parts, we get to know an older, changed version of Kvothe, who runs his own tavern as Kote. He seemingly attempts to leave his past behind and – living far away from any noteworthy cultural centers – to suppress everything that has happened (whatever that might actually be). The reader comes across lines like "as he went through the motions his eyes were far away [...] he did not hum or whistle. He did not sing" (Rothfuss, *Name* 713). This doesn't fit Kvothe's nature at all. His apprentice, Bast, even recommends "not to mention the music. Don't ask him about that" (716). The untypical, unexplained lack of music is further underlined by many explicit statements such as "of course there was no music" (ibid. 28; cf. Rothfuss, *Fear* 1106). These can be found at the beginning and ending of both books. Without music, Kvothe is no longer himself: he becomes Kote.

Similar conclusions can be drawn from his relationship with his lute. This instrument and its sound is of utmost importance to Kvothe. Being shocked after his parents' death, Kvothe decides "to make a shelter for [his] lute" (Rothfuss, *Name* 139). He wants to protect it from bad weather. He even goes so far as to consider the instrument his "baby" (Rothfuss, *Fear* 262) or "hand" (418). It is not astonishing then that Kvothe experiences a "mute stupor" (Rothfuss, *Name* 141) when his lute is damaged. The significance of his musical instrument, which Kvothe "loved like a child, like breathing" (364), becomes most apparent when it is broken. This event seems to be even worse for Kvothe than his father's death (362). The loss is compared to "losing a limb, an eye, a vital organ" (ibid.). Of course, the reunion is equally emotional. Kvothe is shown as "hungry for it, starved" (240) as well as "clutching for it with a white-knuckled fierceness" (362). He considers himself a living dead (ibid.) in this context.

There is no denying the fact that Kvothe also regards music as a link to his own origin and background. His memories of a happy childhood and of his parents are often connected to music. In his early childhood, Kvothe begins to sing with his mother (60). His affection, especially for his mother, is moreover expressed with the help of music-related similes, such as "laughed like bells" (96) or "a voice ... like a flute" (95). Thus, it is not surprising that his memories of the dead are often linked to music: "the image of them gently swaying to the music is how I picture love" (120) and "suddenly remembered things I had avoided for years, my father idly strumming at his lute, my mother beside him in the wagon, singing" (192). This emotionality, this romanticizing, is something that is intertwined with Kvothe's understanding of music and cannot be underestimated. Taking this into consideration it is not surprising that Kvothe's music also has a curative and rejuvenating function. In particular after the murder of his parents, Kvothe plays his lute for weeks and without a break. It is his "only solace" (140). After being wounded, Kvothe plays his music and it seems as if his pain is alleviated (cf. Rothfuss, *Fear* 203) at least to a certain degree. This effect is also underlined by the following lines: "My music always helped. As long as I had my music, no burden was ever too heavy to bear" (715). This effect of music is indeed often referred to in our Primary World as well.

The way the protagonist's music affects his audience is equally remarkable. There is indeed a strong resemblance to Tolkien's concept of enchantment, a state of mind making a reader or listener susceptible to *Faërie*. Right at the beginning, one of the guests at Kote's tavern reminisces about Kvothe's musical abilities (cf. Rothfuss, *Name* 29). He admits that Kvothe's singing made him burst into tears (ibid.). A comparison to the legendary bard of the Edema Ruh, Illien, who is said to have ceased battles by virtue of his music (97), is obviously being made. Kvothe himself in turn claims to have sung "colors to a blind man" (351). Generally, the musician points out that music is the easiest way to enter the listener's heart without making a detour over the mind as in the case of poetry (112). To him it is obvious that "nothing carries more emotion than music" (Rothfuss, *Fear* 828). Thus, a preference for poetry similar to the one in Tolkien's work cannot be attested to in Rothfuss' books. An impressive example of this concept is found on the occasion of Kvothe's performance of the song *The Lay of Sir Savien Traliard* in Imre. This piece and its effect is already alluded to at the beginning of Rothfuss' first book, when the main protagonist mentions the "crowning work" (Rothfuss, *Name* 118) of the legendary Illien. Kvothe stresses that he was enchanted and cried uncontrollably when listening to his parents' performance (ibid.). During his own performance, he enchants his audience in a similar way by means of music that almost seems alive. The music, which had already been described as "a spider web stirred by a gentle breath" (242), moves the audience "like grass against the wind" (401f). People seem to fall into a daydream, weaved by music (403) and referred to as a "spell" (ibid.) by Kvothe himself. Thus, Kvothe and his partner, Denna, succeed in touching their listeners' in such a way that these remain almost emotionally upset (403) as well as crying uncontrollably (407). Music and emotions are apparently linked to each other in the *Kingkiller Chronicles*.

The expressiveness of Kvothe's music is also made clear by his coming to terms with the murder of his parents. After running short of songs to play, Kvothe starts exploring and expressing a deeper level of consciousness with the help of his lute. In doing so, he, for instance, plays *Warm Grass and Cool Breeze* (141) and *Sun Setting Behind the Clouds* (ibid.) as well as *Mother Smiling* (ibid.). In this way, he makes his emotions, impressions, and experiences obvious to and almost tangible for the reader. To him, music works even then, "when words fail us" (Rothfuss, *Fear* 883).

Another aspect that leads us away from this emotionalizing function and closer to Tolkien's use of music in his secondary world is conveyed by the song *Tinker Tanner*. This song matches the concept of folk songs, as it is found in *The Lord of the Rings*, for example among the hobbits. *Tinker Tanner* is characterized by the fact that a famous tune is paired with lines fitting the respective circumstances (cf. Rothfuss, *Name* 29). Furthermore, Kvothe considers the song "older than God" (144) and that everyone seems to know it (460). While the composer remains unknown, *Tinker Tanner* proves to be a drinking song (144), which everyone can sing due to its "simple harmony" (ibid.). This piece of music as well as the plain reference to many different songs such as *Copper Bottom Bot* (570), *Aunt Emme's Tub* (203), *Violet Bide* (Rothfuss, *Fear* 360), and Illien's works have their very own influence on the deepening or broadening of the cultural realm (cf. Wolf 35) of this secondary world.

Likewise, music also aims at deepening and preserving the historical background of a world. It plays an essential role in the oral tradition of knowledge, which is known in our Primary World and also in, for example, Tolkien's works. Kvothe fittingly uses this function in different situations. He e.g. wonders "how […] anyone remembers words that aren't put to music" (Rothfuss, *Fear* 112). The comparison between metal, which is prone to rust, and a song that sticks in your mind (448) serves the same purpose. Songs that take up the topic of the Chandrian emphasize the role of music in preserving knowledge. On the one hand, these songs which every child seems to know (149) reveal pieces of information to Kvothe about how to recognize the ancient murderers of his troupe. For example, it is said that the group of the Chandrian is always close "when the hearthfire turns blue" (Rothfuss, *Name* 568) and metal starts to rust without any reason in a matter of seconds (ibid.). Many of these aspects prove to be true in the course of the story. Hence, some of the songs in Rothfuss' books serve the same instructional purpose as those in Tolkien's. As Bast refers to a nursery rhyme in the context of getting rid of demon carcasses, Kvothe remarks "you'd be surprised at the sorts of things hidden away in children's songs" (39). This becomes obvious in a tragic way after Kvothe's parents are killed by the Chandrian. The motive of this group – to prevent knowledge about them from being spread – is intertwined with the summoning power of Arliden's song. Similar to Tolkien's Tom Bombadil, the Chandrian appear due to a song. The smug Cinder, one of the Chandrian, states that "someone's parents […] have been singing entirely the wrong sort of songs" (127). The double function of the song that Arliden had performed in public for the first time is revealed. On the one hand, the piece of music holds dangerous knowledge, in turn taken from old lore; on the other hand, it works like a beacon that draws the Chandrian close.

One last aspect that needs to be scrutinized in this paper is concerned with the role music plays during Kvothe's encounter with Felurian. This ancient Fae – comparable to a siren – lures her victims by virtue of her supernatural beauty and her own singing. Kvothe feels this strange "pull" (Rothfuss, *Fear* 700) of her voice (699). A battle of minds begins between Kvothe and Felurian, at the end of which Kvothe protects part of his inner self from Felurian's "magic of singing" (700) by means of his own voice. The balance of power shifts, Felurian is subdued, and a corporal relationship starts to grow, the activities of which are often expressed via musical imagery as well: "Our rhythm is like a silent song, like the half-heard thrumming of a distant drum" (701). In this way, music combines several functions: a metaphorical shield, a decoy as well as an anchor in reality and a metaphor for a love act.

To sum up, one might note that both Tolkien's *The Lord of the Rings* and Rothfuss' *Kingkiller Chronicles* assign music a particular range of functions. In both works similarities and differences can be observed.

In Tolkien's books the reader is confronted with a kind of poetry and music that reveals the historical depth of the secondary world while having a two-fold function in terms of the tradition of knowledge in this respect, viz. plain historical knowledge and instructional lore. Furthermore, singing and playing music serves the purpose of entertaining, e.g. the hobbits, and strengthening different characters such as Sam in Shelob's lair. It doesn't come as a surprise that music contributes in a world at war as a call to arms or as a weapon itself, which is shown during Tom Bombadil's battle with the barrow-wights.

Concerning Rothfuss' *Kingkiller Chronicles* the different starting position has to be pointed out again. The main protagonist has an even closer relationship to music and his instrument. To Kvothe, music is an essential element of his own self, of his identity, while he rejects and looks down on poetry at the same time. Music and the lute play a role whenever the boy remembers his parents, his origin, and his childhood. A similar, lesser connection between home and music can also be recognized in Tolkien's hobbits, who – in strange surroundings such as Bree – create a feeling of home in this way. Unlike in Tolkien's works, music exerts its curative effect on Kvothe alone rather than on his audience. To him, music is a medicine alleviating any mental and physical pain. Similar is the concept of enchantment, which is partly transported and expressed by music in Tolkien as well as Rothfuss. While in *The Lord of the Rings* the Elves in particular excel in enchanting their audience with the help of music, Kvothe's performance of *Sir Savien* especially alludes to this effect. His music seems to be quasi-magical just like a living being that bewitches the listeners (and readers). Yet, in the same situation a difference between Tolkien and Rothfuss might be noticed. Kvothe repeatedly succeeds in touching his audience in a way that leaves them emotional and changed by the unforgettable experience. Another contrast to Tolkien can be found in Kvothe's attempt to use music in order to express his own emotions and experiences, whenever words don't suffice. This becomes particularly obvious when Kvothe mourns the murder of his parents and the other members of his troupe. On the other side, one should stress that Rothfuss – just like Tolkien – makes use of music in order to deepen his secondary world. This happens in a cultural as well as historical regard. This becomes apparent in the songs about the Chandrian, which attempt to describe their appearance as well as their origin. At the same time, the songs serve as a way to summon these entities similar to the invocations of Tom Bombadil in *The Lord of the Rings*. The mechanisms and consequences of the Chandrians' appearance admittedly differ in a highly tragic way. Finally, music serves as a shield against the literal loss of one's own self and as a metaphor for a love act, which can be seen during the encounter between Kvothe and Felurian.

Both the analysis of music in Tolkien – which has already been undertaken by Eilmann in an impressive way – as well as the examination of the role and function of music in Rothfuss' works suggest that there is a close relationship between music and fantasy literature in many books. This reveals that – in analyzing literary worldbuilding – music is an essential part of Wolf's cultural realm, and songs and poems contribute to a complexity and verisimilitude of any secondary world.

About the Author

PATRICK SCHMITZ studied History and English at Aachen University. After having worked in Cologne and Aachen, he is currently working as a teacher in the Eifel Region. His main research interests are concerned with New Fantasy Literature, especially focusing on the phenomenon of worldbuilding and connected concepts.

Bibliography

DROUT, Michael. "Introduction – Reading Tolkien's Poetry." *Tolkien's Poetry*. Eds. Julian Eilmann and Allan Turner. Zurich and Jena: Walking Tree Publishers, 2013, 1-9.

EILMANN, Julian. *J.R.R. Tolkien – Romantiker und Lyriker*. Essen: Oldib-Verlag, 2016.

JONES, Diana Wynne. *The Tough Guide to Fantasyland*. New York City, NY: DAW Books, 1998.

KELLY, Mary Quella. "The Poetry of Fantasy: Verse in *The Lord of the Rings*." *Tolkien and the Critics – Essays on J.R.R. Tolkien's The Lord of the Rings*. Eds. Neil David Isaacs and Rose A. Zimbardo. Notre Dame, IL: University of Notre Dame Press: 1972, 170-200.

KOKOT, Joanna. "Cultural Functions Motivating Art – Poems and their Contexts in *The Lord of the Rings*." *Inklings-Jahrbuch* 10 (1992): 191-207.

ROTHFUSS, Patrick. *The Name of the Wind*. New York City, NY: DAW Books, 2008.

The Wise Man's Fear. The Kingkiller Chronicles: Day Two. New York City, NY: DAW Books, 2013.

TOLKIEN, J.R.R. *The Lord of the Rings*. London: HarperCollins, 2007.

"On Fairy-Stories." *The Monsters and the Critics and Other Essays*. Ed. Christopher Tolkien. London: Harper Collins, 1997, 109-161.

WOLF, Mark J.P. *Building Imaginary Worlds – The Theory and History of Subcreation*. New York City, NY: Taylor and Francis, 2012.

Tobias Escher

Of Home Keys and Music Style Guides: Orchestral Scores for Tolkien-based Video Games

Abstract

One medium for literary adaptations often overlooked are video games. Having been graced with large orchestral scores for quite some time now, a large number of Tolkien-based video games extend the Legendarium into a new medium presumably undreamt of by Tolkien himself. Individual composers created coherent scores for these productions, uniquely in the industry tied together by a stylistic unity and the supervision of a head composer. This paper will reveal and discuss musical elements used and compare and contrast them to Tolkien's own writings about music and related subjects.

Composer Chance Thomas has been responsible for a large number of video games in Vivendi/Universal's Tolkien-based franchises. Unique for a video game franchise, Thomas as a Music Director created what he calls a "Tolkien Music Style Guide" with information about the musical characteristics of various cultures in the narrative. He also composed themes for various races and locations, which would later be used by him and other composers in their scores for video games. This thematic unity between otherwise unrelated games produced (and scored) by different people is very unique in the video game industry and allows for a detailed analysis of how an interactive medium adapts descriptions intended for written medium. Thus Tolkien-based games, thanks to the extremely large universe behind the actual narrative, allow for a broad insight into world-building, taking into account Tolkien's views on sub-creation.

Introducion

Video Games based on popular works are often treated as an afterthought – not just by the world of science, but sometimes even by their creators. Tolkien-based video games largely have avoided this fate, at least in the latter category. Using big orchestral scores for quite some time now, a number of such video games extend the Legendarium into a new medium presumably undreamt of by Tolkien himself. Individual composers created coherent scores for these productions, uniquely in the industry tied together by a stylistic unity and the supervision of a head composer.

Video games arguably represent the most intriguing medium for adaptations of Tolkien's works, being the only medium to unite all forms of art: images, moving images, music, sound and quite often even literary works of their own. They are also one of the topics where it is hard to even guess what the author would have thought of. Even if Tolkien was somehow familiar with very early computer games, these in no way were able to suggest the rapid technological advances to come, let alone the introduction of completely new game types (role-playing games with multiplayer capabilities, for example). With rising capabilities of the gaming platforms to create or play back sounds, the acoustic side became an important part of Tolkien-based video games. This paper will reveal and discuss the goals of such music, musical elements used and point out the thought process behind creating it.

Goals of Video Game Music

Music in a video game has a unique place as a "commercial" outlet for creative arts – this, where a creative work is not seen by itself for what it is, but as one part of a larger whole. It shares this distinction with film music, theatre music and all other forms where art serves a purpose other than simply being art. There is one crucial difference, though: Game music needs to react, or even adapt to a flexible narrative that can not be known in advance at the time of composing. With the exception of cutscenes and other movie-like elements, music and sound need to account for the player's decisions and timing. While decisions (or plot developments) can be foreseeable and specific music for it can be written (for example playing a particular piece when an action sequence commences), the timing is more crucial: A player might be in it for the action, thus racing from objective to objective, or spend an hour exploring every nook and cranny of a level. In the first case, the music needs to do its task within mere minutes, while in the second case the experience needs to stay fresh and non-repetitive for hours.

Playing a crucial part in immersing the player in the game world, music becomes particularly important in games that focus on providing a cohesive and immersive world. The Legendarium lends itself to that, not only because of the importance of the world in it, but also because this particular world was itself created through music. Therefore it stands to reason that any adaptation of Tolkien's worldscapes in a video game would put a large focus on music as an integral part of both the world itself, as well as the player experience. A special property of game music is the power the player has over it: While in a movie or an audiobook, the viewer/listener has no choice but to listen to the music, nearly every game allows the player to adjust the music volume or disable music entirely. As composer Chance Thomas puts it: "If someone turns off the music in the game, you've lost the battle" (IUB).

World-building with Music

The primary goal of music in any medium is world-building, which means fleshing out the world portrayed, providing context that cannot be sourced from any other element. A race small in stature like the Hobbits will resort to smaller instruments in their music, validating the instruments used by conforming to their physical appearance. Elves will use harps, which – gathered from the Primary World – the player interprets as a sign of both high class (referencing the Concert Harp), yet a more rural way of living (Elves do not live in big cities, but are very nature-oriented; referencing the Folk Harp tradition). Orcs do not really "play" instruments at all in a musical sense, but rather produce sounds that may have a musical characteristic, but are not intended as artistic performances per se.

The whole world-building aspect of game music relies heavily on prior knowledge and preconceptions on the part of the player. A player who had never heard a single piece of music and did not possess any "general education" would likely not understand the world-building aspect of music. From knowing that some instruments are regarded as more "cultured" or "refined" to understanding the Dwarves as a culture of blacksmiths and craftsmen (and knowing that a blacksmith can create beautiful works of art, not just horseshoes), the player's knowledge and experience from the Primary World forms that foundation of successful world-building. The same of course also applies to non-musical topics.

In the context of a Tolkien-based game with the whole world being created in the First Music, that world-building gets a very active and practical role. As will be seen later in the analysis of the music system in the *The Lord of the Rings* Massively Multiplayer Online Role-Playing Game (MMORPG), music in this world extends the more common task of providing context by association and references to elements known to the player from the Primary World, but actually has active powers in the world of the adaptation. Music is not only a backdrop, building the world by providing atmosphere, stylistic references, etc., but serves to effect changes within the world itself. A song creating an emotive state within the game world; or triggering a certain event; or simply existing as an active thing "to do" within the game, as opposed to just being played back as a backdrop to the gaming experience.

Assisting the Player

While video games generally strive to give the player as much freedom as possible, most games have either a fixed storyline (like a game about *The Hobbit* will most likely loosely follow the book), or have suggested and expected actions (like a MMORPG will expect the player to go on raids with a party every now and then). Most of the time, these storylines or expected actions will require the player to do something at a specific time, like fighting an enemy when he shows up lest the player's character is stabbed in the back, or trying to traverse a certain area as fast as possible to for example avoid suffering damage over time (think of the Midgewater Marshes and the local Neekerbreekers).

For these situations it is imperative that the game makes the player aware that a certain action is required or will be required shortly. Music can aid in this by changing the played music when a foe arrives, or when the player enters a dangerous area. Instead of playing completely different music, the current music can also gain or lose elements to mark the change, like overlaying percussion when a battle is about to commence, or playing a scary, atonal high strings layer when the player is plagued by the aforementioned Neekerbreekers. These are subtle ways to alert the player to required actions and the current game state and provide a much higher immersion than for example a text notification.

For more day to day tasks, music can also tell the player if the current actions or travel direction are correct in terms of story progression. Sierra's 2003 *The Hobbit* adventure game, for example, features a very dynamic music system that will gradually fade the music to silence if the player literally is on the wrong path and is moving away from the mission objectives.

Lastly, by virtue of music being imbued in the whole of Arda through the First Music, music here also serves to aid the player in determining the state of the game world itself, on a higher level than just the player character. Areas inhabited by evil characters will have corresponding sonic soundscapes, tying together world-building (the music is fleshing out the area the player is in) and player assistance (warning the player that this area might not be generally safe), as well as providing a deeper immersion.

Realistic Sounds vs. Emotional Underscoring

As with films, video games also differentiate between diegetic and non-diegetic sound. Diegetic sounds are sounds of any kind that originate directly within the current space, either visibly or implied. The source of diegetic sound usually is directly visible, but one might argue that folk music played in an inn also counts as diegetic music because it is very well possible that a band is playing, even if that band is not currently visible. Non-diegetic sound on the other hand is sound whose source is neither directly visible nor implied. Underscore segments almost always fall into the latter category. There is no obvious source for the music, but it serves to underscore the story/emotional content in the current section.

In silent films, music was the only way to transport auditory information and played a crucial role in fleshing out and explaining the action on screen. With the advent of sound pictures, and also of course in video games, theoretically non-diegetic sound could be left out and instead only actual "realistic" sound be used. This is rarely done, simply because sound and music are extremely effective at world-building and providing aid to the viewer/player. In a nutshell, hardly anyone sees "music that should realistically not be there" as a problem, on the contrary.

With the exception of music games, where music is the primary gameplay element, and music being used within the game as a natural element (like having a car radio in a driving game, or a CD player in a living simulation), music is rarely diegetic and has little actual in-game relevance. Characters inside the game are not aware of it. With the foundation of Tolkien's world being music, games based on the Legendarium stand as a big exception. Here music, regardless whether it is diegetic or non-diegetic, actually can be traced back to an in-universe purpose. The sound of a river indeed can manifest as actual music and it is possible that at least some sound elements not created by a protagonist can be perceived as being audible to the characters in the game. The song of Aerendil the Mariner contains the lines "until he heard on strands of pearl when ends the world the music long" (*LotR* 235; b. 2, ch. 1). On Caras Galadhon, music seems to almost originate from the surroundings themselves: "No folk could they see, nor hear any feet upon the paths; but there were many voices, about them, and in the air above. Ear away up on the hill they could hear the sound of singing falling from on high like soft rain upon leaves" (*LotR* 353; b. 2, ch. 7). Elements of nature are actually directly described with musical features: "At length a silence fell, and they heard the music of the waterfall running sweetly in the shadows. Almost Frodo fancied that he could hear a voice singing, mingled with the sound of the water" (*LotR* 339; b. 2, ch. 6). It is also notable that music or at least musical elements are far more widespread in all of Tolkien's works than is common: When the Fellowship is hunted by the Orcs in the Mines of Moria, the "drums in the deep" announce the imminent danger, very similar to an underscore in a game or movie and assisting the characters in their quest by getting them to be ready for the attack. Nowhere does Tolkien explicitly state that the Orcs were actively playing drums at that time – in fact it would be unwise of them to do so, alerting the fellowship to their presence. Quotes like "there were no more sounds. Even the leaves were silent, and the very falls seemed to be hushed" (*LotR* 345; b. 2, ch. 6) strongly suggest that the numerous mentions of "sound" (125 instances in The Fellowship of the Ring alone) refer to more than just regular ambient noises. In this world, sound and music play a more active role and can change depending on circumstances.

Originally non-diegetic music can still be a part of the in-game universe if it is made an element of the game known to the characters within the game itself. *The Lord of the Rings Online* has a function that allows the player to play back music cues from the game via an "Ambient Music" object when entering their own house inside the game. The selection of available music to play back is originally largely non-diegetic (area themes, themes for the factions, ...) and originally is not necessarily audible or even known to exist to the characters inside the game. This Ambient Music object is placed like any physical object (furniture, plants, ...) and has no direct visible source of sound. The music simply plays when the housing is entered. Still, it is an in-game object audible to every person inside the game (including other players). The music tracks (or "Themes", as *LotRO* calls them) can be purchased for in-game currency from non-player characters, so this music can be regarded as known within the game. The descriptions also allude to this music being of in-game origin, as for example the "Ered Luin Theme" has the description, "A selection of three music Dwarf-make music pieces." [Sic!] (*LotRO* Wiki, Ered Luin Theme), suggesting that these pieces are actual music created, performed and passed on by the characters in the game.

Adaptive Music vs. Interactive Music

Video Game music by the nature of video games as an interactive medium where the player decides what happens (to a point) needs to be able to react to those decisions. Broadly speaking, there are three ways how music can be implemented:

1) Static Music

When static music is used, it is always played in the same way, regardless of player actions. Different areas of a game might have different music, but unless a new level begins/a new area is entered or another special game state is triggered, the player's actions will not have any direct influence on the music. This music is most closely related to film music and other program music, in that it provides a tonal and emotional setting, but one that is fixed and does not change.

2) Adaptive Music

Most games use adaptive music in one form or another. Adaptive music reacts to events within the game; both to changes in game state, as well as directly influenced by the actions of the player. One simple form of adaptive music that ties in with the "assisting the player" motive mentioned earlier, is action music that is played when the game goes from a neutral state to a state of heightened tension, for example if a battle is imminent. Adaptive music can also be tied to the player's character directly, changing with the health of the character or other character attributes. With the exception of battle states, usually a great emphasis of development lies on providing seamless transitions within the music played, so these pieces of music are often closely related to the respective "neutral" music. Ideally the player does not realize that the music just changed.

The line between static and adaptive music is often hard to define, because unless a game simply plays back a single song or playlist in sequence, every change in music motivated by a change in the game narrative in a way is "adaptive". This is why adaptive music is generally seen as music directly reacting to the events within the games on a quite high level and with very complex rules that far exceed simply switching from one musical piece to another, forming reactive soundscapes (see next section).

3) Interactive Music

One special form of music in video games is truly interactive music, that is, music that is directly controlled and, in some way, created by the player. This generally entails that the player's character plays an instrument or sings within the game. In the simplest form, the music thus created is simply played-back pre-recorded audio files or audio files created on the fly by rendering pre-made musical information. In the most complex form, the user himself creates the music by playing the respective instrument(s) within the game with individual notes, creating truly custom and interactive music just like playing a real instrument. This type of game music is described in "the *LotRO* Music System".

Reactive Soundscapes

Regularly what the player perceives as a single piece of music currently playing in the background is composed of multiple layers. String, woodwinds, brass and percussion layers play synchronised to each other. Depending on that game state, layers can change or even fade out completely, or new layers can be added. In a moment of dramatic tension for example the previously subdued percussion layer can switch to a much more driving variation. A heroic battle can use a very epic brass layer – all within the same basic song structure. The composers of the game will create multiple variations of each layers for this which work seamlessly together and can be blended into each other at any time. This allows the music to react directly and within a very short amount of time to player actions and changing game states.

Games use special audio middleware like Wwise or Fmod for handling audio duties, often aided by special adaptive music systems like Elias. Necessitated by the fast-paced gameplay of action-oriented titles, adaptive music (or sound in general) has become a standard in games because the music needs to follow the player actions in a timely fashion. Being able to blend into a new piece or layer only every 10 seconds will introduce a disparity to the action and disrupt the flow of the game.

Constructing the music out of a number of changing layers works very well for any music that has to play continuously for a given time as a background ambience, at least enough time to develop a coherent musical idea. It does not work well when immediate musical reaction to an event is asked for. This is where stingers come into play. Stingers are short musical phrases that are overlaid on the currently playing music, either briefly lowering that music's volume, muting it completely, or playing simultaneously with it. Stingers generally mark major events like level ups, announcements, etc. and are intended to be very noticeable. One major challenge when composing stingers is to make them fit to the currently playing music so that they are not in a completely different key and musically work with the music. To this end stingers generally exist in multiple variations so that the audio engine is able to choose a stinger that fits with the current tonality. A possible solution to this problem of having to create a large number of almost identical musical snippets is to use MIDI files that send playback information to virtual instruments hosted within the game engine.

Adapting the Text

Two broad areas come into focus when creating music for a Tolkien-based video game:

1. How to establish a coherent sound that is rooted in what Tolkien wrote about music in his works.

2. How to give this sound meaning within the game world, relating to the special status music has in the Legendarium.

The starting point in the text have to be direct descriptions of instruments and musical performances, forming the basis for point 1. *The Hobbit* contains the most practical descriptions of instruments and instrumental sounds, beginning with a full Dwarven orchestra brought by Thorin and his company to Bilbo's home. These descriptions have to be taken with some caution, though: Passages like the Dwarves throwing around Bilbo's plates to a quite rude song lean more towards Bilbo venting his frustration and do not necessarily represent actual events. Still – Bilbo has certainly spent a long time with the Dwarves and likely learned a lot of things during his travels and finally in Rivendell, as well. While the Dwarves may not have sung this particular song and may not have brought a full orchestra with them to the Shire, Bilbo very likely still quoted actual Dwarven instrument line-ups as well as musical styles.

The orcs/goblins in *The Hobbit* also seem very inclined to music, breaking into song immediately after capturing the company. The elves as well sing songs quite a lot and later in *The Lord of the Rings* Tolkien also gives specific examples of their instrumentation and vocal qualities. It is these instruments and musical qualities that can be relatively easily read from the text or inferred. As noted before, some of these qualities arise naturally from the surroundings and characteristics of the protagonists. High-cultured Elves would generally not sing coarse drinking songs (though they might of course have them!) while the longing for the Undying Lands will rarely feature in the Green Dragon. For the purpose of creating video game music, all these observations can be taken from the text, which is in fact what composer Chance Thomas did with his "Tolkien Music Style Guide" (see next section).

A more complex topic is the role of music as relating to the origins of Arda in the First Music, which directly ties in focus area 2 mentioned above. If it is accepted that music plays a more active and less re-active role in Arda than it does in the Primary World, in an interactive video game this role needs to be tangibly fleshed out. The question arises: How can music actively shape things here? As we will see on the examples of both the reactive music system in Sierra's *The Hobbit* as well as Turbine's *The Lord of the Rings Online*, the game medium offers music a chance to lead such an active role in the narrative.

The Tolkien Music Style Guide

Chance Thomas explains the content of the Music Style Guide as "Everything Tolkien wrote about each culture's music, I ferreted out, had catalogued and translated into modern music terms. [...] Each race had a home key, or in other words, a tonic tonality defined. Each race had its own palette of instruments, vocal qualities, stylistic traits and signatures, etc." (Spence D. 3).

The content reaches beyond purely musical topics. According to an interview, Thomas also described "production standards and music design recommendations" (Marks 2). Production standards refer to the level of polish of individual pieces are created, including things like the allowed level of ambient or playing noise or artistic mastery of individual elements. A Hobbit drinking song might for example feature generous ambient noise, the occasional buzzing string and its individual lines may have a very "live" feel with subtle tempo changes, avoiding overly rhythmically tight playing, as this would not be realistic for a perceived live pub music situation. Instruments can be left largely untreated, or on the contrary heavily EQ'd and post-processed. A very player-centric locale music with very high production standards denotes a significance of the item this music stands in the game world itself.

Music design is a vast topic in any media production, but especially in game audio, where the player-driven narrative uses music to guide, actively lead and enhance the gaming experience. Music design includes areas like the prevalence of music in a specific section. Frequently, the use of music is not so much about where music is sounding, but rather where it is not sounding. The absence of music, or of sound in general, is among the most powerful tools the composer possesses. Another topic governed by music design is the musical style chosen as well as the fine line between music recognizable as such and sound design that plays into music. Because of the unpredictable nature of video games where it is not known in advance what the player will choose to do, music can be used as part of the ambient sounds and sound effects can become part of the music, especially when they are used rhythmically.

The resulting document – which as of the writing of this paper is not publicly available for legal reasons and whose whole content remains inaccessible save for some information disclosed by Thomas in a magazine article – served as the basis of all music composed for the Tolkien-based games published by Vivendi/Universal, including *The Lord of the Rings Online* with its expansions and *The Hobbit* discussed here. Other titles include *The War of the Ring* (2003), *Middle-earth Online* (which became *LotRO*) as well as the canceled *The Treason of Isengard* (2003) with music by Bread Spear, parts of which made their way into the aforementioned other three titles and also *The Fellowship of the Ring* (2002). (Thomas, *Riffing* 35).

Home Keys, Instrumentation and Culture

Despite the inaccessibility of the Music Style Guide, it is possible to draw a number of conclusions about its contents from both interviews as well as the music created on its basis. In an interview, Thomas says that for the original *LotRO* recordings they had

> an army of acoustic musicians playing ancient and early music folk instruments including the psaltry, the hammer [sic!] dulcimer, the mandolin, the penny whistle, the papoose, the recorder, and three different fiddles. Also included were customized digital samples of Viola di Gamba, Gemshorn and [...] [a] 'golden harp strung with silver' wire-strung harp sample. (Marks 2).

According to Thomas, Virtual Instruments developer Gary Garritan developed the latter specifically for *LotRO*, to represent Dwarven harps that are described to be "strung with silver" by Tolkien (as opposed to Elven harps) (Thomas, *Riffing* 35).

This selection of instruments by its nature of not being in the standard orchestral or band line-up served as a means to "age up" the game world by providing seldom heard sounds to the players. The inclusion of sampled instruments is notable. At the time of these recordings in 2006 and early 2007, virtual instruments were definitely on the rise, but far removed from the current generation of such tools. There was clearly a need felt for these particular instruments to be there instead of replacing them with more easily sourced instruments. This despite Thomas stressing the superiority of live recordings: "There is nothing like recording highly accomplished musicians, pouring their passion, energy and emotion into fine acoustic instruments [...]. Digital synthesis just can't compete with that" (Spence D. 3). For maximum flexibility, all sections of the orchestra were recorded individually during the sessions (Thomas, *Riffing* 37). Thomas writes that "Hobbits' music is voiced by Celtic ensembles, based on the reference that Hobbits play 'pipes and flutes.' But they also played 'horns and trumpets.'" (ibid. 35). Other instruments like clarinets and viols that are also mentioned in the text served to connect the game score to existing scores using classical implementation that the listener base was used to. The "viols as big as themselves" played by the Dwarves also give a rare insight into actual instrument sizes: If Dwarves are accepted to be between 4 to 5 feet tall, that makes instruments the size of a modern Violoncello possible, especially given that "big" can refer to all dimensions. With the average stocky build of Dwarves, these instruments truly need to be quite large to be the same size as their players.

Unified Score Concept

The Tolkien Music Style guide at its heart asked that "a series of main themes be written to reflect the essence of each key race in the story – Elves, Dwarves, Men, Hobbits, and the races of evil, represented by Sauron. These main themes would then be used in every *The Lord of the Rings* game to lay the thematic underpinning for each game score. [...] tying all the scores together with a series of common musical motifs and palettes" (Thomas, *Riffing* 35). Thomas explains that he chose to write an overture for each of these "race themes" and mentions several benefits:

> Not only would this model the style guide's recommendations in a broad range of potential gameplay situations, but it would also provide a plethora of multiple-utility music assets. These assets include dozens of high-quality music cues to

implement directly [...], sectional stems [...] from the live recording sessions [...], MIDI files to start each composer on the right track, and feature-length tracks appropriate for a music CD. (ibid. 36).

This approach is very unique in that it brings one coherent sound to all productions based on the material, with themes or motifs common to every part. In an industry where licensing deals often mean that an officially licensed game adaptation of a franchise is not able to use assets (score, other audio, graphics, etc.) that are an integral part of that franchise in another medium or instalment, this approach gives composers the ability to build on the work done by their colleagues.

Each overture had several parts that combined gave a comprehensive overview on the Style Guide requirements for that race. Thomas mentions the Elves' overture, which features four main Elven themes: "The opening and closing movements, 'From Across the Sea' and 'Return to the Sea,' [...]. The middle three movements underscore the Elven strongholds [...] – Rivendell, Lothlórien, and Mirkwood [...]". (ibid.). Thomas defined the augmented 5th as a harmonic signature for the Elves, with the classical harp as a primary Elven instrument and mentions that the overture is built on these two themes. From this particular overture (and likely also the others), a number of assets could be derived:

- MIDI files that contain the musical information and which can form the basis for showing other composers the musical theory behind the overtures as well as serve as a starting point for their own compositions.
- Stems, which are audio files of a section of the orchestra in isolation, so for example only woodwinds, only brass, etc. These stems are good for analyzing sectional writing and can be directly implemented into a project as layers.
- Full-orchestra cues for use as a showcase and for direct implementation.

All these overtures were then separated into multiple cues (short pieces), in different combinations of stems. Thomas mentions "approaching 100" of these, which were made available to all composers involved. (ibid. 38). These overtures and the resulting individual cues were used in very different ways by different games:

War of the Ring: Composer Lennie More and his team used the MIDI files for 75 to 80% of the compositions (ibid. 38) by "quoting one of the themes, working into a variation of the theme, then going off into a completely original idea." Additional recording sessions were held to record the new material and direct cues from the themes were used for cutscenes and key elements.

Treason of Isengard (canceled): Composer Brad Spear used the MIDI files, but composed more custom material and did not use any of the pre-recorded cues at all. Thomas says that "Nevertheless, it adhered faithfully to the Tolkien Music Style Guide and quoted from the main themes reasonably enough to establish it as a VUG Tolkien game score", thus proving the validity and adaptability of the content of the Style Guide.

Middle-Earth Online (canceled, became *LotRO*): For this game, "developer Turbine Entertainment and composer Geoff Scott prefer sprinkling the game world with the ready-made music cues pulled from the main themes." Thomas then mentions that this approach of using the individual pre-recorded overture elements allowed the composer "to concentrate on creating source music and specialty tunes for the game." This puts a large emphasis on getting diegetic music in the game to a high quality by choosing to spend the recording budget for these situations as well as some additional recordings for "offering grassroots variations for the score" (ibid. 39).

Tales from the Misty Mountains

One anecdote from the scoring process of Sierra's *The Hobbit* tells how the composers showed a battle cue to Music Director Chance Thomas. He replied that "there are no Marimbas in Hobbiton", which meant that this particular instrument could not be used in "Hobbit music" (Abernethy). In this particular case, apart from Marimbas never being mentioned or hinted to at all by Tolkien, the instrument would simply be too big for Hobbits to play. One instance in which the specific recording situation directly influenced the emotional effect of the music is described by Thomas:

> One of the most popular tracks from my early *The Lord of the Rings* work is a piece called 'The Song of the Dwarves." I had a group of about 24 men gathered together to sing the choir parts. They sang the notes correctly, but there was no soul to it. We tried several different approaches, but couldn't seem to convey this idea of ancient chanting in cavernous mines. Finally we tried having the singers slowly swing their heads around and march slowly in place

while they were singing. Magic! It was a total transformation. Suddenly the track was working. It felt like we were no longer in an urban recording studio, but far away in the Misty Mountains. (Gann)

Approaches like this are common in recording situations and frequently different ideas are tried to produce a certain sound or mindset. In this particular case, the physical movements of the singers arguably mirrored the performance situation of the song in-universe, where Dwarves would walk the halls of Khazad-dûm, singing their songs. In practical terms, the change in sound brought by the movement of the singers was probably created by better posture and a focus away from the actual music leading to a freer performance. Still, this anecdote nicely illustrates the impact of the recording situation on the final result, thus validating the time taken to research and implement the "Tolkien Music Style Guide" as actually being beneficial to the end result rather than just providing a generic game score.

Music in *The Hobbit*

The Hobbit is an adventure game published in 2003 by Sierra Interactive. It follows the plot of Tolkien's *The Hobbit* novel, while taking some artistic license, but all in all remaining quite faithful to the book. Like the book it is based on, the game is aimed at a younger audience and therefore the graphics are colorful, the learning curve not very steep and it feels very much like a merry little excursion into Middle-earth. Composed by Rod Abernethy, Dave Adams and Jason Graves, the score is based on the Style Guide's guidelines on the instrumentation, orchestration and style of music in Middle-earth. Like most bigger budget game productions, *The Hobbit* uses live recordings for its score, instead of mainly relying on sampled pieces. Over 75 minutes of music were required, with the pieces split into two categories: "acoustic instrumental for Bilbo's exploration and live orchestral for the action/combat scenes" (Abernethy). A third category of music was composed for the numerous cutscenes and voiceovers between different parts of the game.

Adaptive Soundscapes

The game's technical director Andy Thyssen described the music system: "Another feature on the music side is that we have a pretty complex music logic that blends together the level themes. So we have some very different locales, each with its own melody and theme, and we blend in as you approach certain characters, or as you move in an out of combat or hazardous situations" (IGN 5). The technical properties of the music are a prime example of the implementation of adaptive music. With the game being divided into 11 chapters with 40 scenes,[1] each scene consists of multiple musical cues of 20-30 seconds in varying levels of intensity. These intensity levels can be switched between in any order and there are stingers for "win" and "loose" for each intensity depending on how the player leaves the scene, for example by Bilbo completing the objective or fainting (Abernethy).

As mentioned before, a special feature of *The Hobbit* is its ability to fade out the music if the player is straying from the objectives. While the game is linear in its chapter progression, within a chapter the sections can be traversed freely, so the player has the ability to walk to any point within a section, possibly also in the wrong direction. Using the music – or rather its absence – as a cue to the player that the current direction is wrong, unobtrusively helps the player on the right path and is a prime example how music can fulfil a role as part of the game mechanic.

The Hobbit uses an adaptive system of medium complexity. There are not multiple layers played simultaneously, instead changes in intensity are reflected by switching between multiple versions of the same track. The addition of stingers allows a graceful exit from any game situation. For a fairly linear platformer-type adventure where the player is encouraged to play a pre-defined story line in a suggested order made up of quests and sub-quests, this system is enough to keep things both flexible yet manageable on a technical level.

---

1 The composers speak of six chapters in the article quoted; either this was a mistake, or internally another way of counting was used as the finished game contains 11 playable chapters.

Area Themes and Game State Music

The Hobbit game consists of a number of chapters, which basically are overarching locales that each have sub-sections that are related in graphical style and general story progression. Each section may have its own sub-quests, but all quests ultimately tie into the respective chapter's main quest. The music binds these sections together using a coherent musical language based on the content of the area. Two such locales stand out: The starting locale of Hobbiton and Smaug's Lair in the Lonely Mountain.

Hobbiton – a Warwickshire Village

Tolkien, likening Hobbiton quite pointedly to "more or less a Warwickshire village of about the period of the Diamond Jubilee" (*L* 230), painted an image that is remarkably consistent across adaptations. Other locales may change, characters may come and go, but the Hobbit always live amidst lush, green rolling hills, smoke pipeweed and eat too many meals a day. *The Hobbit* is no different: The musical approach to the Hobbiton chapter, the starting locale, is very much inspired by folk music and emphasizes the rural, cheerful nature of the chapter, as well as the sense of adventure that Bilbo is embarking on.

After Bilbo has been recruited by Gandalf to aid the Dwarves in their quest to Erebor he awakes from a nightmare that serves the battle tutorial with the words "Just a dream. But what an Adventure!" A cutscene greets the player with Bilbo's theme, called "A Hobbit's Tale". This fiddle tune in A-Major accompanied by guitar with background strings coming in on the second part sets the stage for things to come. It is notable that the music fades out after the cutscene and there is no music while Bilbo is still in Bag End.

Only when Bilbo leaves his home and roams the town, an invisible folk band plays "A Walk in the Shire". Dominated by an upbeat flute melody supported by guitar and bass accompaniment, this merry folk tune serves as the backdrop to Bilbo's journey preparations. Set in C-Major instead of the D-Major quite frequently used in such music, the choice of key foreshadows the adventure to come. The music is composed of multiple layers with varying intensity and instrumentation. Hobbiton demonstrates the virtues of the adaptive music system by delicately guiding the player during the chapter. While the linear main quest is to find the Dwarves at the Green Dragon Inn, the player on the way can solve numerous sub-quests all over Hobbiton. In fact, this first level is most similar to general role-playing games where such series of quests are common. Straying from the main goal or going into areas that hold no quest value, the music will gradually reduce in intensity and ultimately completely fade out. When Bilbo sets foot on the right path again, the former upbeat folk theme begins anew.

Smaug's Lair – Golden, Shiny Things

Chapter 9, "Inside Information", shows a wholly different approach to the characters: After an intro cutscene where the Dwarves task Bilbo to steal the Golden Cup, epic brass signals on a steady drum rhythm accompany Bilbo as he makes his way into the lair. This brass signal can be seen as Smaug's Theme and is used whenever Smaug's menace is awaiting Bilbo. The sound abruptly cuts out as Bilbo nears Smaug's chamber, replaced by the dragon snoring.

Entering the chamber, a cymbal roll introduces low, brooding brass and woodwinds playing clusters with high con sordino strings creating tension. After the player gets control, cymbal effects provide atmosphere and draw an auditory connection to the hordes of gold in Smaug's lair. Nearing Smaug, the soundscape gets progressively eerier, with low bass impacts, all very atonal and no melody at all intermingled with Smaug's loud snoring. Steady low woodwinds notes come in the nearer Bilbo gets to Smaug as a higher-intensity level. The composers here chose to forgo almost any tonal elements and do not feature an actual melody for Smaug. The Dragon is represented by his three-note brass call which is used quite effectively for introduction before the player encounters him for the first time and then only in further cutscenes. The use of low woodwind/brass pedal notes marks both a departure from the usual airy orchestration of the score, where there is much space between the instruments and stress the tension aspect of the section, rather than portraying Bilbo's action as heroic. This stands in contrast to for example the encounter with the trolls, which was portrayed much more lightly.

After Bilbo successfully steals the cup, the steady low brass/woodwind clusters with high strings briefly intensify before abating when Bilbo has made his escape. Smaug then wakes up accompanied by his former brass motif. Smaug is angered when Bilbo returns to scout out a weakness and Bilbo has to escape, timing his flight through the lair with pauses in Smaug's attacks, who breathes fire. At start of this action, a stinger-like cue is played blending a triumphant adventure fanfare with bouzouki/mandolin accompaniment. The music emphasizes Bilbo scouting out Smaug's weakness as his heroic act, rather than stealing the Golden Cup before, hinting at both his resistance to the greed for gold – Thorin's tragic flaw – as well as foreshadowing his and ultimately Frodo's role in keeping the One Ring, which he uses quite frequently in this section as opposed to before when stealing the cup. The music here with the use of Hobbit instruments also contrasts Bilbo's Hobbit roots against the "new" Bilbo who comes into his role as a burglar. After this stinger-like cue, the music cuts back to previous ambience, where only ambient effects, low percussion and soft low piano notes play.

Music in *The Lord of the Rings Online*

The Lord of the Rings Online is a MMORPG (*Massively Multi-player Online Role Playing Game*); a fictional, persistent world in which players play their own characters simultaneously with each other and in the same virtual location. Players are able to see each other and interact with each other. Apart from the players, the game world is inhabited by Non-Player Characters (NPCs), which can be interacted with, but are not played by real people. The interaction between players is the driving force of the gameplay. The music for the original release of the game, bearing the subtitle *Shadows of Angmar*, was written by Steve DiGregorio, Chance Thomas and additional composers Geoff Scott, Brad Spears, and Egan Budd. As mentioned before, Thomas also served as Music Director and like with *The Hobbit* was also taken with ensuring musical coherence. Thomas was responsible for the live-recorded parts, while DiGregorio as house composer at developer Turbine created the sampled mockups and later integrated the live recordings into his work (Spence D. 3).

The Challenges of a MMORPG

When contrasting the music required for a MMORPG to a linear single player title like *The Hobbit*, unique challenges become apparent: Because of the vast areas of the game, the amount of music required is staggering and grows with every new expansion. Hundreds of players are active simultaneously and can see each other, so any kind of travel needs to happen in real time to not break the immersion if people would teleport between points. Therefore all ambient music needs to be fairly long, yet unobtrusive to cover long playing times, but not become too repetitive.

Portraying most areas of Middle-earth, *LotRO* relies on musical styles to portray and shape these landscapes. Like visual art is used to distinguish areas, music plays into the player reception by providing an auditory link between different areas. For highly localized and quite famous areas like Rohan in the *Riders of Rohan* expansion, the music style itself becomes a part of the in-game identity of that landscape, intrinsically tied to that particular game area. This is what makes the housing music system mentioned before so emotionally powerful: The player immediately connects the music played upon entering the home with the experiences made playing that particular area/faction.

While every player can be immersed in a unique narrative, all players in the same physical location are still at close proximity to each other and can see each other while playing. This requires the music to not emphasize certain actions or elements too much unless they are completely focused on a player. The music system can easily play a more pronounced element when the player has completed an objective, is entering a specific part, or is doing anything else that links the auditive change directly to the on-screen narrative. The music must not, however, have emphasis in itself not motivated by on-screen action (such as a swell or style change) lest it might collide with something another player is doing and break the immersion. Lastly, players in games like *LotRO* routinely use voice chat to communicate with each other. To avoid the fate of simple being silenced by the player, the music has to remain unobtrusive enough to not interfere with intelligibility of speech, yet interesting enough to not be bland or boring.

Area Themes: Sutcrofts and Norcrofts

Two area themes shall serve as examples on the approach within the game. The *Riders of Rohan* expansion features the Sutcrofts and Norcrofts as two of the new large areas for players to traverse. These adjacent areas both are inhabited by the Rohirrim and feature a similar architectural style, but have subtle differences that show in the music. "You go to the Sutcrofts, and the War hasn't really come there yet. They're sort of in a bubble. So their music is still peaceful – a little naïve, maybe. But in the Norcrofts, the Lord of Norcrofts is secretly in league with Saruman" (Shumway).

Roaming Free (Sutcrofts)

The Sutcrofts appear with lush rolling hills and a very airy atmosphere. The area has a similar vibe to the Shire, though with more rock formations and more spread out hills and more brittle ambiance. The music that is commonly heard is "Roaming Free" and was made available on the game's Youtube channel. The opening rhythmic string pattern evokes a sense of adventure, with a mellow trumpet line giving context to the vast landscape. Strings and lute take over, then the flute with trumpet lead into a self-assured choir part. This part defines the Sutcrofts' inhabitants culturally and mentally with a male chorus chanting to the "Theme for Rohan", composer Chance Thomas' main motif for Rohan. Thomas translated the Old English lyrics in the official *LotRO* Forum:

> We are hardy, We are rugged, We are Rohan, We are free.
> We are hardy, We are rugged, We are Rohan, Standing tall in glory.
> (Thomas, *Forum*)

This part calls into mind a riding Éored on their way through the plains, asserting the Sutcrofts as a land of people proud of their heritage, with sound hearts and a very strong belief that all is well and good. Playing into the naïveté suggested by Thomas, the choir part followed by string accents with Uilleann Pipes reinforces this sturdy (if somewhat wide-eyed) determination. Cutting back to the opening string pattern, a virtuosic fiddle part at the same time can be taken to represent the wild free spirits of the Rohirrim, as well as by its dissonance leading into a slightly melancholic woodwinds and string theme ending the piece to be taken as a sign of things to come to these lands.

Horse Lords of Norcrofts (Norcrofts)

The Norcrofts, despite being inhabited by the same Rohirrim with the same general culture, paint a different picture in both visual style as well as their music. Towns here are heavily fortified, the landscape is plainer, with very large open plains and towns situated high on hills in a position that is easily defensible. The atmosphere is one of readiness for battle and the music represents that. "Horse Lords of Norcrofts" opens with a horn and trombone rendition of the Norcrofts theme, joined by the fiddle later. The male choir representing the Riders of Rohan is present here, too, but instead of proudly chanting the melody itself, it adds single shouted words, all direct references to combat. The following section is aptly described by Thomas: "But then comes a counter theme. Expounded boldly by a large horn section, it seems to announce its warning with gallant melancholy. When continued in the high strings and Bass Recorder it takes on an air of uneasiness and corruption, erasing loyalty from the senses. All the while the incessant tumbling of the riding rhythmic figure keeps things trotting (or galloping) along for the player" (Thomas, *Riders*).

The only sustained choir part in the whole cue is a rendition of "Where now are the horse and the rider? Where is the horn that was blowing?" in Old English over sustained high strings and a percussion bed, emphasizing the Rohirrim's sadness at the times gone by. Thomas mentions "plenty of uncertainty" in the music, referring to the secret alliance between the Lord of the Norcrofts and Saruman. Compared with "Roaming Free", the percussion takes a much more active and prominent role, scaling back in the last third of the cue when a sober brass theme taken over by the strings brings in a melancholy ending foreshadowing the war at hand.

Interactive Music System

Stephen DiGregorio is not only credited as the main music composer, composing most of the ingame music, but also helped create the player-driven interactive music system (Spence D. 3). Players can take to learning an instrument and play custom music, either by playing back pre-made (but user-adjustable) instruction files, or by freely playing whatever notes they choose in real time. The game shows live music by displaying filled-in notes above the players' heads; pre-made music is signaled by not filled-in notes.

Ten different instruments can be played: lute, harp, theorbo, clarinet, horn, pibgorn, cow bell, drum, flute and bagpipes. Harp, lute and cow bell have two different variants each. Each of the different character classes can play at least one of these by default as a passive skill, while the others can be learned. The special minstrel character class can play all of them. With the exception of the minstrel, the sole purpose of instruments is to make music, usually together with other players, making "playing music" a fully integrated optional gameplay element.

Music System for all Classes

If a player owns an instrument and possesses the needed skill for that instrument, Music Mode can be entered, where the player is able to either play pre-made music instructions in the ABC format or play individual notes at will.

ABC Files

The ABC system is a standard for notating basic musical information in a single voice. ABC files (using the file extension .abc) define the name, meter, standard rhythmic duration, tempo and key (as well as optionally other properties) along with note pitches and durations. Each ABC file contains a single part or player, so playing back multiple ABC files at the same time with different players on different instruments allows users to form a virtual band by synchronising the start of playback.

There is a multitude of online resources for such ABC files, with individual websites specifically targeting *LotRO* users. One such example is a transcription of "In Dreams", taken from the *The Lord of the Rings: The Fellowship of the Ring* (2001) film score: (*Lotro ABC*)

    X: 1 (Reference Number)
    T: In Dreams (Title)
    C: Howard Shore (Composer)
    Z: Merecraft of Laurelin (Transcription)
    Q: 1/4=76 (Tempo)

M: 4/4 (Meter)
L: 1/8 (Default note length)

K: C (Key)
z z z z z z cd |e2 g4 de |c4 z2 eg |a3 c' bg z2 |e4 d2 cd |e2 g4 de |c6 eg |a4 g2
e2 |d4 z2 CD |E2 G2 E2 D2 |C4 z2 EG |A2 c2 B2 G2 |E4 D2 CD |E2 G2
E2 D2 |C4 z2 EG |A4 AA GE |D8 |CD E4 CD |E4 z E AB |

c3 d/c/ B2 G2 |E4 D2 CD |E6 CD |E4 z E GB |c4 d3 c/d/ |e4 ec Ac |c2 G6
|_A3 G/F/ _E3 F/G/ |F4 _E2 D2 |C4 _B,3 =B,/B,/ |C6 z F/G/ |E2 G2 E2 D2
|C4 z2 EG |A2 c2 B2 G2 |E4 D2 CD |E2 G2 E2 D2 |

C4 z E AB |c4 d3 c/d/ |e4 ec Ac |c7/2 z9/2 |

The ABC system is routinely used by musicians of all genres to exchange musical information without the need for more complex notation software and is very easy to use, so choosing ABC as the supported format for player-generated music ensures that a lot of users are familiar with it.

Live Music

The heart of *LotRO*'s music system is the ability to play music directly using the computer keyboard. Notes are mapped to the number keys 1-0. Shift plays one octave higher, while Ctrl lowers the pitch by one semitone. The duration of the note is determined by how long the key is pressed. Playing music this way is completely live and every player in the vicinity will be able to hear the created sounds. Players playing together can form a band.

The importance of music in *LotRO* is apparent when noticing the frequency at which players choose to make music this way (or with ABC files). There are even recurring music festivals within the game, the most famous being the *Weatherstock Music Event* (Weatherstock) (named after Woodstock and taking place atop Weathertop every year) as well as *Ales & Tales* (Ales & Tales), a weekly music event at changing locations, usually a tavern. Thus unique music culture shows the importance of music in *LotRO*. One must keep in mind that in a game, using a feature or not is up to the player. While it was the game developers' decision to implement these features, their adoption and continued usage by the user base is a powerful sign that music plays a vital role in the world of Middle-earth, also in the eyes of the recipients.

Music System for Minstrels

The Minstrel is a character class that has the unique ability of being able to use music to affect changes in the game world. Harkening back to the Music of the Ainur, minstrels are able to tap into that power to use music to aid themselves and other players. While all classes are able to play at least one instrument, Minstrels can play all of them and are able to instruct other players in learning to play any instrument; either by direct mentoring, or by writing a manual for a specific instrument. Minstrels possess three so-called stances, which are general mindsets aimed at guiding played music into a specific effect. Dissonance harms enemies, Resonance heals allies, Melody provides a mixture of both. A minstrel uses a three-tiered action system:

- Ballads will apply specific properties to the minstrel (like more attack power, healing power, etc…). Up to three such Ballads can be active at a time.
- Anthems build upon the Ballads and provide additional benefits depending on the anthem chosen. Three Ballads need to be active before an Anthem can be played.
- Codas finally work as a "finisher" ability. They consume the Ballad and Anthem properties and provide one final big effect.

Effects vary depending on Stance, abilities and the combination of Ballads or Anthems. The minstrel class provides a unique way to adapt a music-centric universe into a video game. Minstrels rely on music as their main ability and have this ability grounded in-universe in the First Music, making this player class a natural and believable extension of Tolkien's views about music. *LotRO* here provides a unique way to have music directly affect changes in the game world in a very tangible way.

Conclusion

The Tolkien-based games discussed here as well as the Tolkien Music Style Guide as their foundation are powerful testaments to the status of music in Tolkien's work. They also stand as examples of how a sub-creation can live in a totally new medium, still being faithful to its inspiration. Finally, the Tolkien Music Style Guide is an example of how a coherent artistic vision fitting the source material can be used, adapted and extended by other people (the game composers, in this case) and still remain faithful to its original idea. Modern technology has enabled game music to fulfil the active role that music possesses in the Legendarium by allowing truly adaptive soundscapes that both influence the player (by giving guidance, setting moods, providing a gameplay element) as well as be influenced by the player directly.

About the Author

TOBIAS ESCHER studied Musicology and British Studies at the University of Mainz (Germany) (M.A. 2012) and is currently working on his Dissertation about Worldbuilding through Music in adaptations of J.R.R. Tolkien's works. He holds a diploma in Music for the Media and Cinematic Orchestration as well as a C-Degree in Church Music. He works as a composer, organist and choir conductor, runs a consulting service for media composers and works as a QA Lead, translator and technical writer for music software. He is a member of the German Tolkien Society and has spoken at conferences about Music in Tolkien's works.

List of Abbreviations of Tolkien's Works

H   *The Hobbit*
L   *The Letters of J.R.R. Tolkien*
LotR   *The Lord of the Rings*

Bibliography

ABERNETHY, Rod. "Live Orchestra for The Hobbit." *Mix Online*. 01 Oct. 2003 http://www.mixonline.com/news/films-tv/live-orchestra-hobbit/369083.

Ales and Tales. Facebook Page. https://www.facebook.com/AlesAndTales/.

GANN, Patrick. "A "Chance" Encounter: Interview with Lord of the Rings Online's Chance Thomas." *OSV Original Sound Version*. 02 Mar. 2009. http://www.originalsoundversion.com/a-chance-encounter-interview-with-lotr-onlines-chance-thomas/.

IGN STAFF. "The Hobbit Interview." *IGN US*. 24 Feb. 2003. http://www.ign.com/articles/2003/02/24/the-hobbit-interview-2?page=1.

"Item: 'Ered Luin Theme'." *LotRO Wiki*. 18 February 2017. https://lotro-wiki.com/index.php/Item%3A'Ered_Luin'_Theme.

"Video game music composer Chance Thomas shares techniques, advice." *The Media School Report*. Indiana University Bloomington. 21 Feb 2015. http://mediaschool.indiana.edu/news/video-game-music-composer-chance-thomas-shares-techniques-advice/.

Lotro ABC. Home Page. "In Dreams." http://www.lotro-abc.com.

MARKS, Aaron. "Interview with Chance Thomas, Game Composer." *Gamasutra*. 25 June 2003. http://www.gamasutra.com/view/feature/131243/interview_with_chance_thomas_game_.php.

SHUMWAY, Layton. "Inside the music of LOTRO: The Riders of Rohan." *The One Ring*. 26 July 2012. http://www.theonering.net/torwp/2012/07/26/59937-inside-the-music-of-lotro-the-riders-of-rohan/.

SPENCE D. "Chance Thomas invades Middle-earth." *IGN US*. 23 May 2007. http://www.ign.com/articles/2007/05/23/chance-thomas-invades-middle-earth.

TOLKIEN, John R.R. *The Hobbit*. Boston, MA: Houghton Mifflin, 1987.

The Letters of J.R.R. Tolkien: A Selection. Ed. Humphrey Carpenter with the assistance of Christopher Tolkien. Boston, AM: Houghton Mifflin, 1981.

The Lord of the Rings. 50th Anniversary edition. London: HarperCollins, 2007.

THOMAS, Chance. "Chance Thomas here. Thanks for the love!" *LOTRO.com*. 30 October 2012. https://www.lotro.com/forums/showthread.php?484136-Chance-Thomas-here-Thanks-for-the-love!&p=6501113#post6501113.

"*Lord of the Rings* Online: *Riders of Rohan* Original Music Soundtrack". chancethomas.com. http://www.chancethomas.com/rohansoundtrack.html.

"Riffing on Tolkien: The Conceptualization, Production, and Dissemination of Music in *The Lord of the Rings*." *Game Developer* (Nov. 2003): 34-39.

Weatherstock. Home Page. http://weatherstock.guildlaunch.com.

Walking Tree Publishers
Zurich and Jena

Walking Tree Publishers was founded in 1997 as a forum for publication of material related to Tolkien and Middle-earth studies.

http://www.walking-tree.org

Cormarë Series

The *Cormarë Series* collects papers and studies dedicated exclusively to the exploration of Tolkien's work. It comprises monographs, thematic collections of essays, conference volumes, and reprints of important yet no longer (easily) accessible papers by leading scholars in the field. Manuscripts and project proposals are evaluated by members of an independent board of advisors who support the series editors in their endeavour to provide the readers with qualitatively superior yet accessible studies on Tolkien and his work.

News from the Shire and Beyond. Studies on Tolkien
Peter Buchs & Thomas Honegger (eds.), Zurich and Berne 2004, Reprint, First edition 1997 (Cormarë Series 1), ISBN 978-3-9521424-5-5

Root and Branch. Approaches Towards Understanding Tolkien
Thomas Honegger (ed.), Zurich and Berne 2005, Reprint, First edition 1999 (Cormarë Series 2), ISBN 978-3-905703-01-6

Richard Sturch, *Four Christian Fantasists. A Study of the Fantastic Writings of George MacDonald, Charles Williams, C.S. Lewis and J.R.R. Tolkien*
Zurich and Berne 2007, Reprint, First edition 2001 (Cormarë Series 3), ISBN 978-3-905703-04-7

Tolkien in Translation
Thomas Honegger (ed.), Zurich and Jena 2011, Reprint, First edition 2003 (Cormarë Series 4), ISBN 978-3-905703-15-3

Mark T. Hooker, *Tolkien Through Russian Eyes*
Zurich and Berne 2003 (Cormarë Series 5), ISBN 978-3-9521424-7-9

Translating Tolkien: Text and Film
Thomas Honegger (ed.), Zurich and Jena 2011, Reprint, First edition 2004 (Cormarë Series 6), ISBN 978-3-905703-16-0

Christopher Garbowski, *Recovery and Transcendence for the Contemporary Mythmaker. The Spiritual Dimension in the Works of J.R.R. Tolkien*
Zurich and Berne 2004, Reprint, First Edition by Marie Curie Sklodowska, University Press, Lublin 2000, (Cormarë Series 7), ISBN 978-3-9521424-8-6

Reconsidering Tolkien
Thomas Honegger (ed.), Zurich and Berne 2005 (Cormarë Series 8), ISBN 978-3-905703-00-9

Tolkien and Modernity 1
Frank Weinreich & Thomas Honegger (eds.), Zurich and Berne 2006 (Cormarë Series 9), ISBN 978-3-905703-02-3

Tolkien and Modernity 2
Thomas Honegger & Frank Weinreich (eds.), Zurich and Berne 2006 (Cormarë Series 10), ISBN 978-3-905703-03-0

Tom Shippey, *Roots and Branches. Selected Papers on Tolkien by Tom Shippey*
Zurich and Berne 2007 (Cormarë Series 11), ISBN 978-3-905703-05-4

Ross Smith, *Inside Language. Linguistic and Aesthetic Theory in Tolkien*
Zurich and Jena 2011, Reprint, First edition 2007 (Cormarë Series 12),
ISBN 978-3-905703-20-7

How We Became Middle-earth. A Collection of Essays on The Lord of the Rings
Adam Lam & Nataliya Oryshchuk (eds.), Zurich and Berne 2007 (Cormarë Series 13), ISBN 978-3-905703-07-8

Myth and Magic. Art According to the Inklings
Eduardo Segura & Thomas Honegger (eds.), Zurich and Berne 2007 (Cormarë Series 14), ISBN 978-3-905703-08-5

The Silmarillion – Thirty Years On
Allan Turner (ed.), Zurich and Berne 2007 (Cormarë Series 15),
ISBN 978-3-905703-10-8

Martin Simonson, *The Lord of the Rings and the Western Narrative Tradition*
Zurich and Jena 2008 (Cormarë Series 16), ISBN 978-3-905703-09-2

Tolkien's Shorter Works. Proceedings of the 4th Seminar of the Deutsche Tolkien Gesellschaft & Walking Tree Publishers Decennial Conference
Margaret Hiley & Frank Weinreich (eds.), Zurich and Jena 2008 (Cormarë Series 17), ISBN 978-3-905703-11-5

Tolkien's The Lord of the Rings: Sources of Inspiration
Stratford Caldecott & Thomas Honegger (eds.), Zurich and Jena 2008 (Cormarë Series 18), ISBN 978-3-905703-12-2

J.S. Ryan, *Tolkien's View: Windows into his World*
Zurich and Jena 2009 (Cormarë Series 19), ISBN 978-3-905703-13-9

Music in Middle-earth
Heidi Steimel & Friedhelm Schneidewind (eds.), Zurich and Jena 2010 (Cormarë Series 20), ISBN 978-3-905703-14-6

Liam Campbell, *The Ecological Augury in the Works of JRR Tolkien*
Zurich and Jena 2011 (Cormarë Series 21), ISBN 978-3-905703-18-4

Margaret Hiley, *The Loss and the Silence. Aspects of Modernism in the Works of C.S. Lewis, J.R.R. Tolkien and Charles Williams*
Zurich and Jena 2011 (Cormarë Series 22), ISBN 978-3-905703-19-1

Rainer Nagel, *Hobbit Place-names. A Linguistic Excursion through the Shire*
Zurich and Jena 2012 (Cormarë Series 23), ISBN 978-3-905703-22-1

Christopher MacLachlan, *Tolkien and Wagner: The Ring and Der Ring*
Zurich and Jena 2012 (Cormarë Series 24), ISBN 978-3-905703-21-4

Renée Vink, *Wagner and Tolkien: Mythmakers*
Zurich and Jena 2012 (Cormarë Series 25), ISBN 978-3-905703-25-2

The Broken Scythe. Death and Immortality in the Works of J.R.R. Tolkien
Roberto Arduini & Claudio Antonio Testi (eds.), Zurich and Jena 2012 (Cormarë Series 26), ISBN 978-3-905703-26-9

Sub-creating Middle-earth: Constructions of Authorship and the Works of J.R.R. Tolkien
Judith Klinger (ed.), Zurich and Jena 2012 (Cormarë Series 27),
ISBN 978-3-905703-27-6

Tolkien's Poetry
Julian Eilmann & Allan Turner (eds.), Zurich and Jena 2013
(Cormarë Series 28), ISBN 978-3-905703-28-3

O, What a Tangled Web. Tolkien and Medieval Literature. A View from Poland
Barbara Kowalik (ed.), Zurich and Jena 2013 (Cormarë Series 29),
ISBN 978-3-905703-29-0

J.S. Ryan, *In the Nameless Wood*
Zurich and Jena 2013 (Cormarë Series 30), ISBN 978-3-905703-30-6

From Peterborough to Faëry; The Poetics and Mechanics of Secondary Worlds
Thomas Honegger & Dirk Vanderbeke (eds.), Zurich and Jena 2014
(Cormarë Series 31), ISBN 978-3-905703-31-3

Tolkien and Philosophy
Roberto Arduini & Claudio R. Testi (eds.), Zurich and Jena 2014
(Cormarë Series 32), ISBN 978-3-905703-32-0

Patrick Curry, *Deep Roots in a Time of Frost. Essays on Tolkien*
Zurich and Jena 2014 (Cormarë Series 33), ISBN 978-3-905703-33-7

Representations of Nature in Middle-earth
Martin Simonson (ed.), Zurich and Jena 2015, (Cormarë Series 34),
ISBN 978-3-905703-34-4

Laughter in Middle-earth
Thomas Honegger & Maureen F. Mann (eds.), Zurich and Jena 2016
(Cormarë Series 35), ISBN 978-3-905703-35-1

Julian Eilmann, *J.R.R. Tolkien – Romanticist and Poet*
Zurich and Jena 2017 (Cormarë Series 36), ISBN 978-3-905703-36-8

Binding Them All. Interdisciplinary Perspectives on J.R.R. Tolkien and His Works
Monika Kirner-Ludwig, Stephan Köser, Sebastian Streitberger (Cormarë Series 37),
ISBN 978-3-905703-37-5

Claudio Testi, *Pagan Saints in Middle-earth*
Zurich and Jena 2017 (Cormarë Series 38), ISBN 978-3-905703-38-2

Music in Tolkien's Work and Beyond
Julian Eilmann & Friedhelm Schneidewind (eds.), Zurich and Jena 2019 (Cormarë
Series 39), ISBN 978-3-905703-39-9

Sub-creating Arda: World-building in J.R.R. Tolkien's Works, its Precursors, and Legacies
Dimitra Fimi & Thomas Honegger (eds.), Zurich and Jena 2019 (Cormarë Series 40),
ISBN 978-3-905703-40-5

"Something Has Gone Crack": New Perspectives on J.R.R. Tolkien and the Great War
Janet Brennan Croft and Annika Röttinger (eds.), Zurich and Jena 2019 (Cormarë
Series 41), ISBN 978-3-905703-41-2

Tolkien and the Classics
Roberto Arduini, Giampaolo Canzonieri & Claudio A. Testi (eds.), Zurich and Jena
2019 (Cormarë Series 42), ISBN 978-3-905703-42-9

Deborah A. Higgens, *Anglo-Saxon Community in J.R.R. Tolkien's The Lord of the Rings*
Zurich and Jena 2020 (Cormarë Series 43), forthcoming

Beowulf and the Dragon

The original Old English text of the 'Dragon Episode' of Beowulf is set in an authentic font and bound in hardback as a high quality art book. Illustrated by Anke Eissmann and accompanied by John Porter's translation. Introduction by Tom Shippey. Limited first edition of 500 copies. 84 pages. Selected pages can be previewed on: http://www.walking-tree.org/beowulf

Beowulf and the Dragon
Zurich and Jena 2009 , ISBN 978-3-905703-17-7

Tales of Yore Series

The *Tales of Yore Series* provides a platform for qualitatively superior fiction that will appeal to readers familiar with Tolkien's world:

The Monster Specialist

Sir Severus le Brewse, among the least known of King Arthur's Round Table knights, is preferred by nature, disposition, and training to fight against monsters rather than other knights. After youthful adventures of errantry with dragons, trolls, vampires, and assorted beasts, Severus joins the brilliant sorceress Lilava to face the Chimaera in The Greatest Monster Battle of All Time to free her folk from an age-old curse. But their adventures don't end there; together they meet elves and magicians, friends and foes; they join in the fight to save Camelot and even walk the Grey Paths of the Dead. With a mix of Malory, a touch of Tolkien, and a hint of humor, The Monster Specialist chronicles a tale of courage, tenacity, honor, and love.

The Monster Specialist is illustrated by Anke Eissmann.

Edward S. Louis, *The Monster Specialist*
Zurich and Jena 2014 (Tales of Yore Series No. 3), ISBN 978-3-905703-23-8

Tales of Yore Series (earlier books)

Kay Woollard, *The Terror of Tatty Walk. A Frightener*
CD and Booklet, Zurich and Berne 2000, ISBN 978-3-9521424-2-4

Kay Woollard, *Wilmot's Very Strange Stone or What came of building "snobbits"*
CD and booklet, Zurich and Berne 2001, ISBN 978-3-9521424-4-8

Information for authors

Authors interested in contributing to our publications can learn more about the services we offer on the "services for authors" section of our web pages.

http://www.walking-tree.org/authors

Manuscripts and project proposals can be submitted to the board of editors (please include an SAE):

Walking Tree Publishers
CH-3052 Zollikofen
Switzerland

e-mail: info@walking-tree.org

Walking Tree Publishers, Zurich and Jena, 2019

Lightning Source UK Ltd.
Milton Keynes UK
UKHW020642260919
350494UK00003B/86/P